Sociology

Exploring the Architecture of Everyday Life

Excellence and Innovation for Teaching Introductory Sociology...

THE AUTHOR'S PURPOSE

"I am a sociology teacher first and foremost. So I set out to write a book that is as helpful to the craft of teaching sociology as possible. You will not find a gargantuan summary of every sociological concept, topic, and theory here. Instead, I chose to limit the focus, allowing for a deeper, more thorough, and hopefully more useful analysis of key ideas in the discipline. The book revolves around a sustained theme—the reciprocal relationship between the individual and society—and continually shows the reader his or her active role as creator and shaper of society. I examine the crucial links between people's common, everyday experiences and the broader structural features of their social worlds. Along the way I use a personal style of writing that I think will appeal to students and instructors alike."

David M. Newman
DePauw University

SPECIAL PACKAGES

- Adopt both the Text and its Companion Reader together and your students can get the shrinkwrapped package at a reduced price! (ISBN 0-7619-8521-2)

- Adopt the Text along with George Ritzer's *The McDonaldization of Society*, Revised Edition, and we will shrinkwrap the books together and offer them at a reduced price! (ISBN 0-7619-8549-2)

- Additional packages also available . . . please contact Pine Forge Press for more information!

PINE FORGE PRESS, 2455 Teller Road, Thousand Oaks, CA 91320
tel: (805) 499-4224 ▪ fax: (805) 499-7881 ▪ E-mail: sales@pfp.sagepub.com
http://www.sagepub.com/pineforge

Newman's *Sociology*

Exploring the Architecture of Everyday Life

SECOND EDITION

- Written at the level of *idea* in order to engage students with puzzles and processes—not just terms and theories.

- Helps students become aware of the sociology embedded in everyday life with a wealth of vivid and provocative Visual Essays. (Examples include layouts on gender violence, social change, immigration, stratification, and sexual identity.)

- Features a chapter on power, which includes material from both micro and macro sociological perspectives and helps to link the two halves of the book together.

- Shows students that the relationship between the individual and society is a reciprocal one, in part through "Micro-Macro Connections" placed throughout the text.

- Captures students' interest by speaking *to* them, rather than *at* them, through the author's friendly and conversational style.

- The author uses his compelling ability to tell stories about research studies as a way of developing more thoroughly the treatment of theory and method and how they work together as sociologists engage in their interesting craft. Invites students to actually go out and "do" their own sociology with Your Turn exercises at the end of each chapter.

- The Instructor's Manual, already lauded by some as the best set of instructor's materials available, has an extensive selection of multiple-choice questions, short answer and essay questions, literary and visual resources, as well as exercises to do with your students both in class and outside of class.

Here's what students have to say:

"*This is one of the best books I've ever read. I am glad to have it on my bookshelf . . . it made me enjoy the theories and concepts of sociology. Everyone should include this in their course reading list!*" SANAM TOOSSI, University of Maryland, College Park

"*This is one of the few texts I own that doesn't put me to sleep when I open it! Made me take a look at society in a new way! Thank you.*" MICHELLE L. BALLAN, University of North Dakota

"*Great conversational style of writing; the examples were very helpful to illustrate the points. This is not at all your usual dry textbook. I also really enjoyed the author's frank analyses and criticisms. Bravo!*" SUZANNE MOLEAFONT, Xavier University

"*It seemed as if the author were speaking to me. I really enjoyed this textbook, and I usually dread reading textbooks! It was great to have lots of examples to help explain the theories. I give this book an A!*" GINA MILOVAN, Kent State University

"*This book did a wonderful job explaining sociology using modern examples. I understood the material because I could relate to it! I think David Newman is an amazing writer . . . this book was more of an enjoyment than an assignment for me to read.*" ALISON WEININGER, University of Florida

"*The conversational style is a refreshing change from most books. This is my first sociology course, and my interest in it was heightened by the author's ability to effectively use understandable examples, meshed in with deeper sociological analysis. The whole class seemed to enjoy the text!*" ANGELA M. BUSHEY, University of Southern Maine

A companion anthology entitled

Sociology: Exploring the Architecture of Everyday Life
READINGS

accompanies this book and is available from
your instructor and college bookstore.

Sociology

Exploring the Architecture of Everyday Life

SECOND EDITION

David M. Newman

Department of Sociology and Anthropology
DePauw University

Visual Essays edited by

Douglas Harper

Department of Sociology
Duquesne University

Pine Forge Press

Thousand Oaks, California ■ London ■ New Delhi

Cover photograph by Helen Levitt. Printed by arrangement with Knox Burger Associates Ltd. Reprinted from *In the Street*, published by Duke University Press, © 1987, Helen Levitt.

For information, address:

Pine Forge Press
A Sage Publications Company
2455 Teller Road
Thousand Oaks, California 91320
(805) 499-4224
E-mail: sales@pfp.sagepub.com

Sage Publications Ltd.
6 Bonhill Street
London EC2A 4PU
United Kingdom

Sage Publications India Pvt. Ltd.
M-32 Market
Greater Kailash I
New Delhi 110 048 India

Production Management: Scratchgravel Publishing Services
Copy Editor: Stephanie Prescott
Typesetter: Scratchgravel Publishing Services
Visual Essays Design and Typesetting: Terri Wright
Cover Designer: Lisa Mirski Devenish
Print Buyer: Anna Chin

Printed in the United States of America
97 98 99 00 01 10 9 8 7 6 5 4 3 2 1

Library of Congress Cataloging-in-Publication Data

Newman, David M., 1958–
    Sociology : exploring the architecture of everyday life / David M.
Newman. — 2nd ed.
        p.   cm.
    Includes bibliographical references and index.
    ISBN 0-7619-8518-2 (alk. paper)
    1. Sociology
HM51.N467   1997
301—dc21   96-45366
                                                          CIP

This book is printed on acid-free paper that meets Environmental Protection Agency standards for recycled paper.

For my Dad

PINE FORGE PRESS TITLES OF RELATED INTEREST

Adventures in Social Research: Data Analysis Using SPSS® for Windows™ by Earl Babbie and Fred Halley

Media/Society: Industries, Images, and Audiences by David Croteau and William Hoynes

Exploring Social Issues Using SPSS® for Windows™ by Joseph F. Healey, Earl Babbie, and Fred Halley

Race, Ethnicity, Gender, and Class: The Sociology of Group Conflict and Change by Joseph F. Healey

Race, Ethnicity, and Gender in the United States: Inequality, Group Conflict, and Power by Joseph F. Healey

Sociological Snapshots: Seeing Social Structure and Change in Everyday Life, 2nd Ed., by Jack Levin

Sociology: Exploring the Architecture of Everyday Life (Readings), 2nd Ed., by David M. Newman

Building Community: Social Science in Action edited by Philip Nyden, Anne Figert, Mark Shibley,
    and Darryl Burrows

The Production of Reality: Essays and Readings on Social Interaction, 2nd ed.,
    by Jodi O'Brien and Peter Kollock

The McDonaldization of Society, Rev. Ed., by George Ritzer

Second Thoughts: Seeing Conventional Wisdom through the Sociological Eye
    by Janet M. Ruane and Karen A. Cerulo

Shifts in the Social Contract: Understanding Change in American Society by Beth Rubin

The Pine Forge Press Series in Research Methods and Statistics
Edited by Kathleen S. Crittenden

Investigating the Social World: The Process and Practice of Research by Russell K. Schutt

A Guide to Field Research by Carol A. Bailey

Designing Surveys: A Guide to Decisions and Procedures by Ronald Czaja and Johnny Blair

How Sampling Works by Richard Maisel and Caroline Hodges Persell

Social Statistics for a Diverse Society by Chava Frankfort-Nachmias

Experimental Design and the Analysis of Variance by Robert Leik

Regression: A Primer by Paul Allison

Sociology for a New Century
A Pine Forge Press Series edited by Charles Ragin, Wendy Griswold, and Larry Griffin

Global Inequalities by York W. Bradshaw and Michael Wallace

Schools and Societies by Steven Brint

How Societies Change by Daniel Chirot

Constructing Identities: Race and Ethnicity in the Modern World
    by Stephen Cornell and Douglas Hartmann

Cultures and Societies in a Changing World by Wendy Griswold

Crime and Disrepute by John Hagan

Gods in the Global Village: The World's Religions in Sociological Perspective by Lester Kurtz

Waves of Democracy: Social Movements and Political Change by John Markoff

Development and Social Change: A Global Perspective by Philip McMichael

Constructing Social Research by Charles C. Ragin

Women and Men at Work by Barbara Reskin and Irene Padavic

Cities in a World Economy by Saskia Sassen

Gender, Family, and Social Movements by Suzanne Staggenborg

About the Author

David M. Newman (Ph.D., University of Washington) is an Associate Professor of Sociology at DePauw University. In addition to the introductory course, he teaches courses in research methods, family, social psychology, and deviance. He has won teaching awards at both the University of Washington and DePauw University.

About the Publisher

Pine Forge Press is a new educational publisher, dedicated to publishing innovative books and software throughout the social sciences. On this and any other of our publications, we welcome your comments. Please call or write us at:

Pine Forge Press
A Sage Publications Company
2455 Teller Road
Thousand Oaks, CA 91320
(805)499-4224
E-mail: sales@pfp.sagepub.com

Visit our new World Wide Web site, your direct link to a multitude of on-line resources:

http://www.sagepub.com/pineforge

I'm
Atmosphere
in your/outside
interaction
extroverted vs introverted

note

mood
setting
summer sounds

PREFACE

It was the first day of the fall semester in 1994. I had just finished making the final adjustments to the first edition of this book, which was due to be published the following January. I felt good, like I'd just accomplished something monumental. Even my two children were impressed with me (although not as impressed as the time I dislodged a Frisbee with a garden hose from the upper reaches of a redbud tree). I walked into the first meeting of my Contemporary Society class eager to start teaching wide-eyed, first-year students a thing or two about sociology.

In my introductory comments to the class that day I mentioned that I had just finished writing a book. The panicked look in their eyes—a curious combination of awe and fear—calmed when I told them I wouldn't be using it that semester. I assured them that the process of writing an introductory text helped me immensely in preparing for the course and that I hoped to pass on to them the knowledge I had accumulated.

The next day after class one of the students—a bright, freshly scrubbed, 18-year-old man—approached me. The ensuing conversation would leave a lasting, humbling impression:

Student: Hi. Umm. Professor Newman . . . I called my parents last night to, like, tell them how my first day in college went. I think they were more nervous than I was. You know how parents can be.

Me: Yes, I sure do. I'm a parent myself you know.

Student: Yeah, well, anyway, I was telling them about each of my classes and what all my professors are like. I told them about this class and how I thought it would be pretty cool. I told them you were writing a book. I thought that would impress them, you know, make it seem like they were getting their money's worth.

Me: Well, thanks.

Student: So, they go, "What's the book about?" [He laughed sheepishly.] I told them I didn't know, but I'd find out. So that's what I'm doing . . . finding out.

Me: Well, I'm glad you did. You see, it's an introductory sociology textbook that uses everyday experiences and phenomena as a way of understanding important sociological theories and ideas. In it I've attempted to . . .

Student: Wait, did you say it was a *textbook*?

Me: Why, yes. You see the purpose of the book is to provide the reader with a thorough and useful introduction to the sociological perspective. I want to convey . . .

Student: [quite embarrassed now] Oh. Professor Newman, I'm very sorry. I misunderstood you. I thought you had written a *real* book.

Real book. *Real* book. *Real* book. Those words echoed in my head like some relentless church bell. At first I tried to dismiss the comment as the utterings of a naive kid who didn't know any better. But the more I thought about it, the more I realized what his comment reflected. The perception that textbooks aren't *real* books is pervasive and, sadly, not altogether unwarranted. These books hover on the margins of the literary world, somewhere between respectful, intellectual, trailblazing research and Harlequin romance novels. Historically they've been less than titillating: thick, heavy, expensive, and easily discarded for a measly five bucks at the end-of-semester "book buy-back."

My goal from the start has been to write a textbook that reads like a *real* book. In the first edition I wanted to capture simultaneously the essence of my discipline and the reader's interest. From what reviewers, instructors, and students who've read and used the book have said, I think I've been fairly successful. People like the relaxed tone and appreciate the consistent theme that ties all the chapters together. Many instructors have commented on how the book enables students to truly understand the unique and useful features of a sociological perspective.

Changes in the Second Edition

However, no book, especially a sociology textbook, can be of lasting value if it remains static, locked into a particular style and content. So I've made some changes in this second edition to enhance the features that worked so well the first time.

Visual Essays

This edition includes a larger, improved visual component. Many textbooks have photos, graphs, charts, and so on. But rarely does this material go beyond simply filling up space. I wanted the visual images in this book to paint detailed, informative sociological portraits. To that end, Douglas Harper, one of the foremost visual sociologists in the world today, produced several unique, vivid, and provocative visual essays for this edition. Doug is a master at using photographic images to tell powerful sociological stories. His essays—focusing on such diverse social phenomena as baseball, family photo albums, peasant religious pilgrimages, transsexualism, domestic violence, and illegal immigration—provide a wonderful opportunity for you to "see" many of the concepts and ideas I've written about in the book. As you study the visual essays, you will become a much more visually astute observer of and participant in your own social world.

New Micro-Macro Connections and Research Features

In the first edition I provided several in-depth features that focused either on a specific piece of sociological research or on some issue that illustrates the connection between micro and macro sociology. These extended discussions linked social institutions to personal experiences and, in the process, provided insight into the methods sociologists use to gather information and draw conclusions about how our world works.

Many instructors and students who used the first edition found these features useful tools in generating classroom discussion. So in this second edition, I've updated some and added others. The added features focus on many topics receiving widespread attention in the popular press, such as biases in news reporting, female genital mutilation, religion in the nineties, interpersonal relations in cyberspace, impression management on the streets, the popularity of Prozac, the computerized workplace, gated communities, Afrocentric schools, illegal immigration, and the environmental justice movement.

Updated Examples and Information

As in the first edition, each chapter is peppered with anecdotes, personal observations, and accounts of contemporary events. Many of the examples you will read are taken from today's news headlines; others are taken from incidents in my own life. Throughout the book I've tried to provide the most up-to-date information possible. All of these examples are meant to show you the pervasiveness and applicability of sociology in our everyday experiences in a way that, I hope, rings familiar with you.

One of the greatest challenges I face as a teacher of sociology is trying to get my students to see the personal relevance of the course material, to fully appreciate the connection between the individual and society. The "everyday life" approach in this book uses the examples and personal observations as a vehicle for understanding the relationship between individuals and society. The true value of sociology lies in its unique ability to show the reciprocal connection between the most private elements of our lives—our characteristics, experiences, behaviors, and thoughts—and the cultures, groups, organizations, and social institutions to which we belong.

My purpose is to make the familiar, unfamiliar—to make you critically examine the commonplace and the ordinary in your own life. Only when you step back and examine the taken-for-granted aspects of your personal experiences can you see that there is an inherent, sometimes unrecognized organization and predictability to them. At the same time you will see that the structure of society is greater than the sum of the experiences and psychologies of the individuals in it.

More Material on Social Institutions and Global Issues

The second edition contains significantly more material on the larger structural elements of society and their impact on social life. Here are some examples:

- Chapter 3, Building Reality—a discussion of professional ethics in social research.
- Chapter 4, Building Order—an in-depth analysis of the relationship between social structure and emotions.
- Chapter 5, Building Identity—an examination of how religion in the nineties influences socialization.
- Chapter 8, Building Social Relationships—an expanded discussion of the dynamics of social groups and a structural examination of divorce patterns.
- Chapter 10, The Architecture of Stratification—a look at the media's role in perpetuating perceptions of social class.
- Chapter 15, Architects of Change—an examination of the role of politics in movements for social change.

In addition, you will find enhanced discussions of global processes. One of the most profound trends in the world today is linking heretofore disconnected societies and cultures. It is difficult, if not impossible, to provide a complete picture of sociology and social life without examining how our lives are intertwined with global events and processes. Here are a few examples of this new global emphasis:

- Chapter 7, Constructing Difference: Social Deviance—a detailed discussion of the global drug trade.
- Chapter 9, Building the Structure of Society—an enhanced analysis of the impact of globalization on economics, politics, and religion.
- Chapter 10, The Architecture of Stratification—an expanded examination of global inequality.
- Chapter 12, The Architecture of Inequality: Race and Ethnicity—an examination of worldwide patterns of racism.
- Chapter 14, The Dynamics of Population—a look at the politics of immigration.

New Articles in the Companion Reader

The companion volume to this book is a carefully constructed book of short articles, chapters, or excerpts from other authors. These readings are provocative and eye-opening examples of the joys and insights of sociological thinking. Many of them vividly show how sociologists gather evidence through carefully designed research. The readings examine common everyday experiences, important social issues, or distinct historical events that illustrate the relationship between the individual and society.

Over half of the articles in the companion reader are new to this edition. Instructors and students who used the first edition asked to see more contemporary readings. So I have drawn from the most recent scholarship to glean some selections that touch on such important and relevant sociological issues as credit cards, abortion, lying, the lives of athletes, corporal punishment, hospitals, Disneyland, immigrant nannies, and America's youth.

Teaching Resources to Accompany the Book and Companion Reader

The *Teaching Resources Guide,* available from Pine Forge Press in hard copy or on a disk upon adoption of either the text or its companion reader, provides comprehensive, thorough coverage of the material in each book, including:

Learning Outcomes. An essay written by David Newman that explores the various goals motivating his writing and his teaching, along with suggestions on how to use the guide to achieve these instructional goals.

Chapter Summaries

Class Exercises and Discussion Topics. Suggestions for writing exercises, discussion topics, and student assignments to use both in and outside of class. Also provides suggestions for how to utilize the text's Your Turn activities.

Literary and Visual Resources

Test Bank. Multiple-choice, short answer, and essay questions. The test bank was developed to test students' understanding of the material, so instructors can encourage students to move beyond basic memorization of materials toward application and critique. The multiple-choice questions are separated into Recall Questions and Application Questions. Recall Questions are based more directly on the information presented in the textbook, and Application Questions assess students' comprehension of the material and their ability to apply concepts, theories, and research findings.

Teaching Resource Materials: Annotated Bibliography. An annotated bibliography of resources useful in preparing for and designing classes, suggestions for how to manage teaching interactions and elicit and evaluate student performance, and techniques for handling any challenges that arise in class.

The Architecture of Society

I have chosen the image of architecture in the subtitle to convey one of the driving themes of this book: society is a human construction. Society is not "out there" somewhere, waiting to be visited and examined. It exists in the minute details of our day-to-day lives. Whenever we follow its rules or break them, enter its roles or shed them, work to change things or keep them as they are, we are adding another nail, plank, or frame to the structure of our society. In short, society—like the buildings around us—couldn't exist were it not for the actions of people.

At the same time, however, this structure that we have created appears to exist independently of us. We don't usually spend much time thinking about the buildings we live, work, and play in as human constructions. We see them as finished products, not as the processes that created them. Only when something goes wrong—the pipes leak or the walls crack—do we realize that people made these structures and people are the ones who must fix them. When buildings outlive their usefulness or become dangerous to their inhabitants, people must renovate them or, if necessary, decide to tear them down.

Likewise, society is so massive and has been around for so long that it *appears* to stand on its own, at a level above and beyond the toiling hands of individual people. But here too when things begin to go wrong—widespread discrimination, massive poverty, lack of affordable health care, escalating crime rates—people must do something about it.

So the fascinating paradox of human life is that we build society, collectively "forget" that we've built it, and live under its massive and influential structure. But we are not "stuck" with society as it is. Human beings are the architects of their own social reality. Throughout this book I examine the active role individuals play in planning, maintaining, or fixing society.

A Final Thought

It is my conviction that the teaching/learning experience can and should be a personally relevant, thought-provoking, and enjoyable excursion. Reading a textbook doesn't have to be boring or, even worse, the academic equivalent of a trip to the dentist (although I personally have nothing against dentists). I believe that part of my task as an instructor is to provide my students with a challenging but comfortable classroom atmosphere in which to learn. I want to do the same in this book.

Your instructor has chosen this book, not because it makes his or her job teaching your course any easier, but because he or she wants you, the student, to see how sociology helps us to understand how the small private experiences of our everyday lives are connected to this thing we call society. I hope you learn to appreciate this important message, and I hope you enjoy reading this book as much as I enjoyed writing it.

Good luck,

David M. Newman
Department of Sociology and Anthropology
DePauw University
Greencastle, IN 46135
E-Mail: DNEWMAN@DEPAUW.EDU

ACKNOWLEDGMENTS

A book project such as this one takes an enormous amount of time to develop. I spent thousands of hours toiling away at the computer, holed up in my isolated third-floor office. Yet as solitary as this project was, it could not have been done alone. Many people provided invaluable assistance to make this book a reality. Without their generous help and support, it wouldn't have been written, and you'd be reading some other sociologist's list of people to thank. Because I have revised rather than rewritten this book, I remain indebted to those who helped me with the original edition.

First, I would like to thank the publisher and president of Pine Forge Press, Steve Rutter. He pushed, prodded, and cajoled me into exceeding my expectations and overachieving. The numerous suggestions he offered made this book a better one. For that I am eternally grateful.

Likewise, the staff at Pine Forge—Sherith Pankratz, Jean Skeels, and, for the first edition, Rebecca Holland—must be thanked for helping me through the maze of details and difficulties that crop up in a project of this magnitude. My gratitude goes to Anne and Greg Draus at Scratchgravel Publishing Services for producing a quality book in record time. In addition, Becky Smith and Stephanie Prescott provided firm but kind editorial hands in helping me polish the revised material. I would also like to express my thanks to Mariko Chang and Susanne Monahan for compiling an excellent instructor's manual and to Veronica Oliva for securing copyright permissions.

I appreciate the many helpful comments offered by the reviewers of the first and second editions of this book:

Deborah Abowitz, Bucknell University
Stephen Adair, University of New Hampshire
Rebecca Adams, University of North Carolina, Greensboro
Ron Aminzade, University of Minnesota
George Arquitt, Oklahoma State University
Carol Auster, Franklin and Marshall College
David Bogen, University of North Carolina, Charlotte
Todd Campbell, Loyola University, Chicago
Doug Currivan, University of Iowa
Jeff Davidson, University of Delaware

James J. Dowd, University of Georgia

Charlotte Chorn Dunham, Texas Tech University

Charles Edgley, Oklahoma State University

Rachel Einwohner, University of Washington

Rebecca Erickson, University of Akron

Kimberly Faust, University of Southern Mississippi

Barry Goetz, University of California, Los Angeles

Valerie Gunter, University of New Orleans

Doug Harper, Duquesne University

Susan Hoerbelt, Hillsborough Community College

Valerie Jenness, Washington State University

Kathryn Johnson, Barat College

Tom Kando, California State University, Sacramento

Steve Keto, Kent State University

Peter Kivisto, Augustana College

Marc LaFountain, West Georgia College

Melissa Latimer, University of Kentucky

Fred Maher, St. Michael's College

Benjamin Mariante, Stonehill College

Joseph Marolla, Virginia Commonwealth University

James R. McIntosh, Lehigh University

Jerome McKibben, University of Southern Mississippi

Ted P. McNeilsmith, Adams State College

Melinda Milligan, University of California, Davis

Susannne Monahan, Montana State University

Kelly Murphy, University of Pittsburgh

Elizabeth Ehrhardt Mustaine, University of Central Florida

Toska Olson, University of Washington

Larry Perkins, Oklahoma State University

Bernice Pescolido, Indiana University, Bloomington

Judith Richlin-Klonsky, University of California, Los Angeles

Robert Robinson, Indiana University, Bloomington

Mary Rogers, University of West Florida

Sally S. Rogers, Montgomery College

Michael Ryan, Upper Iowa University

Mark Shibley, Loyola University

Thomas Shriver, Oklahoma State University

Nicholas Sofios, Providence College

Kandi Stinson, Xavier University

Robert Tellander, Sonoma State University

Kathleen Tiemann, University of North Dakota

John Walsh, University of Illinois, Chicago

Gregory Weiss, Roanoke College

Marty Wenglinsky, Quinnipiac College
Janelle Wilson, University of Minnesota
Mark Winton, University of Central Florida
Cynthia A. Woolever, Midway College
Ashraf Zahedi, Santa Clara University
Stephen Zehr, University of Southern Indiana

I also want to express my appreciation to the colleagues and friends who offered cherished guidance throughout the production of this book and who put up with my incessant whining about how hard it all was. Some offered invaluable advice on specific topics; others provided general support and encouragement that helped me retain my sanity. In particular, I'd like to thank Nancy Davis, Rob Robinson, Nafhat Nasr, Tom Hall, James Mannon, Tom Chiarella, Lisa Chiarella, Bizz Steele, Jodi O'Brien, and Peter Kollock.

I would like to express special gratitude to my students who, throughout the years, have kept me curious and prevented me from taking myself too seriously.

Above all, I want to thank my family—Beth, Zachary, and Seth—for putting up with the frequent late nights, long faces, and lost confidences.

■ ■ ■

Additional acknowledgments are made for permission to reprint the following.

Photographs in the visual essays:

"Illustrating Culture: Peasant Pilgrimages of Modern Europe" photos by Marrie Bot, *Miserere: The Great Pilgrimages of Penance in Europe,* Rotterdam, 1985 (English edition).

"Graffiti: Social Deviance or Art?" photos by James Prigoff, in Henry Chalfant and James Prigoff, *Spraycan Art,* New York: Thames and Hudson, 1987.

"The Resolution of Sexual Identity" photo of Jim Morris by UPI/Bettmann; photo of Jan Morris by David Hurn/Magnum.

"Social Stratification: Class, Poverty, and Wealth" photos by Herman LeRoy Emmet, *Fruit Tramps,* Albuquerque: University of New Mexico Press, 1989. Barbara Norfleet, *All the Right People,* Boston: Little, Brown, 1986. Bill Owens, *Suburbia,* San Francisco: Straight Arrow Press, 1973. Eugene Richards, *Below the Line: Living Poor in America,* New York: Consumers Union Press, 1987. Helen Stummer, *No Easy Walk,* Philadelphia: Temple University Press, 1994.

"Gender Violence" photos by Donna Ferrato, *Living with the Enemy,* New York: Aperture, 1991.

"The Sociology of the Contemporary Immigrant" photos by Ken Light, *To the Promised Land,* introduction by Richard Rodriguez, New York: Aperture, 1988.

"Social Change: The Example of the American Ghetto" photos by Camilo José Vergara, *The New American Ghetto,* New Brunswick, NJ: Rutgers University Press, 1995.

Quotations in the visual essay "Graffiti: Social Deviance or Art?":

By Alex Alverez from "In a City of Graffiti, Gangs Turn to Violence to Protect Their Art," by B. Drummond Ayres, Jr., *The New York Times* (13 March, 1994). Copyright © by The New York Times Co. Reprinted by permission.

From "Billboard Hijinks: Graffiti Groups (Pro and Con) Rally Against Chrysler," *San Francisco Bay Guardian* (4 May 1994). Reprinted by permission.

By Richard Rodriguez from *Pacific News Service Newsletter*, published by Pacific News Service. Reprinted by permission.

By Carlos Rolon from "Six Artists Part of February Showing" by Michael Casey, *North Jersey Herald & News* (30 January 1994).

Figures and tables:

Figure 1.1 adapted from a memo prepared by Bettina Huber of The Modern Language Association to the American Sociological Association and several other professional associations, February 1994. Reprinted by permission.

Figure 1.2 from "Proposed Theoretical Relationship Between Potential Suicide and Network Theory of Suicide" by Bernice Pescosolido and Sharon Georgianna, 1989, *The American Sociological Review, 54,* p. 44. Copyright 1989 by the American Sociological Association. Reprinted by permission.

Figure 3.1 from *Word Play* by Peter Farb. Copyright © 1973 by Peter Farb. Reprinted by permission of Alfred A. Knopf Inc. and Brandt and Brandt Literary Agents.

Figure 3.2 adapted from *Pygmalion in the Classroom: Teacher Expectation and Pupil's Intellectual Development* by Robert Rosenthal and Lenore Jacobson (pp. 75 & 76). Copyright © 1968 by Holt, Rinehart and Winston, Inc. Reproduced by permission of the publisher.

Figure 8.1 from *Marriage, Divorce, and Remarriage* by Andrew J. Cherlin (p. 82), Harvard University Press. Copyright © 1981, 1992 by the President and Fellows of Harvard College. Reprinted by permission.

Figure 8.2 from *Marriages and Families: Making Choices and Facing Change* (p. 29) by M. A. Lamanna and A. Reidman, 1994. Copyright © 1994 Wadsworth Publishing Co.

Table 8.1 from *Sharing the Journey: Support Groups and America's New Quest for Community* by Robert Wuthnow (p. 53). Copyright © 1994 by Robert Wuthnow. Reprinted by permission of The Free Press, a division of Simon & Schuster.

Table 11.1 from *New York Times*/CBS News Poll, "Perceptions of the Problem," in "The Homeless at the Heart of Poverty and Policy" by M. Oreskes and R. Toner, 1989, *The New York Times*, 29 January (p. D5). Copyright © 1989 by The New York Times Co. Reprinted by permission.

Table 12.1 from "Income Disparity Between Poorest and Richest Rises" by S. A. Holmes, 1996, *The New York Times*, 20 June (p. A16). Copyright © 1996 The New York Times Co. Reprinted by permission.

Table 12.2 from *Race, Class, and Gender in the United States* (pp. 144–145) by P. S. Rothenberg, 1995. New York: St. Martin's Press. Copyright © P. S. Rothenberg. Reprinted by permission of St. Martin's Press, Inc.

Figure 13.1 from "Housework in Marital and Nonmarital Households" by S. J. South and G. Spitze, 1994, *The American Sociological Review, 59*, pp. 327–347. Copyright © 1994 by the American Sociological Association. Reprinted by permission.

Figure 14.1 from *American Social Problems: An Institutional Analysis,* 2nd ed., by John E. Farley (p. 344). © 1991. Reprinted by permission of Prentice-Hall, Inc., Upper Saddle River, NJ.

Figure 14.2 adapted from *Population: An Introduction to Concepts and Issues* by John R. Weeks (pp. 30, 48), 1994. © 1994 by Wadsworth Publishing Company. Reprinted by permission.

Figure 14.3 from "The Growing Human Population," by Nathan Keyfitz, *Scientific American*, September 1989, p. 122. Copyright © 1989 by Scientific American, Inc. All rights reserved. Reprinted by permission.

Quotations in text:

(Chapter 3) From "Too Late for Prince Charming?" 1986, *Newsweek* (2 June) p. 55. Reprinted by permission.

From Letter to the Editor, 1992, *Greencastle Banner Graphic* (7 March). Copyright 1992 Greencastle Banner Graphic. Reprinted by permission.

(Chapter 7) From "On Being Sane in Insane Places" by D. Rosenhan, 1973, *Science, 179*, p. 253. Copyright 1973 by the American Association for the Advancement of Science. Reprinted by permission.

From "Psychological Warfare" by E. Tims and S. McGonigle, 1992, *Indianapolis Star* (5 April), p. F4. Reprinted by permission of Knight-Ridder/Tribune News Services.

(Chapter 8) From "Court Rules City May Oust Unwed Couple," 1986, *Seattle Times* (16 July). Copyright 1986 by Seattle Times. Reprinted by permission.

(Chapter 11) From "Helping the Homeless" by R. Worsnop, *Congressional Quarterly Researcher*, p. 411, 26 January 1996. Reprinted by permission.

(Chapter 12) From "Black Like Them," by M. Gladwell, 1996, *The New Yorker*, (29 April and 6 May), p. 79. Reprinted by permission of the author.

From "Give Him a Whistle, He'll Love It" by Elaine Viets, 1992, *St. Louis Post Dispatch* (29 November). Copyright 1992. Reprinted by permission of the St. Louis Post-Dispatch.

(Chapter 14) From "Proceeding with Caution" by D. M. Gross and S. Scott, 1990, *Time* (16 July). © 1990 Time Inc. Reprinted by permission.

From "Migrants Create a New Order with Their Feet" by A. Honebrink, 1993, *Utne Reader* (May/June), pp. 46–49. Copyright 1993 by Lens Publishing Company, Inc. Reprinted by permission.

(Chapter 15) From "The End of Innocence" by N. Darton, 1991, *Newsweek* (special summer issue), p. 62. Reprinted by permission.

From "The Abolition of El Cortito, The Short-Handled Hoe: A Case Study in Social Conflict and State Policy in California Agriculture" by D. L. Murray, 1982. © 1982 by the Society of the Study of Social Problems. Reprinted *Social Problems*, Vol. 30, no. 1, pp. 26–29. Reprinted by permission.

Quotations in text from The New York Times:

(Chapter 2) From "Ads on Holocaust 'Hoax' Inspire Campus Debates" by K. Bishop, 25 December 1991, p. A12; "Aging Parents: Women's Burden Grows" by T. Lewin, 14 November 1989, p. B12. (Chapter 5) "In a 90s Quest for Black Identity, Intense Doubts and Disagreements" by L. Williams, 30 November 1991, p. A26. (Chapter 7) "A Shooter as Vigilante and Avenging Angel" by S. Mydans, 12 February 1995, p. A20. (Chapter 11) "The Homeless at the Heart of Poverty and Policy" by M. Oreskes & R. Toner, 29 January 1989, p. D5; "Shift in Feelings on the Homeless: Empathy Turns to Frustration" by I. Wilkerson, 2 September 1991, p. A10; "As the Rich Get Leaner, the Poor Get French Fries" by M. O'Neill, 18 March 1992, p. C6. (Chapter 12) "Service with a Sneer" by J. Kohn, 6 November 1994, *New York Times Magazine*, p. 44; "When Blacks Shop Bias Often Accompanies Sale" by L. Williams, 30 April 1991, p. A14. (Chapter 14) "Stark Data on Women: 100 Million Are Missing" by N. D. Kristof, 5 November 1991, p. C1; "Across the U.S., Immigrants Find the Land of Resentment" by D. Sontag, 11 December 1992, p. A1. Copyright © 1989, 1991, 1992, 1994, 1995 by The New York Times Co. Reprinted by permission.

I

The Individual and Society

What is the relationship between your private life and the social world around you? Part I introduces you to the guiding theme of this book: Our personal, everyday experiences affect and are affected by the larger society in which we live. Chapters 1 and 2 discuss the sociological perspective on human life and the ways in which it differs from the more individualistic approaches of psychology and biology. You will read about what society consists of and get a glimpse into sociologists' attempts to understand the two-way relationship between the individual and society.

CHAPTER 1

Taking a New Look at a Familiar World

- *Sociology and the Individual*
- *The Insights of Sociology*
- *The Sociological Imagination*

Michael and Carole were juniors at a large university. They had been dating each other exclusively for the past 2 years. Both on and off campus they were a loving couple, always reveling in each other's company. By all accounts, the relationship seemed to be going quite well. In fact, Michael was beginning to wonder if it might become more permanent sometime soon. He imagined them getting married and starting a family. Then one day Carole dropped a bombshell. She told Michael she thought the relationship was not going anywhere and perhaps they ought to start seeing other people.

Michael was stunned. "What did I do?" he asked her. "I thought things were going great. Is it something I said? Something I did?"

She said no, he hadn't done anything wrong, they had simply grown apart. She told him she just didn't feel as strongly about him as she once did.

After the breakup Michael was devastated. He turned to his friends for support. "She wasn't any good for you anyway," they said. "We always thought she was a little unstable. She probably couldn't get serious with anybody. It wasn't *your* fault, it was *hers*."

Fred was a model graduate student. His grades were excellent. He got along well with his professors and even collaborated on a published research paper with one of them. During his last 2 years of graduate school, he taught two introductory courses and proved to be a skilled and caring teacher. He completed his dissertation and was granted his PhD. Fred's career script was clear: He would land a job at a top university, establish a national reputation as a top-notch researcher, and become a popular and beloved professor on campus.

But when Fred entered the job market and began applying for faculty positions, he faced a shocking amount of difficulty. No one seemed willing to hire him for a full-time teaching position. The only way he was able to survive was by taking a temporary 1-year replacement job. He became frustrated and began to question his own abilities: "Am I good enough? Do I lack the sort of talent they're looking for? Maybe I'm not trying hard enough. What's wrong with me?" His friends and family tried to encourage him, but some of them secretly wondered if Fred wasn't as qualified as they thought he was.

In both these stories the people involved, as well as outside observers, initially try to explain the situation by focusing on individual characteristics and attributes. Michael wonders what he did wrong to sour his relationship with Carole; his friends question Carole's psychological stability. Fred blames himself for not being able to land a job; others question his motivation and qualifications. Such reactions are not uncommon. We have a marked tendency to attribute people's achievements and failures to their personal qualities (J. Miller, 1984).

It seems perfectly reasonable, for instance, to conclude that something about Michael or Carole or the combination of the two caused their breakup. We tend to view dating relationships—not to mention marriages—as situations that succeed or fail solely because of the traits or behaviors of the two partners: He does something that bothers her, she does something that annoys him, or they're simply incompatible.

But how would your assessment of the situation change if you found out that Donald—to whom Carole had always been attracted—had just broken up with his longtime girlfriend and was now available? Relationships are not exclusively private entities; they are constantly influenced by outside forces. They take place within a larger network of friends, acquaintances, ex-partners, co-workers, fellow students, and persons as yet unknown who may make desirable or, at the very least, acceptable dating partners. When people believe they have no better alternative, they tend to stay with their present partners, even if they are not particularly satisfied. When people think, as Carole did, that better relationships are available, they become less committed to staying in their present ones. In fact, according to recent research, people's perceptions of what characterizes a relationship (such as fairness, compatibility, affection) are less likely to determine when and if it ends than the presence or absence of favorable alternatives (Felmlee, Sprecher, & Bassin, 1990). That is, couples may endure feelings of dissatisfaction until one partner sees a more attractive situation elsewhere.

In addition, the sheer number of potentially available partners—a result of shifts in the birth rate 20 years earlier—could have indirectly affected Carole's decision, increasing the likelihood that she would eventually come across a suitable college-age alternative to Michael. A shortage of such men, however, might have elevated Michael's relative standing in her eyes. Research shows that the risk of a relationship ending increases as the supply of potential alternative relationships increases (South & Lloyd, 1995). In sum, Michael's interpersonal value, and therefore the stability of his relationship with Carole, might well have deteriorated not because he had changed but because of forces over which he had little if any control.

Beyond their immediate dating network, Carole and Michael's relationship was certainly influenced by other social forces. For instance, the very characteristics and features that people consider attractive in the first place are determined by the values of the larger culture in which they live. Fashions and tastes are constantly changing, making particular characteristics (for example, hairstyles, body

Figure 1.1   *Number of Advertisements for Academic Job Openings by Discipline and Year*

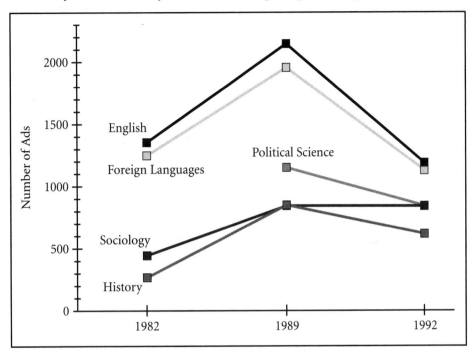

Source: Huber, 1994.

types, clothing), behaviors (smoking, drinking), or life choices (occupation, political affiliation) more or less desirable.

And what about Fred, our highly intelligent, well-trained, talented PhD who can't land a permanent job? Perhaps some inherent, personal flaw is preventing Fred from being employable: lack of ability, lack of drive, laziness, bad attitude, and so on. Or maybe he doesn't come across as particularly friendly during job interviews.

By focusing exclusively on personal "deficiencies," however, we overlook the broader societal trends that can affect a person's job prospects. Twenty-five years ago, faculty positions in higher education were much more abundant (National Center for Education Statistics, 1989). New PhD's had a wealth of occupational choices. But during the recession of the early 1990s, when Fred was looking for a position, many university departments—including English, foreign languages, history, sociology, and political science—were forced to condense their faculty, thereby reducing the number of openings for new PhD's (see Figure 1.1). PhD's in mathematics have the highest unemployment rate ever, despite the fact that the number of new PhD's in the 1994–95 academic year was nearly 16% greater than the number the previous year (Worthington, 1996). So poorly perceived are faculty job opportunities that in a list of "Bottom 10" careers that recently appeared in *USA Today*, "college professor" ranked eighth—ahead of only real estate agent and bartender.

So you see, Fred's employability is as much a result of the economic forces operating at the time as any of his personal qualifications. Had he graduated 25 or even 5 years earlier his prospects certainly would have been much brighter. For that matter, had he graduated 5 or 25 years later his prospects would have been better. Researchers predict that by the turn of the century, as the large number of professors hired in the 1960s reach retirement age, there will be a shortage of university faculty and a subsequent abundance of openings once again.

The moral of these two stories is that to understand phenomena in our personal lives, it is necessary to move past individual traits and examine broader societal characteristics and trends. External features beyond our immediate awareness and control often exert more influence on the circumstances in our day-to-day lives than our "internal" qualities. We can't begin to explain why relationships work or don't work without addressing the broader interpersonal friendship network and culture in which they are embedded. We can't begin to explain an individual's employability without examining current and past economic trends and the resulting job structure. By the same token, we can't begin to explain the ordinary, everyday thoughts and actions of individuals without examining the social forces that influence them.

Sociology and the Individual

Herein lies the fundamental theme of sociology and the theme that will guide you through this book: Everyday social life—our thoughts, actions, feelings, decisions, interactions, and so on—is the product of a complex interplay between societal forces and personal characteristics. To explain why people are the way they are, we must understand the interpersonal, historical, cultural, and organizational environments they inhabit. To understand either individuals or society, we must understand both (C. W. Mills, 1959).

Of course, this is easier said than done. We live in a world dominated by individualistic explanations of human behavior that attempt to understand problems and processes by focusing exclusively on the personality, psychology, or even the physical characteristics of each individual. Consequently, most of us take for granted that what we choose to do, say, feel, and think are fiercely private phenomena. Everyday life seems to be a series of unabashedly free choices. After all, we choose what to major in. We choose what to wear. We choose what and when to eat. We choose our lifestyles, our mates, and so on.

But how free are these decisions? Think about all the times your actions have been constrained by social circumstances. Have you ever felt that, because of your age or gender or race, certain opportunities were closed to you? Your ability to legally drive a car or drink alcohol is certainly constrained by your age. When you reach 70 you might be forced into retirement despite your capacity and desire to continue working. Some occupations, like bank executive and engineer, are still predominantly male, while others, like nurse and secretary, are almost exclusively female. African Americans are conspicuously absent from the highest management positions in professional sports despite their overrepresentation as players.

Likewise, the doctrines of your religion may limit your behavioral choices. For a devout Catholic, premarital sex or even divorce is unlikely. A strict Muslim would not drink beverages containing alcohol. An Orthodox Jew would never drink milk and eat meat at the same time.

Think about why you find certain hairstyles, clothing, or types of music appealing or unappealing. Large-scale marketing strategies can actually create a demand for particular products or images. Your tastes, and therefore your choices as a consumer, are influenced by decisions made in corporate boardrooms all across the country. Furthermore, what you wear is dictated in part by the organizational setting in which you find yourself. For instance, appropriate attire for a stockbroker is very different from that of a college student.

Broad economic trends can also influence your everyday life. You may lose your job as a result of the economic fluctuations brought about by a recession. Or, because of the tightening of the job market, the bachelor's degree that may have been your ticket to a rewarding career 10 years ago may not qualify you for a low-paying, entry-level position today. And even if you do get a job, you may still live at home for years after you graduate—not because you are emotionally incapable of separating from your parents but because you can't earn enough to support yourself. Indeed, according to U.S. Census Bureau statistics, the number of 25- to 34-year-olds who still live at home has increased steadily over the past decade (Quinn, 1993).

Certainly government and politics affect our personal lives as well. A political decision made at the state or national level might result in the closing of a government agency you depend on or reduce the municipal services to which you have grown accustomed. If you are a woman, decisions made by the Supreme Court can increase or limit your options for voluntarily ending a pregnancy or make it easier or more difficult to sue an employer for sexual harassment. If you are homosexual, court decisions can determine whether or not you have the right to legally marry.

Your private life may even be touched by events that occur in distant countries. In 1995 CompuServe, an on-line computer service, cut off all subscriber access to sexually oriented material, a response to the demands of German prosecutors who claimed that the transmission of such materials violated German pornography laws. The ban was eventually lifted, but for a while your choice to view certain computer material was severely restricted because of the influence exerted by a foreign country.

The Insights of Sociology

Our lives, private and personal though they may be, are significantly affected by the people, events, and societal features that surround us. There is a structure and pattern to our lives that often is not immediately apparent. By showing how we can be shaped by *social* processes, and how those processes can in turn be affected by individual action, sociology provides unique insight into the taken-for-granted personal events and large-scale cultural processes that make up our everyday existence.

Other disciplines study human life, too. Biologists study how the body works. Neurologists examine what goes on inside the brain. Psychologists study what goes on inside the mind. These disciplines focus almost exclusively on structures and processes that reside *within* the individual. In contrast, sociologists study what goes on *between* people as individuals, groups, or societies. How do social forces affect the way people interact with one another? How do people make sense of their private lives and the social worlds they occupy? How does everyday social interaction create "society"?

Issues like love, poverty, sex, age, and prejudice are better understood within the appropriate societal context. For instance, we may feel that we marry purely for love, when in fact society pressures us to marry within our social class, religion, or race (P. L. Berger, 1963). Sociology, unlike other disciplines, forces us to look outside the tight confines of individual personalities to understand the phenomena that shape us. Consider the following situations:

■ A young high school girl, fearing she is overweight, begins starving herself systematically in hopes of becoming more attractive.

■ A 55-year-old college graduate, unable to find work for the past 3 years, sinks into a depression after losing his family and his home. He now lives on the streets.

■ A 36-year-old professor kills herself after learning that her position at the university will be terminated the following year.

■ The student body president and valedictorian of the local high school cannot begin or end her day without several shots of whiskey.

What do these people have in common? Your first response might be that they are all suffering or have suffered terrible personal problems—eating disorders, suicidal depression, homelessness, poverty, alcoholism. If you saw them only for what they'd become—an "anorexic," a "homeless person," a "suicide victim," or an "alcoholic"—you might think they have some kind of personality defect, genetic flaw, or mental problem that renders them incapable of coping with the demands of contemporary life. Maybe they simply lack the willpower to pick themselves up and move on. In short, your immediate tendency is probably to focus on the unique, perhaps "abnormal," characteristics of these people to explain their problems.

But we cannot downplay the importance of their *social* worlds. The circumstances described above are all linked to larger phenomena. There is no denying that we live in a society that praises thinness in women, encourages drinking to excess, and values economic success and independence. Some people will suffer under the weight of these conditions. This is not to say, though, that all people exposed to the same social messages will inevitably fall victim to the same problems. Some people are able to overcome wretched childhoods; others can withstand the tragedy of economic failure and begin anew; and some people are immune to cultural images of beauty. But in order to understand completely the nature of human life or particular social problems, we must acknowledge the broader social context in which these things occur.

The Sociological Imagination

We usually don't see the connections between the personal events in our everyday lives and the larger society. In a country like ours, which celebrates individual achievement, we have difficulty looking beyond our immediate situation. When we lose our job, get divorced, or flunk out of school, it's hard to imagine that these experiences are somehow related to massive cultural or historical processes.

The ability to see the impact of these forces on our private lives is what the famous sociologist C. Wright Mills (1959) called the **sociological imagination**.* The sociological imagination enables us to understand the larger historical picture in terms of its meaning in our own lives. Mills argued that no matter how personal we think our experiences are, many of them can be seen as products of societywide, macro-level forces. The task of sociology is to help us view our lives as the intersection between personal biography and societal history, to provide a means for us to interpret our lives and social circumstances.

Unemployment, for example, is a terrible, even traumatic private experience. Feelings of personal failure are inevitable when one loses a job. But if the unemployment rate in an individual's community hovers at 25 or 30%—as it has in many mill and factory towns and inner-city neighborhoods over the past several decades—then we must see unemployment as a social problem that has its roots in the economic and political structures of society. Being unemployed cannot be viewed as a character flaw or personal failure if a significant number of people in one's community are also unemployed. As long as the economy is arranged so that slumps inevitably occur, the social problem of unemployment cannot be solved at the personal level (Lekachman, 1991; C. W. Mills, 1959).

The same can be said for divorce. One can experience divorce as an intimate tragedy, but in a society in which approximately one out of every two marriages ends in divorce, we must view it within the broader historical changes occurring

---

*****Boldfaced** terms are defined in the Glossary/Index at the end of the book.

within the family, the law, religion, the economy, and the culture as a whole. It is impossible to explain significant changes in divorce *rates* in society over time by focusing exclusively on the personal characteristics and behaviors of divorcing individuals. National divorce rates don't rise and fall simply because individual spouses can't get along with one another.

Mills did not mean to imply that the sociological imagination should debilitate us—that is, force us to fatalistically perceive our lives as wholly beyond our control. In fact, the opposite is true. An awareness of the impact of social forces or world history on our personal lives is a prerequisite to any large-scale social change. Without such awareness we fall into the trap of indifference toward both society and one another.

The sociological imagination allows us to recognize that the solutions to many of our most serious social problems lie not in changing the personal situations and characteristics of individual people but in changing the social institutions and roles available to them (C. W. Mills, 1959). Drug addiction, sexual violence, hate crimes, eating disorders, suicide, and so on will not go away simply by treating or punishing the person who is suffering from or engaging in the behavior.

■ ■ ■ ■ ■ ■ ■ ■

ÉMILE DURKHEIM
Sociological Research and the Study of Suicide

Several years ago a tragic event occurred at the university where I teach. On a pleasant night a few weeks into the fall semester, a first-year student shot and killed himself in his dorm room. The incident sent shock waves through this small, close-knit campus. As you would expect in such a situation, the question on everyone's mind was: Why did he do it?

Although no definitive answer was ever obtained, most people simply concluded that his was a "typical" suicide. He must have been despondent, hopeless, unhappy, and unable to cope with the demands of college and the pressures of contemporary social life. I heard students say that no one really knew much about him and that he was a bit of a "loner." In other words, something was wrong with him.

As tragic as this incident was, it was not and is not unique. Since the 1950s the suicide rate (the percentage of people who die through suicide) has almost tripled for people between the ages of 15 and 24, becoming the third leading cause of death, behind accidents and homicides, among young Americans (U.S. Department of Health and Human Services, 1990). Although the suicide rate remains highest among people over the age of 65 (U.S. Bureau of the Census, 1993a), teenagers are the only age group for which suicide rates have increased in the recent past (Basch & Kersch, 1986).

Focusing on individual characteristics like depression and frustration doesn't tell us why so many people in this age group commit suicide, nor does it tell us why there has been such a dramatic increase in youth suicide over the past three or four decades. So, to understand "why he did it," we must look beyond his private mental state and examine the social and historical factors that might have affected him.

Clearly, life in contemporary society is focused on individual achievement more strongly than ever before. Young people are faced with almost constant pressure to "measure up" and define their identities according to standards set by others (Mannon, 1990). Although most can adjust, a growing number of others cannot. The increasing pressure to be beautiful, popular, and successful has taken a particularly heavy toll on young people.

The situation for young people is made worse by other social forces. As the economy grows more unstable and competition for scarce financial resources becomes more acute, young people are likely to experience unprecedented levels of stress and uncertainty about their own futures. As the quest to realize the American dream begins earlier and earlier, the stakes increase.

Within this context we can see that suicide among young people can be linked to certain processes going on in society. Such an explanation occupies a hallowed place in the history of sociology. In fact, one of the classic pieces of sociological research was the first to examine suicide as a sociological rather than psychological issue.

The famous French sociologist Émile Durkheim (1897/1951) argued that suicide is more likely to occur when the social ties that bind people to one another are either too weak or too strong. He saw suicide as a manifestation of the changes going on in modern society that were altering the fundamental bonds that connected people to one another and to their community. In college a close friend of his named Victor Hommay committed suicide. Convinced that there was more involved in Hommay's death than psychological shortcomings, Durkheim began to explore the sociological grounds for suicide.

How does one go about determining whether suicide—perhaps the most private act one can commit—is instigated by the structure of society? Durkheim decided to test his theory by comparing existing official statistics and historical records across groups, sometimes referred to as the **comparative method**. Many sociologists continue to follow this methodology, analyzing statistics such as those compiled by governmental agencies like the U.S. Bureau of the Census, the FBI, and the National Center for Health Statistics to draw comparisons between groups.

For about 7 years Durkheim carefully examined the available data on rates of suicide among various social groups in Europe—countries, religions, ethnic groups, and so on. Instead of simply describing the suicide rates of these different groups, Durkheim sought to discover and explain important social patterns. He thought that changes in the rate of suicide over time or between groups could not be explained through individualistic disciplines like psychology or biology. If suicide is purely an act of individual desperation, he reasoned, one would not expect to find any noticeable changes in the rates from year to year or society to society. That is, the distribution of desperate, unstable, unhappy individuals should be roughly equal across time and culture. If, however, certain groups or societies had a significantly higher rate of suicide than others, something more than individual disposition would seem to be at work.

After compiling his figures, Durkheim discovered that, among other things, suicide rates in all the countries he looked at tended to be higher among widowed, single, and divorced people than among married people; higher among people without children than parents; and higher among Protestants than among Catholics. Did this mean that unmarried people, childless people, and Protestants are more unhappy, depressed, or psychologically dysfunctional than others? Durkheim didn't think so. Instead, he felt that something about the nature of social life among people in these groups increased the likelihood of suicide.

Durkheim argued that when group, family, or community ties are weak, people feel disconnected and alone. If a person lacks family ties and close friends or lives in a community that stresses individualism and de-emphasizes ties to the larger group, then that person is likely to lack the supportive network that could be used as a buffer against personal difficulties. Durkheim pointed out, for instance, that the Catholic church emphasizes salvation through community and binds its members to the Church through elaborate doctrine and ritual; Protestantism, on the other hand, emphasizes individual salvation and responsibility. This individualism, he believed, explained the differences he noticed in suicide rates. Self-reliance and independence may glorify one in God's eyes, but they become liabilities if one is in the throes of personal tragedy and has no supportive community to turn to.

Durkheim felt that life in modern society tends to be individualistic and dangerously alienating. Contemporary sociologists have voiced this same concern (for example, Bellah, Madsen, Sullivan, Swidler, & Tipton, 1985; Riesman, 1950). Many people today don't know and have no desire to know their neighbors. Strangers are treated with suspicion. In the pursuit of economic survival, we have become more willing to relocate, sometimes to areas completely isolated from previous family ties. As we spread out and become more insulated, we become more separated from those who could and would offer support in times of need. One recent study found that membership in voluntary organizations (PTA, Elks Club, Red Cross, League of Women Voters, etc.) has steadily declined over the past several decades. Over the same period the average number of hours a day people watch television has increased (cited in Roberts, 1995). When the structure of our community discourages the formation of ties and bonds to others and to a communal way of life, the likelihood of suicide increases.

It's not surprising, then, that the states with the highest suicide rates today are the sparsely populated mountain states of Nevada, Utah, Idaho, Wyoming, and Montana. In these states divorce rates are also higher than those in other regions,

Figure 1.2   *Proposed Relationship between Potential Suicide and Density of Religious Integration*

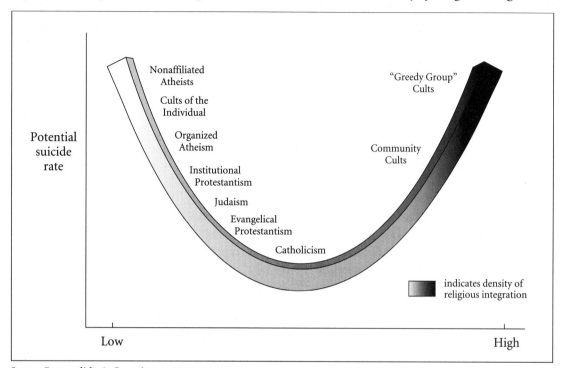

Source: Pescosolido & Georgianna, 1989.

and a larger proportion of new residents are not part of an established community (Doyle, 1994). The greater isolation of people in these regions makes them more individualistic, less likely to seek help or comfort from others in times of trouble, and therefore more susceptible to suicide.

Durkheim also felt, however, that suicide becomes likely when the social ties to one's community are too strong. He suggested that in certain societies individuality is completely overshadowed by one's group membership; the individual literally lives for the group, and personality is merely a reflection of the collective identity of the community. Religious cults, for example, require their members to reject their ties to outside people and groups. Obedience to the values and customs of the community can then become so powerful that when members feel they can no longer contribute to the group and sustain their value within it, they may take their own lives out of loyalty to group norms (see Figure 1.2).

In 1989 four young Korean sisters, ranging in age from 6 to 13, attempted to kill themselves by ingesting rat poison. The three older sisters survived; the youngest died. The eldest provided startling sociological insight into this seemingly senseless act. Their family was poor—the father supported everyone on a salary of about $362 a month. She told authorities that the sisters had made a suicide pact to ease their parents' financial burden and leave enough money for the education of their 3-year-old brother. Within the traditional Korean culture, it is essential that a family be able to send its male children to college; female children are much less important to the family than male children.

The attempted suicides of the young Korean girls clearly illustrates the power of ties to one's cultural values. These sisters attempted to take their lives not because they were depressed or unable to cope but because they felt obligated to sacrifice their personal well-being to the success of their family's male heir.

Just as the suicide pact of these young girls was tied to the social system of which they were a part, so too was the suicide of the young college student at my university. His choices and life circumstances were also a function of the values and conditions of his particular society. No doubt he had emotional problems, but these problems may have been part and parcel of his social circumstances. Had he lived in a society that didn't place as much pressure on young people or glorify individual achievement, he might not have chosen suicide. That's what the sociological imagination helps us understand.

■ ■ ■

Conclusion

As we approach the 21st century, understanding one's place within a cultural, historical, and global context is more important than ever. The world is shrinking. Communication technology and global economies connect us to people on the other side of the planet. The growing attention paid to ecological awareness opens our eyes to the environmental degradations that occur in South American rain forests. The events in the former Soviet Union and Eastern Europe, the unification of Germany, the reawakening of China, and the imposition of black rule in South Africa were perhaps the most significant political events of the late 20th century. The consequences of these colossal changes will continue to be felt around the world for many years to come.

When people's lives are changed by such events—as they sink into poverty or ascend to prosperity; stand in bread lines or work at a job previously unavailable; or find their sense of ethnic identity and sense of self-worth altered—we can begin to understand the personal effects of societal and global changes.

The next chapter will provide you with a more detailed introduction to the theme of the book—that individuals simultaneously influence and are influenced by society. In Part II I will examine how society and our social lives are constructed and ordered. I will focus on the interplay between individuals and the people, groups, organizations, institutions, and culture that collectively make up our society. Part III will focus on the structure of society, with particular attention to the various forms of social inequality.

CHAPTER HIGHLIGHTS

▪ The primary theme of sociology is that our everyday thoughts and actions are the product of a complex interplay between massive social forces and personal characteristics. We can't understand the relationship between individuals and societies without understanding both.

▪ The sociological imagination is the ability to see the impact of social forces on our private lives—an awareness that our lives lie at the intersection of personal biography and societal history.

▪ Rather than study what goes on *within* people, sociologists study what goes on *between* people, whether as individuals, groups, organizations, or entire societies. Sociology forces us to look outside the tight confines of our individual personalities to understand the phenomena that shape us.

YOUR TURN

The sociological imagination serves as the driving theme throughout this book. It's not a particularly difficult concept to grasp in the abstract: Things bigger than us affect our everyday lives in ways that are sometimes not immediately apparent; our personal biographies are a function of social history. Yet what does this actually mean? How can you see the impact of larger social and historical events on your own life?

One way is to find out what events were going on at the time of your birth. Go to the library and find a newspaper and a popular magazine that were published on the day you were born. What major news events took place that day? What were the dominant social and political concerns in the country at the time? What was the state of the economy? What was considered fashionable in clothing, music, movies, and so forth?

Ask your parents or other adults about their reactions to these events and conditions. How do you think those reactions affected the way you were raised and the values in your family? What have been the lasting effects, if any, of these historical circumstances on the person you are today?

CHAPTER 2

Seeing and Thinking Sociologically

- *How Individuals Structure Society*
- *Social Influence: The Impact of Other People in Our Everyday Lives*
- *Societal Influence: The Effect of Social Structure on Our Everyday Lives*
- *Understanding Social Order: Three Perspectives*

In 1994 ethnic violence erupted in the small African nation of Rwanda. The Hutu majority had begun a systematic program to exterminate the Tutsi minority. It wasn't long before gruesome pictures of the tortured and dismembered bodies of Tutsi men, women, and children began to appear on our television screens. Surely, we thought, such horror must have been perpetrated by bands of vicious, crazed thugs who derived some sort of twisted satisfaction from such unspeakable violence. Or maybe these were the extreme acts of angry soldiers, trained killers who were committed to destroying the enemy as completely as possible.

Actually, according to the civil rights organization African Rights, much of the responsibility lies elsewhere, in a most unlikely place. In a 1996 report African Rights provides evidence suggesting that a great deal of the brutality was conceived, planned, and executed by members of the medical profession ("Doctors implicated," 1996). The report details how doctors joined with militiamen to hunt down Tutsis, turning hospitals into slaughterhouses. Some helped soldiers drag sick and wounded refugees out of their beds to be killed. Others took advantage of their position of authority to organize road blocks, distribute ammunition, and compile lists of Tutsi colleagues, patients, and neighbors to be sought out and slaughtered. Many doctors who didn't participate in the actual killing refused to treat wounded Tutsis and withheld food and water from refugees who sought sanctuary in hospitals.

Ordinary, well-balanced people—members of a profession committed to healing and saving lives—had changed, almost overnight, into sadistic killers. How could this have happened?

We can gain some sociological insight into this question by looking back to a remarkable experiment done in 1971 by Philip Zimbardo, a professor of social psychology at Stanford University. Recent prison uprisings had piqued Zimbardo's interest in what it means psychologically to be a prisoner or a prison guard. Why were prisoners so disposed toward violence? Why were prison guards so brutal? The answers, like those initially used to explain the genocide in Rwanda, seemed obvious. Prisoners are violent because of the type of people they are: antisocial criminals who have little regard for other people. Guards are brutal because it takes that type of person to be attracted to such an occupation in the first place.

Zimbardo felt there was more to the dynamics of prison life than the personalities of the individuals involved. He wondered whether the structure of the prison situation played a part in turning prisoners and guards into mean and violent people.

With the help of several colleagues, Zimbardo created a mock prison in the basement of the Stanford psychology building, where he could observe volunteer subjects in the roles of prisoners and guards. Of the 70 or so students who answered his ad for volunteers, Zimbardo chose two dozen mature, emotionally stable, intelligent young men to be part of the study. None had a criminal record. They were, as he put it, the "cream of the crop of this generation" (1971, p. 4). Some subjects were designated as "prisoners" with a flip of a coin; the rest served as "guards."

When it was time for the experiment to begin, the prisoners were unexpectedly picked up at their homes by a city police officer in a squad car, searched, handcuffed, fingerprinted, blindfolded, and taken to the "prison." There they were stripped, given a uniform and number, and placed in a cell with two other inmates. They were told the cell would be their home for the next 2 weeks.

When the guards arrived, they were informed that they had the authority to make up their own rules for maintaining law, order, and respect in the prison and were free to improvise new ones at any time during their 8-hour shifts on duty.

Although the experiment was supposed to last for 2 weeks, it had to be stopped after only 6 days. Zimbardo described the situation as follows:

> What we saw was frightening. It was no longer apparent to most of the subjects (or to us) where reality ended and their roles began. The majority had indeed become prisoners or guards, no longer able to clearly differentiate between role playing and self. . . . In less than a week the experience of imprisonment undid (temporarily) a lifetime of learning; human values were suspended, self-concepts were challenged and the ugliest . . . side of human nature surfaced. We were horrified because we saw some guards treat others as if they were despicable animals, taking pleasure in cruelty, while the prisoners became . . . dehumanized robots who thought only of escape, of their own individual survival and of their mounting hatred for the guards. (1971, p. 4)

Some of the prisoners became severely depressed, confused, or hysterical and had to be released after only a few days. All but three of the remaining prisoners were willing to forfeit all the money they had earned for participating just to get out of the prison. When told they had been "denied parole," however, they returned docilely to their cells. Zimbardo points out that had these individuals been thinking like the college students they were, instead of the prisoners they were playing, they simply would have quit.

Many of the guards became tyrants, arbitrarily using their power and enjoying the control they had over others. Other guards were not as brutal, but they never intervened on behalf of the prisoners and never told the other guards to "ease off."

What Zimbardo so poignantly discovered—and what sheds some light on the role doctors played in the Rwandan genocide—was that individual behavior is largely controlled by social forces and situational contingencies. Just as the prison situation turned nice, ordinary college students into vicious or cowering animals, the circumstances of large-scale ethnic hatred and war transformed well-educated doctors with no previous history of violence into cruel butchers.

In addition, Zimbardo's aborted study illustrated that, given the proper environmental circumstances, individuals can create the very social forces that come to shape their behavior. As the experimenter, he merely provided the physical structure of the "prison" and a few general rules. It was the subjects themselves who created the reality of their roles and therefore defined the power that the prison structure exerted over them.

As you will see, the relationship between individuals and the social environment in which they live is a reciprocal one; each affects the other. In this chapter I discuss, in detail, the process by which individuals construct society and the way people's lives are linked to society.

How Individuals Structure Society

Up to this point I have been using the term *society* rather loosely. Typically, **society** is defined as a population living in the same geographical area who share a culture and a common identity and whose members are subject to the same political authority. Societies may consist of people who share the same ethnic heritage or of hundreds of different groups who speak a multitude of languages. Some societies are highly industrialized and complex; others are primarily agrarian and relatively simple in structure. Some societies are self-sufficient and produce most of the goods and services they need; others rely exclusively on trade with foreign countries for survival.

According to the 19th-century French philosopher Auguste Comte, all societies, whatever their form, contain forces for stability, which he called "social statics," and forces for change, which he called "social dynamics." Many sociologists, however, use the term *society* to mean a "static" entity—a natural, permanent, and historical structure. They frequently talk about society "planning" or "controlling" our lives and describe it as a relatively stable set of organizations, institutions, systems, and cultural patterns into which successive generations of people are born and socialized.

As a result, sociology students are often led to believe not only that society is powerfully influential (which it is) but also that it is something that exists "out there," completely separate and distinct from us (which it isn't). It is tempting to view society simply as a "top down" initiator of human activity, a massive entity that methodically controls the lives of all individuals within it, like a gigantic puppeteer manipulating marionettes. This characterization is not altogether inaccurate. Society does exert influence on its constituent members through certain identifiable structural features and historical circumstances. The concept of the sociological imagination discussed in chapter 1 implies that structural forces beyond our direct control do affect our personal lives.

But this view is only one side of the sociological coin. The sociological imagination also encourages us to see that each individual has a role in forming that society and influencing the course of its history. As people process inputs from their social environments, they respond in ways that may modify the effects and even the nature of the environment (House, 1981). As one sociologist wrote:

> No [society], however massive it may appear in the present, existed in this massivity from the dawn of time. Somewhere along the line each one of its salient features was concocted by human beings. . . . Since all social systems were created by [people], it follows that [people] can also change them. (Berger, 1963, p. 128)

To fully understand society, we must see it as a human construction made up of people interacting with one another. It consists of everyday *microsituations*—what people do, say, feel, and think alone or in groups. When individuals alter their behavior, the nature of society changes (Collins, 1981).

Communication plays an important role in the construction of society. If people couldn't communicate with one another to reach an understanding about society's expectations, they couldn't live together. Through day-to-day communication, individuals construct, reaffirm, experience, and alter the reality of their society. By responding to other people's utterances and gestures in the expected manner and by talking about social abstractions as real things, we help shape society (Shibutani, 1961).

Imagine two people sitting on a park bench who strike up a conversation. Their talk eventually turns to the sour state of the economy—inflation, unemployment, the rising cost of health care, and so on. Whether or not they agree on the causes and solutions to these economic problems, by talking about them they collectively acknowledge their reality. In dealing with and especially talking about these matters, they give shape and substance to society's ideals and values (Hewitt, 1988).

So you see, society is also a "bottom up" phenomenon. It might best be regarded as an ongoing process, a *becoming* rather than a *being*. It is a succession of events, a flow of interchanges among people (Shibutani, 1961, p. 174).

When we view society this way, we can begin to understand our role in altering it. Whenever we modify the expectations or behaviors associated with a social position we occupy, we are simultaneously modifying a part of our society. Individuals who occupy highly visible and influential positions are particularly effective. It is often argued, for instance, that Franklin D. Roosevelt's term as president forever changed the nature of the presidency and the role of the federal government in American life (House, 1981).

It's not only powerful, influential people who can modify society, however. Sometimes the actions of ordinary individuals mobilize larger groups of people to collectively alter some aspect of social life. On December 1, 1955, Rosa Parks, a black seamstress in Montgomery, Alabama, refused to give up her seat to a white man who had boarded the bus after her, as she was required, by law, to do. The incident sparked a year-long citywide boycott of the public transit system and galvanized the entire civil rights movement of the 1950s and 1960s. Ms. Parks was an active member of the NAACP and had challenged the bus segregation laws many times before that day in December. And Montgomery's black community had been demanding changes in the transit system for some time (Kelley, 1996). Nevertheless, this single challenge to the broad societal expectations commonly associated with race at the time helped set in motion a massive restructuring of U.S. race relations. The repercussions continue to reverberate through our economic, educational, and political systems today.

Even something so apparently unchangeable as our collective past can be shaped by individuals. We usually think of history as a fixed, unalterable collection of social events that occurred long ago; only in science fiction can one "go back" and change history. No one would question that the Declaration of Independence was signed in 1776 or that the Civil War took place in the 1860s or that John F. Kennedy was assassinated on November 22, 1963.

Although historical events don't change, their meaning and relevance may. Consider the celebration in 1992 of the 500th anniversary of Columbus's discovery of America. Most of us learned as schoolchildren that Columbus's 1492 voyage represented a triumphant and progressive step forward for Western civilization. However, the increasing sensitivity to the social value of all racial and ethnic groups and the acknowledgment of their past persecution have forced many people to reconsider the historical meaning of Columbus's journey. In fact, some historians now consider it one of the most dismal examples of wanton and deadly prejudice.

We live in a world in which our behaviors are largely a product of societal and historical processes. Society is an objective fact that coerces, even creates, us (Berger, 1963). At the same time, we are constantly creating, maintaining, reaffirming, and transforming society. Hence society is part and parcel of human interaction (Collins, 1981). We create society, then collectively "forget" we've done so, believe it is independent of us, and live our lives under its influence.

Social Influence: The Impact of Other People in Our Everyday Lives

We live in a world with other people. This is not exactly an earth-shattering statement, but it is key to understanding the sociology of human behavior. Our everyday lives are a collection of brief encounters, extended conversations, intimate interactions, chance collisions, and superficial contacts with other people. In our early years we have our parents, siblings, uncles, aunts, and grandparents to contend with. Soon we begin to form friendships with others outside our families. Our lives become filled with connections to other people—teachers, bosses, therapists—who are neither family nor friends but who have an enormous impact on us. And, of course, we have daily encounters with total strangers: the clerk at the supermarket, the server at the restaurant, the woman who sits next to you on the bus. Even when we're alone, we feel the effects of other people. Being alone implies the absence of social contact, and the only way to understand that is to know what being with others is like.

Sociologists tell us that these encounters have a great deal of *social influence* over our lives. Whether we're aware of their doing so or not, other people affect our thoughts, perceptions, and behaviors. We take into account their feelings and concerns before acting. They may be in our immediate presence or hover in our memories. They may be real or imagined, loved or despised. And their effects on us may be deliberate or accidental. Our lives are spent forming or dissolving attachments to other people; we may seek them out one moment, avoid them like the plague the next. As will be discussed in chapters 5 and 6, much of our private identity—what we think of ourselves, the type of people we become, and the images of ourselves we project in public—is derived from our contact with others.

Imagine for a moment what your life would be like if you never had contact with other people (assuming you could survive this long!). Obviously you would be pretty lonely. But beyond that, you'd lack the key experiences that make you a functioning human being. You wouldn't know what love is, or hate or jealousy or compassion or appreciation, for that matter. You wouldn't know if you were wealthy or poor, bright or dumb, witty or boring. You'd also lack some important and basic information. You wouldn't know how much a pound weighed, where England was, or which plants and animals are edible. Furthermore, you'd have no language, and because we use language to think, imagine, and dream, you'd lack these abilities as well.

Contact with people is essential to a person's social development. But there is more to social life than the mere fact that it involves other people. We act and react to things and people in our environment as a result of the meaning we attach to them. A squirrel will instinctively run away at the sight of a dog barreling toward it. A human, however, would not have such an automatic reaction. We've learned from past experiences that some animals are approachable while others aren't. So we're able to think, *Is this a friendly or mean dog? Does it want to play with me or tear me limb from limb?* and respond accordingly. In short, we must interpret events in our environment before we act. To do this, we often look to others to help us define a particular situation.

■ ■ ■ ■ ■ ■ ■ ■

BIBB LATANÉ AND JOHN DARLEY
Why Don't People Help?

In the early morning hours of March 13, 1964, a woman named Kitty Genovese was brutally stabbed to death in front of her New York apartment. As we all know, murders are not uncommon in New York City or any other American city for that matter. But what made this case all the more troubling was the fact that about 40 people either heard her scream for help or watched her being stabbed from their apartment windows. No one called the police until about 35 minutes after the attack had begun (Seedman & Hellman, 1975).

When the story appeared in the newspaper, the public was outraged. How could people be so insensitive to the suffering of another? Why didn't anyone help her? Some newspaper editors and psychiatrists at the time blamed the behavior on "bystander apathy" or growing "urban alienation." The story became a metaphor for modern city life. Others, however, speculated that the failure of people to get involved might be due more to the social influence that bystanders have on each other than to individual callousness.

To test this theory, two social psychologists, Bibb Latané and John Darley (1970), conducted a series of experiments on helping behavior in emergencies. In the first session the room in which subjects were completing written surveys gradually filled with smoke. In the second experiment subjects heard a loud crashing noise from an adjoining room, followed by a woman's screaming, "Oh my God, my foot . . . I . . . I . . . can't move it. Oh my ankle. I . . . can't get this . . . thing off me" (Latané & Rodin, 1969). In the third study subjects were participating in a discussion over an intercom when one of them suddenly choked, gasped, and called out for help. In each situation, the number of individuals present at the time of the emergency was varied so that some subjects were alone and others were with several people. The researchers consistently found that as the number of bystanders increased, the likelihood that any one of them would help decreased. It appeared that people help others more often and more quickly when alone (see Figure 2.1).

This phenomenon, which is often called the *bystander effect,* has a number of sociological explanations. First, the more bystanders present, the more likely it is that we will assume someone else will help. If we are by ourselves when an emergency occurs, we perceive ourselves to be 100% responsible for taking action. However, when there are 10 bystanders, each individual perceives herself or himself to have only 10% of the responsibility. The higher the number of bystanders, the less obligated each individual is likely to feel to intervene.

Second, if we are unsure of our own perceptions and interpretations, or if the situation is ambiguous, we look to others for help in defining what is going on. If others appear calm, we may decide that whatever is happening doesn't require our assistance. Unfortunately, people often try to avoid showing outward signs of

Figure 2.1   *The Diffusion of Responsibility: Percentage of Cases in Which Help Was Given in Emergency Situations*

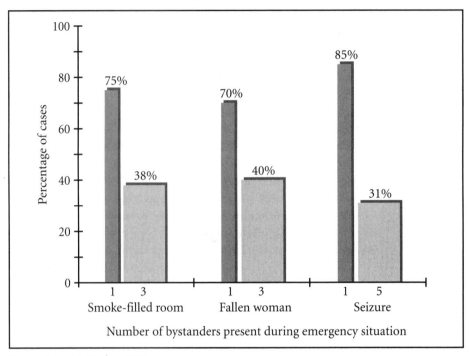

Source: Latané & Darley, 1970.

worry or concern until they see that other people are alarmed. This sort of caution encourages others not to define the situation as one requiring assistance and therefore inhibits the urge to help. The larger the number of people who don't seem concerned, the stronger the inhibiting influence. Obviously, helping will not be inhibited if others are showing visible alarm or if the situation is so unambiguous that one doesn't need to look to the reactions of others—as with a car accident, for instance (Clark & Word, 1972).

Kitty Genovese's neighbors weren't necessarily cruel, cold, or apathetic. They may simply have been victims of social influence, with each looking to others for information, waiting for someone else to define the situation and act. Because *everyone* was waiting for someone else to do something, no one did anything.

■ ■ ■

How Others Influence Our Perceptions

In 1951 social psychologist Solomon Asch devised an experiment that examined the extent to which pressure from other people could affect one's perceptions (S. Asch, 1958). Imagine yourself in the following situation: You sign up for a psychology experiment, and on a specified date you and seven others whom you think are also subjects arrive and are seated at a table in a small room. You don't know it at the time, but the others are actually associates of the experimenter, and their behavior has been carefully scripted. You're the only real subject. The experimenter arrives and tells you that the study in which you are about to participate concerns people's visual judgments.

She places two cards before you. The card on the left contains one vertical line. The card on the right displays three lines of varying length. The experimenter asks all of you, one at a time, to choose which of the three lines on the right card matches the length of the line on the left card. The task is repeated several times with different cards. On some occasions the other "subjects" unanimously choose the wrong line. It is clear to you that they are wrong, but they have all given the same answer. What would you do? Would you go along with the majority opinion or "stick to your guns" and trust your own eyes?

In total, about one third of the subjects who were placed in this situation went along with the clearly erroneous majority. Some of them indicated afterward that they assumed the rest of the people were correct and their own perceptions were wrong. Others knew they were correct but didn't want to be different from the rest of the group. Some even insisted they saw the line lengths as the majority claimed to see them. Asch concluded that it is difficult to maintain that you see something when no one else does. Pressure from other people can make you see almost anything.

How Others Influence Our Actions

Social influence is particularly apparent when it comes to our actions. The presence of other people may motivate us to improve our performance—for example, when the quality of your opponent makes you play the best tennis match of your life. The presence of others may also inhibit us—as when you forget your lines in the school play because your entire family is in the audience.

I'm sure you've been in situations in which other people have tried to persuade you to do things against your will or better judgment. Perhaps a friend convinced you to buy a Ford instead of a Honda. Or perhaps someone persuaded you to steal a candy bar, cheat on your taxes, or disregard the speed limit. On occasion, such social influence can be deadly.

■ ■ ■ ■ ■ ■ ■ ■ ■

STANLEY MILGRAM
Ordinary People and Cruel Acts

If a being from another planet were to read the history of human civilization, it would probably conclude that we are tremendously cruel, vicious, and evil creatures. From countless wars and crusades to ethnic genocides, from backwater lynchings to violent crime and schoolyard bullies, humans have always shown a powerful tendency to ferociously turn on their fellow humans.

The curious thing is that people involved in such acts often show a profound capacity to deny responsibility for their actions by pointing to the influence of others: "My friend made me do it" or "I was only following orders." Can an ordinary, decent person be pressured by another to commit an act of extreme cruelty? Or do cruel actions require cruel people?

Consider the story of Adolf Eichmann, the mastermind behind the Nazi Holocaust during World War II. In 1961 he was found guilty of war crimes and executed in Jerusalem. One would expect someone who had created a meticulous and efficient plan for killing millions of people to look like the devil incarnate or to have a long history of cruelty and violence. Neither was true of Eichmann. Psychiatric evaluations after his capture indicated that he was rather ordinary. He loved his parents, wife, and children (Arendt, 1963). He was an avid horticulturist who would spend hours tending his garden. Eichmann simply claimed that he was doing his job in carrying out the orders of his "boss," Adolf Hitler.

Social psychologist Stanley Milgram (1974) was interested in learning whether ordinary people could be persuaded to commit cruel acts against others. He was familiar with the horrors of Nazi Germany during the 1930s and 1940s. After World War II he witnessed the trials of Nazi war criminals like Eichmann and their repeated attempts to deny responsibility for their actions by claiming that they were merely following orders. Milgram wanted to know how far people would go in obeying the commands of an authority. He set up an experimental situation in which a subject, upon orders from an authoritative figure, flips a switch, apparently sending a 450-volt shock to an innocent victim.

Subjects were told they would be participating in a study of the effects of punishment on learning. On a specified day each subject arrived at the laboratory with another person who, unbeknownst to the subject, was actually an accomplice of the experimenter. Each subject was informed that he or she would play the role of "teacher," while the other person would be the "learner." The teacher was taken to a separate room that held an ominous-looking machine called a "shock generator." The machine had a series of switches ranging from 30 to 450 volts at 15-volt increments and consecutively labeled "Slight Shock," "Danger: Severe Shock," and, ultimately, "XXX." The learner was seated in another room out of the sight of the teacher and was supposedly strapped to an electrode from the shock generator.

The teacher read a series of word pairs (for example, *blue-sky, nice-day, wild-duck*) to the learner. After reading the entire list, the teacher then read the first word of a pair (for example, *blue*) and four alternatives for the second word (for example, *sky, ink, box, lamp*). The learner had to select the correct alternative. Following directions from the experimenter, who was present in the room, the teacher flipped a switch and shocked the learner whenever he or she gave an incorrect answer. The shocks began at the lowest level, 15 volts, and increased with each subsequent incorrect answer all the way up to the 450-volt maximum.

The learner pretended not to be very bright and made many incorrect responses. As instructed, all of the subjects shocked the learner for each incorrect response. As the experiment proceeded and the shocks became stronger, the learner began to cry out in pain. The cries became more blood-curdling, and the learner's pleas to end the experiment became more intense with each increase in voltage. Most of the teachers, believing they were inflicting serious injury on this other person, became visibly upset and wanted to stop. The experimenter, however, ordered them to continue—and they did. At around 300 volts the learner became silent. Some teachers thought they had actually killed the fellow! The experimenter told them to continue, stating that it was essential to proceed and that he, the experimenter, would take responsibility for any harm that might befall the learner. Despite the tortured reactions of the victim, 65% of the subjects complied with the experimenter's demands and proceeded to the maximum, 450 volts.

Milgram repeated the study with a variety of subjects and even conducted it in different countries, including Germany and Australia. In each case about two thirds of the subjects were willing, under orders from the experimenter, to shock to the limit. Milgram showed that one situation, obedience to authority, had the power to cause ordinarily nice people to do terrible things they wouldn't do under other circumstances.

This wasn't a particularly soothing proposition, and Milgram's study generated a tremendous amount of controversy. Indeed, other researchers have found that, when in small groups, people often collectively rebel against what they perceive to be an unjust authority (Gamson, Fireman, & Rytina, 1982). Nevertheless, Milgram's findings are discomforting. It would be much easier to conclude that the brutal acts of inhumanity we read about in our daily newspapers are the products of defective or inherently evil individuals. All society has to do is identify, capture, and separate them from the rest of us. But if Milgram is right, if most of us could become evil given the "right" circumstances, then the only thing that separates us from monsters—whether in Nazi Germany, present-day Rwanda, or a mock prison at Stanford University—is our good fortune and social environment.

▪ ▪ ▪

Societal Influence: The Effect of Social Structure on Our Everyday Lives

Social life is more than just individual people affecting one another's lives. Society also consists of socially recognizable combinations of individuals, such as relationships, groups, and organizations, as well as the products of human action—roles, institutions, history, and culture. A society is more than just a sum of its human parts; it's also the way those parts are put together, related to each other, and organized (Coulson & Riddell, 1980). Although society is dynamic and may change form from time to time, it persists in setting guidelines and influencing our lives, despite the comings and goings of its members. Let's examine some of the important elements that make up a society.

Statuses and Roles

Society is a network of named positions, or **statuses**, occupied by people. "Father" is a status within a network of other statuses—"son," "grandfather," "mother"— that make up a family. "Woman" and "man" are two statuses within a network we call gender. "African American," "Caucasian," "Hispanic," and "Asian" are statuses within a network called race. Professor, uncle, student, shoplifter, brain surgeon, electrician, and alcoholic are other examples of statuses.

Statuses are important sociologically because they all come with a set of expectations that include rights, obligations, behaviors, and duties. These expectations are referred to as **roles**. For instance, a "professor" is expected to teach students, answer questions, be impartial, and dress appropriately. Any out-of-role behavior may be met with shock or suspicion. If your professor consistently showed up for class in a bathing suit, that would certainly violate his or her "scholarly" image and call into question his or her ability to teach.

Each person, as a result of her or his own skills, interests, and interactional experiences, defines roles differently. Students enter a class with the general expectation that their professor is going to teach them something. Each professor, however, may have a different method. Some professors are very animated, others remain stationary behind the podium. Some will not allow questions until after the lecture, others demand constant discussion and probing questions from students. Some are meticulous and organized, others scattered and absent-minded.

We occupy many statuses at the same time. I am a professor, but I am also a husband, son, nephew, uncle, father, friend, consumer, brother, second baseman, homeowner, neighbor, author, and jogger. Because each status has its own set of role expectations, my behavior is dictated to a large degree by the status that is most salient at the time. When I am playing softball, my status as husband or professor is not particularly relevant. On the other hand, if I want to play softball on my wedding anniversary, I may be in trouble!

Statuses often come in pairs or **relationships**. People engage in typical patterns of interaction based on the nature of their relationships. Employers are expected to interact with employees in a certain way, as are dentists with patients and salespeople with customers. In each case actions are constrained by the responsibilities and obligations associated with those particular statuses. We know, for instance, that lovers are supposed to interact with each other differently than with acquaintances or friends. In a parent-child relationship, both members are linked by certain rights, privileges, and obligations. Parents are responsible for providing their children with the basic necessities of life—food, clothing, shelter, and so forth. These expectations are so powerful that not meeting them may constitute the crime of negligence or abuse. Children, in turn, are expected to abide by their parents' wishes. Thus interactions within a relationship are functions not only of the personalities of the two people involved but also of the role requirements of the statuses they occupy.

The power of role expectations is felt most clearly when we occupy two conflicting statuses simultaneously. Sociologists use the term **role conflict** to describe such situations. People may feel frustrated in their efforts to do what they feel they're supposed to do when the demands of one role clash with the demands of another. A parent may have an important business meeting with out-of-town clients (status of business executive) at the same time her 8-year-old son is appearing in the school play (status of parent). Or a high school kid who works hard at his job at the local ice cream shop (status of employee) is frustrated when his buddies come and expect him to give them free ice cream (status of friend).

A few years ago Michael Lowe, the grand dragon of the Texas Knights of the Ku Klux Klan, was being investigated by the Texas Commission on Human Rights to see if he and his organization had unlawfully and violently intimidated four African Americans who had moved into an all-white housing project. The commission sought a court order compelling Mr. Lowe to turn over membership lists, financial documents, and other records of the group. He felt that this order was a violation of his civil rights, because the government cannot compel private groups to divulge information about themselves (Verhovek, 1993). So he contacted the American Civil Liberties Union to defend him. The attorney assigned to his case was Anthony Griffin, a black man. Despite protests from many people in the black community, Mr. Griffin chose to represent Mr. Lowe. Mr. Griffin had to choose between the demands and expectations of his racial status (that is, one should not assist racists who are committed to your destruction) and those of his occupational status (that is, one should protect the legal rights of clients no matter how distasteful they might be). The protests and Mr. Griffin's difficult decision to represent a Klan member illustrate the powerful effects of role conflict.

■ ■ ■ ■ ■ ■ ■ ■
MICRO-MACRO CONNECTION
Caring for Elderly Parents

Role conflict often arises from larger, fundamental changes in society. For instance, the past several decades have witnessed a dramatic shift in the age structure of American society. More people are living into their 80s and 90s (see chapter 14), but at the same time couples are having fewer children (see chapter 8). That is, the American family is expanding *vertically* (more generations living per family) and shrinking *horizontally* (fewer individuals per generation). Thus, as life expectancy increases, fewer siblings are around to share in caring for elderly parents (Sherman, Ward, & LaGory, 1988).

Many people, particularly women in their 40s, 50s, and even 60s, are having to cope with the burden of caring for elderly parents in addition to the usual demands of work and family. More than 6 million elderly Americans now need help with such everyday basics as getting out of bed, eating, dressing, bathing, and using the bathroom (Beck, 1990). Given the high cost of nursing homes, many elderly parents end up moving in with their children. The typical pattern is that sons offer financial assistance, and daughters and daughters-in-law provide the time-consuming, hands-on care.

Almost every woman is going to have to take care of an aging parent or in-law at some point in her life (Lewin, 1989). A survey by the Travelers Corporation in 1985 found that about one out of every five female employees over the age of 30 is currently providing some care to an elderly parent (Lewin, 1989). These caretaking responsibilities can last 10 years or more.

Meeting these obligations often comes at the expense of other family roles. Many women who provide care to elderly parents are forced to spend less time with their husbands and children, leading to resentment and frustration, ultimately threatening the structure of family life. At a time when more families depend on two incomes for survival, many women have had to switch to part-time work, pass up promotions, or quit their jobs altogether. A study by the American Association of Retired Persons estimates that 14% of all part-time adult female workers had left their full-time jobs because of caregiving responsibilities. Of those not employed but who once had jobs, 27% had taken early retirement or simply quit (Lewin, 1989).

With these responsibilities come feelings of guilt, inadequacy, and resentment. A woman who had quit her job to care for her mother, who had developed Alzheimer's disease, echoed the thoughts of many:

> I felt like I was going under. I couldn't do my job because I was pretty much in pieces. I was furious at my brother who didn't help at all. My 15-year-old daughter is mad at me because I am so engaged with my mother. My son has stopped visiting me. And the friends who had been wonderful and supportive through the birth of my babies and my divorce just faded away now that I need them the most. I am alternately so sad about my mother's decline that I can't stop crying and so enraged that my life is being messed up that I want to dump her. I used to think I was good at crises, but this just goes on and on, and I'm falling apart. (quoted in Lewin, 1989, p. B12)

It's important to note that the effects of this sort of role conflict go beyond the emotional difficulties experienced by individual caregivers to the very structure of society. As the elderly population continues to grow and more families are faced with these sorts of dilemmas, the economic structure of society, as well as the fundamental structure of the American family, will be severely strained, necessitating, perhaps, greater governmental involvement in the lives of those affected.

■ ■ ■

Groups

Sometimes networks of many interrelated statuses form well-defined units called groups. A **group** is a set of people who interact more or less regularly with one another and who are conscious of their identity as a group. Families, clubs, and sports teams all constitute social groups. Groups are not just collections of people who randomly come together for some purpose. They have a structure that defines the relationships between members, and each individual occupies some named position—father, president, treasurer, linebacker, and so forth.

A **primary group** consists of a small number of members who have direct contact over a relatively long period of time. Emotional attachment is high in such groups, and members have intimate knowledge of each other's life. Families and close friends would be considered primary groups. A **secondary group**, in contrast, is much more anonymous and impersonal. The group is established for a specific task, such as the production or sales of consumer goods, and members are less emotionally committed to one another. Their roles tend to be highly structured. Primary groups may form within secondary groups, as when close friendships form among co-workers, but in general a secondary group is more formal and goal-driven.

Like societies, groups have a reality that is more than just the sum of its members; a change in a group's membership does not necessarily alter its basic structure. In primary groups change such as that which occurs through divorce or death produces some dramatic effects on the nature and identity of the group. Secondary groups, however, can endure relatively easily despite the fact that some, or even all, individuals leave and new ones enter—for example, when a high school senior class graduates and is replaced the following year by another group of students.

Groups by definition include some people and exclude others. Much of what we do and feel in our everyday lives revolves around our sense of group membership—our feelings of "us" and "them." The term **in-group** refers to the people who constitute the group to which you belong and with whom you identify. **Out-group** refers to people who don't belong. Group membership, then, can become a signifying feature of one's identity and feelings of belonging. It can also be a powerful force behind one's future actions and thoughts. For instance, a girl who is not a member of the popular clique at school but wants to be is likely to structure much of her daily activities around gaining entry into the group.

Social statuses such as race, gender, ethnicity, and religion can serve as important sources of a person's group identity. Although these attributes are not social groups in the strictest sense of the term, they function like groups in that members share certain characteristics and interests. For instance, members of a particular racial or ethnic group may organize into a well-defined unit to fight for a political cause. The feelings of "we-ness" or "they-ness" that are generated by such group membership can be constructive or dangerous, encouraging pride and unity in some cases, anger and hatred in others.

Like statuses and roles, groups come with a set of general expectations. Actions within a group are judged according to a conventional set of ideas about how things *ought* to be. Hence, for example, such family forms as single-parent households, homosexual parents, and childless couples may be seen by others as "abnormal" or "dysfunctional" only because they deviate from the traditional nuclear family.

Organizations

Organizations are larger, more complex networks of statuses. The American Medical Association, General Motors, the International Brotherhood of Teamsters, Microsoft, the National Organization for Women, and the Catholic church are all examples of organizations. Organizations contain groups as well as individuals; some of these groups are transitory, some are more permanent. For instance, a university is composed of individual classes that disband at the end of the semester as well as more permanent groups like the faculty, administration, secretarial staff, maintenance staff, and alumni.

Formal organizations are often characterized by a *hierarchical division of labor.* Each person occupies a position that has a specific set of duties and responsibilities, and those positions can be "ranked" according to power and importance. At Ford Motor Company, for instance, assembly line workers do not make personnel or budgetary decisions, and the vice president in charge of marketing doesn't spray paint the underbodies of newly assembled automobiles. In general, people occupy certain positions in an organization because they have the skills to do the job that is required of them. When one can no longer meet the requirements of a job, that person will be replaced, without seriously affecting the functioning of the organization.

Organizations are a profoundly common and visible feature of everyday social life. You cannot acquire food, get an education, pray, or earn a salary without coming into contact with or becoming a member of some organization. To be a full-fledged member of modern society is to be deeply involved in some form of organizational life (see chapter 9).

Social Institutions

When stable sets of statuses, roles, groups, and organizations form, they provide the foundation for addressing fundamental social needs. These enduring patterns of expectations are called **social institutions**. Sociologists usually think of institutions as the building blocks that organize society. They are the patterned ways of solving the problems and meeting the requirements of a particular society. Key social institutions in modern society include the family, education, religion, politics, and the economy. Some sociologists would add health care and the military to the list.

Family: All societies must have a way of replacing their members; reproduction is essential to the survival of society. Within the institution of family, sexual relations among adults are regulated, people are cared for, children are born and socialized, and newcomers are provided an identity—a "lineage"—that gives them a sense of belonging. Just how these activities are carried out varies from society to society, but family, whatever its form, remains the hub of social life in virtually all societies (Turner, 1972).

Education: New members of a society need to be taught what it means to be a member of that society and how to survive in it. In small, simple societies the family is the primary institution responsible for socializing new members into the culture. However, as societies become more complex, it becomes exceedingly difficult for a family to teach its members *all* they need to know to function within that society. Hence most modern, complex societies have an elaborate system of schools—primary, secondary, college, professional—that not only create and disseminate knowledge and information but also train individuals for future careers and teach them their "place" in society.

Economy: From the beginning of human societies, the problems of securing enough food and protecting people from the environment have persisted (Turner, 1972). Today, modern societies have systematic ways of gathering resources, converting them into goods and commodities, and distributing them to members. In addition, societies provide ways of coordinating and facilitating the operation of this massive process. For instance, banks, insurance firms, stock brokerages, data processing facilities, and accounting firms don't produce goods themselves but provide services that make the gathering, producing, and distributing of goods possible (Turner, 1972). To facilitate the distribution of both goods and services, economic institutions adopt a system of common currency and an identifiable mode of exchange.

Politics and law: All societies face the problem of how to preserve order and avoid chaos. The legal system provides explicit laws or rules of conduct, mechanisms for enforcing those laws, mechanisms for settling disputes, and mechanisms for changing laws that have become outdated or for creating new ones (Turner, 1972). These activities take place within a larger system of governance in which power, authority, and leadership are established and changed. In a democracy the governance process includes the citizens, who have a say in who leads them; in a monarchy kings or queens can claim that their birthright entitles them to positions of leadership. In some societies the transfer of power is efficient and mannerly; in others it is violent. In any case, all societies establish ways to make important societal decisions.

Religion: All societies also face the problem of providing their members with a sense of purpose and meaning. Religion gives individuals a belief system for understanding their existence as well as a network of personal support in times of need. Although many members of a given society—and, in fact, some entire societies—may actively reject religion, it remains one of the most enduring and powerful institutions in human societies. In some societies, it provides enormous comfort to people; in others, it has created irreparable divisions.

Military: To deal with the possibility of attack from outside, many societies maintain an active military defense to protect its citizens from this threat. However, militaries are used not only to defend societies but also, at times, to aggress against others.

Health care: One of the profoundly universal facts of human life is that people get sick. Most modern societies have established a complex system of health care to disseminate medical treatments. Doctors, nurses, hospitals, pharmacies, drug and medical equipment manufacturers, patients, and others all play an active role in the health care institution.

Social institutions are highly interrelated. For instance, although much dissemination of information occurs in the schools, families and churches still play a major role in "teaching" society's members how to get along. Debates over the state of the American health care system make people aware of its links to the economy and politics. Similarly, the family is intimately bound to economic, political, educational, and religious spheres.

To individual members of society, institutions appear to be natural and inevitable. Most of us could not imagine what life would be like without a family. Nor could we fathom what society would be like without a uniform way of establishing governments, a common currency, or a system of schools to educate our children. It is very easy, then, to think that institutions exist independently of people.

We each have a role to play, however, in maintaining or changing social institutions. For instance, in a few years Europe plans to adopt a common form of currency. In the process, many European countries will undergo significant alterations in their economic systems. Travel and trade between and within these countries, as well as the behavior of individual consumers, will surely take on a different look. Although the effects of these changes will be felt on an international level, they are ultimately initiated, implemented, and, most important, experienced by individual people.

Culture

The most ubiquitous element of society is **culture**, which consists of the language, values, beliefs, rules, behaviors, and physical artifacts of a society. Think of it as society's "personality." Culture gives us codes of conduct—the proper, acceptable ways of doing things. We usually don't think twice about it, yet it colors everything we experience.

Culture is particularly apparent when it is questioned or violated. Those who do not believe what the majority believes, value what the majority values, or obey the same rules the majority obeys are likely to elicit reactions from others in the form of punishment, treatment, or social ostracism. (I will discuss the power of culture in more detail in chapter 4.) Two key aspects of culture are thoroughly implicated in institutional, organizational, group, and individual behavior: values and norms.

Values

Perhaps no word in the English language carries more political baggage than *values*. Terms like *moral values, traditional values,* and *homespun American values* are bandied about unthinkingly. Sociologically speaking, a **value** is a standard of judgment by which people decide on desirable goals and outcomes (Hewitt & Hewitt, 1986). Values justify the social rules that determine how we ought to behave. For instance, the law against murder clearly reflects the value we place on human life. Success, independence, efficiency, and equality are seen as important values in this society because they represent general criteria on which our lives and the lives of others can be judged.

Values often come into conflict. The value of privacy ("stay out of other people's business") and the value of generosity ("help others in need") may clash when you are trying to decide whether to help someone who appears to need assistance. Similarly, although the value of cooperation is held in high esteem in this society, when you're taking a final exam in your sociology class, cooperation is likely to be defined as cheating. Sometimes the key values that characterize a particular social institution can come into conflict, causing widespread legal and moral uncertainty among individuals.

■ ■ ■ ■ ■ ■ ■ ■

MICRO-MACRO CONNECTION
Family Privacy and Parental Rights

One such dilemma involves "family values," a vague buzz phrase used by crafty politicians for some time. During the last three presidential campaigns, debate over this term moved to the center stage of national politics, despite the fact that no one could define what it meant.

Although politicians may use the term ambiguously, sociologists are more likely to specify the values that pervade the institution of the family. As we look more closely into this area, we find serious contradictions. One "family value" that has always existed in some form is the ideal of family **autonomy** or privacy. American life is built on the assumption that what a family does in the privacy of its home is its own business. Whether members are treated lovingly or abusively has traditionally been left to the discretion of family members (see chapter 8).

The development of the ideal of family autonomy probably coincided, historically, with the separation of home and work and the growth of cities during the late 19th century (Parsons, 1971). The separation of home from public life reflected not only a growing set of new economic values but also a technological shift toward self-sufficiency (Skolnick, 1987). Such products as the television, telephone, refrigerator, air conditioner, backyard swimming pool, and more recently, the VCR, personal computer, and home shopping network have all increased the privacy and isolation of the American household. Our need to leave home for entertainment, goods, or services has been considerably reduced. The institution of family has become increasingly self-contained.

The large-scale commitment to the value of family autonomy has not been without its problems, however. The negative effects of too much privacy are only beginning to be realized. The value we place on the welfare of children has come into direct conflict with the value of family autonomy. At what point should a state agency intervene and violate the privacy of the family in order to protect the welfare of a child? When, if ever, should the sanctity of the family be sacrificed in the interests of saving a child from potential physical harm? Does it better serve society's interests to protect family autonomy or to protect children?

In 1986 a 3-year-old child named Eli Creekmore was beaten and killed by his father in Everett, Washington. This tragic incident is not unique; thousands of children die at the hands of their parents each year in this country. What made this case particularly disturbing was that the child had been removed from his family because of documented child abuse and placed in foster care on two separate occasions prior to his death. Both times he was sent back home. On each occasion it was determined that, in the interests of protecting the family's right to remain intact and autonomous, the child should be returned to his parents. The case exposed a glaring oversight in many child abuse laws: They are written to protect the rights of parents and the sanctity of the family and not necessarily to protect the welfare of individual children.

We're horrified at the thought of a parent beating his or her child to the point of injury or death. But we're more horrified, it seems, at the thought of the state intervening in the private affairs of families. Since the value placed on privacy *defines* the American way of life, the infliction of severe physical punishment on children by their parents has become an issue of privacy, not an issue of violence. From a sociological perspective, injuring children is simply the extreme outcome of the widely practiced and accepted belief that parents have the right to punish their children as they see fit. A bill, "The Parental Rights and Responsibilities Act," was introduced in Congress in 1996 that would forbid state and local governments from "interfering with or usurping the right of a parent" to direct the upbringing of a child.

Ironically, state intervention in family life is considered appropriate, even necessary, in other situations. For instance, the state is more likely to violate the autonomy of a family when that family's religious or cultural beliefs and values conflict with those of the larger society. In 1990 a Christian Science couple from

Massachusetts was convicted of involuntary manslaughter for refusing medical care for their 2-year-old son, who later died of an obstructed bowel (Margolick, 1990). Similarly, in 1995, an Anderson, Indiana, couple who postponed medical treatment for their 6-year-old son because of their religious beliefs was charged with homicide and neglect of a dependent when he died of streptococcus pneumonia meningitis. The parents are nondenominational Christians who don't attend a church and who choose home-schooling for their children (Labalme, 1995).

In 1996, the U.S. Supreme Court let stand a ruling by the Minnesota Court of Appeals that awarded $1.5 million to the father of an 11-year-old boy who died after his mother, stepfather, and two Christian Science practitioners tried to use prayer to heal his diabetes. In its ruling, the Court stated, "Although one is free to believe what one will, religious freedom ends when one's conduct offends the law by, for example, endangering a child's life" (Greenhouse, 1996a, p. A12).

In addition, concern over increases in juvenile violence have led some cities and states to enact laws that make parents legally responsible for the misbehavior of their children (Applebome, 1996a). In West Virginia, for example, parents of a child caught defacing a public building can be liable for up to $5,000 in fines. In Louisiana, parents can be found guilty of "improper supervision of a minor" and fined up to $1,000 and imprisoned for up to 6 months if their child associates with a convicted felon, drug dealer, or members of a street gang. Implicit in such laws is the belief that parents must be forced, under threat of punishment by the state, to take a more active role in the upbringing of their children.

All of the cases described here illustrate the profound effects of a clash of cultural values on the everyday lives of individuals. Situations like these pit the autonomy of the family against society's institutional responsibility to protect the lives of children or to protect citizens against the threat of crime.

▪ ▪ ▪

Norms

Norms specify what people *should* do and how they should pursue values. Norms are culturally defined rules of conduct. They tell us what is proper or necessary behavior within particular roles, groups, organizations, and institutions. Thousands of norms guide the minute and grand details of our lives, from the classroom to the dining room to the bedroom, from how we should act in elevators to how employees should address their employers.

Norms make our interactions with others reasonably predictable. We know that when we extend a hand to another person, that person will grasp it and a handshake will follow. But what if you held out your hand and didn't know if the other person was going to grab it or spit on it? Norms serve as the fundamental building blocks of social order. Without them, "living with others" in a relatively harmonious way would be utterly impossible (see chapter 4).

Understanding Social Order: Three Perspectives

The question of what holds all these elements of society together and how they combine to create social order has concerned sociologists for many years. Three major theoretical orientations within sociology attempt to address this question: the structural-functionalist perspective, the conflict perspective, and symbolic interactionism. In subsequent chapters I will use all three to examine the relationship between the individual and society.

The Structural-Functionalist Perspective

The structural-functionalist perspective emphasizes how a society is structured to maintain its stability. Society is like an organism. Just as the heart, lungs, and liver work in harmony to keep an animal alive, so too do social institutions work together to keep society alive, maintain social order, and allow us to live together.

According to sociologists Talcott Parsons and Neil Smelser (1956), institutions allow societies to attain national goals, adapt to a changing environment, reduce tension, and recruit individuals into patterned social roles. Economic institutions, for instance, develop ways of adapting to changing physical and human environments, to dwindling supplies of natural resources, or to competition from other societies. Likewise, educational institutions and the family train people for the future roles they will have to play to keep society going. Religions help maintain the existence of society by reaffirming people's core values and maintaining social cohesion (Durkheim, 1915/1954).

Sociologist Robert Merton (1957) distinguishes between manifest and latent societal functions. **Manifest functions** are the intended, obvious consequences of people's activities designed to help some part of the social system. For instance, the manifest function of going to college is to get an education and acquire the credentials necessary to establish a career. **Latent functions** are the *unintended*, sometimes unrecognized, consequences of people's actions that also help the social system. The latent function of going to college is to meet people and establish close, enduring friendships. In addition, college teaches students how to live on their own, away from their parents. It also provides important lessons in negotiating the intricacies of large bureaucracies—registering for classes, filling out forms, learning important school policies—so that students figure out how to "get things done" in an organization. These latent lessons will certainly help students who enter the equally large and bureaucratic world of business after they graduate (Galles, 1989).

From the structural-functionalist perspective, if an aspect of social life does not contribute to society's survival—that is, if it is *dys*-functional—it will soon disappear. Things that persist, even if they seem to be disruptive, must contribute somehow to the survival of society. Take prostitution, for example. A practice so widely condemned and punished would appear to be dysfunctional for society. But prostitution has existed since human civilization began. Functionalists suggest that prostitution satisfies sexual needs that may not be met through more socially acceptable means such as marriage. A customer can have his or her physical needs satisfied without having to establish the sort of emotional attachment to another person that would destroy marriages, harm the institution of the family, and ultimately threaten the entire society (K. Davis, 1937).

The Conflict Perspective

Structural-functionalism was the dominant theoretical tradition in sociology for most of the 20th century. But it has been criticized for focusing on the systematic usefulness of social arrangements without examining how those arrangements are created and maintained. According to the conflict perspective, some groups benefit more from existing arrangements than other groups.

Conflict sociologists see society not in terms of stability and agreement but in terms of conflict and struggle. They focus not on how all the elements of society contribute to its smooth operation and continued existence but on how these elements promote divisions and inequalities between groups. Social order, then, arises not from the societal pursuit of harmony but from dominance and coercion. The family, government, religion, and other institutions foster and legitimate the power and privilege of some individuals or groups at the expense of others.

Karl Marx, perhaps the most famous conflict theorist, focused exclusively on economic arrangements. He argued that the foundations of all human societies are based on the ways those societies develop their primary mode of material production. The individuals or groups who control the means of production—land in an agricultural society, factories in an industrial one—have the power to create and maintain social institutions that serve their interests. Hence, economic, political, and educational systems in a modern society support the interests of those who control the wealth (see chapter 10).

Marx believed that conflict between the "haves" and the "have-nots" is inevitable and creates a situation in which social order must be enforced by those in power. He said that this conflict is not caused by greedy, exploitive individuals; rather, it is a by-product of a system in which those who benefit from structured inequality are likely to act in ways that maintain it.

Contemporary conflict sociologists are interested in various sources of conflict and inequality. Feminist theorists, for instance, focus on gender as the most important source of conflict and inequality in social life. Compared with men, women have less power, influence, and opportunity. But as women seek equality in education, politics, career, marriage, and other areas of social life, they inevitably affect society (see chapter 13 for more detail). Feminist theory enables us to understand the difficulties men and women face in their everyday lives as they experience the changes taking place in our social institutions.

Symbolic Interactionism

The structural-functionalist and the conflict perspectives differ in their assumptions about the nature of society, yet both analyze society mostly at the macro, or structural, level, focusing on societal patterns and the consequences they produce. In contrast, symbolic interactionism attempts to understand society and social structure through an examination of the micro-level, personal, day-to-day interactions of people as individuals, pairs, or groups.

These forms of interaction take place within a world of symbolic communication. The symbols we use—language, gestures, posture, and so on—are influenced by the larger context of a group or society (see chapter 5). Society would be utterly unmanageable if we didn't share a language or agree on what certain gestures meant. But the agreement is never complete. When we interact with others, we constantly attempt to interpret what they mean and what they're up to. Most human behavior, then, is determined not by the objective facts of a given situation but by the subjective meanings people attach to it (Weber, 1947). A gentle pat on the head means one thing if it comes from someone with whom you are romantically involved but something quite different if it comes from your mother.

Society *emerges* from the countless symbolic interactions that occur each day between individuals. By examining how and why we interact with others, symbolic interactionism reveals how the everyday experiences of people help to construct and maintain social institutions and, ultimately, society itself.

Conclusion

Living with others, within a social structure, influences many aspects of our everyday lives. But we must be cautious not to overstate the case. Although the fundamental elements of society are not merely the direct expressions of the personalities of individuals, we must also remember that people are more than "robots programmed by social structure" (Swanson, 1992).

The lesson I want you to take from this chapter—and, in fact, from this book—is that *the relationship between the individual and society is a reciprocal one.* One cannot be understood without accounting for the other. Yes, "society" touches our lives in intimate, important, and sometimes not altogether obvious ways. And yes, this influence is often beyond our immediate control. But society is not simply a "forbidding prison" that mechanically determines who we are and what we do (Berger, 1963). We as individuals can affect the very social structure that affects us. We can modify role expectations, change norms, create or destroy organizations, revolutionize institutions, and even alter the path of world history.

CHAPTER   HIGHLIGHTS

- Although society exists as an objective fact, it is also a social construction that is created, reaffirmed, and altered through the day-to-day interactions of the very people it influences and controls.
- Humans are social beings. We look to others to help define and interpret particular situations. Other people can influence what we see, feel, think, and do.
- Society consists of socially recognizable combinations of individuals—relationships, groups, and organizations—as well as the products of human action—statuses, roles, culture, and institutions.
- There are three major sociological perspectives. The structural-functionalist perspective focuses on the way various parts of society are structured and interrelated to maintain stability and order. The conflict perspective emphasizes how the various elements of society promote conflict and inequality between groups of people. Symbolic interactionism attempts to understand society and social structure through the interactions of people and the ways in which they subjectively define their worlds.

YOUR   TURN

Alcohol occupies an important but problematic place in American society. We decry its evils, yet we are encouraged to turn to it in times of happiness, sadness, disappointment, anger, and worry.

Behavior "under the influence" is a biological consequence of the presence of alcohol in the body. Among the physical effects are vomiting, hangovers, and liver damage. When a person's blood-alcohol level reaches a certain point, that person will have trouble walking and talking; at a higher level he or she will pass out.

But is the social behavior we come to expect from drunken people reducible to a chemical reaction in the body? The traditional explanation for drunken behavior is that the chemical properties of alcohol do something to the brain that reduces inhibitions. If this were true, though, drunken behavior would look the same everywhere. The fact is, social behavior under the influence of alcohol can vary from culture to culture. The way people handle themselves when drunk "is determined not by alcohol's toxic assault upon the seat of moral judgment, conscience, or the like, but by what their society makes of and imparts to them concerning the state of drunkenness" (MacAndrew & Edgerton, 1969, p. 165).

If you know people who grew up in a different culture (for example, foreign students), ask them how people in their native countries behave when drunk. How do these behaviors differ from those you've observed here? You can also ask people from different races, ages, and social classes the same questions. Are there variations in the "drunken experience" even within this society? What do these differences illustrate about the norms and values of these different groups? Have them describe their first drunken experience. Are there similarities or differences in how people are introduced to alcohol?

You might also want to ask some young children to describe how drunk people act. Are there any similarities in the images they have of drunkenness? Where do you think their ideas about alcohol come from?

Use the results of these interviews to examine the role of social and societal influence on people's personal lives. Can your conclusions be expanded to other private phenomena, such as sexual activity or religious experiences?

THE OLD BALL GAME

DOUGLAS HARPER

"…sociology inspires us to see social action from the point of view of the actor. Consider the pitcher, catcher, and batter from this perspective…."

This visual essay tackles the dual themes of "private lives in a social world" and "seeing and thinking sociologically" through the metaphor of professional baseball. The purpose of the essay is to help you see the individual in social structural terms as a member of a culture and as a creator of social life.

Most of us don't normally think of something like baseball in any of these sociological frames; we interpret the world in terms of our own experience. In addition, we "see" photographic and other images in terms that our culture has established and that we have unconsciously internalized.

To be an audience member, for example, is to experience the world both as an individual and as a member of society. This is made more complicated by the fact that there are at least two forms of the baseball audience experience: attending a game in a stadium and viewing the game on television.

If we attend a game, we must construct the audience experience by ourselves. If we are knowledgeable, we watch carefully; perhaps we keep inning-by-inning records, using the arcane symbols of scoring. We understand and enjoy the slow pace of the game as well as the moments of heightened tension and release.

There are, as well, repeated events—called *rituals* in sociological circles—that define the audience experience at the park. Some are specific to an

The boy (or girl) at the game is the means by which a new generation of fans is created. The father (or mother) tries to import his (or her) excitement of the game but is seldom successful. The world of the child can never be fully understood. That baseball, with its slow pace and intricate rules, can be loved by children is itself mysterious. But at every game the children are there.

43

To be a fan at a game is to be involved in one of the few experiences of mass participation left in our culture. There are ironies; for example, the "best" seats—those closest to the field of play—show dramatic details but not the overview. Fans in the cheapest seats also tend to talk to one another and to use one another as entertainment. Each stadium has its particular fan culture. Here at Yankee Stadium, the fans take particular delight in booing the misplays or failed opportunities of their heroes. Because even the best hitters get a hit only one-third of the times at bat, the game provides many opportunities for such fan expression!

individual park; for example, at Yankee stadium the groundskeepers groom the infield while marching in unison to the song "YMCA." Other rituals are universal: Halfway through the seventh inning, in all professional baseball games in America, the crowd stands and sings "Take Me Out to the Ballgame." Like all rituals, it connects the individual with the history of baseball and all viewers who have attended ballgames before. These rituals help define what it means to be an "audience."

If we watch the game on television, TV personalities provide a narrative structure for the game. We are given a range of things to think about; in other words we are told "how to be an audience." The between-inning breaks are filled with commercials (the sponsors hope to convince us to define ourselves as consumers of their products as well as consumers of baseball), and often TV viewers miss the opening moments of each inning so the commercial can be completed. The photographic style used to videotape the game (especially the close-up) emphasizes the individual players and their accomplishments. Thus in watching baseball on TV, we do not see the overview of the game or the participation of several players in most plays.

The baseball game itself seems suspended in time and place. We forget that the action of any individual player is part of a long history, played out in the context of other, larger historical patterns.

Ushers guard the expensive seats from fans with tickets for cheaper seats. But for an hour before the game, fans are allowed to enter the area closest to the field of play, to observe the players practicing and warming up. The fans call greetings and good wishes to their heroes, who seldom look up as they trot toward the dugout. Sometimes, though, a player will toss a ball to a fan. Even more rarely, the players enter the small area where the fan and player spaces intersect—the end of the dugout (see bottom photo, right side)—to sign autographs.

These three images (above and on facing page) were taken from roughly the same vantage point (although in two different parks) but with different camera lenses. The perspectives created by these lenses may be viewed as metaphors for different sociological perspectives.

The photo above represents the "micro" view of social interaction. The photo shows details of a small event: batter and catcher awaiting the ball, with the umpire in judgment. The batter wants to whack it into the outfield; the catcher wants the ball in his mitt after crossing the strike zone. As in many social circumstances (for example, the salesperson and the buyer haggling over the price of a car), the two individuals work closely together to reach different ends. The umpire represents the element of social control, always physically present or imagined.

The top photo on the facing page represents what sociologists call "middle-range" theory. We see the same elements—batter, catcher, and umpire (the batter has let a ball through and hopes the umpire will call it a "ball")—viewed from a wider context, but still not the context of the whole game. We see other social actors—first baseman, runner, first base coach, and another umpire—who are aligning their actions in consort with those of the pitcher, batter, and catcher. We even note an example of norms that violate rules: The first base coach is supposed to stand within the outlined rectangle but typically stands just a few feet outside its border. Middle-range theory seeks explanation of social phenomena at a higher order than interaction but lower than that of the whole system.

The bottom photo on the facing page represents, in our scheme, the structural view. Here the entire game is revealed; we see all the players in relationship to one another. We see the setting of the game (a park) and many of the elements (such as fans and advertisements) that give the game a larger meaning. But it is easy to see that even this photograph does not provide a complete view of the baseball game.

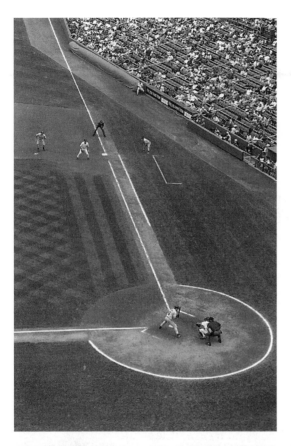

For example, sports are now one of the most integrated aspects of American life. Yet we must recall that although black and white Americans played together on professional baseball teams in the late nineteenth century, the game was segregated by vote of a majority of team owners in 1889. It was not until 1947 that an African American again played in the majors. This history is a sociological tale of social movements and attitudes, struggle and eventual resolution. Indeed, it parallels patterns of racial segregation and integration in the society but tells its own story as well. Today's players, whether African American, Caucasian, Latin, or Asian, all participate in a social landscape that has been battled over for nearly a hundred years.

Because the televised event emphasizes the individual player-as-hero, we see the individual out of the context of his social organization—the team—which gives his heroic actions meaning. The homerun is exciting to witness, but the sacrifice fly may score a run just as meaningful.

The photos above communicate the role of historical symbols in creating meaning. The top photo depicts a statue of Roberto Clemente, a larger-than-life player
for the Pittsburgh Pirates, who played the game like few before him and who
died tragically on an aid mission to Central America. We see fans using the
sculpture for several purposes. For some it is a bench; for others, a point of
nterest; and for still others, we can assume, it is a focal point for their reverence.

The bottom photo is an odd neon sign in a small hallway in Yankee Stadium.
It draws upon a familiar baseball icon—the Great Bambino socking in a homerun—and places it in relationship to the familiar symbols of the Yankees. In
other words, this sign reminds all viewers that the greatest player of all time was,
indeed, a Yankee.

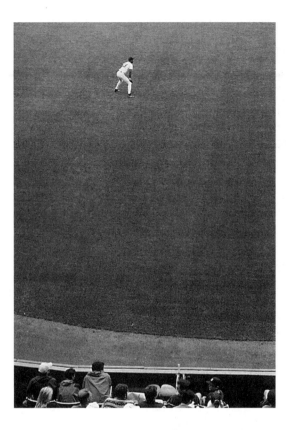

This photo combines several ideas. It suggests a different way to see the player on the field; it shows how photography may lead to new sociological perspectives. The lonely figure in left field is Darryl Strawberry, a player with extraordinary potential whose personal problems have always kept him from the achievements many think should have come easily. He stands alone on the field the way any famous person stands before the public—with little relief from view, with few places to call private. The foreground of this photo reminds us that the fans constitute the basis of this person's entire work world and identity.

Thinking about sociology in this way makes it clear that no single perspective tells the whole story, just as no single photograph by itself reveals the essence of baseball. Each contributes a perspective that, when combined with others, leads to fuller understanding and appreciation.

Finally, sociology inspires us to see social action from the point of view of the actor. Consider the pitcher, catcher, and batter from this perspective. The batter tries to put himself into the mind of the pitcher (and the catcher, who usually directs the pitcher). He guesses fastball high and inside, and if the pitcher throws that pitch, the batter will probably hit it well. Then the sequence begins, like the game of "paper, scissors, stone." Pitcher and hitter try to outguess each other; sometimes as many as twenty pitches are fouled off as the game continues between the two. A player who is routinely successful is likely able to put himself successfully behind the eyes of his opponent, able to predict his next move. To understand the micro dimensions of the sociology of baseball would be to deconstruct this endlessly repeated mental duel.

I photographed baseball for this essay in several parks. I tried to see through the lens as a sociologist rather than as a typical spectator. The photographs show how the stadium recreates heroic myths (see the sculpture of Roberto Clemente at Three Rivers Stadium), and they show some of the background work that makes the game happen. During the lengthy warm-up the players put their muscles and minds in tune and focus their attention on the game ahead. This is also a time in which the most dedicated fans cluster around the dugout, hoping for some interaction with their heroes.

I have photographed the game with several camera lenses, which illuminate some of the issues raised in this essay. The wide-angle lens shows the whole park and the relationship of the players to one another. Telephoto lenses, more common in sports photography, isolate the individuals and concentrate our attention on dramatic moments.

I have also photographed the game from several vantage points—from ground level to the highest reaches of the stands. These camera angles are like the perspectives of sociology—from the intimate look at social interaction to the study of the structure of society.

This visual essay is simply an exercise, for me a pleasure to once again meld my sociological and personal lives.

II

The Construction of Self and Society

Part II examines the architecture of individuals and society: how reality and truth are constructed; how social order is created and maintained; how culture and history influence our personal experiences; how societal values, ideals, and norms are instilled; and how we acquire our sense of self. The tactical and strategic ways in which we present images of ourselves to others are also addressed. You will see how we define "acceptable" behavior and how we respond to those who "break the rules." The section closes with a look into how we form relationships and interact within groups.

CHAPTER 3

Building Reality: The Social Construction of Knowledge

- *Understanding the Social Construction of Reality*
- *Laying the Foundation: The Bases of Reality*
- *Building the Walls: Conflict, Power, and Social Institutions*
- *Appreciating the Art of Social Research*

The year was 1897. Eight-year-old Virginia O'Hanlon became upset when her friends told her there was no Santa Claus. Her father encouraged her to write a letter to the *New York Sun* to find out the truth. The editor's reply—which included the now famous phrase "Yes, Virginia, there is a Santa Claus!"—has become a classic piece of American folklore. "Nobody sees Santa Claus," the editor wrote, "but that is no sign that there is no Santa Claus. The most real things in the world are those that neither children nor men [*sic*] can see" ("Is there a Santa Claus?" 1897).

In his book *Encounters with the Archdruid*, John McPhee (1971) examines the life and ideas of David Brower, one of America's most successful and energetic environmentalists. McPhee recalls a lecture in which Brower claimed that the United States has 6% of the world's population and uses 60% of the world's resources; and that only 1% of Americans use 60% of those resources. Afterward McPhee asked Brower where he got this interesting statistic:

> Brower said the figures had been worked out in the head of a friend of his from data assembled "to the best of his recollection." . . . [He] assured me that figures in themselves are merely indices. *What matters is that they feel right* [emphasis added]. Brower feels things. (p. 86)

What do these two very different examples have in common? Both reflect the fickle nature of "truth" and "reality." Young Virginia is encouraged to believe in the reality of something she cannot and will never perceive with her senses. She will certainly learn a different sort of truth about Santa Claus when she gets older, but for now she is urged to take on faith that Santa Claus, or at least the idea of Santa Claus, exists despite the lack of objective proof. Likewise, David Brower is urging people to believe in something that doesn't need to be seen.

What's important is that the information "feels right," that it helps one's cause even if it is not based on hard evidence.

Such precarious uses of truth might appear foolish or deceitful. Yet much of our everyday knowledge is based on accepting as real the existence of things that can't be seen, touched, or proved—"the world taken-for-granted" (Berger, 1963, p. 147). Like Virginia, we learn to accept the existence of things like electrons, the ozone layer, love, and God, even though we cannot see them. And like David Brower, we learn to believe and use facts and figures provided by "experts" as long as they sound right or support our interests.

How do we come to know what we know? How do we learn what is real and what isn't? In this chapter I examine how sociologists discover truths about human life. But to provide the appropriate context, I must first present a sociological perspective on the nature of reality. How do individuals construct their realities? How do societal forces influence the process?

Understanding the Social Construction of Reality

In the previous chapter you learned that culture, social roles, groups, organizations, and institutions are human creations that provide structure to our everyday lives. These elements of society give us a distinctive lens through which we perceive the world. African Americans, for instance, are likely to see our criminal justice system as less "just" than whites do. In the U.S. labor market, men still are likely to see open career paths where women see restricted roads. Because of their respective occupational training, an architect, a real estate agent, a police officer, and a firefighter can each look at the same building and see different things: "a beautiful example of Victorian architecture," "a moderately priced fixer-upper," "an insecure house," or "a fire hazard."

What we know to be true or real is always a product of the culture and historical period in which we exist. In some cultures the existence of spirits, witches, and demons is a taken-for-granted part of everyday reality. It is hard for us to imagine that what we "know" today—the laws of nature, the causes of certain diseases, and so forth—may not be true for everyone everywhere or may be replaced by different truths tomorrow (Babbie, 1986). Think of all the people who once took for granted that the earth was flat or that cigarette smoking was harmless. Quite possibly people 50 years from now will look back at the end of the 20th century and regard some of our absolute truths to be mistaken, misguided, or downright laughable.

The process through which facts, knowledge, truth, and so on are discovered, made known, reaffirmed, and altered by the members of a society is called the **social construction of reality** (Berger & Luckmann, 1966). This construction starts with the simple foundation of knowledge as a human creation. However, most of us live our lives from a different assumption—that of an objective reality, independent of us. We assume that this reality is shared by others and can be taken for granted as reality (Lindesmith, Strauss, & Denzin, 1991). Trees and buildings don't exist only in our imagination.

Yet there are times when what we define as real seems to have nothing to do with what our senses tell us is real. Picture a 5-year-old child who wakes up in the middle of the night screaming that monsters are under her bed. Her parents comfort her by saying, "There aren't any monsters. You had a nightmare. It's just your imagination." The next day the child comes down with the flu. The child wants to know why she is sick. The parents respond by saying, "You've caught a virus, a bug." "A bug? You mean like an ant or a beetle?" "No. It's the sort of bug you can't see . . . but it's there." Granted, viruses can be seen and verified with the proper equipment, but without access to such equipment the child simply takes the parents' word for it. In fact, most of us accept the reality of viruses without ever having seen them for ourselves. The child learns to accept the authoritative claims of her parents that something that was "seen" is not real, while something that was not seen is real.

Hence, reality may be more a matter of agreement than it is something inherent in the natural world. Sociologists, particularly symbolic interactionists and conflict theorists, strive to explain the social construction of reality in terms of both its causes and its consequences. Their insights help explain many of the phenomena that influence our daily lives.

Laying the Foundation: The Bases of Reality

Symbolic interactionists believe that people's actions toward one another and interpretations of situations are based on their definitions of reality, which are in turn learned from interactions with those around them. What we know to be real we share with other members of our culture. Imagine how difficult it would be to believe in something no one else believed in. Psychiatrists use terms like *hallucination* and *delusion* to describe things experienced by people who see, hear, or believe things others don't. Let's take a closer look at the process by which reality is created both individually and culturally.

Stages of Reality Construction

According to some symbolic interactionists, reality is developed in three stages: externalization, objectivation, and internalization (Berger & Luckmann, 1966). Thinking in terms of stages does not imply that the creation of reality occurs in a neat progression. Instead, the stages provide a general understanding of how the knowledge that guides our conduct is established and how it becomes a part of culture and common sense.

Externalization

The stage at which people construct a piece of cultural knowledge about some aspect of the world is called **externalization**. The process may be formal, as when sociologists develop systematic "theories" to explain a social phenomenon. Or it may be informal, as when someone suggests an explanation for why people act the way they do.

Think of externalization as a sort of "fact marketing" by which certain people try to "sell" a particular explanation to the rest of us. They publish, broadcast, or explain ideas, giving the ideas a form that the rest of us can understand. For instance, until the late 18th century drunkenness was commonly associated with demonic possession, weak will, or sin (Conrad & Schneider, 1980). Today, alcoholism is recognized as a disease by the medical community and the general public. This shift in knowledge didn't occur on its own. Real people—physicians, psychiatrists, and scholars—offered enough compelling theories and evidence about the nature of chronic drunkenness that the public was eventually swayed to look at things their way.

Within academic disciplines like sociology, externalized explanations for social events are usually subjected to logical scrutiny and research to determine their validity. In everyday life, however, they may be accepted as "the way things are" simply because of the perceived expertise, insight, or authority of the individual providing the information. The important point about externalization is that the ideas about why certain things happen are fashioned by human beings.

Objectivation

Externalization leads to the second and most crucial stage of reality construction. **Objectivation** occurs when the "facts" that were originally someone's ideas, speculations, or theories take on an objective reality of their own, independent of the people who first created (externalized) them (Berger & Luckmann, 1966). It has become a self-evident "fact" in the minds of most Americans that alcoholism is, and always was, an illness. As this fact becomes part of the public consciousness and is given life and reinforced in day-to-day conversation, we collectively forget that somebody or some group initially thought it up. The idea becomes a reality that has always existed but was just waiting to be discovered. It becomes what "everybody knows" to be true.

The problem, however, is that ideas are sometimes communicated, externalized, and accepted as truth by the public without any connection between the objectified knowledge and hard facts. We have all heard the stories of Halloween trick-or-treaters receiving apples filled with razor blades or candy mixed with pins. Each year parents are warned not to let their children eat anything that is unwrapped or homemade. Schools train children to inspect treats for signs of tampering. In some cities hospitals, police stations, and other municipal offices make themselves available to examine candy free of charge. California and New Jersey have passed specific laws against food tampering, and some communities have tried to ban trick-or-treating. A 1985 ABC News/*Washington Post* poll found that 60% of parents who planned to allow their children to go trick-or-treating were afraid of tainted candy. "Halloween sadism" has altered the meaning of Halloween and become a symbol for all that is wrong with today's society.

The hard facts are, however, that only two child deaths have been attributed to Halloween sadism. In both these cases the treats were tainted by members of the child's family. Further investigations have concluded that the vast majority of reports have been hoaxes (J. Best, 1990). We are left with an objectified reality that has become an established part of our culture with little if any verifiable support.

Sometimes inaccurate social research becomes objectified, exerting a powerful impact on the entire society. In the mid-1980s the preliminary findings of a study seemed to forecast a dramatic decline in the marriage prospects of well-educated women in their 30s (Bennett, Bloom, & Craig, 1986). The researchers pointed out that women who graduated from college were less likely to marry than women who never attended college. Because the number of women entering college was increasing, the proportion of women who would never marry would also rise. *Newsweek* ran a story—complete with an ominous, plummeting graph on the cover—declaring that successful single women in their 30s had only a 5% chance of ever getting married. By 40 their chances were 1%, meaning that, statistically, they were more likely "to be killed by a terrorist than find a husband." *Newsweek* said the figures "confirmed what everyone expected all along: that many women who seem to have it all . . . will never have mates" (Salholz, 1986, p. 55).

These statistics quickly entered the public consciousness and became objectified reality. *People* magazine ran a story about famous women in their 40s who were still single, further perpetuating the perceived validity of this "cultural fact." Television talk shows dealt with the "stark reality" of grim marriage prospects as if they'd discovered a new terminal illness. Supermarkets across the country began offering "singles nights" in an attempt to reverse the statistical trend.

Unfortunately, the statistics may not have been accurate. Other researchers have reported that college-educated women in their 30s have a 32% to 41% chance, and a 40-year-old has a 17% to 23% chance, of marrying (Moorman, 1987). The original researchers even removed the questionable statistics from the journal article they eventually published.

Nevertheless, in the process of objectifying this distorted piece of information, the study was reaffirming a cultural value—that being married and having a satisfying family life were still essential to personal fulfillment for women who established and maintained successful careers.

Internalization

The process through which people learn the objectified "facts" of a culture and make them a part of their own internal consciousness is **internalization.** Through the ordinary process of socialization (covered in depth in chapter 5), children acquire knowledge without personally going through externalization and objectivation. But to a child who hasn't yet been fully "socialized," certain "facts" about the world that are taken for granted by adults make little sense. We can sometimes glimpse the extent to which we have internalized a certain reality by observing children's thought patterns.

For instance, one study examined the reading tests used by the state of California, which presented a word and a series of three pictures (Mehan & Wood, 1975). Children taking the tests were told to mark the picture that "goes best" with the word. In one item, the word *fly* was followed by pictures of an elephant, a bird, and a dog. Many of the first-grade children marked the picture of the elephant. From an internalized, socially agreed-upon reality, they were clearly wrong. But their answers made perfect sense from the children's perspective: They were all familiar with the Disney character Dumbo, the flying elephant. What was considered incorrect and a sign of incompetence from one perspective could be seen as accurate, even insightful, from another.

The social construction of reality is a process by which human-created ideas become so firmly accepted that to deny them is to deny common sense. We play by the rules so diligently and faithfully that we cannot imagine otherwise.

The Shape of Reality: Culture and Language

We live in a symbolic world and interact through symbolic communication—that is, through language. Language makes people, events, and ideas meaningful. In fact, reality is often determined by the language we speak (Sapir, 1949; Whorf, 1956). The use of words reinforces prevailing ideas and suppresses conflicting ideas about the world.

For instance, all human beings with normal eyesight see the same colors, because all colors exist in the physical world. Color consists of visible wavelengths that blend imperceptibly into one another (Farb, 1983). There are no sharp breaks in the color spectrum that distinguish, say, red from orange. But when we Americans look at a rainbow we see six different colors: red, orange, yellow, green, blue, and purple. Not everyone in the world sees those same colors, though. People who speak non–European-related languages have different ways of partitioning the color spectrum. The Shona of Zimbabwe divide the spectrum into three colors: *cipsuka,* a bluish purple and a reddish orange; *citema*, a greenish blue; and *cicena*, a yellowish green. The Bassa of Liberia have only two color categories: *ziza,* or purplish blue-green, and *hui,* or yellowish red-orange (Gleason, 1961). These basic categories provide convenient labels from which people of

Figure 3.1   *Cross-Cultural Differences in Color Terms*

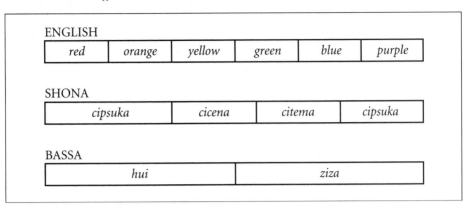

Source: Farb, 1983.

these cultures can describe variants of color. When a Shona says "citema," others know immediately that she is referring to a greenish blue. For the Bassa, purple, blue, and green are different shades of *ziza*, just as pink is a shade of red in English (see Figure 3.1).

Language also reflects the phenomena that have practical significance for a culture. The Solomon Islanders have nine distinct words for "coconut," each specifying an important stage of growth, but they have only one word for all the meals of the day (M. M. Lewis, 1948). The Aleut Eskimos have 33 words for "snow" that allow them to distinguish differences in texture, temperature, weight, load-carrying capacity, and the speed at which a sled can run on its surface (E. T. Hiller, 1933). In Arabic there are approximately 6,000 words that denote the different shapes, functions, degrees of lineage, and attributes of a camel.

Much can be learned about a culture by looking at the categories and linguistic distinctions it makes for certain phenomena. Words reflect aspects of the world that are relevant and meaningful to people's lives. Think of all the English terms for one of the most important elements of our culture: *bucks, moolah, dough, boodle, dollars, sawbucks, C-spot, ten-spot, bills, greenbacks, bones, cash, scratch, long greens, simoleons, beans, dinero*. Then there are all the places where we can put our money: t-bills, certificates of deposit, money market funds, mutual funds, individual retirement accounts.

Some anthropologists (for example, Whorf, 1956), point out that as people learn new languages they come to think differently and therefore perceive reality differently. A fascinating study carried out over 30 years ago illustrates how perceptions of reality can change as language changes. Anthropologist Susan Ervin-Tripp (1964) used as her subjects bilingual Japanese women living in San Francisco who had married American servicemen. The women spoke English with their husbands and children and Japanese with their Japanese friends. A bilingual interviewer carried on two discussions with each subject, one in English and one in Japanese. The two conversations were identical—same location, same interviewer, same topics. The only difference was the language used. Ervin-Tripp found that the attitudes of the women changed when the language changed. In the English conversations, they saw things from a distinctly American perspective—the importance of independence, material wealth, and individual achievement. When speaking Japanese, however, their attitudes reflected the more traditional Japanese approach to life, which stresses community and family obligations. In the following example, one woman completed the same sentences in different ways:

"When my wishes conflict with my family's . . .
. . . it is a time of great unhappiness." (Japanese)
. . . I do what I want." (English)

"I will probably become . . .
. . . a housewife." (Japanese)
. . . a teacher." (English)

"Real friends should . . .
. . . help each other." (Japanese)
. . . be very frank." (English)

Such discrepancies did not occur when subjects were interviewed in English but instructed to give responses typical of Japanese culture. Ervin-Tripp reported that these women became significantly "less Japanese" when they spoke English.

In addition to affecting perceptions of reality, language influences group identity and, consequently, our attitudes toward specific problems and processes (Sapir, 1929). The specialized language of a profession or other group, known as *jargon*, allows members to communicate with one another clearly and quickly. Surfers and cross-country skiers have a specialized vocabulary (not understandable to most nonsurfers or nonskiers) through which they can efficiently convey information about ocean or snow conditions to others. At the same time jargon can sometimes create boundaries and therefore mystify and conceal meaning from outsiders (Farb, 1983). For instance, by using esoteric medical terminology when discussing a case in front of a patient, physicians define the parameters of their "in-group" and reinforce their image as highly trained experts.

Language is sometimes used to purposely deceive. A *euphemism* is an inoffensive expression that is substituted for one that may be offensive. On the surface such terms are used in the interests of politeness and good taste, like saying "perspiration" instead of "sweat." However, euphemisms shape perceptions. Political regimes routinely use them to cover up, distort, or frame their actions in a more positive light. Here are a few examples of euphemisms, followed by their real meanings:

- *opposition research*—digging up dirt on an opposing candidate during an election
- *plausible deniability*—engaging in an illegal or unethical act in a way that enables one's superior to claim a lack of knowledge of the act
- *collateral damage*—civilian deaths during military combat
- *peacekeeper*—MX missile
- *ethnic cleansing*—deportation and massacre of Bosnians by Serbs in Bosnia-Herzegovina
- *tactical redeployment*—retreat during battle
- *economically nonaffluent*—poor
- *revenue enhancement*—tax increase
- *deselected, involuntarily separated, downsized, non-retained, vocationally relocated,* or *de-hired*—fired

Language helps frame or structure social reality and give it meaning. Language also provides people with a cultural and group identity. If you've ever spent a significant amount of time in a foreign country or moved to a new school you know that you cannot be a fully participating member of a group or a culture until you share its language.

Definition of the Situation

We do not respond directly and automatically to objects and situations; instead, we use language to define and interpret them and then act on the basis of those interpretations. Definitions of situations, however, need not coincide with objective reality. As discussed in chapter 2, a person will respond to an emergency situation only if he or she interprets it as such.

If you believe a person is cold and unfriendly, you will act accordingly toward that person whether or not he or she *really is* cold and unfriendly. During the Cold War many Americans saw the Soviet Union as the enemy and the Soviet people as evil and threatening. Today, the Soviet Union no longer exists and its people—the same people we once considered evil—are no longer perceived as a threat. Whether they were ever truly a threat is significantly less important than our collective definition of them as such.

■ ■ ■ ■ ■ ■ ■ ■

HAROLD GARFINKEL

Putting Meaning into Meaningless Situations

People often go to great lengths to establish and preserve meaning, even in situations that may in fact be meaningless (Watzlawick, 1976; McHugh, 1968). Sociologist Harold Garfinkel (1967) designed an experiment in which subjects were led to believe they were taking part in a study of a new approach to counseling.

Each subject was paired with a person who was portrayed as a trainee counselor. The subject was escorted to a room and told to formulate a series of yes/no questions about a personal problem he or she had. The subject then asked the counselor the questions and received either a "yes" or "no" response. After each response, the subject was instructed to comment privately into a tape recorder about what he or she had learned.

The catch was that the answers provided by the "counselor" were completely random and had nothing at all to do with the question being asked. Some answers were confusing and contradictory. A subject might be told "yes" in response to a question about whether someone in whom she or he had a romantic interest would make a suitable mate. But a short time later, when the subject asked whether to continue dating this person, the answer was no.

Although many subjects expressed tremendous frustration and anger, they kept struggling to find a pattern of meaning in the replies. Some subjects thought the counselor had learned something new about them between the two contradictory replies or had discovered some sort of deeper meaning (Wooton, 1975). If the counselor advised against continuing to date a desirable mate, the subject might have concluded that the counselor was telling him or her to "test" his or her love for the other person. The subjects were always able to come up with a "sensible" explanation for the confusing responses they received.

By showing how people can give meaning to an intrinsically meaningless situation, Garfinkel provided insight into the creation and maintenance of reality in everyday life. One of the taken-for-granted assumptions we make in social interaction is that events are relatively orderly and predictable. Even confusing developments "make sense" on further examination. Once a definition has taken hold in our minds, it often becomes irrefutable.

■ ■ ■

Great Expectations: The Power of Self-Fulfilling Prophecies

By acting on the basis of these definitions of reality, we can often create the very conditions we believe actually exist. A **self-fulfilling prophecy** is an assumption or prediction that, purely as a result of having been made, causes the expected event to occur and thus confirms its own "accuracy" (Merton, 1948; Watzlawick, 1984).

In the late 1970s, newspapers on the West Coast began to publish stories of an impending gasoline shortage. People by the millions, fearful of being caught without fuel, started to hoard gas. Photos of long lines of people waiting hours to fill their tanks and any other receptacle they could find further increased the sense of panic and urgency. As a result, the gasoline reserves—which turned out not to be perilously low in the first place—were severely depleted, thereby bringing about the predicted shortage (Watzlawick, 1984). The mere belief in some version of reality creates expectations that can actually bring about a reality that never existed.

Self-fulfilling prophecies can often affect people physically. For years doctors have recognized the "placebo" effect—the tendency for patients to improve because they believe they will. Anthropologists have known for years about the inverse of the placebo effect, the creation of expectancies that make people worse. They have documented numerous mysterious and scientifically difficult-to-explain deaths that follow the pronouncement of curses or evil spells (Watzlawick, 1984). Recently, medical researchers have begun to examine this phenomenon, sometimes referred to as the "nocebo" effect. One study found that heart disease patients who expected their condition to worsen had on average 1.6 times as many episodes of the disease and were 1.5 times as likely to die from it than those patients who had a more positive outlook (cited in Hilts, 1995). In other words, those people who expected to get worse, in many cases, did.

▪ ▪ ▪ ▪ ▪ ▪ ▪ ▪

ROBERT ROSENTHAL AND LENORE JACOBSON
Pygmalion in the Classroom

Self-fulfilling prophecies are particularly powerful when they become an element of social institutions. For instance, Robert Rosenthal and Lenore Jacobson (1968) demonstrated the power of self-fulfilling prophecies in a classroom setting. They had spent much of their careers in education and had become increasingly concerned that teachers' expectations of lower-class and minority children were contributing to the high rates of failure among these students. Such ideas were not without support. In the early 1950s sociologist Howard Becker (1952) found that teachers in slum schools used different teaching techniques and expected less from their students than did teachers in middle-class schools.

Rosenthal and Jacobson's experiment took place in a public elementary school in a predominantly lower-class but not impoverished community. At the beginning of the school year, the researchers gave the students an intelligence test they called "The Harvard Test of Inflected Acquisition." They told the teachers that not only did this test determine intelligence quotients (IQs), but it could also identify those students who would make rapid, above-average intellectual progress in the coming year, whether or not they were currently "good" students.

Before the school year began, teachers received the names of those students who, on the basis of the test, could be expected to perform well. In actuality, Rosenthal and Jacobson randomly picked these names from the class list. The test did not identify "academic spurters" as the teachers were led to believe. Any differences between these children and the rest of the class existed only in the head of the teacher.

A second intelligence test was administered at the end of the year. Those students who had been identified as "academic spurters" showed, on average, an increase of more than 12 points on their IQ scores compared to an increase of 8 points among the rest of the students. The differences were even larger in the

Figure 3.2   *Expectations and Educational Outcomes*

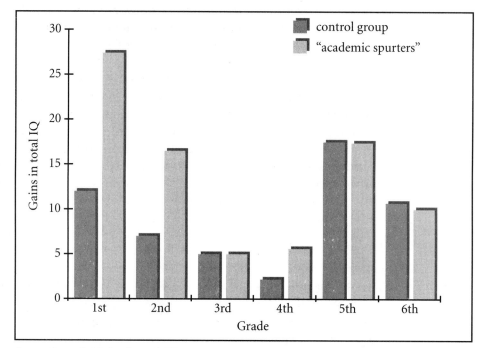

Source: Rosenthal & Jacobson, 1968.

early grades, with almost half of first- and second-grade spurters showing an IQ increase of 20 points or more (see Figure 3.2). Teachers' subjective assessments, such as reading grades, showed similar differences. The teachers also indicated that these special students were better behaved, more intellectually curious, had greater chances for future success, and were friendlier than their nonspecial counterparts.

Rosenthal and Jacobson concluded that a self-fulfilling prophecy was at work. The teachers had subtly and unconsciously encouraged the performance they expected to see. Not only did they spend more time with these students, they were also more enthusiastic about teaching them and unintentionally showed more warmth to them than to the other students. As a result, these students felt more capable and intelligent and performed accordingly.

▪ ▪ ▪

Faith and Incorrigible Propositions

Some features of reality are grounded in physical evidence—fire is hot, sharp things hurt. But, as I mentioned at the beginning of this chapter, reality is often based not on hard evidence but on faith. Have you ever seen a magician saw a person in half and put him or her back together again? Your eyes tell you that this person's body, which was once whole, has now been severed. But your mind tells you that it is impossible for a person to be cut in half and live. You have faith in the fact that what your eyes are seeing is not real but a trick.

You then ask the inevitable question: "How did the magician do it?" In searching for the answer, you are trying to prove that an event you have learned to believe cannot occur was nonexistent, a trick. You are trying to find evidence to reaffirm that your version of reality is right. It's this response that keeps magicians in business. If we all believed that it was possible for people to be cut in half and then put back together, there wouldn't be much interest in magic tricks.

Such assumptions about reality are articles of faith, so dear to us and so important to our lives that when something happens that questions some basic assumption (like an object apparently disappearing into thin air), we are equipped to explain it away. Suppose you leave your house one morning with 75 cents in your pocket. When you arrive at your destination you have only 50 cents. Objectively, 25 cents has disappeared, but you "know better." Even though your eyes tell you that the money has disappeared, you have learned to know that it couldn't possibly have vanished. Rather than abandon that belief, you come up with a series of "reasonable" explanations: "I must have miscounted," "A quarter must have fallen out of my pocket somehow," "Someone picked my pocket." To acknowledge the possibility that the money literally disappeared would be to challenge the reality on which your everyday life is based.

Such an unquestionable assumption, called an **incorrigible proposition,** is a belief that cannot be proved wrong and has become so much a part of common sense that one continues to believe it even in the face of contradictory evidence. By explaining away contradictions with "reasonable" explanations, we strengthen the correctness of the initial premise (Watzlawick, 1976).

Different cultures have different incorrigible propositions. Sociologists Hugh Mehan and Houston Wood (1975) examined the research of the anthropologist E. E. Evans-Pritchard (1937). Evans-Pritchard described an elaborate ritual practiced by the Azande, a small African society located in southwestern Sudan. When faced with important decisions—where to build a house, whom to marry, and so on—the Azande consult an oracle or a high spirit power. They prepare for the consultation by following a strictly prescribed ceremony. A substance is extracted from the bark of a certain type of tree and prepared in a special way during a seancelike ritual. The Azande believe that a powerful spirit enters the potion during this ceremony. They then pose a question to the spirit in such a way that it can be answered either yes or no and feed the substance to a chicken. If the chicken lives, that signals a yes answer from the spirit; if the chicken dies, that means no.

Our Western belief system tells us that the tree bark obviously contains some poisonous chemical. Certain chickens are physically able to survive it, others aren't. But the Azande have no knowledge of the tree's poisonous qualities or of chicken physiology. In fact, they don't believe the tree or the chicken plays a part in the ceremony at all. The ritual that comes from gathering bark and feeding it to a chicken transforms the tree into the spirit power. The chicken lives or dies not because of a physical reaction to a chemical but because the oracle "hears like a person and settles cases like a king" (Evans-Pritchard, 1937, p. 321).

But what if the oracle is wrong? What if an Azande is told by the oracle to build a house by the river and the river overflows its banks, washing away the house? Evans-Pritchard observed several cases of Azande making bad decisions based on incorrect "advice" from the oracle. How can they reconcile these sorts of inconsistencies with a belief in the reality of the oracle?

To us the answer is obvious: There's no spirit, no magic, just the strength of the poison and the health of the chickens. We see these bad decisions as contradictions because we view them from the reality of Western science. We observe this ritual to determine if in fact there is an oracle, and of course we're predisposed to believe there isn't. We are looking for proof of the existence of something of which we are highly skeptical.

For the Azande, though, the contradictions are not contradictions at all. They *know* the oracle exists. This is their fundamental premise, just like our fundamental premise that things don't disappear into thin air or that people can't be sawed in half and put back together again. It is an article of faith that cannot be questioned. All that follows for the Azande is experienced from this initial assumption. The Azande have ways of explaining contradictions to their truths, just as we do. When the oracle fails to provide them with the correct answer, they say, "A taboo must have been breached," or "Sorcerers must have intervened," or "The ceremony wasn't carried out correctly."

Protecting incorrigible propositions is essential for the maintenance of reality systems. By explaining away contradictions we are able to support our original assumptions and live in a coherent and orderly world.

Building the Walls: Conflict, Power, and Social Institutions

We, as individuals, play an important role in coordinating, reproducing, and giving meaning to society in our daily interactions. But our ability to define social reality is limited. We are certainly not completely free to create whatever version of social reality we want to create. We are, after all, born into a pre-existing world of norms, values, roles, relationships, groups, organizations, institutions, and so forth. These features of society always influence our thoughts and deeds and consequently constrain our ability to freely construct our social world (Giddens, 1984). As Karl Marx once said, "[People] make their own history, but they do not make it just as they please; they do not make it under circumstances chosen by themselves, but under circumstances directly encountered, given and transmitted from the past" (K. Marx, 1963).

Marx was particularly interested in how unequal economic conditions shape people's ability to act. Certain people or groups of people are more influential in defining reality than others. Think of all the times you believed something just because someone with more influence, authority, or expertise—like a parent, an instructor, a boss, or a politician—told you it was true.

In any modern society—where classes, ethnic and religious groups, age groups, and political interests struggle for control over resources—there is also a struggle for the power to determine or influence that society's conception of reality (Gans, 1971). Those who emerge successful gain control over information, define values, create myths, manipulate events, and influence what the rest of us take for granted. Conflict theorists therefore argue that reality doesn't simply emerge out of social interaction but is based on the interests and visions of powerful people, groups, organizations, and institutions. People with more power, prestige, status, wealth, and access to high-level policy makers can make their perceptions of the world the entire culture's perception (see chapter 10). In other words, "He who has the bigger stick has the better chance of imposing his definitions of reality" (Berger & Luckmann, 1966, p. 109). That "bigger stick" can be wielded in several ways. Various social institutions and the people who control them play a significant role in shaping and sustaining perceptions of reality.

Moral Entrepreneurs

Certain groups have moral concerns they passionately want translated into law. These **moral entrepreneurs** (Becker, 1963) need not be wealthy or influential individuals. Instead, by virtue of their initiative, access to decision makers, skillful use of publicity, and success in neutralizing any opposition, they are able to turn their interests into public policy (Hills, 1980). Just as a *financial* entrepreneur is in the business of selling a product to the public, the *moral* entrepreneur is in the business of selling a particular version of reality to the public. Groups that seek to outlaw pornography, sexual lyrics in rock music, abortion, gambling, and homosexuality, as well as groups that promote gun control, literacy, or support for AIDS research, are crusading for the creation of a new public conception of morality. For the moral entrepreneur the existing "reality" is not satisfactory: "He [*sic*] feels that nothing can be right in the world until rules are made to correct it. . . . Any means is justified to do away with it. The crusader is fervent and righteous, often self-righteous" (Becker, 1963, pp. 147–148).

Clearly moral entrepreneurship is closely linked to certain social institutions. Religion, for example, provides certain groups of people with values that dictate what is right and wrong, proper and improper, and good and bad (Turner, 1972). These values are sometimes formally written into a religious code (like the Ten Commandments) that provides direct guidance for many people's day-to-day lives.

With the political savvy to insinuate their belief systems into the legislative process, moral entrepreneurs are often capable of using religion to exert significant influence over the definition of reality. In the early 20th century, for instance, the actions of a small group of women, the Women's Christian Temperance Union, led to the passage of the Eighteenth Amendment, which prohibited the use, possession, and sale of alcoholic beverages (Gusfield, 1963). These women used strong, religiously inspired arguments against the "evils" of alcohol to convince legislators it ought to be outlawed.

However, although religious codes of conduct provided the supportive ideology for the temperance movement, it was—upon closer inspection—a political struggle among various interest groups. Alcohol use is a prime example of a consumption habit that distinguishes one group of people from another. The struggle over temperance symbolized the conflict between the values of rural, middle-class Protestants and the values of immigrant, urban, lower-class Catholics (Gusfield, 1963). Alcohol consumption was part of the everyday lives of many new immigrant groups that settled in the industrial urban areas of the country. This lifestyle conflicted sharply with the culture of native-born Protestants.

The temperance movement was thus a symbolic crusade for rural Protestants trying to maintain status in a rapidly changing society. This interpretation is supported by the fact that temperance advocates were less concerned with the enforcement of Prohibition laws than with their passage, which is why the Eighteenth Amendment was eventually repealed. Through issues of reform such as this, a group of moral entrepreneurs can act to defend the dominance and prestige of its perception of reality within the total society (Gusfield, 1963).

The Economics of Reality

Definitions of reality often reflect underlying economic concerns and interests. Ideas that become socially "popular" often reinforce the interests of the economic ruling class and allow it to control the activities of others. The key concerns for conflict sociologists are who benefits and who loses from dominant versions of reality.

Take mental illness, for example. The number of problems officially defined by the American Psychiatric Association as mental diseases and defects increases dramatically each year (Kirk & Kutchins, 1992; Szasz, 1990). The definition of what is and is not mental illness depends on the economic organization of society. We live in a society in which medical services are rarely paid by individuals out of their own pockets. Most of the money for health care comes from the federal and state governments or from private insurance companies. And only if disorders such as alcoholism, gambling, depression, and cocaine addiction are formally defined as illnesses are they eligible for medical insurance coverage.

Economic interests are frequently served by the manner in which language is used to define reality. For example, the Children's Television Act requires local broadcasters to demonstrate their commitment to the educational needs of children in order to have their licenses renewed (Andrews, 1992). The intent of the law was to improve the quality of children's programming. But instead of adding more educational programs, which are traditionally less lucrative, many stations kept the programs that were already in place and simply redefined *educational* and *informational.* A Detroit station, for example, considered the cartoon "Super Mario Brothers" educational because it taught children self-confidence. Another cartoon, "Yo Yogi," in which the main character captures a bank-robbing cockroach, was said to demonstrate the educational value of using one's head rather than one's muscles. Other stations scheduled their educational programs at 5:30 or 6:00 A.M. Because of such lax compliance, a Federal Communications Commission ruling in 1996 tightened the definition of *educational* and required television stations to air 3 hours of educational programming a week between 7:00 A.M. and 10:00 P.M. It is no surprise that with hundreds of millions of dollars at stake, television stations would attempt to redefine reality in order to protect their financial interests.

The Politics of Reality

The institution of politics is also linked to societal definitions of reality. To a great extent, politics is concerned with controlling public perceptions of reality so that people will do things or think about issues in ways that political leaders want them to. We can see attempts to influence public perception during important political campaigns. "Mudslinging," sometimes called "negative campaigning," has become as common an element of the American electoral process as stump speeches, debates, baby kissing, and patriotic songs. As the charges and counter-charges receive more attention and the public begins to believe them, they take on an objectified reality of their own. The actual validity of the claims becomes irrelevant as the accusations are transformed into "fact" and become solidified in the minds of the voting populace.

However, the relationship between politics and reality goes beyond the dirty campaigns of individual candidates. The social construction of reality itself is a massive political process. Governments live or die by their ability to manipulate public opinion so they can reinforce their claims to legitimacy. Information is selectively released, altered, or withheld in an attempt to gain public approval and support. Such shaping of reality is accomplished most notably through the media.

The Medium Is the Message

The mass media—television, radio, books, newspapers, magazines—are the primary means by which we are entertained (Ewen & Ewen, 1982). Furthermore, the messages we receive from the media, particularly television shows, reflect dominant cultural values (Gitlin, 1979). The way characters are portrayed, the topics dealt with, the solutions imposed on fictional problems all link entertainment to the prevailing societal tastes in consumption, the economic system, and the overall political structure.

The media are also our primary source of information about local, national, and international events and people and therefore play a key role in the American political system. The news, for instance, is the means by which political realities are disseminated to the public and is an essential tool in maintaining social order (Hallin, 1986; Parenti, 1986). News broadcasts and newspapers tell us about things we cannot experience directly, making the most remote events meaningful (Molotch & Lester, 1974). The way we look at the world and define our lives within it is shaped and influenced by what we see on the news, hear on the radio, and read in our daily papers.

But what information do we get? Most of us assume that the stories we see are purely factual, an accurate, objective reflection of the "world out there" (Molotch & Lester, 1975). Like everything else, however, news is a constructed reality (Molotch & Lester, 1974). Hundreds, perhaps thousands of potentially newsworthy events occur every day. Yet, if we're lucky, we'll see 10 of them on our favorite evening broadcast. These events exist as news not because of their inherent importance but because of the practical, political, or economic purposes they serve. The news is the product of decisions made by reporters, editors, network executives, and corporation owners, all of whom have their own interests, biases, and values (Molotch & Lester, 1974). The reality we receive from the media is thus an objectified, as opposed to objective, reality.

In some countries—China, for instance—the flow of news information is clearly controlled by the powerful ruling group. Americans rail against such blatant and tyrannical censorship. "Freedom of the press" is a core American value, yet official censorship in this country has been not only tolerated but encouraged in some situations.

Take the media coverage of the Persian Gulf War. Journalists were permitted to cover the war only if they were in organized "pools" escorted by military personnel (Pratkanis & Aronson, 1991). Reporters were never allowed unsupervised access to the battle lines or to the soldiers. Military escorts had the authority to stop any interview or photograph taking if they felt it endangered the operation. Any journalist who attempted to operate independently was subject to arrest. Reporters were completely dependent on official statements and government-issued videotapes. The public, while never being provided the full story, was told that such tight restrictions were necessary to ensure the physical safety of the war correspondents, protect the well-being of our soldiers, and promote the war effort.

Not surprisingly, media reports during the war were congratulatory and optimistic: the low number of allied casualties, the spectacular success of the air campaign and ground attacks, the effectiveness of American high-tech weaponry, the carefully calibrated pressure that kept the Iraqis from unleashing chemical weapons, and so on. Press briefings gave the impression that allied forces were trying hard to maintain a high moral ground in the war (Lopez, 1991).

Such tightly controlled reporting served the interests of the TV networks as well as the military. The Persian Gulf War blurred the boundary between military action and media event, creating what one commentator called "twenty-four-hours-a-day, eye-burning, blood-pumping, high-tech, all-channel" entertainment (Engelhardt, 1992, p. 147). It provided the kind of programming that television networks crave.

Only after the war ended did we hear the other side of the story: the bombing of civilians; the destruction of electric, water, and sewage facilities in northern Iraq; the American casualties due to "friendly fire"; the overstated effectiveness of Patriot missiles in destroying Iraqi Scud missiles (Lopez, 1991). However, the official control of information allowed the public to define the war in terms that were favorable to the military and to the government.

For everyday news stories, such official censorship is usually unnecessary. Because of the economic pressures to attract audiences and keep their attention, TV networks and newspapers censor themselves (Bagdikian, 1991). Reporters pursue particular stories, particular governmental activities, and particular foreign scenes. Less exciting, more complicated stories end up in the wastebasket or on the cutting-room floor.

▪ ▪ ▪ ▪ ▪ ▪ ▪ ▪

MICRO-MACRO CONNECTION
Missing from the News

The problem with the daily distillation of information is not so much what is false but what is missing (Bagdikian, 1991). "What is not [shown] is hardly thought of at all in a world in which [the media] create reality as much as [they] record it" (Solomon, 1988, p. 124). We have no way of knowing what events have not been selected for inclusion in the day's news or what plausible alternatives are kept out of the public eye. As one media critic put it, "editors leave no blank spaces" (Cirino, 1973, p. 42).

Each year Project Censored, a media watchdog group, publishes its list of the top news stories that never made the news and, hence, never came to the public's attention (Jensen & Project Censored, 1995). The most recent list of stories the mainstream media never covered include the following:

▪ Studies carried out in the 1980s by the National Institute for Occupational Safety and Health found that 240,450 American workers were exposed to hazardous materials in the workplace. Of those, about 170,000 were never told about serious health risks from on-the-job exposure.
▪ The world's fishing fleets waste about 60 billion pounds of fish and seafood every year—enough for 120 billion meals.

- Tuberculosis has reemerged as a deadly communicable disease, threatening more people than AIDS, cholera, dengue fever, and other infectious diseases combined—even though it is curable.
- A large oil company quietly pled guilty to three misdemeanor counts of spilling oil off the coast of California. The company agreed to clean up the spill and to pay $1.5 million in fines. The spill was estimated to approach the size of the infamous Exxon Valdez spill in Alaska.
- The U.S. Justice Department rejected a study, which it had originally commissioned, that found that the most popular school-based drug prevention program in the country—Drug Abuse Resistance Education (DARE)—was an extremely expensive failure.

The economic and political motivation for such selectivity becomes apparent when we consider who owns the media. At the end of World War II, 80% of the daily newspapers in the United States were privately owned. By 1990, 80% were owned by corporate chains. Three corporations—Time Warner, News Corp. Ltd., and Hearst—control most of the country's 11,000 magazines (Bagdikian, 1992). About 80% of the daily-newspaper circulation in the United States belongs to a handful of chains like Gannett and Knight-Ridder (Parenti, 1995). Three television networks earn more than two thirds of total U.S. television revenues. Ten business and financial corporations control the three major television networks, 200 cable TV systems, 62 radio stations, 59 magazines, and 58 major newspapers (Parenti, 1986). Many directors of radio, television, and newspaper companies are also partners or directors of banks, big law firms, or other business organizations.

In addition, most journalists come from upper-middle-class families. Almost all have college degrees, and a majority have attended graduate school (see Figure 3.3). Most newspeople earn a salary that puts them in the top 10% bracket (Parenti, 1986). Because common social class interests make for common political perspectives, a remarkable degree of ideological uniformity exists among those responsible for assembling and presenting the news. This is not to say that all the news we receive is knowingly misrepresented. On the contrary, reporters, editors, and producers most likely present the news "as they see it." The problem is that "as they see it" is to some extent determined by their class background and political perspective. Our social institutions are

> the purveyors of [our] cultural myths, values, and legitimating viewpoints. To the extent that news producers—from publishers to reporters—are immersed in that culture, they may not be fully aware of how they misrepresent, evade, and suppress the news. . . . Devoid of the supportive background assumptions of the dominant belief system, the deviant view sounds just too improbable and too controversial to be treated as news, while the orthodox view appears as an objective representation of reality itself. (Parenti, 1986, p. 240)

Figure 3.3 *Background Characteristics of American Journalists*

Source: Based on a 1980 survey of 238 randomly selected journalists at the *New York Times, Washington Post, Wall Street Journal, Time, Newsweek, U.S. News & World Report,* and the news organizations at CBS, NBC, ABC, and PBS.

As the viewing public, our recourse is difficult. Criticism of faulty policies requires good information, which is frequently unavailable. The challenge we face is to recognize the processes at work in the social construction of reality and to take them into account as we "consume" the news. A critical dimension of the sociological imagination is the ability to "read silences"—to be attentive to what the mass media *don't say*. Fortunately, one of the purposes of sociology is to scientifically amass a body of knowledge that we can use to assess how our society really works.

▪ ▪ ▪

Appreciating the Art of Social Research

Research is all around us. Throughout our lives we are flooded with a sea of statistics that are supposedly the result of scientific research: which detergents make clothes brighter, which soft drinks are preferred by most people, which chewing gum is recommended by four out of five dentists. Many of the important decisions we make, from purchasing a car to voting for a candidate, are supported by some sort of research.

In addition, a significant proportion of our lives is spent doing casual research. Every time we seek out the opinions of others, gauge the attitude of a group, or draw conclusions about an event, we engage in a form of research. Say, for example, that you thought your exam scores would improve if you studied with others. You then formed a study group. After the exam you compared your grade with the grade you received on the previous exam to see if there was any significant improvement. If there was, you would likely attribute your better performance to the study group. This is the essence of research: You had an idea about some social process, and you went out and tested it to see if you were correct.

The Nature of Social Research

Although useful and common, personal research like this is fraught with problems. We may make inaccurate or selective observations, overgeneralize on the basis of a limited number of observations, or draw conclusions that protect our own interests (Babbie, 1992). Maybe your exam score would have improved even without the study group because you had a better understanding of the material this time and had a better sense of what the instructor expected.

In contrast to the casual way we carry out our personal research, sociological research helps define reality through a systematic, careful, and controlled process of collecting information and answering questions. Sociological researchers methodically record observations across a variety of situations; they design and choose questions in advance and ask them in a consistent way of a large number of people; they use sophisticated techniques to ensure that the characteristics of the people in a study are similar to those of the population at large; and they use computers to generate statistics from which confident conclusions can be drawn.

Furthermore, sociological research is subjected to the scrutiny of colleagues who will point out any mistakes and shortcomings. Researchers are obligated to report not only their results but also the methods they used to collect data and the conditions surrounding the study. Such detailed explanation allows other researchers to **replicate** a study—that is, perform it themselves to see if the same results are obtained. The more a particular research result is replicated, the greater its acceptance as fact in the sociological community.

The Limitations of Common Sense

A common criticism of sociology is that it is just a fancy version of common sense. Many people feel that social research tells us what we already know. A lot of the things that we think are obvious, however, turn out not to be so straightforward on closer inspection. Consider the following commonsense facts:

- Rape, assault, and murder occur most often between total strangers.
- Because of the high divorce rate in the United States, people are reluctant to get married.
- The high divorce rate means that American children today are more likely to live in a single-parent household than they were 100 years ago.

Most of us probably believe these statements are true. Given what you've read or seen on television, they probably make a lot of sense. But how accurate are they?

- According to the Federal Bureau of Investigation (1991), approximately half of all murder victims each year are related to or know their murderers. Although people close to us provide a great deal of pleasure in our lives, they are also the ones who can frustrate and hurt us the most. Few people can make us as angry as a loved one.
- Close to 90% of Americans marry at least once by the time they're 40. In fact, about two-thirds of divorced women and three-fourths of divorced men eventually remarry (Cherlin, 1992). Although we have become increasingly likely to end a bad marriage, we still tend to place a high value on the institution of marriage itself.
- The percentage of children who live with one parent is roughly the same as it was a century ago. At that time life expectancy was much lower than it is today, so it was highly likely that a child would lose one parent to death before he or she reached adulthood (Kain, 1990).

As you can see, sometimes commonsense "facts" don't hold up under the weight of evidence provided by sociological research.

The Empirical and Probabilistic Aspects of Research

Sociological research, then, is a more sophisticated and structured form of the sort of individual inquiry we use every day. First and foremost, it is an empirical endeavor. **Empirical research** operates on the assumption that questions about human behavior can be ascertained only through controlled, systematic observations in the real world. Great scholars can spend years thinking about human life and developing logical explanations about particular social phenomena. But for most sociologists, the strength of an explanation depends on how much empirical support it has.

Another important characteristic of social research is that it is **probabilistic**. Instead of making predictions, claiming that X always causes Y, most sociologists prefer to state that under certain conditions X will probably cause Y in most people—in other words, that human behavior operates within the laws of probability. Whenever sociologists set out to find the reasons, for example, why people hold prejudiced beliefs, why some religious groups are more opposed to abortion than others, or why some countries have a higher birth rate than others, they are searching for the factors that would explain these phenomena most but not all of the time.

Theories, Variables, and Hypotheses

In addition to being empirical and probabilistic, social research is purposeful. Unlike personal research, which may be motivated by a hunch, whim, or immediate need, most social research is guided by a particular theory. A **theory** is a set of statements or propositions that seek to explain or predict a particular aspect of social life (Chafetz, 1978). Theory is not, as is popularly thought, conjecture or speculation. Ideally, theories concern phenomena as they exist, not morality or ideological preference—that is, they deal with the way things are, not the way they ought to be.

Research and theory closely depend on one another. Research without any underlying theoretical reasoning is simply a string of meaningless bits of information (C. W. Mills, 1959); theory without research is abstract and speculative.

Some theories—like structural functionalism, conflict theory, or symbolic interactionism—are highly general, attempting to explain why social order exists or how entire societies work. Other theories are more modest, attempting to explain more narrowly defined behaviors among specific groups of people. For example, Travis Hirschi (1969) developed a theory of juvenile delinquency called "social control theory," in which he argued that delinquent acts occur when an individual's bond to society is weak or broken. These bonds are derived from a person's attachments to others who obey the law, the rewards one gains by acting nondelinquently, the amount of time a person engages in nondelinquent activity, and the degree to which a person is tied to society's conventional belief system.

The concepts that form the basis of theories are usually abstract and not amenable to empirical observation. You can't directly observe concepts like "social bonds," "conventional beliefs," or "attachments to others." So researchers must translate these concepts into measurable entities called variables. A **variable** is any characteristic, attitude, behavior, or event that can take on two or more values or attributes. For example, the variable "sex" has two categories: male and female. The variable "attitudes toward capital punishment" has categories ranging from very favorable to very unfavorable. The variable "social class" ranges from upper to lower.

Sociologists distinguish between independent and dependent variables. An **independent variable** is the factor that is presumed to cause or influence another variable. The **dependent variable** is the one assumed to depend on, be caused by, or change as a result of the independent variable. If you believe that a person's sex affects his or her attitude toward abortion (that is, women will hold more favorable attitudes than men), then "sex" would be the independent variable and "attitudes toward abortion," the dependent variable.

In his survey of 1,200 boys in grades 6 through 12, Hirschi derived a set of measurable independent and dependent variables from his theoretical concepts. The independent variable, the strength of the social bond, comprised several elements. To determine the degree to which young people are attached to law-abiding others, he measured their attraction to parents, peers, and school officials. To determine the degree to which they derive rewards from acting nondelinquently, he asked them to assess the importance of things like getting good grades. To determine the proportion of their lives spent in conventional activities, he asked them how much time they spent in school-oriented activities. Finally, to determine their ties to a conventional belief system, he assessed questions about their respect for the law and the police.

He measured the dependent variable, delinquent activity, by asking the boys if they'd ever stolen things, taken cars for rides without the owner's permission, banged up something on purpose that belonged to somebody else, or beaten up or hurt someone on purpose. In addition, he used school records and police records to measure acts that had come to the attention of authorities.

To test theories, sociologists must translate abstract theoretical propositions into testable hypotheses. A **hypothesis** is a researchable prediction that specifies the relationship between two or more variables. Hirschi was interested in why juveniles engaged in delinquent behavior. Such a question is far too general to study so he developed a clear, specific, empirically testable prediction: High levels of attachments, commitments, involvements, and conventional beliefs will be associated with low levels of delinquency. The data he collected supported his predictions and therefore strengthened the power of his original theory.

The Modes of Research

Although the answers to important sociological questions are not always simple or clear, the techniques sociologists use to collect and examine data allow them to draw informed and reliable conclusions about human behavior and social life. The most common techniques are experiments, field research, unobtrusive research, and surveys.

Experiments

An **experiment** is typically a research situation designed to elicit some sort of behavior under closely controlled laboratory circumstances. In its ideal form, the experimenter will randomly place subjects into two groups, then deliberately manipulate or introduce changes into the environment of one group of subjects (called the "experimental group") and not the other (called the "control group"). Care is taken to ensure that the groups are relatively alike except for the variable that the experimenter manipulates. Any observed or measured differences between the groups can then be attributed to the effects of the experimental manipulation (Singleton, Straits, & Straits, 1993).

Experiments have a significant advantage over other types of research because the researcher can directly control all the relevant variables. Thus, conclusions about one factor causing changes in another can be made more convincingly. The artificial nature of laboratory experiments, however, may make subjects behave differently than they would in their natural settings, leading some people to argue that experimentation in sociology is practically impossible (Silverman, 1982).

To overcome this difficulty, some sociologists have created experimental situations outside the laboratory. In 1979 Arthur Beaman and his colleagues (Beaman, Klentz, Diener, & Svanum, 1979) conducted an experiment to see whether self-awareness decreases the likelihood of engaging in socially undesirable behavior—in this case, stealing. He set up situations in which children arriving at several homes on Halloween night were sent into the living rooms alone to take candy from a bowl. They were first asked their names and ages and then told, "You may take one of the candies." For the experimental group, a large mirror was placed right next to the candy bowl so that the children couldn't help but see themselves. For the control group there was no mirror. Thirty-seven percent of the children in the control group took more than one candy, but only 4% of the children in the experimental group took more than one candy. The researchers concluded from this experiment that self-awareness can have a significant effect on honesty.

Field Research

In **field research**, sociologists observe events as they actually occur, without selecting experimental and control groups or purposely introducing any changes into the subjects' environment. Field research can take several forms. In **nonparticipant observation**, the researcher observes people without directly interacting with them and without their knowledge that they are being observed. Sociologist Lyn Lofland (1973) studied how strangers relate to one another in public places by going to bus depots, airports, stores, restaurants, and parks and secretly recording everything she saw.

Participant observation requires that the researcher interact with subjects. In some cases the researcher identifies himself or herself. Sociologists Irving Piliavin and Scott Briar (1964) were interested in the importance of demeanor in determining whether juvenile suspects would be apprehended by police. They rode around in the back of police cars and observed the interaction between officers and youths on the street. They found that juveniles who were noncooperative—those who acted nonchalantly, talked back to the officers, and displayed little remorse—were much more likely to be apprehended than those youths who were polite and cooperative.

In more delicate situations the researcher must conceal his or her identity. The researcher attempts to become a member of the group being observed and behave as naturally as possible. In the mid-1950s a social psychologist named Leon Festinger set out to examine how groups protect their beliefs in the face of undeniable contradictory evidence (Festinger, Riecken, & Schacter, 1956). He chose to study a "doomsday cult" that had organized around the belief that a substantial chunk of the Western Hemisphere would be destroyed by a cataclysmic flood on December 21, 1955. He knew that studying such a group would be quite difficult. Highly sensitive to the public's skepticism, members would probably be unwilling to answer an interviewer's questions about their activities and beliefs. So Festinger and his assistants decided to pose as individuals interested in joining the group. Eventually they became full-fledged members, participating in all the group's activities.

When the great flood didn't occur on December 21, the group had to find some way to reconcile their beliefs with the failed prophecy. As the fateful day was ending, their leader began to make importance out of seemingly irrelevant recent news events. For instance, the Associated Press had reported that over the prior few days earthquakes had occurred in Nevada, California, and Italy. The damage brought about by these disasters became "proof" to the group members that cataclysms were actually happening. Members claimed that because of the group's efforts their area had been spared from these upheavals.

Surveys

When it is impossible or impractical to carry out field observations or set up a controlled experimental situation, social researchers use the survey. **Surveys** require that the researcher pose a series of questions either verbally or on paper. The questions should be understood by the respondent the way the researcher wants them to be understood and measure what the researcher wants them to measure. In addition, the respondent is expected to answer the questions honestly and thoughtfully.

All of us have had experience with surveys of one form or another. Every 10 years we are required to fill out questionnaires for the U.S. Census Bureau. At the end of some college courses you have probably filled out a course evaluation. Or perhaps you've been interviewed in a shopping mall or answered questions during a telephone survey.

Surveys typically use standardized formats. All subjects are asked the same questions in roughly the same way, and large samples of people are used as subjects. When sociologists Philip Blumstein and Pepper Schwartz (1983) undertook a massive study of intimate couples in America, they sent questionnaires to people from every income level, age group, religion, political ideology, and educational background. Some of their respondents lived together, others were married. Some had children, others were childless. Some were heterosexual, others homosexual. All couples filled out a 38-page questionnaire that asked questions about their leisure activities, emotional support, housework, finances, sexual relations, satisfaction, relations with children, and so forth. More than 6,000 couples participated. From these surveys Blumstein and Schwartz were able to draw conclusions about the importance of money, work, sexuality, power, and gender in couple's lives.

Unobtrusive Research

All the methods I've discussed so far require the researcher to have some contact with the people being studied: asking them questions, giving them tasks to do in an experiment, or watching them (with or without their knowing that they are participating in social research). The problem with these techniques is that the very act of intruding into people's lives may influence the phenomena being studied. Asking people questions about their voting intentions prior to an election, for instance, may affect their eventual voting behavior. To avoid such influence, sociologists sometimes use another research technique, unobtrusive research, that requires no contact with people at all. **Unobtrusive research** is an examination of the evidence of social behavior that people create or leave behind.

Suppose you wanted to know what exhibits are most popular at a museum (Webb, Campbell, Schwartz, Sechrest, & Grove, 1981). You could poll people, but they might tell you things that make themselves look more intellectual and sophisticated. You could stand there and watch people, but they might become self-conscious of your gaze. Perhaps a better way would be to wait until the museum is empty and check the wear-and-tear on the floor in front of the exhibits. Those exhibits where the carpeting is worn down are probably the most popular. This would be an example of unobtrusive research.

There are several types of unobtrusive research. One type is the analysis of existing statistics. Émile Durkheim used this technique when he examined different suicide rates for different groups to gain insight into the underlying causes of suicide (see chapter 1).

Another form of unobtrusive research, called **content analysis,** is the study of recorded communications—books, speeches, poems, songs, television commercials, and so forth. Suppose you were interested in finding out whether the women's movement has improved the status of women in American society. A good indicator of how well or poorly women are thought of in society might be the nature of their media images. You could identify several influential magazines (*Time, Life, Newsweek*) and examine changes in the depiction of women in ads over the last 10 or 20 years. Or, if you had access to television archives, you could ascertain whether portrayals of women in TV commercials had changed over the years.

A third type of unobtrusive research is **historical analysis,** which relies on existing historical documents as a source of research information. Sociologist Kai Erikson (1966) was interested in how communities construct definitions of acceptable and unacceptable behavior. For his book *Wayward Puritans,* he studied several "crime waves" among the Puritans of the Massachusetts Bay Colony in the late 17th century. Erikson examined diaries, court records, birth and death records, letters, and other written documents of the period. Because a key piece of data was the number of criminal convictions, court records were an important source of information.

Piecing together fragments of information 300 years old was not easy. One problem Erikson faced was the fact that the Puritans didn't observe any consistent rules of spelling. The name of one gentleman was spelled 14 different ways. In some instances it wasn't clear whether two people with similar names were actually the same person. Erikson solved the problem by inspecting birth and death certificates and other records to distinguish one life span from another.

Erikson was able to draw some conclusions about the nature of human life and shifting cultural definitions of reality. He found that each time the colony was threatened in some way—by opposing religious groups, a crisis of faith in the authority of the community leaders, or the King of England's revocation of its charter—the numbers of convicted criminals and the severity of punishments significantly increased. Erikson believed that these fluctuations occurred because the community needed to restate its moral boundaries and reaffirm its authority.

Another form of unobtrusive research that is becoming increasingly popular is **visual sociology**, a method of studying society through photographs, video, and film. Some visual sociologists use these media to gather sociological data—much as documentary photographers and filmmakers do. The visual images they create are meant to tell a sociological story. Other visual sociologists analyze the meaning and purpose of existing visual texts such as sports photographs, film advertisements, and the photographic archives of corporations (Harper, 1996). The visual essays that appear throughout this book use the techniques of this methodology to examine important issues of sociological interest.

The Trustworthiness of Social Research

Most sociologists see research as not only personally valuable but central to human knowledge and understanding. However, as informed consumers we must ask: How accurate is this information? We tend to believe what we read in print or see reported on television. Unfortunately, much of what we see is either inaccurate or misleading. To evaluate the results of social research, we must examine the researcher's samples, indicators, values, and interests. We must also consider the researcher's ethics in conducting the study.

Samples

Frequently, researchers are interested in the attitudes, behaviors, or characteristics of large groups—college students, women, Americans, and so on. It would be impossible to interview, survey, or observe all these people directly. Hence researchers must select from the larger population a smaller **sample** of respondents for study. The characteristics of this subgroup are supposed to approximate the characteristics of the entire population of interest. A sample is said to be **representative** if the small group being studied is in fact typical of the population as a whole. For instance, a sample of 100 students from your university should include roughly the same proportion of first-year students, sophomores, juniors, and seniors that characterizes the entire school population. Sampling techniques have become highly sophisticated, as illustrated by the accuracy of polls conducted to predict election results.

In the physical sciences sampling is not an issue. Certain physical or chemical elements are assumed to be identical. One need only study a small number of test tubes of nitrogen because one test tube is the same as any other. Human beings, however, vary widely on every imaginable characteristic. One could not make a general statement about all Americans on the basis of an interview with one person. For that matter, one could not draw conclusions about all people from observing a sample consisting only of men, whites, or teenagers. Samples that are not representative can lead to inaccurate and misleading conclusions.

Note the sampling problems revealed in the following letter to the editor of a small-town newspaper in the rural Midwest:

> I went to a restaurant yesterday for lunch. I began to feel guilty, when I reached into my pocket for a cigarette. . . . I was thinking of the government figures which estimated cigarette smokers at 26% of the population of the United States. But everywhere I looked inside that room, people were smoking. I decided to count them.

There were 22 people in the room. . . . I was surprised to discover that the government's figures were an outright fabrication. . . . Seventeen people out of the 22 were cigarette smokers . . . that accounts for over 77% of the people in that restaurant. . . . The government's figures are understated by 51% and just plain wrong! (*Greencastle Banner Graphic*, 1992)

This letter writer assumes that the 22 people who frequented a small restaurant in a small, relatively poor rural town on a single day were an adequate representation of the entire population. Such a conclusion overlooks some important factors. Governmental studies show that the lower a person's income, the greater the likelihood that person will be a smoker. Furthermore, people in blue-collar or service jobs are more likely to smoke than people in white-collar jobs. Finally, the prevalence of smoking is higher in the Midwest than in other parts of the country (U.S. Department of Health and Human Services, 1988).

Indicators

One problem sociologists face when doing research is that the variables they are interested in studying are usually difficult to see. What does powerlessness look like? How can you "see" marital instability? How would you recognize alienation or social class? Sociologists thus resign themselves to measuring **indicators** of things that cannot be measured directly. Researchers measure events and behaviors commonly thought to accompany a particular variable, hoping that what they are measuring is a valid indicator of the concept they are interested in.

Suppose you believed that people's attitudes toward abortion are influenced by the strength of their religious beliefs, or "religiosity." You might hypothesize that the more religious someone is, the less accepting he or she will be of abortion rights. To test this hypothesis you must first figure out what you mean by "religious." What might be an indicator of the strength of one's religious beliefs? You could determine if the subjects of your study identify themselves as members of some organized religion. But would this measure tell how religious your subjects are? Probably not, because many people identify themselves as, say, Catholic or Jewish but are not religious at all. Likewise some people who consider themselves quite religious don't identify with any organized religion. So this measure would focus on group differences but would fail to capture the intensity of a person's beliefs or the degree of religious interest.

Perhaps a better indicator would be some quantifiable behavior, like the frequency of attendance at formal religious services. Arguably, the more one attends church or synagogue, the more religious one is. But here too we run into problems. Church attendance, for instance, may reflect family pressure, habit, or the desire to visit with others rather than religious commitment. Furthermore, many very religious people are unable to attend services because they are sick or disabled.

Frequency of prayer might be a better indicator. Obviously people who pray a lot are more religious than people who don't pray at all. But some nonreligious people pray for things all the time. As you can see, indicators seldom perfectly reflect the concepts they are intended to measure.

Surveys are particularly susceptible to inaccurate indicators. A loaded phrase or an unfamiliar word on a survey question can dramatically affect people's responses in ways unintended by the researcher. The National Opinion Research Center asked in an annual survey of public attitudes if the United States was spending too much, too little, or about the right amount of money on "assistance to the poor." Two-thirds of the respondents said the country was spending too little. But when the word *welfare* was substituted for "assistance to the poor," nearly half of the respondents said the country was spending too much money (Kagay & Elder, 1992).

During the Watergate scandal, only 26% of respondents to a survey thought President Nixon "should be impeached." However, more than 50% of respondents felt he should be brought to trial before the Senate. These statements convey the same information; the only difference is that one statement uses the word *impeach*, which many people at the time incorrectly believed to mean a determination of guilt. Note how the wording of questions can change the nature of people's responses and therefore lead to very different conclusions about people's attitudes.

Values and Interests

In addition to samples and indicators, the researcher's own values and interests can influence social research. Ideally, research is objective and nonbiased and measures what *is* and not what *should be*. The study of social events, however, takes place in a particular cultural, political, and ideological context (Ballard 1987; Denzin, 1989). Furthermore, research is sometimes carried out to support a narrowly defined interest, as when tobacco companies fund studies on the relationship between smoking and cancer.

We must remember that sociologists are people too, with their own biases, preconceptions, and expectations. Our values determine from which vantage point information about a particular social phenomenon will be gathered (Eitzen & Baca-Zinn, 1991). If you were conducting research on whether the American criminal justice system is fair, would you seek out criminals, politicians, law enforcement personnel, judges, or victims? Each group would likely provide a different perception of the system. The most accurate picture of reality is likely to be based on the views of all subgroups involved.

In fact, values can influence the questions that researchers find important enough to address in the first place (Reinharz, 1992). For instance, research on the family has historically reflected the interests of men by viewing the female-headed household as deviant and dysfunctional (Thorne & Yalom, 1982). Similarly, the male bias affects the questions that are researched in the study of women's work (Acker, 1978). The term *labor force* has traditionally referred to those working for pay and has excluded those doing unpaid work such as housework and volunteer jobs—areas that are predominantly female. Thus findings on labor force participation are more likely to reflect the significant elements of men's lives than of women's lives.

Ethics in Research

Research, as I mentioned earlier, often represents an intrusion into people's lives—it may disrupt their ordinary activities and often requires them to reveal personal information about themselves. Ethical researchers agree, therefore, that they should protect the rights of subjects and minimize the amount of harm or disruption subjects may experience as a result of being part of a study. Ethical researchers agree that no one should be forced to participate in research, that those who do participate ought to be fully informed of the possible risks involved, and that every precaution ought to be taken to protect the confidentiality and anonymity of subjects.

At the same time, however, researchers must attempt to secure the most accurate information possible. Sometimes this requirement conflicts with ethical considerations. Recall, for instance, the discussion of Milgram's study of obedience in chapter 2. To study such a phenomenon, Milgram had to deceive his subjects into thinking they were actually administering shocks to others. His results would have been severely flawed—and crucial information about the power of authority would have been lost—had he informed his subjects that the fellow "subject" wasn't really being shocked, that it was all a fabrication. The question is always, At what point do the interests of acquiring important sociological knowledge override the obligation to protect subjects?

■ ■ ■ ■ ■ ■ ■ ■

LAUD HUMPHREYS
The Tearoom Trade

Most sociologists agree that the psychological anguish Milgram's subjects experienced was worth the information that was obtained. There is less agreement and more controversy, however, over situations in which researchers misrepresent their identities in order to gather information. Consider Laud Humphreys's 1970 study called *The Tearoom Trade,* a study many sociologists found ethically indefensible. Humphreys was interested in studying anonymous and casual homosexual encounters among strangers. He decided to focus on interactions in "tearooms," which are places, like public restrooms, where male homosexuals go for anonymous sex. (This study was done well before the AIDS epidemic significantly curtailed such activity.)

Because of the secretive and potentially stigmatizing nature of the phenomenon he was interested in, Humphreys couldn't just come right out and ask people about their actions. So he decided to engage in a secretive form of participant observation. He posed as a lookout, called a "watchqueen," whose job was to warn participants of intruders as they engaged in sexual acts with one another in public restrooms. In this way he was able to conduct very detailed observations of these encounters.

Humphreys also wanted to know about the regular lives of these men. Whenever possible he wrote down the license numbers of the participants' cars and tracked down their names and addresses with the help of a friend in the local police department. About a year later he arranged for these individuals to be part of a simple medical survey being conducted by some of his colleagues. He then disguised himself and visited their homes, supposedly to conduct interviews for the medical survey. He found that most of the men were heterosexual, had families, and were rather respected members of their communities. In short, they led altogether conventional lives.

Although this information shed a great deal of light on the nature of anonymous homosexual acts, some critics argued that Humphreys had violated the ethics of research by deceiving his unsuspecting subjects and violating their privacy rights. Some critics also noted that Humphreys might have been sued for invasion of privacy if he had not been studying a group of people rendered powerless by their potential embarrassment. Others, however, supported Humphreys, arguing that he could have studied this topic in no other way. In fact, his book won a prestigious award. But close to 30 years later, the ethical controversy surrounding this study remains.

■ ■ ■

Conclusion

In this chapter I have described some of the processes by which reality is constructed, communicated, manipulated, and accepted. Reality, whether in the form of everyday observations or formal research, is ultimately a human creation. Different people can create different conceptions of reality.

This issue can be raised from a personal level to a global one. Every culture believes that its reality is the paramount one. Who is right? Can we truly believe that a reality in direct conflict with ours is equally valid? If we profess that everyone should have the right to believe what he or she wants, are we acknowledging the social constructive nature of reality or merely being tolerant of those who are not "smart enough" to think as we do? Do we have the right to tell other people or other cultures that what they do or believe is wrong only because it conflicts with our definition of reality? Exasperating and complex, these questions lie at the core of everyday life, international relations, and global survival.

CHAPTER HIGHLIGHTS

■ The social construction of reality (truth, knowledge, and so on) is the process by which reality is discovered, made known, reinforced, and changed by members of society.

■ Language is the medium through which reality construction takes place. It enables us to think, interpret, and define. Linguistic categories reflect aspects of a culture that are relevant and meaningful to people's lives.

■ As social beings, we respond to our interpretations and definitions of situations, not to the situations themselves. If people define situations as real, then the consequences of those situations become real.

■ Not all of us possess the same ability to define reality. Individuals and groups in positions of power have the ability to control information, define values, create myths, manipulate events, and ultimately influence what others take for granted.

■ The purpose of a discipline like sociology is to amass a body of knowledge that provides the public with useful information about how society works. This is done through systematic social research—experiments, field research, unobtrusive research, and surveys.

YOUR TURN

The reality we take for granted is a social construction. This is particularly apparent when we look at the information presented to us as fact through published academic research, word of mouth, or the media. Reality is influenced by the individuals and organizations who are responsible for creating, assembling, and disseminating this information.

Choose an event that is currently making national headlines. It could be a story about the president or Congress, a major tragedy or disaster, or a highly publicized criminal trial. Over the course of a week analyze how this story is being covered by the following:

■ your local newspaper
■ the major national newspapers (*USA Today*, the *New York Times*, the *Washington Post*)
■ mainstream news magazines (*Time, Newsweek, U.S. News & World Report*)
■ alternative magazines (*Utne Reader, Mother Jones, In These Times*, etc.)
■ a local TV station
■ the major networks (NBC, CBS, ABC, CNN)

Pay particular attention to:

- the amount of time or space devoted to the story
- the "tone" of the coverage (Is it supportive or critical? Purely factual or reflective of certain political opinions?)

Summarize your findings. What were the differences in how the story was covered (for example, local versus national media, print versus electronic media, one TV network versus another, mainstream versus alternative press)? What were the similarities?

Interpret your findings. What do these differences and similarities suggest about the people who run these organizations? Whose political or economic interests are being served or undermined by the manner in which the story is being presented to the public? Which medium do you think is providing the most accurate, objective coverage? Why?

CHAPTER 4

Building Order: Culture and History

- *Dimensions of Culture*
- *Cultural Expectations and Social Order*
- *Cultural Variation and Everyday Experience*

In Madagascar, the harvest months of August and September mark the *famadihana*—the "turning of the bones." Families receive messages from their dead loved ones, who may say they are uncomfortable or need new clothes. In an elaborate ceremony that includes feasting and singing, the family digs up the grave of the deceased. The bodies are wrapped in shrouds and seated at the dinner table. Family news is whispered to them and toasts are drunk. Widows and widowers can often be seen dancing with the bones of their dead spouses. The exhumed bones are then oiled and perfumed and laid back onto the "bed" inside the family tomb (Perlez, 1991).

In the late 19th and early 20th centuries, dating and courtship in North America was based on a ritualized system known as "calling." Although the process varied by region and social class, the following general guidelines were involved:

> When a girl reached the proper age or had her first "season" (depending on her family's social level), she became eligible to receive male callers. At first her mother or guardian invited young men to call; in subsequent seasons the young lady . . . could bestow an invitation to call upon any unmarried man to whom she had been properly introduced at a private dance, dinner, or other "entertainment." . . . Other young men . . . could be brought to call by friends or relatives of the girl's family, subject to her prior permission. . . . The call itself was a complicated event. A myriad of rules governed everything: the proper amount of time between invitation and visit (two weeks or less); whether or not refreshments should be served . . . ; chaperonage (the first call must be made on mother and daughter . . .); appropriate topics of conversation (the man's interests, but never too personal); how leave should be taken (on no account should the woman accompany [her caller] to the door nor stand talking while he struggles with his coat). (B. L. Bailey, 1988, pp. 15–16)

How could anybody dig up the body of a dead relative? Why would young men and young women follow such elaborate rules just so they could go on a date? Such practices seem peculiar, silly, or backward to most of us, but to the people involved, they are or were simply the taken-for-granted "right" ways of doing things.

Some of the things you do may look equally silly to an outside observer. For instance, you may not think twice about eating a juicy steak, but someone from a culture that views cows as sacred may be horrified at the thought. You may routinely shave your face, legs, or armpits, but imagine what these practices would look like in a culture where such acts are blasphemous. You may think a Spaniard's fondness for bullfighting is "absurd," yet millions of Americans shell out a lot of money each year to watch large men in brightly colored helmets and uniforms knock each other down while they chase, throw, carry, and kick an object made out of the hide of a dead pig. You may pity the turn-of-the-century woman who squeezed her body into ultra-tight corsets in order to achieve the figure men admired (Ehrenreich & English, 1979). Yet many women today (as well as some men) routinely use makeup, color their hair, have plastic surgery, and even starve themselves in the interests of becoming more attractive.

The legitimacy of certain practices and ideas can be understood only within the unique context of the group or society in which they occur. What is considered abnormal in one case might be perfectly normal, even necessary, in another.

Ancestor worship in Madagascar is a custom that has been around for hundreds of years, impervious to the arrival of Christian churches and Western ideals. To the people who practice it, the ritual of burial and disinterment is more important than marriage. Life is seen as a mere transition. They believe that through one's ancestors an individual can communicate with God. Consequently, the custom is quite rational and beneficial: Their own spiritual salvation depends on it.

Likewise, the practice of "calling" played an integral part in the culture of turn-of-the-century America. It maintained the social class structure by serving as a test of suitability, breeding, and background (B. L. Bailey, 1988). Calling enabled the middle and upper classes to protect themselves from what many at the time considered the "intrusions" of urban life and to screen out the effects of social and geographical mobility that reached unprecedented levels at the turn of the century. It also allowed parents to control the relationships of their children, thereby increasing the likelihood that their pedigree would remain intact.

These phenomena illustrate the important role played by culture and history in creating social order. Whether we're talking about our own ordinary rituals or those practiced by some distant society, the normative patterns that mark the millions of seemingly trivial actions and social encounters of our everyday lives are what make society possible. They tell us what to expect from others and what others should expect from us. In this chapter I examine how order is created and maintained in society by looking at the various taken-for-granted aspects of culture that lend structure to our daily lives. In the process I will compare specific aspects of our culture to others, past and present.

Dimensions of Culture

In common usage, the term *culture* is often evoked only when discussing something "foreign." We rarely feel the need to question why we do certain things in the course of our everyday lives—we just do them. It's *other* people in other lands whose rituals and beliefs need explaining. What we fail to realize is that culture is "doing its job" most effectively when it is unnoticed. It's what we take for granted that we're least likely to speak about; and it's those cultural silences that are most familiar to members and most important for social order to endure (Perin, 1988). Only in times of dramatic social change and moral uncertainty, or when circumstances force us to compare our society to another (for example, when traveling abroad) do we become aware that we, too, are influenced by a set of cultural rules and values.

We are, then, products of the culture and historical epoch in which we reside. From a very young age we learn, with a startling amount of accuracy, that certain types of shelter, food, tools, clothing, music, sports, and art characterize our culture and make it different from others. Without much conscious effort, we also learn what to believe, what to value, and which actions are proper or improper in both public and private.

Material and Nonmaterial Culture

Culture thus consists of both the material and nonmaterial products of a society. **Material culture** includes the physical artifacts that shape the lives of members of a particular society: distinctive clothing, buildings, inventions, food, artwork, writings, music, and so on. Some of the most important elements of material culture are technological achievements, which are the ways members of a society apply knowledge to adapt to changing social, economic, or environmental conditions. For instance, the advent of the automobile in the early 20th century gave people the mobility to take advantage of economic opportunities elsewhere and thereby dramatically changed some of our values and the way we live. Similarly, plastic products introduced later this century provided people with cheaper and more convenient packaging of needed goods—and in the process altered shopping and consumption patterns.

Changes in material culture can also bring about unforeseen problems in the physical environment. The heavy American reliance on the automobile has created several serious problems: air pollution, depletion of fossil fuel reserves, traffic, and overcrowding. These problems, in turn, have created the need for further material developments, such as mechanical devices to reduce pollution, alternative fuel sources, and a more efficient highway system. And the enormous amount of non-biodegradable plastic piling up in overflowing land fills has spawned a vast array of advances in recycling technology.

Although material culture gives a society its distinctive character, it is increasingly becoming more global in nature. Transnational media, global communication and transportation systems, and massive immigration have made "cultural purity" all but obsolete (Griswold, 1994). For instance, what were once unique features of American material culture, the fast-food restaurant and blue jeans, can now be found on nearly every continent. It wouldn't be particularly surprising to find people wearing Levi's in a remote village in the Andes Mountains of Peru or munching on Big Macs in Bangkok.

Nonmaterial culture refers to all the nonphysical products of society that are created over time and shared: knowledge, beliefs, customs, values, morals, symbols, and so on. Nonmaterial culture also includes common patterns of behavior and the forms of interaction appropriate in a particular society. It is a "design for living" that distinguishes one society from another. Like an owner's manual for social life, nonmaterial culture tells us how our society works, what we are to believe is possible, how we are to conduct our everyday lives, and what to do if something breaks down. Without an understanding of a society's nonmaterial culture, people's behaviors—not to mention the symbolic significance of their material world—would be thoroughly incomprehensible.

Subcultures

Sociologists and anthropologists usually speak of culture as a characteristic of an entire society. But culture can also exist in smaller, more narrowly defined units. A **subculture** consists of the values, behaviors, and physical artifacts of a group that distinguishes itself from the larger culture. Think of it as a culture within a culture. Racial and ethnic groups, religions, age groups, and even geographical areas often develop their own distinct subcultures.

Consider life at a university. You are probably well aware of the material and nonmaterial culture that exists on your campus. Perhaps there is some landmark—a bell tower or an ornate archway—that is the defining symbol of the university, or maybe there is an area or a piece of art that occupies a hallowed place in campus life. I'm sure you know what your school mascot is and what the school colors are. When you arrived on campus, you also had to learn a tremendous amount of new information about the nonmaterial culture just to survive—how to register for courses, how to address a professor, where to eat and study, what administrators, faculty, and fellow students expect of you. You may have even been required to learn an entirely new vocabulary of terms that only students at your university understand. Just as you had to learn how to be a member of this society, you had to learn how to be a member of your university subculture.

History: The "Archives" for Everyday Living

Differences between cultures exist *horizontally*—that is, between cultures at the same point in time. But we can also think of cultures differing *vertically*—that is, between past and present in the same society.

Like culture, history is simultaneously ubiquitous and invisible. We rarely see the connection between our personal lives and the larger historical context in which we live. Just as culture tends to be equated with the foreign, history tends to be equated with the past. Thus, we often try to understand the thoughts and actions of people who lived in the past by a particular set of contemporary criteria.

Abraham Lincoln, one of America's most influential proponents of liberty and equality, once said, "There is a physical difference between the white and black races which I believe will forever forbid the two races living together on terms of social and political equality" (quoted in Gould, 1981, p. 35). Similar views of racial separation were voiced by such important historical figures as Benjamin Franklin, Thomas Jefferson, and Charles Darwin. Such comments today would justifiably be taken as indications of a deeply held prejudice. However, we must understand such positions not merely as signs of personal bigotry but as reflections of the dominant belief system of the times. As repugnant as we might find these attitudes, they were taken as undeniable truths by the scientific communities of their era. Innate "racial inferiority" was as much an established "scientific fact" then as the earth revolving around the sun is today.

The norms and values that govern everyday life in a given society are also likely to change over time. According to the Connecticut Department of Education, in 1940 the top disciplinary problems on high school campuses were talking, chewing gum, making noise, running in halls, cutting in line, wearing improper clothing, and not putting trash in the wastebasket. In the 1990s such activities are not likely to elicit harsh punishments from school officials, especially when they are compared to what are now considered to be the most common problems: drug abuse, alcohol abuse, vandalism, assault, teen pregnancy, suicide, gang warfare, rape, and arson.

Some cultural practices that were wholly unacceptable in the past have now become commonplace. Premarital sex and househusbands do not incite the sort of moral outrage and suspicion they once did. On the other hand, many actions have become less acceptable over time, at least among certain subcultures. I read recently that showering after gym class—a mandatory, military-like ritual two decades ago—has become virtually obsolete among U.S. high school students today (Johnson, 1996a). Some cite insecurities about body image, heightened sexual awareness, and lack of time in a busy schedule as possible reasons for a phenomenon that would have been unheard of and even punishable a generation ago.

Other acts have not just become less acceptable, they've become criminal. There was a time when people could smoke cigarettes anywhere and anytime they pleased—in hospitals, supermarkets, restaurants, movie theaters. Now, with the increase in health awareness, smoking in public has been severely restricted and even outlawed in some cities and states.

Historical shifts in the cultural acceptance of certain behaviors involve more than just a societal realization of the danger of such behaviors. In fact, such designations are greatly influenced by social and economic concerns. Take, for instance, the criminalization of opium—the substance from which heroin is derived. During the 19th century, the use of opium was permitted without legal sanction; it was commonly used for therapeutic purposes as a pain reliever, a cold medicine, and a cough suppressant (Inciardi, 1992). The typical "heroin addict" at the time was a white middle-class housewife.

By the early 20th century, however, things had changed considerably. There was a growing fear, particularly on the West Coast, of economic competition from Chinese laborers who had been "imported" to work on the railroads. Chinese immigrants became equated with opium use (Hagan, 1985). What followed must have made perfect logical sense at the time: If a despised group characteristically engages in a particular behavior, there must be something wrong with that behavior. A moral consensus soon emerged that focused on the presumed link between the Chinese and narcotics (Bonnie & Whitebread, 1974). It wasn't long before opium use became the dreaded "Oriental Dope Problem." By 1914 tight legislative controls restricted the distribution of opium to authorized medical prescriptions only. By 1925 it was completely outlawed (Becker, 1963).

Cultural Expectations and Social Order

Despite periodic shifts in the acceptability of specific acts, culture provides people with a common bond, a sense of shared personal experiences. That we can live together at all depends on the fact that we share a tremendous amount of cultural knowledge. This knowledge allows us to predict, with a fair amount of certainty, what most people will do in a given situation. I can assume that when I say, "Hi, how are you?" you will say, "Fine." You probably would not go into some long-winded explanation of your mental, physical, and emotional condition at that precise moment because doing so would violate the cultural rules.

The actions of individuals are not simply functions of personality types or psychological predispositions; rather, they are also a reflection of shared cultural expectations. Culture provides us with information about which of these actions are preferred, accepted, disapproved, or unthinkable at a given time (McCall & Simmons, 1978). You will recall from chapter 2 that norms are the rules that govern the routine social encounters in which we all participate. Although everyday norms are difficult to identify and describe, they reflect commonly held assumptions about conventional behavior: what is considered good and bad, moral and immoral, appropriate and inappropriate. Without norms, individual behaviors in any given situation would vary widely, and a lot more of our time would be spent trying to interpret others' behavior and frame our responses accordingly.

Consider the unspoken norms that emerge in a situation we've all experienced, shopping at the supermarket:

> There is a customer role to be played in grocery stores. There generally is a standard of orderliness. Shoppers are not seen pushing each other out of the way, picking things out of each other's shopping carts, or sitting on the floor eating from a recently opened can. How does one "know" how the role of customer is to be played? Aside

from the "No Shirt. No Bare Feet" sign on the door . . . there is no clear listing of shopping rules.

Evidence of the implied existence of such rules can be found in the way people react to a fellow shopper dressed in a gorilla suit or to someone who violates the norms for waiting in line at the checkout counter. One may feel that rules are being broken when one finds oneself standing in line with melting ice cream behind a grandmother who takes out her grandchildren's photographs to show the clerk. Such behavior violates the norms of universalism (all customers are to be treated equally) and efficiency; the grocery store is not a context in which one shares one's private self with others, particularly anonymous others. (Kearl & Gordon, 1992, p. 274)

Norms can be generalized in similar situations. You can be reasonably certain that grocery store behavior that is appropriate in Baltimore will be appropriate in Houston as well. The grocery store experience itself would be chaotic if there weren't a certain degree of agreement over how we should act. Without such unspoken rules, every situation would have to be interpreted, analyzed, and responded to as if it were an entirely new occasion. Social life would be utterly unmanageable.

■ ■ ■ ■ ■ ■ ■ ■

MICRO-MACRO CONNECTION
Emotions and Social Structure

To illustrate the enormous power of cultural norms, I turn to a common area of social life: emotions. The norms that govern the expression of emotions do not exist in any explicit form. Yet people who instinctively hide or alter their emotions to fit the situation play a significant role in maintaining social order.

Take televised beauty pageants, for example. As the field of contestants is reduced to the final two, the camera zooms in on both of them. Usually they're standing on stage hugging each other in shaky anticipation of the final verdict. When the winner is announced, the runner-up is the picture of grace and charm, all smiles and congratulations. But we all know better. She has just lost the contest of her life on national television and has got to be sad, angry, or at the very least disappointed. Why does the runner-up suppress the urge to show her true emotions? Part of the reason is that she feels compelled to obey the cultural norms regarding the expression of emotions in that context. There's more at stake than her feelings. Imagine what would happen to the economic well-being of the multimillion-dollar beauty contest industry if the losers suddenly began to display their bitterness and discontent on stage—arguing with judges, showing disdain for winners, and so forth.

We have many such unwritten rules about what is appropriate to feel, what is appropriate to display, and how intense the emotional display should be under specific circumstances. For instance, we're supposed to be sad at funerals, happy at weddings, and angry when we are insulted. We're supposed to feel joy when we receive good news but not show too much of it if our good fortune is at someone else's expense. We're supposed to be mildly upset if we get a B– instead of a B+ in a course but not sink into severe depression. In extreme cases the violation of such norms can lead to grave sanctions, such as being diagnosed as mentally ill (Pugliesi, 1987; Thoits, 1985).

Cultural norms about expressing emotions are often linked to organizational concerns and needs. In her book *The Managed Heart*, Arlie Hochschild (1983) describes the *feeling rules* required by occupations in which employees have a great deal of contact with the public. To satisfy these rules, workers must either express or suppress their private feelings on demand. Flight attendants, for example, must constantly be good-natured and calm under dangerous conditions. They must make their work appear effortless and handle other people's feelings as deftly as their own. This ability is not just a matter of living up to social expectations; it is part of their job description. A "smile" becomes an economic asset and a public relations tool.

Likewise, doctors and nurses are trained to show kind concern for their patients but cannot show disgust or alarm. Furthermore, they cannot become too emotionally involved with patients. Because they see pain, suffering, and death every day, however, it is difficult not to become attached to patients. But such emotional outlay would inevitably lead to "burnout," making effective job performance impossible. Doctors and nurses are more successful in their jobs when they are able to keep their emotions under control.

Other occupations may actually encourage excessive emotional display. In the world of professional sports, people tend to show emotions in more exaggerated forms than people in other occupations. Football players engage in elaborate dances when they score touchdowns. Hockey players scream and fight with opponents routinely. Baseball managers argue face-to-face with umpires over controversial calls. Such displays are entertaining to the fans and keep them coming to the games and thus have long-term financial value for the team organizations.

Hochschild warns that such "emotional labor" eventually takes a heavy psychological toll on the workers who are required to adopt a display of emotions that reflect corporate needs and not their own as part of their everyday work lives. These people become increasingly estranged from their true feelings (Hochschild, 1983).

Although it is not surprising that organizations would have an interest in the emotional display of members, it is perhaps less obvious that particular emotions are linked to larger societal concerns like politics and economics, often as a method of social control (Kearl & Gordon, 1992). Fear, for instance, may be used by some political and religious regimes to quell dissent and enforce obedience. Earlier in this century, in response to the increasing political and economic threat posed by African Americans, many white Southerners controlled blacks through the threat of lynching. Similarly, religious leaders will often use the fear of eternal damnation to ensure that their followers will cooperate.

The effectiveness of invoking emotions such as guilt, anxiety, and shame waxes and wanes as social climates change. In the past, when communities were smaller and more interdependent, social behavior could be easily regulated by the threat of shame. If you broke the law or violated some norm of morality, you would bring humiliation upon yourself, your family, and the community at large. But as societies became more complex, such close ties began to disappear. Today, the political control of behavior through emotion is more likely to be directed inward, in the form of guilt and anxiety. For instance, if working mothers are implicated by politicians as contributing to the "breakdown" of the traditional family, more and more mothers will experience guilt when they seek employment outside the home (Berg, 1992). Likewise, more stringent restrictions on abortion would increase the anxiety experienced by women who are considering it.

Norms like those governing the expression of emotions give us a way to communicate and maintain social order. They keep us in line by creating powerful cultural expectations that are difficult to violate.

▪ ▪ ▪

Culture and Institutionalized Norms

Large social institutions are closely related to culture. For one thing, some institutions reflect deeply held cultural values. Our free-market economy, for instance, reflects the values of achievement, competition, material acquisition, and so on. Our democratic government reflects the values of freedom and citizen participation. Other institutions—like education, religion, and family—provide the mechanisms through which culture is transmitted across generations.

Institutions are also strongly supported by cultural norms. When a particular pattern of behavior becomes widely accepted and taken for granted in society, sociologists say that it has become an **institutionalized norm** (DiMaggio & Powell, 1991). For instance, the institutionalized (that is, culturally acceptable) way of becoming financially successful in American society is to get a college degree (and perhaps an advanced degree after that), start out in an entry-level position somewhere, and eventually work your way to the top. Even phenomena that most of us would condemn have, at times, been institutionalized and encouraged by society. American slavery, for example, was for hundreds of years a culturally, politically, and economically "acceptable" practice. Buying and selling of slaves were strongly approved by the nation's most powerful forces (Birenbaum & Sagarin, 1976).

Institutionalized norms constrain people's behavior by making some lines of action unthinkable. But they don't just limit options, they also establish the setting in which people discover their preferences and begin to see the world in a particular way (DiMaggio & Powell, 1991). The orientation and training sessions you are expected to participate in when you start a job, for example, clearly indicate the organization's expectations and your new responsibilities. The fact that other employees accept these expectations as legitimate reinforces the idea that one perhaps shouldn't question organizational norms. Similarly, the military ritualizes the process of becoming a full-fledged member through oaths of allegiance and recognition of the passage from one rank to another. In doing so it ensures conformity to military norms. Religious congregations reinforce "appropriate" lifestyles and downplay inappropriate ones through collective worship services.

When institutions change, so too do institutionalized norms. Changes in the institution of the family, for instance, have created some new expectations: Children are now expected to be more independent; fathers are expected to be more involved in the nurturing of children. In the political realm, shifting public opinion as well as political necessity eventually led to the prohibition of slavery.

Shifts in one institution are often linked to shifts in another. For example, the fact that mothers are no longer expected to be the sole caretaker of children has meant an increase in the number of mothers who enter the paid labor force, which in turn has created higher demand for organized day care. The abolition of slavery meant that the entire economic system of the South had to be restructured, from a plantation economy to one characterized by smaller landholdings and more industry.

Norms and Sanctions

Most norms provide only a general framework of expectations; rarely do they tell us exactly how to act, and rarely are they obeyed by all people at all times. Furthermore, norms may be ambiguous or contradictory. It is no surprise, then, that behavior sometimes departs markedly from normative expectations. When it does, negative **sanctions** may be applied. A sanction is a direct social response that punishes or otherwise discourages violations of social norms and symbolically reinforces the culture's values and morals.

Different norms evoke different sanctions when violated. **Mores** (MORE-ayz) are norms, sometimes codified into laws, that are taken very seriously by society. Violation of some mores can elicit severe, state-sponsored punishment, such as serving time in prison for armed robbery. Other mores may be equally serious but are much less formally stated. Sanctions for violating these norms may be in the form of public ostracism or exclusion from the group, as when one is excommunicated for going against the moral doctrine of one's church.

The vast majority of everyday norms are relatively minor, however; violation of these norms, called **folkways**, carries much less serious punishment. For instance, if you chew with your mouth open and food dribbles down your chin, others might show outward signs of disapproval and consider you a "disgusting pig." You may receive fewer dinner invitations, but you won't be arrested or banished from the community.

According to the structural-functionalist perspective, each time a community moves to sanction an act, it restates its normative boundaries (Erikson, 1966). In the process the rest of us are warned of what is in store if we, too, violate the norms. In the 17th century criminals and religious heretics were executed at high noon in the public square for all to see. The spectacle was meant to be a vivid and symbolic reaffirmation of the community's norms. Today, of course, such harsh sanctions are likely to be hidden from the public eye. However, the publicity surrounding them, as well as the visibility of less severe sanctions of norm violations, serves the same purpose: to declare to the community where the line between acceptable and unacceptable behavior lies. By sanctioning the person who violates a norm, society informs its members of the type of person who *cannot* live "normally" within its boundaries (Pfohl, 1985).

In-groups and Ethnocentrism

As children most of us were taught, explicitly or implicitly, that we live in the greatest country on Earth. We may also have been taught to have pride in our religious, racial, or ethnic group. But the belief that our group is the "best" means that other groups are "not the best." Distinguishing between our in-group and out-groups is not unusual; we all tend to evaluate other cultures in comparison to our own. This tendency is called **ethnocentrism**.

Ethnocentrism is a consequence of the nature of human interaction itself. Much of our everyday lives is spent in groups and organizations. By their very character these collectivities are composed of individuals with some, though not necessarily all, shared interests. The same is true for larger cultures. To the extent that a majority of our time is spent with others "like us," our interactions with others "not like us" will be limited, and they will remain "foreign" or "mysterious" to us. Similarity breeds comfort; difference breeds discomfort.

Another reason for the existence of ethnocentrism is the loyalty we develop to our particular culture. Being part of a group, organization, or culture that we feel positive about encourages a sense of loyalty, which in turn encourages ethnocentrism. Such loyalty obligates us to defend our culture (Charon, 1992). Different values, beliefs, and actions come to be seen not merely as different ways of thinking and doing but as threats to what we hold dear. For example, in 1996 the national convention of Southern Baptists—the largest Protestant denomination in the country—adopted a resolution calling for a major campaign to convert American Jews to Christianity. To some, Christianity is the natural, necessary culmination of Jewish history, making Judaism unnecessary. The persistence of Jews who choose to remain Jews poses a challenge to this idea of inevitability, creating the need for intensive conversion (Garment, 1996).

Cultural loyalty is encouraged by institutional ritual. Saying the Pledge of Allegiance at the beginning of the school day, playing the "Star-Spangled Banner" at sports events, and observing holidays such as Memorial Day and the Fourth of July all reinforce loyalty to American culture. These are the "sacred objects" of our society (Durkheim, 1915/1954). Other rituals and sacred objects elicit loyalty to other groups to which we belong. Religious artifacts and symbols, uniforms and team colors, and distinctive ethnic clothing all foster a sense of pride and identity and hold a community of similar people together, often to the exclusion of others.

■ ■ ■ ■ ■ ■ ■ ■ ■

MICRO-MACRO CONNECTION
Transracial Adoption

Loyalty and pride in one's culture are likely to be felt most powerfully in the face of a perceived threat to the integrity of the culture. Consider the issue of transracial adoption, the practice of adopting children from a different racial group.

Most transracial adoptions take place between white parents and a minority child—African American, Hispanic, or Asian. The assumption is that race is irrelevant and ought to be minimized or ignored in the interests of finding a loving home for the child. In addition, the child, who likely comes from a financially depressed and deprived background, will have better opportunities in a more "advantaged" environment. Advocates argue that transracial adoption has the potential to transform a racially divided society into a racially integrated one. In the late 1960s, when transracial adoptions started to become more common, adoption agencies strongly encouraged white families to adopt children from other races. Today, organizations like the National Committee for Adoption have formally stated that because so many minority children are waiting for adoption, permanency rather than racial matching should be of paramount consideration (Adamec & Pierce, 1991). Recently, the Clinton administration proposed a bill that would make it easier for couples to adopt children of different racial backgrounds.

Transracial adoption has not been without its critics, however. In 1972 the National Association of Black Social Workers (NABSW) passed a resolution, still in effect today, against the adoption of black children by white parents (F. J. Davis, 1991). The group argued that transracial adoptions are harmful to black heritage and that to maintain the integrity of their culture blacks must be loyal to its uniqueness. They pointed out that a black child growing up in a white family will never learn about his or her own culture and will therefore never develop a positive self-image. White parents can never provide a black child with sufficient information about what it is like to be black in a predominantly white society.

Considering the larger historical and political context, we can understand why some groups fear that transracial adoption weakens their racial identity and culture. In the 1960s and 1970s, nearly 30% of all Native American children were removed from their families and put up for adoption. Social workers had deemed thousands of parents unfit because of poverty, alcoholism, and other problems. So devastating to the Native American culture was the removal of these children that the Indian Child Welfare Act was passed in 1978, giving tribes special preference in adopting children of Native American heritage (Egan, 1993). Recently, however, this law has come under attack, after reports of cases in which the adoption by white parents of children with only a minute trace of Indian ancestry has been contested by the tribe. At the time of this writing, an adoption bill is pending in Congress that would limit a tribal court's jurisdiction in adoption proceedings involving children whose biological parents do not maintain "significant social, cultural or political affiliation with the tribe" (Schmitt, 1996a, p. C18).

For African Americans, the civil rights movement of the 1960s instilled an unprecedented pride in their racial identity. The 1970s marked the first generation of black parents in American history that was deeply committed to instilling in their children positive racial self-concepts (Ladner, 1978). At a time when political power seemed to be within reach of African Americans, the possibility that some black children were being raised as white was difficult to tolerate. If it were true that black children adopted by white parents had difficulty identifying with the black culture, then they would be less likely to support black political issues. In this sense, the potential loss of cultural and racial identity could not be separated from broader political concerns.

The opposition to transracial adoption was quite effective. From the mid-1960s to the early 1970s, when transracial adoption reached its peak, approximately 15,000 black children were adopted by white parents (F. J. Davis, 1991). In 1971, 1 out of every 3 black children who was adopted was placed with a white family (Ladner, 1978). But by 1975 (the last year the government collected data on transracial adoption), adoptions of black children by white parents had disappeared almost completely (Adamec & Pierce, 1991; F. J. Davis, 1991). By 1987, 35 states had established policies against cross-racial adoption.

Were the fears of children losing their racial identities borne out? Research on this issue has been somewhat mixed. Some studies have shown that a relatively low percentage of young black children adopted by white families have problems with racial identity (for example, Feigelman & Silverman, 1984). Several studies have found that preschool children involved in transracial adoptions are as well adjusted as children from same-race adoptions (Shireman & Johnson, 1986; Zastrow, 1977). One study followed transracially adopted children and their parents for 20 years and found that despite periodic racial name-calling at school and in other public situations, these individuals do not have problems identifying as black Americans and are functioning successfully as young adults (R. Simon, Alstein, & Melli, 1994).

Beyond the level of individual adjustment, though, the broader problem of cultural heritage remains. White adoptive parents have been known to minimize or ignore the racial identity of their children, considering parenthood and family more important than race (Ladner, 1978). In a study of 30 adolescent black children adopted by white parents, only 10 of them identified themselves as black,

6 said they were "mixed," and the rest tried to avoid a racial identity altogether by saying they were "human" or "American" (McRoy & Zurcher, 1983).

Not only does the issue of transracial adoption provide an interesting example of cultural loyalty and protection, it also shows conflicting institutional functions. Transracial adoption is as much about cultural conceptions of what the family's role in society ought to be as it is about race. Traditionally, one of the important functions of the family has been to offer unqualified emotional support, nurturance, and protection to its members. But the family is also supposed to provide its members with cultural instruction and a sense of racial, ethnic, or religious identity. The difficulty we face as a society in deciding which of these functions should take precedence is at the heart of the debate. The difficulty we face as students of sociology is reconciling our human concern for individual children with our scientific concern for objectivity and acceptance of other points of view.

▪ ▪ ▪

Cultural Variation and Everyday Experience

As our population grows more ethnically and racially diverse and as the people of the world are linked more closely by commerce, transportation, and communication, the likelihood of people from different cultures and subcultures clashing over folkways and mores escalates. Many of the difficulties and tragedies of contemporary society can be traced to a lack of awareness of differences in cultural expectations.

Several years ago, a Chinese immigrant living in New York bludgeoned his wife to death with a hammer after she had confessed she was having an affair. The facts of the case were clear. The man freely admitted he had killed his wife. Instead of being convicted of murder, however, the man was convicted of the lesser charge of second-degree manslaughter. He received a sentence of 5 years' probation.

The judge in the case said he treated the defendant lightly because of testimony regarding Chinese cultural attitudes toward adultery. The defense attorney argued that the man did not intentionally kill his wife. Instead, the overwhelming sense of shame brought on by his wife's adultery put him in a frame of mind in which he could no longer control his actions. According to one anthropologist who testified in the case, adultery in China is an "enormous stain" that reflects not only on the aggrieved husband, but also on his ancestors and all future generations of his family. The judge ruled that his actions, although tragic and unfortunate, were nonetheless understandable from the point of view of the man's cultural training (Bohlen, 1989).

An awareness of cultural differences can be crucial in international relations. Edward Hall (1969), in his classic study of conceptions of space and territory, points out that perceiving the world differently leads to different definitions of what constitutes crowded living, different interpersonal relationships, and even different approaches to both local and international politics. Knowing that Arabs find it acceptable to touch and breathe on one another during casual conversation and that Germans value privacy and distance would be an advantage in business or political negotiations (Karp & Yoels, 1985).

■ ■ ■ ■ ■ ■ ■ ■ ■
MICRO-MACRO CONNECTION
Female Genital Mutilation

Conflict between cultures becomes particularly controversial when one culture's long-held tradition is perceived as brutal and oppressive by members of other cultures. According to the World Health Organization, between 85 and 114 million girls and women worldwide have been subjected to a cultural practice called female genital mutilation (FGM) (cited in Dugger, 1996a). This practice occurs in some form in over 40 countries in Africa and the Middle East, including Saudi Arabia, Iraq, Syria, Kenya, Nigeria, and Egypt. The procedure, which entails the removal of the clitoris and/or the destruction of the labia and vulva, is typically performed by a midwife using a sharp instrument such as a razor blade, scissors, knife, or piece of glass. Antiseptic techniques and anesthesia are generally not used (Sarkis, 1995). The girl's age at the time of the ritual varies from culture to culture, but she is usually between 4 and 10.

This cultural tradition reflects the value of women in these societies. Where FGM exists as a common practice, men have traditionally demanded that their wives be virgins when they marry. Indeed, a girl who has not undergone this procedure may be considered "unclean" or a prostitute by local villagers and therefore unmarriageable. The ritual also serves to regulate women's sexuality.

Ironically women themselves—usually mothers and grandmothers—often enforce the practice, exerting strong pressure on their daughters and granddaughters to abide by the custom (Crossette, 1995). Such pressure is seldom motivated by cruelty. In fact, these older women may have the girls' best interests in mind. If a young woman's marriageability, and therefore her future economic security, requires that she be subjected to FGM, her very survival is at stake:

> In a culture in which men will not marry you unless you have been mutilated and there is no other work you can do and you are . . . considered a prostitute if you are not mutilated, you face a very big problem. Women mutilate their daughters because they really are looking down the road to a time when the daughter will . . . marry and at least have a roof . . . and food. (Walker & Parmar, 1993, p. 277)

Effective change, therefore, can only come about if women's economic and social vulnerability in male-dominated cultures—their poverty, financial dependency, educational disadvantage, and obstacles to employment—is addressed (Gruenbaum, 1993).

International efforts to stop FGM have not gone uncriticized. Some argue that attempting to forbid a practice in another culture that has existed for generations is arrogant. They argue that efforts of international organizations like the United Nations and the World Health Organization to abolish the practice are dangerous examples of ethnocentric meddling.

Others, however, feel that no practice that oppresses a particular group—in this case, women—ought to be tolerated. They cite the influence of international opposition in the dismantling of apartheid in South Africa as an example of how effective global pressure can be used against injustice. They reject the notion that such a physically harmful practice must be understood within the appropriate cultural context and argue that only worldwide demands for change will halt FGM.

The problem of FGM is no longer limited to distant countries. With immigration increasing worldwide, it has become transnational. More and more immigrants from countries where FGM is practiced are bringing the custom with them when they arrive in countries where it was previously unknown. Britain, Sweden, France, and Switzerland have outlawed FGM. Here in the United States some states—Minnesota and North Dakota—have passed laws forbidding the practice; in other states—New York and New Jersey—legislation has been introduced. In 1996 the U.S. Board of Immigration Appeals, a branch of the Justice Department, granted political asylum to a 19-year-old woman from Togo who said she fled her homeland to avoid being subjected to FGM. The ruling represented a formal recognition that FGM is a form of persecution and that women who refuse to undergo the practice face threats to their freedom, physical harm, or social ostracism (Dugger, 1996b).

■ ■ ■

As individuals rooted in a society that does not practice FGM, we can applaud such a stand. But as students of sociology, we must acknowledge that culture and history may make opposing viewpoints equally valid. Comparing our beliefs and behaviors to those of others sheds a great deal of light on the structure and process of society as well as the motivations behind individual behavior. We can also gain insight into why certain rituals, behaviors, and values exist in some cultures but not in others, or in some eras and not others. Such differences can be found in many areas of cultural variation.

Health and Illness

We know that people in some countries live longer and are more healthy than people in other countries, but we usually don't associate health and illness with culture. In this section I describe medical treatment and the sick role, both of which illustrate the enormous influence of culture in our lives and the conflict that can arise over cultural differences.

Medical Treatment

Medical beliefs and behaviors must be consistent with the prevailing cultural values of a particular society (Coe, 1978). Claims of illness are always subject to group or societal validation; that is, you can't claim to have a disease that doesn't exist in your culture.

The way doctors deal with patients and their ailments is also largely determined by cultural attitudes (Payer, 1988). Recall the discussion of the Azande in chapter 3. Because their everyday existence is tied to the supernatural, witchcraft, and sorcery, so too is their practice of medicine. The Azande "doctor" attempts to heal sick people by invoking the power of spirits. What is even more compelling, though, is that dramatic cultural differences in medical activity exist even when we compare societies that share many values, beliefs, norms, and structural elements.

In the United States medical treatment tends to derive from an aggressive, "can do" spirit. American doctors are much more likely than European doctors to prescribe drugs and resort to surgery (Payer, 1988). American women are more likely than their European counterparts to undergo radical mastectomies, deliver their babies by cesarean section, and undergo routine hysterectomies while still in their 40s. Americans see their bodies as machines that require annual checkups for routine maintenance. Diseases are enemies that need to be conquered (for example, "beating" cancer).

In contrast, British medicine is much more subdued. British physicians don't recommend routine examinations, seldom prescribe drugs, and order about half as many X rays as American doctors do. British patients are also much less likely to have surgery. These practices influence the perceptions of patients. People who are quiet and withdrawn—which might be considered symptoms of clinical depression in the United States—tend to be seen by British psychiatrists as perfectly normal.

The French are keenly sensitive to bodily appearance, which is why physicians are more likely to treat breast and other types of cancer with radiation rather than surgery. The French believe that a patient's "constitution," or physical makeup, is as important in the onset of disease as germs and bacteria. They are more likely to prescribe vitamins to bolster the body than antibiotics to fight germs.

The choice of diagnoses and medical treatments is not a science. While scientific research can show us the risks and benefits of a certain course of action, the weighing of those costs and benefits is inevitably made on a cultural scale (Payer, 1988).

The Sick Role

In addition to determining the nature of illness, cultural attitudes determine what it means to be sick. Each society has a **sick role**, a widely understood set of rules about how we're supposed to behave when sick (Parsons, 1951). When you are sick, the illness is considered to be beyond your control, and you are excused from normal social role responsibilities. You are not expected to function in the same capacity you would if you were well.

The sick role entails certain obligations, too. For instance, a sick person is duty-bound to *want* to get better as quickly as possible, to seek technically competent help, and to cooperate in the process of recovery. The obligation to seek technical help is an explicit recognition of the power of the medical profession. In our culture expert assistance almost always involves following a doctor's instructions: taking prescribed medication, resting, exercising, drinking fluids, and so on. Most people in this culture do not go to witch doctors or exorcists for cures. For that matter, most are reluctant to use holistic healers, chiropractors, homeopaths, osteopaths, or any other alternative approach outside the purview of mainstream medicine.

Failure on the part of sick persons either to exercise their rights or to fulfill the obligations of the sick role may elicit sanctions from the group (Coe, 1978). For instance, those who do not appear to want to recover or who seem to enjoy being sick quickly lose certain privileges, such as sympathy.

One may also give up legal rights by not seeking or following expert advice. Parents have been arrested for not acquiring traditional medical assistance for their sick children (see chapter 2). If you are hospitalized and your attending physician doesn't think you ought to be discharged, but you leave anyway, your records will indicate that you have left "A.M.A."—against medical advice. This designation protects the doctor and the hospital from any liability should your condition worsen.

The dimensions of the sick role are, of course, relative to the nature and severity of the illness (Segall, 1987). For certain illnesses we are entitled to stay in bed, free from all our usual obligations. For other illnesses we are expected to carry on with our usual activities. Compare the "rights" of a person with cancer to those of a person with a sore throat.

The sick role is influenced not only by the nature of the illness but also by cultural factors. There is a practice found in parts of Japan, China, India, and Spain called the *couvade,* from a French term meaning "cowardly inactivity." Among anthropologists it is used to describe a custom in which, during childbirth, the *father* experiences labor pains. In some instances he will lie down beside the mother and scream with pain as she is giving birth. Following the birth of the child, the mother is expected to return to her normal duties right away while the father goes to bed, sometimes for up to 40 days! It is the father, not the mother, who is relieved of ordinary social responsibilities and who is eligible for sympathy from the village.

In light of the fact that culture determines conceptions of illness and help-seeking behavior, it is reasonable to assume that subcultural beliefs among different ethnic groups within the same culture will also influence the sick role. One area in which such differences can be seen is in the expression of pain.

■ ■ ■ ■ ■ ■ ■ ■

MARK ZBOROWSKI
The Experience of Pain

On the surface it would appear that pain is physical and universal. But why do people with similar injuries react so differently to pain? Some individuals are better equipped physically to withstand pain than others, but other differences are cross-cultural. Sociologist Mark Zborowski (1952) investigated the meaning people attach to pain, their style of pain expression, and the future expectations derived from it. The groups he chose to study were Jews, Italians, and "Old Americans," whom he defined as white, native-born individuals, usually Protestant, whose grandparents were born in the United States and who did not identify themselves with any foreign group. He interviewed hospital patients from the selected groups, observing their behavior when in pain and discussing their cases with doctors and nurses.

Zborowski found that Jews and Italians tend to have very emotional responses to pain, a finding consistent with the norms among these groups that allow for the open expression of feelings. Both groups felt free to talk about their pain, complain about it, and show their suffering by moaning, groaning, and crying. They complained a great deal, called for help frequently, and expected sympathy and assistance from others.

There were some differences. On the one hand, the Italian patients seemed to be concerned mainly with the immediacy of the pain experience and were disturbed by the actual pain sensation. On the other hand, the Jewish patients focused mainly on the symptomatic meaning of pain and on the significance of pain in relation to their health and welfare.

Among the "Old American" patients, Zborowski found little complaining. They tended to be stoic and to minimize the significance of their experiences. Their complaints focused more on the location and duration of the pain. They indicated there was no point in complaining because "it won't help anybody."

Zborowski noted that not all individuals within each group exhibited the same pain reactions. Furthermore, over succeeding generations, ethnic differences in responses to pain begin to diminish. Nevertheless, he provided strong evidence that a purely physical and private experience like pain can be related to or dictated by one's subcultural expectations, which in turn can influence the sick role.

■ ■ ■

Time

Another interesting area of human life that is very much dictated by culture is the conception of time. Time is the core system of all societies, organizing and synthesizing the activities of our everyday existence (E. T. Hall, 1983). Most of us think of time as uniform and unchangeable. After all, a minute is a minute no matter who you are or where you live.

Time, though, is a human construction. Some units of time, like days, months, and years, parallel natural events, like the movement of the earth and moon. Others, however, are clearly arbitrary. Seconds, minutes, and hours do not exist in nature. The appearance of the 7-day week has been traced to holy numbers, planets, and astrology (Zerubavel, 1985).

Although time is measured in absolute units, it is not perceived the same way in all situations. Think of how time flies when you're on an enjoyable date but drags on when you're in a boring class. The extra 5 minutes of sleep we desire after the alarm goes off in the morning is infinitely more valuable to us than 5 minutes stuck in traffic. In some situations time is structurally irrelevant. Las Vegas casinos, for example, have no windows and no clocks, and they operate 24 hours a day.

It would be a mistake to assume that all members of a large complex society like ours share the same conceptions of time. Different regions have their own time rules. In some areas people are described as "laid back," in others they're "fast-paced" or "always in a hurry."

Conceptions of time are also tied to one's occupation. Work life is often synonymous with the amount of time you spend on the job as well as the time you spend preparing for work, getting there, and getting back. In most jobs people are paid by the hour. Workdays are punctuated by time demands or deadlines. Time has become an economic commodity, something that can be exchanged for money, wasted, shared, or saved (Kearl & Gordon, 1992).

Norms concerning the definition and use of time vary from culture to culture. For example, cultures differ in their orientations toward the future and the past. Phrases like "time heals all wounds" or "that's ancient history" are meaningful only within a culture that makes significant distinctions between the past and the future. To some people such phrases would make neither linguistic nor cultural sense. In many Arab societies there are only three sets of time: no time at all, now (which varies in duration), and forever (too long) (E. T. Hall, 1969). The Hopi of the American Southwest have no tenses in their language indicating past, present, or future (Whorf, 1956). For them time does not proceed in a linear fashion and is not perceived as a series of discrete instances. Life is cyclical, and events such as meals or ceremonies are not unique but are accumulated over time.

Terms like *late, early,* or *on time* are not universal. Americans, for instance, are acutely sensitive to time and timing. Most of us own watches, and our days often consist of a series of precisely scheduled episodes. Your classes meet at specific times of the day. Perhaps you live in a dormitory where meals are served only at certain times. If you work, you have "hours" that you must keep or risk losing your job. A related American ideal is to be punctual or "on time." So valued are the rules of punctuality that if you violate them you are required to provide an apology and an explanation. While there may be individual differences, like the friend who is "always late," or situational differences, like arriving at a party "fashionably late," most of us subscribe to the notion that one should be on time if at all possible.

Other cultures place a very different value on punctuality. Psychologist Robert Levine studied time norms in Brazil. He noted that Brazilians have much more flexible conceptions of time and punctuality than Americans do (Levine & Wolff, 1988). He wrote of an experience he had while he was a visiting professor at a university outside Rio de Janeiro:

> My class was scheduled from 10 until noon. Many students came late, some very late. Several arrived after 10:30. A few showed up closer to 11. Two came after that. All of the latecomers wore relaxed smiles. . . . Each one said hello, and although a few apologized briefly, none seemed terribly concerned about lateness. They assumed that I understood. . . .
>
> Back home in California, I never need to look at a clock to know when the class hour is ending. The shuffling of books is accompanied by strained expressions that say plaintively, "I'm starving. . . . I've got to go to the bathroom. . . . I'm going to suffocate if you keep us one more second." When noon arrived in my first Brazilian class, only a few students left immediately. Others slowly drifted out during the next 15 minutes. . . . When several remaining students kicked off their shoes at 12:30, I went into my own "starving/bathroom/suffocation" routine. Apparently for many of my students, staying late was simply of no more importance than arriving late in the first place. (pp. 78–79)

Such cultural differences in time are not merely amusing or trivial. They tell us a great deal about the nature and values of a particular society. Brazilians tend to believe that a person who is consistently late is probably more successful than one who is consistently on time. Lack of punctuality is a badge of success.

People tend to build ideas of national character around the pace of a particular culture's way of life. We Americans admire the Germans and the Swiss because of their ability to "make the trains run on time." We may characterize some Arab and South American cultures as "lazy" or "apathetic" because of their apparent disregard for timeliness. We see the Japanese as aggressive, partly because their pace of life is quicker than ours and because they are "ahead of us" in other measurable ways (Levine & Wolff, 1988). Appreciating such cultural differences in time sense becomes increasingly important as modern methods of communication put greater numbers of people in daily contact.

Childhood

We can also see evidence of cultural variation in conceptions of childhood. In this case, variations in culture over time are dramatic. In modern Western societies there is a widely held, unquestioned belief that children are fundamentally different from adults. We take for granted that children are innocent and are entitled to nurturance and protection. However, in other cultures (for example,

Japan) children are viewed as much more independent creatures who can act willfully from the earliest moments of life (Kagan, 1976).

We tend to base our belief about the nature of childhood on biological considerations. Young children are thoroughly dependent on adults for their survival. Infants cannot feed themselves or take care of themselves in any way. A 10-month-old child, left on its own, will surely die within days. It is not uncommon for a human to remain dependent on his or her parents for several decades. By contrast, other animal babies are much more self-sufficient. A newborn horse, for example, is able to gallop around when it is only a few minutes old.

It is not surprising, then, that we have laws protecting innocent and defenseless children from dangers like exploitation at work, pornography, neglect, and abuse. It seems inconceivable that the need to protect innocent children is not a fundamental value in all societies, present and past. However, the origin of the Western notion of children as a unique population is relatively recent (Aries, 1962).

Views of Childhood in the Middle Ages

Until the end of the Middle Ages, children were seen as miniature versions of adults. If you look at paintings of the 15th and 16th centuries, you will notice that the children depicted in family portraits look like shrunken replicas of their parents. Their clothes and their bodily proportions are the same as those of adults.

This image goes beyond artistic representation. Because they were seen as miniature adults, they were expected to act accordingly. The notion that children deserve special protection and treatment did not exist at this time. Hence children could be and frequently were punished for social transgressions with the same severity that adults were (Aries, 1962).

This rather "unsentimental" treatment of children probably had something to do with demographic realities. Fatal disease in the Middle Ages was quite prevalent, and infant mortality rates were extremely high. Young children were not expected to live for very long. If one wanted only a few children, it was necessary to have many more in order to "hedge one's bets." As a result, parents couldn't allow themselves to get too emotionally attached to something that was seen as a probable loss. At that time, the death of a baby was probably not the emotional tragedy that it is today. In Spain, for example, when an infant died he or she was likely to be buried almost anywhere on the premises, like a pet cat or dog.

Childhood in the 18th and 19th Centuries

By the 18th century, perceptions of childhood were beginning to change. Children were now seen as innocent and in need of protection. Consequently, though, they were viewed as weak and susceptible to temptation. Along with the notion of protection came the notion of discipline, as parents taught their children to avoid the enticements of their social worlds.

Severe beatings of children in the name of discipline were common occurrences up until the late 18th century and occur in some areas of society even to this day. Such cruelty was often couched in religious terms. One Dutch theologian offered the theory that God had formed the human buttocks so that they could be severely beaten without incurring serious bodily injury (L. Stone, 1979). Heaven was sometimes described to children in Sunday school as "a place where children are never beaten" (Archer, 1985).

Definitions of childhood throughout history have been influenced by social institutions as well. Until the late 1800s, for instance, child labor was commonly practiced and accepted (Archer, 1985). Children worked as long and as hard as adults, sometimes even harder. Because of their small size, they were sometimes given difficult and hazardous jobs, like cleaning out the insides of narrow factory chimneys.

In addition, abandoned children were sometimes recruited by unscrupulous adults for use in robbery and prostitution. Some of them were physically mutilated so they could elicit more sympathy as beggars (L. Stone, 1979). Although there is little evidence of complete social approval or tolerance of these kinds of practices, it is clear that they weren't severely sanctioned either:

> Some had their teeth torn out to serve as artificial teeth for the rich; others were deliberately maimed by beggars to arouse compassion.... Even this latter crime was one upon which the law looked with a remarkably tolerant eye. In 1761 a beggar woman, convicted of deliberately "putting out the eyes of children with whom she went about the country" in order to attract pity and alms, was sentenced to no more than two years' imprisonment. (L. Stone, 1979, p. 298)

Only by the middle of the 19th century did the first child protection organizations emerge. In 1825 the first House of Refuge in America was founded, an institution whose purpose was to provide sanctuary to children who had been abused or neglected. In subsequent years many similar institutions were established.

Even these, however, were not totally sensitive to the welfare of children. Their purpose was not to protect but to prevent children from becoming economic burdens and threats to society. It was widely believed at the time that children who had bad childhoods would grow up to be bad adults. The House of Refuge sought to prevent the potential criminal tendencies of poor urban youths from ever surfacing by removing them from abusive home environments and placing them in institutions. Here they would share a "proper growing up" with other abandoned and neglected youths as well as delinquents who had violated the law (Pfohl, 1977).

The social value of children was also affected by major economic transformations in society (LeVine & White, 1992; Zelizer, 1985). The shift from a predominantly agricultural economy to an industrialized one in the 19th century revolutionized cultural conceptions. On the farm, families were bound together by economic necessity rather than emotions. Children were a crucial source of labor in the family economy, and they were a source of financial support in old age

(LeVine & White, 1992). Consequently, the birth of a child was hailed as the arrival of a future laborer who would contribute to the financial security of the family. In adoption practices, the most desirable child was the teenage male because of his potential value as a laborer (Zelizer, 1985).

20th-Century Childhood

With the advent of industrialization by the middle of the 20th century, however, children were no longer seen as economic necessities. The main source of income was now the parents, or more accurately the fathers, outside the home. As a result, children became economically "useless," and people began to see them as downright costly to raise (LeVine & White, 1992). At the same time, though, their emotional importance was recognized. Today's parents are more likely to look to their children for intimacy and less likely to expect anything tangible in return. The contemporary social value of children is determined not by their labor potential but by the love and care they are thought to deserve. Hence the most desirable child for adoption today is the newborn baby.

Conclusion

Over the span of a year or two, most cultures present an image of stability and agreement regarding the acceptability of certain behaviors. This agreement is illusory, however. From the perspective of a generation or even a decade, that sense of order is replaced by a sense of change (McCall & Simmons, 1978). Behaviors, values, beliefs, and morals fluctuate with startling frequency. Thus comparisons across eras, in addition to comparisons across cultures, can provide rich insight into shifting definitions of acceptability, the nature of everyday life, and ultimately large-scale social change and stability.

The cultural and historical underpinnings of our private lives help us see the relationship between the individual, society, and social order. While different cultures treat illnesses differently or define time and childhood differently, these practices also add continuity and order to social life.

To an individual, culture appears massive and unrelenting, but at the same time it cannot exist without people as a whole. Norms govern our lives, whether we live by them or rebel against them. To fully understand the relationship between the individual and society we must look beyond the fact that culture and history shape our lives; we must see them as human creations as well.

CHAPTER HIGHLIGHTS

■ Culture provides members of a society with a common bond, a sense that we see certain facets of society in similar ways. That we can live together at all depends on the fact that members of a society share a certain amount of cultural knowledge.

▪ Norms—the rules and standards that govern all social encounters—provide order in our lives. They reflect commonly held assumptions about conventional behavior. Norm violations mark the boundaries of acceptable behavior and symbolically reaffirm what society defines as right and wrong.

▪ The more ethnically and culturally diverse a society is, the greater the likelihood of normative clashes between groups.

▪ Over the span of a few years, most cultures present an image of stability and agreement regarding normative boundaries. This agreement is illusory. Over a generation or even a decade, that sense of order is replaced by a sense of change.

YOUR TURN

The acceptability of certain acts or thoughts is *socially constructed*. We as a society decide what is and isn't appropriate, like how to shake hands, how close to stand to someone when conversing, and so forth. These norms form the basis of a taken-for-granted reality that underlies all we do but that remains largely unnoticed and unquestioned. These rules of conduct add predictability and order to our encounters with others. They are so common that they are noticed only when violated. The best proof of the existence of these norms lies in our reactions when they are violated.

The following suggestions for proving the existence of norms are based on an exercise used by Jodi O'Brien at Seattle University. If you like, choose a different unspoken norm that lends order and predictability to daily social interactions.

- Make a purchase in a department store and offer to pay more than the listed price. Try to convince the clerk that you think the merchandise is worth the price you are offering.
- Send a close family member a birthday card months away from his or her actual birthday.
- Talk to yourself in a public place.
- Stand or sit close to a stranger or stand far away from a good friend or lover during the course of an ordinary conversation.
- Select an occasion—going to class, going on a date, going to the library—and dress differently than the expected "uniform." Treat your dress as absolutely appropriate to the circumstances.
- Whenever someone says to you "See you later," ask him or her probing questions: When? Did you have some plans to get together later? What do you mean by "see"? and so on. Or when someone says, "How's it going?" ask: What do you mean by "it"? What do you mean by "going"?
- In a restaurant demand to pay for your meal *before* you order it, or order dessert first, then the main course, then appetizers, then drinks.

It is particularly important that this behavior be neither flagrantly bizarre—like going to class dressed as a chicken—nor a violation of the law. Such acts do not address the power of the subtle, unspoken norms that make social life orderly. Also, do not do anything that might put you in danger. Finally, make sure the norm has something to do with keeping order in face-to-face interactions. For instance, coming to class 10 minutes late is a violation of a social norm, but it doesn't disrupt interactional order when it occurs. *Above all, remember to treat your violation as perfectly normal.* You must give the impression that what you are doing is perfectly acceptable and ordinary.

As you conduct your experiment, record your own feelings and reactions as well as those of the subjects. What were people's initial reactions? What did they do to try to "normalize" your behavior? How did you feel breaching this norm? Was it uncomfortable? If so, why? If possible, try to debrief your subjects afterward: Tell them what you were really doing, and then interview them regarding their interpretations of the experience. This will provide you with information on how people attempt to "explain away" unusual and strange circumstances and how they attempt to restore order to the situation. What are the implications of these sorts of "experiments" for an understanding of human behavior and the nature of social order in this society?

ILLUSTRATING CULTURE
Peasant Pilgrimages of Modern Europe

DOUGLAS HARPER with photographs by MARRIE BOT[*]

"...The modern pilgrimage is an event of a disappearing European peasantry, embodying the marginality of a class that has nearly disappeared under the weight of modernization and industrialization...."

It is impossible to illustrate the concept of culture simply. It is both obvious and subtle, ubiquitous yet transparent. Thus this visual essay looks at a cultural event that is probably far from your own experience, to encourage you to further consider the ideas of this chapter.

While looking at these photographs of peasant pilgrims in Europe, please consider the following issues raised in this chapter:

- Culture exists in all human gatherings. Even though it is universal as a phenomenon, each example of culture is unique.

- Culture is both the objects we surround ourselves with and the beliefs and symbols we share with the group we associate with.

- Culture is a guide for the integration of emotions and social structure, and this pattern has a historical as well as a geographic dimension.

- Culture defines what is normal as well as what is crazy.

[*]Detail in top photograph on this page cropped from photograph by Marrie Bot appearing on page 117.

- We think of our own culture as natural, rational, and the most desirable, but so does everyone else.

Now examine these photographs by the Dutch photographer Marrie Bot. These are from her photographic book, *Miserere* ("Lord have mercy"), a visual study of ten great penitential pilgrimages in six European countries.

The pilgrimage is a cultural event that has emerged from the huge institution of the Chris-

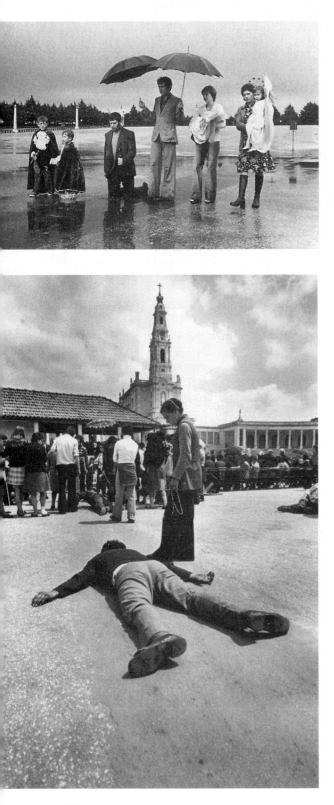

tian church. It has a historical dimension; from the beginning of Christianity the church has encouraged the faithful to visit holy places to obtain remission for their sins. As the social structural contexts of the pilgrimages have changed, however, the meanings of the cultural event have shifted.

Pilgrimages have meanings that are part of the original religious expectations and part of national and regional cultures in which they take place. The pilgrimage of Croagh Patrick, the most important penitential event in Ireland, is sanctioned by the Catholic Church to commemorate St. Patrick's trip to the mountains to seek divine inspiration. Other pilgrimages seek medical cures, the appearance of Mary, or other commemorations of Catholicism. In some periods of history, pilgrimages wrenched people from their social moorings and led them to political revolt. The modern pilgrimage is an event of a disappearing European peasantry, embodying the marginality of a class that has nearly disappeared under the weight of modernization and industrialization.

The European peasants who undertake the long pilgrimages of contemporary Europe engage in behaviors that Dutch sociologist Abram de Swaan says have become forbidden in our culture. We sometimes kiss the hands of those we revere, but we no longer lie prostrate before them. Democracy and modernism require that we transcend such a level of servility. Indeed, modern political movements depend upon a culture that believes in its own potential for meaningful action. The peasants photographed by Marrie Bot belong to a culture of submission and limited aspiration. In the multicultural Europe of today they are remnants of the past.

As you consider these photographs, imagine yourself in this, rather than your own, religious culture. What would happen to the things you take for granted? What new cultural realities would define your reality?

These photographs were taken at Fatima, the largest shrine in Portugal. More than 1.5 million Christians visit the shrine each year. It is the site of the "miracle of Fatima," alleged visitations of the Virgin Mary to three shepherd children in 1917. During the visitation Mary

instructed the children with messages that the Catholic Church still considers significant enough to retain in secrecy.

CHAPTER 5

Building Identity:
The Social Construction of Self

- *Social Structure and the Construction of Human Beings*
- *Socialization and Resocialization: Learning Who We Are*
- *The Structural Context of Socialization*
- *The Socialization of Self*
- *The Socialization of Gender*

My family once lived in a suburb just outside New York City. One day, when I was 9 years old, my parents sat me down and told me that due to financial concerns—which were beyond my understanding—we had to move. They had narrowed down our ultimate destination to two possibilities: Laredo, Texas, and Burbank, California. After some rather intense debate, they chose Burbank. And so we headed "out West," where from age 9 to age 18 I lived in the shadow of the entertainment industry and all its glamour, glitz, and movie stars. It wasn't long before I became a typical sun-worshiping, Frisbee-throwing California kid.

I often wonder how differently I would have turned out if my parents had chosen Laredo and I had spent my formative years in the heart of Texas instead of in the middle of Tinsel Town. Would I have a fondness for 10-gallon hats and snakeskin boots instead of tennis shoes and shorts? Would I have grown up with country music instead of the Beach Boys? Would I have a different accent? Would my goals be different? In short, would I be a different person?

Try to imagine what your life would be like if you had grown up under different circumstances. What if your father had been a harpsichord enthusiast instead of a Cubs fan? What if your family had been Jewish instead of Episcopalian? What if you had had an older brother instead of a younger sister? What if you had lived on a farm instead of in a big city? What if you had been born in the 1940s instead of the 1970s? Your tastes, preferences, and hobbies, as well as your morals, values, ambitions, and aspirations, would no doubt be different. But more profoundly, your self-concept, self-esteem, personality—the essence of who you are—would be altered.

Consider the broader social and historical circumstances of your life. What kind of impact might they have had on the type of person you are? Talk to people who grew up in the 1930s and they will speak of the permanent impact the Great Depression had on them (Elder & Liker, 1982). Imagine spending your childhood as a Jew in Nazi Germany. That couldn't help but shape your outlook on life. The same can be said for growing up black in South Central Los Angeles in the 1990s or white in Beverly Hills during the Reagan presidency. Today's ever-expanding communications technologies, including interactive and virtual-reality computers, information highways, video, and fax machines, will have an unmistakable impact on the kinds of adults you will see in the future (K. J. Gergen, 1991).

Becoming the person you are cannot be separated from the people, historical events, and social circumstances that surround you. In this chapter I examine the process of socialization: how we learn what's expected of us in our families, our communities, and our culture and how we learn to behave according to those expectations. The primary focus will be on the development of identity. **Identity** is our most essential and personal characteristic. It consists of our membership in social groups (race, ethnicity, religion, gender, and so on), the traits we show, and the traits others ascribe to us. Our identity locates us in the social world, thoroughly affecting everything we do, feel, say, and think in our lives. Most people tend to believe that our self-concept, our sense of "maleness" or "femaleness," or our racial and ethnic identities are biologically or psychologically determined and therefore permanent and unchangeable. But as you will discover, these characteristics are as much a product of our social surroundings and the significant people in our lives as they are a product of our physical traits and innate predispositions.

Social Structure and the Construction of Human Beings

The question of how we become who we are has occupied the attention of biologists, psychologists, anthropologists, sociologists, philosophers, and novelists for centuries. Commonly, the issue is framed as an ongoing debate between *nature* (we are who we are because we are born that way) and *nurture* (we are who we are because of our environment). Are we simply a product of our genes and biochemistry, or are we somehow "created" by the people and the social institutions that surround us?

The answer is most likely "both." Most sociologists would argue that human beings are more than just a collection of physical and psychological characteristics. That's not to say that inborn traits are of absolutely no importance. Certainly our physical attractiveness and strength, genetic predisposition to sickness, and so on have some effect on our personal development. Furthermore, there's no arguing that our every thought and action is the product of a complex series of neurological and electrochemical events in our brains and bodies. Males and females obviously differ anatomically and hormonally and may even see the world differently as a result.

The issue is not so much whether these physiological events or innate differences exist; rather, it is whether they are culturally defined as significant. Society can magnify differences or cover them up. We collectively decide which physical traits are socially irrelevant (for example, eye color) and which become embedded in our social institutions (for example, sex and race), giving rise to different rights, duties, expectations, and access to institutional opportunities.

Who we become is also influenced by the behaviors and attitudes of significant people in our lives as well as by cultural and institutional forces. As these things change, so do we. This is not an altogether comforting proposition. It implies that who we are may in some ways be "accidental," the shaky result of a series of social coincidences, chance encounters, decisions made by others, and of political, economic, or historical events that are in large measure beyond our control.

Socialization and Resocialization: Learning Who We Are

The fundamental task of any society—is to reproduce itself to create members whose behaviors, desires, and goals correspond to those that are deemed appropriate and desirable by that particular society. Through the powerful and ubiquitous process of **socialization**, the needs of society become the needs of the individual.

Socialization is a process of learning. To socialize someone is to train him or her to behave appropriately. It is the means by which people acquire important social skills like driving a car, doing long division, speaking the language correctly, or using the little fork instead of the big fork at the right times. But socialization is also the way we learn how to perceive our world; how to interact with others; what it means to be male or female; how, when, why, and with whom to be sexual; what we should and should not do under certain circumstances; what our society defines as good and bad; and so on.

People often assume that socialization is synonymous with child rearing. It is true that the basic, formative instruction of life occurs early on. Young children must be taught the fundamental values, knowledge, and beliefs of their culture. Some of the socialization that occurs during childhood—often referred to as **anticipatory socialization**—is the primary means by which young individuals acquire the values and orientations found in the statuses they will likely enter in the future (Merton, 1957). Paper routes, Little League, dance lessons, dating, and so on give youngsters an opportunity to rehearse for the kinds of roles that await them in adulthood.

Socialization does not end in childhood, however; it continues throughout our lives. Adults must be **resocialized** into a new set of norms, values, and expectations each time they leave behind old social contexts or roles and enter new ones (Brim, 1968; Ebaugh, 1988; Pescosolido, 1986; I. H. Simpson, 1979). For instance, we have to learn how to think and act like a spouse when we marry (Berger & Kellner, 1964), a parent when we have kids (A. Rossi, 1968), or a divorced person when a marriage ends (Vaughan, 1986). Every new group or organization we enter, every new friendship we form, every new life-changing experience we have requires the formation of new identities and socialization into new sets of norms and beliefs.

For certain occupations, resocialization helps entrants abandon their original expectations and adopt a more realistic view of that occupation. Police recruits who believe their job is to protect people must learn that deadly force is appropriate and sometimes necessary (Hunt, 1985). Many medical students' idealistic desires become more realistic as they learn about the exhausting demands of their profession (Becker & Geer, 1958; Hafferty, 1991).

Sometimes adult resocialization occurs forcefully and deliberately in order to meet larger organizational or societal needs. In prisons, mental hospitals, monasteries, military training camps, and other **total institutions** (Goffman, 1961), groups of individuals are cut off from the broader society and lead an enclosed, formally administered life. Previous socialization experiences are systematically destroyed and new ones developed to serve the interests of the group. In an army boot camp, the individual must shed his or her identity as a civilian and adopt the new identity of soldier. He or she must learn to look, act, and think like a soldier and learn to see the world from the soldier's perspective. To aid in this transformation, recruits are stripped of old identity markers (clothes, personal possessions, hairstyle) and forced to take on new ones designed to nullify individuality (uniforms, identification numbers, similar haircuts).

Soon the individual learns to identify with the ideology of the total institution. In the boot camp, the uniformity of values and appearance is intended to create a sense of solidarity among the soldiers and thereby make the military more effective in carrying out its tasks. Part of the reason there has been so much controversy over homosexuals in the military is that their presence allows a diversity of individual lifestyles into a context where, from an institutional perspective, similarity is essential.

We all know of situations in which resocialization in isolation has been tragically exploited: The 1978 mass suicide of 911 members of Jim Jones's People's Temple in Jonestown, Guyana; the 1993 armed standoff and subsequent destruction of David Koresh's Branch Davidian compound in Waco, Texas; and the 1995 sarin gas attack on the Tokyo subway system by members of the Japanese religious group Aum Shinrikyo are three noteworthy examples. Koresh, Jones, and Aum's leader, Asahara Shoko, told their followers that in order to achieve better and more meaningful lives, they would have to isolate themselves, severing all ties to their previous lives—values, relationships, emotional bonds, and so on. The members abandoned their past "disreputable" selves so totally and were resocialized and indoctrinated by their leaders so completely that their ability to make decisions on their own behalf was impaired (Coser & Coser, 1993). When people are physically and emotionally cut off from their friends and family, they lose their personalities and can be influenced, cajoled, or threatened into doing virtually anything, even injuring others or giving up their own lives.

The Structural Context of Socialization

What all types of socialization have in common—whether they occur in childhood or adulthood, whether freely chosen or forced, whether designed to teach specific skills or entire worldviews—is that none can take place in a social vacuum. Think about it: How could you know if you were attractive, smart, or funny unless there were people around to tell you so? Institutions such as the educational system, religious organizations, and the mass media and elements of identity such as race, ethnicity, and social class can exert considerable influence on our self-concept, our values, and our worldview.

Education

In contemporary American society, the most powerful institutional agent of socialization, after the family, is education. According to the functionalist perspective, the primary purpose of schools is the socialization of young people. Children formally enter the school system around age 5 when they begin kindergarten, although many enter earlier in preschool or nursery school. The "personalized" instruction of the family is replaced by the "impersonalized" instruction of the school, where the children will remain for the next 13 years or longer. No other institution has such extended and consistent access to a person's social growth. As a child learns to identify with school, it becomes a key source of influence.

Although schools are officially charged with equipping students with the skills they need to fulfill various roles in society (for example, reading, writing, mathematics), they also teach students important social, political, and economic values. When elementary school students set up simulated grocery stores or banks, for instance, they are learning about the importance of free enterprise and finance in a capitalist society; when they hold mock elections, they are being introduced to a democratic political system.

Even more subtly, schools teach students what they can expect for themselves in the world. Ironically, although individual accomplishment (for example, grades) is stressed, students learn that their future success in society may be determined as much by who they are as by what they achieve. It is in school that children are first exposed to the fact that people and groups are ranked in society, and soon they get a sense of their own relative standing in the social hierarchy. Ample evidence shows that teachers react to students on the basis of race, religion, social class, and gender (Wilkinson & Marrett, 1985).

Some conflict theorists contend that the school's agenda is even more narrowly defined. Early schooling is designed not so much to provide children with factual information and encourage creativity but to produce passive, nonproblematic conformists who will fit into the existing social order (Gracey, 1991). Rules against being late, talking out in class, and arguing with the teacher foster passivity and give students their first taste of formal evaluation and scrutiny by authoritative persons other than their parents. Obeying the kindergarten teacher today prepares the individual for obeying the high school teacher, college professor, and boss tomorrow.

Not all teachers and school systems are overwhelmingly dedicated to fitting every student into a passive role. Some teachers and alternative schools instill values that are at odds with existing social arrangements. The point is that because of the primacy of formal education in the everyday lives of most children, the institutional agenda of a particular school system can have important consequences for the types of people they will eventually become.

Religion

Religion is the social institution that tends to the spiritual needs of individuals and serves as a major source of cultural knowledge. Religion also plays an important socializing role in the formation of people's identities by providing coherence and continuity to the episodes that make up each individual's life (Kearl, 1980). Religious rites of passage, such as baptisms, bar and bat mitzvahs, confirmations, and weddings, reaffirm an individual's religious identity while impressing upon him or her the rights and obligations attached to a new status (Turner, 1972).

Although most Americans identify with some organized religious tradition and three out of four believe in God (Niebuhr, 1996), less than half of adults attend religious services regularly (U.S. Bureau of the Census, 1995a). Some observers of American culture suggest that the large generation of adults in their 30s and 40s—the so-called *baby boom generation*—has almost completely severed its religious loyalties, creating what amounts to a national spiritual crisis (for example, Bellah et al., 1985). Mainline religious groups (Lutherans, Methodists, Episcopalians, Presbyterians, Jews, and so on) have seen their memberships decline steadily over the past several decades (Jacquet & Jones, 1991). Structural changes in society have made religious affiliation more unstable in recent years. Economic circumstances have forced large numbers of families to relocate, loosening connections to extended family and friendship networks. As we become a society of people moving from city to city or state to state, many of the ties that bound us to the same religion are broken. But such a decline does not necessarily mean that religion is losing its influence as a major socializing force in society.

■ ■ ■ ■ ■ ■ ■ ■
WADE CLARK ROOF
Religion and Socialization in the Nineties

According to sociologist Wade Clark Roof (1993a), what has happened is not so much an abandonment of religion as a shift in the way religion is practiced. Over a period of 4 years Roof interviewed and surveyed people in a variety of social settings, including churches, seminaries, folk festivals, airplanes, bars, and ticket lines, about their religious values and goals and their visions for the country.

He found that only about a third of the people have remained actively involved in organized religion. Another quarter dropped out of organized religion for a while but later returned to some form of institutional involvement. The rest, about 42%, remain "dropouts." Yet even among dropouts there is still a significant amount of religious activity and involvement. Some are what Roof calls "believers, not belongers," people who maintain their religious faith but are not involved in any institutional religion. These individuals are likely to express their religiosity privately. Others are "seekers," individuals who choose either mysticism and New Age spiritualism on the one hand or theologically conservative, fundamentalist religion on the other. Indeed, at the same time the membership of mainline religions has declined, that of "evangelical" churches (Church of the Nazarene, Seventh Day Adventist, Assemblies of God, Church of God) has increased (Hunter, 1987; Jacquet & Jones, 1991).

In other words, American religion in the nineties has become remarkably fluid. People move in and out of organized religion with ease and frequency. According to Roof, about half of all Americans will drop out of active religious participation for at least 2 years. Of those, 80% will return at some point, usually to a church or synagogue. Consider the religious biography of this 36-year-old man:

- raised as a Methodist
- dropped out as a teenager, preferring to play Beatles records rather than go to church
- attended a Lutheran church for a while
- dropped out and began attending Buddhist services
- explored the Baha'i faith and attended its meetings
- attended spiritual seminars on Judaism and Hinduism
- currently describes himself as a fundamentalist Christian (Roof, 1993a, p. 175)

Most people don't explore so many religious alternatives, but in general they do feel freer to switch religions than their predecessors did. Some have interpreted this trend to mean that religious loyalties have become superficial and impermanent, with people choosing religion as they would items on a restaurant menu. Roof claims, though, that the people who switch do not do so for frivolous reasons but for moral and religious ones. People want results and are willing to search for a comfortable environment in which to express themselves religiously or spiritually.

Many adults in their 30s and 40s have adopted a uniquely noninstitutional, individualistic approach to religion. Although they still turn to institutional religion during certain life events—birth, marriage, death—they are finding new ways to express their spirituality and traditional human concerns for sharing, caring, and belonging:

Women explore their own spirituality in Goddess groups, but also in home churches; many people, both men and women, find support in adult-children-of-alcoholics meetings and in other 12-step groups but also in evangelical prayer groups; there are meaningful group experiences . . . whether among those spending a week working with Habitat for Humanity or among those exploring the meaning of visualization and dream analysis; there is community and celebration on Jesus Day but also on Earth Day. (Roof, 1993b, p. 167)

A major restructuring of American religion is under way. People's religious and spiritual concerns run deeper than the simple notion of a "return to religion" would imply (Roof, 1993a). Only a small percentage of the population will "return" to the religion into which they were born. The rest will become involved in various types of religious activities. They may or may not describe themselves as religious, and they may or may not view themselves as related to existing establishments. But religion, in whatever form it takes, will still play an important socializing role.

▪ ▪ ▪

Mass Media

Another important institutional socializer is the media. Newspapers, magazines, television, and radio transmit persuasive messages on the nature of reality. They also tell us the type of person we "should" be, from how we should perform our jobs to how different social classes live to what our intimate relationships and families are supposed to look like. The media teach us about prevailing American values, beliefs, myths, stereotypes, and trends (Gitlin, 1979) and provide an avenue through which to learn new attitudes and behavior (Bandura & Walters, 1963). Sociologists, psychologists, and of course, politicians continue to debate to what degree renditions of sex and violence in films and on television can influence behavior, particularly among young people.

But the socializing influence of the media can be much more subtle. Consider the role that televised sports play in teaching us certain cultural values (Gitlin, 1979). Television has reduced the sports experience to a sequence of individual achievements. During the 1995 NBA championship between the Houston Rockets and the Orlando Magic, for example, television announcers defined the series as a battle between the star players of each team: Hakeem Olajuwon and Shaquille O'Neill. It was touted as a "dream matchup." Much of the coverage focused on the comparative performances and personalities of these two players, reducing their teammates to supporting-cast members.

We have grown used to hearing descriptions like "best," "superstar," and "greatest of all time." Praise is heaped not only on individuals and the occasional "dynasty" team, but also on more specific actions: "best jump shot," "best backhand," "best at hitting with two outs and runners in scoring position," "best open field tackler," "best chip out of a sand trap." Such characterizations not only perpetuate the importance of individual achievement—a cultural value on which our entire social structure is based—but also give the impression that it is always possible to find something, however narrowly defined, at which one can be "best" (Gitlin, 1979).

Social Class

Social classes consist of people who occupy similar positions of power, privilege, and prestige (see chapter 10). People's positions in the class system affect virtually every aspect of their lives, including political preferences, sexual behavior, church membership, diet, and life expectancy (M. L. Kohn, 1979). Certainly, given the broad scope of class differences, the values and orientations children learn will be influenced by their parents' class standing.

Sociologist Melvin Kohn (1979) provides evidence to support the contention that social class and socialization are linked. Kohn interviewed 200 working-class and 200 middle-class couples who had at least one child of fifth-grade age. He found that the middle-class parents were more likely to promote such values as self-direction, independence, and curiosity than were the working-class parents. Conversely, working-class parents were more likely to emphasize conformity to external authority. They want their children to be neat and clean and to follow the rules. Of course, not all middle-class parents, or working-class parents, raise their children the same way. Nevertheless, Kohn found that these general tendencies were consistent regardless of the sex of the child or the size and composition of the family.

Class differences in socialization are also directly related to future goals. Working-class parents tend to believe that eventual occupational success and survival depends on their children's ability to conform to and obey authority (Kohn, 1979). Middle-class parents see future success as a result of assertiveness and initiative. Hence, middle-class children's feelings of control over their own destiny are likely to be much stronger.

Racial and Ethnic Identity

Although the issue of racial and ethnic inequality will be addressed at length in chapter 12, it is important to note here that in a race-conscious society such as ours, racial and ethnic differences are widely believed to provide visible clues to other, less visible characteristics like temperament, intelligence, values, morality, sexuality, and tastes. A study by the National Opinion Research Center in 1991 found that three out of four whites believed that African Americans are more likely than whites to prefer living on welfare. Sixty-two percent thought African Americans were less likely than whites to be hardworking; 56% thought they were more violence-prone; and 53% felt they were less intelligent ("Whites retain," 1991). Clearly, we use racial and ethnic categories to impute traits to others, but how are race and ethnicity determined and how do they affect socialization?

Race and Ethnicity: More Than Just Biology

Race is typically viewed as a category of people labeled and treated as similar because of common biological traits, including skin color, color and texture of hair, and shape of eyes, nose, or head. We usually think of race as a fixed and immutable biological characteristic that can easily be used to separate people into distinct groups. But the concept really isn't so straightforward. Australian Aboriginals, for instance, have black skin and negroid facial features but have blond, wavy hair. The black-skinned !Kung of Africa have epicanthic eye folds, a characteristic typical of Asian peoples. Despite obvious differences in physical appearance, Swedes, New Guineans, Japanese, and Navajo are more similar genetically than they are different (Diamond, 1994). Scholars can't even agree on how many human races exist— estimates range from 4 to more than 40.

Different cultures define racial categories differently. Brazil historically has not had a rigid conception of race and thus has a variety of "intermediate" races. In fact, the designation of race is so fluid that parents, children, brothers, and sisters are sometimes accepted as representatives of very different races (M. Harris, 1964). South Africa has four legally defined races—black, white, colored, and Indian—but in Great Britain the term *black* is used to refer to all people who are not white. An African American visiting Tanzania is likely to be considered white by the African blacks there (Njeri, 1990).

In American society we tend to see race in categorical terms: black or white, red or yellow, brown or black. Even when faced with ambiguities, such as mixed-race children, we still try to put people into specific categories. But more and more people of mixed racial heritage are refusing to identify themselves as one race or another. The U.S. Census Bureau has come under attack recently for not providing enough racial categories on the census questionnaire. Organizations representing the interests of people from mixed racial backgrounds have been lobbying the Census Bureau to add a multiracial category to the next census. Currently people who don't feel they fit into one of the present categories— white, black, Asian or Pacific Islander, American Indian, Eskimo or Aleut—are forced to check the unflattering and ambiguous "other" category. Changing a federally mandated document like the census questionnaire may not solve all the problems that people of multiracial backgrounds face, but it would add visibility and legitimacy to a racial identity that has largely been ignored.

But not everyone thinks such a change is a good idea. Civil rights organizations like the National Urban League, the National Association for the Advancement of Colored People, and the National Council of La Raza object to the inclusion of a "multiracial" category. They worry that it would reduce the number of

Americans claiming to belong to long-recognized racial minority groups, dilute the culture and political power of those groups, and make it more difficult to enforce civil rights laws (L. Mathews, 1996). Federal programs that assist minority businesses or that protect minority communities from environmental hazards depend on racial population data from the census. If the percentage of black people in a community goes down because others begin to identify themselves as "multiracial," such programs could be jeopardized.

The complex issue of mixed-race background is not new. Since the earliest humans appeared they have consistently tended to migrate and interbreed. Hence, there is no clear-cut, pure race. Some surveys estimate that at least 75% of American blacks have some white ancestry (cited in L. Mathews, 1996). The famous naturalist Charles Darwin (1871/1971) wrote that despite external differences, it is virtually impossible to identify clear, distinctive racial characteristics because all the races "graduate into each other."

The diversity of physical traits within a racial group is often as great as the diversity between groups. People who consider themselves "white" may actually have darker skin and curlier hair than some people who consider themselves "black." Race is therefore a more meaningful *social* category than it is a *biological* one. That is, the characteristics selected to distinguish one group from another have less to do with physical differences than with what that particular culture defines as socially significant. Although race is a meaningless category biologically speaking, it remains a crucial social category. Along with sex, it is the first thing we notice about one another.

■ ■ ■ ■ ■ ■ ■ ■

MICRO-MACRO CONNECTION
The One-Drop Rule

In Langston Hughes's book *Simple Takes a Wife*, Simple has the following reaction to a story about a man who looked white but was officially declared "colored" by an Alabama court:

> Just one drop of black blood makes a man colored. *One* drop— you are a Negro! Now why is that? Why is Negro blood so much more powerful than any other kind of blood in the world? If a man has Irish blood in him, people will say, "He's *part* Irish." If he has a little Jewish blood, they'll say, "He's *half* Jewish." But if he has just a small bit of colored blood in him, BAM!—"*He's a Negro!*" . . . You can have ninety-nine drops of white blood in your veins down South—but if that other *one* drop is black, shame on you! Even if you look white, you're black. That drop is really powerful. (Hughes, 1958, p. 201)

Despite the movement toward formally recognizing a "multiracial" identity, the United States still adheres to the tradition of the *one-drop rule* for blacks (F. J. Davis, 1991). The term comes from a common law in the South during slavery that a "single drop of black blood" made a person black. The U.S. Census considers a person black if he or she has any known African black ancestry. Anthropologists call this a *hypodescent* rule, meaning that racially mixed people are always assigned the status of the subordinate group (F. J. Davis, 1991).

Walter White, president of the National Association for the Advancement of Colored People (NAACP) from 1931 to 1955, was estimated to be no more than one-sixty-fourth African black. He had fair skin, fair hair, and blue eyes, yet he did not attempt to pass as white—which would have made his life quite a bit easier at that time. The "race" that White represented was the social group with which he identified and not his genetic classification. The black community became outraged only when he married a white woman. He had crossed a major social barrier, if only a minute color barrier.

More recently a Louisiana woman found that although she had always considered herself white (she had twice married white men, and her parents and grandparents had blond hair and blue eyes), she was defined by the state of Louisiana as black. State authorities had traced her ancestry back more than 200 years and found that her great-great-great-great-grandmother was black. She sued the state for $20,000, and the law that defined as black anyone whose ancestry was at least 3% black was eventually repealed (Jaynes, 1982).

Collective anxiety on the part of whites about the number of light-skinned blacks "passing" as white reached a peak in the early part of the 20th century. In the South there was tremendous fear, almost hysteria, over "invisible blackness." Showing a fondness for black culture or voluntarily associating with blacks was sometimes considered proof of blackness even in the absence of known black ancestry (F. J. Davis, 1991).

The one-drop rule and the accompanying issue of racial identity has created racial tensions even within the black community. Color divisiveness among blacks is seen by some within the black community as a worse problem than racial hatred expressed by whites. Light-skinned blacks sometimes are prejudiced against darker-skinned blacks. In turn, darker-skinned blacks sometimes resent light-skinned blacks for using skin whiteners and hair straighteners to conform to white standards of beauty (F. J. Davis, 1991). The entertainer Michael Jackson has been severely criticized for removing most of his "black" physical features.

Reactions to mixed offspring found in other racial and ethnic groups can be quite different. Among Japanese Americans, for instance, mixed marriages were frowned on until recent years. A child who was predominantly Japanese with some white blood was considered white by the rest of the community and not fully admitted into the ethnic group. Among Orthodox Jews, a child born to a Jewish and non-Jewish parent is never considered "half Jewish." If the mother is Jewish, so is the child; if only the father is Jewish, the child is not a Jew. Among white Americans, calling oneself "part Indian" is still less stigmatizing than calling oneself "part black" (Spickard, 1989).

■ ■ ■

Despite the ambiguities and inconsistencies, racial identity remains important because of its connection to **ethnicity**—the learned cultural heritage shared by a category of people. Your history, values, language, tastes, and habits may be more important indicators of identity than skin color or other anatomical features (L. Williams, 1991a). For example, Caribbean blacks are quite different ethnically from African blacks and often take great pains to avoid being identified as "black" (Gladwell, 1996).

The distinction between race and ethnicity is important at the level of individual identity. The debate over what constitutes a black identity was crystallized during the confirmation hearings on Judge Clarence Thomas's nomination to the Supreme Court in the fall of 1991. Some African Americans criticized Thomas for using his race selectively and playing down its importance until he was accused of sexual harassment by Professor Anita Hill. Many questioned his "blackness"—his ethnic loyalty—because he embraces conservative political attitudes and is married to a white woman. Said one observer of the Thomas-Hill hearings: "I saw a black woman, and a white man in black skin" (quoted in L. Williams, 1991a). Such a statement is interesting sociologically because it illustrates that one can be racially black but still have one's ethnic "blackness" called into question for beliefs, actions, and attitudes that don't conform to those of most group members. To many, the very survival of the group depends on a shared ethnic identity.

Race and Socialization

The day after the Los Angeles riots in May 1992, students in my introductory sociology class became embroiled in a heated discussion of the incident. One student, who was white, expressed concern that young children of all races would now grow up mistrusting or even hating the police. As a child she had been taught that the role of the police is to help people and that if she were ever in trouble or lost she could approach an officer for help. She never questioned whether or not the police could be trusted. She then speculated how awful life would become for kids without the sense of safety and certainty she had been socialized to take for granted.

A few of the African-American students in class immediately pointed out to her that their socialization experiences had been quite different. Parents and others in their neighborhoods had taught them never to trust the police because officers were just as likely to exploit and harass them as to help them. They were taught to turn to neighbors if they ever needed help. To them the police were not knights in shining armor but bullies with badges. Indeed, in a 1994 survey of 227 blacks in South Central Los Angeles, 55% felt that unnecessary force by the Los Angeles Police Department was increasing; many respondents felt that it could have easily been them being beaten instead of Rodney King (Murty, Roebuck, & Armstrong, 1994).

Although the two perspectives of my students are not representative of every white or every African-American person in this country, the interchange illustrates the stark impact race can have on socialization. For white children, the values they are taught when growing up are likely to mirror those of the wider society. Chances are that schools and religious organizations will reinforce the socialization messages expressed to them in their families—for example, "hard work will pay off in the long run."

For racial minorities, however, socialization occurs within a larger social environment that is often incompatible with their own experience (Taylor, Chatters, Tucker, & Lewis, 1990). These children must become knowledgeable of the dominant white culture as well as their own simply to survive. Minority children must also be socialized to deal with the realities of racism in a society that has been and still is set up to ignore or actively exclude them (Staples, 1992). For instance, minority children are more likely than white children to be taught that "hard work" alone might not be enough to get ahead in this society. Even minority children from affluent homes in integrated neighborhoods need reassurances about the racial issues they will encounter (Comer & Poussaint, 1992).

The Socialization of Self

Whether a person is rich or poor, black or white, the most important outcome of the socialization process is the development of a sense of self. *Self* refers to the unique set of traits, behaviors, and attitudes that distinguishes one person from the next. Social scientists, however, have a more complex concept of what self is, and they take particular interest in the process through which a person develops a sense of self.

The Nature of Self

The **self** is both the active source of behavior and the passive object of behavior (G. H. Mead, 1934). As an active source, the self can initiate action that is frequently directed toward others. Curt and Mary are having dinner in a restaurant. Mary has a self that can perceive Curt, talk to him, evaluate him, perhaps even try to manipulate or persuade him to act in a way that is consistent with her interests. Mary also has a self that is a potential object of others' behavior: She can be perceived, talked to, evaluated, manipulated, or persuaded by Curt.

Mary can also direct these activities toward herself. She can perceive, evaluate, motivate, and even talk to herself. This is called **reflexive behavior.** To have a self is to have the ability to plan, observe, guide, and respond to one's own behavior (G. H. Mead, 1934).

Think of all the times you have tried to motivate yourself to act by saying something like, "All right, if I read 20 more pages of this boring textbook, I'll give myself a hot fudge sundae." To do this you must simultaneously be the motivator and the one being motivated; the seer and the seen.

At this very moment you are initiating an action: reading this book. But you also have the ability to be aware of your reading behavior, to observe yourself reading and even evaluate how well you are doing. This sounds like some sort of out-of-body experience, but it isn't. Nothing is more fundamental to human thought and action than the capacity for self-awareness. It allows us to control our own behavior and interact smoothly with other self-aware individuals.

The philosopher William James (1890) labeled the active source of behavior the "I" and the passive object of behavior the "me": "*I* perceive *me*," or "*I* talk to *me*." George Herbert Mead (1934) went one step further and described the "I" and the "me" as alternating phases of every action that involves the self.

Mead felt that the "I" is the part of the self that responds directly to outside events. It is impulsive and not subject to control at first. The "I" can be seen in situations where we react spontaneously without assessing possible consequences of our actions. You may have told yourself, for example, "It's such a beautiful day . . . the heck with studying for this stupid sociology exam, I'm going to the beach!"

The "me" represents society within the individual. It is the self-reflective, conventional aspect of the self that incorporates society's values, norms, ideals, and expectations. The "me" represents the internalization of the attitudes and group standards of others. If you reconsider your beach trip in light of its possible outcome, you are invoking the "me": "No, I'd better not go to the beach. I may fail the exam and the course."

According to Mead, the "I" and "me" are alternating elements of a constant process of thought and action. One moment we are responding directly to environmental stimuli. The next moment we direct our conscious attention inward and become aware of our conduct: "Wow, I can't believe how angry I am at Tom." This process allows us to alter our behavior to bring it in line with social conventions ("I shouldn't be so angry at him . . . I'll apologize and act like everything's OK"). Then this behavior becomes the object of our own scrutiny ("I wonder if he thinks I'm still mad").

The ability to carry on this internal dialogue enables us to incorporate the perceptions and expectations of other people. Sociologically, the crucial aspect of the self is that it allows us to transform, modify, and control our behavior when we interact with people in various circumstances. As we become aware that different people expect different things, we can tailor our behavior to meet the demands of each situation.

The Acquisition of Self

The capacity for humans to control their own conduct rests on the development of the self. Because we can act toward ourselves as objects, we can imagine alternate lines of conduct and choose from among them. But how do we acquire a self? How is the newborn infant transformed into a self-aware, self-controlled member of society? Unlike other animals, human babies cannot care for themselves. Moreover, they possess no sense of self at birth, have no capacity for reflexive behavior, and lack the ability to consciously control their actions.

This is not to say that infants don't act. Anyone who has been around babies knows that they have a tremendous ability to initiate action ranging all the way from Kodak-moment cute to downright disgusting. They cry, eat, sleep, play with squeaky rubber toys, and eliminate waste, all with exquisite panache and regularity. They respond to the sounds, sights, smells, and touches of others from the very first days of life.

But this behavior is not characterized by the sort of self-consciousness that characterizes later behavior. Babies cannot say to themselves, "I can't believe how loud I can cry" or "I wonder if Mom will feed me if I scream." As children grow older, though, they begin to exert greater control over their conduct. Part of this transformation is biological. As they mature they become more adept at muscle control. But physical development is only part of the picture. Humans must acquire certain cognitive capacities through interactions with others, including the abilities to differentiate between self and others, to understand and use symbolic language, and to take the roles of others.

The Differentiation of Self

To distinguish between oneself and others, one must be able to recognize oneself (Michener, DeLamater, & Schwartz, 1986). The first step in the acquisition of self, then, is learning to distinguish our own faces and bodies from the rest of the physical environment. Surprisingly, we are not born with this ability. Not only are newborns incapable of recognizing themselves, they also cannot even discriminate the boundaries between their bodies and the bodies of others. An infant will pull its own hair to the point of excruciating pain but will not realize that the hair it's pulling and the hair that it feels being pulled is the same hair.

With cognitive growth and social experience, the infant gradually recognizes itself as a unique physical object. Most studies in this area indicate that children usually develop this ability at about 18 months (for example, Bertenthal & Fischer, 1978). If you make a large mark on a child's forehead with a washable marker, hold the youngster up to a mirror, and observe whether the child reaches up to wipe away the smudge, you can tell if the youngster knows that the image in the mirror is its own.

Language Acquisition and the Looking-Glass Self

The next important step in the acquisition of the self is the development of speech (Hewitt, 1988). Mastery of language is critical in a child's efforts to differentiate itself as a distinct social as well as physical object (Denzin, 1977). Most parents talk to their children from the start. Gradually, children learn to make sounds, imitate sounds, and use sounds as symbols for particular physical sensations or objects. The child learns that the sounds "Mama" and "Dada" are the sounds associated with two important objects in its life. Soon the child learns that other objects—toys, animals, foods, Aunt Donna—have unique sounds associated with them as well.

This learning process provides the child access into the preexisting linguistic world in which the child's parents and others live (Hewitt, 1988). The objects that are named are not only those that are recognized within the larger culture, but also those recognized within the family's particular social group (race, class, religion). The child learns the names of concrete objects (balls, buildings, furniture) as well as abstract ideas that cannot be directly perceived (for example, God, happiness, idea).

By learning that people and other objects have names, a child also begins to learn that these objects can be related to one another in many named ways. Depending on who is talking to whom, the same person can be called several different names. The object "Daddy" is called, by various other people, "David," "Dave," "Dr. Newman," "Professor Newman," "Honey," and "Dummy." Furthermore, the child learns that different people can be referred to by the same name. All those other kids at the park have someone they also call "Mama."

Amidst these monumental discoveries young children learn that they too are objects that have names. A child who learns that others are referring to her when they use the word "Nancy," and that she too can use "Nancy" to refer to herself, has taken a significant leap forward in the acquisition of self. The child is now able to visualize herself as a part of the named world and the named relationships to which she belongs.

The self that initially emerges from this process is a rather simple one. "Nancy" is just a name associated with a body, which explains why very young children just learning to form sentences will refer to themselves by their name instead of the first-person pronoun (for example, "Nancy is hungry" instead of "I am hungry"). A more sophisticated sense of self is derived from the child's ability to learn the *meaning* of this named object.

Children learn the meaning of named objects in their environment by observing the way other people act toward them. Children learn what "chair" means by observing people sitting in it. They learn that a "hot stove" is something to be avoided. Similarly, they learn the meaning of themselves by observing how people act toward them. People treat children in a variety of ways: care for them, punish them, love them, teach them. If parents, relatives, and other significant people perceive a child as smart, they will act toward him or her that way. Thus the child will eventually come to *believe* he or she is a smart person. Sociologist Charles Horton Cooley (1902) referred to this process as acquisition of the **looking-glass self**. We use the actions of others toward us as mirrors in which we see ourselves.

How the child-as-named-object is defined by others is linked to larger societal considerations as well. Every culture has its own way of defining individuals at various stages of the life cycle. As we saw in chapter 4, children in past cultures were not always defined as a special subpopulation that requires nurturance and protection but rather as miniature adults (Aries, 1962). They were expected to behave like adults and were held accountable for their actions just as adults would be. Hence a 5-year-old's self-worth might have been derived from how well he or she contributed economically to the family, not from how cute or playful he or she was. Moreover, every society has its own standards of beauty and success. If thinness is a culturally desirable characteristic, a thin child is more likely to garner positive responses and develop a positive self-image than a child who violates this norm (that is, an obese child).

The Development of Role Taking

Different people expect or desire different things from us. A child eventually learns to modify his or her behavior to suit different people. Four-year-old Robbie learns, for instance, that his 3-year-old sister loves it when he sticks green beans up his nose, but he also knows that Dad does not find this behavior at all amusing. So Robbie will avoid such conduct when Dad is around but will proceed to amuse his sister with this trick when Dad is gone. The ability to use other people's perspectives and expectations in formulating one's own behavior is called **role taking** (G. H. Mead, 1934).

Role-taking ability is developed gradually, paralleling the increasing maturation of linguistic abilities. G. H. Mead (1934) identified two major stages in the development of role-taking ability and, ultimately, in the socialization of the self: the play stage and the game stage. The **play stage** occurs when children are just beginning to acquire language. Most 3-year-olds are able to imitate the characteristics and behaviors associated with others in particular roles. They can play at being a Mommy, a firefighter, a soccer player, an astronaut, and so on. This sort of play is marked by its transient, unorganized quality. Children at the play stage commonly drift from one role to another in no logical sequence. Mead pointed out that this trait is the definitive characteristic of childhood. You cannot count on a child. You cannot assume that what a child does now will determine what he or she will do a minute from now.

More important, role taking at the play stage is quite simple in form, limited to one other person at a time. Young children cannot see themselves from different perspectives simultaneously. They have no idea that certain behaviors may be unacceptable to a variety of people across a range of situations. They know only that this particular person who is in their immediate presence will not approve of this conduct. Children cannot see that Mom's disapproval of public nose picking reflects the attitudes of a larger group. This more sophisticated form of self-control develops at the next stage of the socialization process.

The **game stage** occurs when children first begin to participate in organized activities like school events and team sports. The difference between role taking at the play and game stages parallels the difference between childhood play behavior and game behavior. Play is not guided by a specific set of rules. Play has no ultimate object, no clearly organized competition, no winners and losers. Children playing baseball at the play stage have no sense of strategy and may not even be aware of the rules and object of the game. They may be able to hit, catch, and throw the ball but have no idea how their behavior is linked to that of their teammates. If a little girl is playing third base and the ball is hit to her, she may throw the ball to the left fielder, not because this will help her team win the game but because that's where her best friend happens to be.

At the game stage children do have a sense of the object of the game. They realize that each player on the team is part of an organized network of roles determined by the rules of the game. Children know they must continually adapt their behavior to the team's needs in order to achieve a goal. To do so, they must predict how both their teammates and the opponents will act under certain circumstances.

The ability to imagine the group's perspective characterizes the game stage of development. With regard to social behavior, not only does the child learn to respond to the demands of many people, but he or she can also respond to the demands of the community or even society as a whole. The perspective of society and its constituent values and attitudes is known as the **generalized other.**

To take the role of the generalized other is to perceive one's behavior from the point of view of the group, not just one particular person. "Mommy doesn't like it when I pick my nose in restaurants" (play stage) becomes "It is not acceptable to pick one's nose in public" (game stage). This ability is crucial because it makes it possible to resist the influence of specific people who happen to be in one's immediate presence. The boy who defies his peers by not joining them in an act of petty shoplifting is showing the power of the generalized other. During the game stage, the attitudes and expectations of the generalized other are incorporated into one's self-concept, forming the "me."

Real life is not that simple, though. The perspective of society is not the same for everyone. People from markedly different backgrounds are likely to internalize different sets of group attitudes and values. Granted, the generalized other becomes larger as a child matures, growing to include family, peer group, school, and finally the larger social community. But as societies themselves grow and become more complex, so does the generalized other.

Groups, organizations, and communities have their own sets of norms, values, and beliefs. A Catholic contemplating divorce, for instance, is taking the role of a different generalized other than an atheist contemplating divorce. Likewise, the social worlds and social standards of men and women are different, as are those of children and adults, parents and nonparents, middle-class and working-class people.

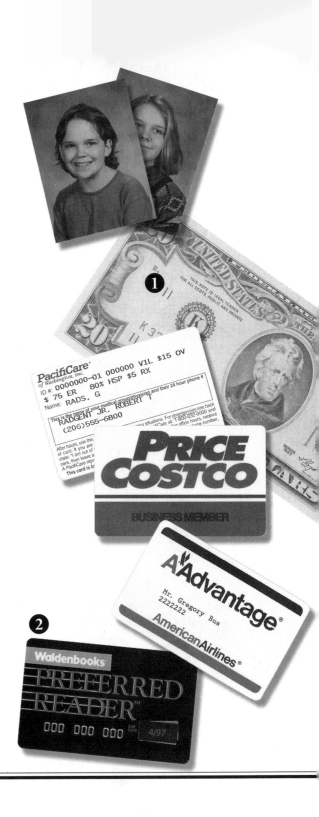

Take out your wallet. Even better, ask a friend for his or her wallet. Dump the contents out on the table. What can you tell about a person simply by looking at this collection of cards, photos, notes, and so on? More important, what can you tell about the larger society and the role it plays in our lives? Think of all the indicators of group or organizational membership that we have in our wallets. Think of the artifacts of friendships, families, and social class that we carry with us. If you've ever lost your wallet, you know the gnawing panic that results. To lose a wallet is to lose tangible evidence of your personal identity and your connections to the social structure. As you look at the wallet contents on these pages, reflect on the importance of groups, organizations, and institutions in your life.

❶ Depending on whom you talk to, money is either "the root of all evil" or "what makes the world go 'round." There's no denying that money is vitally important in the lives of Americans. The entire structure of our society is built around it. But the money in our wallets has no intrinsic value. It is merely paper. It is valuable only because we, as a collective, agree to give it symbolic value. In fact, the dollar bill is one of the most internationally recognized symbols, readily accepted throughout the world.

We need identification cards to utilize the services of many of the organizations and groups to which we belong. Forget your membership card and you can't work out in your local gym; forget your meal card and you can't eat in your campus dining hall; forget your video store card and you can't rent that movie you were dying to see. Some office buildings, in the interest of security, have even issued identification cards with a magnetic strip that employees must pass through a machine just to get into their offices.

Most of us carry a variety of credit cards for department stores or other retail outlets. But credit cards do more than simply enable us to make purchases without having to pay cash right away. They represent power, status, and prestige. Credit card companies have created a whole system of hierarchy and privilege. If you have a regular credit card, you're just a regular citizen; own a silver card and you have access to more privileges; a gold card puts you at the top of the heap, giving you even more opportunities. Other organizations have tried to use this status system. The Preferred Reader card ❷ you see here is an example of this credit card irony.

Your driver's license ❸ is the most frequently asked-for identification card. What does this say about the cultural importance of automobiles in our lives? What are some of the reasons people ask to see our driver's licenses? The necessity of having this identification card has caused many people who don't need or want to drive to take a driving test.

The library card ❹, like many identification and credit cards, has a bar code on it. Magnetic strips and bar codes connect you to huge organizations of data banks that keep track of your credit worthiness and your record of payments (not to mention whether you have any overdue books). These data banks also sell your name to marketing organizations who profile your patterns of consumption—maybe not always accurately—for future marketing campaigns. The catalogs that multiply in your mailbox can probably be traced back to an identification strip on one of your cards.

The contents of a wallet reflect important sociological ideas. As you make your way through this book, notice how concepts such as social identity, deviance, socialization, power, organizations, institutions, race, gender, class, and family can be "seen" by taking a peek inside your wallet.

As we move from one institutional context to another, we adopt the perspective of the appropriate group and can become, for all intents and purposes, a different person. At work we behave one way, at church another, at a family reunion still another. We are as many different people as there are groups and organizations of which we are members. Because role taking is the process of imagining another person's attitudes and intentions and thereby anticipating that person's behavior, it is essential for everyday social interaction. Through it we are able to envision how others perceive us and what their response may be to some action we're contemplating. Hence we can select behaviors that are likely to meet with the approval of the person or persons with whom we are interacting and avoid behaviors that might meet with their disapproval.

By imagining others' reactions, we are able to "rehearse" social encounters prior to engaging in them. If we can predict their responses to our conduct, we are in a better position to devise a plan of action to meet both their expectations and our needs. Role taking is thus a crucial component of *self-control*. It is fundamental in the development of a social being who is capable of behaving in ways that conform to the wishes and expectations of others. Moreover, role taking becomes a means of social control to the extent that such behavior conforms to broader societal expectations. In this way it is the means by which culture is incorporated into the self.

The Self in Structural Context

When we imagine how others will respond to our actions, we choose from a limited set of alternative lines of conduct that are a function of the wider culture. In the United States, the self is likely to incorporate key American virtues such as self-reliance and individualism. Hence personal goals often take priority over allegiance to groups (Bellah et al., 1985). Americans readily change their group membership as it suits them—switching churches, leaving one employer for another, moving from neighborhood to neighborhood, and so on (Goleman, 1990). In most non-Western countries, however, the self is more likely to be *collectivist*; that is, personal identity is completely subsumed under group identity (K. J. Gergen, 1991). A high value is placed on preserving one's public image so as not to bring shame upon one's family, tribe, or community (Triandis, McCusker, & Hui, 1990). Overcoming personal interests and temptations to show loyalty to one's group and other authorities is to be celebrated.

In individualistic cultures like ours, one's personal accomplishments are a key ingredient of one's self-concept. The amount of respect you deserve is determined in large part by your level of expertise. For example, a lecturer will be introduced to her audience as "a distinguished scholar, a leader in her field" along with a list of her scholarly achievements. In Asia, however, such pronouncements would be considered self-centered and egotistical. Asian lecturers usually begin their talks by telling the audience how little they know about the topic at hand (Goleman, 1990). Not only does this example show some interesting cultural differences in "appropriate" public behavior, it also illustrates vast differences in how people see themselves and the worlds they inhabit.

When we acquire a self, we are simultaneously acquiring a repertoire of behaviors that are culturally defined. Our cultural belief systems determine whether we see ourselves as a bundle of individual traits and accomplishments or as an extension of a dense network of social relations and group affiliations.

To fully understand how we become who we are, we must understand our position in the social structure. We must know the norms and values of our society, family, peers, co-workers, and so forth. We must know the attitudes taken toward us by people in socializing institutions. We must know that our race, social class, and religion set limits on the kinds of social relationships we can and will form and therefore limit our ability to take the roles of people who are different from us.

The Socialization of Gender

An analysis of socialization would be incomplete without examining the process by which we develop our gender. Gender, along with race and ethnicity, is one of the primary elements of our social being. Our everyday behavior, our tastes and desires, our experiences in intimate relationships, our health and well-being, our career choices, and our political beliefs are linked directly or indirectly to gender.

Sex Versus Gender

Before discussing how individuals acquire gender, it is necessary to distinguish between gender and sex. **Sex** is used to refer to a person's biological maleness or femaleness. **Gender** designates psychological, social, and cultural aspects of maleness and femaleness (S. J. Kessler & McKenna, 1978). This distinction is important because it reminds us that male-female differences in behaviors or experiences do not spring naturally from biological differences between the sexes (Lips, 1993). In addition, this distinction allows us to separate masculinity from maleness and femininity from femaleness, which makes it possible for people to deviate from cultural notions of gender without having any impact on their sex.

We usually think of sex as being determined at the time of conception. If you asked someone how to distinguish between males and females, the response would probably focus on observable physical characteristics—body shape, hair, voice, facial features, and so on. When scientists distinguish between the sexes, they, too, refer to physical traits: chromosomes (XX for female, XY for male), sex glands (ovaries and testes), hormones (estrogen and testosterone), internal sex organs (uterus and prostate gland), external genitalia (vagina and penis), reproductive capacities (pregnancy and impregnation), germ cells produced (ova and sperm), and secondary sex characteristics (hips and breasts, facial hair and deep voice).

These characteristics, and hence the two biological sex categories, male and female, are assumed to be universal, exhaustive (that is, there's no third sex), and mutually exclusive (that is, a person cannot be both or be neither). There may be differences across time and cultures as to how we expect the two sexes to act and look, but every society has some way of determining who is male and who is female. As a result, we cannot and perhaps should not be fully comfortable with any ambiguity:

> [People] are either one or the other, zero or 100 percent. We may modify our decision ("He is an effeminate man"), but we do not usually qualify it ("Maybe he is a man"). If we should have to qualify it, then we seek further information until the qualification is no longer necessary. (S. J. Kessler & McKenna, 1978, p. 2)

Yet things aren't always so clear-cut. Hermaphrodites, for instance, are individuals in whom sexual differentiation is either incomplete or ambiguous. They may have the chromosomal pattern of a female but the external genitalia of a male, or they may have both ovaries and testicles. According to one prominent biologist, instead of two sexual categories, there are many gradations of sex running from female to male, and along that spectrum lie at least *five* sexes (Fausto-Sterling, 1993). In addition to males and females, there are "true hermaphrodites," people who possess one testis and one ovary; "male pseudohermaphrodites," people who have testes and some aspects of female genitalia but no ovaries; and "female pseudohermaphrodites," people who have ovaries and some aspects of male genitalia but no testes.

It is interesting to note that the medical response to hermaphrodites supports the cultural reality of sex. Hermaphroditism is usually defined by biologists as a combination of the two existing categories and not as a third, fourth, or fifth category unto itself. Furthermore, upon the diagnosis of hermaphroditism, a decision is always made to define the individual as either male or female. In societies with advanced medical technology, surgical and chemical means may be used to establish consistency between anatomy and the social label.

Such drastic intervention is undertaken not because the infant's life is threatened, but because our entire social structure is organized around the fact that there are two and only two sexes (Lorber, 1989). The male-female dichotomy in our culture is so essential to our way of life that those who challenge it are considered either crazy or cultural heretics who are being disloyal to the most fundamental of biological "facts." To suggest that the labels "male" and "female" are not sufficient to categorize everyone is to threaten the entire institutional order of social life.

But some cross-cultural evidence indicates that not every society has two and only two sexes.

- In traditional Navajo culture, one could be male, female, or *nadle*—a third sex assigned to those whose sex-typed anatomical characteristics were ambiguous at birth (M. K. Martin & Voorhies, 1975). Physically normal individuals also had the opportunity to choose to become *nadle* if they so desired. *Nadle* were allowed to perform the tasks of both men and women. Again we see that sexual characteristics need not be consistent with socially defined gender.

- Among the Hua of Papua New Guinea, gender is thought to change throughout a person's life (Gailey, 1987). The Hua believe that women lose some of their femininity each time they have a child. After three births a woman has lost enough femininity to be allowed to participate in the discussions and rituals of men and to share their higher status and authority. Men gradually lose their masculinity by giving it to young boys during developmental rituals. Consequently, older men come to acquire the same social status as young women (Gailey, 1987).

- The Hijras in India are neither men nor women. They are born as men, but they undergo an operation in which their genitals are surgically removed. This transforms them not into women, but into Hijras, who live as women—dressing, standing, walking, and sitting as women. There are many such figures in Hindu mythology, who are neither male nor female. Hence, Indian culture not only accommodates the Hijras but views them as meaningful, even powerful beings (Nanda, 1990).

These cross-cultural examples illustrate that our beliefs about sex and gender are not held worldwide. In other societies sex and gender are neither dichotomous nor permanent. Likewise, there are situations in U.S. society in which one's gender doesn't line up with one's sex. *Transsexuals*—those who have the normal biological characteristics of one sex but the gender identity of the other—sometimes go so far as to have their biological sex altered through "corrective" surgery to bring it in line with their psychological gender. In other words, it's easier for them to alter their sex than to alter their gender.

The Structural Context of Gender Roles

Gender is a social role. Like other social roles, it implies a set of rights, expectations, obligations, and privileges commonly associated with that gender. In our society the gender dichotomy is a major way in which everyday life and larger social institutions are organized.

Religious doctrines, for instance, frequently reinforce status and power differences between men and women. The traditional Judeo-Christian ideology incorporates beliefs that have historically given men special rights and privileges over women:

Unto the woman [God] said, I will greatly multiply thy sorrow and thy conception; in sorrow thou shalt bring forth children, and thy desire shall be to thy husband, and he shall rule over thee. (Gen. 3:16)

For a man . . . is the image and glory of God; but the woman is the glory of man. For the man is not of the woman, but the woman of the man. Neither was the man created for the woman, but the woman for the man. (1 Cor. 11:7–9)

Blessed art Thou, oh Lord our God, King of the Universe, that I was not born a woman. (Orthodox Jewish morning prayer)

Other social institutions, too, afford different rights and privileges to men and women. The American political system has long excluded women from the highest levels of its decision-making process. Economic discrimination and exploitation in terms of both access to certain careers and low wages is well documented (see chapter 13). Family life has always been clearly delineated along gender lines, with men and women holding distinct and differently valued familial obligations.

Many of these institutions are in the process of changing, however. The last decade has seen more women's participation in the clergy, the paid labor force, and national politics. Marital and parental roles are slowly becoming more balanced. Yet while our society creeps toward gender equality, the impetus to keep the genders ideologically separate and their respective expectations different prevails.

The Language of Gender

We live in a society in which virtually all institutions, organizations, and day-to-day interactions are built on fundamental differences between boys and girls, men and women, and masculine and feminine. Consider the gender distinctions in our language. Although English is not so grammatically gendered as, say, French or Spanish, gender pervades the language, as in the traditional use of the inclusive male pronoun *he* and the generic *man* in referring to both genders. Such words make females appear as exceptions. Female terms are often created as mere extensions of existing male terms by adding an *ess* or *ette* (for example, po-et*ess*, steward*ess*, major*ette*) or by using the words *lady, female,* or *woman* as noun modifiers (for example, *lady* doctor, *woman* lawyer, *female* engineer).

Even the use of nongendered terms like *congressperson* or *spokesperson* implies that the individual being referred to is female. The fact that women's job titles are modifications of traditional male terms reinforces the cultural belief that most occupations are still the man's domain, with the woman being an exception to the rule. There's no need to call a man a *male* engineer or a *male* doctor, because the terms themselves already imply a male occupant.

Our gender-biased vocabulary reflects and perpetuates underlying societal beliefs about the relative roles of men and women. To "mother" a child is to nurture, coddle, and protect that child; to "father" a child is simply to fertilize an egg.

Similarly, a "governor" is an elected official who acts as the head of a state; a "governess" is one who cares for other people's children. In common usage, a "master" is one who rules over others; a "mistress" is a woman with whom a man has an extended extramarital affair (Richardson, 1987).

Men and women also differ in the ways they use language. Apparent gender differences in communication parallel gender differences in existing social arrangements. The common belief that women's speech tends to be more emotionally expressive than men's reflects the deeper cultural belief that women are the ones who are supposed to tend to relationships (Lakoff, 1973). However, one of the consequences of disclosing a great deal of information about yourself or openly showing your emotions is that it makes you less powerful (P. M. Blau, 1964). By linguistically overexposing themselves, women perpetuate the preexisting power differences between men and women. Some researchers (for example, Kollock, Blumstein, & Schwartz, 1985) argue that certain gender-typed conversational behaviors, such as men interrupting more than women, are actually the result of power imbalances rather than inherent gender differences.

Social Institutions and the Acquisition of Gender Roles

These sorts of gender distinctions are far from trivial; they have serious educational, political, and economic implications. Different expectations create unequal opportunities. One's identity as male or female has a profound impact on one's self-development, determining paths chosen, decisions made, and treatment received at the hands of others.

How are all these ideas, expectations, and values transmitted to children? How do children come to be masculine or feminine in a way that is consistent with larger cultural dictates? The gender socialization process begins the moment a child is born. A physician, nurse, or midwife immediately starts that infant on a career as a male or female by authoritatively declaring whether it is a boy or girl. In most hospitals the infant boy is wrapped in a blue blanket, the infant girl in a pink one. From that point on the developmental paths of males and females diverge. The subsequent messages that individuals receive from families, books, television, and schools not only teach and reinforce gender-typed expectations but also influence the formation of their self-concepts.

Family

Parents are their children's first source of information about gender. If you asked parents whether they treated sons any differently from daughters, most would probably say no. Yet there is considerable evidence that what parents do and what they say they do are two different things (Lips, 1993; Lytton & Romney, 1991; Renzetti & Curran, 1989). Gender-typed expectations are so ingrained in

American parents that they are often unaware that they are behaving in accordance with them (Goldberg & Lewis, 1969; Will, Self, & Datan, 1976).

In one study, 30 first-time parents were asked to describe their recently born infants (less than 24 hours old). They frequently resorted to common gender stereotypes. Those with daughters described them as "tiny," "soft," "fine-featured," and "delicate." Sons were seen as "strong," "alert," "hardy," and "coordinated" (J. Z. Rubin, Provenzano, & Luria, 1974). Parents also tend to engage in rougher physical play with infant sons than with infant daughters and use different subtle tones of voice and pet names, like "Sweetie" versus "Tiger" (MacDonald & Parke, 1986; Tauber, 1979).

New parents, understandably proud of their new parental status, can be very sensitive about the correct identification of their child's sex. Even parents who claim to consider sex and gender irrelevant will nevertheless spend a great deal of time ensuring that their child has the culturally appropriate physical appearance of a boy or girl. This is not surprising given the centrality of sex and gender and the cultural distaste for ambiguity that I described earlier. Others' misidentification of the sex of their baby can be an embarrassing, even painful experience for some parents, which may explain why parents of a girl baby who has yet to grow hair (a visible sign of gender in this culture) will often tape pink ribbons to the bald baby's head. In many Latin American countries, families will have baby girls' ears pierced shortly after birth to provide an obvious indicator of the child's sex.

Beyond its importance to parents, proper identification of babies has a lot to do with maintaining social order. When my elder son was an infant, I dressed him on several occasions in a pink, frilly snowsuit in order to observe the reactions of others. (Having a sociologist for a father can be rather difficult from time to time!) Invariably someone would approach us and start playing with the baby. Some variation of the following interchange inevitably ensued:

"Oh, she's so cute! What's your little girl's name?"
"Zachary."
"Isn't 'Zachary' a boy's name?"
"He's a boy."

At this point the responses would range from stunned confusion and awkward laughter to dirty looks and outright anger. Clearly they felt that I had emotionally abused my son somehow. I had purposely breached a fundamental gender norm and thereby created, in their minds, unnecessary trauma (for him) and interactional turmoil (for them).

According to most developmental psychologists, by the age of 3 or so most children can accurately answer the question "Are you a boy or a girl?" (for example, Kohlberg, 1966). But to a young child, being a boy or a girl means no more than being named Bobby instead of Betty. It is simply another characteristic, like having brown hair or 10 fingers. The child at this age has no conception that gender is a category into which every human can be placed (S. J. Kessler & McKenna, 1978).

At around age 5 the child begins to see gender as an invariant characteristic of the social world—something that is fixed and permanent. Likewise, these young children exhibit a high degree of gender typing in their preferences for particular activities (Kohlberg, 1966). Children at this age express statements such as "men are doctors" and "women are nurses" as inflexible, objective "truths." Only later will the child be able to realize that gender roles are not as inflexible as once believed.

These early lessons of gender are provided by parents, siblings, and other significant people in the child's immediate environment. Often these individuals serve as observational models whom the child can identify with and ultimately imitate. Other times the lessons are more purposive and direct, as when parents provide their children with explicit instructions on proper gender behavior, like "Big boys don't cry" or "Act like a young lady."

Evidence suggests that the instructions for boys are particularly rigid and restrictive during childhood (Franklin, 1988). Indeed, the social costs for gender-inappropriate behavior are disproportionately severe for boys. The "sissy" in American society will have much more difficulty during childhood than the "tomboy." This discrepancy is clearly linked to the different social value ascribed to men and women and will be discussed in more detail in chapter 13.

As children grow older, parents tend to encourage more gender-typed activities. One study found that household tasks differ along gender lines. Boys were more likely to mow the lawn, shovel snow, take out the garbage, and do the yardwork, whereas girls tended to clean the house, wash dishes, cook, and babysit the younger children (White & Brinkerhoff, 1981).

Parents also influence their children's conceptions of sex and gender through the things they routinely purchase for them, such as clothes and toys. Not only do clothes inform others about the sex of an individual, they also send messages about how that person ought to be treated and direct behavior along traditional gender lines (Shakin, Shakin, & Sternglanz, 1985). Frilly dresses do not lend themselves easily to rough and dirty play. Likewise, it is difficult to walk quickly or assertively in high heels and tight miniskirts. Clothes for boys and men rarely restrict physical movement in this way.

Toys, too, serve to distinguish between the sexes. War toys, competitive games of strategy, and sports paraphernalia have been long-standing staples of the toy industry's boy market. The words *hero, warrior, battle*, and *speed* characterize boys' toys. Dolls, makeup kits, and toy kitchens continue to be profitable items for girls. The vocabulary of girls' toys consists of terms like *nurturing, love*, and *magic* (Lawson, 1993). Sex-specific toys foster different traits and skills in children and thereby serve to further segregate the two sexes into different patterns of social development. Boys' toys encourage invention, exploration, competition, and aggression. Girls' toys encourage creativity, nurturance, and physical attractiveness (C. L. Miller, 1987).

In some cases manufacturers have attempted—only half-heartedly—to blur the lines between boy and girl toys. The Hasbro toy company has tried to interest boys in troll dolls, which are traditionally popular among girls. What they came up with were old-fashioned action figures in the shape of a troll with names like "Troll Warrior" and "Battle Troll" (Lawson, 1993). Other companies have tried to sell girls on action figures and dinosaurs, which are typically the province of boys. But here, too, there is a drift into traditional sex stereotypes. Meritus Industries' "Darlin' Dinos," for example, are pink and have full heads of hair that can be combed. Mattel's "Wonder Woman" action figure fights not with swords or machine guns but with a wand that sprays bubbles.

Moreover, toy manufacturers are still quick to exploit the gender-distinct roles children are encouraged to pursue when they become adults. "My Bundle Baby," manufactured by Mattel, is a 10-inch infant doll in a padded pouch that can be worn around a child's abdomen. By pressing a button hidden inside the pouch, the child can feel the baby inside "kick" and can hear its heartbeat (Lawson, 1992). The "Judy" doll, manufactured by the Judith Corporation, looks like any other 11-inch doll except that she is pregnant. She comes with a distended tummy that, when removed, reveals the presence of a cute baby nestled comfortably inside the doll's plastic uterus. The baby can be bloodlessly removed and a flat, nonpregnant tummy inserted in its place. The advertisement reads, "Judy is more than a toy, she's a natural way for your child to learn while playing." Hence the Judy doll teaches young girls the cultural value of motherhood.

Mass Media

Children receive gender lessons from other sources as well. Children's books, for instance, teach children what other little boys or girls do and what is expected of them. In the early 1970s, Lenore Weitzman and her colleagues studied the portrayal of gender in popular preschool books (Weitzman, Eifler, Hodada, & Ross, 1972). They found that boys played a more significant role in the stories than girls by a ratio of 11 to 1. Boys were more likely to be portrayed in adventurous pursuits or activities that required independence and strength; girls were likely to be confined to indoor activities and portrayed as passive and dependent.

The prevalence of gender stereotypes in children's books has decreased only slightly over the past several decades (S. B. Peterson & Lach, 1990). Males still tend to be portrayed as adventurous, competent, and clever, while females are depicted as fearful, incompetent, and dependent (A. J. Davis, 1984). In addition, recent attempts to neutralize the stereotypical portrayal of gender through nonsexist children's books have had little impact on the overall market.

These images of males and females have a strong influence on children's perceptions and behaviors. One study found that children's own writing reflects the same sort of gender stereotypes found in the books they read. In stories written by 180 boys and girls in the first through sixth grades, male characters predominated. Further, the male characters were depicted in stereotypically male occupations: doctor, astronaut, dentist, professor, police officer. Female characters were shown largely in traditional female occupational roles: cook, teacher, babysitter, nurse (Trepanier & Romatowski, 1985).

Another important source of gender information is television. Despite some notable exceptions (for example, "Sesame Street"), most children's television shows continue to portray males and females in stereotypical gender roles (Signorielli, 1990). In cartoons, male characters outnumber female characters 4 or 5 to 1 (M. Morgan, 1982). Furthermore, male characters dominate the activities depicted and are more likely than female characters to be shown as holding positions of power (M. Morgan, 1987).

The portrayal of gender on prime time television also remains rather traditional and stereotypical (Signorielli, 1990). From 1969 to 1985, prime time television was populated by two to three males for every female. Although fewer women are portrayed as housewives than in the past, close to half cannot be classified by occupation (Signorielli, 1990). Men tend to be portrayed as powerful and unemotional, while women express emotions much more easily and are significantly more likely to use sex and charm to get what they want. Physical attractiveness continues to be the preeminent quality for women on television (see also chapter 13).

Children who watch a lot of television are more likely to hold stereotypical attitudes toward gender, exhibit gender-related characteristics, and engage in gender-related activities (M. Morgan, 1987; Signorielli, 1990). In one study, girls who did not have stereotypical conceptions of gender to begin with showed a significant increase in sexist attitudes after 2 years of heavy television watching (M. Morgan, 1982). In another study, 4- to 6-year-old children refused to play with a particular toy after watching two Muppets on TV who said the toy was OK only for the other sex (Cobb, Stevens-Long, & Goldstein, 1982).

Schools

In addition to the family and the media, an important institutional setting for gender socialization is the school. In school, children learn the intellectual and social skills for roles played by adults of their gender (Grant, 1984). Like parents, however, teachers are often unaware of the differential treatment they give to their male and female students. Many contemporary teachers still physically segregate boys from girls by, for example, asking them to line up by gender, pitting the boys against the girls in classroom competitions, or keeping them separated on the playground. It is not uncommon for teachers to ask boys to run the film projector or rearrange desks and ask girls to water the plants or dust the tables (Thorne & Luria, 1986). In fact, gender in schools has been found to account for more segregation than race (Schofield, 1982).

Teachers are also likely to treat their female students differently. A nationwide survey of 3,000 boys and girls between the ages of 9 and 15 found that boys received far more attention from teachers than girls. Teachers were also more likely to encourage assertive behavior in boys (American Association of University Women, 1991). This differential treatment is often reinforced by textbooks and other curricular materials that frequently consign women to stereotypical roles in American society (for example, nurse, spouse) or ignore their contributions to the shaping of history.

The gender-differentiated socialization that occurs in education extends male experiences by encouraging curiosity, independence, and initiative, and restricts female experiences by discouraging exploration and stressing "proper" behavior (Block, 1983). The result is that both boys and girls acquire a sense of their relative social positions. When third graders were asked what they wanted to be when they grow up, boys typically identified such occupations as football player, spy, firefighter, and motorcycle racer. Girls' responses included mother, teacher, and "plain old woman" (R. Best, 1983).

Consequently, boys have higher expectations and higher self-esteem than girls, a gap that widens with each passing year in the school system. According to one study, around the ages of 8 and 9, about two-thirds of both boys and girls report feeling confident and positive about themselves. By high school, however, the percentage drops to 29% for young women (Freiberg, 1991). As girls make the transformation from childhood to adolescence, they are faced with a conflict between the way they see themselves and the way others, particularly teachers, see them (Gilligan, 1990). Concern over these tendencies has led some school districts around the country to create sex-segregated classrooms—particularly in math and science—where girls are able to work without the anxiety and threats to esteem they often feel in sex-mixed classrooms (Hancock & Kalb, 1996).

Similar gender-typed patterns continue through high school. Teenage boys derive their prestige almost exclusively from athletics. They are also likely to be encouraged by counselors and teachers to formulate ambitious career goals. Prestige and popularity for teenage girls is more likely to come from their physical appearance and from having a boyfriend (Lott, 1987). As you might expect, girls' career aspirations tend to be lower than those of their male classmates (Bridges, 1988) despite girls' academic achievement, which is usually higher than that of boys.

College isn't much different. Most notably, the choice of major appears to be linked to gender. Despite their growing presence in master's, doctoral, and professional programs, women remain concentrated in fields like nursing, literature, home economics, certain of the social sciences, education, and library science. Men continue to dominate areas such as mathematics, the physical sciences, engineering and architecture (M. F. Fox, 1989). College professors, like their elementary school counterparts, may treat men and women differently in the classroom as well. Disparaging comments about women, the use of sex-stereotyped examples, and the use of the generic "he" are some examples (R. M. Hall & Sandler, 1985).

Even as more and more colleges move to mixed-sex living arrangements, gender stereotypes persist. Anthropologist Michael Moffatt (1989) spent several years living among college students in a Rutgers University coed dorm. He concluded that the price women have had to pay for being treated as near-equals in this setting is that they must act more like men in order to be accepted. Here, too, the male standard of behavior predominates.

Conclusion

Becoming the people we are is a complex, social process. Those intimate characteristics we hold so dear—our self-concept, our gender, and our racial and ethnic identity—are reflections of larger cultural attitudes, values, and expectations. Yet we are not perfect reflections of society's values. With all the powerful socializing institutions that pull our developmental strings, we continue to be and will always be individuals.

Sometimes we ignore our generalized others and strike out on our own with complete disregard for community standards and attitudes. Sometimes we form self-concepts that contradict information received from significant others. Sometimes we willingly violate the expectations associated with our gender or our race. Societal influence can go only so far in explaining how we become who we are. The rest—that which makes us truly unique—remains a mystery.

CHAPTER HIGHLIGHTS

▪ Socialization is the process by which individuals learn their culture and learn to live according to the norms of that particular society. It is how we learn to perceive our world, gain a sense of our own racial or ethnic identity, and interact appropriately with others. It also tells us what it means to be a man or a woman, and what we should and should not do across a range of situations.

▪ Socialization occurs within the context of several social institutions—schools, religious institutions, the mass media, and the family.

▪ Socialization is not just a process that occurs during childhood. Adults must be resocialized into a new galaxy of norms, values, and expectations each time they leave or abandon old roles and enter new ones.

■ One of the most important outcomes of socialization for an individual is the development of a sense of self. The ability to modify our behavior to meet the expectations of other people and society in general rests on the development of the self.

■ Humans are not born with a self. To acquire a self, children must learn to recognize themselves as unique physical objects, master language, learn to take the role of others, and, in effect, see themselves from another's perspective.

■ We learn our gender and the social expectations that go with it through socialization. Whereas sex refers to biological characteristics, gender designates the psychological, social, and cultural aspects of maleness and femaleness.

YOUR TURN

This chapter has focused on the construction of self and gender. Many social institutions assist in the process of socialization in ways that are sometimes not immediately apparent.

To see firsthand how this sort of socialization works, visit a local shopping mall. Most malls today have a children's clothing store. If yours doesn't, go to one of the large department stores and find the children's clothing section. Start with the infant clothes. Note the differences in the style, color, and texture of boys' clothes versus girls' clothes. Collect the same information regarding clothes for toddlers, preschool, and school-age children.

After collecting your "data," try to interpret the differences you noticed. Why do they exist? What do these differences say about the kinds of activities in which boys and girls are expected and encouraged to engage? For instance, whose clothes are "dainty"? Whose are "rugged"? How do these clothing differences reinforce our cultural conceptions of masculinity and femininity?

The next stop on your sociological shopping trip is the toy store. See if you can tell when you've entered the "boy" section or the "girl" section. How did you know? How did the toys differ? Note the differences in color, sound, and types of material used.

What sorts of interactions with other children do the toys encourage? Competition? Cooperation? Which sex's toys are designed for active play? Which encourage passive play? For what sorts of adult roles do the toys prepare children?

Finally, find a bookstore that has a children's book section. Are there "boy" books and "girl" books? How can you tell? What are the differences in the sorts of characters and plots that are portrayed?

Use your findings to discuss the role that consumer products play in socializing people into "appropriate" gender roles. Why is there so much sex-typing in these products? Are manufacturers simply responding to market demands (that is, they make sex-specific products because that's what people want), or do they have a role in creating those demands?

THE RESOLUTION OF SEXUAL IDENTITY

DOUGLAS HARPER

"…Because our society so discourages ambiguous sexual or gender definitions, people who define themselves in a way that is inconsistent with their biological definitions are usually seen as deviants…."

This chapter has stressed the relationship between the social and physical bases for identity. This relationship is, indeed, complex. You have learned that in our society the separation of people of different sexes (physical characteristics) and genders (psychological, social, and cultural aspects of maleness and femaleness) is strongly enforced.

Because our society so discourages ambiguous sexual or gender definitions, people who define themselves in a way that is inconsistent with their biological definitions are usually viewed as deviants. They have failed at the roles set by biology. It is possible to redefine one's sexual identity through surgery and hormone treatment, but the shift in an individual's identity is usually hidden from public view.

The case of Jim and Jan Morris is unusual. A well-known and respected travel writer, Morris lived into his adulthood as Jim. He then became "Jan" through a process that was both surgical and social. Jan's professional life continued the career begun by Jim; the transformation was public and unabashed.

UPI/BETTMANN

DAVID HURN/MAGNUM

While we typically view events such as these from the social perspective, sociologist Harold Garfinkel studied the physical transformation of an individual's sexual identity to define the unrecognized practical reasonings that constitute daily life. In other words, we each experience the world as a man or a woman, but we can only guess at how we might perceive the same flow of life as a member of the other sex or gender. The individual who has made this transition may help us understand the most basic ways in which the world is experienced based on our gender and sexual identities.

CHAPTER 6

Building Image: Individual and Organizational Identities

- *Forming Impressions of Others*
- *Managing Impressions: Actors on a Social Stage*
- *Mismanaging Impressions: Spoiled Identities*

On Christmas Day, 1981, I met my soon-to-be wife's family for the first time. Entering this group of important strangers, I knew I had to be on my best behavior and try to say and do all the right things. I wanted to make sure the impression they formed of me was that of a likable fellow who would make a fine addition to the family.

As family members busily opened their presents, I noticed the wide and gleeful eyes of my wife's 14-year-old sister as she unwrapped what was to her a special gift: her very own basketball. Being the youngest in a family of eight kids, she didn't have much she could call her own, so this was a significant moment for her. She had finally broken away from a life filled with hand-me-downs and communal equipment. She hugged that ball as if it were a puppy.

I saw my chance to make the perfect first impression. *I'm not a bad basketball player,* I thought to myself. *I'll take her outside to the basketball hoop in the driveway, impress her with my shooting skills, become her idol, and win family approval.* "Hey, Mary," I said, "let's go out and shoot some hoops." After we stepped outside I grabbed the new ball from her. "Look at this," I said, as I flung it toward the basket from about 40 feet away. We both watched as the ball arced gracefully toward its destination, and for a brief moment I actually thought it was going to go in. But that was not to be.

As if guided by the taunting hand of fate, the ball struck an exposed bolt that protruded from the base of the supporting pole of the hoop. There was a sickeningly loud *pop,* followed by a hissing sound as the ball fluttered to the ground like a deflated balloon. It sat there lifeless, never having experienced the joy of "swishing" through a net. For that matter, it never even bounced on the ground in its short-lived inflated state.

For a few seconds we both stood numb and motionless. Then I turned to apologize to the 14-year-old girl whose once cheerful eyes now harbored the kind of hate and resentment usually reserved for ax murderers. In a flash she burst into tears and ran into the house, shrieking, "THAT GUY popped my ball!" It was hardly the heroic identity I was striving for. As the angry mob poured into the backyard to stare at the villainous and still somewhat unknown perpetrator, I became painfully aware of the fragile nature of the self-images we try to project to others.

We all have been in situations—a first date, a job interview, a first meeting with a girlfriend or boyfriend's family—in which we are compelled to "make a good impression." We try to present a favorable image of ourselves so that others will make positive judgments of us. This phenomenon, referred to as **impression management**, is not only an important and universal aspect of our personal lives but a key element of social structure as well.

In this chapter I examine the social creation of images. How do we form impressions of others? What do we do to control the impressions others form of us? I also discuss broader sociological applications of the principles of impression management. What are the institutional motivations behind individual impression management? How do groups and organizations present and manage collective impressions? How is impression management linked to social order? Finally, what happens when impression management fails and images are spoiled, as mine was in the above story?

Forming Impressions of Others

When we first meet someone we form an immediate impression based on observable cues (Pryor & Ostrom, 1981). These cues consist of social group characteristics (age, race, sex), individual attributes, and verbal and nonverbal expressions. Keep in mind that the importance of this information—the value attached to a certain age, race, or sex; the particular traits that are defined as desirable; the meaning of certain expressions—varies from culture to culture. Hence the impressions people form of others—good, bad, or indifferent—must always be understood within the appropriate cultural context.

Social Group Membership

Age, sex, race, and, to a certain degree, ethnicity can often be determined by looking at a person's physical features; religion and social class are less obvious but are sometimes known early in an encounter with another person, through the person's language, mannerisms, or dress. All of these attributes help us form an initial assessment of the identities of other people. As you saw in the previous chapter, our socialization experiences provide us with a sense of the cultural significance of being male or female, young or old, black or white, upper class or working class, and so on. Moreover, we have learned to expect certain things from certain types of people. For instance, if all you know about a person is that she's female, you're likely to assume that she's probably compassionate, emotional, and nurturant. Likewise, if all you know about a person is that he or she is 85 years old, you might predict that this person has low energy, poor memory, and conservative political attitudes. Think about how you are likely to react when you know someone is from a different country. Or, for that matter, from a different region of the United States. Such predictions are rarely completely accurate. Nevertheless, we begin social interactions with these culturally defined conceptions of how people from certain social groups are likely to act, what their tastes and preferences might be, and even what values they are likely to hold.

This information provides the initial backdrop to all social encounters between people who have little if any prior knowledge of one another. It is so pervasive and so quickly processed that we usually notice it only when it isn't there. Imagine how difficult it would be to form a friendship or even carry on a conversation if you didn't know whether you were dealing with someone of the same sex or opposite sex.

From a person's readily observable social characteristics, we form a preliminary judgment of that individual as a representative of a group about whom we have already formed certain behavioral expectations. These expectations need not be positive or negative. But when this information is the only thing we know about an individual, we structure our impressions around it.

Individual Attributes

Impressions based on social group membership are not final. We confirm or modify our impressions when we gain additional information that is unique to a particular person (Berndt & Heller, 1986). To do this, we assess other characteristics that are easily perceivable: physical appearance, clothing, and so on. But even then, our impressions are influenced by our cultural background.

Physical Appearance

A quick glance at the latest magazine or television advertisements attests to the enormous importance of physical appearance in American society. Everywhere we turn, it seems, we are encouraged to believe that if our skin isn't free of blemishes, if we are too short, if we are over- or underweight, if our hair isn't stylish, if our clothes don't reflect the latest fashion trend, we have fallen short of the important cultural standard of attractiveness. Although we readily acknowledge that using a person's physical attractiveness to form an impression is shallow and unfair, we do it anyway.

Research shows that in our culture physical appearance dramatically affects our perceptions and judgments of others. Attractive men are perceived to be more masculine and attractive women more feminine than their unattractive counterparts (Gillen, 1981). We assume that physically attractive people possess other desirable traits like sensitivity, kindness, strength, and sexual responsiveness (Dion, Berscheid, & Walster, 1972). The impressions adults form of young children are heavily influenced by the child's physical attractiveness (Clifford & Walster, 1973; Dion, 1972). Even research on juries suggests that attractive people are treated better (for example, receive shorter jail sentences) than unattractive people (Stewart, 1980).

Physical appearance has considerable impact on our own feelings of self-worth as well. According to one study, 85% of women and 72% of men are dissatisfied with at least one aspect of their looks (cited in Goleman, 1991a). Such dissatisfaction can have long-lasting effects. People who don't like the way they look report higher levels of overall unhappiness than people who are satisfied with their appearance (Berscheid & Walster, 1974).

So important is the ideal of physical attractiveness that a psychiatric diagnosis called *body dysmorphic disorder* has become more common over the last decade or so (Goleman, 1991a). Psychiatrists estimate that between 2% and 10% of the population have this "disorder." These individuals are so self-conscious about their looks that their lives are constricted in some significant way, from feeling inhibited during lovemaking to becoming homebound or suicidal.

In our society physical appearance is a more crucial determinant of self-worth for women than it is for men. Throughout history different parts of the female anatomy have been used to symbolize a woman's femininity and sexuality. Consider a young woman's breast development: "Parents and relatives mark their appearance as a landmark event, schoolmates take notice, girlfriends compare, boys zero in; later a husband, a lover, a baby expect a proprietary share. No other part of the human anatomy has such semipublic, intensely private status" (Brownmiller, 1984, pp. 40–41). Given the amount of social attention, it is not surprising that many women are self-conscious about their breasts. The "Wonderbra"—a push-up bra designed to increase bust size—reached sales of $120 million in 1994 and was named one of the top 10 products in America by *Time, Newsweek, USA Today*, and *Fortune* (DeCoursey, 1995). Choosing a more permanent course, an estimated 150,000 women a year in the United States undergo breast implant surgery (S. M. Wolfe, 1991). Although some of these surgeries are performed for medical reasons, the vast majority—about 80%—are performed for cosmetic reasons. In the early 1990s, breast implants ranked second only to liposuction (a procedure that siphons away body fat) as the most popular form of cosmetic surgery (L. Williams, 1992a).

But gender differences in the importance of physical appearance are not limited just to individual parts of the anatomy. The cultural norms used to evaluate overall female beauty continue to be so narrow and unrealistic that many women have a sense of perpetual deficiency as a result (Schur, 1984). Women have more money, political clout, and legal recognition today than ever before, but they are continuously encouraged to define themselves almost exclusively in terms of their physical appearance. At the individual level such an emphasis devalues a person's other attributes and accomplishments; at the institutional level it plays an important role in the nation's economy by sustaining several multibillion-dollar industries, including advertising, fashion, and cosmetics (Schur, 1984).

■ ■ ■ ■ ■ ■ ■ ■
MICRO-MACRO CONNECTION
Obesity

The negative effects of a lack of physical attractiveness on impression formation are perhaps felt most strongly by those whose body size does not meet cultural standards. Those who are noticeably overweight tend to be evaluated quite negatively (Allon, 1982; English, 1991). The phenomenal growth and success of the multibillion dollar diet "industry"—low-calorie foods, dieting books, weight-loss organizations, and so forth—provide clear evidence of the obsession with weight in this country. The number of readers of *Weight Watchers Magazine* is the same as that of the *New York Times* ("Harper's Index," 1996).

Fatness carries tremendous symbolic meaning in this society. An overweight person may be judged by others as lacking in willpower and as being self-indulgent, personally offensive, and even morally and socially unfit (Millman, 1980). The following story appeared several years ago in newspapers across the country:

> UPI reports that majorette Peggy Ward will be barred from Friday's football game. The reason? Ms. Ward is 1–2 pounds overweight. She is 5 foot 4 and 127 pounds. This weight exceeds the guidelines established by the band director. The school superintendent supports the band director, but Ms. Ward is fighting back by fasting to make the limit in time for the game. But the event has been psychologically costly for the majorette. "The pressure and intense publicity surrounding the controversy apparently became too much at one point for Ms. Ward, who telephoned her mother . . . in tears and asked to be taken home from school." (quoted in E. E. Jones et al., 1984, p. 1)

Obesity can affect economic opportunities as well. A recent study of young women in Britain found that those in the heaviest 10% of their age group earned 7.4% less than their nonobese peers; and those in the heaviest 1% earned 11.4 percent less (cited in "Physical traits," 1994). In high-visibility occupations such as modeling, public relations, and sales, companies often regard overweight people as unemployable because they fear they will project a negative image of the company. In one California city, hiring policies once specified that teachers could not be more than 25% overweight (Laslett & Warren, 1987).

While our society's distaste for obesity applies to everyone, it is again felt particularly strongly by women. Cultural standards have idealized increasingly thinner female bodies since the 1920s (Freedman, 1986). In one study 70% of college women felt they were overweight, although less than 40% actually were (T. M.

Miller, Coffman, & Linke, 1980). Furthermore, women are becoming weight conscious at increasingly younger ages. A 1987 survey of 500 elementary school children found that more than half the girls thought they were too fat, even though only 15% were actually heavier than the norm (Goleman, 1991a). At any one time, half of American women are on a diet; and half of all 9-year old girls have been on a diet at least once in their lives ("The facts," 1996).

These are not merely the trivial misperceptions of individual women. Unnecessary concern over weight shows how powerful cultural beliefs are in the formation of self-concepts. At best, the failure to meet broad cultural standards of thinness can generate antagonism toward one's own body and lowered self-esteem. At worst, it can lead to life-threatening eating disorders (Chernin, 1981). And, of course, female weight concern has macro-level implications because of the role it plays in supporting the many large businesses that sell weight-loss products and programs.

■ ■ ■

Clothing and Body Adornment

The way people dress and decorate their bodies is also important in forming impressions and communicating feelings, beliefs, and group identity to others. We make assessments of ethnicity, social class, age, cultural tastes, morality, and political attitudes on the basis of people's clothes, jewelry, hairstyles, and so on. A common T-shirt can

> speak over the din of a concert, a party, or a sport event. It can carry a concise and lucid message in ways body and behavior cannot. . . . The tee shirt is the modern equivalent of the poster in prerevolutionary France, wall graffiti in Latin America, or the flaming cross in antebellum South. . . . The wearing of brand names, of exotic place names, of expensive tee shirts . . . [says] to all who will look that the wearer is well located in the class system. (Young, 1993, pp. 147–148)

The emphasis on clothing and body adornments can be found everywhere. Business people are acutely aware of and usually conform to a rigid corporate dress code. Most high-profile politicians now employ fashion consultants to advise them about the right clothes or haircut for particular occasions. And, as you are well aware, fashion is a significant element of the student culture on most college campuses (Moffatt, 1989). In short, Americans tell one another who they are and what they stand for by what they wear.

Clothing and body adornment are important in understanding impression formation because—unlike age, race, gender, and, to a certain extent, physical attractiveness—they can be purposely managed and manipulated to influence the impressions others form of us. People can dress to convey the impression that they are worthy of respect or, at the very least, attention (Lauer & Handel, 1977). Children often signal their entry into the world of adolescence by wearing the clothing of their peers and refusing to wear the clothing chosen by their parents (G. P. Stone, 1981). The purveyors of rap, hip-hop, and grunge music use clothing and hairstyle as an expression of subcultural identity and even social rebellion.

Many people also see clothing—and the image it conveys—as a tool for success in the working world. Graduating college students who aspire to a "serious" job, for instance, will often rush out to acquire a "power suit" for job interviews. An organization in Chicago, called "The Bottomless Closet," helps get women off welfare and into the work force by providing them with outfits to wear on job interviews, free of charge, from a supply of donated clothing.

Verbal and Nonverbal Expressions

Another important piece of information we use in forming impressions of others is what people express to us verbally or nonverbally. Through talk, movement, posture, and gestures, people provide cues about their values, attitudes, sentiments, personality, and history (G. P. Stone, 1981). Most of us are quite proficient at "reading" even the subtlest nonverbal messages. We learn early on that a raised eyebrow, a nod of the head, or a slight hand gesture can mean something in a social encounter. So important is this ability that a deficiency in it is considered by some psychologists to be a learning disability akin to severe reading problems (Goleman, 1989).

As we obtain information from others in order to form impressions, we also communicate information about ourselves to them. We do so through physical expressions such as a shaky voice, flushed face, and trembling hands, which are difficult to control, or through words, which can be purposely used to express certain emotions, desires, attributes, or attitudes.

We can strategically furnish or conceal information. On a first date, you might hide the fact that this is the first date you've had in 2 years. On the same date, however, you may casually drop a line about your family's vacation home in Aspen. In both cases you've attempted to communicate or conceal information that will maximize your perceived desirability in this person's eyes.

People form impressions of others and manage impressions of themselves at the same time. The ability to manage impressions is the defining feature of human interaction.

Managing Impressions: Actors on a Social Stage

In social encounters individuals must decide what sort of self-image they want to present and what sort of image they will allow the other person to claim. Erving Goffman (1959), the sociologist most responsible for the scholarly examination of impression management, portrays everyday life as a series of social interactions in which a person is motivated to "sell" a particular image to others.

A person can occupy various identities: student, sibling, child, employee, wealthy person, trusted friend, future lawyer. As a general rule, the more important an identity is to an individual's overall self-concept, the more time he or she will spend on activities expressing that identity (McCall & Simmons, 1978). For instance, if you aspire to be a marriage counselor, you may spend a great deal of time listening to people's problems or commenting on people's relationships.

The primary goal of impression management is to project a particular identity that will increase the likelihood of obtaining favorable outcomes from others in particular social situations (E. E. Jones & Pittman, 1982; Stryker, 1980). This sometimes requires advertising, exaggerating, or fabricating your positive qualities and concealing behaviors or attributes that you believe others will find unappealing.

Goffman argues that impression management is not used just to present false or inflated images of ourselves. Many attributes we possess are not immediately apparent to others or may be misinterpreted. Imagine yourself taking the final exam in your sociology course. You look up from your paper and make brief eye contact with the instructor. You are not cheating, but you think the instructor may interpret your wandering eyes as an indication of cheating. Chances are you will consciously overemphasize your noncheating behavior by acting as though you're in deep thought or by glancing at the clock, in order to maintain your "law-abiding" image.

Obtaining favorable outcomes through impression management is usually associated with social approval—that is, being respected and liked by others. However, different circumstances may require projecting different identities (E. E. Jones & Pittman, 1982). Perhaps you've been in situations where you tried to appear helpless in order to get someone else to do a task you really didn't want to do, or maybe you tried to be as powerful and fearsome as you could to intimidate someone into doing something. Perhaps you "played dumb" to avoid challenging the status of a superior (Gove, Hughes, & Geerkin, 1980). As social beings we have the ability to tailor our images to fit the requirements of a particular situation.

■ ■ ■ ■ ■ ■ ■ ■

MICRO-MACRO CONNECTION
Managing Impressions in Cyberspace

Within the past few years the Internet—the vast global network linking some 10 million host computers—has evolved from an obscure tool of professors, government officials, and computer scientists to a popular "mainstream" communications medium for the general public. In fact, many social observers feel the Internet will eventually be the backbone of an emerging global information economy and transform social institutions as profoundly as the telephone, radio, and television did (Chapman, 1996). While the political and economic implications of the Internet are astounding, what is particularly interesting is its effect on the way people perceive and interact with others and electronically manage impressions.

People use the Internet for two reasons: to find information and to communicate with others. Electronic mail, for example, is a common way for people to send messages to one another. Other elements of the Internet—newsgroups and bulletin boards—foster open discussions on a wide variety of topics, such as television shows, infectious diseases, vegetarianism, and sexuality. Users range from highly technical experts to computer novices, from teenagers fooling around with their parents' computer to homebound elderly people seeking social contact (Donath, 1997). Some discussion groups are close-knit and friendly; others are angry and confrontational; and some are simply repositories of knowledge where information is impersonally exchanged.

In any face-to-face interaction, our first impressions play a key role. The social categories in which we place a new acquaintance shape future interpretations of his or her motives and behaviors. Ultimately the identity we've ascribed to someone determines the trustworthiness of the information he or she provides. If I make authoritative statements about which California wine to serve with shellfish or how to stay in shape or where holes in the ozone layer are forming, you would want to know if I have the expertise to make such claims. Furthermore, if I claim to be a young, attractive Native American woman, it might be useful for you to physically verify such information. In the disembodied world of electronic communication, however, identity is difficult to prove (Donath, 1997). Without access to physical features, facial expressions, tone of voice, body language, clothing, biographical information, or any other interactional cues that aid in forming impressions, Internet participants must rely on words alone for information about a person's trustworthiness (Rheingold, 1994; Sproull & Kiesler, 1991).

In some ways these informational limitations make interactions more honest and straightforward. People often end up revealing far more about themselves than they would be inclined to do without the protection of the anonymous computer screen. In a university study, 3% of students who filled out a paper-and-pencil version of a survey admitted using illegal drugs at least once a week for recreational purposes. Of those who received the same survey via electronic mail, 14% made the same admission (Sproull & Kiesler, 1991). Ironically, people seem to feel less certain about the privacy and confidentiality of their responses when answering on paper even though technically anyone answering a computer survey can be traced. Internet discussion groups are particularly popular among gay men and lesbians who feel they can openly discuss issues of importance to the gay community or even "come out of the closet" without being condemned or harassed by neighbors and co-workers ("Gay men and lesbians," 1996).

Moreover, people with physical characteristics that might impede face-to-face interactions or negate their authority can communicate effectively over the Internet without immediately being judged by others. Thus computer interaction has the capacity to eliminate or at least reduce people's social advantages over one another. As one participant in a computer conference system bluntly put it:

> All messages have an equal chance because they all look alike. The only thing that sets them apart is their content. If you are a hunchback, a paraplegic, a woman, a black, fat, old, have two hundred warts on your face, or never take a bath, you still have the same chance. (quoted in Zuboff, 1988, p. 371)

But although computers allow people to interact without risking prejudgement because of their obvious social characteristics, computers also allow people to lie about who they are. At first blush the identities people can claim in computer discussion groups or other anonymous electronic communication appear unlimited: one person can create multiple identities, a man can create a female identity, a high school dropout can claim to be a senior citizen surviving on social security. A person "can have any physical description and will be responded to as a function of that description. The plain can experience the self presentation of great beauty; the nerdy can be elegant; the obese can be slender" (Turkle, 1994, p. 162).

The more technologically sophisticated interactive environments even let people communicate using two- or three-dimensional graphical, cartoon-like representations of themselves known as *avatars*. A San Francisco software company, for instance, has built an on-line environment called "Alpha World" that is an electronic version of a cocktail party where guests can select an avatar to represent themselves and then chat with other avatars (Flynn, 1996). Visitors to interactive environments may select from a wide variety of existing images, or they can create their own custom avatar. Some avatars have a full range of gestures that allow users to express themselves more fully. Of course, the image you choose to represent yourself says a great deal about how you want to be seen by others; all this comes without the inconvenience of actually *being seen* by others.

Ironically, while deceptive impression management is clearly easier in the virtual world of computers than in the physical world, the medium itself contains institutionalized methods of limiting identity deception. For instance, all posted messages contain a header that includes an "account" or "user" name and a "domain" or address. Although all identifying information can be stripped from a message so it can be sent anonymously or with a pseudonym, many user groups frown on anonymous postings. The domain name, which indicates the organization that provides the account from which the person is writing, functions very much like company letterhead. It can tell you whether a person is writing from a university, a research lab, a private corporation, a government agency, or a commercial on-line service. Hence it may provide contextual information about the writer, such as his or her educational status or occupation. And while there aren't yet any recognized "wealthy" virtual neighborhoods, it's probably only a matter of time until exclusive on-line domains become symbols of social status (Donath, 1997).

The contents of a message may also include identity-related information that makes deception difficult. A man may write, "I am a female," but using a "female voice" and providing convincing responses would be quite difficult for a man to do over time (Donath, 1997). Since gender affects language patterns, perspective, and interpretations of experiences, "passing" as the opposite gender for any length of time would be difficult. Because language is an important indicator of group identity, the idiosyncratic language style people use on-line—jargon, phrases, and abbreviations common to particular groups or communities—may either reinforce or negate a claimed identity.

The Internet is a world of complex interactions, unmatched in its ability to bring together people from different real-world cultures. It holds the possibility of reducing differences between social groups by de-emphasizing information about race, ethnicity, occupation, gender, and other social statuses. One can only imagine what the cultural and institutional implications will be as large numbers of people manage impressions, form relationships, and do business outside the traditional physical, geographical, political, racial, and ethnic constraints that have always governed human interaction. At the same time, however, without these constraints we must figure out how to deal with information that can be unreliable, hard to verify, and perhaps even deceptive.

▪ ▪ ▪

The Role of Norms in Impression Management

Whether impression management takes place face-to-face or over a computer, it is governed by powerful but unspoken cultural norms (Crittenden & Wiley, 1985). For instance, self-promotion may help us present ourselves in the most favorable light, but too much of it can have decidedly negative consequences. The brazen self-promoter or braggart often is perceived as a socially inept individual with suspicious motives. We are thus culturally obligated to inject some modesty into the statements we make about ourselves. Under certain conditions, such as performing an act of extreme bravery, an individual's interests might best be served by not demanding personal credit for positive outcomes (Bradley, 1978).

Cultural norms also define which attributes are valued and thus which ones people will try to project. In a culture that values mental prowess over physical agility, impression-management strategies are likely to demonstrate intelligence rather than strength.

Impression management norms cannot be separated from broader socioeconomic factors. In a capitalist society like ours, workers must be careful to communicate support and respect for their superiors or risk losing their jobs (Welsh, 1984). The importance we attach to weekends, holidays, vacations, and all those times when we can "act naturally" illustrates the extent to which the economic structure constrains the rest of our lives.

Altercasting

In addition to managing our own impressions, sometimes we try to place another person in a particular identity. Using verbal strategies to impose a certain image on others is called **altercasting** (Weinstein & Deutschberger, 1963).

We cast others into roles that are to our advantage. The applied identity then forces people to act "voluntarily" in ways that are consistent with our interests. Saying "After all the things I've done for you, the least you could do is let me borrow your car," immediately places on the recipient of the comment the identity of "obligated friend" and compels him or her to reciprocate a favor. Similarly, when a teacher tells a student, "I know you can do better," the student is compelled to live up to an identity of competence.

The use of altercasting is demonstrated in a study by sociologist Philip Blumstein (1975) on social interaction in a dating situation. Women in the study were instructed to claim a "healthily assertive" identity by altercasting their dates into a submissive role. They would say things like, "I've been dating this one guy, but we broke up because he would never let me have any say about what we do. You wouldn't treat me that way, would you?" Or, "I like guys who don't come on like they own me, but let me take some initiative." While some of the men rejected the attempts, most allowed their dates to claim the assertive identity by presenting themselves in a way that was consistent with the identity into which they had been cast (for example, "Sorry I've been so pushy. Whatever you say goes").

This research has obvious implications for interpersonal power relations, showing how people can manipulate the behavior of others. It also sheds light on the strength of the particular identities that make up one's self-concept. Most of the men who resisted the altercasting attempts had indicated earlier in the study that dominance was an important aspect of their own self-concept. The men who rated dominance as unimportant were more likely to accept the submissive identity. Blumstein concluded that we tend to reject altercasting attempts that threaten an identity central to our overall self-concept.

Dramaturgy: Social Interaction as Theater

"All the world's a stage, and all the men and women merely players. They have their exits and their entrances, and one man in his time plays many parts," wrote William Shakespeare in *As You Like It*. The study of social interaction as theater is called **dramaturgy**. Goffman (1959) argued that people in everyday life are like actors on a stage. The "audience" consists of people who observe the behavior of others, the "roles" are the images people are trying to project, and the "script" consists of their communications with others. The goal is to enact a performance that is believable to a particular audience and that allows us to achieve the goals we desire. Every aspect of social life can be examined dramaturgically, from the ritualized greetings of strangers to the everyday dynamics of our family, school, and work lives.

Front Stage and Back Stage

A key structural element of dramaturgy is the distinction between front stage and back stage. In the theater, front stage is where the performance takes place. In contrast, back stage is where makeup is removed, lines are rehearsed, performances are rehashed, and people are able to fall "out of character."

In social interaction, **front stage** is where people maintain the appropriate appearance as they interact with others. In a restaurant, front stage is the dining room where the customers (the audience) are present. Here the servers (the actors) are expected to present themselves as upbeat, happy, competent, and courteous. **Back stage**, however, is the region where people can knowingly violate their impression management performances. In the restaurant, back stage is the kitchen area where the once-courteous servers now shout, shove dishes, and even complain about or make fun of the customers.

The barrier between front and back stage is crucial to successful impression management because it blocks the audience from seeing behavior that would ruin the performance. During a therapy session (front stage), psychiatrists usually appear extremely interested in everything their patients say and show considerable sympathy for their problems. At a dinner party with colleagues or at home with family (back stage), however, they may express total boredom and disdain for the patients' disclosures. If patients were to see such back-stage behavior, not only would the performance be disrupted, but the psychiatrist's professional credibility and reputation would suffer as well. One study found that beneath their mask of neutrality, many psychiatrists report harboring strong and professionally inappropriate feelings—including hatred, fear, anger, and sexual arousal—toward their patients (Goleman, 1993).

Props

Successful impression management also depends on the control of identity objects, called *props*, in the environment. In the theater, props must be handled deftly for an effective performance. A gun that doesn't go off when it's supposed to or a chair that collapses can destroy an entire play. The same is true in social interaction. For instance, you might make sure your school books are in clear view and beer bottles disposed of as you prepare for an upcoming visit from your parents. Similarly, you may spend a great deal of time setting a romantic mood for a dinner date in your apartment—the right music, the right lighting, pictures of former lovers hidden from view, and so on. Clearly, the mishandling of these props can severely disrupt the performance and, ultimately, the impression you wished to convey.

Social Influences on Impression Management

Up to this point I've described dramaturgy and impression management from the point of view of individual people driven by a personal desire to present themselves in the most favorable light possible. But people do not exist in a social vacuum. A person's social group identity—most notably gender, race and ethnicity, social class, and occupational status—influences others' immediate expectations and impressions. And because expectations can be self-fulfilling, social group membership may also influence the sorts of images a person presents in social interaction.

Gender

Expectations based on gender are powerful. People who want to be judged positively by others may be forced to present themselves in ways that are consistent with the appropriate gender stereotypes (Crittenden, 1991; Spence, Deaux, & Helmreich, 1985). Traditionally, women have been more likely to present themselves as weak or dependent, whereas men have been more likely to project power and competence (Gruber & White, 1986; Instone, Major, & Bunker, 1983; P. Johnson, 1976).

Such images, however, depend on the perceived expectations of others. In a study by von Baeyer, Sherk, and Zanna (1981), female subjects played the role of job applicants who were to be interviewed by a male "employer." The women who believed their interviewer held traditional views of women were much more likely to present themselves in a stereotypically feminine way. They wore more makeup and clothing accessories, talked less, made less eye contact, and gave more traditional answers to questions about marriage and children than the women who saw their interviewers as nontraditional. In another study, men were more likely to present themselves as strong, independent, and stereotypically masculine when they thought others in the study expected them to fit the stereotype (Eagly, Wood, & Fishbaugh, 1981).

A conflict perspective on these impression management tactics emphasizes the influence of a social structure in which men and women have traditionally been assigned different positions of power (Howard, Blumstein, & Schwartz, 1986). As women gain more power and as gender stereotypes lose their legitimacy, the images people present of themselves in social situations might also change.

Race and Ethnicity

Like gender, race and ethnicity influence the images people project. People of racial or ethnic minorities are often forced to present self-images that are consistent with the expectations or stereotypes of others. In a society in which race is a primary source of inequality, living up (or down) to such expectations may be one of the few means by which people can participate actively in public life while retaining their own cultural identity. Individuals from oppressed groups may appear to fit common racial or ethnic stereotypes in public (front stage), but an analysis of private (back stage) behavior often indicates that they are keenly aware of the roles they have been forced to play. Impression management is obviously an important survival tactic.

■ ■ ■ ■ ■ ■ ■ ■

ELIJAH ANDERSON
The Code of the Streets

Throughout the 1980s sociologist Elijah Anderson carried out observational research in a racially, ethnically, and economically diverse area of Philadelphia he called Village-Northton. The area was home to two communities: one black and very poor, the other middle- to upper-income and predominantly white. Anderson was particularly interested in how young black men—the overwhelming majority of whom were civil and law-abiding—managed public impressions to deal with the assumption of Village residents that young black men are dangerous.

Anderson discovered that a central theme for most of the residents was maintaining safety on the streets of the Village and avoiding violent and drug-related crime. Incapable of making distinctions between law-abiding black males and others, people relied for protection on broad stereotypes: Whites are law-abiding and trustworthy; young black men are crime-prone and dangerous.

Residents of the area, including black men themselves, were likely to defer to unknown black males on the street. Women—particularly white women—clutched their purses and edged up closer to their companions as they walked down the street. Many pedestrians crossed the street or diverted their eyes from young men who were seen as unpredictable and menacing.

Some young black men in the Village developed certain interactional strategies to overcome the immediate assumption that they were dangerous. For instance, they often used friendly greetings as a kind of preemptive peace offering, designed to advise others of their civil intentions. Or they went to great lengths to behave in ways contrary to the presumed expectations of whites:

> I find myself being extra nice to whites. A lot of times I be walking down the streets ... and I see somebody white. . . . I know they are afraid of me. They don't know me, but they intimidated. . . . So I might smile, just to reassure them. . . . At other times I

find myself opening doors, you know. Holding the elevator. Putting myself in a certain light, you know, to change whatever doubts they may have. (E. Anderson, 1990, pp. 185–186)

Such impression management requires an enormous amount of effort and places responsibility for ensuring social order on this man. He feels compelled to put strangers at ease so he can go about his own business. He understands that his mere presence makes others nervous and uncomfortable. He recognizes that trustworthiness—an ascribed characteristic of whites—is something blacks must work hard to achieve.

Other young black men, less willing to bear the burden of social order, capitalized on the fear they knew they could evoke. Some purposely "put on a swagger" or adopted a menacing stance to intimidate other pedestrians. Some purposely created discomfort in those they considered "ignorant" enough to be unnecessarily afraid of them.

According to Anderson, law-abiding youths have an interest in giving the impression that they are dangerous: It is a way to keep others at bay. The right looks and moves ensure safe passage on the street. Notice how this young man used such a strategy as a protective device:

When I walk the streets, I put this expression on my face that tells the next person I'm not to be messed with. That "You messing with the wrong fellow. You just try it. Try it." ... I'll put my hand in my pocket, even if I ain't got no gun. Nobody wants to get shot. ... Some guys go to singing. They try to let people know they crazy. 'Cause if you crazy [capable of anything], they'll leave you alone. And I have looked right in they face [muggers] and said, "Yo, I'm not the one." Give 'em that crazy look, then walk away. ... They catch your drift quick. (E. Anderson, 1990, p. 177)

The irony of such survival tactics is that they make it even more difficult for others to distinguish between those who are law-abiding and those who are crime-prone. By exhibiting an air of danger and toughness, the young black man may avoid being ridiculed or even victimized by his own peers, but he risks further alienating law-abiding whites and blacks. Thus, whether they attempt to contradict the stereotype or embrace it, members of racial or ethnic minorities face special dilemmas in impression management.

▪ ▪ ▪

Social Class

Social class can also influence impression management. Like the young black men in Anderson's study, some working-class youths, frustrated by their lack of access to the middle-class world and their inability to meet the requirements of "respectability" as defined by the dominant culture, may present themselves as malicious or dangerous. A tough image helps them gain attention or achieve status and respect within their group (Campbell, 1987; A. K. Cohen, 1955).

Conversely, those who occupy the dominant classes of American society receive the most attention (Derber, 1979). People cater to them in restaurants, shops, and other public settings. They monopolize the starring roles in politics and in the workplace and also claim more than their share of attention in ordinary interaction.

Generations of social strivers have known that attention can be "purchased" through impression management. By displaying the symbolic props of material success—large homes, tasteful furnishings, luxury cars, expensive clothes—individuals can attract the attention of others and thereby reinforce their own sense of worth and status.

Occupational Status

In the world of work, occupational status is often exploited as a means of getting attention. Company presidents and chief executive officers need not disclose their high status because it is already known to people with whom they interact regularly. Their occupational status is a permanently recognized "badge of ability" (Derber, 1979, p. 83). Other people, however, must consciously advertise their occupation to receive the attention to which they feel they are entitled. For example, physicians may wear beepers and white coats outside their work environment to communicate their high-status identity to others. Female doctors will often wear white coats in hospital settings to ensure that they will not be mistaken for nurses. For business managers or other professionals, status information surfaces in conversation through blatant or subtle verbal disclosures.

Because of the primacy of work in American society, those who have no way of exhibiting an occupational badge or whose occupation is seen as inferior find their social worth constantly in question, particularly in interactions with high-status others. They must resort to alternative strategies, like talking constantly or shifting the conversation to a topic about which they have some expertise, simply to prevent others from withdrawing attention and to reduce the fear that they might be completely disregarded (Trudgill, 1972).

Impression management plays a prominent role in the socialization process within many occupations (Hochschild, 1983). Managers and CEOs in large companies, for instance, are acutely aware of the corporate image they must exude through their dress and demeanor. If you've ever worked as a salesperson, you know the economic importance of presenting yourself as knowledgeable, trustworthy, and, above all, honest. Medical school students must learn how to manage their emotions in front of patients and present the image of "competent physicians." New teachers must learn what images are most effective in getting students to comply. One teacher described the importance of impression management:

You can't ever let them get the upper hand on you or you're through. So I start out tough. The first day I get a new class in, I let them know who's boss. . . . You've got to start off tough, then you can ease up as you go along. If you start out easygoing, when you try to be tough, they'll just look at you and laugh. (Goffman, 1959, p. 12)

Collective Impression Management

We often find ourselves in situations that require a "couple" image, a "group" image, or an "organizational" image of some sort. These impressions are more complex than individual ones, and their management often requires the help and cooperation of others.

If you have ever seen a political party's national convention, you have witnessed the careful and strategic staging of a collective event designed to manage the image of a particular candidate. Gala political occasions like these are designed to promise a prosperous culture and a better society (Mayo, 1990). If the attention of the audience depended solely on the speeches of the politicians, conventions would be a dismal failure. The props must be cleverly and meticulously controlled. Music, balloons, lighting, colors, even individual delegates are all transformed into stage props that are manipulated to project images of patriotism, unity, organization, and effectiveness.

The candidate must also personally present an image that will appeal to the public, even if it's not an image he or she particularly likes. For example, during the presidential campaign of 1996, the Republican candidate, Bob Dole, made a conscious effort to alter his public image as a stiff, political insider by resigning from the Senate and adopting a somewhat more casual wardrobe.

Political impression management continues past election day. The president, with the help or hindrance of the media, must play simultaneously to an external and internal audience (P. Hall, 1990). The external audience is composed of foreign allies and adversaries, who must be convinced of his authority and his ability to fulfill commitments. The internal audience is the voting public, whom he must impress through the portrayal of "presidential character": good health, decisiveness, a stable home and family life, and so forth. Like all politicians, a president must be prepared to use impression management to get a favorable result in an opinion poll or a desired vote in Congress.

Teamwork

Goffman uses the term **performance team** to describe those individuals who intimately cooperate in staging a performance that leads an audience to form an impression of one or all of the team members (Goffman, 1959). For example, a political candidate's advisers try to present a coherent, unified message. Parents often present a united front and a joint image of authority to their children.

Team members are highly dependent on one another and must show a fair amount of trust and loyalty, because each member has the power to disrupt or "give away" the performance at any moment. Individuals who cannot be trusted—like political advisers who have worked for another party or small children or people who are emotionally unstable—thus make poor teammates.

One of the most obvious teams is the married couple. Couples frequently must create or sustain a collective impression for others, whether they are entertaining friends at home, attending the office holiday party, or dining at a restaurant. The couple is socially obligated to present a believable and cooperative image, particularly if the audience does not know them very well. Nothing is more uncomfortable than being present when a couple is fighting, bickering, or putting each other down. We, as the audience, feel as if we are watching something not meant for our eyes. Cultural norms dictate that couples are supposed to convey the message that all is well between them. If the teamwork is cohesive and the performance believable, a couple can give the impression that they are happy and content even if they have had a bitter fight moments before going out in public. The cultural value of marriage—and, by extension, the institution of family—is publicly reinforced by the ability of couples to project contented images of their relationship.

Like individual impression management, successful teamwork depends on maintaining the boundary between front and back stage. This boundary is especially fragile and always in danger of being breached by poor teamwork. In addition, the intrusion of third parties can also expose the back-stage aspect of impression management. For instance, young children who can speak but are not yet schooled in the social conventions of everyday interaction represent a particular peril to successful front-stage teamwork. Imagine a dinner guest being informed by a precocious 4-year-old that "Mommy and Daddy wanted someone else to come over, but she couldn't come. So they invited you." From the dramaturgical perspective, children are not trustworthy performance teammates. They are often too honest to maintain a front. They are naturally inclined to let audiences back stage, thereby disrupting both the order of the situation and the identities the actors have attempted to claim.

The ability to go back stage periodically is critical to the maintenance of a sound team relationship. Not only does it give the team a place to rehearse public performances, but it also provides a refuge from public scrutiny. For married couples, tensions can rise if they must constantly be "on" for an audience. This is precisely why out-of-town guests become a burden after a long visit or why living with one or the other partner's parents becomes so difficult. The couple has no back stage, no chance for privacy, no place to go to escape the demands of audience expectations.

We often find ourselves in situations where we must depend on others for the successful performance of the roles we play. Without teamwork many performances would fail, interactions would fall apart, and, ultimately, society would be threatened (Henslin, 1991). Successful teamwork may also have financial implications. Some professional situations—like a gynecological examination, for instance—require individual and team impressions to be managed with finesse so that clients do not become embarrassed, humiliated, or threatened and take their business elsewhere (Henslin & Biggs, 1978).

Organizational Impression Management

Organizations must carefully manage their impressions, too, particularly if they depend on public approval for their survival (S. J. Taylor & Bogdan, 1980). Individual impression management and organizational impression management are governed by the same principles (Hochschild, 1983). Take, for instance, the management of physical space. The walls of a hospital are usually lined with soothing paintings designed to calm, not agitate; children's wards are often filled with colorful images of familiar cartoon characters. Airplanes are meticulously designed to manage a collective impression that distracts passengers from the potential danger:

> The Muzak tunes, the TV and movie screens, and the smiling flight attendants serving drinks are all calculated to "make you feel at home." Even fellow passengers are considered part of the stage. At Delta Airlines, for example, flight attendants in training are advised that they can prevent the boarding of certain types of passengers—a passenger with "severe facial scars," for example. The instructor elaborated: "You know, the other passengers might be reminded of an airplane crash they had read about." The bearer of a "severe facial scar," then, is not deemed a good prop. His or her effect on the emotions of other money-paying passengers might be all wrong. (Hochschild, 1983, pp. 51–52)

For some organizations, collective impression management is the defining feature of the services they provide. Organizations with a dubious history or a negative public perception must be acutely vigilant of the images they present to the public. One obvious example is the funeral industry.

■ ■ ■ ■ ■ ■ ■ ■

RONNY TURNER AND CHARLES EDGLEY
Mortuary Performances

> Perhaps no other industry is as concerned with public image as the funeral industry. Use of the term *funeral director* instead of *undertaker* attests to the importance of performance and impression management. Funeral directors must present themselves as sincere, sympathetic, and understanding. Because of the extreme emotions involved in their work, every aspect must be tightly controlled down to the last detail.

Ronny Turner and Charles Edgley (1976) observed funeral services, interviewed directors, and studied the manuals of 15 mortuaries in three cities. They examined the manner in which mortuary employees manage the circumstances of the funeral ritual in order to establish the legitimacy of their work. The director, for instance, must stage the performance so that the grieving family and friends will attribute dignity and sincerity to the mortuary. Turner and Edgley write: "A successful funeral is a sequence of activities performed by the funeral director and his staff that are later seen by the bereaved as a respectful, appropriate tribute to the life and memory of the deceased" (p. 287).

The maintenance of a separate and completely hidden back-stage area is essential to the performance. The corpse preparation room is physically separated from the public areas of the funeral home. The procedures used—washing, shaving, slicing, powdering, embalming—would shock the friends and family of the deceased. So would the jokes, racial slurs, sexual comments, insults, and other activities that are commonplace back stage. The "casket" becomes the "stuffing box"; the "dearly departed" becomes the "cold one"; "embalming" becomes "pickling," and so on.

Such back-stage behavior, while seemingly distasteful and inappropriate, is not meant to be callous. Look at it as an institutionalized means by which employees manage stress and psychologically distance themselves from a potentially repulsive and gloomy aspect of their occupation. Similar lightheartedness can be found among medical students who, in the course of their clinical training, must observe the dissection of cadavers (Hafferty, 1991). By going back stage, one is able to maintain composure in highly emotional situations, thereby protecting the stability of the overall occupational structure.

You can see how witnessing the preparation of the body for the funeral would destroy the front-stage impression so essential to the industry. The body is never touched by mortuary personnel in front of family and friends. The deceased is transformed from an object back stage to a respected human being front stage.

As for the management of the setting, funeral homes always present themselves as warm, soothing places with white columns, lots of flowers and grass, and meticulous indoor decorations. Black is never seen. Many hearses are now gray, white, or blue instead of the traditional black. The chapel, where the memorial service is held, is designed to facilitate a successful performance. Here, music is tactfully used to set the mood.

For their part, the audience actively participates in the drama. The family has no intention of going back stage; they want little if any knowledge of bodily preparations or other arrangements. They too have a stake in impressions being maintained and the event flowing smoothly.

▪ ▪ ▪

Mismanaging Impressions: Spoiled Identities

We sometimes fail miserably in our attempts to project favorable images of ourselves to others. We may mishandle props, blow our lines, allow the audience back stage, or otherwise destroy the credibility of our performances. Some of us manage to recover from ineffective impression management quite well; others suffer an extended devaluation of their identities. What happens when impression management is unsuccessful? What do we do to regain identities and restore social order?

Embarrassment

A common emotional reaction to impression mismanagement is **embarrassment**, the spontaneous feeling we experience when the identity we are presenting is suddenly and unexpectedly discredited in front of others (Gross & Stone, 1964). An adolescent boy trying to look "cool" in front of his friends may have his tough image shattered by the unexpected arrival of his mother in the family station wagon. We can see his embarrassment in the fixed smile, the nervous hollow laugh, the busy hands, and the downward glance that conceals the eyes from the gaze of others (Goffman, 1967). Embarrassment can come from a multitude of sources: lack of poise (for example, stumbling, spilling a drink, inappropriate bodily exposure), intrusion into the private settings of others, improper dress for a particular social occasion, and so on.

Embarrassment is sociologically important because it has the potential to destroy the orderliness of a social situation. Imagine being at your graduation ceremony. As the class valedictorian is giving the commencement address, a gust of wind blows her note cards off the podium. As she reaches down to collect them, she knocks over the microphone and tears her gown. In front of hundreds of people she stands there, flustered, not knowing what to say or do. The situation would be uncomfortable and embarrassing not only for her, but for you and the rest of the audience as well.

Because embarrassment is disruptive for all concerned, it is in everyone's best interest to cooperate in eliminating it. To respond to such an act may be as embarrassing as the original episode itself, so we may pretend not to notice the faux pas (Lindesmith, Strauss, & Denzin, 1991). By suppressing signs of recognition, we make it easier for the person to regain composure (Goffman, 1967). A mutual commitment to supporting others' social identities, even when those identities are in danger, is a fundamental rule of social interaction.

At times, however, embarrassment is used strategically to disrupt another person's impression management. Practical jokes, for instance, are intentional attempts to cause someone else to lose identity. On a more serious note, groups and organizations may use embarrassment or the threat of embarrassment (for example, hazing) to encourage a preferred activity or discourage behavior that may be damaging to the group. Such embarrassment reasserts the power structure of the group, since only certain people can legitimately embarrass others. A low-status employee has much less freedom to embarrass a superior than vice versa.

Groups and organizations, as entities, may also be embarrassed. Many of America's most successful companies have had to deal with tarnished images caused by insensitive, negligent, or criminal behavior: ValueJet following a recent crash of one of its planes; A. H. Robins following injuries caused by the Dalkon Shield birth-control device; the Jack-In-The-Box restaurant chain following sickness and death caused by tainted hamburger meat; Dow Chemical following the lingering ill health caused by the defoliant Agent Orange used during the Vietnam War; Rockwell, GTE, General Electric, and other military contractors following disclosures they had overcharged the government for supplies; and so on. Most governments and large corporations have public relations departments that carefully manage the corporate image by controlling negative publicity (E. Gross, 1984). There is even an insurance company that, as part of its corporate liability policy, pays policyholders up to $50,000 for the emergency hiring of an image consultant to help manage such public relations disasters (Landler, 1996).

Sometimes a single rumor causes massive corporate embarrassment. In 1993 a rash of reports surfaced around the United States from people who claimed to have found hypodermic needles and syringes in cans of Diet Pepsi. Investigators eventually found the claims to be unsubstantiated. Nevertheless, stores in many parts of the country began to pull the product off their shelves or offer refunds to worried customers. Even the Food and Drug Administration advised consumers to buy Pepsi in glass or plastic bottles. The phenomenon was a public relations nightmare for Pepsi. Facing severe financial losses, the company mounted a massive and expensive media campaign—which included TV commercials, talk show appearances, full-page newspaper ads, and a toll-free consumer hotline—to counteract the embarrassment and costly fallout of a spoiled public image.

Remedies for Spoiled Identities

While organizations and governments can enlist the aid of experts to overcome the debilitating effects of negative images, individuals are left to their own devices to restore tarnished identities. But fixing a spoiled identity is not easy. The mere knowledge that we are being evaluated negatively can impede our thought, speech, and action. Nevertheless, the major responsibility for restoring order lies with the person or group whose actions disrupted things in the first place. The embarrassment that results from failure in claiming an identity is not a trivial matter. Social life requires that we protect each other so that we can carry on the business of living (L. H. Lofland, 1971). The two main ways of preserving social order in such cases are aligning actions and intentional identity transformations.

Aligning Actions

An **aligning action** is something that returns order to a situation that has become disordered and that restores a spoiled image (Stokes & Hewitt, 1976). Sometimes aligning can be done easily and quickly. If you step on a person's foot while standing in line at a cafeteria, a simple apology may be all that's needed to bring back order. By apologizing you acknowledge the wrongfulness of the act and send the message that you are not ordinarily a breaker of such social norms. Other situations, however, call for more detailed repairs, in the form of an account or a disclaimer.

Under certain circumstances we may be called on not only to apologize but also to explain our motives (C. W. Mills, 1940; M. Scott & Lyman, 1968). An **account** is a verbal statement designed to explain unanticipated, embarrassing, or unacceptable behavior. Accounts can take two forms: excuses and justifications.

An *excuse* is an acknowledgment of the wrongfulness of the act but a denial of responsibility. The person is saying, "I know what I've done looks bad, but for the following reasons you should not consider me blameworthy." Perhaps the individual will cite events beyond his or her control ("I was late for the wedding because there was a lot of traffic on the highway") or blame others ("I spilled my milk because so-and-so pushed me").

A *justification* is an admission of responsibility that contains a persuasive attempt to define the behavior as appropriate under the circumstances. Justifying an act asserts its acceptability despite claims to the contrary and attempts to convince others that the act shouldn't be considered threatening. Such verbal strategies are not limited to "embarrassing" acts. People use several common justifications for rather serious "offenses" (Sykes & Matza, 1957), such as denying that anyone was hurt by the act ("Yeah, I stole the car, but no one got hurt"), claiming that the victim deserved to be victimized ("I beat him up, but he had it coming"), or claiming higher, unselfish motives ("I stole food, but I did it to feed my family").

To illustrate the role that accounts play in warding off threats to identity, Diana Scully and Joseph Marolla (1984) interviewed 114 convicted rapists to see what sorts of accounts they used to explain themselves and their violent actions. Although some of the men admitted they had raped their victims, many either denied they were guilty or defined their actions as essentially "nonrapes." Some attempted to justify their behavior by presenting the victim in a light that made her appear responsible, regardless of their own actions. Some of the men defined women as seductresses, by claiming that women said no when they meant yes or that they actually enjoyed being raped and by stating that nice girls don't get raped. These justifications are buttressed by a cultural environment that views women as sexual commodities and that trivializes and sometimes even condones rape.

To be acceptable, accounts must fall within the range of believable explanations within a given society. Citing "family problems" as a cause of one's depression and listlessness can work as an excuse only if the audience understands what the term implies. Some societies, like the Azande discussed in chapter 3, have no conception of coincidence or chance. Thus an Azande would be unlikely to explain an identity-threatening, disruptive act as "accidental."

Some accounts may be so overused (for example, "The dog ate my homework") that they are immediately considered unreasonable, even if they are true. Others are deemed illegitimate because the seriousness of the infraction exceeds the credibility of the account. If you cite blocked vision as the reason you ran over a neighbor's tomato plant with your car, that account might be accepted. However, if you ran over the neighbor's child, such an account would fall far short of acceptability.

The acceptability of accounts, then, is specific to particular groups or situations. A group is able to maintain the loyalty of its members in part because it provides a context in which they can talk about the reasons for their conduct and have their reasons confirmed by others. For instance, if you didn't do your homework, "I was hungry, so I went for pizza" may be a legitimate excuse among your friends but would fail if you tried to use it with your instructor (S. Bernstein, 1990). A company president who explains the low salaries he or she pays by citing market pressures and profit margins may be supported by business colleagues but scoffed at by his or her employees.

Another type of aligning action, the **disclaimer**, is a verbal assertion given before the fact to forestall any complaints or negative implications (Hewitt & Stokes, 1975). The anticipatory nature of disclaimers requires knowledge of the potential wrongfulness or harmfulness of an act or statement. If we think something we are about to do or say will threaten our identity or be used by others to construct a negative judgment of us, we may employ a disclaimer. Phrases such as "This may sound crazy to you, but . . ." or "I probably don't know what I'm talking about, but . . ." or "This may sound racist, but . . ." introduce acts or expressions that ordinarily might be considered undesirable. As long as a disclaimer is provided, a person claiming to be nonracist feels he or she can go ahead and make a racist statement, and a self-proclaimed nonexpert can pretend to be an expert.

At the individual level, disclaimers keep others from making negative judgments and destroying our public images. At the corporate level, they can protect an organization financially, ethically, and legally, as in television messages that warn "The following may not be suitable for young children" or in warning labels on potentially dangerous products.

Accounts and disclaimers are an important link between the individual and society. We use them to explicitly define the relationship between our questionable conduct and prevailing cultural norms. By using accounts and disclaimers, we publicly reaffirm our commitment to the social order that our conduct has violated and thereby defend the sanctity of our social identities and the "goodness" of society.

Identity Transformations: Cooling Out

Some socially undesirable acts are so major or happen with such frequency that aligning actions are no longer effective. Others may cease to help violators restore spoiled identities and may in fact deliberately destroy the identities of those who fail repeatedly and glaringly.

One technique for transforming a person's identity is called **cooling out** (Goffman, 1952). The term comes from con artists who "cool the mark out," or make the victim of a con feel as though she or he hasn't been conned. In the context of social interaction, cooling out means gently persuading someone who has lost face to accept a less desirable but still reasonable alternative identity. People engaged in cooling out seek to persuade rather than force offenders to change. It is an attempt to minimize distress. The challenge is to keep the offender from realizing that he or she is being persuaded.

Cooling out is a common element of social life; it is the major function of consumer complaint personnel, coaches, doctors, and priests. Cooling out also plays a major part in informal relationships. A partner who terminates a dating or courting relationship might persuade the other person to remain a "good friend," thereby gently pushing the person into a lesser role without completely destroying his or her identity.

Some individuals are involuntarily placed in the "cooler" role not because of their job or relationship, but because of who they are. Women, for instance, must constantly deal with the unsolicited comments and advances of men in public situations (Snow, Robinson, & McCall, 1991). Most women who have been in bars or nightclubs have faced the problem of unwanted male attention. In an attempt to escape from the encounter without disrupting the orderliness of the situation, women may offer polite excuses, advertise their unavailability, or otherwise "let him down easily." Successful, trouble-free public life for women is contingent on their ability to cool men out. For their part, men are obligated to respond to the cooling-out lines in a cooperative manner, leave the encounter without too much fuss, and preserve the order of the situation.

Cooling out is often motivated by institutional pressures. Consider the environment of higher education. The aspirations of many people in American society are encouraged by open-door admissions policies in some universities and most community colleges (Karabel, 1972). There is a widely held cultural belief that higher education is linked to better employment opportunities and that anyone can go to college. Discrepancies, however, inevitably arise between people's aspirations and their ability to succeed. If educational institutions adopted a "hard response" and simply kicked unqualified students out of school, the result would likely be widespread public pressure and anxiety over the system itself.

Hence, most community colleges opt for the "soft response" of cooling out the unqualified student (B. Clark, 1960). A counselor may direct a poor student toward an alternative major that would be easier but is still "not that different" from the student's original goal (for example, nurse's aide instead of registered nurse). Or the counselor might encourage the student to seek employment after graduation from a two-year program rather than transfer to a four-year university. The student is being gently persuaded to redefine himself or herself.

The important sociological consequence of this process is that society is able to continue to encourage students' maximum effort without any major disturbances from unfulfilled expectations. By cooling out "failed" students, society is able to avoid massive public discontent with the entire institution of education.

Institutional cooling-out processes like these are inherent in an educational system that doesn't have clear selection criteria. In the United States, acceptance into college is based on achievement (tests, grades), aptitude (standardized test scores), and personality traits (interviews, letters of recommendation). In contrast, educational selection in Japan is based on a single criterion: achievement on grades and exams. Selections are made upon admission to senior high school. National universities do not allow any exceptions. Because career paths are clearly and quickly defined, Japanese higher education has no need for an institutionalized cooling-out process (Kariya & Rosenbaum, 1987).

Stigma

When the identity of a valuable or competent person has been tarnished, the assumption is that it ultimately can be corrected. In some situations, though, a person's identity can be permanently spoiled. For this individual, social interaction becomes an obstacle to overcome or avoid. And the impression management task is not so much to recapture a tarnished identity as to minimize the social damage.

Permanent identity spoilage is called **stigma**. A stigma is a deeply discrediting characteristic, widely viewed as an insurmountable obstacle, that prevents competent or morally trustworthy behavior (Goffman, 1963). Stigmas spoil the identities of individuals regardless of other attributes those individuals might have. According to Goffman, three types of stigma are defects of the body (for example, scars, blindness, paralyzed or missing limbs), defects of character (for example, dishonesty, weak will, unorthodox beliefs inferred from a known record of mental illness, imprisonment, or substance abuse), and membership in particular social groups, such as races, religions, or ethnicities that are devalued in society.

The Social Construction of Stigma

Each society creates its own hierarchies of desirable and undesirable traits. Sometimes the motivation is clear, as when an individual is stigmatized as a "hardened criminal" for repeatedly breaking society's laws. Other times the designation of a stigma seems rather arbitrary. For instance, in our culture the use of one mechanism to compensate for a sensory deficiency (eyeglasses) is far less stigmatizing than the use of another (hearing aid).

The nature of stigma can vary across time and culture. Being a Christian in the 1990s is very different from being one in A.D. 10, and being a Christian in the United States is different from being one in the Middle East (Ainlay, Becker, & Coleman, 1986). Obesity is stigmatized in contemporary Western societies but was seen as desirable, attractive, and symbolic of status and wealth in the past (Clinard & Meier, 1979).

Some stigmatized attributes have remained remarkably stable in the face of major social changes. While divorce has become more commonplace and even acceptable in contemporary society, divorced people often still feel discredited in the eyes of others (Gertsel, 1987). Many divorced people believe they are perceived as failures and are targets of informal sanctions like exclusion, blame, and devaluation. Some even come to believe that their married friends and acquaintances see them as misfits who could not maintain a stable marriage.

Interactions between the stigmatized and the nonstigmatized—called **mixed contacts**—are often uneasy. We have all felt uncomfortable with people who are "different" in appearance or behavior. Stigma initiates a judgment process that colors impressions and sets up barriers to interaction (E. E. Jones et al., 1984).

Whether intentionally or not, nonstigmatized individuals often pressure stigmatized people to conform to the inferior identities being placed on them. A person in a wheelchair who is discouraged from undertaking certain activities or a blind person who is dissuaded from venturing out of the house alone is never given the chance to develop important skills and is subsequently kept dependent.

The anticipation of discomfort can lead people to arrange their lives so as to avoid mixed contacts (Goffman, 1963). Research shows that people terminate interactions sooner, are more inhibited, and are more rigid when interacting with a physically disabled person than with a physically normal person (Kleck, 1968; Kleck, Ono, & Hastorf, 1966). Such discomfort probably stems from uncertainty as to what behavior is appropriate. On the one hand, the nonstigmatized may fear that if they show direct sympathy or interest in someone's condition they will be regarded as rude or intrusive. On the other hand, ignoring it may make the interaction artificial or create impossible demands (Michener, DeLamater, & Schwartz, 1986).

As for people with stigmatizing conditions, Goffman argues that they usually have some sense that others are evaluating them negatively, whether in the form of disgust, anger, or pity. In one study a group of subjects was led to believe that a large scar had been applied to their faces with stage makeup, stigmatizing them in the eyes of people with whom they were to interact. Another group was led to believe that their interaction partners knew they had a mild allergy—a nonstigmatizing condition (Kleck & Strenta, 1980). Actually, the interaction partners had no knowledge of either condition: They weren't told of the allergy, and no artificial scar had been applied. Nevertheless, the "facial scar" subjects perceived their partners as more tense, more patronizing, and less attracted to them than did the "allergic," nonstigmatized subjects. Videotapes of the interactions showed no evidence of stigmatization in the actual conversations. The people who believed they were stigmatized simply perceived that others were relating to them negatively.

Strategies for Coping with Stigma

Whether their perceptions are accurate or not, people with stigmatizing conditions often use drastic coping strategies to establish the most favorable identity possible. One strategy is to try to hide the stigmatizing condition. People who are hard of hearing, for instance, may learn to read lips or otherwise interact with people as if they can hear; those with bodily stigmas may opt for surgical remedies.

Michael Petrunik and Clifford Shearing (1983) studied the coping strategies used by people who stutter. They observed and took part in weekly therapy groups over a period of 13 years. In addition they conducted in-depth interviews with stutterers, their families and friends, speech therapists, and other medical practitioners. Common public reactions to stutterers include pity, condescension, ridicule, and impatience. Some stutterers hide their stigma by avoiding speaking situations or by not using particularly troublesome words. Others structure situations so that someone else does the talking. For example, in a restaurant stutterers may encourage others to order first. As soon as an acceptable item is mentioned, they simply duplicate the order by saying, "Me too" or "Same here."

Of course, not all stigmas can be hidden. Some individuals can only minimize the degree to which their stigmas intrude on and disrupt the interaction. One tactic is to boldly call attention to their condition by mastering areas thought to be closed to them (such as mountain climbing for an amputee) or by organizing a movement to counter social oppression (such as demanding legislation outlawing discrimination against the disabled). Others will use self-deprecating humor to relieve the tension felt by the nonstigmatized. Still others may try to focus attention on attributes that are unrelated to the stigma. A person in a wheelchair may carry around esoteric books in a conspicuous manner to show others that he or she can perform well in other areas.

Some stigmatized individuals, particularly those whose conditions are not immediately observable, use a policy of selective disclosure and concealment. Sociologist Charlene Miall (1989) interviewed and surveyed 70 infertile women to see if they felt stigmatized. Nearly all the respondents categorized infertility as something negative, an indication of failure, or an inability to function "normally." Furthermore, most of the women were concerned that an awareness of their infertility would cause others to view them in a new and damaging light. Consequently, most of these women engaged in some form of information control. Many simply concealed the information from everyone except medical personnel and infertility counselors. Others used medical accounts, saying "It's beyond my control." Some disclosed the information only to people they felt would not think ill of them. Some even used the disclosure of their infertility to gain control of a situation by deliberately shocking their "normal" audience (Miall, 1989).

Just as aligning actions and cooling out maintain social order, so do coping strategies used by stigmatized individuals. By successfully managing their stigmas in public interactions, they are able to avoid the embarrassment of indelicate questions and gain acceptance. The interaction becomes smooth-flowing. The nonstigmatized also benefit because they are saved from facing the true pain and injustice suffered by stigmatized people, thus alleviating their own sense of discomfort and guilt.

Overcoming the problems created by stigma cannot be accomplished solely through individual impression management. Improvements can be accomplished only at the societal level through the alteration of cultural beliefs about the nature of stigma (Link, Mirotznik, & Cullen, 1991). As long as we hold stigmatized individuals solely responsible for overcoming their condition, social problems will continue to be perceived only in individual terms.

Conclusion

People consciously manufacture images of themselves that allow them to achieve some desired goal. There's no denying that most of us go through life trying to create the impression that we're attractive, honest, competent, and sincere. To that end we carefully manage our appearance, present qualities we think others will admire, and hide qualities we think they won't. When caught in an act that may threaten the impression we're trying to foster, we will strategically use statements that disclaim, excuse, or justify it. At times we will even force other people into identities that suit our needs and interests (that is, altercasting).

After reading this chapter, you may have an image of human beings as cunning, manipulative, and cynical play-actors whose lives are merely a string of phony performances carefully designed to fit the selfish needs of the moment. If you act one way with your friends and another way with your parents, which is the real you? The impression manager comes across as someone who consciously and fraudulently presents an inaccurate image in order to take advantage of a particular situation. Even the person who seems not to care about his or her appearance may be consciously cultivating the image of "not caring."

Do people freely change their images to suit the expectations of a given audience, or does something more stable characterize them across all situations?

If you are aware that the impression you are managing is not you, then you must have some knowledge of what is you. And what you are may, in fact, transcend the demands of particular situations. Is there a basic, pervasive part of your being that allows you to choose from a repertoire of identities the one that best suits the immediate needs of the situation?

As you ponder these questions, realize that the answers you come up with not only indicate your feelings about impression management but also reflect your beliefs about the nature of individuals and the role society and others play in our everyday lives.

CHAPTER HIGHLIGHTS

▪ A significant portion of social life is influenced by the images we form of others and the images others form of us.

▪ Impression formation is based initially on our assessment of social group membership (race, gender, etc.), personal attributes (for example, physical attractiveness), and verbal and nonverbal messages.

▪ While we are gathering information about others to form impressions of them, we are fully aware that they are doing the same thing. Impression management is the process by which we attempt to control and manipulate information about ourselves to influence the impressions others form of us. Impression management can be both individual and collective.

▪ Impression mismanagement can lead to the creation of damaged identities that must be repaired through aligning actions and cooling out in order to sustain social interaction.

YOUR TURN

In this chapter we have examined the importance of impression management. For most of us, impression management is a tool we use to present ourselves as likable people. Occasionally, however, our attempts fail. Survey several friends or classmates and have them describe their most embarrassing moment. What were the circumstances surrounding the incident? What were the identities they were trying to present? How did the attempt to claim this identity fail? What were their immediate physical and behavioral reactions to the embarrassment? What did they do to try to overcome the embarrassment and return order? Did they offer some sort of account? Were the consequences of the failed impression management temporary or permanent? What did the witnesses to the embarrassing incident do? Did their reactions alleviate or intensify the embarrassment?

Once you've gathered a substantial number of stories (about 12 or 15), see if you can find some common themes. What are the most frequent types of embarrassing situations? What are the most frequent reactions?

Sociologists Edward Gross and Gregory Stone wrote, "In the wreckage left by embarrassment lie the broken foundations of social transactions" (1964, p. 2). What do you suppose they meant by that? Discuss the sociological importance of embarrassment (and, more important, the reactions to embarrassment) in terms of the maintenance of interactional and social order.

CHAPTER 7

Constructing Difference: Social Deviance

- *Defining Deviance*
- *Explaining Why People Become Deviant*
- *Power and the Social Construction of Deviance*

In 1936 a 29-year-old woman named Gladys Burr was diagnosed as psychotic. Later that year she was also declared mentally retarded and shortly thereafter was committed to the Mansfield Training School for the Retarded in Connecticut. From the beginning of her stay there, she never felt that she deserved to be institutionalized. She wrote several letters to state officials asking that they reconsider her placement, but to no avail (Brooke, 1985). Little note was taken of the fact that she had completed 2 years of high school and a 3-month business course.

Six months after being committed, doctors declared her "cured," and several intelligence tests revealed her IQ to be in the normal range or slightly above. Despite these developments, which would seem to indicate that she did not need to be institutionalized, Gladys Burr remained in a series of state-run hospitals, training centers, and group homes until her release in 1978—42 years after her initial commitment! In 1985, after a prolonged legal battle, she was awarded $235,000 in compensation and damages. She died in 1990.

Why did this happen? How could she have failed to persuade the authorities that she was normal? According to Burr's lawyer, the reason was clear and simple: They forgot about her. In large bureaucracies such as state mental health systems, someone is bound to be overlooked or ignored every once in a while.

But perhaps something more was going on—something about the way people perceived Burr and the impressions they formed of her. As you know, our responses to other people are based on our expectations of them. Could it be that because Gladys was authoritatively pronounced "psychotic" and "mentally retarded" she could not convince people otherwise?

We may never know in Gladys Burr's case. But what we do know is that such labels and what they imply in people's minds can overshadow everything else about a person. Gladys had been officially tagged a deviant by others and publicly degraded. From that point on, nothing she did or said could overcome that label.

Being denied one's freedom for 42 years as a result of a designation of deviance is an extreme and rare occurrence. Keep in mind, though, that the process of affixing deviant labels and judging people on the basis of them can be found not only in systems like mental hospitals and criminal courts but in social interchanges as well. Perhaps there have been times in your life when you acquired some sort of reputation that you could not shed.

In this chapter I focus on several questions that have been addressed by many sociologists but are still met with widespread disagreement: What is deviance? How do people become deviant? Who gets to define what is and is not deviant? What are the consequences of being identified as deviant by others?

Defining Deviance

For the most part, deviance refers to socially disapproved behavior: the violation of some agreed-upon norm that prevails in a community or in society at large. Staring at a stranger in an elevator, driving over the speed limit, talking to yourself in public, wearing clothes that are outlandish, robbing a bank, or intentionally taking someone's life can all be considered deviant acts. Most of us occupy statuses or engage in behaviors that could be regarded by others as deviant (see Figure 7.1).

The determination of which behaviors or characteristics constitute deviant activity, however, is more complex. We usually assume that people agree about what and who is deviant. For instance, no one would challenge the notion that child abuse is bad and that child abusers ought to be punished. But the level of agreement within a given society over what is deviant—what specific acts constitute child abuse—is subject to much disagreement and even overt conflict. What is a method of discipline to one parent is a form of abuse to another.

To make the issue more complex, some functionalist sociologists (for example, Durkheim, 1958; K. Erikson, 1966) argue that deviance is not always bad for society and may actually serve a purpose. As you recall from chapter 4, norm violations help define the moral boundaries that distinguish right from wrong, increase feelings of in-group togetherness for those who unite in collective opposition to normative threats, and encourage society to revise itself and respond to new concerns. At the surface level, acts of deviance are disruptive and generate varying degrees of social disapproval, but at a deeper level, they can contribute to the maintenance and continuity of every society.

Before examining the theoretical explanations and social implications of deviance, let's look at two different approaches to defining it: absolutism and relativism.

Absolutism

According to **absolutism**, there are two fundamental types of human behavior: that which is inherently proper and good and that which is obviously improper, immoral, evil, and bad. The distinction is clear and identifiable. The quality of deviance can be found in the very nature of the act. Right and wrong exist prior

Figure 7.1   *Adults in the United States in Various "Deviant" Statuses*

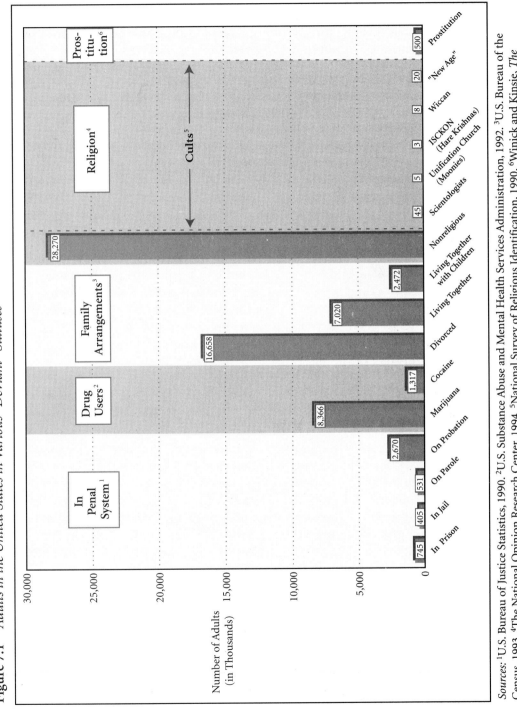

Sources: [1]U.S. Bureau of Justice Statistics, 1990. [2]U.S. Substance Abuse and Mental Health Services Administration, 1992. [3]U.S. Bureau of the Census, 1993. [4]The National Opinion Research Center, 1994. [5]National Survey of Religious Identification, 1990. [6]Winick and Kinsie, *The Lively Commerce: Prostitution in the United States,* 1971.

to and independent of socially created rules, norms, and customs (E. Goode, 1994). Deviance is a malfunction, a potentially destructive force that society needs to eliminate or, at the very least, keep under control.

The absolutist believes that members of society do or should agree on the basic goals people ought to pursue. No normal, decent person would willingly violate norms and participate in a deviant lifestyle, be it violent crime, drug use, or nontraditional sexuality. Consider the following letter to the editor from an irate citizen protesting the discussion of homosexuality in a college English course:

> Homosexuality is one of the most vile blasphemies against God. . . . [I]t is not society that is sick, it is those whose life-styles debase the sacred purpose of the sex act. Homosexuality is not part of the "total human experience" which a healthy, well-balanced human being can ever accept. The practice of homosexuality is an abomination of the natural order. . . . It is not love; it is undisciplined lust, drawing man down to the level of animals. (quoted in Hills, 1980, p. 9)

Behavior that does not fit the tight values of the absolutist is self-evidently "sick," "disturbed," or "detestable." Deviance is not something in which a healthy, well-adjusted person would engage; rather, it is seen as comparable to malignant cells in an organism, something to be eliminated, treated, and contained (Hills, 1980). It matters little whether the source of the behavior lies in the individual's own makeup or in the environment within which he or she lives.

An absolutist definition of deviance implies something about the person committing the act as well. To many people, deviant individuals are morally, psychologically, and even physically different from ordinary, conforming people. The attribute or behavior that serves as the basic reason for defining a person as deviant in the first place is pervasive and essential to his or her entire character (Hills, 1980). Respectable, conventional qualities become insignificant. It doesn't matter, for instance, that the "sexual deviant" has an otherwise ordinary life, that the "schizophrenic" has recovered, or that the violent act of the "murderer" was completely atypical of the rest of his or her life.

In short, the deviant act or trait becomes a sort of moral identity, signifying a judgment about the overall worth of the individual (J. Katz, 1975). Being defined as deviant means being identified as someone who cannot and should not be treated as an ordinary human being. Often this sort of absolute disapproval has less to do with specific offending acts than with the kind of person one is thought to be (Schur, 1984).

This is where the absolutist approach runs into some problems. Absolute beliefs about deviants and deviance are often guided by powerful and emotionally laden stereotypical imagery. If you ask someone to imagine what a typical drug addict looks like, chances are the response will describe a dirty, poor, strung-out young man living on the streets and resorting to theft to support his habit. The image probably wouldn't be one of a middle-class alcoholic housewife or a clean-shaven, hardworking physician hooked on prescription drugs, even though these groups constitute a higher percentage of drug addicts than any other in American society (Hills, 1980). Likewise, the image of the typical rapist is usually that of a psychotic stranger lurking in the bushes or masquerading as a door-to-door salesman, and not a classmate, fellow employee, dating partner, or longtime family friend, even though these types of people account for the majority of rapes committed in this country (Warshaw, 1988).

When absolute beliefs about what deviants look like are held by people within the criminal justice system—police, judges, attorneys, juries—decisions about whom to apprehend, their guilt or innocence, and the severity of their punishment reflect these biases as much as they reflect the nature of the act committed. In other words, stereotypical conceptions of race, age, religion, gender, physical appearance, and so on can influence a person's chances of being processed through the system and "becoming" a deviant. For example, sociologists William Chambliss and Richard Nagasawa (1969) compared the arrest rates of white, African-American, and Japanese-American youths in Seattle, Washington. They found that ethnic stereotypes led police to overestimate the involvement of African Americans in criminal activities and underestimate the involvement of Japanese Americans.

In U.S. society, the consequences of these stereotypes fall heavily on African Americans. The Sentencing Project, a nonprofit research and advocacy organization, found that one in three black men in their 20s is under the supervision of the criminal justice system—prison, probation, or parole—on any given day. Although some might see such a figure as clear evidence of higher rates of black involvement in crime, other statistics seem to suggest something different. For instance, African Americans make up 12% of the nation's population and constitute roughly the same percentage (13%) of all illegal drug users; yet they represent over 40% of arrests for drug possession, 56% of all convictions for drug possession, and 74% of all prison sentences for drug possession (Butterfield, 1995a; U.S. Bureau of Justice Statistics, 1993). Figure 7.2 shows the black/white disparity in arrests, convictions, and length of sentence for different types of crime. Such biases can distort the official records regarding who makes up the population of deviants in this country and can reinforce public perceptions of what deviants look like (Archer, 1985; Pfohl, 1985; Reiman, 1990).

No matter what the behavior, oversimplified images of the typical deviant will always fall short of accounting for every individual. The vast majority of African Americans do not commit crimes, just as the majority of Italians are not involved in the Mafia. Nevertheless, the degree to which images like these are thought to characterize an entire group is important insofar as it determines individual and societal responses. If affluent housewives or businesspeople who abuse drugs are not considered typical drug addicts, they will never be the focus of law enforcement attention, collective moral outrage, political rhetoric, or public policy.

Figure 7.2   *Racial Differences in Arrests, Convictions, and Length of Sentences*

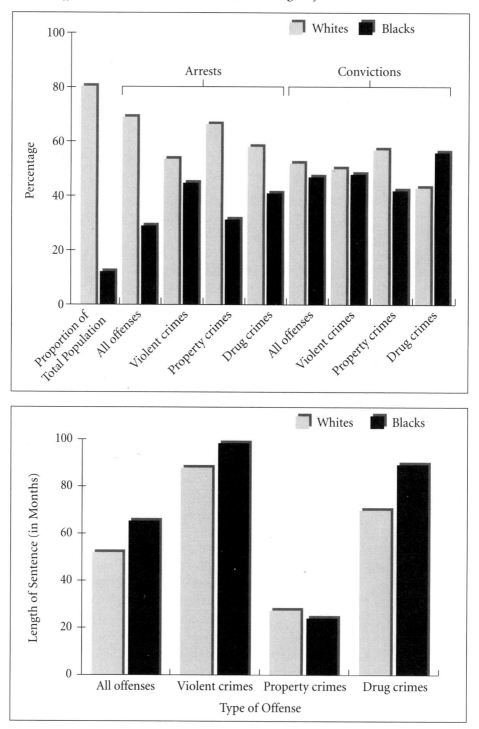

Source: U.S. Bureau of Justice Statistics, 1993.

Relativism

An absolutist definition of deviance can lead to narrow and often inaccurate perceptions of many important social problems. For the relativist, complex societies consist of different groups with different values and interests. Sometimes these groups agree and cooperate to achieve a common goal, as when all segments of society join together to fight a foreign enemy. But more often than not there is conflict and struggle between groups to realize their own interests and goals. In **relativism**, life cannot be seen in terms of absolute right and wrong. Drawing from symbolic interactionism, deviance is not a property inherent in any particular act, belief, or condition; instead, it is socially created by collective human judgments and ideas. Like beauty, deviance is in the eye of the beholder.

Not surprisingly, different observers can have dramatically different interpretations of the same event. In 1995, a 35-year-old white man named William Masters was taking his usual armed, late-night walk through a barren neighborhood in Los Angeles when he came upon two young Hispanic men spray-painting graffiti beneath a freeway overpass. He wrote down the license number of their car on a small piece of paper. When the men saw him and demanded the paper, Mr. Masters pulled out a 9-millimeter pistol and shot them—wounding one and killing the other. He told police that the men threatened him with a screwdriver and that he acted in self-defense, even though both were shot in the back. He was not charged with murder. Eventually he was found guilty of one count of carrying a concealed gun in public and one count of carrying a loaded gun in public—charges that carried a maximum of 18 months in jail and a $2,000 fine.

Shortly after his arrest, Mr. Masters claimed that his actions shouldn't be defined as deviant. In fact, his statements indicated that he felt the killing should be seen as appropriate, even desirable: "People were relieved that here was a murder victim who was not murdered. Instead, one of the murderers died. Where are you going to find 12 citizens to convict me?" (quoted in Mydans, 1995, p. 10).

Many people agreed. One caller to a radio talk show said, "I don't care if he's Looney Toons or what, but we need more guys like him around." Another said, "William, you're not a hero to me, you're a saint." A letter to a local newspaper echoed these sentiments: "Kudos to William Masters for his vigilant antigraffiti efforts and for his foresight in carrying a gun for self-protection" (all quoted in Mydans, 1995, p. 10).

Others defined the event and Mr. Masters quite differently, expressing dismay at the verdict and arguing that he was simply a racist out looking for trouble. They felt he was not a considerate fellow who was doing his part to clean up the streets but a deviant who literally got away with murder.

Was William Masters a "hero" or a "killer"? An "avenging angel" or a "dangerous deviant"? The answers to these questions lie not in the act itself but in the way it was defined and responded to by others.

To fully understand the societal and personal implications of deviance designations, we must look at how these definitions are created and perpetuated. From a relativistic approach, one of the key factors in determining the deviant nature of an act is who is doing the defining. If an act is deviant only because someone sees it that way, then the definition of deviance becomes rather arbitrary. One person's crime is another person's act of moral conscience; one group's evil is another group's virtue; one culture's freedom fighter is another culture's terrorist. When we try to see certain acts from another group's perspective, even our most solidly held ideas about deviance become perplexing.

Definitions of deviance are relative to particular cultural standards. In Singapore, a young vandal is a serious deviant (punishable by caning), as is a person who leaves chewed gum where it can be stepped on. A blasphemer in an Islamic society may be severely punished for saying something we in this country would probably consider innocuous. Making a large profit on a business transaction is highly acceptable in the United States but, until recently, was considered "profiteering" in China—a crime punishable by death (G. Stephens, 1994).

Even within the same country one community's standards can differ from another's, creating conflict. For example, the sacramental use of peyote—a cactus that contains the hallucinogenic substance mescaline—has been a part of the religious rituals of certain Native American groups for centuries. In 1990 the Oregon State Supreme Court ruled that the First Amendment's protection of free exercise of religion allowed the use of peyote for religious purposes. The U.S. Supreme Court later overturned this ruling, stating that governmental policies and laws must be upheld even to the disadvantage of some religious groups. Justice Antonin Scalia stated that criminalizing this religious practice was an "unavoidable consequence of democratic government [which] must be preferred to a system in which each conscience is a law unto itself" (quoted in Greenhouse, 1990). Thus, although those who used peyote for religious purposes didn't consider themselves deviant, they were defined and treated that way by the dominant culture.

Although the absolutist approach assumes that certain individual characteristics are typical of all deviants, the relativist approach acknowledges that there is no typical deviant. In fact, the same objective act committed by two different people may be defined very differently. For example, street prostitutes are regularly harassed, arrested, and jailed by the police. In the 1980s, however, Sydney Biddle Barrows, a wealthy descendant of an original Plymouth colonist, established a high-class brothel as a business enterprise and became known as the "Mayflower Madam." Instead of spending time in prison for breaking the law, she made the talk-show circuit and wrote a best-selling book. Clearly her socioeconomic status and pedigree influenced public definitions regarding the deviant nature of her activities. When *she* did it, somehow it wasn't so bad.

Immediate situational circumstances can also influence definitions of deviance. Drinking liquor in a bar is more acceptable than drinking in your college classroom; drinking on the weekend is more acceptable than drinking during the week; drinking in the evening is more acceptable than drinking in the morning.

Even acts of extreme violence may be defined as acceptable under certain circumstances. Killings committed under the auspices of the government—shooting looters during a riot, killing enemy soldiers during wartime, or capital punishment—fall outside the category of behaviors deemed deviant and problematic in society. Under certain circumstances, then, the act of purposely taking a human life might even be seen as humane by certain groups or cultures (E. Goode, 1994).

■ ■ ■ ■ ■ ■ ■ ■

MICRO-MACRO CONNECTION
Mercy Killing

To some in the United States, the right to die with dignity is the most fundamental and inalienable of all human rights. But what about helping another person commit suicide or, in the extreme, taking the life of a person who is terminally ill or suffering? Are these acts of deviance or acts of compassion? Murder or mercy killing?

Over the last decade or so we have witnessed a tremendous increase in controversial ethical and legal battles over this issue. All you have to do is pick up the newspaper to read about a family fighting to take a loved one off life-support equipment or a husband putting his wife "out of her misery" because he can't stand to see her suffer any longer. One of the most highly publicized cases was that of Roswell Gilbert. In 1984 Gilbert, then 76 years old, fatally shot his wife, who suffered from Alzheimer's disease, in their Fort Lauderdale condominium. Gilbert was arrested, convicted of murder, and sentenced to life imprisonment. In 1990 his sentence was commuted to 5 years. Some felt he acted out of love for his wife; others thought he was a cold-blooded killer.

In 1991 Derek Humphry, founder of the Hemlock Society, wrote a controversial book called *Final Exit*. The Hemlock Society is an organization committed to protecting and promoting people's right to die a dignified death. Humphry's book provides practical, step-by-step guidance for those who wish to take their own lives or assist others in doing so. It gives advice on choosing the most efficient and painless technique; finding a physician who will help; skirting the law; acquiring, storing, and using lethal drugs; and taking care of life insurance policies and other financial considerations. Humphry even provides a checklist of things one ought to attend to before dying and a table showing lethal dosages of common and readily available prescription drugs. Despite the vociferous opposition to the publication and sale of the book, it remained on the *New York Times* best-seller list for several weeks.

One of the most controversial figures in recent years has been Dr. Jack Kevorkian. A retired Michigan physician, Kevorkian invented a machine that allows people to inject lethal doses of drugs into themselves. On June 4, 1990, he wrote a letter to the *New York Times* in which he talked freely about helping a woman suffering from Alzheimer's disease kill herself the day before. Desiring a gentle and certain death, she had sought out Kevorkian and his machine. To date, he has helped more than 30 people commit suicide. On several occasions Kevorkian has been arrested and charged either with first-degree murder or violations of state laws against assisted suicide. So far, he has been acquitted on all charges.

To the absolutist, a person purposely taking the life of another person, even if motivated by love and sympathy, is and always will be a murderer. A person who writes a book on how to do it is an accomplice to murder. To the relativist, however, the situational circumstances are the *only* relevant factors. The value of life itself must be weighed against other values, like the personal freedom to be active, freedom from suffering, and control over one's life (Finlay, 1985). Requiring a suffering, terminally ill person to live would be the moral equivalent of a crime. Putting an end to his or her misery would be the acceptable thing to do under certain circumstances.

The controversy over mercy killing goes beyond the moral and ethical debate over individual actions and definitions of deviance. The issue is intimately tied to the broader structure of the medical profession and its place in society. Because people can now be kept alive artificially for indefinite periods, the very definition of death is more problematic than it was in the past (Finlay, 1985). Answering the question of when a person ought to die is relevant because medical technology is sophisticated enough to allow physicians to intervene and keep that person alive.

How the controversy over mercy killing is ultimately resolved will in turn have a dramatic impact on the practice of medicine. Fifty years ago, the task of a doctor or a nurse was clear: Keep the patient alive as long as possible. However, a recent survey of 852 intensive-care nurses found that 16% had performed euthanasia or helped terminally ill patients commit suicide. Some reported engaging in these practices without the request or advance knowledge of a physician or others (D. A. Asch, 1996).

The Netherlands has recently legalized physician-assisted suicide. According to the law, a physician can help a patient die if the following strict guidelines are met: The patient must make the decision voluntarily after being informed of all alternatives, the patient's condition must be "unbearable" and "hopeless," the physician must consult a colleague who does not have a professional or family relationship with either the patient or the doctor, the doctor whenever possible should have patients administer the fatal drugs to themselves, and the procedure must be documented and subjected to a professional investigation (Simons, 1995). Dutch physicians must now make decisions not only on how to keep their patients well, but also on how to let them die.

In this country the movement to legalize physician-assisted suicide is gaining momentum. Federal appeals courts in California and New York have overturned bans on assisted suicide and ruled that mentally competent, terminally ill adults have a right to get help in ending their lives. The issue is certain to reach the U.S. Supreme Court sometime soon.

But assisted suicide is not simply a legal matter. It has important institutional implications. Imagine how the medical profession would change if euthanasia and assisted suicide ever became a common, legally acceptable solution to the problem of human suffering. The practices and beliefs underlying the entire medical establishment—from the training of medical students to the structure and purpose of hospitals—would have to be altered. Perhaps certain physicians would choose to specialize in assisted suicide. Furthermore, the entire economic structure of the health care system would have to adapt. How, for instance, would medical insurance cover assisted suicide? How would families change? Would some terminally ill people feel an obligation to die to avoid becoming a burden to their loved ones? Finally, within the culture itself we would no doubt have to engage in philosophical reevaluation of the meaning of life and death.

■ ■ ■

In sum, to a relativist, the main concerns in defining deviance are who commits the act, who labels it, and where and when it occurs, as much as what is committed. Some people have the wherewithal to avoid having their acts defined as deviant. Definitions of deviant behavior change over time, and certain acts are acceptable to some groups and not others. But despite the relativist nature of conceptions of deviance, *every* society identifies certain individuals and certain behaviors as bothersome and disruptive and therefore justifiable targets of social control, whether through treatment, punishment, spiritual healing, or correction.

The Elements of Deviance

Given the complex and controversial issues covered so far, the general definition of deviance we're left with goes something like this: **Deviance** is an individual's or group's behavior (how people act), ideas (how people think), or attributes (how people appear) that some people in society find offensive, wrong, immoral, sinful, evil, strange, or disgusting. This definition consists of three elements (Aday, 1990):

■ *Expectation.* Some sort of behavioral expectation must exist, a norm that defines appropriate, acceptable behavior, ideas, or characteristics. The expectations may be implicit or explicit, formal or informal, and more or less widely shared.

■ *Violation.* Deviance implies some violation of normative expectations. The violation may be real or alleged; that is, an accusation of wrongdoing may be enough to give someone a reputation of deviance.

■ *Reaction.* An individual, group, or society must react to the deviance. The reaction is likely to lead to some sort of response: avoidance, criticism, warnings, punishment, or treatment. The reaction may accurately reflect the facts, or it may bear little resemblance to what really happened, as when people are punished or ostracized for acts they did not commit.

Explaining Why People Become Deviant

The question of *how* people come to be defined as deviant is different from the question of *why* people commit deviant acts. Most sociological theories assume there is agreement as to what acts are deviant and proceed directly to an examination of the characteristics of people who commit them.

Sociological Models

The structural-functionalist perspective tells us that it is in society's interest to socialize everyone to strive for success so that the most able and talented people occupy the most important positions. In this way, people who aren't satisfied with what they have will be motivated to do better.

Sociologist Robert Merton (1957) was interested in how these structural conditions affected the likelihood of people engaging in deviant acts. He argued that the probability of committing deviant acts increases when people experience a contradiction between the culturally defined goals that we are all socialized to strive for (for example, wealth and success) and access to the legitimate means by which they can achieve those goals (for example, education, good jobs, and family influence). Those who believe that being wealthy and achieving the "American Dream" are important goals, but who have no money, no employment opportunities, and no access to higher education, Merton argued, are more inclined than others to achieve the goal of success through *illegitimate* means, such as theft or the sale of illegal goods and services. In this sense, people who sell, say, stolen TVs to get rich are motivated by the same desires as people who sell real estate to get rich. Sometimes people who lack access to the legitimate means reject the culturally defined goals of wealth and success and retreat from society altogether. According to Merton, vagrants, chronic drunks, drug addicts, and the mentally ill fall into this category.

Another sociologist, Edwin Sutherland (Sutherland & Cressey, 1955), based his theory of deviance upon the symbolic interactionist principle that we all interpret life through the symbols and meanings we learn through our interactions with others. Sutherland argued that individuals learn deviant patterns of behavior from the people with whom they associate on a regular basis: friends, family members, peers. Through our associations with these influential individuals we learn not only the techniques for committing deviant acts (like how to pick a lock or how to snort cocaine) but also a set of beliefs and attitudes that justify or rationalize the behavior (Sykes & Matza, 1957). In order to commit deviant acts, we must learn how to perceive those acts as normal.

Other sociologists have turned away from the issue of why some people violate norms to the issue of why more people don't (for example, Hirschi, 1969). Their concern is with the mechanisms society has in place to control or constrain people's behavior. *Deterrence theory* concentrates on identifying the most effective punishment to prevent deviance. It assumes that people are rational decision makers who calculate the costs and benefits of behavior before they act. If the benefits of a deviant act (for instance, monetary wealth or psychological satisfaction) outweigh the costs (for instance, the severity of punishment or the likelihood of getting caught), we will do it. Conversely, if the costs exceed the potential benefits, the theory predicts that we'll decide it's not worth the risk (van den Haag, 1975).

The current controversy surrounding capital punishment is, essentially, a debate over its capacity to deter potentially violent criminals. Opponents of the death penalty argue that violent offenders are often under the influence of drugs or alcohol or are consumed by passion when they commit an act of violence. Hence they may not be thinking rationally (that is, weighing the benefits of the act against the cost of punishment) at the time of the crime. The threat of being condemned to death may not deter them. Researchers have indeed found little empirical support for the argument that the publicized threat of capital punishment reduces killings (W. C. Bailey, 1990). In fact, one study found that the murder rates in states with the death penalty are actually higher than rates in other states (W. C. Bailey & Peterson, 1989). Nevertheless, the majority of Americans continue to favor the death penalty and believe it is a useful tool in fighting crime. Recent legislative efforts to increase the number of offenses punishable by the death penalty and reduce the number of "death row" appeals an offender can file reflect this popular belief.

Labeling Theory

These theories help us explain why some people engage in deviant acts while others don't, but they bypass the question of why certain acts committed by certain people are considered deviant in the first place. To find the answer, we must examine the social and interpersonal processes through which acts, attributes, and beliefs become deviant (for example, Becker, 1963; Lemert, 1972). Such an approach, often called *labeling theory*, doesn't analyze what causes people to commit deviant acts. Instead, it attempts to explain how cultural and individual perceptions create and sustain deviant identities. According to this theory, deviance is the consequence of the application of rules and sanctions to an offender. A deviant person, then, is not someone who is fundamentally different from a nondeviant but rather someone—like Gladys Burr—to whom the label "deviant" has been successfully applied (Becker, 1963).

Although deviant labels can be used for therapeutic purposes in some situations, such as the use of the "alcoholic" label by members of Alcoholics Anonymous (Trice & Roman, 1970), labeling theorists assume that most deviant labels are harmful. The process of being singled out, defined, and reacted to as deviant changes a person in the eyes of others and has important life consequences for that individual. It may alter his or her self-concept, taint face-to-face interactions with nondeviants, and increase the probability that the behavior itself will stay the same or become worse (Archer, 1985). For example, the actual or imagined reactions of others can determine a mental patient's self-image, create "deviant" patterns of behavior, and lead to social rejection after the illness is "cured."

Whatever psychological distress may actually be present, the labeling of mental illness necessarily involves an interpretation. Consider two people, Person A and Person B, who are suffering from an incapacitating depression in which they display identical symptoms. They are overwhelmingly sad, can't eat, can't sleep, and are unable to carry out their customary roles in life. Person A's wife has just died, he's unemployed, the bills are piling up, and he sees no likelihood of a change in his circumstances. Person B shows all the same symptoms of depression as Person A, but no one can figure out why. He has a satisfying and high-paying job and a loving wife and family. Person A probably would not be considered mentally ill because his depression has a logical and culturally acceptable explanation. Person B, on the other hand, is likely to be regarded as sick because his social circumstances do not explain his problems. Clearly the diagnosis of mental illness depends on a process of social interpretation (R. Turner & Edgley, 1983). Although some mental illnesses may be caused by biological or chemical processes, such conditions are considered disorders in the first place because their symptoms violate the norms of everyday life.

The Dramatization of Evil

The historical roots of the concern over the effects of labeling date back to a book called *Crime and Community*, written in 1938 by sociologist Frank Tannenbaum. Tannenbaum was primarily interested in male juvenile delinquents, although his ideas can be applied to many different deviant groups. He believed that most acts of delinquency—breaking windows, petty theft, truancy, and so on—are a normal part of adolescent street life. Kids engage in these activities for fun, adventure, and excitement. The community at large, though, is likely to see such activities as evil or annoying and may demand some sort of control over the situation (that is, punishment).

If delinquent behavior becomes more visible and frequent, the situation gradually becomes redefined. There is a shift from the definition of specific acts as "evil" to a definition of the individual as "evil." All the boy's acts become suspect. His companions, hangouts, speech, clothes, conduct, and everything about him become an object of scrutiny and further "proof" of his delinquent nature. From the community's point of view, the basically "good" individual who used to do mischievous things has been transformed into a bad and useless human being.

Because first impressions are important in determining how others see us and, consequently, how we see ourselves, this "delinquent" label can have a tremendous impact on the young boy's life. What concerned Tannenbaum in particular was the effect the label would have on the boy's self-concept. The boy is likely to be overwhelmed by the community reaction and begin to think of himself as the type of person who would do such things. Over time the label becomes a self-fulfilling prophecy. The juvenile becomes bad because he is *defined* as bad by others.

Tannenbaum called this process the *dramatization of evil*, and it plays a greater role in the making of a deviant than perhaps any other experience. The reactions of others, no matter how compassionate the intent, may perpetuate the deviance they seek to get rid of by trapping individuals in a role from which they cannot escape. They now live in a different world. They have been "tagged" (Tannenbaum, 1938). In the eyes of others, the person who steals *is* a thief, the person who kills *is* a murderer.

The Stickiness of Labels

Like stigmas (see chapter 6), deviant labels are difficult to overcome. The motives, actions, and character of the "deviant" are assumed to be typical of others who possess the label. The criminal is "cold-blooded and ruthless," the mental patient is "dangerous," the alcoholic is "weak-willed," the prostitute is "dirty and immoral." Thus the label suggests that the deviant is someone who is habitually given to certain kinds of undesirable behavior and who can be expected to behave in this way in the future. It influences the kinds of feelings others have and the behaviors others direct toward the person: rejection, suspicion, withdrawal, fear, mistrust, and hatred (A. K. Cohen, 1966).

Deviant labels can impair the individual's eligibility to enter a broad range of socially acceptable roles. Consider the impact on convicted sex offenders of the 1994 Federal Crime Bill. It requires states to register and track convicted sex offenders for 10 years after their release from prison and to privately notify police departments when criminal sex offenders move into their communities. Two years later the U.S. Senate approved a measure requiring all states to make *public* notifications of the whereabouts of paroled sex offenders in the community. These are men who have "paid their debt" to society by serving their prison sentences. However, under this law convicted sex offenders can never fully shed their deviant identity and be above suspicion.

All ex-convicts experience the stickiness of labels to some degree. Potential employers, for instance, often refuse to hire ex-convicts, even when the crime has nothing to do with the job requirements. Employers are part of the public that widely believes that prisons do not rehabilitate but actually make convicts more deviant by teaching them better ways to commit crime and providing social networks to criminal activity on the outside (R. Johnson, 1987). We do in fact know that a great many ex-convicts return to prison. An estimated two-thirds of all adult inmates in the United States have been in prison before (Petersilia, 1985; U.S. Bureau of Justice Statistics, 1983). Roughly 35% of convicted robbers, 43% of convicted burglars, and 22% of people convicted of homicide are convicted of second crimes (Wallerstedt, 1984). Thus, stigmatization due to fear of future criminal activity may be rational.

What is not so rational is the fact that a mere *charge* of criminal activity conjures up suspicions of tainted character. The labeling process is powerful enough, even in the absence of wrongdoing, to produce a durable loss of status for the individual (Schwartz & Skolnick, 1962). Not only does labeling challenge the important legal contention that one is "innocent until proven guilty," it also suggests that the negative effects of being labeled a criminal cannot be reduced simply by diverting offenders away from prison (Erickson & Goodstadt, 1979). For someone who has a record of past criminal activity, or even simply of arrest on suspicion of crime, every act might be interpreted as an expression of his or her "criminal tendencies."

Similarly, former mental patients often have trouble resuming a nondeviant role. Although community reactions to former mental patients are not as negative as they once were (Cockerham, 1992; Torrey, 1988), some of these individuals may still experience discrimination, abuse, and suspicion. A significant proportion of the public still sees former mental patients as dangerous and is reluctant to interact with them (Link et al., 1987).

■ ■ ■ ■ ■ ■ ■ ■

DAVID ROSENHAN
Being Sane in Insane Places

In 1973 sociologist David Rosenhan designed a clever study to examine the difficulty people have shedding the "mentally ill" label. He was particularly interested in how staffs in mental institutions go about processing information about patients in light of their diagnosed condition. He decided that the best way to get this information was from the inside through participant observation. Rosenhan and seven associates had themselves committed to different mental hospitals by complaining that they were hearing voices (a symptom commonly believed to be characteristic of schizophrenia). The staff did not know the "pseudopatients" were actually part of a field experiment. They assumed they were patients like any others and had no reason to believe the reported symptoms were fake.

Beyond the alleged symptoms and a falsification of name and occupation, the important events of the pseudopatients' life histories were presented as they had actually occurred. Furthermore, prior to the study, Rosenhan instructed them to act completely normal upon admission into the hospital. That is, they were not to act "crazy" in any way. In fact, Rosenhan told them that acting normal was the only way they could get out.

Despite the fact that they did nothing out of the ordinary, the pseudopatients remained hospitalized for an average of 19 days, from a low of 9 days to a high of 52. Their sanity was never detected except, ironically enough, by the actual patients in the hospitals. All of Rosenhan's associates retained the deviant label even after being discharged. Their schizophrenia was said to be "in remission," implying that it was dormant and could possibly resurface. At no time during their stay in the hospital was the legitimacy of their schizophrenic label ever questioned. It was simply assumed that they were schizophrenic; after all, why else would they have heard voices?

Everything they did and said was understood from this premise. Normal behaviors were overlooked entirely or profoundly misinterpreted. Minor disagreements became deep-seated indicators of emotional instability. Boredom was interpreted as nervousness or anxiety. Even the act of writing on a notepad was seen by the staff as a sign of some deeper psychological disturbance.

Furthermore, even though there was nothing "pathological" about the pseudopatients' past histories, these records were reinterpreted to be consistent with the schizophrenic label. One patient, for instance, had had a close relationship with his mother but a remote one with his father during early childhood. As he matured he became closer to his father while his relationship with his mother became more distant. He had a warm and loving relationship with his wife and children, although there were occasional fights and friction. In short, there was nothing particularly unusual about this person's history. But notice how this history was translated into something troubled and psychopathological by the attending psychiatrist:

> This white 39-year-old male . . . manifests a long history of *considerable ambivalence in close relationships*, which began in early childhood. A warm relationship with his mother cools during his adolescence. A distant relationship to his father is described as becoming very intense. *Affective stability is absent.* His attempts to control emotions with his wife and children are punctuated by angry outbursts and, in the case of the children, spankings. And while he says that he has several good friends, one senses considerable ambivalence embedded in those relationships also [emphasis added]. (Rosenhan, 1973, p. 253)

Just as behavior was interpreted in light of the label, the facts of this man's past were distorted to achieve consistency with what was generally believed to be true about the family dynamics of schizophrenics.

Rosenhan didn't conclude that the staffs at these hospitals were incompetent or dishonest. In fact, he argues that there was no conscious effort to misconstrue the evidence to fit the label. They were doing their jobs effectively. He reasoned that the labels were so powerful that they profoundly affected the way information was processed and perceived. Had the same behaviors been observed in a different context, without the perceptual effects of the preexisting label, they no doubt would have been interpreted in an entirely different fashion.

▪ ▪ ▪

Power and the Social Construction of Deviance

Because deviance is socially defined, the behaviors and conditions that come to be called "deviant" can at times appear somewhat arbitrary. However, the definition of deviance is often a form of social control exerted by more powerful people and groups over less powerful people and groups. Let's examine this process from a conflict perspective. Prior to the 17th century, people who were "insane" were not necessarily separated from the general population. Like poor people and other "undesirables," they freely roamed the countryside. Responsibility for their care rested with the family or the local community. Madness at the time was a public matter, out in the open and part of everyday life. As long as the people weren't dangerous, they weren't considered particularly troublesome.

As cities began to grow, so did the population of roaming vagrants and mad people. Their presence and visibility became increasingly bothersome to the rest of the population. In 1657 King Louis XIII of France issued a royal decree forbidding all people from begging on the streets of Paris. It wasn't long before the French army began to hunt down street people and herd them into an institution euphemistically called the Hôpital Général (Foucault, 1965). There, mad people were confined with beggars, vagabonds, street thieves, the poor, the unemployed, and anybody else who could not support himself or herself. It is estimated that at its peak the hospital held 1% of the entire population of Paris (Conrad & Schneider, 1980).

The General Hospital wasn't the kind of hospital we have today. There were no medical treatments, doctors, nurses, or medical equipment. It was more like a pauper's prison that symbolically represented society's distaste for idleness and laziness. More important, it served the interests of the growing ruling class of landowners, merchants, and businesspeople. In periods of economic prosperity, the inhabitants of the hospital provided a limitless pool of cheap labor. In slow economic times, the hospital reabsorbed these individuals so they wouldn't be a nuisance to the more affluent citizens.

As capitalism began to flourish and the need for a competent workforce increased, the ruling class thought it best to separate the hospital inhabitants who could work from those who couldn't (that is, the insane). A more specialized institution, the madhouse, was established to house only the insane. This separation occurred not to provide the insane with more effective psychiatric treatment but to protect others from the "contagion" of madness (Foucault, 1965). Their presence disrupted the reserve labor pool, so they had to be segregated. The madhouse quickly grew in popularity, evolving into the more humanitarian insane asylum of the 19th century and the more therapeutic mental hospital of the 20th century. Thus, a new deviant category (the insane) and a new way of dealing with them (confinement in specialized institutions) were created by the state primarily for economic and social reasons (Chambliss, 1974).

In our society, the predominant means of controlling deviants—those whose behavior does not conform to the norms established by the powerful—are criminalization and medicalization. Labeling people as either criminals or as sick people gives the socially powerful a way to marginalize and discount certain people who challenge the status quo. Criminalization and medicalization also have economic and other benefits for certain powerful groups.

The Criminalization of Deviance

One of the most important constructed realities is that determining what we regard as legal or illegal behavior. Certain acts are defined as crimes because they offend the majority. We come to trust our legal institutions—legislators, courts, and police—to regulate social behavior in the interest of the common good.

Conflict theorists argue that the contemporary U.S. criminal justice system works to ensure that the offenders who wind up in prison are members of the lowest socioeconomic class (Reiman, 1990). Police treat poor communities as if they are enemy territory: "They drive around it in patrol cars looking for troublemakers to arrest; friendly contact with the inhabitants is often negligible, and citizens respond by regarding the police as an occupying army" (G. Stephens, 1994, p. 27).

In our society, which values achievement, the deviants are those who don't succeed. Indeed, poor people are more likely to get arrested, be formally charged with a crime, have their cases go to trial, get convicted, and receive harsher sentences (Parenti, 1995). This imbalance is not simply the result of prejudice against the poor. If that were the case, the situation would be relatively easy to deal with. Instead, it occurs because the actions of poor individuals are more likely to be **criminalized**—that is, officially defined as crimes. Poor people happen to commit acts—car theft, burglary, assault, illegal drug use, and so on—that fit commonly held definitions of what a crime is. As a result, they become "typical criminals."

The Social Reality of Crime

Conflict theorists point out that powerful groups often try to foster a belief that society's rules are under attack by deviants and that official action against them is needed. The tactic has worked well. In polls taken in the 1980s and early 1990s, an average of 83% of respondents felt that the justice system was not harsh enough in dealing with criminals (Gaubatz, 1995). Governments at the state and federal level have responded to the popular mandate by getting tough on crime— lengthening prison sentences and building more prisons. According to the Justice Department, the number of inmates in U.S. prisons has tripled since 1980 (cited in Butterfield, 1995b).

According to conflict theorists, the law is not a mechanism that merely protects good people from bad people; it is a political instrument used by specific groups to further their own interests, often at the expense of others. The law is created by economic elites who control the production and distribution of major resources in society (Chambliss, 1964; Quinney, 1970). Law is, of course, determined by legislative action. But legislatures are greatly influenced by these powerful segments of society via lobbying groups, political action committees, individual campaign contributions, and so on (see chapter 10). The acts that conflict with the economic or political interests of the groups who have the power to influence public policy are more likely to be criminalized:

> Two wealthy contractors, who pocketed $1.2 million in government contracts for work they never did, were ordered to pay $5,000 in fines and do 200 hours of community service. But a Norfolk, Virginia, man got ten years for stealing 87 cents; a youth in Louisiana received fifty years for selling a few ounces of marijuana; a Houston youth was sentenced to fifty years for robbing two people of $1 as they left a restaurant; a five-time petty offender in Dallas was sentenced to *one thousand* years in prison for stealing $73. A man caught trying to break into a house in Florida, thus violating his probation for shoplifting a pair of shoes, was sentenced to life in prison. (Parenti, 1995, p. 127)

Through mass communication, dominant groups expose the public to ideas that force us to look at crime in ways that are favorable to them. The selective portrayal of crime plays an important role in shaping public perceptions of the "crime problem" and therefore its "official" definition. When politicians talk about fighting America's crime problem, or when news shows report an increase in crime rates, they are almost always referring to street crimes (illegal drug use, robbery, burglary, murder, assault, etc.) rather than corporate crimes, governmental crimes, or crimes more likely to be committed by people in positions of power:

> Press coverage focuses public attention on crime in the streets with scarcely a mention of "crime in the suites," downplaying such . . . crimes as briberies, embezzlements, kickbacks, monopolistic restraints of trade, illegal uses of public funds by private interests, occupational safety violations, unsafe consumer goods, and environmental poisonings. (Parenti, 1986, p. 12)

Furthermore, how crime is defined and reported is largely determined by the race and social class of the victim and victimizer. Affluent victims receive more press coverage than poor victims, leaving the public with the impression that most crime victims are from middle- and upper-class backgrounds. Conversely, racial minority and low-income lawbreakers are more likely to be publicized as criminals than are wealthy corporate leaders whose law-breaking activity may actually be more harmful to the common good (Parenti, 1986).

Such exposure creates a certain way of perceiving crime that becomes social reality. We accept the objectified fact that certain people or actions are a threat to the well-being of the entire society and therefore a threat to our own personal interests. Thus the enactment and enforcement of laws against some acts and not others represent not only a legal victory but a victory in the struggle to control social reality and perpetuate power differences.

White-Collar Crime

We take for granted that street crime is our worst social problem and that white-collar crime is not as dangerous or as costly (Reiman, 1990). However, unsafe work conditions; dangerous chemicals in our air, water, and food; faulty products; unnecessary surgery; and shoddy emergency medical services put us in constant and imminent physical and economic danger:

> Every year roughly 28,000 deaths and 130,000 serious injuries are caused by dangerous products. At least 100,000 workers die from exposure to deadly chemicals and other safety hazards. Workplace carcinogens are estimated to cause between 23 and 38 percent of all cancer deaths. . . . Fraud costs the nation's businesses and individuals upwards of $100 billion each year. The Senate Judiciary Committee has estimated that faulty goods, monopolistic practices and other such violations cost consumers $171 to $231 billion. . . . The dollar cost of corporate crime in the United States is more than 10 times greater than the combined total from larcenies, robberies, burglaries and auto thefts. (Mokhiber, 1989, p. 14)

The individuals responsible for these dangers rarely show up in police or prison records. Although antitrust violations, false advertising, price fixing, unfair labor practices, embezzlement, and fraud cost society more money and pose a greater danger to the public safety than ordinary street criminals, the people who commit these white-collar crimes seldom receive heavy punishment (Reiman, 1990). Their offenses tend not to be treated as "real" crimes.

Furthermore, the crimes of large corporations usually go through less visible civil procedures rather than embarrassing criminal trials. For example, in 1992 the U.S. Justice Department accused Teledyne, Inc., of systematically falsifying tests on an electrical component used in the construction of sophisticated weapons and spacecraft. The suit asserted that Teledyne was essentially selling the government a $6 part for $20. These practices, which went on for about 7 years, defrauded the government of about $250 million (Stevenson, 1992). Moreover, three years earlier Teledyne had pleaded guilty to overcharging the Defense Department. Twice before, their shipping operations had been suspended by the Pentagon because of overcharging. Despite all this, the company continues to do business with the government today. If you had stolen $250 million dollars from a bank, would you be allowed to carry on with life as usual or do business with the very company from which you had stolen?

In 1994, six U.S. airlines—American, Delta, Northwest, TWA, Alaska, and Continental—settled federal antitrust charges that they had collaborated illegally to raise airline ticket fares between 1988 and 1992. The price-fixing arrangement cost consumers some $4 billion in excess fares. No criminal charges were filed, however, and the airlines received no formal punishment. Under the settlement, they simply agreed not to use a computerized fare system to negotiate ticket-price changes anymore.

Activities like these take place every day without much public outcry, moral panic, or legislative action. Yet at the same time massive law enforcement efforts are directed at "typical" street criminals like street beggars, thieves, and drug dealers.

The War on Drugs

The United States has been in an ill-defined and undeclared but highly publicized "war" for many years: the War on Drugs. There is a widespread feeling on the part of the public that many of our social ills are created by the moral failure of a specific group of individuals: drug users and drug dealers. They are the enemy, they are destroying our country, and they need to be stopped (E. Goode, 1989). Not surprisingly, three-quarters of the prisoners incarcerated in the United States since 1980 are drug offenders (Parenti, 1995).

The United States has been described as a *temperance culture* (Levine, 1992)—one in which self-control and industriousness are perceived as necessities for economic survival. In such a culture, drug-induced states of consciousness are likely to be perceived as a *loss* of control and thus inordinately feared. It is not surprising then that "drugs" have become a generic scapegoat in American culture, "a folk devil on which to blame a range of bizarre behaviors or other conditions [people] find troubling but difficult to explain in other terms" (Reinarman, 1994, p. 99).

Many sociologists argue that antidrug campaigns and legislative activities are also motivated by economic and political interests (E. Goode, 1989). The war on drugs in the United States has increased social control over groups perceived to be threatening and mobilized voter support for candidates who profess to be "tough" on drugs. Capitalizing on the "drug menace" as a personal and societal threat is a common political tactic in our society (Ben-Yehuda, 1990). It is relatively easy to generate moral panic from phrases like "Drugs destroy young minds" or "Drugs destroy the future of our country." Indeed the term *drugs* itself is an easy and safe scapegoat on which to focus collective hatred.

The Drug War is also big business. More than $60 billion is spent each year at all levels of the criminal justice system to fight the drug menace (Gottfredson & Hirschi, 1989). Not surprisingly, law enforcement and some drug fighting organizations portray the drug problem as ever worsening, meaning that the fight against it needs more funding. Such portrayal is not altogether unwarranted. Recent figures from the National Household Survey on Drug Abuse, for instance, show that drug use among youths ages 12–17 has increased dramatically since 1992, though it still remains far below the peak reached in the late 1970s. Monthly marijuana use among youths has doubled and cocaine use has more than doubled over the past five years. Among adults, however, the number of illicit drug users has not changed since 1992. This follows more than a decade of steady decline (U.S. Department of Health and Human Services, 1996).

Furthermore, when we hear the phrase "the War on Drugs," we all know that the drugs in question are the illegal ones: marijuana, crack, heroin, cocaine, and so forth. The assumption is that illegal drugs are the most dangerous substances and the ones that must be eradicated. However, the difference between legal and illegal drugs is not necessarily a function of their relative danger. The National Commission on Marijuana and Drug Abuse defines a drug as any chemical that affects the structure and function of a living organism (cited in Fine, 1990). Such a definition would include alcohol, nicotine, caffeine, and perhaps even salt and sugar. These substances, even though they can be harmful, are either completely legal or legal under certain age restrictions.

Tobacco, for example, is a clearer health risk than either alcohol or marijuana but has only recently been discussed in terms of drug abuse. Not counting the death and sickness caused by inhaling second-hand smoke and by chewing it, tobacco is estimated to kill approximately 400,000 Americans annually—the equivalent of three fully loaded jumbo jets crashing each day (Paulos, 1995). For every American who dies from illegal-drug use, 21 die from smoking-related illnesses ("Harper's Index," 1996). Knowing the hazards of cigarette smoking has not prompted our society to outlaw it entirely, as we have outlawed marijuana smoking and cocaine use.

In 1996, the Clinton administration apparently reversed this trend by imposing strict regulations on the marketing and sale of cigarettes and chewing tobacco. But these restrictions were aimed almost exclusively at children, not adults. Some critics fear that framing the campaign against tobacco as a problem of youth implicitly condones adult smoking, sending the message that young people should avoid smoking not because it causes serious health problems but because they're not old enough to do it (Glantz, 1996).

The legality or illegality of a drug may be more a function of who sells it and who uses it than how dangerous it is. Marijuana and crack are sold by "pushers";

cigarettes and alcohol are sold by "businesspeople." You will recall from chapter 3 that addiction to opium was not defined as a problem until it became associated with Chinese immigrants rather than middle-class housewives.

Why don't abusers of legal drugs elicit the same frenzied, warlike public reaction as "illegal" drug users? One reason is that substances like tobacco and alcohol represent multibillion-dollar industries. Criminalizing tobacco would certainly have an impact on the economies of several states that depend on this crop.

Another reason has to do, again, with public perceptions of "typical" drug addicts. They are assumed to be irresponsible and dangerous and to look dirty and unkempt. But society does not stigmatize and scorn "respectable" people addicted to legal substances. Police don't harass people who abuse prescription drugs, ransack their homes, or develop creative ways of apprehending and arresting them. Yet such tactics may be used against "typical" addicts, even if such measures cross the line of ethics and individual, constitutional rights.

Consider a law enforcement method called the "drug courier profile." The profile is a set of characteristics that are innocent in and of themselves, but when used together they serve as clues to identifying drug smugglers in public facilities such as airports, train stations, bus depots, and interstate highways. Officers look for people who are obviously in a hurry, have bought a one-way ticket or paid for the ticket with cash, have changed travel plans at the last minute, are the first to get off the plane, or fly to or from Miami or Detroit or any other city with heavy drug traffic. The Supreme Court ruled in 1989 that such factors, as well as a person's physical appearance, can amount to a "reasonable suspicion." Law enforcement officers are allowed to stop and interrogate people who fit the profile. It is estimated that hundreds of people are stopped each week as they are boarding, arriving, or simply passing through an airport (Belkin, 1990).

Other people who fit the "drug swallower profile" have been forcibly taken to local hospitals to be X-rayed to see if they had swallowed pouches filled with drugs. In 1990, 348 people were X-rayed in New York, Miami, and Houston. Of those, 161 (or 46%) were found to be carrying drugs (Belkin, 1990). Notice that more than half were not. The Drug Enforcement Administration nonetheless says that the success rate justifies the practice. In other words, the price of wrongly accusing and inconveniencing innocent people is acceptable if guilty people are caught in the process.

Critics argue that the success of the practice is not the issue. They suggest that stereotypes, particularly racial ones, are a key element of the drug courier and drug swallower profiles. In 1989 the *Mississippi Sun Herald* examined police files on people stopped and searched on a major interstate highway. Of 57 stops, 55 involved Hispanics or African Americans who drove cars with Texas or Florida license plates. A Rutgers University statistician found that on a stretch of the New Jersey Turnpike, only 4.7% of all traffic consisted of late-model cars with out-of-state license plates driven by African-American men. However, more than 80% of the cars that were stopped and interrogated on the highway fit that description (cited in Belkin, 1990).

You can see that the "enemies" in the war on drugs are principally individual drug dealers and users. Little has been done to stop the laundering of drug money through established financial institutions, even though there are laws against it (Parenti, 1995). For decades, the U.S. government has tried to stop the flow of illicit drugs into the country (Bullington, 1993). But waging a war against international drug suppliers is especially difficult because it is a global enterprise run by massive crime organizations that wield tremendous economic power and political influence.

■ ■ ■ ■ ■ ■ ■ ■

MICRO-MACRO CONNECTION
Global Deviance and the International Drug Trade

As social life becomes more global, certain forms of deviance begin to take on a more international flavor. Recent global trends like the growing diversity of populations, higher immigration rates, realignment of national borders, deteriorating economic conditions, democratization of governments, and improving computerization and communication technology have all helped to create major international organized crime networks (Godson & Olson, 1995; G. Stephens, 1994). Except for military expenditures, the global illegal drug trade is the largest industry in the world (United Nations Research Institute, 1995). Major crime rings from Colombia, China, Italy, Korea, Jamaica, Russia, Japan, and Southeast Asia do business in the United States today. International criminal organizations (ICOs) can threaten the stability of governments, hinder economic development, and even challenge a superpower (Godson & Olson, 1995).

In the early 1990s, for instance, the Medellin drug cartel launched a full-scale terrorist assault in Colombia. Public facilities and newspaper offices were bombed. Members of leading families were kidnapped. A leading candidate for the presidency was assassinated. Hundreds of police officers were murdered. A national airline flight was blown up in midair. The cartel's aim was to force the government to share power with the drug traffickers.

ICOs don't rely on violence alone to influence governments. The fantastic sums of money generated by illegal activities, especially drug production, gives ICOs the ability to employ bribery to achieve their goals. In 1994 the president of Colombia was accused of accepting $6 million from drug dealers to help him win the election. He was eventually acquitted of all charges, but many in Colombia and elsewhere were highly skeptical of his innocence.

The global connections established by ICOs allow them to create whole new drug markets. The introduction of "crack" in the United States in the mid-1980s revolutionized the cocaine market here. International networks also enable ICOs to adapt quickly to law enforcement efforts. When U.S. agencies shut off the flow of heroin from Turkey, new sources quickly developed in Southeast and Southwest Asia. When enforcement efforts were increased in Florida and the Caribbean, cocaine was simply routed through Central America and Mexico. Mexican organized crime was enlisted to run the network of local landing strips, safe houses, and corrupt government officials necessary to sustain the operation. The Colombian cartels have explored similar contacts with the Sicilian Mafia in hopes of expanding the European drug market (Godson & Olson, 1995). ICOs even establish connections with terrorist groups, which provide armed protection for landing fields, production facilities, and operations in exchange for cash.

Unlike the more traditional national or ethnicity-based criminal groups, like the American Mafia or ethnic street gangs, ICOs are massive business enterprises, often with transnational political and financial connections. The Colombian drug cartels, for example, have tens of thousands of specialized employees and associated businesses worldwide. Although the more traditional crime organizations may also develop international ties and suppliers, ICOs are organized for the express purpose of engaging in large-scale criminal activities across international borders (Godson & Olson, 1995).

The profits earned by ICOs dwarf those of traditional crime organizations:

> The Colombian cartels alone probably make more in a week than the American Mafia does in a year. The Colombian cartels now outperform most Fortune 500 companies. A conservative estimate of illegal drug sales at the retail, or user, level in the United States alone is $50 billion. [The] cartels are estimated to make a profit of about $20 billion annually from these revenues. . . . The combined budgets of the governments of Colombia, Bolivia, and Peru is only about $9 billion annually. (Godson & Olson, 1995, p. 23)

Furthermore, although traditional, nationally based criminal organizations may pose a variety of threats to society, they are in no position to challenge the sovereignty and integrity of an entire government. But where governments are unable to deliver needed social services and economies are deteriorating, the appeal of powerful international crime organizations can overwhelm respect for the law. In some areas—like small villages in the Peruvian Andes—ICOs are the only form of authority many people have ever known. In fact, in circumstances where governmental authority is weak, powerful ICOs may see themselves as the legitimate political authority (Godson & Olson, 1995).

In sum, these crime organizations are powerful enough to challenge, destabilize, and perhaps someday completely control small countries. Hence they represent a threat to international security that no single country can control alone.

■ ■ ■

The Medicalization of Deviance

Given the fact that deviance designations are related to the economic and political power arrangements in society, how does a particular way of thinking about deviance become dominant? In chapter 3, I described the actions of moral entrepreneurs—people or groups of people who crusade to have their versions of reality accepted by society at large. Moral entrepreneurs are interested in a single issue, be it abortion, drunk driving, child abuse, or offensive art. Occasionally, however, certain institutions become particularly influential in constructing an entire belief system that proposes causes of and solutions to a wide range of social problems. Instead of fighting for one particular issue, some institutions create an entire worldview.

Perhaps the most obvious and powerful force in defining deviance today is the medical establishment. The field of medicine has been extremely successful in presenting a conception of deviance that equates it with illness. Each time we automatically refer to bizarre or troublesome behavior as "sick," we help to perpetuate the perception that deviance is diseaselike. **Medicalization** is the definition of behavior as a medical problem or illness and the mandating or licensing of the medical profession to provide some type of treatment for it (Conrad, 1975). Many physicians, psychologists, psychiatrists, therapists, insurance agents, and the entire pharmaceutical industry benefit from a medicalized view of deviant behavior.

Conduct that was once categorized simply as misbehavior is now redefined as a psychiatric disease, disorder, or syndrome. Between 1952 and 1986 the number of mental disorders recognized by the American Psychiatric Association increased from 110 to 210 ("Harper's Index," 1986). To accommodate the growing number of "illnesses," the number of psychiatric professionals and the number of people seeking psychiatric help have almost tripled over the last two decades. The U.S. government has estimated that the economic cost of mental health care is close to $55 billion a year (Kirk & Kutchins, 1992). Experts estimate that between 20% and 33% of Americans suffer from some sort of mental disorder (Robins & Regier, 1991). Along with alcoholism, drug addiction, and mental illness, these disorders now include overeating, undereating, learning disabilities, shyness, violence, child abuse, addiction to the Internet, and excessive gambling, shopping, and sex.

Why has the medical view of deviance become so dominant? One reason is that medical explanations of troublesome social problems and deviant behaviors are appealing to a society that privileges individualistic rather than sociological explanations. It is comforting when a researcher tells us that violence is the result of a dysfunction in the brain; it then becomes a problem of defective, violent individuals, not of the larger societal context within which violent acts take place. Likewise, it is a relief when our doctor or therapist tells us our anxiety, depression, crabbiness, and insecurity will vanish if we take an antidepressant drug. By looking inside the individual, we are spared the difficult task of looking at the structure of our society. The depressed person is the problem, not us.

The medicalization of deviance also appeals to our humanitarian values. The designation of a problem as an illness removes legal and moral scrutiny or punishment in favor of therapeutic treatment (Zola, 1986). The alcoholic is no longer a sinner or a criminal but a victim, someone whose behavior is an "illness," beyond his or her control. Children who have trouble learning in school aren't disobedient and disruptive, they are "sick." If people are violating norms because of a disease that has invaded their bodies, they should not be held morally responsible. Medicalization creates less social stigma and condemnation of people labeled deviant.

Despite its enormous appeal, our tendency to medicalize deviance has serious social consequences (Conrad, 1975). These include the use of medicine as a means of social control, the individualization of complex social issues, and the depoliticization of deviance.

Exerting Social Control through Medicine

The medical profession is a powerful establishment. To become a physician, one must undergo years of rigorous training and be licensed by the profession's governing body. Because special expertise is acquired in this area, we assume that admission into the ranks must be carefully controlled. Physicians enjoy a tremendously high status in American society. "Plumber's orders," "accountant's orders," or even "sociologist's orders" do not carry the same influence and authority that "doctor's orders" carry. Consequently, physicians are able to claim jurisdiction over the label of illness and anything to which the label can be attached, regardless of whether or not they can deal with it effectively (Friedson, 1970).

Decisions regarding diagnosis and treatment of a host of problems are almost completely controlled by the medical profession. No other profession has such extensive access to a person's body or mind as physical and psychiatric medicine (Conrad, 1975). And the consequences of medical professionals' decisions reach far beyond the health and well-being of an individual patient. Plastic surgeons have helped define or at least perpetuate cultural standards of beauty. Any psychiatrist who prescribes drugs for a person's emotional suffering alters our cultural conceptions of what conditions we need not tolerate. Organ transplants have redefined our notions of death and dying (Zola, 1986).

The more behaviors that are defined as illnesses, the larger the legitimate domain of the profession:

> The increasing acceptance of technical [medical] solutions . . . results in the withdrawal of more and more areas of human experience from the realm of public discussion. For when drunkenness, juvenile delinquency . . . and extreme political

beliefs are seen as symptoms of an underlying illness or biological defect the merits of such behaviors or beliefs need not be evaluated. (Reynolds, 1973, p. 200)

Defining a problem as medical removes it from the public arena and places it where only medical people with medical expertise can talk about it (Conrad, 1975).

In addition, medicalizing deviance justifies certain intrusive procedures to be performed on individuals not only in the name of "treatment" but also in the interests of the common good. When health professionals attempt to eradicate a disease or a behavior, we all supposedly benefit. According to one critic, a larger, more sinister motive may also be behind the use of medical techniques to shape and control the behavior of deviants:

> [A]uthorities have moved beyond clubs, bullets, and eavesdropping devices and are resorting to such things as electroshock, mind-destroying drugs, and psychosurgery. Since the established powers presume that the present social system is virtuous, then those who are prone to violent or disruptive behavior, or who show themselves to be manifestly disturbed about the conditions under which they live, must be suffering from *inner* malfunctions that can best be treated by various mind controls. (Parenti, 1988, pp. 150–151)

Medical social control goes beyond "curing" problems or alleviating behavior defined by certain groups as troublesome. In some cases, treatments, particularly drugs, have become so popular they've shaped the entire culture.

■ ■ ■ ■ ■ ■ ■ ■

MICRO-MACRO CONNECTION
Prozac and the Pharmaceutical Personality

Since its introduction in 1987, the antidepressant drug Prozac has been taken by close to 20 million people worldwide. Almost as soon as it hit the market, it was being hailed as a miracle drug. Not only was it effective in treating depression and easy to prescribe, it was relatively free of side-effects—weight gain, low blood pressure, irregular heart rhythms, and so on—common to other drug treatments. By 1990 it had become the nation's top-selling antidepressant, a position it continues to hold. In 1995 it became the world's first prescription mental health drug to bring in over $2 billion in annual receipts (Burton, 1996).

Prozac has grown to be more than just a treatment for depression, however. It is now regularly prescribed for people with eating disorders, obsessive-compulsive disorders, anxiety disorders, social phobias, obesity, gambling addiction, family problems, and premenstrual syndrome. Some people use it to enhance job performance, improve their alertness and concentration, overcome boredom, think more clearly, become more assertive, or get along better with their mates. The number of children between the ages of 5 and 10 for whom Prozac was prescribed or recommended increased from 61,000 in 1992 to 220,000 in 1994 (Brophy, 1995). It's even used to treat the behavior problems of dogs and cats.

Clearly Prozac's initial realm of clinical depression has expanded to include more of what were once thought of as ordinary life stresses. In his book *Listening to Prozac,* psychiatrist Peter Kramer—an avid proponent and energetic prescriber of the drug—argues that Prozac can (and perhaps should) also be used to remove aspects of our personality we find objectionable. He likens the use of Prozac in overcoming undesirable psychological traits to the use of cosmetic surgery in overcoming undesirable physical ones.

Most people who have benefited from the drug describe it in adoring, almost worshipful terms. They weren't healed, they were transformed. Shy introverts report turning into social butterflies; mediocre workers turn into on-the-job dynamos; the bored become interested and alert; even the unattractive begin to feel more beautiful. One woman, referring to this apparent change in physical appeal, reported that "people on the sidewalk [now] ask me for directions!" (Kramer, 1993, p. 8). Some people see Prozac as nothing short of a divine creation:

> As my husband and I watched the results of Prozac, we knew that the medication was God's gift to us. Breakthroughs . . . like Prozac are evidence of His grace. I now *feel* God's love for me as I never have before. . . . I believe that it is helping me be more true to the person God created me to be [emphasis in original]. (quoted in "Christian faith," 1995, p. 17)

According to Kramer, his patients feel "better than well" shortly after taking the drug. They report experiencing noticeable improvement in their popularity, business sense, self-image, energy, and sexual appeal (Kramer, 1993). One patient was having trouble at work and had recently broken up with her boyfriend. Kramer prescribed Prozac. Within weeks she was dating several men and handling her job demands smoothly. She even received a substantial pay raise. So enthusiastic was her loyalty to the drug that she happily referred to herself as "Ms. Prozac."

Prozac is appealing for economic reasons as well. Because traditional psychotherapy (patients talking to therapists about their problems) is time-consuming and expensive, efforts to cut health care costs work against its use. A psychiatrist might charge $150 for an hour-long session. Prozac, which is one of the most expensive antidepressants, costs only about $15 a week. Many prepaid health care plans have begun to limit or exclude extensive talk therapy in their coverage, thereby indirectly encouraging greater use of drugs like Prozac (Cooper, 1994).

In light of these benefits, we should perhaps not be surprised that Prozac has become a cultural icon. It pops up in magazine cartoons and David Letterman jokes. In 1993 a picture of the pill made the cover of *Newsweek.* A popular cocktail drink is called "Cranzac" (Prozac and cranberry juice for those unable to tolerate full doses of the drug). Even the word "Prozac" has become a metaphor for a quick-relief, cure-all. Commenting on the effectiveness of job training programs in helping unemployment and underemployment, the editor of the *Washington Post* recently said, "Employment training programs are no Prozac for an anxious age" (quoted in Sorohan, 1995, p. 11). One writer noted that, "Prozac has attained the familiarity of Kleenex and the social status of spring water" (Cowley, 1994, p. 41).

The popularity of Prozac raises fundamental sociological questions about the role drugs ought to play in everyday life. Critics fear that Prozac—as well as other drugs that can modify character—is aimed not so much at "sick patients" as at people who already function at a high level who want enriched memory, enhanced intelligence, heightened concentration, and a transformation of bad moods into good ones (Begley, 1994).

If Prozac does make people "better than well," how might social life be affected? In a fast-paced, achievement-oriented society like ours, the motivations for gaining a competitive edge—whether in school, on the job, or in interpersonal relations—are obvious. Those who earn higher grades, sell more cars, or come across as more charming and attractive can reap enormous financial and social benefits.

But once people begin to use a drug to chemically enhance performance, those who do not use the drug—whether for reasons of principle or because they can't afford it—risk losing out and becoming the less-rewarded and less-valuable members of the community (D. J. Rothman, 1994). Would we, as a society, have to resort to legal regulation—much like the ban on athletic performance enhancers like anabolic steroids—to prevent a desperate race to keep up?

On a more profound level, if we can use existing pharmaceutical technology to chemically eradicate sadness and despair—to create a world in which pain can be "erased as easily and fully as dirty words on a school blackboard" (Mauro, 1994, p. 46)—why would anyone ever put up with emotional discomfort? In the past, people simply assumed that despair was part of the human condition. Suffering made us stronger. Just as physical pain prevents us from burning ourselves if we get too close to a fire, perhaps mental pain, too, serves a purpose, such as motivating us to change life situations that are getting us into trouble. People today are more inclined to believe they have a right not to be unhappy. Sadness is inconvenient and prevents us from reaching our potential. Yet, do we want a society free of undesirable emotions, where people are "shiny and happy" all the time?

Questions like these are, of course, hypothetical. Prozac hasn't yet completely redefined society. Surely depression, unlike polio or smallpox, will never be totally eradicated. But the technological possibilities raise important issues about the role of medicine in controlling behavior, constructing personality, and ultimately determining social life and the culture that guides it. As Kramer says at the end of his book, "Once we have witnessed the effects of Prozac, it is impossible to imagine the modern world without [it]" (1993, p. 300).

▪ ▪ ▪

Individualizing Complex Social Issues

Our society often emphasizes the individual over the social system. Depression, alcoholism, eating disorders, and so on are "diseases" that lie within the person and hence can be remedied only through actions aimed at the individual (Kovel, 1980). Instead of seeing certain deviant behaviors as symptomatic of a faulty social system—blocked economic opportunities, neighborhood decay, repressive social institutions, or unattainable cultural standards—we see them as expressions of individual traits or shortcomings. The heavy reliance on Prozac, for example, focuses on individual symptoms rather than addressing the conditions that lead people to seek help in the first place.

Individualistic medical explanations of deviance are not necessarily wrong. Many violent people do have brain diseases, and some schizophrenics do have chemical imbalances. But when we focus exclusively on these explanations, the solutions we seek focus on the perpetrator alone, to the exclusion of everything else.

Consider the problem of hyperkinesis, or attention deficit hyperactivity disorder. A child who is "hyperactive" is difficult to deal with at home and in the classroom. He or she fidgets and squirms, has difficulty remaining seated, can't sustain attention in tasks or play activities, can't follow rules, talks excessively, and is easily distracted (American Psychiatric Association, 1987).

Forty years ago these children were considered bad or troublesome and would have been subjected to punishment or expulsion from school. Today, however, most hyperactive behavior is diagnosed as a symptom of a mental disorder, and drugs are prescribed to treat it. It is estimated that over 2 million children in the United States are taking drugs to curb their overactivity or inattentiveness (Merrow, 1995). Production of Ritalin, the most popular of these drugs, has increased by nearly 500% in the last five years (Kolata, 1996). Despite occasional adverse side effects, the drugs are generally successful in quieting unruly and annoying behavior (Whalen & Henker, 1977). In this sense, the medicalization of hyperactivity is useful. As Conrad (1975) writes, everyone involved benefits from the medical diagnosis and treatment of the problem:

> Both the school and the parents are concerned with the child's behavior; the child is very difficult at home and disruptive in school. No punishments or rewards seem consistently to work in modifying the behavior; and both parents and school are at their wits' end. A medical evaluation is suggested. The diagnoses of hyperkinetic behavior leads to prescribing . . . medications. The child's behavior seems to become more socially acceptable, reducing problems in school and at home. (p. 19)

But are we ignoring the possibility that these actions may be an adaptation to the child's social environment? Hyperactive behavior may be a response to an educational system that is set up to discourage individual expression (Conrad, 1975). Narrowly defined norms of acceptable behavior make it difficult if not impossible for children to pursue their own desires and needs. Consequently, the illness label conveniently diverts attention away from the school system as a potential cause or contributor to the problem and focuses attention exclusively on the individual child.

I'm not suggesting that all children who are diagnosed with attention deficit hyperactivity disorder are disruptive because they are bored in school or because their individual creativity has been discouraged. The point is that from an institutional perspective, the labeling of disruptiveness as an individual disorder serves the interests of the school system by protecting its legitimacy and authority. The institution could not function if disruptiveness were tolerated (Tobin, Wu,. & Davidson, 1989). When unruly behavior is translated into a sickness, medical remedies (that is, drugs) become a convenient tool for enforcing conformity and upholding the values of the system. If our educational system promoted and encouraged free individual expression instead of obedience and discipline, overactivity wouldn't be considered disruptive and wouldn't be a problem in need of a solution.

Depoliticizing Deviant Behavior

The process of individualizing and medicalizing social problems depoliticizes deviant behavior. The legitimacy of disruptive or threatening behaviors and statements is automatically destroyed when they are seen as symptoms of individual defects or illnesses. One need not pay attention to the critical remarks of an opponent if that opponent is defined as mentally ill. If we want to consider a person insane, we need not "drive" him mad; we can simply "declare" him mad (Szasz, 1984, p. 158). Historically, political opposition has often been quelled by the tactical use of medical labels. Political dissidents in totalitarian countries are often declared mentally ill and confined to hospitals in an attempt to quiet dangerous political criticism (Medvedev & Medvedev, 1971).

Such practices are not found only in foreign countries. In 1945 the famous American poet Ezra Pound, who was living in Italy, was brought back to the United States to stand trial for treason. He was accused of making anti-American radio broadcasts from Rome during World War II. But the court, prosecution, and defense, together with several psychiatrists, agreed that he was mentally unfit to stand trial. He was committed to St. Elizabeth's Mental Hospital in Washington, D.C., where he remained for the next 13 years. Although some have argued that confining Pound in a mental hospital helped him avoid an almost certain prison sentence, others suggest that declaring him "mentally ill" not only punished him for subversive conduct but also allowed the government to discount statements he had made that attempted to undermine the United States' war effort.

Nor is the political use of medicalization restricted to past history. A *Dallas Morning News* investigation discovered that high-ranking military commanders have tried to discredit and intimidate subordinates who report security and safety violations or military overpricing by ordering them to undergo psychiatric evaluations or by sending them to a mental ward (Timms & McGonigle, 1992). One West Point cadet spent a month in a psychiatric ward for reporting widespread illegal drug use at the academy. He met officer patients in the ward who had objected to Army policy and who were involuntarily receiving electric shock treatments. A chief petty officer in the Air Force contends that his forced hospitalization was part of a retaliation for reporting payroll abuses at Dallas Naval Air Station. He insightfully describes the power of medical labels to discredit his political criticism: "What happened was nobody would speak to me. Let's face it. After someone has gone to a mental ward, you kind of question what's going on. It was a nice ploy, and it worked. What they did was totally neutralize me" (quoted in Timms & McGonigle, 1992).

Portraying deviants as sick people who must be dealt with through medical therapies is a powerful way for dominant groups in society to maintain conformity and the status quo. The seemingly merciful medical labels not only reduce individual responsibility but also reduce the likelihood that such potentially contagious political behavior will be taken seriously (Hills, 1980).

Conclusion

When we talk about deviance, we usually speak of extreme forms: crime, mental illness, substance abuse, and so on. These activities are indeed troublesome, but for most people they remain comfortably distant phenomena. I think most of us would like to cling to the belief that deviants are "them" and normal people are "us."

The lesson I want you to take away from this chapter (and previous ones as well) is that the issue of deviance is, essentially, an issue of social definition. As a group, community, or society, we decide which differences are benign and which are devalued. Standards and expectations change. Norms come and go. The consequence is that each of us could be considered deviant to some degree by some audience. We have all broken unspoken interactional norms; many of us have even broken the law. To a lesser degree, we are all potential Gladys Burrs who can be erroneously labeled deviant and treated unfairly as a result. Given the right—or wrong—circumstances, all of us run the risk of being negatively labeled or acquiring a bad reputation.

This chapter has examined deviance as both a micro- and macro-sociological phenomenon. While sociologists are interested in the broad social and political processes that create cultural definitions of deviance, they are also interested in how these definitions are applied in everyday life. Societal definitions have their most potent effect when expressed on a face-to-face level. We can talk about powerful institutions like medicine creating definitions of deviance that are consistent with broader political or economic interests, but if these definitions aren't accepted as appropriate to some degree by most of us, they will be ineffectual. Again, we see evidence of the sociological imagination, the complex interplay between individuals and the culture and community within which they live.

CHAPTER HIGHLIGHTS

▪ According to an absolutist definition of deviance, there are two fundamental types of behavior: that which is inherently proper, good, and acceptable and that which is inherently improper, bad, and unacceptable. In contrast, a relativist definition of deviance suggests that deviance is not a property inherent in any particular act, belief, or condition. Instead, it is a definition of behavior that is socially created by collective human judgments. Hence, like beauty, deviance is in the eye of the beholder.

▪ According to conflict theory, the definition of deviance is a form of social control exerted by more powerful people and groups over less powerful ones.

▪ The labeling theory of deviance argues that deviance is a consequence of the application of rules and sanctions to an offender. Deviant labels can impede everyday social life by forming expectations in the minds of others.

▪ The criminal justice system and the medical profession have had a great deal of influence in defining, explaining, and controlling deviant behavior. Criminalization is the process by which certain behaviors come to be defined as crimes. Medicalization is the depiction of deviance as a medical problem or illness and the mandating or licensing of medical professionals to provide some kind of treatment for it.

YOUR TURN

People's perceptions of deviant acts and individuals are a crucial element of our understanding of deviance. From a conflict perspective, these perceptions are usually consistent with the goals and interests of those in power. But what exactly are people's perceptions of deviance?

Retype the list below and make copies. Find 20 to 30 people who would be willing to read the list and answer a few questions. Try to get an equal proportion of males and females and younger and older people. Have each person rank the following "deviant" acts in order from 1 to 15, with 15 being the most serious and 1 the least serious. Do not define for them what is meant by "serious."

- catching your spouse with a lover and killing them both
- embezzling your employer's funds
- robbing a supermarket with a gun
- forcibly raping a stranger in a park
- selling liquor to minors

- killing a suspected burglar in your home
- practicing medicine without a license
- soliciting for prostitution
- hitting your child
- selling cocaine
- manufacturing and selling cars known to have dangerous defects
- forcibly raping a former spouse
- being drunk in public
- killing a person for a fee
- fixing the prices of machines sold to businesses

After the volunteers are finished, ask them how they decided on their selections. What criteria did they use for judging the seriousness of each act? Where did their perceptions come from? Why do they think the "less serious" acts on the list are against the law?

After collecting all of your data, compute the average ranking for each of the 15 items. The larger the average score, the more the perceived seriousness of that act. Which acts were considered the most serious and which the least serious? Was there a fair amount of agreement among the people in your sample? Were there any differences between the ratings of men and women? Between older and younger people? Between people of different racial or ethnic groups? Using the conflict perspective, discuss the role these perceptions play in the nature and control of deviance.

[Note: The 15 items in this exercise are adapted from P. Rossi, E. Waite, C. E. Bose, and R. E. Berk, "The seriousness of crimes: Normative structure and individual differences," American Sociological Review, 39, *224–237, 1974.]*

GRAFFITI
Social Deviance or Art?

Photographs and concept by JAMES PRIGOFF

"…Sometimes as a form of deviant behavior becomes more common and sophisticated, it becomes part of the mainstream culture.…"

Most people would consider graffiti an ugly and harmful form of deviant expression that wantonly defaces property. Yet the deviant nature of graffiti is a matter of human judgment and evaluation. As you will see in the following pages, the identity of the individual or group responsible for creating graffiti may be more relevant to it being called "deviant" than the painted drawings or words themselves.

The world of the graffiti writer is a diverse subculture with its own well-defined language, roles, and standards of excellence. New York–style graffiti, and its artistic outgrowth, spraycan art, which originated in the train yards of New York City in the 1960s, has come to communicate

This mural is by "Twist" (Barry McGee), a graffiti artist in San Francisco.

Mural by Omega in Psycho City, 1991, San Francisco. Artists are Omega, Hex, Raevyn, Crayone, Picasso, Toons, Benz, and Ink.

Lask with his mural "Wine," 1985, Staten Island, New York.

everything from simple group identity and political ideology to messages about power, anger, and rebellion.

Is graffiti always deviant? What is the difference between the graffiti sprayed on a garbage truck, a commissioned mural carrying the name of a political candidate during a campaign, and a soft drink advertisement painted on the side of a city bus? Who gets to write and draw on public property?

Murals by Chico on the Lower East Side, New York City.

"I'm not out here to change the world. I just say what's on my mind. I see the whole city as my canvas. Wherever there is a wall, I just love to paint it."

—CARLOS "DZINE" ROLON, one of six artists featured in a graffiti artists' show in a museum in New Jersey

Painted by Apolonari, in Oakland, California.

> *"Kids call it tagging. To most adults, it is nothing but ugly, hostile graffiti, as unavoidable as a scream . . . insistent and rude as rap from a boom box. . . . Whatever else it is, this is lettering on public display, far different from the dismal scrawlings on a public toilet. This is script as stylized as the uniform of teen urban life—the bandanna, the baseball cap worn backwards, the Raiders football jacket."*
> —RICHARD RODRIGUEZ

> *"I write my name up there and then maybe paint a little extra picture around it and— KA POW!—I'm famous. It's a real rush."*
> —ALEX ALVAREZ, GRAFFITI PAINTER

Sometimes as a form of deviant behavior becomes more common and sophisticated, it becomes part of the mainstream culture. Here you can see how a graffiti artist who was once considered the prototypical urban vandal is now recognized and celebrated by the commercial art

Neon at the Oakland Amtrak line.

Phresh with his mural, 1984, Oakland, California.

The work of Twist on display at the San Jose Art Museum (1994) and on the wall of a building in San Francisco (see also the first image of this essay).

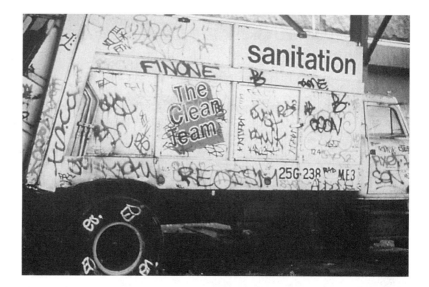

Youths without permission practice their calligraphy and design capability on this sanitation truck.

Jerry Brown commissioned Frame, a spraycan artist, to paint his name and a mural on the bus to advertise his presidential candidacy in 1991.

Corporate "graffiti": A Pepsi ad completely covers this San Francisco bus.

world. His work has been featured in San Francisco art shows and galleries.

Cities and private groups still try to fight graffiti, while conflicting messages are sent by mainstream culture. Graffiti, once the visual scourge of neighborhoods, has become another weapon in the financial arsenal of the corporate world.

Who has the right to write and draw on public property?

Cities and private groups still fight graffiti, while conflicting messages are sent by mainstream culture.

Chrysler created its own "graffiti": altered ads for its Plymouth Neon. The ads started out with a plain white background, an image of the car, and the simple message "Hi." In subsequent weeks, advertisers added letters, graffiti-style, to spell out "Hip" and "Chill." The outcry from anti-graffiti organizations prompted the public relations manager for the Chrysler corporation to issue a formal statement: "We don't promote or condone graffiti or the destruction of property. The campaign [has been] successful. It's given the car a personality."

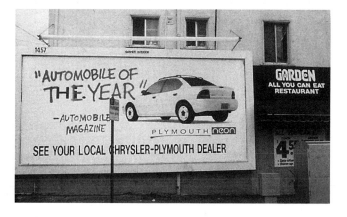

CHAPTER 8

Building Social Relationships: Groups and Families

- *Life in Groups*
- *Intimacy and Family*
- *Family and Social Structure*
- *Family Dilemmas*

So far, the 1990s have been a strange and highly public decade for social relationships. Over the past few years a number of events have aroused controversy and challenged social norms and values:

- Celebrities such as Jack Nicholson, Eddie Murphy, Madonna, and Warren Beatty, as well as one-fourth of all single American women between the ages of 18 and 44, became unwed parents.
- A South Carolina judge ordered a 15-year-old girl with a history of delinquency to be chained to her mother 24 hours a day, 7 days a week, for a month.
- In 1993 a Virginia woman made national headlines for months when she sliced off her husband's penis after he had allegedly repeatedly raped her. That same year, 3 to 4 million women were battered by their husbands.
- A 25-year-old Cincinnati man pleaded no contest to charges of "domestic violence" for punching his girlfriend in the mouth. As part of his sentence, the judge ordered the man to marry her within 9 months or risk jail. Said the judge, "I happen to believe in traditional American values. Boy meets girl, boy asks girl out, boy and girl go steady, boy and girl get married, and then boy and girl start raising a family. Maybe somebody needs to nudge them along to get married."
- A Texas mother who speaks only Spanish to her 5-year-old daughter at home was ordered by a judge to speak English to the child or risk losing custody.
- A 12-year-old boy hired a lawyer to sue his negligent parents for "divorce" and initially won, only to have the decision reversed on appeal.
- Several cities passed domestic partnership laws granting homosexual and cohabiting couples some of the same legal rights previously reserved for married couples. But in Richmond, Virginia, a mother lost custody of her 2-year-old son because she was a lesbian.

Some people see these events as proof of the demise of the "traditional" family and the breakdown of American society; others see them as a sign of the redefinition of family and other relationships in light of changing societal circumstances.

Like every other aspect of our individual lives, relationships must be understood within the broader contours of our society. We often fail to realize that laws, customs, and social institutions regulate what we can and can't do with our partners, relatives, friends, and associates (Cherlin, 1978). This chapter takes a sociological peek into the private and public aspects of social relationships. Specifically, it explores the role social relationships, including family, play in our daily lives and some of the social processes that take place within small groups. How are these relationships established? Why are they so important to us? How do societal factors like social institutions, gender, race, and social class affect our perceptions of intimacy and belonging? And why are the desirable aspects of these relationships so often outweighed by the negative, such as group conflict and family violence?

Life in Groups

Being a social being implies that groups play an important role in our lives. Most of us have a powerful need to belong. Consequently, much of our lives are spent with other people. We live with them, eat meals with them, learn with them, work with them, and often entertain ourselves in their presence. But for sociologists, just being in the company of others does not, in and of itself, constitute a group. The crowd that gathers to watch a street performer or watch police and paramedics tend to the victims of a car accident isn't really a group.

Most sociologists agree that groups have several features that distinguish them from other collections of people. First, members of a group usually have common goals and interests. Members of a Neighborhood Watch group, for instance, have the common goal of achieving safe streets. Second, group members interact with one another on a relatively regular basis. The interaction is usually face-to-face, but can be written or electronic. Third, groups have an identifiable structure consisting of statuses, relationships among statuses, norms, mechanisms for social control, and perhaps some form of leadership. Finally, groups provide members with a sense of identity and the feeling of belonging to something larger than a collection of people randomly interacting. The support and companionship we experience within groups helps explain their appeal as well as their influence on our thoughts and actions.

Desires and Difficulties in Social Relationships

Social relationships—whether they are between associates, friends, or family members—are the standard against which many of us judge the quality and happiness of our lives (Campbell, Converse, & Rodgers, 1976). We spend a tremendous amount of time worrying about present relationships, contemplating new ones, obsessing over past ones, or fretting over the fact that we are currently not part of one. Indeed, the search for a sense of belonging and intimacy has become one of the prime obsessions of the nineties. Popular magazines, self-help books, advice columns, supermarket tabloids, and television talk shows overflow with advice, warnings, and pseudoscientific analyses of every conceivable aspect of a relationship: forming new relationships, dealing with the people at work, maintaining relationships, finding the right mate, raising well-adjusted children, resolving conflict, ending relationships, and so on.

Ironically, at a time when we hunger for closeness and will sometimes pay tidy sums of money to get it, our social relationships are fraught with difficulty. In our complex, urban, and industrial society, we have become less integrated and connected to others. We're more mobile in our careers, more likely to relocate, and thus more likely to break ties with friends and fellow members of religious, sports, and social groups. The proportion of Americans who socialize with neighbors more than once a year has steadily declined over the last two decades. Membership in church-related groups, civic organizations (such as the Red Cross, Boy Scouts, and PTA), and fraternal organizations (such as the Lions, Elks, and Shriners) has likewise decreased. Between 1980 and 1993 the total number of bowlers in the United States increased by 10%, but team bowling in organized leagues *decreased* by 40% (Putnam, 1995). During the same period, the number of American adults living alone almost doubled; single people who have never married now make up about one-fourth of the adult population in this country (U.S. Bureau of the Census, 1994).

Some sociologists talk about how our culture's emphasis on individualism has taken away our sense of community, diminishing our ability to establish ties with others and making it easier for us to walk away from groups that we see as unfulfilling (Bellah et al., 1985; Sidel, 1986). In a national poll, 25% of Americans said that for $10 million they'd abandon their entire family (J. Peterson & Kim, 1991). The high value contemporary society places on individual achievement and success sometimes makes social relationships, even family relationships, seem expendable. Yet we still seem to value belonging and intimacy.

■ ■ ■ ■ ■ ■ ■ ■ ■
ROBERT WUTHNOW
The Quest for Community

Wanting to learn more about the ways people establish connections to others in such a potentially alienating environment, sociologist Robert Wuthnow conducted a national survey and face-to-face interviews with people who were deeply involved in small voluntary groups, such as special interest clubs, community associations, weight-control groups, Bible study groups, and book discussion groups (as well as a comparable sample of people who were not). He discovered that the depiction of Americans as "a society of lonely, self-interested individualists suffering from isolation, disrupted families, a lack of friends, difficulty in establishing intimate relationships, and the demeaning anonymity of large-scale institutions" does not provide a complete picture of contemporary social life (Wuthnow, 1994, p. 12).

Although it might be true that our family ties have become looser and that we're, perhaps, more inclined to fear our neighbors than to feel a common bond with them, we have been able to find meaningful relationships and a sense of community elsewhere. Wuthnow found that 40% of adults 18 and older living in the continental United States (roughly 75 million individuals) claim to be involved in "a small group that meets regularly and provides caring and support for those who participate in it" (p. 45). Thirty-eight percent of them are involved in at least two or three groups, and half have been involved for five years or more.

These small, intimate gatherings meet a variety of needs (see Table 8.1). Small groups have thus become a significant feature of what holds society together:

> [They] draw individuals out of themselves, pull them out of their isolated personal lives, and put them in the presence of others where they can share their needs and concerns, make friends, and become linked to wider social networks. Small groups provide a way of transcending our most self-centered interests; they temper our individualism and our culturally induced desire to be totally independent of one another. . . . Even amidst the dislocating tendencies of our society, [we] are capable of banding together in bonds of mutual support. (Wuthnow, 1994, p. 12)

Wuthnow points out that these groups function very much like families. Indeed, there are some obvious similarities between the two. Both involve relatively few people who interact intimately, both can involve strong emotional bonds, and both help to shape people's identities. But they are also different. Small group members typically don't share the heritage, physical traits, or personality characteristics that connect people in families. In addition, members of small groups don't bear legal responsibility for feeding, clothing, sheltering, educating, and providing medical support for others.

Small voluntary groups are also different from other social connections that have traditionally given people a sense of belonging, such as neighborhoods, ethnic groups, tribes, and so forth. These other forms of community generally have an important physical dimension: People live in the same area, see each other a lot in the course of their everyday lives, and identify themselves with various aspects of material culture such as buildings, streets, parks, food customs, and distinctive clothing. In the small groups Wuthnow studied, people from various locations and perhaps different subcultures come together regularly (on average, once a week) for group meetings.

So the sense of community we derive from membership in small groups, unlike families and neighborhoods, is something over which we have a great deal of

Table 8.1   *Meeting the Need for Community (Percentage of small-group members who have [A] felt each need and [B] met each need fully)*

	A	B
Having neighbors with whom you can interact freely and comfortably	93	43
Being able to share deepest feelings with someone	94	57
Having friends value the same things in life you do	98	58
Having people in your life who give you deep emotional support	98	66
Being in a group where you can discuss your most basic beliefs and values	90	50
Having friends you can always count on when you're in a jam	97	64
Having people in your life who are never critical of you	83	29
Being part of a group that helps you grow spiritually	90	53
Having cooperation rather than competition with people at work	85	31
Having people you can turn to when you feel depressed or lonely	96	62
Knowing more people in your community	95	32

Source: Wuthnow, 1994, p. 53.

control: It is intentional and voluntary. After all, we choose which groups we want to join, and we choose whether or not to attend a meeting. We may feel an obligation to provide emotional support and may even donate a lot of money and time to the group, but there are no serious, formal, legal responsibilities to do so.

Small voluntary groups have become an important element within established social institutions. Religious organizations, alarmed by shrinking memberships have made small groups a vital part of their programs. Many Jewish communities, for example, are experimenting with *havurot,* small informal gatherings in private homes, as a way of bringing people who have become disenchanted with traditional religious services back to the congregation. The more intimate settings of Bible study groups, support groups, youth ministries, and retreat centers are effective ways of encouraging both spiritual renewal and a sense of belonging.

Similarly, small supportive groups have sprung up in the workplace. Work is a sphere of life where we spend an increasing share of our waking hours. If we're lucky, we may have a few close friends there. But with work becoming more automated and computer-based, employees often don't even work in the same physical location anymore. The intentional formation of small groups helps to overcome feelings of loneliness and isolation. Some meet to discuss issues of common interest; others gather to accomplish specific tasks; still others provide emotional and spiritual support among co-workers.

In small voluntary groups, Americans seem to have found the sense of belonging and intimacy that is harder to come by these days from more traditional sources like families, civic organizations, and neighborhoods. While they are not perfect substitutes for such attachments, these groups have been able to grow in number and popularity, providing a source of intimacy, friendship, and support for millions of people.

■ ■ ■

Group Pressures toward Conformity

One of the ways in which groups exert influence on the actions of individuals is through the norms that develop within a group. Perhaps you've expressed an opinion or engaged in some behavior that met with disapproval from your friends or classmates. Or maybe you expressed an unpopular political sentiment at the dinner table, or dated someone your parents despised. If so, you certainly know the discomfort of standing out and violating the group's standards. Think of how others in the group showed their disapproval. Did they try to persuade you to think or behave otherwise, or did they simply ignore you and make you feel like an outcast?

In socializing members to a set of norms and values, groups often pressure their members to conform. Whenever a member says or does something that is out of line with group norms, other members may increase their communication with that person in an effort to change her or his mind (Rodin, 1985). If majority members lack the capability or desire to apply pressure to the person who is out of line, they may simply reject him or her, either blatantly or subtly (Schacter, 1951). Rejecting the "deviant" is a means of reestablishing equilibrium within the group and ensuring that its values and perceptions remain dominant. In so doing the group not only rids itself of a "troublemaker," it also reinforces the goodness of its beliefs.

Group Decision Making

Sometimes these sorts of group dynamics lead individuals to make terrible decisions. We've all had the experience of trying to come to a decision or solve a problem within a group setting. Maybe you were a member of the planning committee for the school prom or for the homecoming game festivities. Or maybe you've been in a club that had to come up with a budget. It would seem that a group of people working together would make effective, rational decisions. After all, the many viewpoints expressed by group members enhance the possibility of exploring the potential consequences of all options and weighing the relative value of each. The group can take advantage of the special expertise or knowledge of each member so that the best decision is ultimately reached.

But decision making doesn't always function so smoothly. Sometimes not all opinions are heard, or one or two people dominate the discussion. Or sometimes pressures to reach agreement and maintain good feelings lead the group to adopt a faulty decision that is promoted by a powerful and vocal individual whom the rest of the group members don't want to cross. All of these conditions are likely to create a situation in which a compromise is reached that satisfies no one.

Psychologist Irving Janis (1991) uses the term **groupthink** to describe the process whereby pressures to achieve a unanimous decision overwhelm individual members' motivation to weigh alternatives realistically. In an effort to achieve consensus, maintain good feelings among the group, or appease a leader, group members neglect critical thought and the weighing of pros and cons. Janis argues that groupthink is likely to occur when there is a crisis situation, when the group is tight-knit, when the members are insulated from the criticisms of qualified outsiders, and when a powerful leader actively promotes his or her favored solution. The group then comes to an unwise decision that might have been avoided had there been more discussion.

Some of the worst political decisions in history may have resulted from the harmful consequences of groupthink. President John F. Kennedy's failed Bay of Pigs invasion in 1961, Richard Nixon's Watergate cover-up, and Ronald Reagan's Iran-Contra scandal are examples of situations in which a small group of presidential advisers unfortunately suppressed their desire to disagree in favor of group unanimity and cohesiveness. One of the most striking and tragic cases of groupthink was the ill-fated decision to launch the space shuttle *Challenger*.

■ ■ ■ ■ ■ ■ ■ ■

GREGORY MOORHEAD, RICHARD FERENCE, AND CHRIS NECK
The Challenger *Disaster*

On January 28, 1986, the space shuttle *Challenger* was launched from Kennedy Space Center in Florida. The temperature that morning was in the mid-20s, well below the lowest temperature at which the rocket booster engines had been tested. Seventy-three seconds after lift-off, the shuttle exploded, killing all seven passengers—six astronauts and one civilian.

The presidential commission investigating the incident concluded that flawed decision making during meetings the night before was the primary contributing cause of the accident. How could such smart, well-intentioned people make such a disastrous decision? Researcher Greg Moorhead and his colleagues (Moorhead, Ference, & Neck, 1991) reviewed the notes of these meetings to see if groupthink had played a part.

The meetings took place throughout the day and evening of January 27. Those involved—known as "The Level I Flight-Readiness Review Panel"—consisted of NASA representatives from the Johnson Space Center in Houston and the Kennedy Space Center in Florida and engineers from Morton Thiokol, Inc., in Utah (manufacturers of the crucial O-ring seals). At 8:45 P.M. the Morton Thiokol engineers on the panel, fearful of a malfunction under untested temperatures, recommended not to launch. Usually such expressions of doubt would have been enough to postpone the mission. But their warnings went unheeded, and through the ensuing discussions, the fateful decision to launch was made.

Was groupthink responsible? One of the conditions under which groupthink occurs is that the group is close and highly cohesive. Although much of the deliberation occurred over the telephone and some panel participants were new to the process, others had worked together before. They knew each other quite well and had worked their way up the ranks of the space program together. There was a high level of esprit de corps among them.

A second condition is that there is a group leader (or leaders) who energetically states and defends his or her position. In this case two top-level managers from NASA actively promoted their pro-launch opinions in the face of any opposition. They had a preferred decision in mind and promoted it rather than critically weighing the alternatives. They tended to focus on supportive information and ignore any information that may have reflected negatively on their position. In addition, they constructed elaborate rationalizations that discounted the earlier warnings, ultimately convincing themselves and the rest of the panel that the engineers' data were inconclusive.

Finally, groupthink is likely to occur when those promoting the opposing position are effectively neutralized. The Morton Thiokol engineers who made the negative recommendations were not even present or consulted when the final decision to launch was made. Neither did the panel seek the opinions of others outside the group who may have had expertise in the area. Curiously, the role the engineers played was quite different from their role in past launch-readiness meetings. Ordinarily they would be called on to prove with 100% certainty that the shuttle was ready. The slightest doubt would be sufficient to postpone the project. In this case, however, the engineers were forced to show beyond all doubt that the booster rockets were unsafe. That is, they were told to prove with 100% certainty that the rockets would fail. Without the appropriate data—remember, the engines had not been tested at temperatures this low—they could not prove conclusively that a failure would occur. Hence their objections were dismissed.

Other external circumstances enhanced the groupthink effect. The panel was under strong pressure from the public and the government to launch on time. A delay would have been a public relations disaster. The launch had already been postponed once, and the window of opportunity for another launch was closing fast. Panel members feared that further delays could actually affect future congressional funding for the entire space program. Under such pressures to make a decision quickly, the groupthink effect was magnified.

The decision to launch the *Challenger* can be classified as a groupthink situation, although with some modifications. It wasn't necessarily a strong group desire for agreement that led to the tragic decision. Instead it was the system, the organization, the political pressures, and the culture surrounding high-risk technology that created an environment in which the possibility of a flawed decision was high (Vaughan, 1996). This analysis has important implications for all group decision-making situations. Powerful group pressures and norms can induce members toward agreement and away from rational debate.

▪ ▪ ▪

Intimacy and Family

Groups are obviously important to social functioning. But of all the groups in our lives, the most important is the family. Family, considered one of the major social institutions, provides the relationships that give us a sense of identity and personal history. Perhaps no facet of human existence is more familiar to us or occupies more time, effort, and emotion. Most of us spend our childhood and adolescence in some kind of family, go through the sometimes painful rituals of dating, fall in love, and become spouses, parents, and grandparents. Many of us have seen the dark side of these relationships, too: divorce, abuse, and violence.

Historical Trends in Family Life

Many functionalist sociologists have voiced concern over the current state of the American family as an important social institution. Over time, they argue, the family has been losing many, if not all, of its traditional functions (Lasch, 1977). Historically, the family was the center of many important activities. It was where children received most of their education and religious training. It was where both children and adults could expect to receive emotional nurturance and support. It was the institution that regulated sexual activity and reproduction. And it was also the economic center of society, where family members worked together to earn a living and support one another financially.

But as our economy shifted from a system based on small, privately owned agricultural enterprises to one based on massive industrial manufacturing, so did the role of the family. Economic production moved from the home to the factory, and families became more dependent on the money that members earned outside the home. The teaching of skills and values that were once a part of everyday home life began to take place almost exclusively in the schools. Even the family's role as a source of emotional security and nurturance disappeared as it became less able to shield its members from the harsh realities of modern life (Lasch, 1977).

For all these reasons many people in this country, from research scholars to politicians to everyday people on the street, are concerned about the survival of the contemporary American family. As anxiety over the future of the American family escalates, calls for a return to the "good ol' days" of family life become louder. The belief in a lost "golden age" of family has led people to depict the present as a period of rapid decline and inevitable family breakdown (Coontz, 1992; Hareven, 1992; Skolnick, 1991). However, although concern over the state of the family is particularly acute today, it is important to realize that each succeeding generation of Americans from the time of the Puritans to the late 20th century has been concerned about a "crisis of the family" (Hareven, 1992; Skolnick, 1991).

According to sociologist William Goode (1971), the traditional family of the past that we speak so fondly of and want to re-create never existed. He calls our idealized image of the past "the classical family of Western nostalgia":

> It is a pretty picture of life down on grandma's farm. There are lots of happy children, and many kinfolk live together in a large rambling house. Everyone works hard. Most of the food to be eaten during the winter is grown, preserved, and stored on the farm. . . . Father is stern and reserved and has the final decision in all important matters. . . . All boys and girls marry, and marry young. . . . After marriage, the couple lives harmoniously, either near the boy's parents or with them. . . . No one divorces. (p. 624)

Like most stereotypes, this one is not altogether accurate. Because 19th-century adults had a shorter life expectancy than adults today, children were actually more likely to live in a single-parent home at that time due to the death of a parent (Kain, 1990). Although more than 20% of American children live in poverty today, about the same proportion lived in orphanages at the turn of the century, and not just because their parents had died. Many were there because their parents simply couldn't afford to raise them. Rates of alcohol and drug abuse, school dropouts, and domestic violence were all higher a century ago than they are today (cited in Coontz, 1992).

Perhaps the most pervasive myth is that of the **extended family**—several generations living under the same roof. Today's more isolated **nuclear family**, consisting only of mother, father, and children, is often compared unfavorably to the image of the huge, happy family of the past with its massive and perpetually available support network. Research shows, however, that the American family has always been fairly small (Blumstein & Schwartz, 1983; W. J. Goode, 1971; Hareven, 1992). There is no strong tradition in this country of large extended families. In fact, the highest proportion of extended family households ever recorded in this country was only around 20%, between 1850 and 1885 (Hareven, 1978). Because people didn't live as long as they do today, most died before ever seeing their grandchildren. Even in the 1700s the typical family consisted of a husband, a wife, and approximately three children.

When households of the past were large, it was probably due to the presence of nonfamily members: servants, apprentices, boarders, and visitors. The reduction in household size over the last several centuries was not due to a decline in the number of extended relatives but to a decrease in nonfamily members, a reduction in the number of children in a family, and an increase in young adults living alone (Kobrin, 1976).

As people immigrated to the United States from countries like China or Italy that did have a tradition of extended families, their first order of business was to surrender their extended families so they could create their own households. Reducing the size of their families was seen as a clear sign that they had "become" Americans. Large, multigenerational families simply didn't make economic sense anymore. Being geographically mobile with a family of 12 would be next to impossible.

In addition, it's not at all clear that today's family is as isolated as some people make it out to be. More Americans than ever have grandparents alive, and the ties between grandparents and grandchildren may be stronger than ever. Today, most adults see or talk to a parent on the phone at least once a week (Coontz, 1992). Extended family members may not live under the same roof, but they do stay in contact and provide advice, emotional support, and financial help when needed (Cicirelli, 1983).

Another oft-cited indicator of the demise of the American family that is based on faulty conceptions of the past is the current high divorce rate. Most of us assume that the divorce rate in this country was always very low until it accelerated with unprecedented speed during the 1960s and 1970s. To many observers it seemed that the intact middle-class lifestyle depicted in 1950s television shows like "Ozzie and Harriet," "Father Knows Best," and "Leave It to Beaver" had crumbled away forever. The rise in the divorce rate was attributed to the free love movement of "swinging singles, open marriages, alternative lifestyles, and women's liberation" (Skolnick, 1991). True, this era was a revolutionary period in American history. Norms governing all aspects of social life were certainly changing.

What these conclusions overlook, however, is the longer historical trend in American divorce. People were comparing divorce rates in the 1960s and 1970s to the abnormally low rate of the 1950s—the so-called baby boom years. From this narrow perspective the divorce rate did, indeed, shoot up. But divorce in this country had been increasing steadily since 1900. It rose sharply right after World War II, most likely because of short courtships before the young men shipped out and the stress of separation. In the 1950s the rate dropped just as sharply. The high divorce rates of the 1960s and 1970s, then, represented a return to a national trend that had been developing since the turn of the century (see Figure 8.1).

Furthermore, the rate of "hidden" marital separation a hundred years ago was probably not that much less than the rate of "visible" separation today (Sennett, 1984). For financial or religious reasons, divorce was not an option for many people a century ago. A significant number turned to the functional equivalents of divorce—desertion and abandonment—which have been around for centuries. Although the divorce rate may have been lower in the past, families found other ways to break up.

Figure 8.1   *Historical Trends in American Divorce (Annual divorce rate, United States: for 1920–1988, divorces per 1,000 married women aged 15 and over; for 1860–1920, divorces per 1,000 existing marriages)*

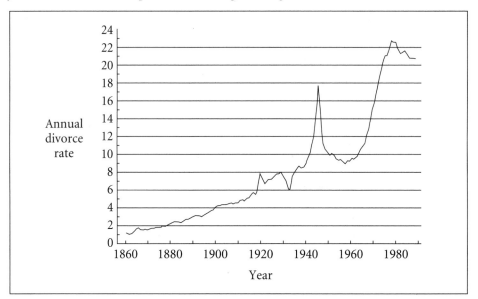

Source: Cherlin, 1992.

In sum, the image of a warm, secure, stable family life in past times is at odds with the actual history of the American family (Skolnick, 1991). We have a heritage of challenge and crisis. By glorifying a mythical and idealized past, we artificially limit ourselves to an inaccurate image of what we think a "normal" family ought to look like.

The Culture of Intimacy and Family

Family attitudes and behaviors are also influenced by culture. Families can be found in every human society, and they are all designed to address similar societal needs: regulating sexual behavior, creating new members of society to replace those who die, and protecting and socializing the young. The way families go about meeting these needs—their structure, customs, patterns of authority, and so on—differ widely across cultures. Thus our own definition of what constitutes a family is culturally determined.

Cultural Variation in Family Practices

Most of us take for granted that **monogamy**, the marriage of one man and one woman, is the fundamental building block of the family. Some families do exist without a married couple, and some people may have several spouses over their lifetimes. But there is no denying that the monogamous marriage is an integral part of our image of the family.

Monogamous marriage continues to be the only adult intimate relationship that is legally recognized, culturally approved, and endorsed by the Internal Revenue Service. It is still the one relationship in which sexual activity is not only acceptable but expected. Monogamous marriage, like the family in general, is an institution, a patterned way of life that includes a set of commonly known roles, statuses, and expectations:

> People know about it; they can describe it; and they have spent a lifetime learning how to react to it. The *idea* of marriage is larger than any individual marriage. The *role* of husband or wife is greater than any individual who takes on that role [emphasis in original]. (Blumstein & Schwartz, 1983, p. 318)

No other relationship has achieved such status. Despite its current state of disrepair and public concern with its disintegration, monogamous marriage remains the pinnacle of committed intimacy. It is the cultural standard against which all other types of intimate relationships are judged. For instance, the campaign to legally recognize permanent homosexual relationships is, in essence, a campaign to elevate those unions to the status of marriage.

It is hard to imagine a society that is not structured around the practice of monogamy, but many cultures allow an individual to have several husbands or wives at the same time. This type of marriage is called **polygamy**. Some anthropologists estimate that about 75% of the world's societies prefer some type of polygamy, although few members within those societies actually have the resources to afford more than one spouse (Murdock, 1957; Nanda, 1994). Even in the United States, certain groups practice polygamy. Approximately 50,000 members of a dissident Mormon sect in Colorado, Utah, and Arizona live in households made up of a man with two or more wives (D. Johnson, 1991).

Cultures differ in other taken-for-granted facets of family life. Take living arrangements, for example. In our society, families tend to be **neolocal**—that is, we expect young married couples to establish households separate from their respective families when financially possible. Cross-culturally, however, this arrangement is somewhat uncommon. Only about 5% of the world's societies are neolocal (Murdock, 1957; Nanda, 1994). In most societies married couples live with or near either the husband's relatives (**patrilocal residence**) or the wife's relatives (**matrilocal residence**).

The belief that members of a nuclear family ought to live together is not found everywhere either. Among the Kipsigis of Kenya, for instance, the mother and children live in one house while the father lives in another. The Kipsigis are polygamous, so a man might have several homes for his several wives at one time (Stephens, 1963). Among the Thonga of southern Africa, children live with their grandmothers once they stop breastfeeding. They remain there for several years and are then returned to their parents. On the traditional Israeli kibbutz, or commune, children were raised not by their parents but in an "infants' house," where they were cared for by a trained nurse (Nanda, 1994).

Child-rearing philosophies vary cross-culturally as well. As I discussed in chapter 4, most Americans believe that young children are inherently helpless and dependent. We feel that if parents attend to the child's drives and desires with consistency and affection, that child will learn to trust them, adopt their values, develop a sturdy self-concept, and turn out to be a well-rounded, normal individual. In contrast, the traditional Japanese parent views the young infant not as dependent and helpless, but as a willful creature whose natural instincts need to be tamed (Kagan, 1976). Any excitement on the part of the child must be suppressed. In the highlands of Guatemala, parents believe that their child's personality is determined by the date of birth. The parents are almost entirely uninvolved in the child's life, standing aside so he or she can grow as nature intended. In many societies—Nigeria, Russia, Haiti, the Dominican Republic, and Mexico, to name a few—parents think the best way to teach children to be respectful and studious is to beat them. In contrast, most American child development experts believe that hitting children can deaden the child's spirit and lead to violence later in life (Dugger, 1996c). Despite these dramatic differences, most children in all these cultures grow up equally well adapted to their societies.

The American Definition of Family

In our society the *official* definition of family, as used by the U.S. Census Bureau, is "two or more persons, including the householder, who are related by birth, marriage, or adoption, and who live together as one household." If we accept this narrow definition, then other arrangements—homosexual relationships, nonmarital cohabitation, and various forms of group living—cannot be considered families in the strict sense of the word. They become deviant lifestyles that require condemnation, alternative arrangements that require tolerance, or sociological curiosities that require explanation. Nevertheless, the structure of American households is quite diverse, as shown in Figure 8.2.

This definition has many practical implications. Things like inheritance rights, insurance coverage, eligibility to live in certain apartment complexes, savings from joint tax returns, and even visitation rights in prisons and hospital intensive care units are determined by marital or family status. Members of other kinds of relationships are not eligible. In 1990 a woman whose lesbian partner had died of cancer charged AT&T (her deceased lover's employer) with discrimination for refusing to pay her the same death benefits it would have paid to a surviving spouse. In her suit she claimed that her relationship was as much a marriage as any heterosexual union. She and her lover had even formalized their relationship in a 1977 ceremony where they exchanged vows and rings in the company of parents and friends. They bought a house together where they raised

Figure 8.2   *Diversity of American Households*

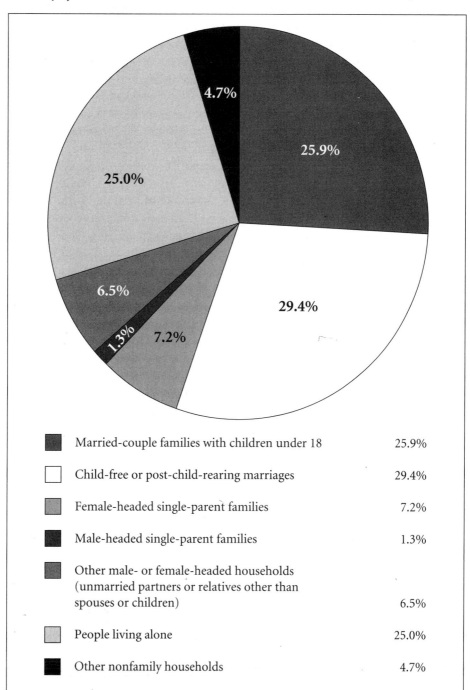

■	Married-couple families with children under 18	25.9%
□	Child-free or post-child-rearing marriages	29.4%
■	Female-headed single-parent families	7.2%
■	Male-headed single-parent families	1.3%
■	Other male- or female-headed households (unmarried partners or relatives other than spouses or children)	6.5%
▨	People living alone	25.0%
■	Other nonfamily households	4.7%

Source: Lamanna & Riedmann, 1994.

her children from a previous marriage. AT&T said its benefits were for legal spouses only, and since the law did not recognize homosexual unions, neither did the company (Lewin, 1990).

Most Americans still perceive homosexual unions as a threat to the "family" (Weston, 1991). According to a recent poll, nearly 70% of Americans oppose homosexual marriages (cited in "Marriage and divorce," 1996). Currently no state legally recognizes them. In 1995, Utah passed a law banning same-sex marriages. Delaware and South Carolina followed suit in 1996, and similar bills were considered by legislatures in several other states. Hawaiian courts were asked to decide the constitutionality of the state's policy of refusing to issue marriage licenses to same-sex couples. A similar case in Florida was on hold, pending the outcome of the Hawaii case. At the national level, in 1996 the U.S. Congress approved a measure formally reaffirming the definition of marriage as the union of one man and one woman, authorizing all states to refuse to accept same-sex marriages from other states if they ever became legal, and denying federal pension, health, and other benefits to same-sex couples.

Nevertheless, there have been some noteworthy attempts at the local level to recognize homosexual unions. In San Francisco, gay couples can register their relationships with the city and declare that they have "an intimate, committed relationship of mutual caring," that they live together, and that they agree to be responsible for each other's basic living expenses. Similar laws have been enacted in the state of Vermont and in cities such as West Hollywood, California; Ithaca, New York; and Madison, Wisconsin. The city of Seattle, Washington, extends full medical, dental, and life insurance benefits to the "domestic partners" of city workers. In addition, several large organizations, including Sony, Walt Disney, Ben & Jerry's, Lotus, Apple Computer, the University of Chicago, and the American Sociological Association now grant "domestic partners" the same benefits traditionally granted to spouses, such as health insurance, pension benefits, employee discounts, and health club membership (J. L. Griffin, 1993). In 1996, a circuit court judge in Oregon ruled that a university was guilty of discrimination for denying medical, life, and dental insurance benefits to the domestic partners of three gay employees.

Heterosexual cohabitors have also faced difficulty. Between 1970 and 1993 the number of cohabiting couples increased 600%, growing from 523,000 to 3.5 million (U.S. Bureau of the Census, 1994). But although public attitudes have grown more tolerant of unmarried adults living together (Spanier, 1989), the law has been slower to adjust. In 1986 a state appeals court in St. Louis ruled that a couple could be ousted from their jointly owned house, citing an ordinance prohibiting an unmarried man and woman from living together. The court stated, "There is no doubt that there is a governmental interest in marriage and in preserving the integrity of the biological or legal family" ("Court rules city," 1986).

Obviously, whatever a culture decides to define as the legitimate characteristics of a family has important consequences for people's lives.

Family and Social Structure

As a social institution, family is connected to other institutions in important ways. The legal, political, economic, and religious forces that shape society influence and are influenced by the actions of individuals within family relationships. In addition, issues of gender and social diversity are strongly related to family relationships.

Law and Politics

The relationship between the family and the law is obvious. Marriage, for instance, is a legal contract. Each state determines the legal age at which two people can marry, the health requirements, the length of the waiting period required before marriage, rules determining inheritance, and the division of property in case of divorce (Baca-Zinn & Eitzen, 1996). In the case of homosexual unions, the law's power to either forbid or grant family rights and privileges is especially obvious.

Politics and family are interconnected in other ways as well. Many of today's most pressing political issues—affordable child care, parental leave, teen pregnancy, the aging population, abortion, homelessness, poverty—are fundamentally family problems. For example, abortion didn't become a significant political issue until the late 1960s, when it became part of the larger movement for women's rights and reproductive freedom. Later the right-to-life movement framed the abortion debate not only as a moral and political issue but also as a symbolic crusade to define (or redefine) the role of motherhood and family within the larger society (Luker, 1984).

Family has taken on enormous symbolic importance in social life and has become a highly emotional political buzzword. Over the past two decades many politicians have defined as one of their primary goals the restoration of "traditional family values." In the 1996 presidential election, debate over the needs of families became the focus of national politics. What exactly "traditional" or "family" means in the context of such debates is never made clear.

Strictly speaking, the term "traditional family" refers to persons living together who are related by blood, marriage, or adoption. Politically, however, the term usually has more to do with family authority, the moral obligations of parenting and marital commitment, and sexual expression (Hunter, 1991). Conservative critics deplore not only the greater visibility of cohabiting and homosexual couples but also the increasing numbers of single and working mothers and rising rates of divorce. Despite all the political rhetoric, however, women are still raising children alone, wives and mothers still remain in the workplace, sex has not been confined to marriage, and gays have not returned to the closet (Skolnick, 1991).

Religion

The fundamental purpose of religion is to constrain or at the very least encourage members to act in certain ways. This normative aspect of religion has important consequences for people's family experiences. Almost universally, religions prohibit sexual relations outside marriage. Some religions prohibit divorce or don't permit remarriage after divorce. Some oppose the use of contraceptives and encourage large families. In highly religious families, the Bible may serve not only as a source of faith but as a literal guidebook for every aspect of family life (Ammerman, 1987).

But the link between religious beliefs and actual family behavior may not be as strong as we might think. Even in highly religious families, the practical demands of modern life make it difficult to subscribe to the teachings of the Bible. For instance, although Fundamentalist Christians believe wives should stay at home and submit to the authority of their husbands, many fundamentalist women do work outside the home and exert powerful influence over family decisions (Ammerman, 1987). Moreover, although many religions stress the value of keeping families intact, increased religious involvement does not do much to strengthen troubled marriages. Recent research has found little support for this idea (Booth et al., 1995). Increased religious involvement does seem to slightly decrease thoughts about divorce, but it doesn't enhance marital happiness or stop spouses from fighting.

Economics

The world of economics affects virtually every aspect of family life, from the amount of money coming in to the day-to-day management of finances and major purchasing decisions. Money matters are closely related to feelings of satisfaction within intimate relationships. When couples are disappointed with how much money they have or how it is spent, they find all aspects of their relationships less satisfying (Blumstein & Schwartz, 1983).

Such financial problems are not just private troubles. Rather they are directly linked to larger economic patterns. Major alterations in an economy almost always have a profound impact on the family. The average wage for full-time male workers dropped from $34,048 in 1973 to $30,407 in 1993. Yet children need ever-more-costly educations for ever-longer periods of time. No wonder it has become increasingly difficult to support a family. About a third of all men between the ages of 25 and 34 don't earn enough to keep a family of four out of poverty (Thurow, 1995).

In addition, many contemporary economists say that in order to sustain a viable national economy, we as a nation must "tolerate" a certain amount of unemployment (see Lekachman, 1991). Although this policy may make good economic sense, it does nothing for those who lose their jobs and are without sufficient income to support their families.

At the global level, the competitive pressures of the international capitalist marketplace have forced many businesses and industries to make greater use of so-called disposable workers—those who work part-time or on temporary contract. These jobs offer no benefits and no security and therefore import instability directly into family life (Kilborn, 1993; Uchitelle, 1993). Other companies are reducing costs by cutting salaries, laying off workers, or encouraging early retirement. Some businesses are relocating either to other countries or to other parts of the United States where they can pay lower wages (see chapter 10 for a more detailed discussion). More than 1,100 U.S.-owned manufacturing plants, including some run by Ford, General Motors, RCA, and Zenith, are now located in northern Mexico (Baca-Zinn & Eitzen, 1993). The companies obviously benefit, but displaced American workers and their families do not.

Financial uncertainty makes a stable family life very difficult. It is nearly impossible to sustain a supportive, nurturant family environment without adequate income or health insurance. When economic foundations are weak, the emotional bonds that tie a family together can be stretched to the breaking point (Newman, 1988).

▪ ▪ ▪ ▪ ▪ ▪ ▪ ▪
MICRO-MACRO CONNECTION
Dual-Earner Parents

One of the most significant economic facts to emerge in the late 20th century is that in most families both partners must work. The financial strains of modern living make it virtually impossible for young couples to survive on only one income. In 1990, 54% of families with at least one child under the age of 6 had two working parents. That figure is up from 32% in 1976. Of those families with children between the ages of 6 and 10, 68% consist of an employed mother and father (U.S. Bureau of the Census, 1991a). The dual-earner family is now the most common type of American family. Only about 14% of American families include married couples that have only one worker outside the home (Kain, 1990).

Nevertheless, society, for the most part, is still built around the outdated belief that only one partner (typically the father) in a couple should be working. Hence affordable child care and maternity and paternity leave are woefully inadequate to serve the needs of most young working couples who are just beginning their families. As recently as 1990, only 52% of the nation's largest companies had some form of maternity leave guaranteeing that an employee would not lose her job by taking time off to have a baby (Aldous & Dumon, 1990). Even those couples in which both partners have successful careers must come to grips with both the demands of the organization that employs them and the lack of social support for family relationships (Hertz, 1986). A recent survey of 1,000 people in dual-earner families found that 28% of them had made a voluntary lifestyle change involving a drastic reduction in earnings, such as moving to a less stressful job or turning down a promotion (cited in Smolowe, 1996).

The dilemma is felt most strongly when parenting and work responsibilities come into conflict. For example, a 32-year-old Minnesota woman was fired from her job as an accounting clerk at a computer company because she had to stay home from work frequently to care for her sick baby, who had a series of illnesses. The company stated that she missed almost half the work time from January to May of 1990. The state commissioner of jobs and training said she was not eligible for unemployment benefits because she had "voluntarily" put family interests ahead of her employer's interests, a choice amounting to misconduct (Lewin, 1991). The woman's husband was unable to care for the child, and all her nearby relatives worked. In addition, she said, most day care providers do not accept sick children and the cost of bringing somebody into the home to care for the child was far too expensive. Eventually an appeals court overturned the denial of benefits, ruling that her absenteeism was beyond her control and therefore did not amount to misconduct.

In 1993 President Clinton signed into law a bill that guarantees workers up to 12 weeks of unpaid family leave per year to care for a new child or a sick relative. This law represents a noteworthy shift in the government's position on the dual-earner family, but it has some important qualifications that seriously limit its applicability to a significant proportion of the population. First of all, the law covers only workers who have been employed continuously for at least one year and who work at least 25 hours a week. As a result, temporary contract workers would not be eligible. In addition, the law exempts companies with fewer than 50 workers; hence, only about 40% of the American workforce is covered. Some critics fear that companies with exactly 50 employees might be motivated to dismiss a single employee to avoid the requirement. Finally, the law allows an employer to deny leave to any employee who is in the highest-paid 10% of its workforce, if allowing that person to take the leave would create "substantial and grievous injury" to business operations.

By comparison, the United States' two major economic competitors, Germany and Japan, have family leave policies with no such conditions. Each country guarantees a minimum of 3 months of paid family leave to all employees regardless of the size of their employer. Additional unpaid leave is available if it is needed (Shanker, 1990). In Sweden, pregnant women are given 8 weeks of paid leave *before* the baby is born, and either parent can remain at home for up to 9 months after the child is born while drawing 90% of his or her salary (Kamerman, 1985; Sidel, 1986). Swedish parents are allowed to take time off, with pay, to care for sick children up to the age of 12 (B. Cohen, 1991).

▪ ▪ ▪

Gender

We cannot talk about historical, cultural, and institutional influences on the family without discussing the role of gender. Gender roles in the family are certainly changing. But men and women are still likely to enter relationships with vastly different expectations, desires, and goals. Gender explains a variety of phenomena in intimate relationships, such as the way people talk to one another, how they express themselves sexually, how they deal with conflict, and what they feel their responsibilities are. As a result, gender influences how men and women go about creating, maintaining, and thinking about family relationships.

It is often argued that the traditional gender-role socialization of women emphasizes sensitivity, the expression of affection, and the revelation of weakness, whereas men are taught to be competitive, strong, and emotionally inexpressive. Research has consistently shown that women have more close friends than men and are more romantic in their intimate relationships (Perlman & Fehr, 1987). Furthermore, there is a great deal of support for the contention that women are more concerned about, attentive to, and aware of the dynamics of their relationships than men are (for example, Fincham & Bradbury, 1987; Rusbult, Zembrodt, & Iwaniszek, 1986). They even think more and talk more about their relationships than men do (Acitelli, 1988; Holtzworth-Munroe & Jacobson, 1985).

Ironically, such attentiveness and concern do not necessarily mean that women get more out of family relationships than men do. In fact, the opposite may be true. According to one sociologist, every marriage actually contains two marriages: "his" and "hers"—and "his" seems to be the better deal (Bernard, 1972). Married men derive more satisfaction from marriage than married women do (Skolnick, 1981). Marriage even seems to benefit men's health and well-being. Married men get sick less, live longer, and have fewer emotional problems than single men (Gove, Style, & Hughes, 1990; Ross, Mirowsky, & Goldstein, 1990).

Women's family experiences can be quite different. Because of the continued pressures of gender-typed family responsibilities, women are more likely than men to experience the stresses associated with parenthood and running the house. Three times as many married as single women show signs of anxiety, depression, and emotional distress (Carr, 1988). Wives are more likely to suffer some loss of identity. Not only do most women still change their names upon marrying but their careers often become secondary to those of their husbands. In most states, husbands still have the legal right to decide where the couple will live after marriage (Renzetti & Curran, 1989).

Social Diversity

Another influential factor in people's family lives is their membership in important social groups. Religious, racial and ethnic, and social class differences in family structure, sexual division of labor, child rearing, and so on have been well documented (for example, L. Rubin, 1976; Shon & Ja, 1992; Staples & Mirande, 1980).

The increasing ethnic diversity of the American population is likely to alter our conceptions of the "typical" family in the years to come. Whether American families in the future become more similar or more diverse depends on whether the formation of families across racial, religious, or social class lines becomes more common than it is today.

Unlike some countries, such as India and Pakistan, where marriages are arranged by families with little thought given to the compatibility or shared affection of the partners, the choice of marital partners in the United States is supposedly more open, a matter of personal preference. Most of us assume that we have the freedom to become attracted to whomever we please and that love is all that is needed to establish a fulfilling, long-lasting relationship. But our intimate choices are far from free and private. The choices we make regarding whom to date, live with, or marry are governed by two important social rules that limit the field of eligible partners: exogamy and endogamy.

Exogamy specifies that an individual must marry outside certain groups. In almost all societies, exogamy rules prohibit people from marrying members of their own nuclear family—siblings, parents, and children. Rules of exogamy extend to certain people outside the nuclear family to include cousins, grandparents, and, in some societies, stepsiblings.

Less obvious are the rules of **endogamy**, which is marriage within one's social group. The vast majority of intimate relationships in this country occur between people from the same religion, race, and social class. Although these similar backgrounds increase the likelihood that the two people will share common beliefs, values, and experiences, rules of endogamy reflect our society's traditional distaste for relationships that cross group boundaries.

Religion

Today, approximately 20% of all marriages occur between people of different religions (Glenn, 1982). Most religions actively discourage interfaith marriages out of a concern that such marriages may weaken people's religious beliefs and values, lead to the raising of children in a different faith, or take religion out of the family entirely. Religious leaders are often concerned about the bigger problem of maintaining their ethnic identity within a diverse and complex society (M. M. Gordon, 1964).

Among those religions whose numbers are already small, the phenomenon of interfaith marriage is particularly urgent and troublesome. It is perceived as a dangerous and ever-growing force that threatens to destroy a culture and heritage. For instance, it is estimated that about 40% of American Jews marry non-Jews, up from 6% in the early 1960s (Krantowitz & Witherspoon, 1987). Many Jewish leaders fear that the outcome of this growing trend will be not only the shrinking of the Jewish population but also the erosion and perhaps extinction of an entire way of life. They believe that the survival of American Jewry itself depends on maintaining the integrity of traditional Jewish values and institutions. Interfaith marriage is not just a matter of individual prerogative but a shirking of one's responsibility to the larger group.

Race and Ethnicity

In the United States, race and ethnicity are associated with some differences in family structure. For example, compared to African-American and Hispanic families, white families tend to have a higher household income, fewer children, and a higher proportion of two-parent households (Baca-Zinn & Eitzen, 1993). African-American and Hispanic families, however, have greater access to emotional and economic support from extended family and friendship support networks than do white families (R. J. Taylor et al., 1990; Vega, 1990). This society has a particularly strong aversion to relationships that cross racial lines. Although not always enforced, laws forbidding marriage and sexual contact between whites and other racial groups—Asian Americans, African Americans, and Native Americans—existed in most states until 1967, when the Supreme Court ruled that they were unconstitutional (Spickard, 1989). Usually, the interracial marriages would simply be declared null and void, but in certain cases couples were imprisoned, sometimes for 2 years or more.

Although still infrequent—they constitute a little over 1% of all marriages—interracial marriages have more than tripled since 1970, according to the U.S. Bureau of the Census (Mathews, 1996). However, we still experience massive discomfort over the thought of interracial relationships. Some couples, fearful of family ostracism, never tell their own parents that they are married and have children. Others suffer blatant indignities such as being spat on or refused services. According to one researcher, "Interracial relationships have not passed the 'no blink' test. It's clear that the majority of whites are not prepared to accept this as just another couple. The minimum you get is a look and a stare" (quoted in Wilkerson, 1991a). One in five whites still believes interracial marriage should be illegal. Sixty-six percent say they would oppose a close relative's marriage to a black person. Only 4% say they would favor it.

Social Class

There are also strong pressures on people to marry within their social class (Carter & Glick, 1976; Kalmijn, 1994). Even if two individuals from different races or religions marry, chances are they will have similar socioeconomic backgrounds. Certainly some people do marry others from different social classes, but the classes tend to be adjacent ones—for instance, an upper-class woman marrying a middle-class man. Marriages that take place between people of vastly different class rankings are quite rare. The reason is that individuals from similar social classes are likely to come into contact and share values, tastes, goals, expectations, and educational background.

Our education system plays an important role in bringing people from similar class backgrounds together. Neighborhood high schools tend to be homogeneous in social class, and students tend to rank themselves according to their parents' socioeconomic status. College continues class segregation. People from upper-class backgrounds are considerably more likely to attend costly private colleges, whereas those from the working class are most likely to enroll in community colleges. These structural conditions increase the odds that the people whom you meet and form intimate relationships with will come from a similar class background.

The role that social class plays in people's intimate lives is particularly apparent when we look at differences in family functioning. In many ways all families must face the same issues: work, leisure, child rearing, and interpersonal relations (L. Rubin, 1976). But beneath the similarities we see dramatic differences in how these issues are handled. Because of heightened concern over class boundaries, ancestry, and maintenance of prestige, upper-class parents exert much more control over the dating behaviors of their children than lower-class parents (Domhoff, 1983; M. K. Whyte, 1990). Upper-class families are also better able to use their wealth and resources in coping with some of the demands of family life. Finding adequate child care arrangements will probably not pose much of a dilemma to parents who can afford a full-time, live-in nanny. The picture for working-class families, though, is quite different.

▪ ▪ ▪ ▪ ▪ ▪ ▪ ▪

LILLIAN RUBIN
Working-Class Families

To examine class differences in family life, sociologist Lillian Rubin (1976) conducted in-depth interviews with 50 working-class families. For purposes of comparison she also interviewed 25 professional middle-class families. The differences she found give a personal face to the effects of social class on family life in American society. Among the differences she discovered were that working-class people are more likely than middle-class people to marry early, have large families, have premarital pregnancies, and experience marital unhappiness and divorce.

Working-class youth, living in the confined space of their parents' homes, must often forgo college and make significant economic contributions to the family. For them, marriage often represents an attractive escape from the hardships and restrictions of their lives with their parents. But the women Rubin interviewed were almost unanimous in their beliefs that many of the troubles in their marriages came from marrying too early. Many expressed hope that their daughters would not make "the same mistake" they had made.

Another noticeable characteristic of working-class marriages is a severe split between masculine and feminine cultures. Working-class couples tend to be more traditional in their perceptions of gender roles. Working-class wives seem to be more willing than middle-class wives to grant legitimacy to their husbands' authority. Furthermore, Rubin found little communication between working-class husbands and wives, especially regarding personal or emotional matters:

> They talk *at* each other, *past* each other, or *through* each other—rarely *with* or *to* each other. He blames her: "She's too emotional." She blames him: "He's always so rational."... The problem lies in the fact that they do not have a language with which to communicate, with which to understand each other. [emphasis in original] (p. 116)

In perhaps the most telling illustration, Rubin asked the wives what they valued most in their husbands. The professional, middle-class subjects tended to focus on such issues as intimacy, sharing, communication, and the comforts and prestige that their husbands' occupations provided them. Working-class wives were more dismal in their assessments, focusing on the absence of such problems as unemployment, alcoholism, and violence. As one 33-year-old housewife put it:

> I guess I can't complain. He's a steady worker; he doesn't drink; he doesn't hit me. That's a lot more than my mother had, and she didn't sit around complaining and feeling sorry for herself, so I sure haven't got the right. (L. Rubin, 1976, p. 93)

This is not to say that working-class women are not concerned with the emotional side of their marriages. When the material aspects of life are problematic, they become dominant, all-consuming issues that require immediate solutions. Thus to understand the private experiences of family life, we must take into consideration the position of a particular family in the larger structure of society.

▪ ▪ ▪

Family Dilemmas

Given all the pressures on families from the society around them, it should be no surprise that some families experience problems. Those problems include divorce and its aftereffects, and family violence. Experts project that close to one out of every two marriages that begins in a given year will eventually end in divorce (T. C. Martin & Bumpass, 1989). More and more people are delaying marriage, choosing to remain single, or cohabiting instead of marrying. Every day in this country, four women are killed by their spouses or lovers; and in any given year more women are abused by their husbands than get married in the same period. One in seven Americans claims to have been sexually abused as a child and one in six claims to have been physically abused (cited in Coontz, 1992). Half of all children will spend a part of their childhood in a single-parent home.

Divorce

Most of us have seen the end of a marriage, either our own or that of someone close to us. In an average year there are about 1.2 million divorces in the United States, a rate of roughly 21 divorces per 1,000 existing marriages (U.S. Bureau of the Census, 1994). This rate has more or less stabilized over the past few years, but it is still quite high considering that the rate was about 14 per 1,000 marriages in 1970. The projection that roughly one out of every two marriages that begins this year will end in divorce terrifies people who are about to enter a "lifetime" relationship and distresses those already married who want some sense of permanence for their children (Blumstein & Schwartz, 1983).

The Normalization of Divorce

Why has divorce become such a prevalent feature of family life in this society? One reason is a cultural shift in the perception of marriage. Marriage has become a *voluntary contract system* that can be ended at the discretion of either spouse. In the past, marriage was predominantly an economic agreement, a joining of the financial resources of two families. Today the only thing that is exchanged is emotional gratification (Furstenberg & Cherlin, 1991). In the absence of emotional satisfaction and happiness, marriage is difficult to maintain. When economic needs—not to mention such constraints as parental expectations or religious norms—held couples together, people "made do" with loveless, unsatisfying marriages because they had to. But, when these constraints do not exist, people are less willing to make do (Skolnick, 1996). Particularly for women, increasing earning power and decreasing economic dependence on men have made it easier to end a marriage that is unsatisfying.

In addition, people's overall attitudes toward divorce have become more accepting since the 1960s (Thornton, 1989). Thirty years ago a divorced politician didn't stand a chance of being elected. But in the 1980s Ronald Reagan's divorce and remarriage didn't prevent him from being elected—twice. In the past, parishioners wouldn't tolerate a divorced minister. But people now recognize that a divorce may be preferable to an unhappy marriage.

Changing perceptions of marriage and changing cultural attitudes toward divorce have been accompanied by other structural changes. Modifications of divorce laws in the past two decades, for instance, have made it easier for people in an unsatisfying marriage to end it. In the past, evidence of wrongdoing—adultery, desertion, abuse, and so forth—was required for courts to grant a divorce. But in the past 25 years every state has adopted a form of *no-fault divorce*. No-fault laws have eliminated the requirement that one partner be found guilty of some transgression. Instead, marriages are simply declared unworkable and are terminated. The laws have also redefined the responsibilities of husbands and wives. The husband is no longer automatically considered the head of the household and the wife is no longer considered solely responsible for the care of the children. Financial awards—alimony and child support—are based on the spouses' ability to work. If neither spouse is unable to work, courts usually assume that both are equally capable.

Many critics argue that these laws have made divorce too easy and too quick, leading to an increase in divorce-related problems like poverty and juvenile delinquency. As a result, we seem to be experiencing a shift back toward less tolerant public attitudes toward divorce. A recent survey found that 55% of Americans favor making it harder to leave a marriage when one partner wants to maintain it (cited in Leland, 1996). In some states—Iowa, Idaho, Georgia, Pennsylvania, to name a few—there is talk of toughening divorce laws. In Michigan, a measure is being debated that would revoke the no-fault provision in cases where one spouse opposes the divorce. A divorce would not be granted unless the spouse seeking the divorce could prove that the partner had been abusive, had a problem with alcohol or drugs, had committed adultery, had deserted the home, or had been sentenced to prison (D. Johnson, 1996b).

The Personal Experience of Divorce

While scholars, politicians, and pundits argue over what to do about our high divorce rate, several million people will continue to experience the ending of a marriage each year. Despite the fact that it's so common, divorce is not the sort of experience that many of us prepare or train for. Prenuptial agreements may spell out in advance the settlement conditions if a marriage ends, but they address only the economic and legal facets of breakups, not the emotional, interpersonal, and social ones.

The "spoiling" of a close relationship can be emotionally devastating. It can create deep wounds akin to those associated with the death of a loved one (McCall, 1982). We may experience a wide range of emotions, including anger, bitterness, sadness, self-pity, self-doubt, guilt, and shame. When a relationship ends, so do the benefits that came with it. We lose the partner on whom we came to depend, and we lose contact with friends and acquaintances whom we came to know through that partner.

The ending of a relationship requires a transformation of identity. Becoming an ex-spouse or ex-lover means exiting one social role and entering another (Ebaugh, 1988). People whose relationships have ended must remove themselves from the norms and expectations associated with the old role and learn new ones. They must begin to see the world from a single person's perspective and not the couple's perspective. In addition, the entire history of the relationship requires redefinition. Those once-pleasant rituals, in retrospect, become annoying habits. The good times get reinterpreted as bad; the bad times are seen as more typical, indicative of the eventual breakup.

Further complicating the process of role exit is the social stigma associated with the termination of an intimate relationship. Like most things in our achievement-oriented society, relationships—particularly marriages—tend to be viewed in success/failure terms. Although studies consistently show a clear decline in disapproval of divorce as a general category, disapproval of divorced *individuals* continues (Gertsel, 1987). These individuals may come to feel demoralized and rejected by married friends and experience diminishing self-esteem. Friends and family close to the couple can increase feelings of stigma by passing judgment and taking sides. The stigmatizing effects of divorce illustrate, again, the social nature of intimate relationships.

The failure of a marriage has broader societal implications because it threatens the ideal cultural images of love and romance (Blumstein & Kollock, 1988). A divorce calls into question the entire moral code of intimacy. Friends may begin to question the stability of their own relationships. The disengaging couple is socially obligated to inform others that although commitment to this particular relationship has deteriorated, commitment to the idea of relationships has not, as reflected in the fact that an estimated 90% or more of today's young adults will marry at some point in their lives (Norton, 1987). Such commitment is also reflected in the high percentage of people who remarry after divorce.

Remarriage and the Reconstituted Family

Half of all marriages today involve at least one partner who was previously married (Bumpass, Sweet, & Castro Martin, 1990). Overall, four out of every five divorced individuals in this country are likely to remarry (Norton, 1987). These statistics suggest that although people are quite willing to escape a bad marriage, they have not necessarily given up on the concept of marriage.

Although they are common, remarriages are not without their problems. The divorce rate for remarriages is actually higher than the rate for first marriages (Sweet & Bumpass, 1987), perhaps because remarriage is an "incomplete institution" (Cherlin, 1978). Remarriage disrupts the conventional family structure so that the traditional roles, relationships, and norms no longer apply. We have no set of institutional expectations for relationships between former and current spouses, between stepparents and stepchildren, between step- and half-siblings, and with extended kin (Ahrons & Rodgers, 1987). Laws and customs have been slow to catch up. For instance, do stepchildren have legal claims to their stepparents' property? Do incest rules apply to stepsiblings? An increasing number of people face such issues, finding themselves in a marital structure quite different from the kind with which they are familiar (Goetting, 1982).

The family relationships produced by remarriage can be complex and confusing. Consider the knotty but not uncommon situation of one family:

When Ellen was eight and David ten, their parents separated. They continued to live with their mother, Nancy, spending weekends and vacations with their father, Jim. Two years after the divorce their father married Elaine, who was the custodial parent of her daughter, Jamie, aged six. Ellen and David lived in a one-parent household with their mother for three years, at which time their mother remarried. Their new stepfather, Craig, also had been divorced, and he was the joint-custodial parent of two daughters, aged six and eleven. His daughters spent about ten days each month living in his house. Within the next four years, Ellen and David's father and stepmother had two children of their own, a son and a daughter. When Ellen and David are 15 and 17, their family looks like this: They have two biological parents, two stepparents, three stepsisters, a half-brother and a half-sister. . . . They have two sets of stepgrandparents, two sets of biological grandparents, and a large network of aunts, uncles, and cousins. (Ahrons & Rodgers, 1987, p. 279)

Remarriage is particularly difficult when children are involved. When a new parent enters the former single-parent family, the entire system may be thrown out of balance. Rules and habits change and, for a time, confusion, resentment, and hostility may be the norm. While conflict is common in all types of families, issues like favoritism, divided loyalties, the right to discipline, and financial responsibility are particularly likely to occur in the reconstituted family.

The high divorce rate of remarriages and the high levels of conflict within some reconstituted families are not simply an outgrowth of people's psychological inability to sustain intimate relationships, as some analysts have claimed. It is the fact that remarriages are not fully institutionalized that makes them susceptible to failure. The lack of clear role definitions, the absence of established societal norms, and the increased complexity of the family structure itself increase the likelihood of tension and turmoil. Perhaps in the future, as our culture develops standard ways of defining and coping with these families, remarriage might become more institutionalized and less problematic. But as long as parents and children are separated from one another and as long as other adults (that is, the one who marries a remarried spouse) are expected to take on parental role responsibilities without being able to legitimately expect the rewards (for example, the loyalty and love of someone else's child), there will continue to be a great deal of tension and confusion. The structure of reconstituted families continues to grow more complex, making the lack of institutional guidelines even more serious.

Children, Divorce, and Single Parenting

While remarriage is certainly common, only about half of children whose parents divorce are likely to ever live with a stepfather (Bumpass & Sweet, 1989). The rest will spend their childhoods after the divorce with only one parent. From 1970 to 1993 the proportion of American families headed by a single parent increased

Table 8.2   *Families with Children under 18 by Type and Race*

	1970	1994
All Races:		
Two-parent families	87%	69%
One-parent families (mother)	12	27
One-parent families (father)	1	4
Whites:		
Two-parent families	90%	75%
One-parent families (mother)	9	21
One-parent families (father)	1	4
Blacks:		
Two-parent families	64%	35%
One-parent families (mother)	33	60
One-parent families (father)	3	5
Hispanics (may be of any race):		
Two-parent families	NA	64%
One-parent families (mother)	NA	31
One-parent families (father)	NA	5

NA = Not available
Source: U.S. Bureau of the Census, 1995a.

from around 13% to 30%; nearly 87% of single-parent families are headed by women. If the divorce rate remains high and out-of-wedlock birth continues its upward trend—nearly 25% of never-married women between the ages of 18 and 44 have children (U.S. Bureau of the Census, 1994)—perhaps as many as 60% of children born in the 1990s will live in a single-parent family before the age of 16 (Furstenberg & Cherlin, 1991). Moreover, the odds of growing up in a single parent family are higher for some racial groups than others (see Table 8.2).

Although divorce can be traumatic for adults, most recover after a period of years. Children, however, have a more difficult time adjusting. For them, divorce sets a series of changes in motion, each with the potential to disrupt their lives. They may have to move to a new home in a new neighborhood, make new friends, and go to a new school. Because the overwhelming majority of divorced children live with their mothers, they may also experience a decline in their standard of living because the earning capacity of women is lower than that of men, and because noncustodial fathers do not always pay child support (see chapter 10). In about two-thirds of divorces, fathers are required to pay child support. Of these, 51% pay the full amount, 24% pay a partial amount, and 25% pay nothing (U.S. Bureau of the Census, 1994). This means that about half of divorced mothers don't receive any child support at all. In addition, the relationship children have with their noncustodial parent diminishes over time. One study found that only 40% of children living with their mothers had seen their fathers in the past month. Thirty-five percent of them hadn't seen their fathers in over five years (cited in Brody, 1991).

What are the effects on children of living in single-parent families? A review of recent research on this question shows that compared to children from two-parent families, children from single-parent families are more likely to:

- earn poorer grades in school
- be absent from school
- drop out
- commit delinquent acts and engage in drug and alcohol abuse
- be poor, and when they reach adulthood, have lower earnings
- marry early, have children early, and divorce (McLanahan & Booth, 1991)

These differences are typically attributed to factors such as the absence of a father, increased strain on the custodial parent to keep the household running, and emotional stress and anger associated with the separation. However, it seems that the causes are more likely to be factors that can also be found in two-parent families: low income, poor living conditions, and lack of parental supervision (Cherlin, 1992).

These behavioral problems may not be caused by the divorce itself but by exposure to conflict between ex-spouses. If we look at kids whose parents are unhappily married or whose families experience a great deal of conflict, we find that differences in the frequency of problems between children of divorce and children in intact families disappear (Furstenberg & Cherlin, 1991). In fact, children who grow up in intact families that exhibit frequent conflict may actually have *more* problems. In short, the simple fact of growing up in a single-parent family may not be as important in the development of a child as the way parents relate to one another and to the child.

Family Violence

Throughout this chapter I have discussed the vital role of family and intimacy in our everyday lives. These relationships, it seems, are the havens to which we ought to be able to escape when life becomes overwhelming. No matter how lousy your day was or how much you hate your job, you can still look forward to spending the evening with your loved one. At least you'll get some much-needed nurturance, warmth, and compassion from him or her, right? Certainly you won't get screamed at, emotionally belittled, punched in the face, or physically threatened simply because you came home too late or said the wrong thing at the wrong time.

But that is precisely the conduct that awaits a large number of people, especially children and adult women, in this country. Nothing is more opposed to our image of the loving family than the idea of domestic violence. The tragic irony is that, outside of wars and riots, the home—that loving place that nourishes us when the outside world has sucked away our life energy—is the most violent place in American society.

Although it would be comforting to believe that domestic violence is rare and occurs only in families that harbor a "sick" parent or spouse, the fact is that it happens with alarming frequency and is likely to be committed by people we would otherwise consider normal. Spouse abuse, elder abuse, and child abuse are found in every class, race, and religion. Domestic violence is not a deviant aberration; it is a fundamental characteristic of the way we relate to one another in family settings.

The American Medical Association estimates that as many as one in three women will be assaulted by a partner in her lifetime—4 million in any given year (cited in Blackman et al., 1994). Half of the victims are beaten at least three times a year (Straus, Gelles, & Steinmetz, 1980). There are more than two million *reported* cases of child abuse each year, and in a given year 1,300 children will die of abuse or neglect (Gelles & Cornell, 1990; U.S. Bureau of the Census, 1994). Because of the private nature of this violence and the desire of family members to keep it hidden, all of these figures are almost certainly underestimates.

Public Tolerance of Domestic Violence

To understand why domestic violence is so common in this country, we must look at public perceptions and attitudes toward it. In a national survey, one in four wives and one in three husbands said that hitting a partner was "necessary, normal, or good." When the same sample was asked about "slapping or spanking" a 12-year-old child, the figure rose to about 75% (Straus, Gelles, & Steinmetz, 1980).

Being violent with a stranger in public has clear, definite, and punishable consequences. But being violent with a family member in the privacy of one's own home has few. People hit their "loved ones" simply because they can (Gelles & Straus, 1988). Traditionally we have perceived domestic violence, particularly wife abuse, as somehow less bothersome and more tolerable than other types of violence.

To investigate public tolerance of family violence, psychologists Lance Shotland and Margaret Straw (1976) performed an experiment that involved staging what appeared to be heated altercations between a man and woman as they emerged from an elevator. They set up two scenarios that were identical except for one important detail. In the first, the woman, who is the object of the man's verbal and physical threats, shouts, "Get away from me! I don't even know you!" In the second (with identical actors and identical behaviors), she says, "Get away from me! I don't know why I ever married you!" In the first situation, bystanders intervened 65% of the time (that is, they attempted to stop the apparent fight). In the second, bystanders intervened only 19% of the time. Clearly the second case was being defined by observers as a domestic dispute between spouses, conjuring up a different set of norms that stopped them from "getting involved" in the private affairs of a couple. The perception of an intimate relationship prevented most people from seeing the incident as a potentially violent and dangerous situation.

Similar perceptions exist at the organizational level. Police departments have historically been reluctant to get too involved in domestic disputes. Some have arrest policies called "stitch rules," which specify how serious an injury a victim must sustain, measured by how many stitches are required, to justify an arrest of the assailant (Gillespie, 1989). One study found that the majority of domestic disputes and family violence incidents reported to the police resulted in no arrest; either the police did nothing or the offender was referred to other agencies (Bell & Bell, 1991). Given this sort of response, it is not surprising that only about 15% of battered women ever contact the police (Straus & Gelles, 1986).

But things are starting to change. Many police departments around the country have revised their unspoken "hands-off" policies toward domestic violence cases. In Indianapolis, for example, where the number of domestic violence cases doubled between 1990 and 1991, officers are now required to make an arrest even if they don't directly witness the assault. In addition, officers must have 30 hours of in-service domestic violence training each year. In other cities, domestic violence victims are prohibited from dropping assault charges once they are filed.

Family Violence in Cultural Context

Individual-level factors such as economic frustration, stress, and alcohol and drug use are frequently implicated as major causes of domestic violence. To some analysts, batterers are either psychopaths or people who are just plain prone to violence. But to fully understand domestic violence, we must take a look at some important characteristics of our society.

We live in one of the most violent industrialized countries on earth. The United States is fundamentally committed to the use of violence to achieve desirable changes (Straus, 1977). It is in our streets, our schools, our movies, our television shows, our toy stores, our spectator sports, and our government. It's even in our everyday language: we *assault* problems, *conquer* fears, *beat* others to the punch, *pound* home ideas, and *shoot down* opinions (Ewing, 1992). For many, violence is the appropriate means by which to resolve certain problems. It is not surprising, then, that such cultural patterns of violence would spill into the American family.

We also live in a society dominated by and built around the interests of men. Men occupy the high-status positions, exercise decision-making and political power, tend to be dominant in interpersonal relationships, and occupy the roles society defines as most valuable (Frieze, Parsons, Johnson, Ruble, & Zellman, 1978). Domestic violence not only is a consequence of male domination, it reinforces it:

> The act of violence is many things at once. At the same instant it is the individual man acting out relations of sexual power; it is the violence of a society—a hierarchical, authoritarian, sexist, class-divided . . . crazy society—being focused through an individual man onto an individual woman. . . . These acts of violence are like a ritualized acting out of our social relations of power: the dominant and the weaker, the powerful and the powerless . . . the masculine and the feminine. (Kaufman, 1987, p. 1)

Male dominance has a long and infamous history (Gelles & Cornell, 1990). Roman law, for instance, justified a husband's killing of his wife for reasons such as adultery, wine drinking, and other so-called inappropriate behaviors (Steinmetz, Clavan, & Stein, 1990). The "rule of thumb" in English common law recognized a husband's right to beat his wife with a stick that was no bigger than the circumference of his thumb.

This heritage has sometimes led to a double standard of acceptable violence. In 1994, a Maryland man who killed his wife with a hunting rifle 4 hours after finding her in bed with another man pleaded guilty to voluntary manslaughter and was sentenced to 18 months in prison. The sentence was half as long as the prosecution recommended. The judge in the case said afterward that he wished he didn't have to send the man to prison at all. A day after this case, another judge handed down a 3-year sentence to a woman who pleaded guilty to voluntary manslaughter for killing her husband after 11 years of abuse. Her sentence was *three times longer* than what the prosecutors in that case had sought (Lewin, 1994).

If it is true that some men beat their partners because they feel that such behavior is appropriate, then some wife beaters are not psychotic, deranged, "sick" individuals. Rather, they are men who believe that male dominance is their birthright. Men who assault their wives are actually living up to cultural prescriptions that are cherished in Western society—aggressiveness, male dominance, and female subordination (Dobash & Dobash, 1979).

The problem of domestic violence is all the more insidious because it represents an extreme extension of norms dictating suitable spousal treatment. There is a deeply entrenched cultural tendency to perceive domestic violence as "normal" violence, as something that, while not necessarily desirable, is not surprising or unexpected either. As a result, much of the research in this area has focused on the victim's response to the situation.

Responses to Abuse

One question that has captured the attention of many marriage and family researchers is: Why do women stay in abusive relationships? During the 1960s the *masochism thesis*—that is, women liked being humiliated and hurt—was the predominant reason offered by psychiatrists (for example, Saul, 1972). Even today, many psychiatrists believe masochism—or self-defeating personality disorder, as it is now called—should be a "legitimate" medical explanation for women who stay in abusive relationships. Other contemporary explanations focus on the woman's character flaws, such as weak will or pathological emotional attachment.

All of these explanations wrongly focus on the victim while paying little attention to her social situation. In a culture that is still reluctant to punish abusers, it is not surprising that many women perceive there to be no alternatives available and feel physically, economically, and emotionally trapped in their relationships. Women who are unemployed and cannot support themselves financially are significantly less likely to leave an abusive marriage than women who are employed and therefore have their own source of income (Strube & Barbour, 1983).

The cultural context of abusive relationships can even affect the beliefs of the victims. Kathleen Ferraro and John Johnson (1983) were participant observers at a shelter for battered women in the Southwest. They gathered information from 120 women, ranging in age from 17 to 68, who came to the shelter over the span of a year. From this information they identified several common techniques that battered women use to justify or neutralize the violence their partners direct toward them. Unfortunately, these tactics may inhibit a sense of outrage and efforts to escape the abuse. Some women had convinced themselves that they must endure the abuse while helping their "troubled" partners return to their "normal," nonabusive selves. Others claimed that their abusive partners were "sick" and that their actions were beyond their control; their partners were also victims. Finally, many women blamed themselves, taking the responsibility away from their spouses.

The lengths to which these women went demonstrate the powerful allure of family life. Despite the problems and changes in the institution of family, we still tend to regard it as the epitome of group life, the best place to achieve a sense of intimacy and belonging. We still prefer living in families to living alone.

Conclusion

Social relationships form the center of our personal universes. Life in groups provides us with the sense of belonging that most of us need. Although these relationships are the principal source of identity, community, happiness, and satisfaction for many, they can be the source of tremendous anguish and suffering for others.

Perhaps the most important group to which we belong is family, a public as well as a private institution. True, most intimate and family behavior occurs away from the watchful eyes of others; we alone have access to our thoughts, desires, and feelings regarding someone with whom we are intimately involved. But other people do care about what goes on in our relationships. People around us, the government, even society as a whole, have a vested interest in what happens in our intimate lives.

The social institutions and culture that make up our society also shape the very nature and definition of "family." Today the boundaries of that definition are being pushed by rapidly increasing numbers of "nontraditional" families: dual-earner couples, single-parent households, cohabitation, voluntary singlehood, same-sex couples, and so on.

Every family relationship, whether it violates or conforms to current social norms, reflects the dominant ideals and beliefs about what a marriage or a family ought to look like. Each relationship is unique. However, this uniqueness will always be bounded by the broader constraints of our cultural, group, and institutional values.

CHAPTER HIGHLIGHTS

▪ In this culture, social relationships are the standard against which we judge the quality and happiness of our everyday lives. Yet in a complex, individualistic society like ours, they are becoming more difficult to establish and sustain.

▪ By nature, groups exert pressures on individual members to conform to the group norms. Their structure may also encourage faulty decision making (that is, groupthink).

▪ Many people in this society long for a return to the "golden age" of the family. But our image of the family of the past is largely a myth.

▪ Although the monogamous marriage is the only sexual relationship that has achieved widespread cultural legitimacy in this society, other forms of intimacy (for example, extra- and premarital sex, polygamy) are considered legitimate in other societies.

▪ Although we like to think that the things we do in our family relationships are completely private experiences, they are continually influenced by large-scale political interests and economic pressures. Furthermore, our choices of romantic partners are governed to some degree by cultural rules that encourage us to form relationships within certain social groups and outside others.

▪ Divorce is not a solely private experience. It occurs within a cultural, historical, and community context. The high rate of remarriage after divorce indicates that Americans still view the institution of marriage as desirable.

▪ Instead of viewing domestic violence (spouse abuse and child abuse) as a product of "sick" individuals, sociologists are likely to view it as the product of a culture that tolerates violence in a variety of situations, traditionally grants men authority over women in family roles, and values family privacy and autonomy over the well-being of individual members.

YOUR TURN

There is no universal definition of "family." Our ideas about what a family is lie in sharp contrast to those of people in other cultures. Within our culture, there is also tremendous debate over what a family is and which groups get to be defined as a family.

With so much disagreement, it would be interesting to find out how people actually define a family. Go to a spot on campus where there is a lot of foot traffic and ask passersby for their definition of the word *family*. See if you can find any patterns in their responses. Is there a tendency to focus on blood relations, or is the emotional component of family more important? Is the presence of children necessary to their definitions of a family?

To delve deeper into the diversity of family definitions and experiences, pose the following questions to several friends or classmates. Try to talk to people from different racial, ethnic, religious, gender, and age groups:

How many brothers and sisters do you have?

If they are younger, did your parents expect you to help take care of them?

Did you share a room with any of them while you were growing up?

How many different houses did you live in while growing up?

How often do you see your grandparents?

Did you ever have grandparents or other relatives live in your house?

Do you address your relatives by family terms ("Uncle Bob," "Aunt Beth," "Grandpa," "Grandma") or by first name?

Do you expect to help support your parents when you are older?

Examine the various responses. How do you explain these differences? What do people's responses say about the structure of their families?

FAMILY PHOTOGRAPHY
One Album Is Worth 1000 Lies

RICHARD CHALFEN

"...family members who take pictures of themselves and organize the photographs into family albums are simultaneously making statements about themselves...."

Something new is happening in the history of the human configuration recognized as the family. Family members have new opportunities and abilities to keep track of one another, to remember one another, to hold onto details of life lived together. In addition to the now-common 35mm cameras, point-and-shoot cameras, and instant cameras, families often own a video camera. Family members can now duplicate their off-camera lives in real time with a symbolic on-camera counterpart, recorded in color, with sound, and with "special effects." Ordinary people can make pictorial statements about personal and family life that were virtually impossible as recently as 100 years ago. What's going on and how significant is it all? What are some of the special effects in both literal and metaphoric terms? What can we learn about American families from their photograph albums? Answers to these questions rely on what we know about photographic representation in general and family album representation in particular. Issues of pictorial representation and visual communication are at the heart of family photography.

We may safely assume that virtually every family in the United States takes and/or keeps its own pictures. Although family members

Composition of "the family" often includes members of the "canine extended family" as in this 1972 snapshot. Family albums often illustrate the place of dogs and cats as surrogate children or as child-companions, but definitely as members of the family.

may value their photograph collection as a perfect representation of their family and family life, we should understand that in reality these artifacts are a preferred version of family life. Selective perception and "happiness filters" produce an upside composite image, one that is

Cape Cod
July 1983

MERRY CHRISTMAS

Matthew 10½
David 4
Alexander 2½
The Rogers!

Family photos illustrate the family in its harmonious best—"the way we looked" in the sunshine, smiling, and on vacation. Some examples may be sent to as many as 100 relatives and friends as in this 1983 photo Christmas card.

socially and culturally approved. If, as some insist, a picture is worth a thousand words, then the words associated with family snapshots are all favorable ones. But, as one family friend commented to me, "Who could tell from these [family album] pictures that in three months they [husband and wife] would be divorced and living on opposite sides of the country?" How have we come to this situation?

When one asks, "Why did you take so much time and effort to make this family album?" the first response is usually, "We just wanted to remember how we looked!" A simple answer to a simple question, both seemingly based on commonsense knowledge. But common sense is less an answer than a problem, making it important to dig further and explore layers of human behavior behind family photography and photographic representation.

First, the phrase "how we looked" contains an interesting and provocative ambiguity. On one hand, of course, there is the unproblematic sense

The arrival of a baby promotes the purchase of a new camera. Snapshots of "smiling babies" are preferred to "crying/wailing babies" and "crying baby" is much preferred to "crying adult."

of "how we looked" when we were babies, young children, teenagers, newlyweds, parents, senior citizens, and the like. That is, we occasionally like to "show off" and produce a documentation of

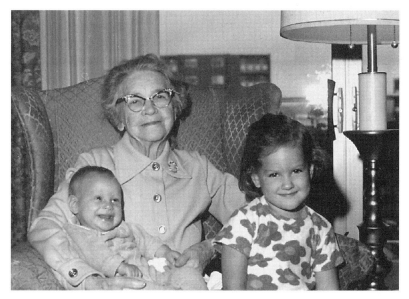

As family members age, they may become shy of the camera. An important exception is when grandparents and grandchildren are photographed together, providing nice examples of family continuity. Especially important are three- and now, more common, four-generation photographs.

Some calendar holidays, such as Christmas, are family times. The day before Christmas is the day of highest film sales. Snapshots celebrate a sense of family unity as in this 1961 example showing uncle, nephew, and niece.

Graduation shapshots are a must. They provide evidence of achievement, of making progress, of doing things right, and they are an expression of family pride in its members. But we find virtually no pictures of classroom activities, studying in libraries, or teachers.

physical appearance—hair styles, makeup, preferences for dress (including a sequence of uniforms), strength, prowess, and the like.

Second, and more interesting, is the sense of "how we looked at the world"—both with and without cameras—with specific reference to our immediate surroundings and especially family life. This second meaning offers much more to consider, including how we preferred to look at life and what we felt was appropriate to retain as legitimate memory. We might start with the often used gambit: What would explorers from outer space learn about family life if they arrived on this planet and excavated a family's photograph collection? What could be learned about earthling family life? How would this artifact be classified and understood? Would it matter where on Earth our visitors

arrived, or would all photographic samples from all parts of Earth be the same?

In most simple terms, family members who take pictures of themselves and organize the photographs into family albums are simultaneously making statements about themselves. This activity is a form of social communication and brings up two important questions. What are families saying about themselves as they take, preserve, and display these pictures? And to whom are such statements being made?

These questions raise related questions. How well does a photo album represent, reflect, or even mirror a family and family life? How does it represent information, and what does it *re*present to viewers in photographic form? What kinds of structural comparisons can be made to autobiographies, diaries, personal journals, and

Snapshot images of family gatherings often fail to include one member, namely the male head of household. Fathers are missing because they tend to take family pictures more than either mothers or children. Here we see four sandwiches but only three people are shown.

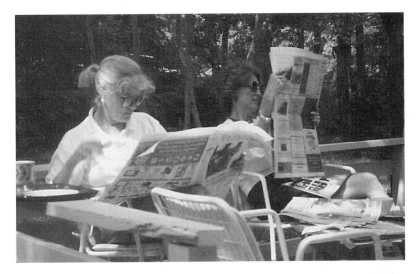

Off moments of family life may be more frequent but are seldom photographed. Scenes of people reading the newspaper, sleeping, watching television, or washing the dishes are not considered appropriate images for the family photograph collection—seriously limiting this view of family life.

even memoirs? If we acknowledge family photography as a form of social communication, we must begin to ask questions such as: Who in the family made the pictures? Who later organized the album? Are these pictorial records demo-cratic—are these group expressions where everyone in the family has an equal "voice"? Or are they idiosyncratic expressions and personal visions of family life? According to what is known from examples in American culture, adult family

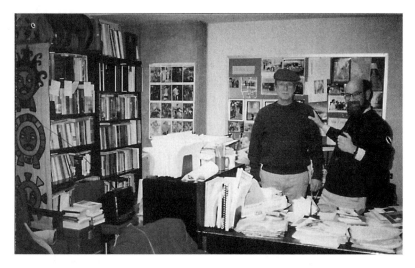

Snapshots of family members at work or in some workplace are rare as in this 1984 picture of a colleague and the author (right) in his university office. Illustrations of play/leisure prevail over work/labor in the family album portrait of life.

members contribute more to the album than do children; husbands and fathers tend to use the camera more whereas wives and mothers tend to put together the photograph albums. Thus, a division of labor related to family politics takes place.

We should also ask about motivations and intentions: What do family photographers and album makers expect to accomplish? Can anything be said about personal, social, and/or cultural effects? Marketing reports cite two factors that regularly promote the purchase of a new camera: having a baby and taking a trip. Studies indicate that adult family members feel strongly about capturing views of young children because the children change so quickly and will never look the same again. Documenting change in a culturally approved, positive direction is very important.

Other motives include "holding onto the special moment" and "otherwise we might forget what happened." Travel photography is very popular. People want to bring home a piece of their vacation—which provokes the quip that

tourists don't know where they have been or if they've had a good time until they get their pictures back from the drugstore.

Interestingly, family members often use a financial metaphor to explain their motivations for taking photographs. They feel they are "contributing to their memory banks," that "interest will grow with time," and that "investing their time to take family pictures will pay off in the long term." In general, the key point is that these photographs are meant to last, to be saved, and to make people feel good.

If family members can be said to look at themselves with cameras, what do they say about themselves through this medium? What are the contents of these pictures, and what is being expressed about family life in these collections? Are all events included, or can a pattern of inclusion/exclusion be detected?

What is the intended audience or destination of family picture collections? Who is meant to see these photographs? Family pictures are part of home media and what has been called the "home mode of pictorial communication." This

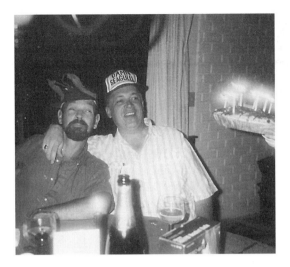

Birthday parties for family members are not restricted to young children as in this 1990 snapshot that celebrates two birthdays of fictive uncles on same day.

implies that the pictures are meant for personal use by members of the nuclear and extended family (including future members) and perhaps by close friends. They are not created to be published in newspapers or magazines, for advertising or other commercial purposes.

Other questions focus on how family pictures are displayed, organized, stored, and preserved. Organizing an album is both organizing a display of pictures and metaphorically organizing a progression through life. There is a sense of creating order and coherence, of bringing organization to chaos, of putting the best face on family life. Family members will confess to feeling guilty about not organizing their pictures in albums, even if it is merely putting them all in a chronological order. Showing off family accomplishments—including graduations, confirmations, and weddings—by framing and displaying certain family photographs in particular household spaces provides a sense of "look how we are doing things right."

Finally, we can ask, "What do family photographs do for people?" The overriding message might be: "At one point in time, we were together as a family unit. We may be in different places now, but this is how it was." In some cases, family pictures socialize children, when the pictures answer their questions about the past: "What did mommy and daddy look like when they were young?" "Where did we live when I was a child?" In these situations the photo album promotes group identity in the family. Perhaps the most telling characteristic of the pictorial documentation of family life is revealed when we consider what is included and what is excluded from the camera's lens and the picture collection—what Erving Goffman and others have called "image management." In this way, family members exert a control of information about themselves. What are some of the dimensions of this managed version of family life? We find, for instance, more photographs surrounding births than those related to deaths, photographs of play and leisure times and almost none of work or labor. We see pictures associated with engagements and weddings and none associated with separations or divorces. We see family members when they are healthy but not those who are sick or terminally ill. We favor photographs of people when they are young over those of very old family members. We find pictures that celebrate the results of school life, such as graduations, but virtually no records of daily school life or teachers. We tend to photograph beginnings and new things rather than endings or old things. Family members could take pictures of the "down side" of family life. Advertisements for the latest camera technology stress the ability to "capture" anything, at any time, from any perspective, with automatic f-stops, self-adjusting focus, zoom lenses, and the like. If we all took advantage of these technological advances, we could take a more complete look at family life. But we don't.

Social and cultural filters kick in. Our decisions not to photograph many situations and events are taken for granted. We tend not to take pictures when a family member is angry, when someone is emotionally upset or visibly sick, when children are physically fighting with one another, when members of the family are naked, when they are using the bathroom, and during other culturally defined "unphotogenic" moments. In fact, however, such situations are much more common in our lives than "Kodak moments." So the family album is really not a very complete record of family life.

Value-laden statements are contained within the photo album. The album is biased toward what is appropriate and right and, in general, the way things ought to be. The snapshot version of life favors the sunny rather than the seamy side of life; it promotes moments of victory rather than the agonies associated with defeats. Illustrations of progress are very important to the composite view of family album life.

The majority of these comments come from observations of Anglo-American middle-class culture. Does this mean that family members from all sectors of American culture and all parts of the world behave in similar ways? Do family members from different societies and cultures, using similar cameras, do the same things? Studies conducted among ethnic peoples in the United States as well as France, Hungary, the Netherlands, and Japan are helping to answer these questions. Initial findings indicate that culture plays an important role in what people do with similar camera technology.

This brings us back to the question posed earlier: What can be learned about a family from their photographs? Probably the most direct use of family album imagery comes from health care specialists known as photo therapists. In marriage and family therapy, clients are asked to bring their own family pictures to their sessions or to make new ones of their family life. In many cases therapists use the photographs as "reality checks," comparing verbal comments and feelings to what is seen in the family photographs. Photographs are used to stimulate insights and therapeutic discussions. Often therapists notice great discrepancies between the positive views expressed in the album and the negative comments made by family members.

Family album pictures are like all other representational forms: They never include everything; they are biased and highly selective. In short, a family album is a construction, one of many that we as humans deal with on a daily basis.

The pictures in photo albums are usually grounded in some form of verbal accompaniment, such as a caption or a narrative. The relationship of the images to memory is problematic. Just as memories can change, so can the meaning of individual snapshots. In short, photographs do not, by themselves, "speak to us." People say things about, and in conjunction with, pictures. In fact, the significance of family pictures lies in what people have to say about them. Without the right people, family photographs can be rendered meaningless; these are the ones we find abandoned in flea markets and sidewalk trash cans.

The stories we tell about ourselves, to ourselves, are highly selective and carefully managed. Our job, as Clifford Geertz suggests, is to develop a theory of fictions that, in turn, contributes to a more comprehensive notion of communicative competence. It may indeed be true that family album representation may teach us more about patterns of human representation than about the details of family life.

III

Social Structure, Institutions, and Everyday Life

Up to this point you have learned how our everyday lives are constructed and ordered. But this is only part of the picture. What does social life look like from the top down? Once the architecture is constructed and in place, what influence does it exert on our everyday lives? In answering these questions we investigate the organizational and institutional pressures on everyday life and the various sources of structural inequality in society: social class, wealth, race and ethnicity, and gender. Population trends are another structural influence on everyday life. These facets of society may seem ominous and impenetrable. However, you will see that our lives don't completely fall under the control of the social structure. The collective actions of individuals often bring about fundamental changes in society.

CHAPTER 9

Building the Structure of Society: Organizations and Social Institutions

- *Social Structure and Everyday Life*
- *Social Dilemmas: Individual Interests and Structural Needs*
- *The Structure of Organizations*
- *Organizations and Institutions*
- *Globalization and Social Institutions*

In the early morning hours of May 21, 1992, two buses carrying members of the California Angels baseball team were on their way from New York to Baltimore for a weekend series with the Orioles. The players and coaches had just settled in for the 2-hour trip when they were jolted from their seats as one of the buses careened out of control, crashed through a guard rail, and landed on its side in a ravine. Fortunately, only a few of the players and coaches were injured. As the shock of this potential disaster faded, baseball fans and sportswriters began to wonder what would have happened had all or most of the team been severely injured or killed.

The incident brought to light a little-known rule euphemistically called the "rehabilitation plan." Since 1965, major league baseball has had a procedure for immediately replacing teams that lose players to some tragedy. If a few players are disabled or killed, a team supplements its roster by promoting minor league players. However, in the event of a wide-scale tragedy—that is, when a team loses six or more players to death or disability—the rehabilitation plan goes into effect. The team would be allowed to select replacement players through a draft from healthy teams. The league president would decide how many players each remaining team could "protect" from being drafted (Eskenazi, 1992).

Other professional sports leagues have similar disaster plans. The National Basketball Association has a plan that goes into effect if five or more players on a team die or are dismembered. Remaining teams could protect up to five of their players. The rest would be available for a draft. The National Football League has two plans, one for a disaster and one for a near-disaster. A near-disaster is defined as the loss of fewer than 15 players in one accident. The team would be required to replace these players through the signing of free agents—players who are not, at the time, under contract with another team. But if a quarterback is among those lost, the team would be allowed to draft up to two replacement quarterbacks from other teams. If more than 15 players are lost, the team decides whether to cancel the rest of the season. If it decides to continue, the near-disaster plan goes into effect. If it cancels, the disaster plan goes into effect, and the team would be able to draft players from other teams the following year (Eskenazi, 1992).

What do all these arrangements have to do with the creation of social structure? They illustrate an important theme of this chapter: that organizations and institutions are something more than the people who happen to make them up. They usually don't cease to exist if their constituent members are lost. The California Angels would have continued even if that accident had been much worse.

Even though organizations and institutions exist at a level above that of the individual or the social group, they are still human creations. One of the great sociological paradoxes of human existence is that we are capable of producing a social structure that intrudes on virtually every aspect of our daily lives. We then experience this structure as something other than a human product. It is ironic that in a society that so fiercely extols the virtue of rugged individualism and personal accomplishment, we spend most of our lives either within or responding to the influence of larger structural entities. This chapter focuses on our relationship with the social structure we create and maintain. This focus will require an examination of the structure not only from the individual's perspective but also from the macro-sociological perspective of the organizations and institutions themselves. Many important social issues look quite different depending on the perspective we use to understand them.

Social Structure and Everyday Life

As you will recall from chapter 2, social structure is the framework of society that exists above the level of individuals and provides the social setting in which individuals interact with one another to form relationships. The concept of structure is important because it implies a patterned regularity to the way societies work.

All scientific disciplines have some notion of structure: Chemists assume the existence of *atomic* structure; microbiologists rely on *molecular* structure; physicians couldn't practice medicine if they didn't have a sense of *anatomical* structure; even astronomers take for granted the structure of the universe (Smelser, 1988). There may be uncertainty about its nature, but members of these disciplines do not abandon the concept of structure.

Likewise, structure occupies an important place in sociology. Although sociologists may disagree about its origin, constituent elements, or power over everyday life, few would argue that **social structure**—the social institutions, organizations, groups, statuses and roles, values, and norms that add order and predictability to our private lives—doesn't exist at all. It would be impossible to draw any meaningful conclusions about human behavior if we started with the notion that society is haphazard and that things happen by chance alone.

Consider, for instance, the components of social structure that affect the experience of going to high school in this society. Within the broad American educational system there are organizations (the National Education Association, National Teacher's Association, state teachers' associations, local school boards, local administrative boards, etc.), groups (faculty, student body, classrooms, cafeteria staff, etc.), statuses (teacher, student, principal, custodian, coach, librarian, etc.), and roles (teaching, learning, disciplining, making and taking tests, coaching, etc.). Moreover, there are institutionalized beliefs that support the structure. Education is highly valued in this society: It is seen as the principal means of achieving financial success, and it makes possible a complex division of labor. Without education a technologically advanced society would be impossible. Finally, there is a set of institutionalized norms that govern educational activity, among them the expectation that everyone attend school until the age of 16. There are also a multitude of school rules that determine acceptable behavior (not running in the halls, not screaming in class, staying on the school grounds until classes are over, etc.) (Saunders, 1991).

The massive structure of the educational system is a reality that determines life chances and choices. You may choose what classes to take in high school, whether to go on to college, and what to major in once you get there, but the availability of jobs to people without a college education and the admissions policies of potential colleges are factors beyond your control. You're reading this book right now not because of your fondness for fine literature but because of the structural requirements of being a college student. You know you must graduate in order to get a good job. To do so you must get good grades in your classes. To get good grades in your classes, you must keep up with the material so you are prepared for exams. You may rather be doing a number of other things right now—reading a *better* book, swimming, making love, watching TV, doing nothing, sleeping—but these personal preferences must take a back seat to the more immediate structural demands of college life.

Although social structure is an essential element in the organization of everyday life, it can at times create problems. Mistakes are often the end result of a chain of events set in motion by a social structure that either induces errors or makes them difficult to detect. The *Challenger* disaster discussed in chapter 8 probably had as much to do with the competitive environment and organizational culture of NASA (for example, an institutionalized pattern of putting economic and political interests above safety considerations) as it had with the effects of groupthink on the decision-making process (Vaughan, 1996).

What appear to be obvious errors in human judgment are often, on closer inspection, linked to broader system failures. Take, for example, medical mistakes. It's estimated that 1.3 million people are injured by medical errors each year in the United States (Leape et al., 1995). We've all heard about patients who are prescribed the wrong drug, have the wrong kidney removed, or have the wrong leg amputated. The tendency to sue individual doctors for malpractice in such cases demonstrates our overwhelming cultural perception that such errors are caused by individual incompetence. But a recent analysis of 334 drug errors in hospitals found that system failure (for example, poor dissemination of drug knowledge to doctors, inadequate availability of patient information, faulty systems for checking correct dosage, and inefficient hospital procedure) was responsible for most of them (Leape et al., 1995).

Social Dilemmas: Individual Interests and Structural Needs

Although social structure can clearly affect the lives of individuals, individual actions can also have an enormous effect on the structure and stability of an entire group or community. We often take for granted that groups of individuals with common interests will attempt to further those interests. Let's say residents want to make sure that their neighborhood is free of crime. It follows logically that each individual would, as a rational person, act to achieve that objective. For instance, everyone would volunteer at some point to "patrol" his or her street at night, or neighbors might all chip in money to improve street lighting.

In actuality, though, the opposite appears to be true (Cross & Guyer, 1980; Messick & Brewer, 1983; Olsen, 1965). People often do not voluntarily act to achieve the common objective unless some sort of coercion or other device forces their behavior. Instead, they act to ensure their own personal interests. For example, they may not donate money for a new street light because they believe others will do so. Such a phenomenon is known as a **social dilemma** (Messick & Brewer, 1983). When each person in a group pursues his or her own self-interests, the result may be ruin for everyone. If each person individually decides not to donate money, the new street light is never purchased, and everyone suffers.

The phenomenon of social dilemmas illustrates how individual actions can have disastrous consequences for larger collectivities. Major social problems like pollution can be understood as stemming, at least in part, from the decisions made by people acting in their own interest as opposed to the collective interest. My flinging one bag of trash onto the highway may not seem so significant or destructive. But large numbers of people doing the same thing would be very destructive. If we think of nations as individual actors and the planet as the community to which they belong, many situations that have global significance—including inadequate recycling, failure to conserve energy, and species extinction—can also be understood from this perspective. Two important types of social dilemmas are the tragedy of the commons and the free-rider problem.

The Tragedy of the Commons

The term *commons* was originally used to describe the pasture ground that was often located in the center of colonial New England towns where herders brought their animals to graze. The land was a public good available to anyone. Used in moderation by everyone, the commons worked. The grass was allowed to regenerate, resulting in a perpetual supply of food for the herds (Hardin & Baden, 1977).

However, each herder could personally benefit by increasing the size of his or her herd and letting the animals eat as much as they wanted. Each animal represented a profit to the individual herder, while the cost of grazing them was shared by all the herders. Responding to such an incentive, each herder might rationally decide to increase his or her herd. But when all the herders allowed their growing herds to eat as much of the grass as they wanted for as long as they wanted, the grass in the commons could not regenerate fast enough to feed them all. The tragic conclusion was that the commons would collapse and the herds that grazed on it would be destroyed. Tragedy ensued when the short-term needs of the individual overshadowed the long-term collective needs of the group.

In this illustration, the common resource was grass, and the group was relatively small. However, the "tragedy of the commons" model can be applied to any situation in which common resources can be used by a number of people and are available to all: air, food, fuel, water, and so on.

The situation becomes particularly dangerous when the community adopts a crisis mentality. In the summer of 1993 several Midwestern states were beset by a series of destructive floods. When a river overflowed its banks in Des Moines, Iowa, it wiped out a filtration system and made the municipal water system unsafe. People were unable to use running water for weeks and were without drinkable water for longer than that. In order to restore full water service, the system had to be refilled with clean water. Local officials asked everyone to voluntarily refrain from using water in their homes and businesses for a few days. The situation was urgent. Without full water pressure in the city's water pipes, not only were residents without regular water service, but fire engines weren't able to use hydrants.

If all the city's residents had done as they were asked, everyone in the community would have had water within a couple of days. For some individuals, however, the temptation to use water secretly in the privacy of their own homes was too hard to resist. So many residents violated the city's rules that the resumption of full water service was delayed for many more days (Bradsher, 1993). As a result of individuals seeking their short-term benefits, the entire community suffered.

Why do such dilemmas occur? Part of the problem is a lack of communication and a lack of trust among individual members of a community. I may want to conserve water by using it sparingly, but if I think that my neighbors are hoarding, I too will hoard to make sure I don't go without. Hence I am induced to follow a line of action that results in a positive outcome for me but that may eventually have negative outcomes for the community. In the end we will all be worse off. In dire circumstances, immediate gratification is enticing. A "sensible" strategy—that is, one of moderation and conservation—is quite easy to abandon at the first sign of someone else satisfying his or her short-term gains.

The problem is made worse when individuals are fooled into thinking that meeting their individual needs will not have an effect on the community. "Is the cost of my using an extra gallon of water really going to harm the community?" From my point of view the answer is no. The dilemma arises, however, when everyone, or at least a substantial number of people, arrives at the same conclusion. As we collectively ignore or downplay the consequences of our actions, we collectively overuse the resource and pave the way for disasters that none of us has caused individually (Edney, 1979).

The Free-Rider Problem

Social dilemmas can also occur when people refrain from contributing something to a common resource when the resource is available anyway. To put it another way, why pay for something you can use for free? For example, it is irrational, from an individual's point of view, to donate money to public television. I can enjoy "Sesame Street" and "Masterpiece Theater" without paying a penny. My small, personal donation wouldn't be more than a tiny drop in public television's budgetary bucket and would have no noticeable impact on the entire amount needed to run a network anyway. From my perspective, there is no incentive for me to incur any costs when I don't have to. If everyone acted this way, however, we would all keep our money, but we'd eventually lose the resource. If public television depended solely on voluntary donations—corporate grants and sponsorships actually keep it going—it would have disappeared a long time ago.

Sociologists sometimes refer to this situation as the **free-rider** problem (Olsen, 1965). As the term implies, a free rider is an individual who acquires a good or service without risking any personal costs or contributing anything in return. Free ridership can be seen in a variety of everyday activities, from reading a magazine at a newsstand without buying it to photocopying a chapter from a book without buying the book. We all enjoy the benefits our tax dollars provide us—police, firefighters, smooth roads, and other municipal services. But if taxes were voluntary, would anyone willingly pay for these services?

We can see evidence of the free-rider problem at the institutional level. People often talk about children as a vital resource on whom the future of the country and the planet depend. The care and education of these children can be seen as a public resource. All of society benefits when children are in good physical, social, and psychological health. Yet most members of society are not willing to pay for the services necessary to ensure the well-being of children. It is difficult to convince people that increasing their taxes to improve schools, raise teachers' salaries, or hire more social workers will benefit them in the long run.

Solutions to Social Dilemmas

The tragedy of the commons and the free-rider problem can be solved or at least decreased in several ways (Messick & Brewer, 1983). Establishing communication between individuals helps, because it allows people to know what others are up to. When individual actions are identifiable, feelings of personal responsibility are likely to increase (Edney & Harper, 1978). However, this solution is not very practical when the group or community is quite large, like an entire country, for instance.

Another solution is to use coercion through restrictive rules or laws to prevent people from seeking their self-interested goals. Requiring people to pay taxes is one example. Another example is setting up union "closed shops," meaning that in order to work at a company an employee must join the union and pay union dues. Without this requirement, individual employees would be able to enjoy the benefits provided by the union—higher wages, better working conditions—without having to pay anything for them.

The city of Des Moines used a form of coercion to ensure compliance with its water-use rules. City officials set up an emergency hotline where people could call and anonymously turn in violators of the water rules. A work crew would go to a reported home or business and check for unauthorized water use. If the crew found the water meter running, the valve at the curb would be turned off for a week. No appeals were allowed, and water users were never told who turned them in. In addition, the offenders' names and addresses were immediately made known to reporters under Iowa's open records rules and spread across the state by newspapers, radio, and television (Bradsher, 1993).

The Structure of Organizations

Organizations are a defining structural feature of a complex society. We are all, to varying degrees, organizational creatures. We're born in them, educated in them, spend most of our adult lives working for them, and will most likely die in them (E. Gross & Etzioni, 1985). Think about all the things you do in the course of a typical day that are touched by some larger organizational system. Organizations design, produce, and market the alarm clock that wakes you up, the sheets and pillow cases you sleep on, the toothpaste you sleepily use, the showerhead whose spray jolts you into consciousness, the clothes you put on, the coffee you can't begin the day without, the newspaper you read, the car you drive, the computer you use at work, the bed you return to, and so on.

Organizations are responsible for the food that graces your table. The farm where the food is produced is probably a huge organization, as are the unions that protect the workers who produce the food and the transportation companies that bring it to your local stores. And all this is controlled by a vast network of financial organizations that sets prices and by governmental agencies that ensure the food's safety.

In order to prepare the food that is produced, delivered, and sold, you have to use products made by other organizations: a sink, a refrigerator, a microwave, a stove. To use those appliances you have to make arrangements with other organizations like the department of water and power, the gas company, and the electric company. And in order to pay these bills, you have to use still other organizations: the U.S. Postal Service, your bank, and credit companies.

Where does the money to pay the bills come from? Most likely your job. If you are employed, you probably work for yet another organization. When you receive a paycheck, the Internal Revenue Service and the Social Security Administration step in to take their share.

Now think of the car you use to get to that job. It was no doubt manufactured in a huge corporation and sold to you by a local dealership. The fuel that makes it run is produced by huge multinational corporations. The roads you travel to get to your destinations are built and maintained by massive organizations within the state and federal governments. You can't even drive unless you are covered by insurance, which is available only through an authorized company.

What if things aren't going well? Say you become sick, or you have an accident, or you have a dispute with someone else. Here, too, organizations come into play. You have to make use of hospitals, insurance companies, police departments, and courts.

You get the picture? Life in a complex society is a life touched by public and private organizations at every turn. In such a society things must be done in a formal, planned, and unified way. For instance, the people responsible for producing our food can't informally and spontaneously make decisions on what to grow and when to grow it. The people responsible for selling it to us can't make its availability random and unpredictable. Imagine how chaotic your life would be if you didn't know when your local supermarket would be open or what sorts of foods would be available for purchase. What if one day it sold nothing but flour, the next day only plums, and the day after just packaged lunch meats?

In a small-scale community where people grow their own food and the local mom-and-pop grocery store provides everything else, the lack of structure might not be a problem. But such an informal arrangement can't work in a massive society. We must have a relatively efficient and predictable system of providing goods and services to large numbers of people. The tasks that need to be done just to keep that system going are too complex for a single person: accounting, sales, marketing, research and development, public relations, insurance, maintenance, shipping and receiving, and so on. This complexity is what makes bureaucracy necessary.

Bureaucracies: Playing by the Rules

A **bureaucracy** is a large hierarchical organization that is governed by formal rules and regulations and that has a clear specification of work tasks. According to the famous 19th-century sociologist Max Weber (VAY-ber) (1946), a bureaucracy is the most efficient means of managing large groups of people. Weber felt that in a bureaucracy all decisions are made purely on the basis of what will accomplish the organization's goals.

Today, however, we tend to see bureaucracies as impersonal, rigid machines that trespass into our personal lives. Bureaucracies conjure up images of rows of desks occupied by faceless workers, endless lines and forms to fill out, and frustrations over "red tape." Indeed the word *bureaucrat* has taken on such a negative connotation that to be called one is the highest order of insult.

Characteristics of Bureaucracies

Bureaucracy refers to a specific type of organization with certain important characteristics:

- *Division of labor:* The bureaucracy has a clear-cut **division of labor**, which is carefully specified by written job descriptions for each position. The bureaucracy theoretically becomes more efficient because it employs only specialized experts, with every one of them responsible only for the effective performance of his or her narrowly defined duties (Blau & Meyer, 1987). The division of labor enables large organizations to accomplish larger goals than would be possible if everyone acted independently. Tasks become highly specific, sometimes to the point that it is illegal to perform someone else's task. For instance, in hospitals, which are highly complex bureaucracies, orderlies don't prescribe drugs, nurses don't perform surgery, and doctors don't help patients with their insurance forms. All groups play an important role in keeping the hospital going so that sick people can get better. But all must sacrifice the freedom to do any task they want in the interests of efficiently meeting the organization's goals.

- *Hierarchy of authority:* Not only are tasks divided in a bureaucracy, they are also ranked in a **hierarchy of authority** (Weber, 1946). Most bureaucracies are organized in a pyramid shape with a few people at the top who have a lot of power and many at the bottom who have virtually none. People at one level are responsible to those above them but can exert authority over those below. Authority tends to be attached to the position and not to the person occupying the position, so that the bureaucracy will not stop functioning in the event of a retirement or a death. Bureaucratic authority is also supposed to be honored despite the personal characteristics of the person occupying the position. When President Bill Clinton took office in 1993, he automatically became the commander-in-chief of the military. Because of his lack of military service, many in the armed forces resented him. Some high-ranking military officials privately expressed their mistrust of him. And yet those officers never questioned their obligation to follow his directives. The hierarchy of authority in bureaucracies not only allows some people to control others but it also justifies paying some people higher salaries than others.

- *Impersonality:* Bureaucracies are governed by an elaborate system of rules and regulations that ensure a particular task will be done the same way by each person occupying a position. With a system of rules, people don't have to "reinvent the wheel" each time a problem arises. The rules can govern everything from personal appearance and simple tasks like filing documents to complex issues like financial or political decisions of international significance. Furthermore, rules help ensure that bureaucrats perform their tasks impartially and impersonally. There is no place for the expression of strong feelings about superiors, subordinates, or clients. Ironically, the very factors that make the typical bureaucrat unpopular with the public—an aloof attitude, lack of genuine concern—actually allow the organization to run more efficiently. We want the person administering our driver's license examination to acknowledge us and care about us, but to do so would seriously impede the smooth functioning of the entire system. Think of how you'd feel if the road-test examiner had decided to stop for a cup of coffee with the person who was taking his or her driver's test before you.

Your university is a clear example of a bureaucracy. It has a definite division of labor that involves janitors, secretaries, librarians, coaches, professors, and administrators. The tasks people are responsible for are highly specialized. Professors in the Spanish department don't teach courses in biology. In large universities the specialization of tasks is even more narrowly defined. Sociology professors who teach social deviance probably don't teach demography.

Although the power afforded different positions varies from school to school, all universities have some sort of hierarchy of authority. Usually this hierarchy consists of students at the bottom (sorry!), followed by staff employees, teaching assistants, part-time instructors, professors, and department chairs. At the administrative level are associate deans, deans, vice presidents, and ultimately the president of the university and the board of trustees.

In addition, the university is governed by a strict set of rules regarding when and how students can register for classes, when grades must be turned in by the professor, graduation requirements, and university policies. Strict adherence on the part of university employees to these rules and policies, sometimes to the chagrin of the frustrated student who can't register for the one political science class he or she needs to graduate, is likely to give the university its final bureaucratic characteristic: impersonality.

Problems of Bureaucracies

Although he stressed the functional necessity of bureaucracies in complex Western societies, Weber warned that they could take on a life of their own, becoming impersonal "iron cages" for those within them. He feared that bureaucracies might one day dominate every part of society, locking people into a system that allows movement only from one dehumanizing bureaucracy to another.

In a classic bureaucracy the emphasis on conformity and routine inhibits the rational exercise of judgment. Bureaucratic life is precise. Personal discretion is minimized. People are expected to arrive at work at a given time, perform a pre-determined set of activities, rest at a certain time, and resume work until the day is over. In some companies, one shift of workers will replace another so that work can continue uninterrupted around the clock. Many bureaucracies are designed like machines, and the people within them are expected to behave as if they were parts of a machine. The mechanistic definitions of job responsibilities often encourage organizational members to adopt mindless, segmented attitudes about their jobs: "I do what I'm told," "It's not my responsibility."

As workers are fit into roles that completely determine their duties, responsibilities, and rights, they often become rigid and inflexible and are less concerned with the quality of their work than with whether they and others are playing by the rules. Hence, people become oriented more toward conformity than toward problem solving and critical thinking. They are the source of frustrating red tape, procedures and practices that often seem designed to prevent things from happening (G. Morgan, 1986).

Weber's fears have been largely realized. The bureaucratic model pervades every corner of modern society. The most successful bureaucracies not only dominate the business landscape, they have come to influence our entire way of life. Take, for instance, large fast-food restaurant chains. It is difficult for most of us to imagine what life would be like if we weren't able to go to the drive-thru and grab a quick bite to eat on the run. More than providing convenience, these restaurants have become a key piece of American culture.

■ ■ ■ ■ ■ ■ ■ ■

GEORGE RITZER
The McDonaldization of Society

Sociologist George Ritzer (1993) uses the McDonald's restaurant chain as a metaphor for some of the harmful effects of bureaucratization on society. Each day 7% of the U.S. population eat at McDonald's (Drucker, 1996). In 1995 alone, McDonald's cash registers rang up about $30 billion in sales. The 11,000 McDonald's restaurants in the United States and 7,000 in 89 other countries can be found in every corner of life: from airports, shopping malls, movie theaters, and college campuses across the United States to the main thoroughfares in major foreign cities such as London, Paris, and Moscow. Dining cars on the Swiss Federal Railroads serve McDonald's meals. There are 63 restaurants in China, even though only 10% of the population can afford a Big Mac. Because of its international appeal, McDonald's fed all the 1996 Olympic athletes in Atlanta (Drucker, 1996).

McDonald's phenomenal success has spawned countless other fast-food chains that emulate its model: Kentucky Fried Chicken, Taco Bell, Domino's

Pizza, Long John Silver's, and so on. Its fast-food formula has also influenced other types of businesses, among them Toys "R" Us, *USA Today*, Econo-Lodge motels, Pearle Vision Centers, Jiffy Lube, and Blockbuster Video.

But the success of McDonald's is more than just a story about hamburgers, profits, and business savvy. McDonald's has become a sacred institution, occupying a central place in popular culture. As you know, the "golden arches" of McDonald's are among the most identifiable symbols in society today. They're everywhere. When we're not driving past them in town or on an interstate highway, we see them on television. A 1986 survey found that 96% of schoolchildren were able to identify Ronald McDonald (Greenhouse, 1986). McDonald's appeals to us in a variety of ways:

> The restaurants themselves are depicted as spick-and-span, the food is said to be fresh and nutritious, the employees are shown to be young and eager, the managers appear gentle and caring, and the dining experience itself seems to be fun-filled. We are even led to believe that we contribute, at least indirectly, to charities by supporting the company that supports Ronald McDonald Houses for sick children. (Ritzer, 1993, p. 6)

According to Ritzer, McDonald's has been so successful primarily because it fits Weber's model of the classic bureaucracy. It has a clear division of labor and a uniform system of rules that make it highly efficient and predictable. No matter where you are, you know what to expect when you go into a McDonald's. You know that the ketchup will always be in the same place on the sandwich. French fries cook in precisely 3 minutes and 10 seconds; hamburger patties in 108 seconds. As one observer put it, McDonald's customers "are not in search of 'the best burger I've ever had' but rather 'the same burger I've always had'" (Drucker, 1996, p. 47).

In addition, if you've ever watched the workers behind the counter, you know that they each have specialized tasks that are narrowly defined:

> By combining twentieth-century computer technology with nineteenth-century time-and-motion studies, the McDonald's corporation has broken the jobs of griddleman, waitress, cashier and even manager down into small, simple steps. . . . The corporation has systematically extracted the decision-making elements from filling french fry boxes or scheduling staff. . . . They relentlessly weed out all variables that might make it necessary to make a decision at the store level, whether on pickles or on cleaning procedures. (Garson, 1988, p. 37)

McDonaldization will continue for several reasons. First, it is impelled by economic interests. Profit-making enterprises will go on emulating the McDonald's bureaucratic model because it leads to higher profits and lower costs. When McDonald's reaps greater efficiency and therefore higher profits through the increased use of nonhuman technology or the uniformity of its product, others quickly follow suit.

Second, McDonaldization has become a culturally desirable process. We live in a culture that treasures efficiency, speed, predictability, and control. Our desire for these values often blinds us to the fact that fast foods, as well as their domestic equivalent, microwaved foods, actually cost us more financially and nutritionally than meals we prepare ourselves. For many people the commitment to McDonald's is more emotional than economic. We all have memories of McDonald's: It's where we went after Little League games, it's where we hung out as teenagers, it's where we stopped on the way to the hospital for the birth of a first child, and so on. Because of the hallowed place it occupies in our society, people are willing to overlook its disadvantages.

Finally, McDonaldization parallels other changes occurring in society. With the increasing number of dual-earner couples, and therefore the increasing number of workers in general, there is less likely to be someone in the family who has the time or the desire to buy the ingredients, prepare the meal, bring everyone together to eat it, and clean up afterward. Furthermore, a society that emphasizes mobility is one in which the fast-food mentality will thrive.

But there is a downside to this model. Although the efficiency, speed, and predictability of McDonaldized systems may be appealing and comforting to some, the system as a whole has made social life more homogeneous, more rigid, and less personal. The smile on the face of the employee taking your order is a requirement of the position, not a sign of sincere delight in serving you. The "fast food" model has robbed us of our spontaneity. Our creativity and desire for uniqueness have been reduced, trapping us in Weber's "iron cage"—a bureaucratic culture that requires little thought and leaves virtually nothing to chance.

■ ■ ■

The Hierarchical Makeup of Organizations

Given the previous descriptions, you might think that everyone within a bureaucracy feels alienated, depersonalized, or perhaps even exploited. But a person's experience in a large bureaucracy depends in part on where he or she fits in the overall hierarchy of the organization. While some people are dehumanized by their place in the hierarchy, others may actually benefit from theirs.

The Upper Echelons

People at the top of large organizations have come the furthest within the bureaucracy, are the fewest in number, and get the most out of their position.

One interesting and disturbing characteristic of American bureaucracies is that executives tend to be extremely homogeneous; that is, they are similar to one another in terms of relevant social characteristics (DiMaggio & Powell, 1983; Kanter, 1977; W. H. Whyte, 1956). They are almost exclusively male, white, and middle- or upper-class (Zweigenhaft, 1987). Within Fortune 500 companies, for example, women and minorities hold fewer than 5% of senior management posts (Reskin & Padavic, 1994). In addition, their educational, social, and familial experiences are remarkably similar (Kanter, 1977; C. W. Mills, 1956). This homogeneity is due not only to historical prejudices in hiring and promotion practices but also to the nature of top-level jobs.

The higher one's place is in the bureaucracy, the more ambiguous one's job description becomes. Upper-level executives don't have clearly bounded jobs with neatly defined responsibilities. The executive must be prepared to use discretion and be flexible enough to deal with a variety of different problems at all times. Ironically, however, while discretion is the defining feature of an executive's position, the bulk of his or her time is not spent in making major decisions, creating, and planning, but in attending meetings, writing memos, responding to phone messages and faxes, and participating in company-related social gatherings.

Because the role of the executive is, by nature, a vague one, there are no clear-cut criteria by which to evaluate whether a person is performing her or his job effectively. Things like sales and production records or profit margins can provide only indirect indicators of an executive's competence. When asked what makes an executive effective, top-level employees identified such vague factors as the ability to communicate and win acceptance as the most important criteria (Kanter, 1977).

In such an environment, rapid communication, common language, and common understanding are important. Executives are therefore forced to spend a great deal of time with other executives whom they have come to trust and with whom they can communicate most smoothly and readily. From the perspective of the organization, the most efficient way to ensure acceptance and ease of communication is to limit top-level jobs to people who are similar to one another, who have had similar experiences, and who come from similar backgrounds. People like to include in their groups people "like" themselves and exclude those who are "different." This is why many male executives report feeling uncomfortable communicating with women: "You never knew where you stood. They changed their minds all the time; I never knew what they'd do from one minute to the next" (Kanter, 1977, p. 58). The result is a closed circle of executives who resemble one another but who are insulated from the rest of the organization. The structure of their occupational roles makes it more comfortable to try to exclude people seen as different, such as racial and ethnic minorities and women.

A self-fulfilling prophecy is embedded in this structure as well. The more closed and exclusive the network of executives, the more difficult it is for "outsiders" to break in. Their very difficulty gaining access to the top level of the organization is then perceived as a sign of their incompetence and an indicator to the insiders that they were right to close their ranks in the first place.

The Middle Ground

The view from the middle is quite different. The middle is in some ways the most discouraging part of an organization (Kanter & Stein, 1979). Those at the top set the organizational agenda and dictate policy, and those at the bottom solely follow orders and directives from above. The people in the middle are caught between those below, whose cooperation they need, and those above, who selectively grant them the authority to implement organizational policy. Hence middle-level employees are sometimes trapped in a world of conflicting role expectations.

Often the morale of people in the middle is sustained by the belief that they have a shot at the top. If I believe that in the future I will be promoted, my boring and unfulfilling job as a middle-level manager will hold different meaning for me than it would if I expect to remain in the same position forever (McHugh, 1968). It becomes a step on the ladder of success, a necessary but temporary stage in my upward mobility. Unpleasant tasks may be minor inconveniences, but they are the price I have to pay. This hope of future promotion may drive people in the middle to concentrate on accumulating bits of status and privilege so they can make enough of an impact to gain recognition from those above.

For many middle-level employees, however, the hope of upward mobility is just that, hope. Because of the pyramid structure of most bureaucracies, the vast majority of middle-level employees will not move up. Many simply fail in the increasingly competitive push for advancement into the upper echelons of the organization. Others are stuck in jobs that provide little or no opportunity for advancement. Some people are able to develop a comfortable niche in the middle (Kanter & Stein, 1979), but others are likely to harbor a bitterness that creates feelings of alienation and anger and may manifest itself in attempts to retaliate and punish the company.

Because of the structure of most large organizations, middle-level managers are forced to become cautious in their approach to their jobs. Unwilling to jeopardize the limited privileges they have attained, middle-level managers often become controlling, coercive, and demanding in their relationships with the people they supervise, ruling their narrow domain with an iron hand:

> Getting everything right, and demanding that subordinates do the same, is the response of those who lack other ways to impress those above them or to secure their position; and in turn, they demand this kind of ritualistic conformity from subordinates, like a school teacher more concerned about the neatness of the paper than its ideas. (Kanter & Stein, 1979, p. 95)

For some people in the middle, membership in the organization becomes their life, often to the detriment of other roles and relationships. Almost four decades ago sociologist William H. Whyte (1956) described how the personal lives of rising young executives were often overshadowed by their desire to succeed in the corporate world. Large organizations instilled in their employees a corporate social ethic, a belief that "belongingness" to the group was the ultimate need of the individual. Such beliefs encouraged total commitment to the organization, making a person's private life irrelevant for smooth organizational functioning.

Whyte's depiction of the private costs of organizational life ring true today. Organizations still value team players, middle-level employees who place organizational interests above their own (Jackall, 1988). To be a good team player one must avoid expressing strong political or moral opinions, sacrifice one's home life by putting in long hours, and be forever obedient to one's superiors. Being seen as a loyal and effective group member and sticking to one's assigned position are also important. Striking, distinctive characteristics, such as being abrasive or pushy or not knowing when to back off, are dangerous in the bureaucratic world. According to one study, one of the most damaging things that can be said about a middle-level manager is that he or she is brilliant. This judgment usually signals that the individual has publicly asserted his or her intelligence and is perceived as a threat to others (Jackall, 1988).

Interestingly, while organizations still value the ideal of team play, individuals today seem to be less willing to sacrifice their personal lives and beliefs for the organization. Two sociologists, Paul Leinberger and Bruce Tucker (1991), interviewed the sons and daughters of the original "organizational men" that Whyte interviewed more than 30 years earlier. They found that these individuals were very different from their parents in their values and attitudes. They tended to be individualists, more inclined to pursue self-fulfillment than a feeling of belongingness to the organization. Given recent social trends, this finding is not surprising. In an era when corporate mergers, relocations, and periodic layoffs are commonplace, the concept of organizational loyalty has become all but extinct.

Although few desire to go back to a past when middle-level employees sacrificed everything for their career aspirations, Leinberger and Tucker point out that today's cultural emphasis on individualism has also created other problems, such as feelings of isolation, the inability to commit to others, and the absence of a sense of community.

The Lower Echelons

A discussion of the everyday experience of bureaucracy would be incomplete without discussing what it looks like from the bottom. Those who stand lowest in the organization's hierarchy are paid the least, valued the least, and considered the most expendable (Kanter & Stein, 1979). The real sign that you are at the bottom is the degree to which you are controlled by others. People at the bottom don't have the right to define their occupational tasks themselves. They have little discretion, little autonomy, little freedom, and little influence. In the university bureaucracy, for example, students usually don't have much say over the content of their courses, the curriculum of their major, or the requirements necessary for graduation.

Most American corporations are still organized in terms of ideas developed in the early 1900s. The fundamental principle is that a highly specific division of labor increases productivity and lowers costs. Hence the low-level work tasks in a bureaucratic organization are usually subdivided into small parts that can be performed repetitively by unskilled workers. This structure provides management with the maximum control over workers' jobs while the workers themselves become "an indistinguishable swarm" (Kanter & Stein, 1979, p. 178).

Often technological advancements coincide with the subdivision of low-level jobs and a decrease in the skill levels required to do them (Hartmann, Kraut, & Tilly, 1989). For example, in the insurance industry, the skilled work of assigning risks and assessing people's claims has been increasingly incorporated into computer software programs. What once required a great deal of human judgment and discretion is now almost completely routinized. Less-skilled, less-experienced, and lower-paid clerks can now perform the work once performed by skilled workers and professionals (Hartmann, Kraut, & Tilly, 1989).

This process, called **de-skilling**, creates jobs that require obedience and passivity rather than talent and experience. De-skilling provides the organization with clear financial benefits but creates low levels of job satisfaction among the employees. Dull and repetitive tasks that offer little challenge, such as assembly-line work, account for a substantial amount of the discontent experienced by workers at the bottom of large bureaucracies (U.S. Department of Health, Education and Welfare, 1973). In one study, assembly-line workers in textile and automobile plants were compared to skilled technicians in the chemical industry. Because the skilled workers had jobs that involved the exercise of judgment and initiative, they were much less alienated and found their jobs much more rewarding than did the assembly-line workers (Blauner, 1964).

Attempts at enriching the otherwise dull work lives of people at the bottom have been somewhat successful. Workers at the Motorola Company had to assemble a portable telephone beeper that consisted of 80 small parts. In the traditional way, each worker made a small change and passed the unit on to the next worker. In the revised procedure, each worker assembled an entire unit, and the worker's name appeared on the completed beeper. Although the assembly costs were higher, the company claimed that the quality of the product was also higher and absenteeism and turnover rates were lower (cited in E. Gross & Etzioni, 1985).

Without such workplace innovations, the task facing many workers at the bottom is to make their occupational lives tolerable by exerting some kind of control over the work they do. It would appear, from the previous discussion, that the top-down flow of authority in bureaucratic organizations would make such a task relatively impossible. In reality, though, lower-level employees are not completely powerless and can be somewhat autonomous, even creative, in their positions.

For one thing, the sheer size of large corporations makes it next to impossible for middle- and upper-level managers to supervise directly and therefore exert continuous authority over lower-level workers. Substantial opportunities exist, even in the most highly structured and repetitive jobs, for workers to either redefine the immediate nature of their tasks or willingly and secretly violate the expectations and orders of superiors. For instance, one study found that clerical, service, and manual workers often exerted autonomy in the workplace by figuring out ways to do required chores in less than the time alotted by management. They could then spend the rest of their time doing why they wanted. As one night shift worker in a chemical plant described it:

> You can disappear in [the] plant and never be seen, especially if you are on the night shift where there aren't many people. . . . We have intercoms, but you don't have to answer the intercom if you don't want to. Some sleep, some rest. . . ; some have girlfriends or boyfriends come down and they'll disappear with them out in the plant somewhere, or sit out in the parking lot. (Hodson, 1991, p. 63)

In sum, lower-level workers are not necessarily powerless automatons whose lives are totally structured from above. In fact, the authority of middle-level managers is thoroughly dependent on their subordinates' willingness to cooperate and abide by management's directives. People who don't care about the organization because they feel it doesn't care about them can allow mistakes to go through, put in the minimum amount of time possible, or engage in deliberate sabotage. Such worker resistance can be disastrous for the manager and for the organization as a whole (Armstrong, Goodman, & Hyman, 1981). When organized, lower-level workers can even exert tremendous influence over the policies of a company, through strikes, slowdowns, and collective bargaining arrangements (see chapter 15).

The Creation of Organizational Reality

Organizations are more than just structure, rules, policies, goals, job descriptions, and standard operating procedures. As in society as a whole, their formal, structural characteristics are created, maintained, and changed through the everyday actions of their members (G. Morgan, 1986).

The language of an organization is one of the ways it creates its own reality. At one level, new members must learn the jargon of the organization in order to survive within it. To function within the navy system, for example, a recruit must learn the meaning of a dizzying array of words, phrases, acronyms, abbreviations, slang, sounds, and symbols that are unintelligible to outsiders (Evered, 1983). More important, language helps to generate and maintain the organization by marking boundaries between insiders and outsiders.

The organizations that work well are those in which everyone internalizes the same rules, values, and beliefs. The best-selling managerial book *In Search of Excellence* states that building a strong corporate culture requires "shaping norms," "instilling beliefs," "inculcating values," and "generating emotions" (Peters & Waterman, 1982). Corporate slogans like "Quality is job 1" (Ford), "Progress is our most important product" (General Electric), and "No surprises" (Holiday Inn) communicate the values around which organizations build and symbolize important aspects of the corporate philosophy (G. Morgan, 1986). In some organizations new members are told stories about the founding of the organization, its charismatic leaders, or some other significant event that becomes a metaphor for the culture of that organization.

Whatever the official rules, beliefs, and values of the organization, people have their own ideas and may develop their own informal structure within the larger formal structure of the organization (Meyer & Rowan, 1977). For example, restricting output is one norm that frequently emerges in factory settings (P. Thompson, 1989). Employees collectively decide, implicitly or explicitly, not to produce as much as they are physically capable of producing. This informal system of productivity norms develops partly out of a mistrust in management and the belief that increased productivity would result in higher expectations, not higher rewards (Roethlisberger & Dickson, 1939). Those who produce too much or who work too quickly are considered "rate busters," deviants within the factory subculture. Indeed, rate busters are likely to be employees whose skill and seniority place them in relatively strong positions. Only a worker with such status can escape the sanctions of fellow workers (Burawoy, 1979).

Restricted output can also be seen in the college classroom. Most instructors tell their students that classroom discussion is important and may even use it as a criterion for assigning a final grade. Yet rarely does every student in a class, or even a majority of students, participate. Most college students know that a small group of people—perhaps 3 or 4 in a class of 40—can be counted on to respond to questions asked by the professor or comment on any issue raised in class. These students relieve the remainder of the class from the burden of having to talk in class (Karp & Yoels, 1976). But although these talkative students are carrying the discussion for the entire class, they tend to be disliked by others. There is a strong norm among many students that people shouldn't talk too much in class (Karp & Yoels, 1976). Such linguistic "rate busting" upsets the normative arrangement of the classroom and, in the students' eyes, may increase the instructor's expectations, thereby hurting everyone in the long run. Other students indicate their annoyance by audibly sighing, rolling their eyes, rattling their notebooks, or openly snickering when a classmate talks too much.

At a higher level, an organization may substitute, for its formally stated goals, others for which it was not originally created (E. Gross & Etzioni, 1985). Most organizations are established to serve a specific purpose. But some organizations often displace their original goals with the informal goal of maintaining their own well-being. Consider social welfare agencies that seek to rehabilitate the blind. Their stated goal is to help blind people become independent, functioning members of society. The vast majority of blind people are old or severely handicapped in other ways, but agencies pay little attention to these people. Instead, they prefer the "desirable" blind—young people who have employment prospects—because it is easier to raise money for them (R. Scott, 1967). However, there aren't enough "desirable" blind people to go around, so agencies are forced to compete with one another to get such clients. They then attempt to keep their blind clients dependent on the agency, rather than make them independent, self-sufficient members of society. So while the formal goal of the organization is to help people, the more immediate goal is to survive.

One of the fascinating ironies of large organizations is that if everyone followed every rule exactly and literally, the organization would self-destruct. For example, the goal of the highly bureaucratized criminal court system is to ensure justice by punishing those who have violated society's laws. Each person accused of committing a serious crime is constitutionally guaranteed a trial by a jury of peers. The jury trial is the epitome of justice and has been played out in movies and television so often that we all know what it looks like even if we haven't directly experienced it ourselves. However, the day-to-day operations of the criminal court system bear little resemblance to this common media image. Public defenders, district attorneys, private attorneys, and judges actually work closely together to move offenders through the system in an orderly fashion (Sudnow, 1965). Only a tiny percentage of criminal cases—between 10% and 20%—ever go to trial (D. C. Gibbons, 1992). The rest are either dismissed or, more commonly, settled through plea bargaining, an arrangement whereby, in exchange for a less severe punishment, the accused pleads guilty to a less serious crime than the original charge.

If judges and attorneys followed the procedural rules to the letter and provided all their clients with the jury trial that is their constitutional right, the system would break down. The courts, already overtaxed, would be incapable of handling the volume of cases. The informal system of plea bargaining has taken root, allowing the courts to continue functioning. Those individuals who play exclusively by the rules, like the young idealistic public defender who wants to take all of his or her cases to trial, are subject to informal sanctions by judges and superiors, such as inconvenient trial dates or heavier caseloads.

In sum, organizational life is a combination of formal structural rules and informal patterns of behavior. Codified rules are sometimes violated and new, unspoken ones created instead. Stated organizational goals often conflict with the real ones. Although there may appear to be a clear chain of command, the informal structure—friendships, coalitions, and so on—often has more of an impact on how things are done.

■ ■ ■ ■ ■ ■ ■ ■
MICRO-MACRO CONNECTION
Virtual Organizations

One of the unspoken assumptions underlying the sociological discussion of organizational reality is that the managers, supervisors, and employees who belong to an organization and who help to shape its culture work in physical proximity to one another. This point seems obvious, but it is not always true. Certain businesses have never relied on having all employees in the same place at the same time. Journalists and traveling salespeople, for example, have always been able to do their work away from a centralized location.

With recent advances like E-mail, voice mail, fax machines, cellular phones, and sophisticated computer technology, such arrangements may soon become the norm. About 3 million employees of U.S. companies perform all or part of their work away from their offices, and their numbers increase some 20% each year (Bjerklie, Cole, & Cray, 1995). As the technology becomes more efficient and convenient, the trend is likely to accelerate dramatically. In fact, more and more businesses are completely abandoning the traditional assumption that common physical space is the defining feature of an organization.

In the past, you could always count on a company's phone number being linked to a specific location. But today, if you call a major airline's toll-free reservations desk to make flight arrangements, for example, you may talk to someone in San Diego or Fargo or New York or Honolulu. The office as a "home" for the phone—with a real person to answer it—may soon become a relic of the past (Handy, 1995).

The decreased reliance on physical space means that maintaining an office may soon become an enormously expensive luxury (Handy, 1995). A few years ago, IBM reduced office space in its Denver facility from nine floors to four—saving a projected $6 million over the next several years—by providing employees with a computer, printer, and fax-modem so they could work away from the office. At one large accounting firm, employees who find themselves in need of physical space must reserve a room at least one day in advance. In 1995, a large advertising agency in California made headlines when it got rid of its executive offices, secretary cubicles, and file cabinets. The only spaces employees can now call their own are lockers where they can stow personal belongings. They move wherever their work takes them, whether in the building, at home, or on the road. Along with personal space, paper too has all but vanished. Faxes and memos arrive on personal computer screens. Phone messages are recorded on voice mail. Important documents are available only electronically on computer terminals scattered around the building.

"Virtual organizations"—those organizations that link employees and clients electronically rather than physically—are not just limited to businesses. Students at the Open University in Great Britain can participate in classes from their homes or places of work via E-mail, mobile phones, and videoconferencing. They will never be in the same place at the same time. The Open University's business school is the largest in Europe, although few students have ever met the faculty or any of the other students (Handy, 1995). Recently in this country, the governors of 10 western states agreed to fund a massive virtual university in which students from the region could take courses and earn degrees by computer (Cushman, 1996).

Economically, the virtual organization offers several advantages. It may be a solution to the clash between material growth and environmental degradation. Electronic information, after all, doesn't take up very much of the earth's resources. A less-urgent need for office space means fewer skyscrapers and fewer people commuting to work. Moreover, employment in these new, free-floating organizations appeals to the younger generation of potential workers, who have grown up alongside the technology that has made virtual organizations possible.

But with economic advantage comes disadvantage. These new forms of business organization, coupled with the new generation of sophisticated technology, are forcing people out of work. Automated technologies have been reducing the need for human labor in manufacturing for years and within 10 years less than 12% of all U.S. workers will work in factories (Rifkin, 1996). But the service sector of the economy is also beginning to automate. In banking, insurance, and wholesale and retail trades, companies are replacing the white-collar workforce with small, highly skilled work teams aided by state-of-the-art technology.

Another troubling economic consequence of our growing organizational reliance on computer technology is that access to information is quickly becoming the new divide between the "haves" and the "have-nots." Wealthier school districts already have equipment that is unavailable to poorer ones. And although computers and peripheral technological gadgets get cheaper each year, they are still priced well out of the reach of many people. The higher a family's income, the more likely it is that the family will own or use a computer (see Table 9.1). Millions of Americans don't even have the phones upon which high-speed information services depend. In an effort to alleviate the problem, some communities—like Santa Monica, California—have public electronic networks that provide computer terminals in banks, community centers, and grocery stores that anyone can use ("A new divide," 1995).

As organizations become ever more dependent on information technology and less dependent on face-to-face interaction, new managerial and personal dilemmas arise as well. For instance, how do you manage people who aren't there? No longer will a co-worker be just down the hall, available for a spontaneous, unscheduled meeting or a quick check on his or her progress. With heightened efficiency comes a loss of direct control and a greater dependence on trust.

How does an organization disseminate its culture, give direction and purpose, and set its course when people are scattered all over the place? What becomes of workers' loyalty to the organization?

Table 9.1   *Computer Use and Family Income*

Annual Family Income	Uses Computer Anywhere	Has Computer at Home
Less than $10,000	11.4%	6.8%
$10,000–14,999	15.2	8.4
$15,000–19,999	23.0	12.5
$20,000–24,999	27.7	15.3
$25,000–34,999	36.5	21.2
$35,000–49,999	46.3	31.3
$50,000–74,999	60.3	45.9
$75,000 and over	65.4	61.7
Income not reported	24.4	20.2

Source: U.S. Bureau of the Census, 1995b, p. 1.

> Organizationally, we have to wonder whether a company is, in the future, going to be anything more than the box of contracts some companies now seem to be. Is a box of contracts a sustainable basis for getting the work done in our society, or is it not, in fact, a recipe for disintegration? (Handy, 1995, p. 41)

People may not be willing to give a significant amount of their lives, time, and talent to an organization they work for but don't spend any time in, one that is owned, run, and managed by people they don't know and perhaps have never met.

How will loss of visibility, lack of access to the "office grapevine," and the reliance on self-motivation affect the employee who works alone at his or her computer terminal at home? For employees whose social life revolves around co-workers, such a transition can be difficult. The problem with communicating electronically is that it is "deliberate communication." That is, if Employee A wants to "talk" to Employee B, she or he must think about what needs to be said and how best to say it. Employee B can compose a response to ensure a particular reaction. The informal, unplanned, free-ranging conversations that take place in traditional organizations are fast becoming obsolete (M. O. Kirk, 1996).

In response to these potential problems, some companies have returned to more conventional modes of organization. A large engineering firm in Philadelphia, for example, recently reopened its headquarters and moved many of its suburban employees back. A computer software company that offers virtual services holds quarterly wine and cheese receptions for its employees and clients. Said the president of the company, "They want to see each other. And they want to see us, our equipment, our staff, and make sure we are real" (quoted in M. O. Kirk, 1996, p. 10).

▪ ▪ ▪

Organizations and Institutions

Understanding the influence of organizations on our everyday lives tells only part of the story. Organizations themselves exist within a larger structural context, acting as a sort of liaison between people and major social institutions. The major social institutions include the economic system, government, religion, health care, education, and family. As you recall from chapter 2, institutions are stable sets of statuses, roles, groups, and organizations that provide the foundation for behavior in certain major areas of social life. They are patterned ways of solving the problems and meeting the needs of a particular society.

In a complex society, much of our individual and organizational behavior is institutionalized—that is, governed by the common, taken-for-granted expectations associated with various social roles (Berger & Luckmann, 1966). The actions of parents and children within a family, teachers and students in a classroom, representatives in Congress, and workers and supervisors in a factory are examples of institutionalized behavior. Much of what occurs in these settings is fairly repetitive and predictable. If a problematic situation arises—a death in the family, a breakdown of factory machinery, a national political crisis—there is usually a precedent or at least some agreement on how people ought to act. The actions of corporations, political parties, and other types of organizations are also institutionalized to a certain degree.

Institutions are more than just systems of routine behaviors. Each individual is unique and brings a personal touch to institutional behavior. Some parents are more strict than others in raising their children; some factory supervisors are more flexible than others; some students talk and argue in class; some legislators are more active than others in trying to change laws. Institutionalized behavior is always a combination of the structurally defined expectations of a social position and the characteristics of the particular person occupying it (Zucker, 1991).

Individuals aren't the only ones influenced by large social institutions. Organizations, too, must operate within an institutional context. Individuals constitute organizations, and the structure of these organizations exerts tremendous influence over our day-to-day experiences. But this is only part of the picture. Some social phenomena can be understood only if we take a step back and treat organizations and institutions as the objects of analysis.

Organizational Networks within Institutions

Like individual people, organizations are born, grow, become overweight, slim down, migrate, form relationships with others, and die. They interact with one another, too, cooperating on some occasions and competing on others depending on the prevailing economic and political winds. Just as we can talk about a hierarchy of people or groups within an organization, we can also talk about a hierarchy of organizations within an institution. As with people, some organizations are more powerful than others and can dictate the manner in which others live their lives. When giant corporations like General Electric, Microsoft, Coca-Cola, and IBM change their operations or come up with an innovative new product, it immediately influences the practices of other organizations throughout their respective industries. If one of these titans decides to downsize or expand its operations, the effects are felt throughout the entire financial community.

But even powerful organizations like these cannot stand alone. Massive networks of organizations are linked by common goals and needs. The networks are often so complex that organizations from very different fields find themselves dependent on one another for survival. Our experiences with major institutions, then, are often mediated by organizations.

Consider the American health care system, a major institution. Think about the vast network of organizations necessary for a single hospital to operate. First of all, it is tightly linked to all the other hospitals in the area. A change in one, such as a reduction in the number of patients treated or the opening of a new state-of-the-art trauma center, would quickly have consequences for all the others. The linkage between hospitals makes it possible for equipment, staff, and patients to be transferred from one hospital to another when necessary.

The hospital must also be linked to formal socializing organizations like medical schools, nursing schools, and teaching hospitals. It couldn't function if it didn't have connections to organizations responsible for the professional training of its staff. These organizations, in turn, are usually affiliated with larger universities, thus expanding the links in the network.

To survive financially, the hospital must also have connections to funding organizations. Hospitals have traditionally been owned and operated by a variety of governmental, religious, nonprofit, and for-profit organizations. They must operate under a set of strict regulations, which means they must also be linked to the city, state, and federal governmental agencies responsible for certification, such as the Joint Commission on Accreditation of Hospitals (Perrow, 1986). Add to these the links to the medical equipment industry, the drug industry, insurance companies, the legal profession, charities, and patients' rights groups, and the system becomes even more complex. Given such complexity, it's not surprising that health care spending has nearly doubled over the past two decades (see Figure 9.1).

When you consider that each of these parts of the health care system is a part of its own complex bureaucratic network, it begins to boggle the mind. Despite this institution's size and importance, in the end people make the whole system work, and people can change it. There is an ongoing debate at the highest levels of government about how to change the nation's health care system. If changes

Figure 9.1   *Trends in Spending for Health Care in the United States, 1970–1990*

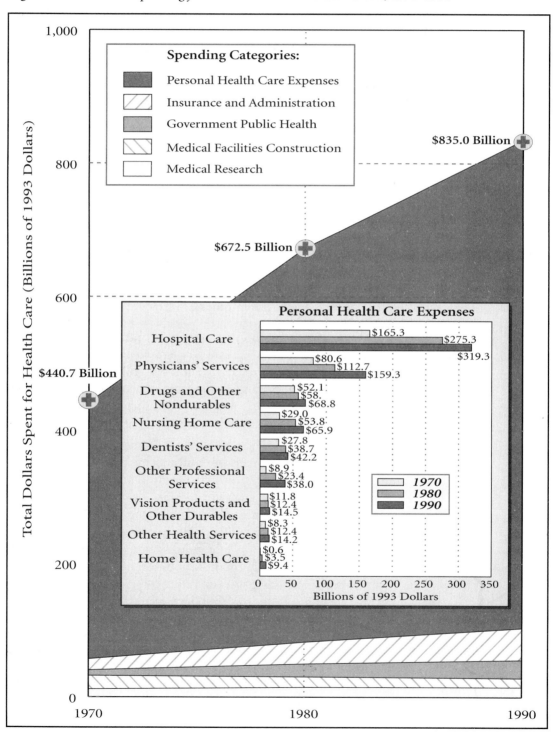

occur, the whole institutional network will sink or swim on the actions of the individual people who represent business, medical, governmental, and consumer interests.

To have a sociological imagination—to fully understand how our lives are affected by social forces—we have to know something about how the organizations to which we belong affect one another and how they are influenced by the larger institutional context in which they exist.

Institutional Pressures toward Similarity

If you think about how many varieties of organizations there are in the world, it is tempting to focus on their diversity. Some are large, others small. Some are formal and complex, others informal and simple. Some have a pyramid-shaped chain of command, others are more egalitarian (E. Gross & Etzioni, 1985). Sociologists have long been interested in the unique ways different organizations adapt to changing political, economic, cultural, or environmental circumstances. However, organizations seem to be more similar than different and even tend to imitate one another's actions as they become established in a particular institution (DiMaggio & Powell, 1983).

Organizational similarity is not really that surprising. Because of the nature of the problems organizations in the same industry have to address, they come to adopt similar methods of dealing with them. For instance, NBC, ABC, and CBS go about trying to attract viewers in much the same way. As you well know, the perceived success of a certain type of television show, such as the miniseries or the reality-based docudrama, creates an avalanche of similar shows on other networks.

In short, instead of adjusting directly to changes in the social environment—such as the shifting tastes of the television viewing public—organizations end up adjusting to what other organizations are doing (DiMaggio & Powell, 1983). The surprising fact is that the imitated practices are not necessarily more effective. After once-innovative new strategies have spread throughout an industry, they no longer improve the organization's performance. Viewers eventually get sick of "real life" cop shows or emergency rescue shows. The net effect of the imitations is to lessen diversity within the industry.

The tendency for organizations to emulate one another is heightened in times of institutional uncertainty (DiMaggio & Powell, 1983). When new technologies are poorly understood, when there are dramatic changes in the physical environment, or when local, state, and federal governments create new regulations or set new agendas, there is likely to be some confusion about how things ought to be done. Just as individuals look to one another to help define ambiguous situations and determine an appropriate course of action (see chapter 2), so do organizations.

Take changes in the field of higher education, for instance. The pool of potential college students—18-year-old high school graduates—has been decreasing over the last several years because of a drop in the birth rate in the mid-1970s. In addition, costs of college tuition have been steadily increasing. As a result, many colleges and universities across the country are being forced to address the problem of how to attract more students. The problem is particularly acute among private colleges that depend on tuition money.

Such was the case at the university where I teach. As enrollment shrank, administrative panic began to set in. An outside consultant was called in to design a new marketing strategy for the school. I was one of several professors asked to meet with the consultant and provide him with information about the school and what it was like to teach here. He had some clear strategies for "packaging" the school's image to make it more attractive to prospective students, despite the high cost. The ideas sounded interesting: redesigned brochures, a new recruitment video, state-of-the-art bulk mailing techniques, and so on.

After our meeting I asked him how many other schools he worked for. He said between 15 and 20, several of which were schools like mine competing for the same shrinking pool of students. Although he was quick to point out that each school's situation was unique, he admitted that many of the "novel" strategies he advised us to use were things other universities were already using. We were addressing a new and uncertain dilemma by replicating the practices of other organizations in the network.

Organizations also resemble one another because those who run them, particularly professionals, tend to come from similar training backgrounds. In many institutions the professional career track is so closely guarded that the individuals who make it to the top are virtually indistinguishable from one another (DiMaggio & Powell, 1983). Medical schools are important centers for the development of organizational norms among doctors. Furthermore, the fact that most doctors belong to the American Medical Association creates a pool of individuals with similar attitudes and approaches across a range of organizations. When these doctors become administrators, they will likely bring this common approach to running a hospital.

Certain organizational forms dominate not necessarily because they are the most effective means of achieving goals, but because social forces like institutional uncertainty and the power of professions to provide individuals with a single normative standard create pressures toward similarity. Such similarity makes it easier for organizations to interact with one another and to be acknowledged as legitimate and reputable within the field (DiMaggio & Powell, 1983). But it is not without its costs. When organizations replicate one another, institutional change becomes difficult, and the iron cage of bureaucracy becomes harder to escape. Moreover, when organizations model each other they may imitate responses that are inadequate, harmful, or maybe even catastrophic. One such situation involves the AIDS epidemic.

■ ■ ■ ■ ■ ■ ■ ■

MICRO-MACRO CONNECTION
The AIDS Epidemic

We usually don't think of the spread of deadly diseases as an organizational or institutional issue. Epidemics occur because people infect one another with a disease that has no cure. AIDS (acquired immunodeficiency syndrome) is a deadly infectious disease that has reached epidemic proportions. By 1994 more than 250,000 people, mostly men between the ages of 25 and 44, had died from it (U.S. Bureau of the Census, 1995a). AIDS has become the leading cause of death among this segment of the population in close to 40% of America's large cities.

Although the epidemic was first identified in 1981 (Shilts, 1987), it really wasn't taken that seriously by the government or the scientific community until several years later. By the time President Ronald Reagan first spoke of the disease publicly—in 1985, after actor Rock Hudson's death—more than 20,000 people had already died from it (Shilts, 1987). That year the federal government allocated only about $100 million for AIDS research; the total provided by the states for research, patient care, and education amounted to about $9 million. In contrast, 10 years earlier President Gerald Ford authorized $135 million dollars for a nationwide inoculation program against the swine flu. By the time that program ended, only 107 cases of swine flu had been reported, and 58 people had died from it (Eitzen & Baca-Zinn, 1989).

Today, of course, AIDS funding is in the billions and the disease is recognized for what it is: a chronic, deadly virus that has infected more than a million people and will be a part of the human condition for a long time to come (Fee & Fox, 1992). All state governments, including the District of Columbia, now provide funds for AIDS treatment and research. Virtually every public school system and every university has a form of AIDS awareness education.

Why did it take so long for the magnitude of the epidemic to be recognized by the public, the government, and the scientific community? Part of the reason was the stigmatized identity of the majority of the victims—gay men, intravenous drug users, and so on. Fear, hostility, and discrimination certainly prevented massive public outcry and a quick and effective response from the scientific community. To many citizens AIDS was self-inflicted, the product of unnatural and repugnant behavior. Images of rampant promiscuity among the gay male population only added to the widespread rejection of homosexuality and, therefore, shaped the unsympathetic public response to AIDS. Even among the scientific community in the mid-1980s there was little prestige to be gained in studying a "homosexual disease" (Fee & Fox, 1992; Shilts, 1987).

While homophobia no doubt played a role, sociologists Charles Perrow and Mauro Guillen (1990) argue that this explanation is insufficient. They point out that if intolerance were all that mattered, the repression of homosexuals and intravenous drug users would have been fiercer than it had been and wouldn't have required an epidemic to increase it. These individuals are not executed or placed in concentration camps as a matter of public policy as they are in some countries, such as Cuba (Perrow & Guillen, 1990). Certainly discrimination exists in this country. But it is not officially and overtly sanctioned. Furthermore, public health and government officials have gone to great lengths to reassure the gay community that everything possible is being done for them.

Perrow and Guillen offer a more pervasive, although not immediately apparent, explanation: organizational failure. The organizational structure that was set up at the time—the government, medical research firms, hospitals, and so on—was ill equipped to deal with the AIDS epidemic. Inaction, slowness, and outright denial became the normative responses that organizations copied from one another.

Ironically, the essential facts about the disease—that it is a blood-borne virus infecting men and women whether gay or straight, that it can be passed on by a mother to her unborn child, and that it can be prevented by relatively cheap measures (for example, condoms)—were well known early on. Yet for several years, the government, the medical community, and even the gay community mounted no public education campaign. In those early years, most of the at-risk population was visible, accessible, and geographically concentrated in small areas of major cities such as New York and San Francisco. It would have been relatively easy and cheap to implement a massive educational effort to stop the spread of the disease (Perrow & Guillen, 1990). But 2 years after the epidemic began, the total of the government's attempts to prevent the spread of AIDS among gay men was two sentences of guidance: "Sexual contact should be avoided with persons known or suspected to have AIDS. Members of high-risk groups should be aware that multiple sexual partners increase the probability of developing AIDS" (Shilts, 1987, p. 242).

Budget considerations played a major role in the federal government's response to AIDS. These budgetary decisions were politically as well as economically motivated. There is no denying that feelings about gay people and IV drug users influenced the government's response. The Reagan administration aligned quite clearly with religious, conservative groups such as the Moral Majority. Had this epidemic affected nonstigmatized citizens, it would have been fought with greater resources and less government denial (Perrow & Guillen, 1990).

The response of the medical community was also ineffective. The United States spends more money on health care but gets fewer results in terms of good overall health statistics than any industrialized country (Perrow & Guillen, 1990). It is a system characterized by fragmented services, poor leadership, and a complacent public. AIDS came along at a time of high inflation and massive federal cutbacks in health care services. With reduced revenues, hospitals had a hard time dealing with the surge of AIDS patients that began knocking on their doors in the mid-1980s.

Part of this problem is institutional. American medicine's emphasis on treatment over prevention (see chapter 4) has made hospitals the major focus of our health care system. Because controlling costs is the chief goal of health policy and treating AIDS patients is costly, it is not surprising that the response to this epidemic was inadequate. Some hospitals with special "AIDS units" experienced a mass defection of non-AIDS patients who went elsewhere. For others that admitted large numbers of AIDS patients, the resulting shortage of beds meant jammed emergency rooms and long waiting periods. This inefficiency had an economic effect on the entire community. Many business owners, for example, pointed to the lack of hospital bed space as a reason for moving their companies to other cities, thereby reducing the number of jobs available in the community.

In addition, the process of reviewing and publishing medical research in the most prestigious scholarly journals may have also delayed public acknowledgment of the seriousness of the epidemic. These journals are the primary means by which information is disseminated in the medical community. Also, publishing articles in these journals is the primary means by which individual researchers can enhance their reputations. The process of reviewing, revising, and publishing, however, can take up to a year, and virtually all journals have an iron-clad rule about the secrecy of material that is being considered for publication: If there is any leak whatsoever to the popular press about the research prior to publication, the journal will not publish the article (Shilts, 1987).

These operating procedures delayed the publication of information about the disease. The first article on AIDS appeared in June 1981 in the *Morbidity and Mortality Weekly Report*, a newsletter published by the Centers for Disease Control (CDC) that is far less prestigious but has a much shorter publication time than the top journals. Even when the article was published, the CDC dropped all references to homosexuality from the title and placed it inconspicuously on the second page of the report, not wanting to offend homosexuals or inflame prejudice against them (Shilts, 1987).

The many organizations that compose the nation's blood industry were also slow to respond. No national program for testing blood or screening blood donors existed until several years after the epidemic began. As early as July 1982, the CDC warned the blood industry of its suspicion that the disease was transmitted through blood and asked that blood banks not accept blood from high-risk groups. It also recommended that the Public Health Service test all blood.

The opposition to such recommendations was strong. The gay community strongly opposed screening for high-risk groups on civil rights grounds and the fear of further discrimination against gays. The blood industry, fearing for its own livelihood, continued to deny there was any danger (Perrow & Guillen, 1990). As late as 1984, the Red Cross refused to acknowledge that AIDS could be transmitted through blood transfusions. Blood banks finally began screening the blood supply in March 1985. However, it wasn't until July of that year that they bothered notifying the donors that they were infected. Many people continued to pass on the virus unknowingly to others. By 1989 several thousand cases of AIDS due to blood transfusion had been reported, and hundreds of lawsuits had been filed against the blood banks.

The National Hemophilia Foundation also found that AIDS blood screening conflicted with its goals and weakened its ability to do its job. Hemophiliacs lack the substance that clots blood. A blood-clotting product made of donated blood was increasing the life span of many hemophiliacs to near normal up until 1985 when blood screening for AIDS was finally in place. But because of the earlier lack of screening, hemophiliacs who received blood transfusions prior to 1985 had an infection rate between 65% and 95% (Perrow & Guillen, 1990).

In sum, the AIDS crisis is tied to organizational and institutional failure. The federal, state, and local governments failed to fund education and research, the research community failed to respond quickly enough, the health care system failed to respond effectively enough, and the blood industry failed to ensure the safety of their product. To make matters worse, organizations replicated each other's ineffectiveness and inaction. The sad conclusion is that the magnitude and seriousness of the epidemic could have been avoided had the organizational response been different.

■ ■ ■

Globalization and Social Institutions

A discussion of social structure would not be complete without addressing how social institutions are influenced by globalization in today's world. **Globalization** is the process through which people's lives all around the world become economically, politically, environmentally, and culturally interconnected. Many of today's most pressing societal problems—widespread environmental devastation, large-scale wars, and so on—are global in scope.

Television, film, computers, and telecommunications give people worldwide immediate access to other cultures, making it practically impossible for societies to exist in complete isolation. To some sociologists, the outcome of globalization will be nothing short of a single "global culture" where traditional geographic, political, economic, and cultural boundaries will eventually become obsolete (Featherstone, 1990). Clearly, societies are becoming more alike or at least becoming highly interdependent. But various local cultures are reasserting themselves—with sometimes dramatic results, as we've seen in the former Yugoslavia and former Soviet Union.

Economics

The next time you stroll through a shopping mall, notice all the products that are made in other countries: clothes, shoes, food, cooking utensils, computers, stereo equipment, sporting goods, toys, and so forth. Sitting in my office, I see that my telephone, radio, and computer were made in Japan, my watch in the Philippines, my stapler in Great Britain, my calculator in Taiwan, my shoes in Korea, my pants in Hong Kong, my bottled water in France, my picture frame in Thailand, and my briefcase, paper clips, and tea kettle in China.

If a product wasn't made in another country, chances are some of its component parts were (for example, computer chips). Almost 40% of all the parts used in American manufacturing are imported from foreign countries (Cetron, Rocha, & Luckins, 1991). The production of the Ford Escort, for example, involves parts assembled in 16 countries on three continents (Braun, 1991). Such global connections are often quite invisible. For instance, most of the lace that goes into making Western shawls, curtains, doilies, and undergarments is imported through a vast network of traders and exporters. Yet the fabric itself is produced by a small group of poor "housewives" in a few secluded villages in India who work 8 hours a day making the lace in addition to the 8 hours they spend each day doing housework (Mies, 1982). When you think of the enormous number of international transactions and interactions that must take place for all these things to arrive in your local stores, you get a good sense of how economically interdependent the world has become.

In many ways the world has become a single economic unit. Cultural differences aside, most countries today share a similar language, the language of money (Bradshaw & Wallace, 1996). Even the most remote rural villagers are linked to the world economy as they send and receive goods around the world. Businesses that had once operated exclusively in their home country now extend their markets and production facilities globally. These **multinational corporations**—companies that have manufacturing, production, and marketing divisions in many countries—don't owe their allegiance to any one country's political authority or culture. At the same time national governments and international financial organizations like the World Bank and the International Monetary Fund loan money to countries all over the world to finance development and reconstruction projects.

The influence of the global economy is far-reaching. Economic pressures in distant countries can have serious ramifications for our private lives here. For example, the *Calophyllum lanigerum* tree, which grows in the rain forests of Malaysia, produces a substance that may destroy the HIV virus. Thus the Malaysian rain forests may contain the cure for AIDS. But logging companies are fighting with pharmaceutical companies, international medical researchers, and the Malaysian government to continue highly profitable heavy cutting in these rich forests (Bradshaw & Wallace, 1996). A medical treatment that could possibly benefit hundreds of thousands of people in this country, and perhaps millions worldwide, is being destroyed as people and companies in another country carve out their piece of the economic pie.

Furthermore, the prospect of international economic competition is fostering change in our educational system. Students in other countries consistently outperform American students in fields like math and science, causing alarm among many educational experts and political leaders. American children spend an average of 180 days a year in school, compared to 210 in Germany, 211 in Russia, 222 in Korea, and 243 in Japan (National Center for Education Statistics, 1993; World Monitor, 1992). Japanese schools, in particular, are famous for producing high-achievers. Even 3-year-olds may spend hours a day memorizing stories, learning vocabulary, making calendars, and taking achievement tests. Their goal is to pass the grueling entrance exams to get into the best elementary schools, which in turn serve as gateways into the top high schools and universities (WuDunn, 1996). Few people, however, would argue that we should emulate the pressurized Japanese educational model. In fact, some critics feel we already place far too much emphasis on performance and achievement in this society (Mannon, 1990). Nevertheless, concern over our ability to compete in the global marketplace has led to nationwide calls for such educational reforms as heavier emphasis on math and science, more time spent on foundational skills like reading and writing, increased computer literacy, and training in political geography and international relations.

A global economy has its everyday advantages. Goods and services manufactured abroad are less expensive for consumers. Universally accepted credit cards like Visa and MasterCard make international travel more convenient. Global economic influence has enabled a significant portion of the world's population to be healthier, eat better, and live longer than the royalty of past civilizations (Kurtz, 1995). But as we'll see in more detail in the next chapter, not everyone is an equal player in the global economy. Globalization has fostered some serious social problems, including higher levels of domestic unemployment, the exploitation of workers in poor, developing countries, and a worldwide system of inequality.

Religion

Another institution influenced by globalization is religion. Considering the enormous variety of cultures and ethnicities that exist today, it's startling that more than half the world's population belongs to just a few major religions—Christianity, Buddhism, and Islam—that have successfully crossed national boundaries for centuries (see Table 9.2).

Technological advances have made many of the world's religions even more international. Indeed, global religion has become a high-tech enterprise:

> Jews from around the world can now fax their prayers to the Wailing Wall in Jerusalem. Fortunetellers in China provide computer-generated astrological charts. . . . American television offers its viewers Christian preachers and Buddhist teachers.
> (Kurtz, 1995, p. 1)

Worldwide religious movements have sometimes created dramatic social changes. According to Max Weber, the spread of Protestant beliefs throughout

Table 9.2   *World Religions*

Religion	Number	Percentage of Total
Christians	1,901,148,000	33.6
Muslims	1,033,453,000	18.3
Nonreligious	923,104,000	16.3
Hindus	764,000,000	13.5
Buddhists	338,621,000	6.0
Atheists	239,111,000	4.2
Chinese folk religion	149,336,000	2.6
New religionists	128,975,000	2.3
Tribal religionists	99,150,000	1.8
Sikhs	20,204,000	0.4
Jews	13,451,000	0.2
Other	49,280,000	1.0

Source: U.S. Bureau of the Census, 1995a.

Europe made the growth of modern capitalism possible. Protestantism maintained that a person's entry into heaven is predestined by God. Evidence of such predestination is revealed through successful worldly achievements like the accumulation of wealth through hard work. But early Protestants also believed that God frowns on vulgar displays of wealth—big houses, fancy clothes, and so forth. So people were motivated to save and reinvest their wealth rather than spend it frivolously. You can see how such beliefs made large-scale and long-term economic growth possible (Weber, 1904/1977).

Increased access to the world's religions sometimes carries immediate political implications. In the 1960s, Americans saw television pictures of Buddhist monks setting themselves on fire in Vietnam to protest the war there. Such images of religious opposition fed the growing antiwar movement in this country. In the 70s and 80s we watched Catholic priests and nuns challenging government policies in Central and South America, provoking a heightened awareness of the plight of indigenous people there.

The globalization of religion has also created crises for religious communities. Exposure to competing worldviews challenges traditional beliefs. In some cases, the religious have reacted with a forceful revitalization of ancient, fundamentalist traditions (Kurtz, 1995). Witness the growing trend toward governments defining themselves in narrow religious terms. The ascension of fundamentalist Islamic governments in Iran and Afghanistan, the growing influence of orthodox Jews in Israeli politics, and the continuing conflict between Christian and Muslim Serbs in Bosnia attest to the fact that many people today believe religion cannot be separated from a nation's social and political destiny.

In sum, globalization has had a dramatic impact on our major social institutions. The nature of economics and work, the structure of educational systems, and the practice of religion have all been touched by global forces. These forces affect us all and will surely help determine the role the United States will play in the 21st century.

Conclusion

More than three centuries ago, John Donne wrote, "No man is an island, entire of itself; every man is a piece of the continent, a part of the main." The same can be said of contemporary social life. We are not isolated individuals whose lives are simply functions of personal characteristics and predispositions. We are social beings. We are part of aggregations of other social beings. We have a powerful need to belong to something larger than ourselves. As a result, we constantly affect and are affected by our associations with others, whether face-to-face or in well-structured groups, massive bureaucratic organizations, or all-encompassing social institutions.

Throughout Part II of this book I discussed the relationship between the individual and society in terms of how society and culture affect everyday experiences and how those experiences help to construct and maintain social order. The development of self and self-controlled behavior, the influence of cultural norms, responses to deviance, and so on are all topics that provide insight into how we are able to live together in a relatively orderly and predictable way. In this chapter, however, we begin to see that the social structure, although created and maintained by the actions of individuals, is more than just the sum of those actions. Organizations interact at a level well above the individual; institutions are organized in a massive, global system.

Social structure is bigger than us, exerts enormous control over our lives, and is an objectified reality that appears to exist independent of us. But it cannot exist without us. I'm reminded of a skit from the old British comedy show "Monty Python's Flying Circus," in which a high-rise apartment building stood erect only because its inhabitants believed in it. When they doubted its existence, it began to crumble. Like this building, social structure requires constant human support. Once we as a society are no longer able to sustain our organizations or believe in our institutions, they fall apart.

CHAPTER HIGHLIGHTS

- Social structure is both a source of predictability and a source of problems in everyday life. Sometimes individual interests coincide with structural needs; other times they conflict.
- By virtue of living in society, we are all organizational creatures. We are born in organizations, educated in them, spend most of our adult lives working in them, and will probably die in them.

▪ A common form of organization in American society is the bureaucracy. A bureaucracy is a large hierarchical organization that is governed by a system of rules and regulations, has a clear specification of work tasks, and has a well-defined division of labor.

▪ The everyday experience of bureaucratic organizations is determined by where one fits into the hierarchical structure. Bureaucracies look very different depending on whether one is situated at the top, middle, or bottom.

▪ Organizations are more than structures, rules, policies, goals, job descriptions, and standard operating procedures. Each organization, and each division within an organization, develops its own norms, values, and language.

▪ Organizations exist within highly interconnected networks. In times of institutional or environmental uncertainty, organizations tend to imitate one another, adopting similar activities, policies, and goals.

▪ As national borders become increasingly permeable, cultures and social institutions become more global in nature.

YOUR TURN

One of the major criticisms of contemporary society is its routine and overwhelming, sometimes dehumanizing, way of life. To see such routinization firsthand, visit several fast-food restaurants close to your home (McDonald's, Taco Bell, Kentucky Fried Chicken, Long John Silver's, and the like). Observe the overall structure of the establishment. How is the work area situated in regard to the customer area? Are the cooking facilities hidden from public view? Note the number of employees and the gender configuration of the staff. Observe the way the customers are processed. Can you detect a "script" that the employees follow? How do they address customers? How are orders filled? Is there any room for "ad-libbing"? Does each worker seem responsible for a single task (grilling burgers, bagging french fries, operating the cash register, cleaning tables)? Do male employees seem to work in different areas than female employees? Is there an apparent hierarchy among the workers? What is the manager's role? Were you able to detect the ways in which ordinary workers "resist" on a daily basis (rate-busting norms, sabotage, labor-management conflicts, etc.)?

Compare your findings across the different restaurants you observed. How much similarity in routine is there? Does there seem to be a common procedure that is characteristic of all fast-food restaurants, or does each restaurant have a unique way of running? How do things like diversity and creativity fit into the procedure?

Drawing from this chapter's discussion of the features of bureaucracies and the notion of McDonaldization, discuss how the systems employed in these restaurants maximize efficiency at the cost of dehumanizing the people involved, both workers and customers.

CHAPTER 10

The Architecture of Stratification: Power, Class, and Privilege

- *The Nature of Stratification and Inequality*
- *Social Class in Everyday Life*
- *Stratification and Power in Everyday Life*
- *The Impact of Institutional Power*
- *Global Development and Inequality*

High in the crow's nest of the luxury liner *Titanic*, lookout Frederick Fleet peered into the dazzling night. It was calm, clear, and bitterly cold. There was no moon, but the cloudless sky blazed with stars. The Atlantic Ocean was like polished plate glass; people said later that they had never seen it so smooth.

> Suddenly Fleet saw something directly ahead, even darker than the darkness. At first it was small, . . . but every second it grew larger and closer. Quickly Fleet banged the crow's nest bell three times, warning of danger ahead. (Lord, 1956, quoted in Sidel, 1986, p. xiii)

The iceberg Fleet saw drew closer and closer. At the last second the ship steered clear of it, and for a brief moment it seemed that disaster had been avoided. However, the grinding sound that seemed to come from somewhere deep inside the hull of the vessel indicated that the ship had, in fact, struck the deadly iceberg.

The *Titanic* was the most magnificent vessel of its time. It had every amenity and comfort: Turkish baths, the finest orchestras, intricately tiled walls, the best cuisine. What it didn't have were enough lifeboats. There was room for only 1,178 out of the 2,207 passengers and crew members on board. Over the next 2 hours on that cold April night in 1912, as the "unsinkable" ocean liner was engulfed by the frigid waters of the north Atlantic, more than 1,500 people lost their lives.

All this is fairly well known. What is less well known is that some of the passengers actually had much better survival chances than others. The percentage of people saved from the wealthy first-class deck (over 60%) was much higher than the percentage saved from the second-class deck (36%), which was higher than the percentage of the lowest, or "steerage," class passengers who were saved (24%). The figures were even more striking for women and children, who, by virtue of chivalrous tradition, were entitled to be spared first. Ninety-seven percent of the women and children in first class and 89% of those in second class survived. However, only 42% of the women and children in steerage were saved (W. Hall, 1986).

One of the reasons so many of the wealthier passengers survived was that access to the lifeboats was from the higher first- and second-class decks. The locked doors and other barriers that kept the third-class passengers from venturing up to the upper decks during the cruise were not removed when disaster struck. In addition, there is evidence that little effort was made to save the people in steerage. Some were even forcibly kept down by sailors standing guard.

For the passengers on the *Titanic,* social inequality meant more than just differences in the comfort of their accommodations or the quality of the food they ate. It literally meant life or death. This situation is a metaphor for what many people face in today's society. Those at the top have easy access to various "lifeboats" in times of social or economic disaster, others face locked gates, segregated decks, and policies that make mere survival exceedingly difficult (Sidel, 1986).

Let's turn the clock ahead to 1995 when a record-setting summer heat wave took the lives of over 700 people in Chicago. Most of the victims were poor and elderly people who were found suffocated in their closed, stifling apartments. Most couldn't afford air conditioners or fans. Some died behind boarded windows, afraid of being invaded by prowlers and thieves in their high-crime neighborhoods if they left their windows open (Terry, 1995). Furthermore, the city's heat emergency plan was inadequate to deal with poor communities where large numbers of people had no way of escaping the heat. Again we see how the lack of economic resources can have direct, physical consequences for people's lives.

The next several chapters will examine the various aspects of social inequality. In this chapter I look at the issues of inequality and stratification. Why does inequality exist? How is it related to power, and how is that power expressed at the individual and institutional levels? Finally, what does inequality look like at the global level? In subsequent chapters I explore other facets of inequality: poverty, race, and gender.

Before I begin, let me point out that the approach of these chapters is more top-down than the previous ones, as I examine the larger social structures and institutions that create and perpetuate inequality. Keep in mind, however, that individuals both create these social structures and live under their influence. Inequality, as well as the power of social structure, is often felt most forcefully and reinforced most effectively in the chain of day-to-day interactions that constitute our ordinary private experiences (Collins, 1981). People bring with them into all social encounters different levels of conversational, emotional, physical, institutional, and cultural resources that create and enforce the status differences between them. Although social inequalities exist at a level "above" the individual, they are not fixed and unyielding. They ultimately derive from the actions of real people.

The Nature of Stratification and Inequality

Inequality is woven into the fabric of all societies through a structured system of **stratification**, the ranking of entire groups of people that perpetuates unequal rewards and life chances in a society. Just as geologists talk about strata of rock that are layered one on top of another, the "social strata" of people are arranged from low to high. All societies, past and present, have had some form of stratification, although societies may vary in the degree of inequality between strata.

One of the most persistent historical forms of stratification was slavery. **Slavery** was an economic form of inequality in which some people were legally the property of others. One could become a slave in a variety of ways: through birth, military defeat, debt, or, as in the United States, capture and commercial trade (Kerbo, 1991). Because slaves were considered possessions, they were denied the rights and life chances other people took for granted.

In some societies today, such as India and Pakistan, stratification is created by a **caste system** in which heredity ensures that a person of one caste cannot become a member of another caste. One's caste, which determines one's lifestyle, prestige, and occupational choices, is fixed at birth and cannot be changed. Cultural rules specify that people should take the occupation of their parents and marry within their caste (Weber, 1970). The rights and duties associated with membership in each caste are clear. In India, "untouchables"—members of the lowest caste—are required to hide or, if that's not possible, bow in the presence of anyone from a higher caste. Some members of the higher castes fear they would suffer ritual pollution if they touch or otherwise come in contact with an untouchable.

Another form of stratification is the **estate**, or **feudal system**, which develops when high-status groups own land and have power based on their noble birth (Kerbo, 1991). In medieval Europe the highest "estate" in society was occupied by the aristocracy, who derived their wealth and power from large-scale land holdings. The clergy formed the next estate. Although they had lower status than the aristocracy, they still claimed considerable status because the Church itself owned a great deal of land and exerted influence over people's lives. The last, or "third," estate were the commoners: serfs, peasants, artisans, and merchants. Movement between estates was possible, although infrequent. Occasionally a commoner might be knighted or a wealthy merchant might become an aristocrat. Estate systems were most commonly found in preindustrial societies.

Stratification systems in contemporary industrialized societies are likely to be based on social class. Throughout this book I have talked about the effects of social class on a variety of experiences—socialization, deviance, family, and so forth. But social class is more than a characteristic that distinguishes one group's pattern of behavior from another's. It is a means of ranking people or groups that determines access to important resources and life chances. **Social class** refers to any group of people who share a similar economic position in society based on their wealth and income.

Closely related to the concept of class is socioeconomic status. In chapter 2, I defined *status* simply as a social position. But with regard to stratification, **socioeconomic status** refers to the prestige, honor, respect, and lifestyle associated with different positions or groups in society (Weber, 1970). Socioeconomic status is obviously correlated with wealth and income but can also be derived from achieved characteristics such as educational attainment and occupational prestige and from ascribed characteristics such as race, ethnicity, gender, and family pedigree. Hence it is possible for a person's class ranking to be different from his or her socioeconomic status. For instance, the occupational prestige of high school teachers is far higher than that of carpenters, plumbers, and mechanics (J. A. Davis & Smith, 1986), yet teachers' incomes are often substantially lower. Organized criminals may have a lot of money but lack status—that is, prestige and honor. Some of our most influential and powerful politicians—Bill Clinton and Bob Dole, to name two—come from rather modest class backgrounds.

Class systems are different from other systems of stratification in that there are no legal barriers to **social mobility**, the movement of people or groups from one level to another. In practice, however, mobility between classes may be quite difficult. Much as we'd like to believe otherwise, the opportunities to move from one class to another are not available to all members of society. Often the families we're born into exert as much or more influence on our class standing as our personal achievements. Likewise, race and gender have historically determined a person's access to educational, social, and employment opportunities.

The Structural-Functionalist View of Stratification

Sociologists have long been interested in figuring out why societies are stratified. From a structural-functionalist perspective, the answer lies in a society's inevitable need for order. Because social inequality is found in some form in all societies and is apparently unavoidable, it must somehow be necessary for societies to run smoothly.

As with bureaucracies, the efficient functioning of society requires that various tasks be allocated through a strictly defined division of labor. If the tasks associated with all social positions in a society were equally pleasant, were equally important, and required the same talents, it wouldn't make any difference who got into which position. But functionalists argue that it does make a difference. Some occupations, such as teaching and medicine, are more important than others and require greater talent and training. Society's dilemma is to make sure that the most talented people perform the most important tasks. One way to ensure this distribution of tasks is to assign higher rewards—better pay, greater prestige, more social privileges—to some positions in society so that they will be attractive to the people with the necessary talents and abilities.

Presumably, if these talented people were not offered sufficiently high rewards, they would have no reason to take on the difficult and demanding tasks associated with those important positions. Why would people go through the agony and costs of many years of medical school without some promise of compensation and high prestige? Those who rise to the top are seen as the most worthy and deserving because they're the ones who can do the most good for society (K. Davis & Moore, 1945).

But the functional importance of a position is not enough to warrant a high place in the stratification system. If a position is easily filled, it need not be heavily rewarded, even though it is important (K. Davis & Moore, 1945). Imagine what our society would be like without people who remove our trash. Not only would our streets be unsightly, but our collective health would suffer too. Therefore, garbage collectors serve a vital social function. They don't get paid very much, however, and trash removal certainly isn't a highly respected occupation.

Why aren't garbage collectors higher up in the hierarchy of occupations? According to the structural-functionalist perspective, it is because there is no shortage of people who have the skills needed to collect garbage. Physicians also serve the collective health needs of a society, but because of the skills and training needed, society must offer rewards high enough to ensure that qualified people will want to become doctors.

The structural-functionalist perspective gives us important insight into how societies ensure that all positions in the division of labor are filled. Every society, no matter how simple or complex, differentiates people in terms of prestige and esteem and possesses a certain amount of institutional inequality. Critics argue, however, that this explanation doesn't address the fact that stratification can be unjust and divisive, a source of social *dis*order (Tumin, 1953).

One look at the salary structure in our society reveals that many highly rewarded positions are not as functional as positions that receive smaller rewards. Entertainers and professional athletes are among the highest-paid people in American society. The heavyweight boxer, Mike Tyson, for example, can make several million dollars for a few minutes' worth of punching someone else's face. Comedians such as Bill Cosby and singers such as Barbra Streisand are among the wealthiest of Americans. You might say that their careers serve important social functions by providing the rest of us with a recreational release from the demands of ordinary life, and there's no denying that the best entertainers and athletes have rare skills indeed. However, it seems that society probably can do without another record album, TV show, starting pitcher, or heavyweight prizefighter more easily than it can do without competent physicians, scientists, computer programmers, teachers, or even trash collectors.

Furthermore, the functionalist argument that only a limited number of talented people are around to occupy important social positions is probably overstated. Many people have the talent to become doctors. What they lack is access to training. Why is it that some people—women and racial minorities—are paid less for or excluded entirely from certain jobs? The debates over equal employment opportunity (see chapter 12) and comparable worth (see chapter 13) are essentially debates over how the functional importance of certain positions is determined.

Finally, when functionalists claim that stratification serves the needs of society, we must ask, Whose needs? A system of slavery obviously met the needs of one group at the expense of another. In a class-stratified society, those individuals who receive the greatest rewards have the resources to make sure they continue receiving such rewards. Over time, the competition for the most desirable positions will become less open and less competitive. The offspring of "talented"— that is, high-status—parents will inevitably have an advantage over equally talented people who are born into less successful families. Social background and not personal aptitude may become the primary criterion for filling important social positions (Tumin, 1953).

The Conflict View of Stratification

Conflict theorists argue that social inequality is neither a necessity nor a source of social order. They see it as a reflection of the unequal distribution of power in society and as a primary source of conflict, coercion, and unhappiness. Stratification ultimately rests on the unequal distribution of resources—some people have them, others don't. Important resources include money, land, information, education, health care, safety, and adequate housing. Those high in the stratification system can control the resources because they are able to set the rules that limit challenges to their positions by others. A system of stratification allows members of the dominant group to use those in subordinate positions as consumers, renters, employees, and so on, thereby reinforcing their own superiority over others.

Stratification virtually guarantees that some groups or classes of people (those who have less) will always be competing with other groups or classes (those who have more). The stratification system serves the interests of those at the top and not the fundamental survival needs of the entire society. The dominant classes can manipulate the economic and political system to maintain advantages over others and to protect their interests. What the conflict perspective gives us that the structural-functionalist perspective doesn't is an acknowledgment of the interconnected roles economic and political institutions play in creating and maintaining a stratified society.

The Marxian Class Model

According to Karl Marx and Friedrich Engels (1848/1982), societies are divided into conflicting and stratified classes on the basis of two criteria: ownership of the **means of production**—land, commercial enterprises, factories, and wealth—and

Table 10.1   *Marxian Model of Class*

	Controls labor of others	Does not control labor of others
Owns means of production (land, factories, etc.)	CAPITALISTS	PETITE BOURGEOISIE
Does not own means of production	WORKERS	WORKERS

the ability to purchase and control the labor of others. Marx and Engels felt that in modern societies, two major classes emerge: **capitalists** (or bourgeoisie), who own the means of production and are able to purchase the labor power of others, and **workers** (or proletariat), who neither own the means of production nor have the ability to purchase the labor power of others. Workers, instead, must sell their own labor power. Some workers, including store managers and factory supervisors, may control other workers, but their power is minimal compared to that exerted over them by those in the capitalist class. Marx and Engels supplemented this two-tiered conception of class by adding a third, the **petite bourgeoisie**, which is a sort of transitional class of people who own the means of production but don't purchase the labor power of others. This class would consist of self-employed skilled laborers and businesspeople who are economically self-sufficient but don't have a staff of subordinate workers (Robinson & Kelley, 1979). (See Table 10.1.)

Capitalists have considerable sway over what will be produced, how much will be produced, and who will get how much of it. Such influence allows them to control other people's livelihoods, the communities in which people live, and the economic decisions that affect the entire society. In such a structure there is an inevitable tendency for the rich to get richer, to use their wealth to create more wealth for themselves, and to act in ways that will protect their interests and positions in society.

Ultimately, the wealthy gain the ability to influence important social institutions: the government, the media, the schools, and the courts. Those in power have access to the means necessary to create and promote a reality that justifies their exploitive actions. This version of reality is so influential that even those who are harmed by it come to accept it. Marx called this phenomenon **false consciousness**. False consciousness is crucial because it is the primary means by which the powerful classes in society prevent protest and revolution. As long as large numbers of poor people continue to believe in the American Dream—that wealth and success are solely the products of individual hard work and effort rather than structured inequalities in society—resentment and animosity toward the rich will be minimized because the inequalities will be perceived as fair and deserved (Robinson & Bell, 1978).

Other Conflict Models of Stratification

For Marx, economic inequality was the only important factor in creating a system of stratification. If private ownership of property were ever to be abolished, all other forms of inequality and conflict would disappear. He was not interested in the power and authority relations between workers and those who directly controlled them.

In Marx's time, the mid-19th century, ownership of property and control of labor in a capitalist system were synonymous. It made sense to lump all those who didn't own productive resources into one class and all those who did into another. However, the nature of capitalism has changed a lot since then. Today corporations have become much larger and more bureaucratic, with a long, multilevel chain of command. Ownership of the largest corporations often lies in the hands of stockholders who have no connections at all to the everyday workings of the business. Thus ownership and management are separated. The powerful people who run businesses and control workers on a day-to-day basis are frequently not the same people who own the businesses.

As a result, other sociologists (for example, Dahrendorf, 1959) have argued for an explanation of class stratification that focuses primarily on different levels of authority. What's important is not just who owns the means of production, but whether some people are able to exercise authority over others. **Authority** is the possession of some status or quality that compels others to obey (Starr, 1982). A person with authority has the power to order or forbid behavior in others (Wrong, 1988). Such commands don't require the use of force or persuasion, nor do they need to be explained or justified. Rulers have authority over the ruled, as do teachers over students, employers over employees, and parents over children. These authority relationships are not fixed, of course: Children fight with their parents, students disagree with their teachers, and workers protest against their bosses. But while the legitimacy of the authority may sometimes be called into question, the ongoing dependence of the subordinates maintains it. The worker may disagree with the boss, and the student may disagree with the teacher, but the boss still signs the paycheck and the teacher still assigns final grades.

According to Ralf Dahrendorf (1959), social classes are distinguished on the basis of their relation to authority. Whereas Marx lumped all those who didn't own the means of production in the same worker class, Dahrendorf lumps together all those who exert authority over others, whether or not they own the means of production, into the **command class** (Robinson & Kelley, 1979). The command class includes not only capitalist owners but all levels of managers and supervisors as well. On the other end are members of the **obey class**, workers who are subject to the authority of others but exercise none themselves. Finally, there is what Dahrendorf called the **classless group**, self-employed people who neither exercise authority nor are subject to it. The Dahrendorf model is shown in Table 10.2.

Table 10.2   *Dahrendorf Model of Class*

	Exercises authority	Does not exercise authority
Owns means of production	COMMAND CLASS	CLASSLESS GROUP
Does not own means of production	COMMAND CLASS	OBEY CLASS

Like Marx, Dahrendorf believed that relations between classes inherently involve conflicts of interest. But by emphasizing authority, Dahrendorf argued that stratification is not an exclusively economic phenomenon. Instead, it derives from the social relations between people who possess different degrees of power.

Sociologist Erik Olin Wright (E. O. Wright, 1976; E. O. Wright, Costello, Hachen, & Sprague, 1982; E. O. Wright & Perrone, 1977) has developed a model of class stratification that synthesizes the ideas of Marx and Dahrendorf, incorporating both the ownership of means of production and the exercise of authority over others. The capitalist and petite bourgeoisie classes in the scheme are identical to Marx's. What is different is that the class of people who do not own society's productive resources (Marx's worker class) are divided into two classes: managers and workers (see Table 10.3).

Wright's approach gives us a sense of the complexities of conflict and social class that Marx's and Dahrendorf's do not. We can see that social class is not simply a reflection of income or the extent to which a group exercises authority over another. Lawyers, plumbers, and cooks, for instance, may own their own businesses and hire assistants (which would place them in the capitalist class), work for a large company without any subordinates (placing them in the worker class), work for a large company and have subordinates (placing them in the manager class), or work alone (placing them in the petite bourgeoisie class) (Robinson & Kelley, 1979).

Table 10.3   *Wright Model of Class*

	Exercises authority	Does not exercise authority
Owns means of production	CAPITALISTS	PETITE BOURGEOISIE
Does not own means of production	MANAGERS	WORKERS

Class conflict is also more than just a clash between rich and poor. There are, in fact, multiple lines of conflict—economic, political, administrative, or social. Some positions, or what Wright calls *contradictory class locations*, fall between two major classes. These positions make it difficult for individuals to identify with one side or the other. Managers and supervisors, for instance, often must struggle over where their allegiances should lie. They can ally with workers because both are subordinates of capitalist owners. Yet because they can exercise authority over some people, they also share the interests and concerns of owners. Coaches of professional sports teams also must struggle with the dilemma of whether they represent the interests of the owners or the players.

Social Class in Everyday Life

When most of us think of social class in our everyday lives, it is not in terms of broad occupational classes like capitalists, petite bourgeoisie, managers, and workers. We are more likely to define class in crude relative terms (that is, from upper to lower) using a combination of such outward signs as speech patterns, material possessions, mannerisms, and style of dress (Domhoff, 1983).

To rank people on the basis of class, contemporary sociologists usually compile information on quantifiable factors like income, wealth, occupational status, and educational attainment. This is certainly a clearer and more systematic way of defining class than relying on outward appearances, but the boundaries between classes still tend to be rather fuzzy. Some have argued that there aren't any discrete classes with clearly defined boundaries at all, but rather a socioeconomic continuum on which to rank individuals (P. M. Blau & Duncan, 1967).

Nevertheless, class designations remain a part of everyday thinking and social research. The "upper" class is usually thought to include owners of vast amounts of property and other forms of wealth, owners of large corporations, top financiers, and members of prestigious families. The "middle" class is likely to include managers, supervisors, executives, small business owners, and professionals (for example, lawyers, doctors, teachers, engineers). The "working" class includes industrial and factory workers, office workers, clerks, and farm and manual laborers. Finally, the "poor" consist of people who work for minimum wages or are chronically unemployed. They are sometimes referred to as the "underclass." These are the people who do society's dirty work, often for very low wages (Walton, 1990; E. O. Wright et al., 1982).

"Class" implies more than just economic position. People's social class standing provides them with an understanding of the world and where they fit into it. A description like "middle class" or "working class" may not mean much when applied to a single person. It does tell us something, however, about the broader system of stratification and how people are clustered at different levels of comfort, status, and control over their lives (Ehrenreich, 1989). "Class" is also a statement about culture that defines an entire way of life:

It's composed of ideas, behavior, attitudes, values, and language; class is how you think, feel, act, look, dress, talk, move, walk; class is what stores you shop at, restaurants you eat in; class is the schools you attend, the education you attain; class is the very jobs you will work at throughout your adult life. Class even determines when we marry and become mothers.... We experience class at every level of our lives; class is who our friends are, where we live ... even what kind of car we drive, if we own one.... In other words, class is socially constructed and all-encompassing. (Langston, 1992, p. 112)

Thus when we talk about social class, we are making broad generalizations about large groups of people regarding what they look like and how they live. Class is a statement about self-worth and the quality of one's life (Langston, 1992). It determines your life chances, including access to education and high-paying jobs (Della Fave, 1980; Mantsios, 1995; Reiman, 1990). As you recall from chapter 7, working-class and poor people are significantly more likely to get arrested, get convicted, go to prison, and receive the death penalty than are upper-class people (Reiman, 1990). Research also shows that those at lower levels of the stratification system are more likely to die prematurely as a result of homicide, accidents, or inadequate health care than are people at higher levels (Kearl, 1989). The death rate for Americans with family incomes of less than $9,000 a year is three times higher than that of people with family incomes of more than $25,000 a year (Pear, 1993a). Lack of health care causes three times more deaths than AIDS (Navarro, 1992).

■ ■ ■ ■ ■ ■ ■ ■
MICRO-MACRO CONNECTION
Mass Media and the Images of Social Class

In chapters 3 and 5 you saw that the mass media play a significant role in socialization and the shaping of reality. It shouldn't be surprising, then, that the media help to foster people's conceptions of class, wealth, and poverty (Mantsios, 1995).

Even though over 50% of the adult working population are manual, unskilled, or semiskilled workers (Navarro, 1992), the media tend to ignore the poor and the working class (Mantsios, 1995; Parenti, 1996). In the affluent, middle-class worlds of television and film, poor and working-class people typically are depicted in such minor roles as waiters, service people, attendants, and the like (Parenti, 1996). In the news media, too, stories about poor people are rare. Fewer than 1 in 500 articles in the *New York Times* and 1 in 1,000 articles in the *Readers Guide to Periodic Literature* are on poverty (Mantsios, 1995).

When the news media do turn attention to the poor, the portrayals are often negative or stereotypical. Frequently the poor are portrayed in grouped, statistical terms, such as annual fluctuations in the numbers of people in poverty or on welfare. Such coverage ignores the individual suffering and personal indignities of poverty (see chapter 11). The more detailed stories about poor people tend to focus on welfare cheats, drug addicts, or greedy panhandlers.

Such images reinforce a perception that poverty is an aberration from the American way of life or something caused by poor people themselves (Mantsios, 1995). The message is often that we ought to blame those below us in the class structure for our society's most pressing problems. We learn to fear being victimized by the poor, and we learn to resent "welfare mothers" and blue-collar unions for our declining purchasing power and economic insecurity.

In contrast, the media tend to focus much of their attention on the concerns of the wealthy and the privileged. For instance, although relatively few people actually own stock, the news media devote a significant amount of broadcast time and print space to daily business news and stock market quotations (Mantsios, 1995). Some cable networks report exclusively on these issues. International news and trade agreements are reported in terms of their impact on the business world, not on ordinary working people. Further, in the "style" sections of most large newspapers the focus is typically on high-priced fashion, costly vacation spots, reviews of expensive restaurants, and etiquette for lavish, formal dinner parties.

The media also regularly provide information on individuals who have achieved super success. We hear and read regular reports about the multimillion-dollar contracts of professional athletes. Society pages and gossip columns keep those in the upper class informed of one another's doings and entice the rest of us to admire their achievements.

A popular television show of the 1980s and early 1990s was called "Lifestyles of the Rich and Famous." Each show was a 60-minute celebration of affluence, vanity, and materialism. Wealthy people flaunted their riches, portraying their lifestyles as healthy and desirable. Viewers were encouraged to pursue their own "champagne wishes and caviar dreams." No place on earth was too far away or too inaccessible for the show's host to reach by private jet, track down one of the world's "beautiful people," and salivate at the sight of his or her palatial home and ostentatious lifestyle. Rags-to-riches success stories were particularly popular. The show's seductive appeal lay in its underlying message that all of your problems—indeed all the world's problems—would recede into insignificance if you simply had enough money.

When members of the upper class are portrayed negatively—like the real estate investor Donald Trump or the Cincinnati Reds owner Marge Schott—they are depicted as isolated, atypical deviations. They are "bad apples"—individuals who are victims of their own personality flaws, not inevitable products of a much larger system of inequality.

In sum, the mass media shape how people think about each other and the nature of society. By celebrating the lifestyles of the upper and middle class the media create the impression that the interests and worries of the well-off are, or should be, important to everyone. Consequently, class differences and conflicts are concealed or rendered irrelevant. It's true, for instance, that we're all concerned about economic issues. But whether that concern revolves around profit margins and stock dividends, job security, or the source of your next meal clearly depends on your class standing.

■ ■ ■

Class Consciousness

To fully understand the phenomenon of class in American society, we must go beyond differences in objective economic conditions and life chances. We must look at people's subjective beliefs about what class they belong to and their feelings and attitudes about social stratification.

Marx felt that **class consciousness**—people's awareness of their true class identity—would eventually create a revolutionary movement on the part of the proletariat to eliminate class differences. However, Americans traditionally have been profoundly reluctant to recognize class differences and to identify themselves in terms of class (Domhoff, 1983; Langston, 1992). The willingness of people to place themselves in social classes would, in itself, be an open recognition of class inequalities, which the American society is not supposed to have. Moreover, media images blur class boundaries. Some sociologists have concluded that Americans aren't particularly class conscious: They don't recognize the class system, they don't think of themselves in terms of class membership, and they don't define their lives in class-related ways (for example, Hurst, 1979).

Research suggests, however, that Americans are in fact acutely aware of class distinctions and are quite willing to identify their position within the class system. Sociologists Mary and Robert Jackman (1983) asked a national sample of more than 1,900 American adults the following question: "People talk about social classes such as the poor, the working class, the middle class, the upper-middle class and the upper class. Which of these classes would you say you belong to?" (p. 14).

They found that all but 3.5% of the sample identified themselves with one of the class categories provided. However, only 7.6% perceived themselves as poor, and a little more than 9% perceived themselves either as upper-middle or upper class. The vast majority of people considered themselves either working class (36.6%) or middle class (43.3%). The respondents did not identify themselves with a particular class only because they were forced to give an answer. About 80% of the respondents indicated that they felt strongly about their class identification.

People's perception of where they are in the system affects their beliefs about the nature of inequality. Those at the lower end are likely to see stratification as unfair (Robinson & Bell, 1978) and may even express animosity toward those above them (Halle, 1984). However, upper-class people are likely to see stratification as a hierarchy of positions in which opportunities for success and advancement are equitably distributed. One of the ideological cornerstones of middle-

and upper-class America is the belief that all people are created equal and that so-cial class should not impede a person's progress in everyday life. In other words, your ambition, effort, and intellect alone are responsible for your success.

▪ ▪ ▪ ▪ ▪ ▪ ▪ ▪

SUSAN OSTRANDER
Upper-Class Consciousness

To more closely examine the issue of class consciousness, sociologist Susan Ostrander (1980) conducted in-depth interviews with 38 upper-class women in a large midwestern city. These women belonged to distinctly upper-class clubs, lived in the wealthiest areas of the city, had husbands who worked in the top ech-elons of business, and had children who attended private schools. They showed an obvious sense of "we-ness," a sense of belonging, and a feeling of cohesiveness with other wealthy individuals. Their daily activities, which included volunteer and charity work, were clearly organized around class-related behaviors and val-ues. Nevertheless, when asked directly whether they considered themselves upper class, they quickly rejected the use of the term with comments like:

> I hate [the term] upper class. It's so *non*-upper class to use it. I just call it "all of us," those of us who are well-born.

> I hate to use the word "class." We're responsible, fortunate people, old families, the people who have something.

> I wouldn't classify anyone as upper class, just as productive, worthwhile people.

> We're not supposed to have layers [in our society]. I'm embarrassed to admit to you that we do, and that I feel superior at my social level. I like being part of the upper crust.

Ostrander concluded that class consciousness is not a matter of how people identify themselves but a matter of how people act. Despite an unwillingness to call themselves upper class, the activities of these wealthy women clearly indicate that they are. The implications are profoundly important: If those at the top are reluctant to acknowledge that a class structure exists, then any strategy to elimi-nate class inequality will be seen as unnecessary and receive little attention.

Downward Mobility and the Disappearing Middle Class

In discussing the American class system and class consciousness, it is tempting to focus attention on the very top or the very bottom, overlooking the vast chunk of the population that falls somewhere in the ill-defined middle (B. Ehrenreich,

1990). But those who are neither exceedingly wealthy nor destitute are experiencing increasing economic instability in today's society.

The term *middle class* has become particularly important in defining American culture: its moods, political direction, lifestyles, values, habits, and tastes. During the first half of the 20th century, middle-class parents were more strict with their children than were working-class parents. Child development experts advised all parents that the key ingredient in bringing up a child was a firm hand and strong discipline. By the 1960s, however, middle-class parents had become more permissive. Experts began advising parents to be warm and affectionate while giving their children "room" to explore and grow (Goleman, 1991b). In short, the middle class is taken as a social norm against which every other class is measured and judged. It is a universal class, a class that supposedly represents everyone (Ehrenreich, 1990).

Given the lofty cultural status of the middle class in American society, two recent scholarly examinations of this class, Katherine Newman's *Falling from Grace* and Barbara Ehrenreich's *Fear of Falling*, have aroused great interest. The "falling" metaphors are apt in light of the increase in what sociologists term *downward social mobility* among members of the middle class. Instead of playing out the American Dream and rising through the class structure via hard work and perseverance, many are falling and falling hard. They are losing their jobs, struggling to make ends meet, and confronting the sort of prolonged economic hardship that in the past had been confined to the poor.

The Fall of the Middle Class

The traditional pattern of mobility in this country has always been that present generations of people would exceed the standard of living of previous ones. Nothing was more typically American than the expectation that children, once grown and in careers of their own, would eventually surpass their parents' financial well-being and quality of life. But today many young people are coming to the realization that their lives will probably be worse than that of their parents. A *Newsweek* poll in 1991 showed that only 62% of Americans are satisfied with their current standard of living, the lowest level since 1963 (M. Levinson, 1991).

These subjective reports of dissatisfaction are bolstered by government statistics that showing average family income declined by more than 5% between 1991 and 1993 (U.S. Bureau of the Census, 1995a) (see Table 10.4). Between 1973 and 1991, the average hourly wage for nonsupervisory workers decreased 13% after adjusting for inflation (M. Levinson, 1991). A recent survey found that 1 in 10 adults—about 19 million people—acknowledged that a lost job in their household had precipitated a major crisis in their lives (cited in Uchitelle & Kleinfield, 1996). Most people who lose a job eventually find another one. But the nature of those replacement jobs has deteriorated. Between 1963 and 1978, only 23% of the

Table 10.4   *Median Family Income, 1991 to 1993* (Median means half of families earn more than this figure, and half less)*

	1991	1992	1993
All families	$38,129	$37,914	$36,959
White	40,085	40,074	39,300
Black	22,861	21,794	21,542
Asian and Pacific Islander	43,471	43,830	44,456
Hispanic origin (of any race)	25,351	24,616	23,654

*In 1993 dollars.
Source: U.S. Bureau of the Census, 1995a.

new jobs that were created paid poverty-level wages; however, during the 1980s and early 1990s, more than half of the new full-time jobs that were created were unskilled, unstable positions paying below the poverty line (B. Harrison & Bluestone, 1988; J. E. Schwarz & Volgy, 1993). Recent Labor Department statistics show that only about 35% of laid-off full-time workers end up in equal- or better-paying jobs when they return to work (Uchitelle & Kleinfield, 1996).

Not only are people earning less, but what they do earn can't buy what it used to. In 1985 the National Association of Homebuilders determined that a family needs an income of approximately $37,000 to afford an average-priced home. The average family income that year was $27,735, almost $10,000 short (cited in Ehrenreich, 1990). More than half of all families today can't afford to buy a home (Gergen, 1991).

Downward Mobility and Self-Concept

So unexpected and "foreign" is downward social mobility to most middle-class Americans born after the Great Depression that anthropologist Katherine Newman (1988) likens it to living in a different culture. She conducted anthropological field interviews with 150 "downwardly mobile" people in a variety of settings. She discovered that in the face of downward mobility, people lose their feelings of security and find themselves suddenly powerless and unable to control the direction of their lives. The experience of the downwardly mobile middle class is quite different from that of the officially poor. These are people who once had it made. They have skills, education, and years of steady work experience. Many are homeowners. But their American Dream has become a nightmare. As a result, they must contend not only with the financial hardships but with the psychological and social consequences of "falling from grace."

Nowhere are the consequences of downward mobility more striking than in the unique problems of identity. At one time the downwardly mobile were successfully middle class. They enjoyed the trappings and apparent stability of a reasonably comfortable life. They became accustomed to power, to deference, and to the middle-class norms of consumption. But they have lost all that and must now venture into a work world that offers no autonomy, no authority, and no feelings of self-importance (Newman, 1988). They are caught between two selves, one highly valued and the other not. Consequently, many continue to cling to previous occupational identities:

> Even after hundreds of interviews fail to rescue them from a bottom-level job, after the family home has been sold to pay off debts, after the sense of self-assurance fades to be replaced by self-recrimination, the torture of two selves endures. For the kids' sake, for the [spouse's] sake, or simply for the sake of one's own sanity, it is hard to ditch yesterday's honored identity in order to make room for today's poor substitute. (Newman, 1988, p. 10)

In other areas of life, society has institutionalized some of the roles that result from dramatic changes in personal circumstances: the divorced spouse, the recovering alcoholic, the retiree (Ebaugh, 1988). But there are no guidelines for the downwardly mobile to assist them in shedding the old self; there is no legitimate role for the ex-breadwinner. Without a coherent identity they have lost their place in the social landscape. Although massive layoffs, such as the 29,000 workers laid off by General Motors in 1986, may create feelings of collective tragedy and allow one to attribute cause for the downward mobility to external forces, it is little solace to the person who has lost not only a career and a lifestyle but a valuable identity as well.

Downward Mobility and the Family

Downward mobility wreaks havoc on the institution of family by destroying the economic foundations of life and stretching emotional bonds to the breaking point (Newman, 1988). The reduction in income has far-reaching social and economic consequences, from residential moves to inferior housing. It means drastically less money for recreation and leisure and more pressures due to inadequate time and finances. The sudden financial strain also causes social dislocation through the loss of familiar friendships and emotional support networks.

Women are particularly vulnerable to downward mobility. Some plunge after the loss of a job. But for most, the main cause is divorce. In the United States, divorced men experience an average 10% increase in their standard of living; divorced women (and their children) experience a 27% decrease (R. R. Peterson, 1996).

A divorced woman faces a world in which her earning capacity is less than a man's simply because she is a woman (see chapter 13 for more details). If she did not work outside the home during her marriage, she also must deal with the toll those years away from her career path have taken on her ability to earn a living. Even today, marriage still imposes disadvantages on a woman's employment prospects, particularly if she is awarded custody of minor children. After a divorce, men become single and women become single *parents* (Weitzman, 1985). This responsibility further restricts a woman's job opportunities by limiting her work schedule and job location, her availability to work overtime, the freedom to take advantage of special training, travel, and other opportunities for advancement.

Children are hard hit by downward mobility as well. Their values and future plans are threatened. Once "invincible" parents become mere shells of their former middle-class selves. The parental authority that sprang from their financial control disappears. A 15-year-old girl describes the sad transformation of the father she once idolized after he lost his job as a successful show business promoter:

> He just seemed to be getting irrational. He would walk around the house talking to himself and stay up all night, smoking cigarettes in the dark. . . . All I perceived is that somebody who used to be a figure of strength was behaving strangely: starting to cry at odd times . . . hanging around the house unshaven in his underwear when I would bring dates home. . . . In the absence of any understanding of what was going on, my attitude was one of anger and disgust, like "Why don't you get your act together? What's the matter with you?" (Newman, 1988, p. 96)

For some children, downward mobility makes economic stability a doubtful concept. As children become adults, many cannot trust the appearance of success because they fear failure may be lurking around the corner: "The higher they climb, the more urgently they sense they are about to fall" (Newman, 1988, p. 142).

The problems of economic instability are not unique to people at the very bottom of the stratification system. Today, more and more people are having difficulty making ends meet. With so many different types of people from different backgrounds and circumstances suffering financially, we can no longer contend that they have only themselves to blame.

Stratification and Power in Everyday Life

Through class and status inequality, social stratification creates an unequal distribution of power. **Power** can be defined as the capacity to follow a line of action despite interference or resistance from others (Weber, 1968). More important, power is the ability to intentionally influence others to act in a way that is consistent with your wishes (Wrong, 1988) or even to change their beliefs, emotions, behaviors, and identity.

Those who own businesses, who are highly educated, who occupy prestigious positions in society, and who are connected to one another through upper-class social and family ties have the ability to make major decisions that profoundly influence the lives of others. If you work for General Motors and the board of directors decides to discontinue a line of trucks manufactured at your plant, you may be out of a job. Similarly, if the owner of the computer software company where you work decides to move the office from Los Angeles to Phoenix because it's not as expensive to run a business there, you might be forced to relocate if you want to keep your job. Or maybe you live in an area that is economically dependent on a big company. If that company decides to move, you may feel a ripple effect of small businesses disappearing, schools closing due to shrinking enrollments, and home values collapsing.

Compare the effects of these high-level decisions to the decisions made by ordinary people. If you buy a Ford instead of a Chevrolet or decide to move across the country, those actions will have virtually no effect on the lives of your superiors.

Power is rarely absolute, though. It's not very often that someone or some group or organization has total control over all aspects of your life. Even in the most lopsided power relationship, the person or group in the disadvantaged position is still able to influence the behavior of superiors: Workers strike, peasants revolt, children manipulate their parents by throwing tantrums or giving them the silent treatment. In some situations the outward signs of a power relationship obscure a much more complicated scenario. The office secretary, for instance, wields a tremendous amount of hidden power by controlling the flow of information to his or her boss, managing the boss's public impressions, and making sure the entire office runs smoothly. While a doctor's formal power over nurses is undeniable, many nurses learn how to take the initiative and make recommendations to doctors in a way that appears deferential (Stein, 1967).

Power is felt most forcefully in the multitude of interactions that characterize our lives (Collins, 1981). When we first hear the word *power,* we think of it in terms of orders, threats, and coercion. But noncoercive forms of power are much more common. These can be seen in the subtle cues—such as nonverbal gestures, the use of time and space, and conversational behaviors—that signal power and assert dominance (Henley, 1977). The humiliation of being powerless is felt when people are ignored or interrupted, are intimidated by another's presence, are afraid to approach or touch a superior, or have their privacy freely invaded by another. These often unnoticed details of ordinary social encounters—the signs and symbols of dominance, the subtle messages of threat, or the gestures of submission—can reveal a great deal about one person's power over another and that person's place within the larger stratification system.

The interpersonal expression of power is embedded in the very structure of a stratified society. Stratification systems persist and acquire legitimacy when a large majority of the people in the society reproduce the unequal distribution of power, wealth, and prestige in their everyday activities.

Power and Role Taking

As discussed in chapter 5, a key element in the development of the self is mastering the ability to take the role of others. It is something we all must learn to do in order to be functioning members of society. But from an institutional perspective, some roles command more respect than others, and some people face much less pressure to engage in role taking than others.

People in superior positions have the "luxury" of being insensitive and indifferent to the desires of subordinates. Therefore they will not find it necessary to take the role of people who are less powerful. In the political arena, low-level White House staffers must have thorough knowledge of the president's likes and dislikes in order to avoid a misjudgment of his conduct that might get them into trouble. The president, however, doesn't have to conform his behavior to the wishes and desires of underlings. This is not to say that he is mean or inconsiderate of his staff. Rather, the institutionalized structure of the White House does not require awareness to flow from top to bottom.

The less powerful a person is in any sort of relationship, the more dependent he or she is on that relationship (Emerson, 1962). If a less powerful person has a greater stake in the continuation of a relationship, then he or she must be more aware of the more powerful person's preferences and interests. Powerless individuals thus use role taking as a management strategy (Thomas, Franks, & Calonico, 1972).

Common sense suggests that people who have greater knowledge and experience would be better role takers (for example, parents should be more sensitive to their children's views than vice versa, since they were children once themselves). However, given the conditions of power and dependence, this is not the case. First-year college students are much more aware of the actions and interests of upper-class students than vice versa. Low-level employees must be sensitive to the behaviors and preferences of their superiors in order to achieve occupational success and mobility. It could even be argued that powerless nations must have heightened sensitivity to the activities of more powerful neighboring countries. I have heard some Canadians complain that they are "required" to know virtually everything about the United States—its culture as well as its economic and political systems—whereas most people in the United States tend to be rather oblivious to even the most accessible elements of Canadian society and culture.

Hurry Up and Wait

In chapter 4 I described the social norms that govern the use and perception of time. Although time is experienced under rather strict cultural guidelines, it is also profoundly influenced by power. At the interpersonal level, time can be used as a means of social control. If you have ever been to summer camp, either as a camper or a counselor, you know how tightly time is controlled. Most camps schedule events throughout the day, keeping campers' free time to an absolute minimum, to reduce the likelihood of their getting into trouble. All parents know the importance of controlling when their children eat, sleep, and play. Children's time is of no significance. They are made to do things when it is convenient for their parents.

Powerful people also have the ability to control the timing, length, and nature of interactions. The powerful share as little of their time with the powerless as possible, while the powerless must give up time as the powerful demand it (Henley, 1977). Waiting is an important means by which power can be created, maintained, and legitimated (B. Schwartz, 1973). The least powerful people in society can be approached at will, but the most powerful can be seen only "by appointment." If you have ever been kept waiting in a doctor's office past the scheduled time of your appointment, you are aware of the frustration that comes from knowing that your time is being defined as less important than the doctor's.

Waiting is experienced differently by different social classes. The organizational lives of poor and working-class people are filled with waiting—in hospital emergency rooms, for unemployment or welfare benefits, for food stamps, in courts, in long check-out lines at discount stores. What's more, because of the nature of their jobs, they are often unable to take time off to go to places whose services aren't available during nonworking hours, like the bank or the gas company.

Some of the waiting is caused by a demand for goods and services that are in limited supply. You may be forced to wait for a rare part for your foreign car because it is not kept in stock and must be obtained elsewhere. In other situations, though, waiting may be used strategically and purposely to express power and keep others in their place. To be kept waiting is to be sent a message that your time (and therefore your social worth) isn't as valuable as the time and worth of the person imposing the wait. Waiting provides a sense of subordination. To the powerful person, the fact that others are willing to wait for him or her merely serves to reinforce the sense of importance and domination associated with his or her position.

Strength in Words

Power is also expressed in the way people talk to one another. Because we live in a symbolic world, the terms we use to refer to ourselves and others convey a great deal of information about who and what we think we are. The fact that an uncle calls me "Davey" is irritating not because I don't like the name but because it doesn't fit with my professional self-concept. The terms we use to address others—Ms., Ma'am, Sir, Mr., Doctor, Senator, and so on—may on the surface appear simply to be forms of etiquette. On closer inspection, however, the norms that govern the use of such terms reflect underlying power differences.

Forms of address are governed by the relative statuses of the individuals involved. The conversations that take place between friends or siblings are commonly marked by the mutual use of informal terms like first names or nicknames. When status is different, though, the lower-status person is often required to use terms of respect and formal pronouns like sir or ma'am. In the South in years past, every white person had the privilege of addressing any black by first name and receiving the respectful form of address in return. These differences are clearly institutionalized in some languages. In Spanish, *tu* is the familiar word for "you," which is used when one is talking to a subordinate or to a person of equal status. *Usted* also means "you," but it is the formal version, used when one is addressing a person of superior status.

Conversational style is also affected by power differences. Ordinarily, conversations are organized to ensure that one speaker talks at a time and that speakers trade off. Speakers are usually expected to respect and obey the rules of taking turns or risk some form of informal punishment. For instance, the person who always butts in and never lets another get a word in edgewise will soon gain a reputation as ill-mannered and uncouth.

The power derived from differences in social status gives certain people more freedom than others to violate and ignore these rules. To interrupt someone in midsentence is not only rude but a clear expression of power, for it immediately makes the other person stop talking. Often politicians in debates will attempt to gain the upper hand by frequently interrupting their opponents, thus preventing them from getting their message across unchallenged.

Sociologists Peter Kollock, Phil Blumstein, and Pepper Schwartz (1985) examined taped conversations between intimate partners in heterosexual, gay male, and lesbian couples to see if positions of power influenced people's conversational behavior. They were particularly interested in such conversational norm violations as interrupting, talking over the other person, and monopolizing the conversation. They found that regardless of the sexual composition of the couple—the factor that in past research had been used to explain differences in conversational behavior—people in positions of power interrupted more, overlapped their partners more, and talked for longer periods of uninterrupted time than those people with less power. In other words, power can create a conversational division of labor.

The Impact of Institutional Power

Stratification doesn't just affect individuals, it also shapes the nature of social institutions and the way those institutions interact. Inequality is produced and reproduced in families, economic relations, political activity, and the educational system. Once established and in place, practices and programs are supported by those individuals, groups, and organizations that benefit from them. For example, wealthy school districts are likely to acquire and retain more innovative and expensive educational programs than are poorer districts.

Those at the top of the class structure are both the architects and the products of the institutional expectations that eventually become a taken-for-granted part of our society (Powell, 1991). They further consolidate their power by assuming authority within institutions.

Institutionalized Authority

The power derived from authority is a key feature of institutional relationships. Within the family, the educational system, and all other institutions, someone has the power needed to get everyone acting in the "normal manner." Many historical battles for freedom and justice have revolved around the issue of authority. The institution of slavery was "justified" by slave owners with the argument that whites, by virtue of their race, had authority over blacks. Similarly, the historical subordination of women in families as well as in the workforce has long been justified by the argument that men are physically, genetically, and maybe even spiritually endowed with authority. Mutinies, revolutions, and other movements for change are challenges to conceptions of authority within political, economic, religious, and other institutions.

Prerequisites for Institutional Authority

Institutional authority is based on dependence and legitimacy. Legitimacy rests on the belief that you should obey the directives of an authority; dependence is based on the undesirable consequences that await you if you don't.

Dependence is directly related to the unequal distribution of economic resources. Such inequalities enable certain individuals or groups to exercise tremendous power over others. If I control something you need in order to survive or have become accustomed to, our relationship can easily become one of exploitation. I may force you to act as I wish by dangling before you the resources you need. Dependence is built into many institutional roles: Children depend on parents for their physical needs, employees depend on employers for their financial needs, students depend on teachers for their educational needs.

The crises that sometimes lead people to consult professionals—doctors when we're sick, lawyers when we're in legal trouble, accountants when we have money problems—create greater possibilities for dependence than other authority-subordinate relationships. In a large complex society, professionals often act as gatekeepers between people and the benefits they desire or the penalties they fear (Starr, 1982). Teachers certify those who are eligible to graduate from school; judges determine who will and will not go to prison. The authority of professionals is enhanced by our need for them.

The dependency, power, and trust that exist between clients and professionals is influenced by one's position in the larger class system. On the one hand, wealthy individuals are likely to see professionals under voluntary conditions and are more likely to pay for sessions in private settings. Furthermore, they are likely to share the same beliefs and values as the professionals they consult. On the other hand, when poor or working-class people encounter professionals it is more likely to be involuntary or take place in public institutions.

Legitimacy refers to the generally acknowledged right to command and the acknowledged obligation to obey (Wrong, 1988). It is the source of the command rather than its content that endows it with legitimacy. By nature of their institutional positions, generals, presidents, queens, kings, and other leaders can issue commands that will be obeyed by others simply because of who they are. The norms that grant one person legitimate authority over another are shared by the larger community and culture to which the two people belong. Legitimate authority allows an individual to exert influence in those areas of life in which the people involved agree that such influence is proper and right (Huston, 1983).

The costs of disobeying legitimate authority are socially prescribed and enforced by the community. It would come as no surprise if your boss fired you for consistently disobeying his or her commands. You may think your boss is a dolt, consider the commands unreasonable, or feel the reaction was extreme, yet you still would acknowledge that the boss certainly had the right to respond that way.

Legitimate authority may also be based on perceived competence. For example, you will likely obey the directives of someone if you believe in his or her expertise to decide on a line of action that is in your best interest (Wrong, 1988). "Doctor's orders" is the prototype of legitimacy derived from cultural definitions of competence. The doctor who tells a patient, "Stop smoking or you will die within a year," is not threatening to kill the patient, nor is he or she appealing to the patient's sense of moral obligation to obey. He or she is simply saying, "I'm the expert here. I have been trained to identify causes of illness. I have the appropriate credentials. Hence I am qualified to tell you how you can become healthier."

The Authority of Professions

Institutionalized authority is a defining characteristic of professions. A **profession** is an occupation that requires extensive training and that is governed by a code of ethics. Professionals become powerful because we depend on their knowledge and competence. They are able to claim authority not necessarily because of their personal charm and intelligence, but because they are members of a social group that has had its competence legitimated by the culture (Starr, 1982). If they violate the standards of the community, as when a physician or lawyer commits malpractice, their authority becomes illegitimate.

The phenomenon of exercising power by requiring someone to wait is more than just an individual tactic for gaining the upper hand. It often derives from structural conditions that characterize the profession. Because a significant number of people fail to keep their appointments, for instance, doctors overbook—that is, schedule several people at the same time. The waiting room is an institutionalized response to a common problem in the profession. That most of us quietly tolerate waiting says more about the power behind the profession than the power of that individual physician.

Professionals not only advise us to act in certain ways, they also provide a collective interpretation of reality. The church, for instance, makes authoritative judgments about the nature of the world. In a highly specialized society, different professional communities come to rule different aspects of reality, such as the structure of the atom, the elements of the law, the nature of the universe, or the process of disease (Starr, 1982). Such authority is so extensive that it transcends individual people, residing in cultural objects like the Bible, dictionaries, maps, mathematical tables, or written laws.

The Pluralist Perspective

Institutional power and authority are most apparent in the political sphere. From an early age we learn about the democratic character of the American political system. We are taught that we have a government "of, by, and for the people," and we learn to favorably contrast our system of government with that of others. Our political system is one in which the will of the majority always prevails, in which there is equality for everybody under the law, and in which policy decisions are made to maximize the common good. Even schoolyard disputes are often settled by the democratic declaration, "Majority rules!"

At the heart of **pluralism**—or the pluralist perspective—is the notion that power in American society is evenly distributed among a number of diverse interest groups (Dahl, 1961). These groups represent a variety of constituencies from all corners of society: farmers, women, laborers, business and industry, gun owners, religious, racial, age, or ethnic groups, and so on. These groups, although they are made up mostly of "ordinary" Americans, have access to government officials because of their numbers. They compete with one another to influence political decisions. Those groups that are well organized are able to neutralize attacks on their interests.

Because their interests are narrow, no single group is concerned with all issues of national policy. Hence no group is capable of dominating at all times. In this way, power is constantly shifting and, in the long run, is balanced. On occasion diverse interest groups will even form curious alliances when some common interest is threatened, as when radical feminists and fundamentalist Christians fight together against the "evils" of pornography.

According to sociologist David Riesman (1950), the federal government in a pluralist society is a neutral body that is responsive to all interests and dominated by none. The president and Congress simply make decisions based on the wishes of a particular interest group that happens, at that time, to have the largest amount of support from the people. In this way the political system is democratic. Decisions of national and international significance are made in the interests of those groups that have the most popular support. People are free to join or otherwise support the groups that promise to best represent their interests. Power, then, is ultimately in the hands of the people.

Although Riesman felt that interest groups fit into a democratic system of government by representing the needs of the people, he could not have foreseen the enormous power and influence these groups have attained in their own right. While they certainly ensure that a variety of interests will be represented at the highest levels of the government, it's not clear whether the average citizen has much influence over them or is able to have his or her interests represented by them.

The most controversial type of interest group on the political landscape today is the **political action committee** (PAC). PACs are organizations formed to represent narrowly defined special interests, including big business (tobacco growers, banks, real estate, electronics, construction); professions (teachers, lawyers, physicians); labor unions (autoworkers, teamsters, sheet metal workers, postal workers); or ideological positions on single issues (gun control, human rights, Social Security, abortion).

PACs were born out of political necessity in the 1940s. When labor unions were prohibited from spending union treasury money on candidates for federal office, they came up with the idea of pooling donations and presenting that money to the candidates. The idea caught on with business and ideological groups. By 1974 there were approximately 500 PACs. Today there are close to 5,000 PACs representing the whole political spectrum, from liberal environmentalists to the National Rifle Association (Makinson, 1993).

PACs are allowed to collect funds from their members and make contributions much larger than those allowed individual contributors. The amount of money PACs spent on political campaigns increased from $60 million in 1979 to nearly $190 million in 1990 (Makinson, 1995). In 1994, about 23% of money donated to political campaigns came from union PACs, 10% from single-issue PACs, and 67% from corporate PACs (Henwood, 1994).

Although financial contributions made by PACs have dropped slightly in recent years, these interest groups still exert tremendous control over candidates and the entire electoral process. That PACs have influenced the way our government makes decisions is undeniable. In the early 1980s, for instance, 92% of Congress members who received contributions from PACs supporting the construction of a nuclear breeder reactor voted for it. Only 29% of those who received no contributions voted for it (Green, 1984). In 1982 a PAC called the National Automobile Dealers' Association opposed a bill that would have required used-car dealers to tell prospective buyers about known defects in their cars. The association distributed campaign contributions in excess of $840,000 to senators and

Figure 10.1   *PAC Contributions to House and Senate Candidates*

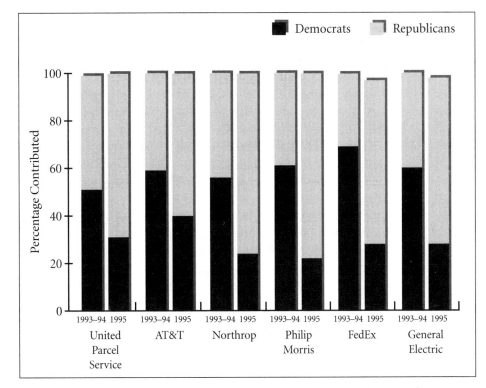

Source: Adapted from *New York Times Magazine,* January 7, 1996, p. 12. (Information from Pac-Track, a diskette reference published by Sunshine Press Services, Washington, D.C.)

representatives. Eighty-five percent of those who received these contributions voted against the legislation. And in 1988, $8.4 million was given to candidates for the House of Representatives who were running unopposed (Eitzen & Baca-Zinn, 1991).

Political ideology doesn't stand in the way of PACs' attempts to buy influence and ensure access to elected officials. Common Cause, a reform group that frequently criticizes the influential power of PACs, studied seven Senate races in 1988. It found that 274 PACs gave money to both Democratic and Republican candidates in the same races. Federal Express Corporation, for instance, contributed to all 14 candidates in these races (Minzesheimer, 1989). What seems to matter to PACs is not the candidate's political affiliation but his or her power to affect legislation. Thus, the Republican takeover of Congress in 1994 dramatically altered the political direction of PAC contributions (see Figure 10.1).

Given the power of PACs, how accurate is it to describe the American political system as pluralistic? Compared with many other nations, the United States does have well-established formal rules to put "the little guy" on equal footing with the rich and powerful. After all, a poor person's vote counts as much as a wealthy person's. But the everyday experiences many Americans have with the political system have led them to doubt its "democratic" character. Many people feel that government and the political power that comes with it has been concentrated in the hands of a very few people who are primarily concerned with their own interests and not the interests of the people.

The Ruling-Class Perspective

According to sociologists G. William Domhoff (1983) and C. Wright Mills (1956), political and economic power rest not in the hands of competing interest groups but in the hands of a small, socially cohesive **ruling class**. They feel that pluralism is a myth, reflecting what we might like American society to be and not what it really is. They argue that, instead of being a pure democracy, the United States is a society dominated by a small group of people—men and, in very rare cases, women—who hold the highest political and economic positions in the country.

Influential interest groups do exist, but only at a secondary level of power. The real power to make decisions of local, national, and global significance is at a level above and beyond their reach. It is the ruling class alone that makes economic and policy decisions that chart the course of American society.

Composed of rich businesspeople and their families, America's ruling class is an exclusive group that occupies the highest levels of status and prestige. As evidence of their existence, social registers are maintained in many major American cities. These registers are telephone-book–like volumes that contain information about America's elite. Individuals and families are listed in them by virtue of their family pedigree and their economic standing. Furthermore, the American ruling class is perpetuated through a set of clubs, resorts, charitable and cultural organizations, and social activities that provide members with a distinctive lifestyle and perspective on the world that distinguishes them from the rest of society.

More important, the ruling class is able to run the political and economic institutions in this country by controlling the executive branch of government, both major political parties, large corporations, the majority of privately held corporate stock, the media, universities, councils for national and international affairs, and so on (Domhoff, 1983). Hence members of the ruling class enjoy political and economic power to a degree not available to members of other classes.

The ruling class can work in a couple of ways to ensure that their interests are met. First, it may directly participate in national government. Pierre Du Pont of Delaware, John D. Rockefeller IV of West Virginia, and John Danforth of Missouri are heirs to immense fortunes and have served or are serving as U.S. senators or representatives. Perhaps the most obvious examples of the meshing of economic power and political aspirations came in 1992 and 1996 with the presidential campaigns of H. Ross Perot and Steve Forbes. These multibillionaires made no bones about the fact that they intended to use their tremendous financial resources to try to get elected.

Second, the ruling class can also participate in the political process by making financial contributions to the campaigns of politicians who support their interests or who are sympathetic to their views. Because successful campaigns cost so much money to run, candidates for office often must mold their views to be consistent with the views of those providing financial support.

The idea that a small group of privileged people is able to dominate politics and the economy violates our country's fundamental pluralistic values. Keep in mind, however, that the existence of an American ruling class doesn't necessarily imply that other classes in society are totally powerless (Domhoff, 1983). Even the most powerless people can develop the capacity to disrupt the system. Under certain circumstances the voting masses have placed legislative restraints on the actions of the ruling class. "Ruling class" doesn't necessarily mean total control and domination. Instead, it refers to the ability to set the terms and define the rules under which other groups and classes must operate.

You can see how this approach echoes a general notion of the conflict perspective described earlier—that political power in a stratified society is based on the unequal distribution of wealth, information, and other resources. Implicit in this explanation of society's political and economic power structure is the notion that those with wealth and authority can structure other social institutions to ensure that their personal interests are met and that the class itself endures.

Like other social structures, the names and faces of the ruling class may change, but the institutions that perpetuate it stay virtually intact over time.

Wealth, Class, and Education

Consider the role of the educational system. Education plays not only a key socializing role (see chapter 5) but also an important role in perpetuating or reproducing the American class structure. In public schools, working-class and poor kids are taught their place in authority relationships so that they will be prepared for the subordinate work positions they will probably occupy in the future (Bowles & Gintis, 1976). Many members of the ruling class on the other hand, spend their childhoods in private schools, their adolescence in boarding schools, and their college years in heavily endowed private universities (Domhoff, 1983).

Such schools provide very different lessons for children of the ruling class. Elite private schools have been called "educational country clubs" where children from families like the Rockefellers, Kennedys, and Vanderbilts go to get socially polished for admission to exclusive colleges (Cookson & Persell, 1985). In addition to the standard curriculum, these schools teach "vocabulary, inflection, styles of dress, aesthetic tastes, values and manners" (Collins, 1971).

In boarding schools, required attendance at school functions, participation in esoteric sports such as lacrosse, squash, and crew, the wearing of school blazers or ties, and other "character-building" activities are designed to teach young people the unique lifestyle of the ruling class. In many ways, boarding schools function like total institutions (Goffman, 1961), isolating members from the outside world and providing them with routines and traditions that are highly effective agents of socialization.

Peter Cookson and Caroline Persell (1985) studied more than 60 elite boarding schools in the United States and Great Britain. They accumulated hundreds of hours of interviews and conversations with prep school heads, teachers, students, and alumni and distributed questionnaires to thousands of students and teachers. They observed classes, assemblies, chapel services, sports contests, cultural events, meals, and other school activities and were given access to catalogs, curriculum listings, brochures, SAT scores, and grade-point averages.

The researchers found that the philosophies, programs, and lifestyles of boarding schools help transmit power and privilege. The schools act as gatekeepers into prestigious universities. After attending these universities, boarding school graduates connect with one another in the financial and governmental world. The prep school experience forms an everlasting social, political, and economic bond. Institutional and interpersonal ties exist at the highest levels of business, finance, and government. Said the director of development at Choate, an elite prep school in Connecticut:

> There is no door in this entire country that cannot be opened by a Choate graduate. I can go anywhere in this country and anywhere there's a man I want to see . . . I can find a Choate man to open that door for me. (quoted in Cookson & Persell, 1985, p. 200)

The privileged social backgrounds that are produced and maintained through the elite educational system are similar to one another but highly unrepresentative of the American population as a whole. This standing practically guarantees that members of the ruling class who occupy key political and economic positions will form a like-minded, cohesive group that bears little resemblance to the majority of Americans whose lives depend on their national and international decisions.

Class Connections

The homogeneity of the ruling class provides members not only with opportunities for social contacts but also with opportunities for the sharing of knowledge and mutually beneficial financial and governmental activities (Eitzen, Jung, & Purdy, 1982). Retired government leaders are often appointed to corporate boards. Government officials frequently call on business leaders for advice. Persons of wealth are routinely invited to become U.S. ambassadors. Former cabinet members become highly paid business consultants. Top corporate executives are often given cabinet posts or other advisory positions within the government. Such traffic in personnel has become so heavy that Congress had to pass a law setting time limits and restricting permissible contact between ex-government officials and their successors.

Certain prestigious professions have also been able to take advantage of class connections. In response to reports that doctors' incomes were falling, several bills were introduced in Congress that would give doctors new ways to make money (Gottlieb, 1995). One bill would relax restrictions on doctors' ability to operate laboratories and own companies they can refer patients to and would allow them to set their own fees for Medicare patients. Another limits the amount of money malpractice victims could be awarded in lawsuits against doctors. Ironically, at the same time Congress was attempting to improve the financial well-being of middle- and upper-class physicians, it was fighting to block a bill that would increase the minimum wage.

Members of the ruling class often act as **corporate interlocks**, serving on the boards of directors of several large corporations simultaneously (Useem, 1978). In a study by a Senate subcommittee on governmental affairs, of the top 245 large corporations in the United States, 123 were interlocked through at least one common board member with an average of 62 of the remaining 122 corporations. For instance, Morgan Bank shared directors with such corporations as Ford, Eastman Kodak, IBM, Procter and Gamble, Sears Roebuck, General Motors, General Electric, Bethlehem Steel, and Prudential Insurance (U.S. Senate Committee on Governmental Affairs, 1978). These individuals are in a position to exercise influence over several major firms simultaneously. Because credit is a crucial resource for most large corporations, for instance, the inclusion of a banking executive on their boards of directors can help ensure adequate financing in the future (Useem, 1978).

Although people are forbidden by law to serve on the boards of competing corporations—Ford and General Motors, for instance—corporate interlocks still can have a substantial impact on the economy and subsequently our personal lives. Interlocks reduce competition among corporations in general. Thus, a relatively small number of corporate giants with various ties have come to dominate the economy. Through this domination they have obtained tremendous political and economic influence. What is important about this inner circle from an institutional perspective is that instead of being concerned with the interests of a single organization, these companies are unified in their concern for the long-term interests of business as a whole. They come together as a community, sharing similar values and goals (Domhoff, 1983). When individual members of this inner group find their way into positions of political influence, they can speak for the interests of the entire corporate world rather than the narrowly defined interests of one corporation.

■ ■ ■ ■ ■ ■ ■ ■
MICRO-MACRO CONNECTION
Gated Communities

The homogeneity and cohesion of the ruling class is also enhanced by residential patterns. One such phenomenon that has grown in popularity over the last 10 years is the "gated community." Gated communities are residential areas with restricted access designed to privatize normally public spaces, like streets, footpaths, and parks (Blakely & Snyder, 1995). Perhaps three to four million Americans—mostly on the East and West Coasts and in Texas—seek this type of residence to escape crime and other problems associated with urban and suburban life.

The phenomenon of gated communities is not new. Ancient cities commonly had walls around them to keep out undesirables or foreign invaders. The first contemporary gated communities that appeared in the 1980s were either retirement villages—like "Sun City" in Florida and "Leisure World" in Los Angeles—or the secure closed neighborhoods of the super rich. Today, however, the majority of gated communities are inhabited by middle- and upper-middle-class residents. Even many traditional neighborhoods—that is, those with open access—are asking city governments to fence off streets or declare them "private" so they can isolate and protect themselves and limit contact with outsiders.

Gated communities illustrate the nation's larger pattern of residential separation by income and economic opportunity. Neighborhood segregation along class lines is as common as segregation along race lines, if not more so (Frisbie & Kasarda, 1988). Fearful of the increasing level of crime and pessimistic about the government's ability to address it, many affluent suburban residents are seeking separation, exclusion, and protection (Blakely & Snyder, 1995; D. J. Kennedy, 1995). Neighbors who heretofore had been complete strangers suddenly experience an intense sense of community when it is rumored that a low-income housing project is about to be built nearby or that their school district is to merge with a poorer one.

The key feature of gated communities is the shared socioeconomic status of the residents (Blakely & Snyder, 1995; Reich, 1991). The educational backgrounds and consumer tastes of people who live in these communities, where everyone earns about the same amount of money, are likely to be similar, as well. In addition, affluent neighbors tend to share the same concern with maintaining and upgrading their property values.

The feelings of solidarity within the gated community are enhanced by the often strict rules, conditions, and restrictions all residents must abide by. These rules can dictate house colors, shrubbery heights, and types and number of pets; they may prohibit things like basketball hoops attached to garages, flagpoles, visible clotheslines, satellite dishes, streetside parking, and tall grass (Egan, 1995).

But the matter of residential segregation is more than just a matter of who lives where, near whom, and under what conditions. The middle- and upper-middle-class residents of gated communities have, in effect, withdrawn their money from the support of public institutions shared by everyone and dedicated that money to their own private services. While public parks and playgrounds are allowed to deteriorate, private health clubs, golf courses, tennis clubs, skating clubs, and every other type of recreational association in which costs are shared among members have grown phenomenally (Reich, 1991). While complaining about property taxes, members of gated communities will readily give money to maintain *their* roads, mend *their* sidewalks, repair *their* streetlights, and hire security guards to protect *their* lives and property. In one Los Angeles gated community, residents pay $360 a month for private security guards (National Public Radio, 1995). A community in Florida spends over $1 million a year on helicopters and canine patrols (Dillon, 1994, p. 8). Furthermore, gated communities are able to benefit from state expenditures on their behalf. Their streets, fire hydrants, streetlights, and so forth were initially paved, installed, and constructed at public expense (D. J. Kennedy, 1995).

Although the private funding of security, street maintenance, parks, garbage collection, and other services is beneficial in that it relieves taxpayers of additional burdens, it has some unintended negative consequences. Residents of gated communities may become less interested in participating in tax programs that would increase funding for public schools, streets, police, or other city and county services. In addition, contact with unknown neighbors is reduced considerably. In fact, gated communities often purposely restrict the freedoms of nonmembers, who must forfeit their right to live in certain areas, their right to move about freely, and their constitutional guarantee of equal protection (D. J. Kennedy, 1995). The resulting loss of connection between residents inside and outside the gates weakens the bonds of mutual responsibility that once held communities together.

In sum, gated communities are fostering a residential, financial, and social gap between the more affluent and the rest of society that is "widening into a chasm." The withdrawl of the affluent from the population at large raises fundamental questions about the future of American society. Life inside and life outside the gated community become two different worlds in terms of services, citizenship, governance, financial responsibilties, and property rights (D. J. Kennedy, 1995). As increasing numbers of the more affluent members of society isolate themselves in these serene walled fortresses, it becomes more difficult to convince people that they have any abiding obligations to citizens outside their walls:

> What is the measure of nationhood when neighborhoods require armed patrols and electric fencing to keep out other citizens? When public services and even local governments are privatized and when the community of responsibility stops at the subdivision gates, what happens to the function and the very idea of democracy? (Blakely & Snyder, 1995, p. 10)

▪ ▪ ▪

Global Development and Inequality

The perpetuation of the American class structure must be understood within the context of a global system of inequality. The trend toward globalization may have brought the world's inhabitants closer together (see chapter 9), but it has not occurred evenly or fairly. Structured inequalities exist not only within national boundaries but within a worldwide system of stratification. Because different nations have differing amounts of power to ensure that their interests are met, the industrialized, developed countries of the world and the less developed, so-called Third World countries experience inequalities in wealth and standards of living.

The Global Economic Gap

In 1994, the average per capita yearly income in the wealthy, industrialized countries of Western Europe, the United States, Canada, and Japan was about $22,000; in the less-developed countries of South America, Asia, and Africa it was a little over $300 (Bradshaw & Wallace, 1996). These wealthy countries thus constitute 20% of the world's population but account for 65% of the world's income. In contrast, Third World developing countries account for 67% of the world's population but only 18% of its income (McMichael, 1996). In addition, wealthy countries consume 85% of the world's supply of paper, 79% of its steel, and 80% of all commercial energy (Kerbo, 1991; Schor, 1991). Grains fed to U.S. livestock equal the amount of food consumed by the combined populations of India and China (McMichael, 1996).

The gap in the quality of everyday life between people in rich and poor countries is particularly striking. Only about 20% of school-aged children in poor countries are enrolled in secondary school, compared to 90% in affluent countries. In wealthy countries, 40% of college-aged people go to college; in poor countries only 3% do. The number of children who die before the age of five is nearly 20 times higher in poor countries than in rich ones (Bradshaw & Wallace, 1996). Life expectancy in rich countries approaches 80 years; in poor countries it is barely above 50.

Let me express the discrepancies in another way: In the space of a day passengers flying from Japan to Uganda leave the country with the world's highest life expectancy—nearly 80 years—and land in one with the world's lowest—a little over 36 years. A flight between France and Côte d'Ivoire takes only a few hours, but it spans over 30 years of life expectancy. A short air trip between Miami, Florida, and Haiti represents a life-expectancy gap of over 31 years (U.S. Bureau of the Census, 1995a).

Because of their access to better technology, wealthy nations are able to produce higher-quality goods at lower prices than are poor nations (D. A. Smith, 1993). This advantage allows them to have a more favorable balance of trade and ultimately gives them greater control of the world's financial resources (Wallerstein, 1974). Powerful nations, like powerful ruling classes, seek to retain their favored positions while keeping other nations in their place. Just as upper-class people can exploit and exercise power over lower-class people within a society, so too can wealthy countries exploit poor ones in a global context.

As the gap between rich and poor nations continues to grow, so does the gap between rich and poor people within the same country. The United States has the greatest income inequality between its poor and wealthy citizens of any industrialized nation (see chapter 11 for more detail). But such inequalities are even worse in developing countries, where the wealthiest and poorest people live in increasingly separate worlds. For example, the richest 10% of Mexicans control 41% of the country's wealth, while the bottom half controls only 16% (DePalma, 1996b). The national average income in Brazil is about $5,370 per year, 10 times higher than the average income of the poorest 20% of the population ($564 per year). Similar disparities exist in other Latin American countries and in most of sub-Saharan Africa. In contrast, the national average income in Japan is only twice as high as the average income of the poorest 20% of its population (United Nations Development Program, 1996).

Explanations for Global Stratification

How has such global inequality come about? Earlier in this chapter we saw how the conflict perspective explains stratification within a society. We can also use this perspective to explain stratification *between* societies. One way a country can use its power to control another is through **colonization**—the process by which a powerful country invades and establishes control over a weaker country and its people in order to expand markets. Typically, the native people of the colony are considered lower in status and forced to give up their culture. Labor, cultural treasures, and natural resources are extracted to enhance the power and wealth of the colonizing country. The colonies serve as a source of raw materials and a market for high-priced goods. Much of North and South America, Africa, and Asia were at one time or another under the colonial control of European countries like Great Britain, France, Spain, Holland, and Portugal. The United States once controlled territories in Central and South America.

Although the direct conquest and subjugation of weak countries is rare today, wealthy countries are still able to exploit them for commercial gain. They can set prices for manufactured goods and control the international markets where raw materials from poor countries are purchased. Because their economic base is weak, poor countries often have to borrow money or buy manufactured goods on credit from wealthy countries. The huge debt they build up locks them into a downward spiral of exploitation and poverty. As a result, they cannot develop an independent economy of their own and thus remain dependent on wealthy ones for their very survival (Frank, 1969).

Multinational Corporations

Global stratification has been made more complex in recent years by the growth of massive multinational corporations. Because of their access to economic and political resources, wealthy companies in the United States and elsewhere are able to go outside their country's borders to pursue their financial interests if domestic opportunities aren't promising. They can invest their money in more lucrative foreign corporations or, with assistance from the government, establish their businesses or factories abroad.

Economic globalization has meant that countries all over the world are connected by social, political, and economic processes that have made national boundaries all but irrelevant. Some of the largest American corporations, such as Exxon, IBM, Mobil, and Dow Chemical, have branches or production facilities in other countries and earn well over half of their revenues from foreign sales (Braun, 1991). At the same time, foreign firms and individuals have increasingly invested in American companies. These multinational corporations do not fall under the governance of any one country. Their decisions reflect corporate goals and not necessarily the well-being or interests of any particular country. In fact, the largest multinational corporations are wealthier than most *countries* in the world (see Table 10.5).

From a functionalist perspective, an American company locating a factory in a poor country would seem to benefit everyone involved. The host country benefits from the creation of new jobs and a higher standard of living. The corporation, of course, benefits from increased profits. And the country in which the corporation is based benefits from lower consumer prices for the products that are manufactured abroad and sold in the home country. Furthermore, the entire planet benefits because these firms have allegiances to many different countries and therefore might help pressure them into settling their political differences peacefully.

Multinational corporations are indeed a valuable part of the international economy. However, conflict theorists argue that in the long run multinationals can actually perpetuate or even worsen global stratification. One common criticism of multinationals is that they exploit local workers and communities. The employees who work in foreign plants or factories work under conditions that we wouldn't tolerate in this country. The most obvious intolerable condition is the wage they earn. Whereas the hourly wage of an auto worker in the United States is over $20, the wage of a worker in Taiwan or South Korea is less than $3 (Braun, 1991). Nike, for instance, recently came under attack for its treatment of workers in foreign manufacturing plants. More than a third of Nike's products are manufactured in Indonesia, where workers are paid the minimum wage of $2.20 a day—a wage level it took 4 years of violent struggle to achieve. However, now Nike considers its labor costs in Indonesia too high and intends to move its facilities to Vietnam, where the minimum wage is $30 a *month* (Herbert, 1996).

Table 10.5   *The Fifty Richest Economic Entities, Excluding Highly Industrialized Wealthy Countries*

Entity	Millions of U.S. Dollars (1992)*	Entity	Millions of U.S. Dollars (1992)*
1. China	$506,075	26. PHILIP MORRIS	$50,621
2. Russian Federated Rep.	$387,476	27. IRI	$50,488
3. India	$214,598	28. SIEMENS	$50,381
4. GENERAL MOTORS	$133,622	29. Colombia	$48,583
5. Indonesia	$126,364	30. VOLKSWAGEN	$46,312
6. Thailand	$110,337	31. CHRYSLER	$43,600
7. Iran, Islamic Rep.	$110,258	32. Pakistan	$41,904
8. FORD MOTOR	$108,521	33. UNILEVER	$41,843
9. Turkey	$99,696	34. Chile	$41,203
10. EXXON	$97,825	35. NESTLE	$38,895
11. ROYAL DUTCH/SHELL GROUP	$95,134	36. MYANMAR	$37,749
12. Ukraine	$94,831	37. ELF AQUITAINE	$37,016
13. TOYOTA MOTOR	$85,283	38. HONDA MOTOR	$35,798
14. Poland	$83,823	39. Algeria	$35,674
15. HITACHI	$68,581	40. ENI	$34,791
16. INTERNATIONAL BUSINESS MACHINES	$62,716	41. FIAT	$34,707
17. MATSUSHITA ELECTRIC IND.	$61,385	42. SONY	$34,603
18. GENERAL ELECTRIC	$60,823	43. TEXACO	$34,359
19. DAIMLER-BENZ	$59,102	44. Egypt, Arab Republic	$33,553
20. Malaysia	$57,568	45. NEC	$33,176
21. MOBIL	$56,576	46. E. I. DU PONT DE NEM	$32,621
22. NISSAN MOTOR	$53,760	47. CHEVRON	$32,123
23. BRITISH PETROLEUM	$52,485	48. PHILLIPS ELECTRONICS	$31,666
24. Philippines	$52,462	49. DAEWOO	$30,893
25. SAMSUNG	$51,345	50. PROCTOR & GAMBLE	$30,433

*Figure represents annual multinational sales for corporations and Gross Domestic Products for countries.
Source: Bradshaw & Wallace, 1996, p. 49.

In addition, environmental regulations and occupational safety requirements, such as protection against dangerous conditions or substances, which drive up the cost of products in this country, sometimes don't exist in other countries. Hence local workers might become sicker and the environment more polluted when foreign manufacturers set up facilities (Satchell, 1991).

The exploitation of foreign workers need not even take place in *foreign* countries. In 1995, it was discovered that 72 illegal immigrants from Thailand had been beaten and subjected to forced labor in a garment factory in El Monte, California. They worked from 7 A.M. to midnight, 7 days a week for a little over $1 an hour. They were locked up and guarded each night and threatened with harm or death if they tried to escape. All mail was censored and phone calls were monitored. Everything they bought came from the company store, which marked up prices 200% to 500%. Some of the Thais had worked at the factory for as long as 7 years. The products they made were sold in large department stores like Macy's, Mervyn's, and Neiman-Marcus (Scheer, 1995).

The money that multinational corporations earn is rarely reinvested in the host country. Eighty-five percent of the profit from exported products ends up in the hands of the multinational corporations, bankers, traders, and distributors (Braun, 1991). For example, in Brazil, one of the world's largest agricultural exporters, shipments abroad of fruits, vegetables, and soybeans over the past several decades grew considerably. During the same period, however, the number of Brazilians who are undernourished grew from one-third to two-thirds of the population during the same period of time (Braun, 1991).

Not all multinationals are hard-hearted organizations that don't care about the physical well-being of workers abroad or about the financial well-being of the workers at home whose jobs are exported to other countries. From the perspective of many multinationals, relocating manufacturing facilities in another country where labor is less expensive is a necessary response to global economic pressures. But those processes that drive corporate decisions do sometimes drive individuals out of work and contribute to environmental problems.

Conclusion

In chapter 1, I pondered the question of how free we really are to act as we wish. I described some of the personal, interpersonal, and structural considerations that limit or constrain our choices. In this chapter we have seen that this fundamental issue is affected by social stratification and inequality. Certain groups of people have a greater capacity to control their own lives than others. Your position in the stratification system can determine not only your ability to influence people and exert authority, but a whole host of life chances as well, from financial stability to housing, education, and health care. The unequal distribution of resources, most notably wealth, at both the national and international levels has created a seemingly indestructible culture of haves and have-nots.

Power and inequality are also obvious in the social institutions and political decision-making processes that guide our existence and in the relationships between countries in the global marketplace. These processes might seem distant from your private experiences. But it is in the minute details of our lives that power and inequality derived from these processes touch us tangibly and personally. Our routine interactions sometimes reflect the constraints as well as the privileges that are bestowed on us by virtue of our social positions; our access to jobs and careers sometimes reflects economic processes at the international level.

That profound imbalances in wealth, power, and prestige are the defining feature of this society is nothing short of ironic given how loudly and frequently we sing of our cultural commitment to the values of equality and justice. Nevertheless, our system is set up, by and large, to promote, enhance, and protect the interests of those who reside at or near the top of the stratification system. Authority, wealth, and influence grant rights unseen and unknown to the vast majority of people, who have fewer structural advantages.

CHAPTER HIGHLIGHTS

- Stratification is a ranking of entire groups of people, based on race, gender, or social class, that perpetuates unequal rewards and life chances in society.
- The structural-functionalist explanation of stratification is that the stability of society depends on all social positions being filled—that is, there are people around to do all the jobs that need to be done. Higher rewards, such as prestige and large salaries, are afforded to the most important positions, thereby ensuring that the most qualified individuals will occupy the highest positions.
- Conflict theory argues that stratification reflects an unequal distribution of power in society and is a primary source of conflict and tension.
- Social class is the primary means of stratification in American society. Contemporary sociologists are likely to define one's class standing as a combination of income, wealth, occupational prestige, and educational attainment.
- Social class is more than an economic position; it is a way of life that affects how we experience every facet of our lives. The middle class has been particularly influential in defining American culture and its moods, politics, lifestyles, and tastes.
- Stratification is most vividly felt in the everyday expression of interpersonal power: role taking, conversation, and the use of time and space.
- Sociologists are also concerned with how power and authority are distributed within our economic and political institutions. The pluralist perspective, which emphasizes the role of competing interest groups, and the ruling-class perspective, which emphasizes the role of a small group of wealthy individuals, are two competing explanations of institutional power.
- Stratification exists not only among different groups within the same society, but also among different societies within a global community. Wealthy nations are better able to control the world's financial resources than poor nations.

YOUR TURN

Social stratification can be based on more than just individual achievement. Your family can determine your access to certain opportunities and life chances. Furthermore, the American Dream of upward mobility—enjoying a quality of life superior to that of your parents—is becoming for many a nightmare of downward mobility.

To understand how your life has been and continues to be influenced by the lives of people in your family, construct a family tree. You may need to ask your parents, grandparents, and other relatives about distant ancestors. Go back as far into the past as you can. For each person in the tree, identify his or her occupation and the highest level of education achieved. Is there a pattern of upward or downward mobility in your family? To what extent has family helped or hindered individuals' mobility? Is there a career legacy that has been handed down from generation to generation? How do the occupational and educational paths of men and women differ in your family? What are your own career aspirations? How do they compare to those of your ancestors? If you have or expect to have children, what are your career and educational aspirations for them? Does your family experience support the contention that social class is "hereditary"?

CHAPTER 11

The Architecture of Disadvantage: Poverty and Wealth

- *The Distribution of Economic Resources*
- *The Consequences of Poverty*
- *Why Poverty Persists*
- *An Institutional View of Poverty and Wealth*

Luther Place Memorial Church in Washington, D.C., is a beautiful red sandstone structure that was built in 1870 to commemorate the end of the Civil War. Today, the church provides counseling, shelter, and meals to homeless people in the community. Whereas the shelter and food provide immediate relief, the counseling programs offer long-term skills that will, it is hoped, make recipients more self-sufficient. Senior Pastor John Steinbruck says of his church:

> In [this] environment of love and care, healing can take place. People are shown how to reach a better place in life. We try to provide an exit route from homelessness to independence. It's not our goal to provide just three "hots" and a cot. . . . [The people who use our services] aren't straggling around outside, nor are they a problem to the community. Our block is . . . probably the most drug-free block in Washington. (quoted in Worsnop, 1996a, p. 75)

With all the talk these days about the futility of tax-supported government handout programs to assist the poor, and about the necessity of getting poor people to support themselves, you'd think that such a place would receive substantial community support. Instead Luther Place is fighting for its life. For years it has faced harassment and periodic attacks from zoning and licensing agencies and neighborhood residents worried about erosion of property values. Objections from neighbors forced Luther Place to lop two stories off a 10-story building offering affordable housing for the homeless that was being constructed in an adjacent parking lot. Steinbruck estimates that the church has spent hundreds of thousands of dollars in court simply defending its right to exist (Worsnop, 1996a).

The story of Luther Place is not unique. All across the country, providers report concerted, sometimes vicious, efforts to stop their activities. A report from the National Law Center on Homelessness and Poverty cites 61 examples between 1993 and 1995 of government and residential opposition to the siting and operation of homeless services (cited in Worsnop, 1996a). Of these, 21 projects were halted, 6 private facilities and 5 government-run facilities were forced to close, 2 were forced to move, and 9 cases are still pending. Only 18 providers were able to establish the opposed programs largely intact. The report concluded that the prevalence of such reactions to housing and services for homeless people not only exacts a horrible human toll on those who can't get the things they need but ironically perpetuates the problem opponents want to avoid: people living on the streets.

This situation underscores the strange paradox in our country regarding poverty. As the number of people who are hungry, homeless, and sick increases, poverty becomes a more visible part of our everyday lives. In a 1991 survey, 68% of urban Americans said they saw homeless people during the course of their daily lives, up from 54% four years earlier (DeParle, 1991). Yet public attitudes toward poverty and poor people frequently remain indifferent or even hostile.

Chapter 10 introduced you to the structural inequalities of American society and the world and explained how these inequalities provide some nations and people with a disproportionate amount of power and privilege. In this chapter I examine the economics of the social stratification system, especially poverty. How are economic resources distributed in our society? How do we tell who's rich and who's poor? What are some of the everyday consequences of being poor? What are the cultural and institutional forces that perpetuate the unequal distribution of economic resources?

The Distribution of Economic Resources

Poverty is a word that has become all too common in the English language. Politicians typically include it in their laundry lists of issues they say they plan to address if elected. Social researchers devote their careers to examining and explaining whom it affects and why it occurs. People point to it as the major cause of other social problems, like violent crime and drug abuse.

But what exactly is poverty? In common usage, poverty is usually conceived in subsistence terms, as the lack of sufficient money to ensure adequate functioning. Sociologists, though, often make a distinction between absolute and relative poverty. **Absolute poverty** refers to the minimal requirements a person needs to sustain a reasonably healthy life. **Relative poverty** refers to one's economic position compared to the living standards of the majority in a given society. Absolute poverty means not having enough money for adequate food, clothing, and shelter, but relative poverty is more difficult to define. It reflects culturally defined aspirations and expectations. An annual family income of $5,000, which would constitute abject poverty in our country, is perhaps five times higher than the average income in many developing countries. Life in an American slum might be considered luxurious compared to the plight of tens of millions of starving people in other parts of the world. In Bangladesh, for example, 55% of the population are without access to health facilities, 51% are without access to safe water, and overall life expectancy is only about 51 years (Institute on Hunger and Development, 1992).

The Gap between Rich and Poor

What makes the lives of the American poor particularly difficult then is their standing relative to more affluent Americans. The wide economic gap between the richest and poorest segments of the population has grown even larger in recent years. In 1994, the income of the top 20% highest-paid American households (with an average annual income of $105,945) accounted for 46.9% of all before-tax income in the United States, up from 41.5% in 1980. That same year the annual income of the 20% lowest-paid households (averaging $7,762 per year) accounted for only 4.2% of before-tax income, down from 5.2% in 1980 (U.S. Bureau of the Census, 1995a). Between 1968 and 1994, the average income for the highest-paid 20% of the population increased 44%. In contrast, the bottom 20% saw their income increase a mere 7% during the same period (Holmes, 1996). An additional two million children fell into poverty during the late 1980s and early 1990s, but the number of millionaires increased by 1400%, from 4,414 to 63,642 (Farhi, 1992). The income gap between the rich and the poor is the widest it's been since World War II.

Even more striking are the relative disparities in wealth, which are reflected in ownership of durable consumer goods like cars, houses, and furniture and in financial assets like stocks, bonds, savings, and life insurance. In 1994, the most prosperous 20% of American households held 78% of the nation's wealth (up from 76% in 1984). Their average net worth was about $871,463. And the wealthiest 1% of American households owned 40% of the wealth (Bradsher, 1995a). At the same time, the average family in the poorest 20% of the population had a net worth of –$7,075, meaning the family *owed* more than it *owned*. This debt was twice as large as it was in 1984. The average family's share of the nation's wealth was actually below zero (–0.64%) (Bradsher, 1996).

The United States is one of the most economically stratified of all industrial nations. In Great Britain, for example, the wealthiest 1% of the population owns only 18% of the wealth (compared to 40% in the U.S.), despite that country's long tradition of an elite aristocracy. In Finland, the lowest-earning 20% earn 11% the country's income (compared to 4.2% in the U.S.). In Japan, chief executives in manufacturing companies earn 10 times more than their workers do; in the United States, executives earn 25 times more (Bradsher, 1995b).

The large economic gap between rich and poor in the United States challenges the notion that we live in a society based on equality. As disparities in income and wealth grow, so too does relative poverty, or the gap in quality of life between those at the top of society and those at the bottom.

The Poverty Line

Although such relative comparisons are important, for practical purposes there is an official cut-off point to distinguish the poor from everyone else. The U.S. government uses an absolute definition of poverty to identify those people who need assistance. The official **poverty line** identifies the amount of yearly income a family requires in order to meet its basic needs. The figure is adjusted each year to account for inflation. In 1960 the official poverty line for a family of four was an annual income of $3,000; in 1995 it was $15,455.

To measure the success of its efforts to relieve poverty, the government also tracks the official **poverty rate,** the percentage of Americans whose income falls below the poverty line. In 1960 the poverty rate in this country was over 22%. It reached a low of 11.1% in 1973 and peaked again at 15.1% in 1993. In 1994, the rate actually decreased a bit to 14.5%, meaning that a little over 38 million Americans live in poverty (Bradsher, 1995a; U.S. Bureau of the Census, 1995a) (see Figure 11.1).

The government bases its definition of poverty on pretax money income only and does not include food stamps, Medicaid, public housing, and other noncash benefits (Renwick & Bergmann, 1993). If these benefits were included as part of a person's income, approximately 5 million fewer people would officially be defined as poor (U.S. Bureau of the Census, 1995a). However, according to experts at the National Academy of Sciences, if certain other expenses—out-of-pocket medical expenses, taxes, child care costs, work expenses—were subtracted from a person's income, the number of poor people could increase by five to seven million (cited in Pear, 1995).

The cutoff line established by the U.S. Department of Agriculture is computed from something called the Thrifty Food Plan. This plan is used to calculate the cost of a subsistence diet, which is the bare minimum a family needs to survive. The plan does not identify a healthy, nutritious diet but one on which people are likely to become malnourished if it becomes long-term (Beeghley, 1984).

In the early 1960s an obscure civil servant working for the Social Security Administration took the Thrifty Food Plan and multiplied it by 3, since research at the time showed that the average family spent one-third of its income on food each year. The resulting amount was adopted in 1969 as the government's official poverty line. The line does vary according to family size, but the formula itself and the basic definition of poverty have remained the same for over three decades (DeParle, 1990; Ruggles, 1990).

The Face of Poverty

The poverty line and the national poverty rate are useful statistics for policy makers, economists, and sociologists. But when used to describe national trends in poverty, they obscure important differences among subgroups of the population.

Figure 11.1   *Historical Trends in the American Poverty Rate*

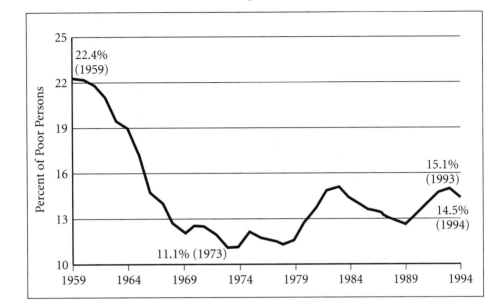

Source: U.S. Bureau of the Census, 1995c, p. 1.

Although two out of every three poor people in this country are white, the poverty rate for non-Hispanic whites—that is, whites of European descent (12.2%)—is considerably lower than that for Hispanics (30.6%) and African Americans (33.1%). Southern states have the highest rate of poverty (17.1%), and the Northeast has the lowest (13.3%). Finally, poverty is higher in rural areas (16.8%) than in cities (13.9%) (U.S. Bureau of the Census, 1995a; "America's poor showing," 1993).

Although racial and ethnic minorities have consistently been rated among the poorest Americans, other groups have seen their status change over time. Before Social Security was instituted in 1935, many of the most destitute Americans were those over 65. As recently as 1970, 25% of Americans over the age of 65 fell below the poverty line. Today, only 12.2% of the people in this age group are poor (see Figure 11.2 and chapter 14).

Taking their place, however, are women and children. In 1993 the poverty rate for families headed by a single mother was 38.7%, compared to 13.6% for all other families (U.S. Bureau of the Census, 1995a). Over 80% of people in poor families are women and children (Harris, 1996). Perhaps the most striking feature about the increase of women in poverty is that they are largely people who were not born into poverty but were instead forced into it by unemployment, illness, and especially divorce (Sidel, 1986).

Figure 11.2   *Historical Trends in Poverty by Age*

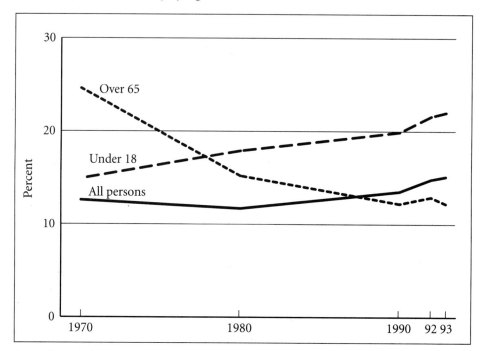

Source: "America's poor showing," 1993.

A study in 1988 of eight industrialized countries (the United States, Canada, Australia, Germany, Norway, Sweden, Switzerland, and the United Kingdom) found that the United States had the highest proportion of children living in poverty (Smeeding, Torrey, & Rein, 1988). The poverty rate for children under the age of 18 has increased from 15% in 1970 to 22% in 1993 (Figure 11.2). Children under 18 represent 26% of the American population but constitute 40% of those living in poverty. Most poor children live in single-parent families. The Census Bureau estimates that about 60% of children born in 1983 will spend some part of their childhood in a single-parent home; others feel the figure is closer to two-thirds (Hofferth, 1983). Whichever estimate is correct, it is clear that a significant proportion of the current generation of American children will spend some part of their lives financially impoverished.

The Poor and the Near-Poor

Many policy makers, sociologists, and concerned citizens question whether the current poverty line provides an accurate picture of the poor and the nonpoor in this country. Several things have changed since a family's basic needs were last defined in the early sixties. By 1990, for instance, food costs had dropped to one-sixth of the average family's budget because the price of other things, such as housing and medical costs, had inflated at much higher rates (Cloward & Piven, 1993). Today, most people spend almost half their income on housing alone (Ruggles, 1990). In addition, there were fewer dual-earner or single-parent families in the past, meaning that fewer families had to pay for child care at that time. In short, today's family has many more expenses and therefore probably spends a greater proportion of its total income on nonfood items. The consequence is that the official poverty line, based on outdated spending patterns, is probably too low and therefore underestimates the extent of poverty in this country.

how have they changed

Interestingly, while the government is likely to downplay the problem of poverty or even claim that the poverty rate is overestimated (see DeParle, 1990), at the same time it seems to agree implicitly that the poverty line is too low. The Census Bureau defines as **near-poor** individuals or families who earn between 100% and 125% of the poverty line, resulting in an overall "near-poverty" rate of 20% (U.S. Bureau of the Census, 1995a). Families are eligible for food stamps if they earn up to 130% of the poverty line. Pregnant women and children younger than the age of 6 are eligible for Medicaid if their families earn up to 133% of the poverty line (DeParle, 1990).

Deciding who is and isn't officially poor is not just a matter of semantics. When the poverty line is set too low, we fail to recognize the problems of many families who do not have enough money to survive but who earn more than what the government thinks is sufficient and hence are not officially defined as poor. A needy family making slightly more than the poverty line still may not qualify for a variety of public assistance programs, such as housing benefits, education aid, or Aid to Families with Dependent Children. As a result, their standard of living may not be as good as that of a family that earns slightly less and therefore qualifies for these programs.

who is responsible?

In addition, the poverty line income does not by any means define a comfortable standard of living. Consider the $15,455 pretax poverty line income for a family of four in 1995. Is that enough to meet a family's costs? Let's calculate a minimum subsistence budget for a hypothetical family with two preschool children. They live in a working-class neighborhood. Both parents are employed. That family would have to spend a minimum of about $350 a month on food (Renwick & Bergmann, 1993). A decent two-bedroom apartment in this neighborhood would rent for no less than $350 a month. Utilities—gas, electric, water, sewage, telephone—add up to about $170 a month. If this fictitious neighborhood has no public transportation and the family must own a car, count on $100 a month in transportation and insurance costs. What about health care? According to the National Health Care Expenditure Survey, the average monthly medical expense for a family of four is roughly $100 (Renwick & Bergmann, 1993). Because both parents work, full-time day care for the two children would cost about

$500 a month (Renwick & Bergmann, 1993). Clothing runs about $100 a month if we include the purchase of clothes and shoes as well as the costs of doing laundry at a laundromat. The cost of personal care and miscellaneous items—haircuts, toiletries, shaving cream, toothpaste, sponges, house cleansers, diapers for the children—would be about $50 a month.

The total comes out to about $1,720 a month, or $20,640 a year—and we haven't even taken out taxes yet or allowed for other incidental costs like furniture, household repairs, and entertainment. This amount is over $5,000 above the official poverty line. And it might even be a somewhat conservative estimate: Others have calculated the minimum amount of money needed by a family of four to be closer to $22,000—over 40% higher than the current poverty line (Ruggles, 1990; J. E. Schwarz & Volgy, 1993).

You might think that it is not so difficult for two working adults to earn $22,000 a year. But at the current minimum wage, which is $4.75 an hour (and which will increase to $5.15 an hour in 1997), two adults working year-round, full-time would make only $19,760 before taxes. Obviously, the minimum wage is not intended to bring a worker's income above the poverty line. The family that makes $18,000 or $19,000 a year is not officially considered poor but doesn't earn enough to adequately meet its expenses and provide a comfortable life for its members.

Life on the edge of poverty is precarious. Imagine being a poor single mother with a sick child. One trip to the doctor might cost an entire week's food budget or a month of rent. If you depend on a car to get to work and it breaks down, a few hundred dollars to fix it might mean not paying the electric bill that month and having less money for other necessities.

In sum, in addition to the 38 million officially poor Americans, a significant number of others fall into the category of near-poor. That is, their incomes are too high to be officially poor but so low that any slight drop—caused by the loss of a job, a serious illness, disability, or some other major unforeseen expense—would send them into poverty. The near-poor are a huge but largely unnoticed segment of the population. It has been estimated that about one-quarter of Americans hovering above the poverty line will fall below it at some point in their lives.

Although calls for a revision of the poverty line can be heard from economists and advocates for the poor, there are institutional obstacles to doing so. Think of the implications of raising the poverty line and therefore dramatically increasing, by perhaps tens of millions, the number of officially poor people in this country. A sudden increase in the poverty rate not only would bring the obvious political costs to whatever administration happens to be in office but would certainly bring on the demand for increased spending on social welfare programs, something few people in government are willing to consider, given the ongoing public pressure to reduce government spending.

The Consequences of Poverty

Poverty, of course, is more than just a phenomenon of income figures, statistical rates, and political liabilities. You've heard the old saying, "Money can't buy happiness." The implication is that true satisfaction in life is more than just a matter of having a lot of money. Yet such a saying provides little solace to those people who can't pay their bills, don't know where their next meal is coming from or whether their job will exist tomorrow, suffer from ill health, or have no home. Poverty pervades every aspect of an individual's life. The entertainer Pearl Bailey perhaps summed it up best: "I've been rich and I've been poor. Rich is better."

Homelessness

The most publicly visible consequence of poverty is homelessness. No one knows for sure exactly how many homeless people there are in the United States. Estimates range from 324,000 (Jencks, 1994) to 2 million (National Alliance to End Homelessness, 1995).

In the past homelessness was unseen and was confined mostly to skid-row areas of large cities or hobo villages beside train tracks. The typical "vagabond" or "vagrant" was an unemployed, alcoholic male over the age of 50 (Siwek, 1992). Today, the American homeless population is considerably more diverse. According to a 1995 survey of 29 major cities, 46% of homeless people are single men, 14% are single women, 36.5% are families with children, and 3.5% are children on their own. One out of every four homeless people is a child, one out of five is employed, and fewer than half are substance abusers (cited in Worsnop, 1996a).

Furthermore, homeless people today aren't found only in skid-row sections of major cities. We see them in suburban parks, in train and bus stations, in abandoned buildings, and on the sidewalks of trendy neighborhoods. Shelters are available, but they are few and far between, overcrowded, and plagued by drugs, violence, and crime. An estimated 24% of requests for emergency shelter by homeless families go unmet each year (Worsnop, 1996a). In rural areas homelessness is just as prominent, though much less visible. Here homeless people might sleep in sheds, barns, and cars or stay temporarily with family or friends (Fitchen, 1992a).

The Institutional Causes of Homelessness

In a national poll conducted in 1989, 82% of the respondents believed that homelessness was the fault of mental hospitals for releasing patients who couldn't lead normal lives. Drug and alcohol abuse was blamed by 90% of the sample (cited in A. B. Johnson, 1990). These results reflect a common but largely inaccurate perception about the nature of homelessness: that all homeless people are mentally ill. Such a belief is appealing because it suggests that individuals are responsible for their own fate and explains why an affluent society like ours cannot provide something so simple and basic as housing for all its citizens (A. B. Johnson, 1990). Furthermore, if the homeless are all crazy, we have an obvious solution: Treat and cure their mental illness, and the problem of homelessness will go away.

But the number of mentally ill homeless people has been grossly exaggerated (A. B. Johnson, 1990). Sociologist David Snow and his colleagues conducted a field study of homeless people in Austin, Texas, over a 20-month period (Snow, Baker, Anderson, and Martin, 1986). They found that only about 15% of the homeless are mentally ill. In addition, only 10% of the homeless in the study had any previous history of psychiatric hospitalization. The authors concluded that far from being mentally ill, most homeless people had been caught in low-paying, dead-end jobs without much hope of advancement. They were unable to build up enough money to cope with disasters like illness, fire, or eviction. When the money ran out, they were forced to leave their homes. Although some found less-expensive housing, most could not.

The most obvious and important reason for homelessness, then, is an institutional one: the national decline in affordable housing (P. Rossi, 1988). During the 1980s and 1990s most of the country's largest cities experienced massive reductions in low-income housing (rooming houses, single-room occupancy hotels, and the like) ranging from 12% to 58%. In the nation as a whole, half a million units of low-income housing are lost every year to condominium conversion, abandonment, arson, and demolition. In Boston between 1982 and 1984, over 80% of housing units that were renting for $300 or less disappeared, while those going for $600 or more doubled. Between 1981 and 1986 federal support for low-income housing dropped from $28 billion to $9 billion (Kozol, 1988).

Compounding the problem are zoning laws that prevent the construction of multifamily dwellings in "fashionable neighborhoods." Many residents in these neighborhoods fear a decrease in their property values should low-income residents move in. As one high school teacher in suburban Chicago put it, "People want to do something about [homelessness], but not if it's on their doorstep" (quoted in Oreskes & Toner, 1989).

Economic forces have also diminished families' ability to absorb homeless relatives. In 1987, 2.6 million extremely poor adults aged 22 to 59 were living in their parents' homes; an additional 677,000 were living with siblings or grandparents (P. Rossi, 1988). But research shows that even family members tend to wear out their welcomes after about 4 years (P. Rossi, 1988). Furthermore, as economic conditions force more families to slip into poverty or near-poverty themselves, fewer have the resources to support an additional member.

Public Attitudes and Intolerance

A fair amount of evidence suggests that the public's tolerance of homelessness is wearing thin (Smolowe, 1993). More and more cities are imposing harsher restrictions on homeless people in an effort to reduce their visibility and force them to go elsewhere (Wilkerson, 1991b). Consider these examples:

- In the months leading up to the 1996 Summer Olympics, the city of Atlanta stepped up its efforts to remove homeless people from the streets. The city increased enforcement of existing antiloitering laws and passed a new ordinance that allowed police to arrest people "acting in a manner not usual for law-abiding individuals" in parking lots and garages (Smothers, 1996, p. A8).
- The District of Columbia closed two emergency shelters and announced plans to eliminate half the beds in the remaining shelters. Voters there repealed a 1984 law that required the city to shelter all people in need (Smolowe, 1993).
- In many areas, city planners "sleep-proof" or "bum-proof" benches—for instance, by nailing pieces of wood to the bench or shaping benches like barrels so people can't lie down—to discourage homeless people from sleeping in bus shelters.
- In a Los Angeles park, a sprinkler system comes on at random intervals throughout the night to prevent homeless people from sleeping there. Janitors in New York's Grand Central Station accomplish the same thing by spreading ammonia on the floor.
- In Burlington, Vermont, a group of business owners formed an organization called "Westward, Ho!" to buy one-way plane tickets for their downtown's most visible beggars (Blau, 1992).
- Santa Barbara, California, banned homeless people from sleeping on public streets, beaches, or sidewalks. This measure left the homeless with one place to sleep—a public lot surrounded by trees where they are kept out of sight of downtown businesses. Said the president of Santa Barbara's Chamber of Commerce:

> Our goal is to make things as uncomfortable for them as we can so they can move on. When you look at these characters sitting out in the middle of the day when everybody else is working just to survive, you don't get a lot of sympathy. (quoted in Wilkerson, 1991b, p. 10)

This sort of municipal intolerance is not universal. In 1993 a federal judge declared as unconstitutional the city of Miami's practice of arresting homeless people for "harmless, involuntary, life-sustaining acts" in the city's streets and parks. The ruling prompted the city to impose a 1% tax on restaurant meals to finance programs for the homeless, such as medical treatment, job training, low-cost housing, and temporary shelters (Rohter, 1993). The program was estimated to generate about $7.5 million in its first year. In 1996, the mayor of San Francisco dismantled a controversial crackdown policy on the homeless enacted by the previous mayor. The policy had required police to arrest people sleeping, camping, drinking, or relieving themselves in public. Shortly thereafter, a municipal judge

Table 11.1   *Perceptions of Causes of Homelessness*

| | Amount of Effect on Homelessness | | |
Reason	A Lot	Some	Hardly Any
Local government failing to take care of people in need	30%	52%	14%
Homeless people being unwilling to work	37%	50%	11%
Mental institutions releasing patients who aren't able to live normal lives	44%	38%	12%
The domestic policies of the federal government	24%	52%	18%
Alcohol and drug abuse by the homeless	50%	40%	7%

Source: Oreskes & Toner, 1989.

dismissed 40,000 citations and arrest warrants that had been issued to homeless people since 1993 (C. Goldberg, 1996).

Such policies are rare, however, and increasing citizen apathy, decreasing public sympathy and patience, and a decline in political concern have further contributed to the problem (Worsnop, 1996a). A *New York Times*/CBS News poll in 1992 showed widespread indifference to the homeless despite the fact that increasing numbers of people have personally seen homeless people in their communities or on their way to work. Fifty-five percent of the respondents said that most people have become so used to seeing the homeless that they are no longer upset by the sight (Steinfels, 1992). Another survey found that 87% of the respondents felt the unwillingness of homeless people to work was at least partly to blame for the problem of homelessness (see Table 11.1) (Oreskes & Toner, 1989).

The growing public intolerance for and resentment of homelessness may be more the result of feelings of frustration and powerlessness than callousness. Such is the paradox of the sociological imagination. The frustration may indicate that some people are abandoning individualistic explanations of homelessness, talking instead about the root causes of poverty: lack of affordable housing and a changing economy that has all but eliminated entire classes of well-paying, low-skilled jobs. Yet such institutional causes are commonly seen as problems far beyond the reach of the individual citizen, who may be quite concerned about the problem but feel a kind of "compassion fatigue" and hopelessness.

Health Issues

Related to homelessness and poverty is the problem of physical health. According to the World Health Organization (1995), poverty is the single greatest cause of ill health in the world today:

Poverty is the main reason why babies are not vaccinated, why clean water and sanitation are not provided, why . . . drugs and other treatments are unavailable and why mothers die in childbirth. It is the underlying cause of reduced life expectancy, handicap, disability, stress, suicide, family disintegration, and substance abuse. (p. 1)

In this country, about 12% of the general population is in poor health. That figure rises to 32% for the poor and 44% for the homeless. Poor people, and in particular homeless people, are more likely to suffer from such medical problems as trauma, infection, chronic disease, and malnutrition (Siwek, 1992). In addition, poor people go to the hospital more often and stay longer than others. For families with incomes under $14,000, the hospitalization rate in 1989 was 131 per 1,000; for families with incomes over $50,000, the rate was 72 per 1,000; and the poorer group spent twice as many days in hospital as the affluent group (National Center for Health Statistics, cited in Colburn, 1992).

At the same time, the medical treatment received by poor people is generally worse than it is for others. About 30% of poor people have no medical insurance (U.S. Bureau of the Census, 1990b). A 1991 report by the Center for Health Policy Studies at Georgetown University found that hospital patients without medical insurance die at up to three times the rate of similar patients with insurance ("Uninsured hospital patients," 1991). Even when they have insurance, poor people receive less preventive medical care and less effective management of chronic diseases than wealthy people (Leary, 1996).

Poor people also die younger. At age 25, women with incomes above $50,000 can expect to live 4 years longer than women with incomes below $5,000. For men, the difference is 10 years. Advances in medical technology that have increased life expectancy affect mainly the middle and upper classes, not the poor (Colburn, 1992; Pear, 1993b).

The infant mortality rate, an important indicator of the general health of a population, has been decreasing worldwide—from 115 per 1,000 live births in 1980 to 87 per 1,000 in 1993 (World Health Organization, 1995). The U.S. rate (8.5 deaths per 1,000) is quite low in global comparison, but it is relatively high compared to other industrialized nations. Among these nations, the United States ranks 18th in infant mortality. Countries like Japan, Sweden, Great Britain, Finland, Spain, Singapore, and Hong Kong have significantly lower infant mortality rates. Some 700 babies born in the United States each day suffer from low birth weight, which is mainly due to the mother's poor health and a lack of prenatal care. Seventy-two of those babies will die before one month; 110 will die before their first birthday. Incidentally, our national infant mortality rate masks discrepancies between subpopulations. In 1992, the rate for black babies was 16.8 infant deaths per 1,000 live births; the rate for white babies was 6.8 (*World Almanac*, 1996). The rate is 13.5 for women living in poverty ("Infant deaths," 1995). Some of the poorest areas of the United States show higher rates of infant mortality than less-developed countries like Cuba, Jamaica, Panama, and Costa Rica (J. L. Brown, 1987).

Hunger and Malnutrition

One of the crucial reasons why poverty adversely affects physical health is poor nutrition. There seems to be a clear link between income and the nutritional value of one's diet. The Agriculture Department has found that while the average weekly grocery budget rose slightly in middle- and upper-income households during the eighties, food spending fell 13.1% in the nation's poorest households (O'Neill, 1992). Poor people simply cannot afford the sorts of healthy foods available to more affluent individuals and therefore don't have the luxury of choosing food items that are nutritionally sound.

This society's heightened concern with diet and fitness over the past several years has only amplified the disparity between the rich and the poor. The more health concerns shape the country's most expensive cuisine and the higher the prices rise on "healthful" vegetables, pastas, fish, and other fat-reduced food products, the more healthful eating drifts beyond the reach of poor people (O'Neill, 1992).

Interestingly, throughout history the foods that characterized upper- and working-class lifestyles have completely reversed. Anthropologist Nan Rothschild (1990) studied excavations in New York City that helped reveal the way of life in the 18th century. She found that wealthy areas could be identified by the remains of heavy meat bones, while poorer neighborhoods were indicated by cheap vegetables and fish. By 1984, however, that pattern had completely reversed. Apparently, in contemporary society, the lighter the food one eats, the higher one's status. Because of poor grocery distribution in low-income neighborhoods, fresh fruits and vegetables in these neighborhoods are typically more expensive than those in suburban stores, driving healthy foods further beyond the reach of the poor.

Dietary concerns have become one of the great dividers between poor people and the rest of society. As one senior vice president for a market research firm in New York put it: "When I hear the words, 'I don't care if it's good for me or not,' I know that I am talking to somebody poor. Almost nobody above the poverty level says that anymore" (cited in O'Neill, 1992, p. C6).

Poverty affects not only the quality of food but the quantity as well. For the vast majority of Americans concerned with weighing too much, the reality of not having enough to eat is a distant one. When most of us hear the word *hunger* we are likely to conjure up images of famine-ravaged countries in sub-Saharan Africa or destitute villages in Latin America or Southeast Asia where naked, dusty children, stomachs bloated with the telltale signs of malnutrition, plead for scraps of food. The World Health Organization (1995) estimates that at least 2 billion people worldwide are undernourished, despite the fact that annual food production is adequate to feed every person on earth. Almost a third of the world's children under the age of five are underweight for their age. Every day more than 40,000 children throughout the world die from hunger-related causes (N. A. Lewis, 1988).

A common misconception we have about hunger is that there isn't enough food to feed people because of natural factors such as droughts and soil erosion.

But the world food shortage is only partly caused by environmental conditions. Politics and economics play an even bigger role. Many developing countries, like India and Brazil, export huge amounts of food while millions of their people are starving or malnourished. In an attempt to modernize, they often spend a dispro-portionate amount of money on building up cities and industrializing their economies. As a result, farmers in rural areas aren't provided the incentives to grow as much food as they could. In some areas, civil wars and border disputes also take up a significant proportion of revenue that might otherwise go to do-mestic food production. Ethiopia, for instance, spends 42% of its budget on de-fense (J. Matthews, 1989). Corrupt governments and warring factions sometimes prevent food supplies from reaching the neediest people.

Whatever its cause, as long as the image of hunger remains a foreign one, we can continue to convince ourselves that it is a distant tragedy, one that we can comfortably address from afar with benefit concerts and charity events. But sooner or later we will be forced to acknowledge the magnitude of the problem in this country. No one can agree on the figures, but estimates on the hungry popu-lation in the United States range from 5 million to 30 million (Barringer, 1992).

The Psychological Impact of Poverty

Even if a poor person has a home to live in and doesn't suffer from ill health or hunger, the consequences of poverty can still be psychologically damaging. A spe-cial governmental task force on work in America once found that lower-class, blue-collar workers have

> an almost overwhelming sense of inferiority: the worker cannot talk proudly to his children about his job, and many workers feel they must apologize for their status. Thus the working-class home may be permeated with an atmosphere of failure— even of depressing self-degradation. (cited in Neubeck, 1986, p. 176)

In a society that measures individual worth in terms of occupational achieve-ment and accumulated wealth, feelings of self-worth tend to be based on one's ability to amass and consume material goods. According to Thorsten Veblen (1899/1953), the wealthy do not acquire wealth in order to consume goods con-spicuously; rather, they consume goods in order to display their accumulation of wealth to others. Poor and working-class people are unable to indicate their so-cial worth to others because by and large they have no goods to display.

■ ■ ■ ■ ■ ■ ■ ■
RICHARD SENNETT AND JONATHAN COBB
The Hidden Injuries of Class

> Sociologists Richard Sennett and Jonathan Cobb (1972) interviewed working-class men to examine the lives and conflicts of people near the bottom of the oc-cupational scale. These men were employed and not officially poor. However,

their economic situations were sufficiently insecure to create in them the sorts of identity conflicts experienced by many poor people. Listen to how one garbage collector defined his failures as the result of his own inadequacies:

> Look, I know it's nobody's fault but mine that I got stuck here where I am, I mean . . . if I wasn't such a dumb ———— no, it ain't that neither . . . if I'd applied myself, I know I got it in me to be different, can't say anyone did it to me. (p. 96)

To survive in this world of perceived failure and self-blame, these people must somehow defend themselves and restore dignity and value to their lives. They begin to see their work as meaningless and irrelevant to their core identity and define it instead as a sacrifice they make for their families rather than a reflection of self-worth. Instead of focusing on the dreariness of their dead-end jobs or the insignificance of their work performance, working-class men come to view their work self-righteously as a noble act of sacrifice; thus they are provided an alternative source of esteem. A bricklayer put it simply: "My job is to work for my family" (p. 135).

Defining a job as sacrifice solves the problem of powerlessness in several ways. First, in return for their sacrifice, working-class men can demand a position of power within their own families: "In exchange for my sacrifice, you will obey and respect me." Second, framing degrading work as sacrifice allows these men to slip the bonds of the present and orient their lives toward the future, which gives them a sense of control they can't get through their jobs.

Ironically, framing work as sacrifice causes other hidden injuries. Most American parents want for their children what they themselves could not attain. They are more than willing to work two or even three jobs, go without many of life's luxuries, and even forgo medical care or insurance in order to give their children more. Even upper- and middle-class parents want to see the struggles of their adult lives redeemed through sacrifice for their children.

However, there are differences in the nature of the sacrifice between upper-class and working-class parents. The balancing act of working-class parents is much more treacherous. On the one hand, they want to spend time with the children and show concern for them. On the other hand, they know that the only way they can provide a "good home" for their family, which, in turn, will give their own lives greater meaning, is to work longer hours at an unfulfilling job and be absent from home more frequently. Unfortunately, from the perspective of the child, parental absence is precisely what constitutes a "bad home."

In addition, it is more difficult for working-class parents to sacrifice "successfully." Upper-class parents make sacrifices so that their children will have a life like theirs. Working-class parents sacrifice so that their children will *not* have a life like theirs. Their lives are not a "model" but a "warning." Hence the sacrifice does not end the conditions that made the parents prey to feelings of shame and inadequacy in the first place. The danger of this type of sacrifice is that if the children do fulfill the parents' wishes and rise above their quality of life, the parents may become a "burden" to them.

The everyday experience of class thus goes well beyond financial stability or instability. People who struggle to make ends meet are caught in a vicious trap. Their work offers no glory or pride—as culturally defined—unless framed as future- and family-oriented sacrifice. But by making such sacrifices, other painful wounds are opened up, including resentment, hostility, and shame.

▪ ▪ ▪

Why Poverty Persists

Now that we have a sense of what poverty is and how it affects individuals, let's take a look at it from a more macro-sociological perspective. As I mentioned in the previous chapter, every society has a system of stratification, meaning that there will always be a group of people at the top and a group at the bottom. Even in the best of times, our prosperous country has had a sizable population of poor people. Why is it that in such an affluent country, poverty for millions of people is a permanent fixture on the social landscape? To explain the persistence of poverty, we must look at the structural role poverty plays in larger social institutions as well as the dominant cultural beliefs and attitudes that help to support it.

Functions of Poverty

In chapter 10, I discussed the structural-functionalist assertion that stratification and inequality are necessary because they ensure that the most qualified and valuable people in society will occupy the most important positions. Social conditions exist and persist only if they are functional to society in some way. But functional for whom? If you were to survey people on the street and ask them if poverty was a good or bad thing, they would all, I'm sure, say "bad." Yet according to sociologist Herbert Gans (1971, 1996), we must face the fact that within a free market economy and competitive society like ours, poverty plays a necessary institutional role. Although functionalism has often been criticized for its propensity to justify the status quo, Gans combines it with conflict thinking to link poverty and class. To that end, he identifies several economic and social "functions" played by poverty that benefit all other classes in this society.

Struct. function. View of poverty

Economic Functions

Economically, poverty benefits the rest of society in a variety of ways. First, poverty provides a ready pool of low-wage laborers who are available to do society's "dirty work." Poor people will work at low wages primarily because they have little choice. They will do the dangerous, undignified, or menial jobs that others won't do but that are necessary to keep businesses running, such as housekeeping, hospital cleaning, garbage collection, and manual labor. When large numbers of poor people compete for scarce jobs, business owners have the luxury of paying low wages.

Poverty also creates occupations and services that either serve the poor or protect the rest of society from them: police officers, penologists, social workers, lawyers, pawnshop owners, and so on. Even drug dealers and loan sharks depend on the presence of a large population of poor people willing to pay for their illegal services.

On an organizational level, the welfare system has supported a vast network of private sector businesses that make enormous profits by providing the system with a wide range of goods and services. When you hear people use the term *welfare dependency*, they are probably referring to the alleged long-term reliance of some welfare recipients on programs like Aid to Families with Dependent Children or food stamps. But we can also talk about people or organizations whose livelihood depends on the existence of this vast welfare system. For instance, everyone who works in the system needs to have an office or clinic space in which to work, as well as supplies, equipment, and furnishings. Bankers, real estate developers, office system suppliers, computer manufacturers, and the construction and building industries profit each time a new welfare office, mental hospital, jail, unemployment office, or public housing project for the poor is needed (Bedard, 1991). Some government assistance programs provide things to poor people that must be purchased from private industry. For instance, approximately one-third of all the infant formula manufactured in this country is purchased by the U.S. Department of Agriculture for its Women, Infant, and Child (WIC) nutrition program. In 1988, WIC accounted for half a billion dollars' worth of sales for the infant formula industry (Novac, 1988).

Another economic function of poverty is that poor people purchase goods and services that would otherwise go unused: secondhand goods; day-old bread, fruits, and vegetables; deteriorated housing; dilapidated cars; incompetent physicians; and so forth. Consider the following example of a company benefiting from its ability to sell a faulty product to the poor:

> At regular intervals, pineapple juice canneries must clean out the pipes that carry the juice from the crushing to the canning rooms. To do this, a salt solution is forced through the pipes and then flushed out before the new canning process starts again. A few years ago, one large cannery went through this cleaning operation and began running juice again before it was discovered that the pipes had not been totally purged of the salt solution. But, by that time, thousands of gallons of pineapple juice, all of it slightly salty, had already been processed and canned.
>
> The cans were sold, unlabeled, at a very low price to a food distributor who specializes in handling off-brand and reject merchandise for sale in poor neighborhoods and communities. The distributor put labels on the cans and retailed them for

about half the usual price for that size, making a very good profit for himself. Across the label was printed "No Sweetener Added," certainly an accurate statement of the juice's condition. (Jacobs, 1988, pp. 123–124)

Clearly, this merchandise would have had little or no monetary value outside the poverty market.

Social Functions

The poor also serve several less-obvious social functions. They act as a visible reminder to the rest of society of the "legitimacy" of the conventional values of hard work, thrift, and honesty. By violating, or seeming to violate, these mainstream values, the poor reaffirm their virtues. If poor people are thought to be lazy, their presence reinforces the ethic of hard work; if the poor single mother is condemned, the two-parent family is legitimated as the ideal (Gans, 1996).

In truth, the poor are just as moral or law-abiding as anyone else. For instance, the proportion of welfare recipients who cheat is actually far lower than the percentage of taxpayers who cheat (Funicello, 1993). However, the poor are more likely to get caught and punished when they participate in deviant acts (Reiman, 1990). They lack the political and cultural power to correct the stereotypes others have of them as being lazy, dishonest, promiscuous, and unworthy of sympathy. As a result, they provide "living proof" that moral deviance does not pay.

Furthermore, poverty guarantees the status of those who are not poor. The poor provide a reference point against which others can compare themselves. Charity events allow upper- and middle-class people to symbolically demonstrate their concern and philanthropy and reinforce their feelings of moral superiority. Finally, the poor provide the manual labor that enables societies to produce many impressive achievements, from railroads to national parks.

Political Functions

When large numbers of poor people are considered "unworthy" or "undeserving," they can sometimes serve as institutional scapegoats for society's problems. The alleged laziness of the jobless poor and the anger aimed at street people and beggars take the heat off the failure of the economic system to adequately deal with the needs of all citizens. Likewise, the alleged personal shortcomings of slum dwellers and the homeless deflect attention away from the housing industry (Gans, 1996).

Furthermore, once poor people are declared "undeserving," they lose their political legitimacy and influence. Many of the poor do not vote, because they think politicians are unmoved by their concerns. But even if the poor did vote or mobilize, elected officials could not possibly satisfy their demands for economic justice.

As a result, the political system focuses its attention on the easier-to-meet demands of more affluent constituents.

It's easy to dismiss this functionalist explanation of poverty as cold and heartless. We certainly don't want to admit that poor people and the welfare system allow the rest of us the opportunity to live comfortable and pleasant lifestyles. Yet this explanation is quite compelling. Just as society needs talented people to fill its important occupational positions, it also needs a stable population of poor people to fill its "less-important" positions. After all, someone needs to clean toilets or work the night shift at McDonald's. What would society be like if there was full equality? Who would do the dirty work?

If we are truly serious about getting rid of poverty, we must find alternative ways of performing the functions it currently fulfills. But such a change will assuredly come at a cost to those of us who are now able to take advantage of poverty's presence. In short, poverty will be eliminated only when it becomes dysfunctional for people who aren't poor.

The Ideology of Competitive Individualism

Poverty also persists because of cultural beliefs and values that support the economic status quo. An important component of this value system is the belief in **competitive individualism** (Feagin, 1975; M. Lewis, 1978; Neubeck, 1986). As children, most of us are taught by our families and schools that nobody deserves a free ride. The way to be successful is to work hard, strive for goals, and compete well against others. We learn that we are fully responsible for our own economic fates. Stories of people like Abraham Lincoln and Henry Ford, who rose above terrible conditions to make it to the top, reinforce the notion that anybody can be successful if he or she simply has the desire and puts in the necessary effort.

The belief in competitive individualism is fostered by the economic socialization children receive in school. Sociologists Scott Cummings and Del Taebel (1978) surveyed children from grades 3 through 12 to see how they learned about economic life and stratification in this country. They found that even young people can articulate the idea that private ownership and individual productivity are necessary components of a smooth-flowing economy. As one ninth-grader put it:

> People that own their own businesses will work harder because they want to make more money; if no one can own anything they aren't going to work so hard and so nobody will make much money and then the economy falls apart. (Cummings & Taebel, 1978, p. 205)

Although younger children enthusiastically support the idea that the government ought to do more to help poor people, by the 12th grade many of them have come to hold the individual responsible for his or her own economic destiny. Character flaws and motivational deficiencies are often seen as the causes of poverty and economic insecurity:

> People are rich because they have the know-how and the opportunity, and to an extent most of them are wealthy because of some type of motivation that causes them not to settle at one step or one degree; they wanted to reach higher heights. . . . People are poor because they are not educated enough to know that there is something for them out there; that they can make money. . . . They are ignorant and uneducated; a lot of them just don't care . . . they're happy the way they are . . . if you really want to have some money, you can get it no matter how poor you have been. (Cummings & Taebel, 1978, p. 207)

This study shows the dark side of cultural beliefs about poverty: When we internalize the belief in competitive individualism, we are also adopting an explanation of why rewards are distributed unequally and why there is poverty. If people who are financially successful deserve to be there because of their individual hard work and desire, then the people who fail and are suffering financially must equally deserve their plight because of a lack of hard work and desire. However, such a belief system doesn't take into consideration that the competition itself is perhaps not fair. Opportunities to learn a trade, skill, or profession are assumed to be available to everyone. Every person is supposed to have the chance to "be all that he or she can be." But as we saw in chapter 10, the system may be rigged to favor those who already have power and privilege.

Nevertheless, competitive individualism allows us not only to explain inequality but also to maintain our belief that the world is a fair and just place (J. Huber & Form, 1973; Lerner, 1970). We have an intense need to believe that we live in a world where good things happen to good people and bad things happen to bad people. People will get what they deserve. When used to explain poverty, however, this future-oriented belief often gives way to a past-oriented belief that people deserve what they got. If a poor person is suffering, he or she must have done something to deserve it, and that "something" is either a lack of ability, a defective trait, or a lack of desire to succeed. People get unequal rewards because some are born smarter, stay in school longer, or work harder.

The belief in competitive individualism also gives people the sense that they can control their own fate. Because we are all supposedly created equal, no one should be inhibited from exercising his or her ambitions to the fullest extent (M. Lewis, 1978); individual opportunity is the presumed birthright of every American. So while grudgingly acknowledging the existence of unequal outcomes, Americans can justify the situation by emphasizing equal chances. To take or not to take advantage of these chances is up to the individual. In this way the cultural ideology of poverty both explains and justifies the system of stratification.

▪ ▪ ▪ ▪ ▪ ▪ ▪ ▪

JOAN HUBER AND WILLIAM FORM
Why the Rich Are Rich and the Poor Are Poor

The ideology of competitive individualism is not equally accepted by all Americans, according to sociologists Joan Huber and William Form (1973). Wealthy and middle-class individuals see themselves as deserving of their status. They are likely to explain wealth and poverty in individualistic terms, such as the personal characteristics of ability, thrift, or effort. The poor, however, are more likely to emphasize structural forces in their lives, such as the failure of private industry to provide sufficient jobs or the failure of society to provide adequate schooling (see also Feagin, 1975). In other words, the belief in competitive individualism should be most attractive to those receiving the highest rewards from the stratification system.

To test their hypothesis, Huber and Form interviewed 107 poor, 200 middle-income, and 47 rich individuals in Michigan. They bluntly asked their subjects, "Why are rich people rich and why are poor people poor?" They found that about twice as many rich people as poor people cited personal attributes as the cause of both wealth and poverty. Here is a response typical of those offered by the wealthy subjects:

> If you have to generalize, it's the self-discipline to accumulate capital and later to use that capital effectively and intelligently to make income and wealth. The poor? I don't think the average person on the lower economic scale wants to assume the responsibilities and obligations necessary to become rich. He doesn't want to be bothered. . . . The rich acquire wealth by their own effort. The poor lack the ability to rise above their class situation. There's no lack of opportunity but lack of ability. (p. 102)

Compare this response to one made by a poor subject in the study:

> The rich stepped on other people's toes to acquire what they got or they were born with it. The poor? It was handed down through the family. . . . They lacked opportunity. (p. 103)

Higher-income respondents were also more likely to think that poor people don't work as hard as rich people and to believe that a lack of motivation accounted for their lack of success. The great majority of poor people felt that they worked just as hard as anybody else even though their rewards have been low. They tended to think that the opportunity structure in society prevented them from becoming successful. Such perceptions have enormously important implications for governmental policy. If those in power tend to believe that poor people lack motivation, then poverty programs will focus on reducing people's dependence on government subsidies. But if poverty is viewed as the result of structural problems, then policymakers will focus on increasing educational and occupational opportunity for everyone (Morris & Williamson, 1987).

▪ ▪ ▪

The Culture of Poverty

If it is true that poor people perceive the causes of poverty very differently from those who are better off, can we then say that poor people have their own belief system—a unique "culture"—that influences their lives and persists over generations? A variation of the belief in competitive individualism is the argument that the poor as a group possess beliefs, norms, values, and goals that are significantly different from the rest of society and that perpetuate a particular lifestyle that keeps them poor.

Oscar Lewis (1968), the chief proponent of this **culture of poverty** thesis, maintained that poor people, resigned to their position in society, develop a unique value structure to deal with the improbability that they will become successful in terms of the values and goals of the larger society. This culture is at odds with the dominant middle-class culture because it downplays the importance of self-discipline and hard work. Although it may keep people trapped in what appears (to the outside observer) to be an intolerable life, it nevertheless provides its own pleasures. Street life in the ghetto is exhilarating compared to a world where jobs are dull, arduous, and difficult to obtain and hold (P. Peterson, 1991). It is more fun to hang out, tell exaggerated stories, and exhibit one's latest purchases and conquests than it is to work and struggle in the "conventional" world. This extreme "present-orientedness"—the inability to live for the future (Banfield, 1970)—and not the lack of income or wealth is the principal cause of poverty. Thus the culture of poverty is an adaptation and reaction of the poor to their position in a stratified society (O. Lewis, 1968).

Once the culture of poverty comes into existence, Lewis argued, it perpetuates itself. This way of life is remarkably persistent: You can take the child out of the ghetto, but you can't take the ghetto out of the child. Furthermore, it is passed down from generation to generation. By age six or seven, most children have absorbed the basic values and attitudes of their subculture, rendering them unable to take advantage of any opportunities that may present themselves later in life. Others have argued that a poor family with a history of welfare dependence will tend to raise children who lack ambition, a solid work ethic, and self-reliance (Auletta, 1982).

Critics of the culture of poverty thesis point out that to generate such a persistent culture of poverty, a society must have a large group of permanently poor. However, government statistics show that only a little over half of the individuals living in poverty in a given year are found to be poor the next, and considerably less than one half remain poor over many years (Duncan, 1984; Sherraden, 1988). In 1990 and 1991, only 4.5% of all poor people were poor for the entire 24 months. Moreover, the average duration of poverty is 4 months (U.S. Bureau of the Census, 1995a). In short, people tend to move in and out of poverty, making it difficult to sustain a single, long-standing, poverty-based lifestyle and value system.

Contrary to popular belief, not all poor people are on welfare either. Only about 27% of persons below the poverty level receive cash assistance in the form of Aid to Families with Dependent Children, 43% receive food stamps, 41% participate in Medicaid, and 19% receive some kind of housing assistance (U.S. Bureau of the Census, 1995a). Most people are only on welfare for about 2 years at a time (Bedard, 1991; K. M. Harris, 1996). However, it's estimated that between 34% and 40% of welfare recipients are "recidivists"—people who've returned to welfare after being off it for a period of time (Bane & Ellwood, 1983). Nevertheless, as in poverty, there is a great deal of movement in and out of welfare, making it difficult to sustain a tradition of dependence across generations.

Critics of the culture of poverty approach also contend that the behavior of poor people is largely due to institutional impediments, such as a tradition of racial or ethnic prejudice and discrimination, residential segregation, limited economic opportunities, and occupational obstacles against advancement (Wilson, 1980). Any cultural values that exist must emerge from specific social and historical circumstances that reflect one's class, race, and ethnicity. Consider poverty among racial minorities. In a racially stratified society, the class position of individual minorities is heavily influenced by their racial history. The African-American experience, for example, still bears the mark of slavery and Jim Crow laws.

Today, the argument that hard work is the tried and true way from poverty to wealth dominates much of the debate. Many feel our welfare system makes the problem worse by breeding a cycle of dependency. After all, if poverty is a "way of life," then giving poor people enough money to raise them out of poverty is not the answer; changing their troublesome culture is. Says one sociologist sarcastically, "By liquidating the lower-class culture we can liquidate the lower class, and, thereby, bring an end to poverty" (Ryan, 1976, p. 123).

Indeed, there is a strong perception among politicians as well as the public that welfare creates, rather than fights, poverty. Surveys show that most people think spending on welfare ought to decrease rather than increase (Dowd, 1994). A recent national poll found that fewer than 30% of adult Americans believe welfare recipients truly need the aid, and 68% believe they are cheating the system ("Welfare mistrust," 1996). Ironically, the amount of money the government spends on welfare programs is less than half the amount it spends on assistance programs that go to predominantly middle-class recipients, such as Social Security, disability insurance, unemployment insurance, Medicare, and so on (U.S. Bureau of the Census, 1994). Nevertheless the 1995 federal budget cut welfare spending by $81.5 billion while leaving other assistance programs largely intact.

Congress and the White House also worked together to overhaul the current welfare system. In 1996, President Clinton signed into law a bill that effectively ended the federal guarantee of cash assistance for the poor that had been in place for over 60 years. The law gives states the power to run their own welfare and work programs with lump sums of federal money. It establishes a lifetime limit of

5 years of welfare payments to any family and requires most adults to work within 2 years of receiving aid. The law also reduces food stamp benefits and abolishes Aid to Families with Dependent Children, which had provided cash benefits to more than 8 million poor children. The clear assumption underlying this reform is that the behavior of poor people is the primary source of the nation's economic problems.

The culture of poverty explanation obviously remains popular despite the lack of supportive evidence. Many people strongly believe that the poor live by a different set of moral standards and therefore will remain in poverty unless forced to change their values. Like competitive individualism, this ideology protects the nonpoor, the larger social structure, and the economic system from blame.

An Institutional View of Poverty and Wealth

The overarching goal of welfare reform is a good one: to reduce poverty. And where earlier programs were tested—in California, for instance—they showed moderately encouraging results in making some individuals less reliant on government assistance (Passell, 1993). From a sociological perspective, however, welfare reform overlooks important institutional factors that may in the long run make them ineffective. As long as we affix the blame for poverty on the poor people themselves—their aberrant subcultural values, reproductive habits, and lack of effort, skill, and intelligence—the structural causes of poverty will remain unchallenged and unchanged.

Work and Occupational Structure

The overall structure of occupations in this country is a major institutional cause of poverty. The United States has what is called a **segmented labor market,** meaning that the economy is divided into two job sectors that have different characteristics and payoffs (D. M. Gordon, Edwards, & Reich, 1982; Piore, 1994). The primary sector includes large bureaucratic organizations with relatively stable production and sales. Jobs in this category require high-level skills, are highly paid, provide good benefits, and have good working conditions. Within this sector there are both upper-tier jobs (high-status professionals and managers) and lower-tier jobs (such as white-collar clerical and blue-collar skilled workers). These lower-tier jobs tend to be rather monotonous, and mobility is limited. But because they are likely to be unionized, they still tend to be relatively secure.

The secondary sector is composed of firms that are marginal because demand for their products is unstable. The welfare of these companies springs directly from the well-being of primary companies (Braun, 1991). As a result, the jobs here, which include low-level clerical and unskilled blue-collar occupations, have considerably lower pay, far less job security, poorer working conditions, and fewer prospects for advancement. The secondary sector is particularly vulnerable to business slowdowns and technological changes that can lead to abrupt and widespread unemployment. For instance, many of the factory jobs that most Americans in the past could reasonably expect to get, even if they weren't well educated or well trained, are disappearing as companies automate, move their facilities elsewhere, or simply go out of business.

But as the economic system expands and contracts, even primary sector companies are touched by larger economic pressures. *Downsizing*—the process whereby companies reduce the work force in size and redundancy—has come to exemplify the economic worries of the 1990s. Many of the largest and best-known primary-sector companies in the United States have announced or carried out the elimination of huge numbers of jobs over the past several years. Between 1992 and 1996, AT&T, IBM, General Motors, and Boeing cut their workforces by 30% or more (Uchitelle & Kleinfield, 1996).

It's easy to see how business cycles and trends can produce unemployment and thereby maintain poverty. But as with official definitions of poverty, the official definition of "unemployed" may also underestimate the magnitude of the problem. According to the Bureau of Labor Statistics, in order to be officially considered unemployed you must be out of work, must be available for work, and must have actively sought work in the past 4 weeks (Herbert, 1993). The unemployment rate in the United States is actually lower today than it has been in 6 years. Nevertheless, on average, somewhere between 8 million and 9 million people are considered officially unemployed at a given time.

This figure doesn't account for the millions of "discouraged" workers who want a good job but have become so disheartened that they've stopped looking. In addition, some 30 million people—over a quarter of the U.S. labor force—are employed in part-time or temporary jobs. A substantial proportion of them would prefer permanent, full-time jobs but cannot find them. These workers are six times more likely than full-time workers to receive the minimum wage and much less likely to receive health and pension benefits (Cloward & Piven, 1993). And what about the large, unmeasurable group of "underemployed" who are working in jobs for which they are overqualified, like college graduates and other professionals who deliver pizza or drive cabs to make ends meet?

There is little reason to think that a substantial number of unemployed poor people, who probably have few marketable skills, can become self-sufficient when the growing millions of currently employed people cannot. When the labor market is saturated with people either looking for work or seeking to improve their employment situation, and when the only jobs that are available are low-paying ones, mandatory job-training programs and limitations on benefits will not be very effective in reducing dependence on welfare (Cloward & Piven, 1993). One study found that none of these programs succeed in raising earnings more than $2,000 above what recipients receive in welfare payments. Only a handful of people in welfare-to-work programs achieve a stable source of income and job-related benefits that adequately cover medical expenses. Not surprisingly, a substantial number of people who find jobs end up reapplying for welfare because they cannot survive on their earnings (Cloward & Piven, 1993).

The American occupational structure has an impact on communities as well as individuals. Where jobs are scarce and prospects for industrial development are low, pockets of poverty persist. For instance, a corporation is unlikely to open a manufacturing facility in a run-down area of a large city that has a high crime rate. A high-tech corporation is more likely to locate where it can hire well-educated workers and where executives' families will feel comfortable. The movement of manufacturing jobs out of the inner city to the suburbs leaves urban residents isolated and without any realistic prospects for work (Wilson, 1987).

Most people in the inner city don't have the resources to live in the areas where the jobs are, so those who want to work must find a way to get there. But public transportation is not always available, and the cost of purchasing and operating a car might be too much (Kasarda, 1989). Ironically, the stability of the inner city is further undermined when those people who do have job skills and who can serve as positive role models—teachers, professionals, merchants, and the like—move out of the neighborhood and into areas where the jobs are located. The urban poor become isolated from the rest of society economically, socially, and geographically.

In rural areas, because of the loss of manufacturing facilities, local jobs tend to be low-paid, part-time, and temporary. What makes matters even worse is that poor people from urban areas, squeezed out by high rents in the city, often end up in rural towns, where the subsequent competition for a shrinking number of jobs becomes even tighter. Also, the housing market is worse in rural areas. Approximately 42% of the rural poor currently spend more than half their income on housing (Fitchen, 1992b).

The institutional structure of employment in the United States has had a dramatic impact on the distribution of economic resources. Millions of good jobs no longer exist, and the ones that remain offer little security. At the same time, executive pay has increased far faster than inflation. As you can see, broad economic processes that no single individual or group caused or controls can significantly affect the livelihood of American workers and thereby perpetuate the economic gap between rich and poor (Granovetter & Tilly, 1988). The problems are not likely to disappear without major changes in the American occupational structure and the nature of jobs that are created.

Education

In a society where status is usually based on credentials, chances of success in life are strongly determined by educational attainment (Jencks et al., 1979). You are probably taking this class and reading this book because you assume that getting a college education is a prerequisite for having a successful career. But although education is necessary for all of us to get ahead, it is not equally available to all segments of the population.

As addressed in chapter 10, the probability of getting a good education is closely tied to family and class background. In poor neighborhoods, where children seldom have the opportunity to interact with people in middle-class, professional jobs, they have little understanding of the relationship between schooling and career success (Wilson, 1987). Poverty also adversely affects the development of linguistic, educational, and job-related skills necessary for the world of work in the mainstream economy. Teachers become frustrated and do not teach; children become cynical and do not learn. Children from the lowest 10% in socioeconomic status are only one-twelfth as likely to complete college as the highest 10%, averaging about 5 fewer years of education (Bowles & Gintis, 1976).

In the Chicago school system, of the 39,500 students who enrolled in the ninth grade in 1980, only 18,500 (or 47%) graduated 4 years later; of these, only about 6,000 (15%) were capable of reading at or above the national 12th-grade level. Of the 25,000 African-American and Hispanic students who were enrolled in these segregated, nonselective schools, only 2,000 (or 8%) both completed high school and could read at or above a level considered average for the rest of the country (Wilson, 1987).

Both elite private schools and poor public schools serve to legitimate inequality. For many people, the worst schools can produce feelings of powerlessness that continue throughout their lives (Bowles & Gintis, 1976). Discipline and hierarchy, two crucial requirements for a free-market economy, are taught early on in the education system. The "successful" students are the ones who learn to submit to authority. But poor children's prior socialization—their manner of speech, dress, and action—do not fit with those of the teacher and the school administration at large, and so they are subtly made to feel inadequate. Instead of developing as competent, hopeful members of society, many poor young people become resigned to their fate.

The educational deck clearly seems to be stacked against poor people. With very few exceptions, the quality of elementary and high school education for the poor is inferior to the quality of education available to children in the middle and upper classes. Even if they graduate from high school, most poor children cannot afford to attend college. Those who do are more likely to attend community colleges or state universities, which lack the quality and prestige of their more expensive counterparts (A. M. Cohen & Brawer, 1982).

Conclusion

This chapter has examined economic aspects of the American Dream. It's rather shocking that in a country as wealthy as this one, a comfortable and stable life is well beyond the reach of tens of millions of people. The constant images we see of wealth and power remind poor, working-class, and, for that matter, downwardly mobile middle-class people that they are outsiders who can only watch and long to be part of that golden world (Sidel, 1986).

Culture and social institutions justify and perpetuate social inequality, but there is also the personal side. We speak of the poor as if they are an unchanging and faceless group to be pitied, despised, or feared. To talk of "the poverty problem" is to talk about some depersonalized, permanent fixture on the American landscape. But poverty is people. It's people standing in soup kitchen lines and welfare lines. It's people living in rat-infested projects. It's people sleeping on sidewalks. It's people struggling to acquire things the rest of society takes for granted. It's people coming up short in their quest for the American Dream.

When we look at the institutional causes of poverty, we see that the personality or "cultural" traits often associated with poverty—low ambition, rejection of the hard work ethic, inability to plan for the future—might be better understood as consequences of poverty rather than causes of it. As long as the structural obstacles to stable employment, adequate wages, and a decent education continue to exist, so will the characteristic hopelessness associated with poverty.

For those of us fortunate enough never to have been hungry or homeless or on welfare, these are easy issues to ignore. When we cross the street to avoid coming face-to-face with a "street person," we are engaging in a futile attempt to return the problem of poverty to its once-comfortable home of concealment. As long as poverty remains invisible, it remains someone else's problem. As long as poverty is seen as the "fault" of poor people, it remains someone else's responsibility. And as long as it remains someone else's problem and someone else's responsibility, it becomes virtually impossible to ignite the kind of public compassion necessary to solve it.

CHAPTER HIGHLIGHTS

■ The face of American poverty has changed somewhat over the last several decades. Single mothers and their children have seen their economic status deteriorate while that of people over age 65 has improved somewhat. What hasn't changed is the ever-widening gap between the rich and the poor.

■ The official poverty line, the dollar cutoff point that defines the amount of income necessary to provide minimal subsistence living, may actually be set too low, thereby underestimating the proportion of the population that is suffering financially.

■ Poverty persists because in a free-market and competitive society it serves economic and social functions. In addition, the ideology of competitive individualism—that to succeed in life all one has to do is work hard and win in competition with others—creates a belief that poor people are to blame for their own suffering. Finally, poverty receives institutional "support" in the form of segmented labor markets and inadequate educational systems.

▪ Traits commonly associated with poor people—low ambition, failure to subscribe to the ethic of hard work, inability to plan for the future, and so on—might be better understood as the consequences of poverty rather than the causes of it.

YOUR TURN

Economic stress is no longer a way of life only for people who fall under the official poverty line. Even people whose income is well above the poverty line find that their ability to make ends meet has been steadily deteriorating.

Imagine a family of four living in your hometown. Suppose that both parents work, that one child is 7 years old and in elementary school, and that the other is 3 and must be cared for during the day.

Make a list of all the goods and services this family will need to function at a minimum subsistence level—that is, at the poverty line. Be as complete as possible. Consider food, clothing, housing, transportation, medical care, child care, entertainment, and so on.

Estimate the minimum monthly cost of each item. If you currently live on your own and must pay these expenses yourself, use those figures as a starting point (but remember that you must estimate for a family of four). If you live in a dorm or at home, ask your parents (or anyone else who pays bills) what their expenses are for such goods and services. Call the local day care center to see what it charges for child care. Go to the local supermarket and compute the family food budget. For those expenses that aren't divided on a monthly basis (for example, clothing, household appliances), estimate the yearly cost and divide by 12.

Once you have estimated the total monthly expenses, multiply by 12 to get the family of four's subsistence budget. If your estimate is higher than the government's official poverty line (around $15,455), what sorts of items could you cut out of the budget for the family to be defined as officially poor and therefore eligible for certain governmental programs? By cutting expenses from your minimal subsistence budget you will get a good sense of what poverty is like.

Describe the quality of life of this hypothetical family that makes too much to be officially poor and too little to sustain a comfortable life. What sorts of things are they forced to do without that a more affluent family might simply take for granted (for example, annual vacations, a second car, eating out once a week)? What would be the impact of poverty on the lives of the children? How will the family's difficulty in meeting its basic subsistence needs translate into access to opportunities (education, jobs, health, etc.) for the children later in life?

[NOTE: This exercise is adapted from M. V. Miller, "Poverty and its definition," in R. C. Barnes and E. W. Mills, Techniques for Teaching Sociological Concepts, *Washington, DC: American Sociological Association, 1985.]*

SOCIAL STRATIFICATION
Class, Poverty, and Wealth

DOUGLAS HARPER

"...consider how people in different social locations experience some of the same things...."

The aim of this essay is to portray life in different classes in the United States. It is the longest visual essay in the book both because its topic is central in the study of sociology and because it applies to chapters 10 and 11. This essay does not tell us how social classes came into existence, nor does it reinforce one theory over another regarding the functional or dysfunctional aspects of social classes. Instead, the images can help you put yourself in the circumstances being portrayed, to consider how people in different social locations experience some of the same things.

Poverty exists in several settings in our society, including the inner city, isolated rural areas, and the mobile lives of migrant workers. Although many of the poor are unemployed, many others, such as the migrant workers portrayed on these pages, work most of the time and in physically demanding situations. We must also remember that the minimum wage is below the poverty line, and thus great numbers of people seem on the surface to be leading middle-class lives but are actually struggling in low-paying jobs to maintain a stable life.

Helen Stummer's photographs of Newark, New Jersey, are published in a book called *No Easy Walk*. The setting is an urban area like many in the United States, devastated by the riots of the late 1960s that led to an exodus of businesses and middle-class residents. The people who remained had few employment opportunities and scant urban services such as transportation or trash removal. Housing is poor or nonexistent. Because their schools are funded by local taxes, the residents have few resources. People in these settings are isolated from the social mainstream and marginalized.

Eugene Richards photographed several poverty settings in the United States for his book, *Below the Line: Living Poor in America*. The images from his book selected for this essay document the conditions in a dilapidated house in the American South and in a homeless shelter on Long Island, New York.

The final images of poverty are of a family of migrant workers, Linda and L. H. Tindal, reprinted from Herman LeRoy Emmet's book, *Fruit Tramps*. Emmet worked with the Tindal family for more than ten years, traveling with them from Florida to New York. He actually

Detail in top photograph taken from photograph by Barbara Norfleet appearing on page 407.

387

HELEN STUMMER

Playing dress-up on Eagle Street, September 1980.

became one of the migrant workers in the fields to be "their voice" through his camera, documenting their lives and showing how their children are integrated into the work of migrant laborers from an early age. Emmet's photographs remind us that one can work very hard and still be poor.

The portrayal of middle-class, suburban life, is from a 1972 book, *Suburbia,* by Bill Owens. Owens, a newspaper photographer, took a course in visual anthropology at a local university and then returned to his own neighborhood to photograph the things he had lived with all his life. Although some of the clothes and furnishings now appear dated, his photographic study remains the single best visual ethnography of suburban America. Note a sense of impermanence in the housing and possessions; things take care of people's needs but look like they might wear out quickly. People appear content

and focused on their immediate community but perhaps isolated from the larger forces of society. It is a way of life that many of us have known.

Finally, sociologist Barbara Norfleet photographed the leisure lives of the rich in many U.S. locations for her book *All the Right People.* The rich live in exclusive suburbs or enclaves; they spend leisure time on yachts, in private clubs, and in pursuits such as fox hunts that symbolize their real or imagined royal European roots. These are the wealthy Americans who make many of the decisions that create (or eliminate) economic opportunity for other Americans. Their power and influence make them difficult subjects to study. Norfleet's photographs offer a peek at a world that is usually private.

As you look at all these photographs, first compare the settings of these three class locations. Examine what people wear and what possessions surround them. Try to infer from the

388

"This is Valerie's world in miniature. She makes it what she wants it to be ...without war, racial hate, or misunderstanding. Ken and Barbie (dolls) are man and woman rather than Mom and Dad. They enjoy living, and having a camper truck is the good life. Today Valerie has the chicken pox and can't go out and play."

BILL OWENS

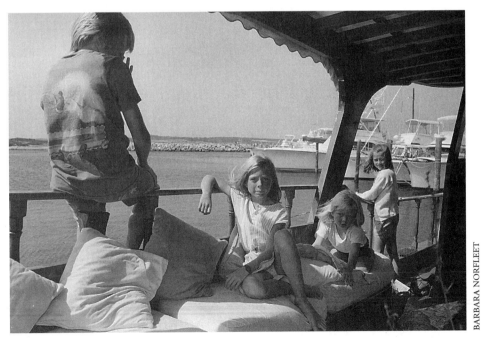

BARBARA NORFLEET

Private junk, Martha's Vineyard, Massachusetts, 1985.

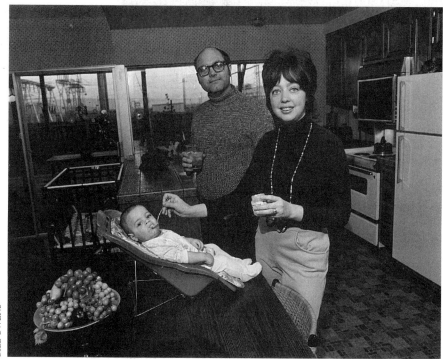

BILL OWENS

"We're really happy. Our kids are healthy, we eat good food, and we have a really nice home."

photographs what the typical activities of these groups are. Consider particularly the lives of the children. What have these children already learned about their social roles? What would happen if the children from one setting were placed into the other class locations? Study the body language of the people in the three class settings. How do they face the camera and each other? Do posture, expression, and emotion seem to be functions of class?

America is often billed as a society in which mobility is open to all who apply themselves. As you consider these photographs, ask yourself whether effort would be sufficient to move people from one of these class locations to another.

Finally, as you look at these photographs, think about the social structural and historical forces that have created these contexts for class experience.

Calvin Tindal emptying citrus pick sack while Shannon watches oranges fall into plastic tub, in Loxahatchee, Florida.

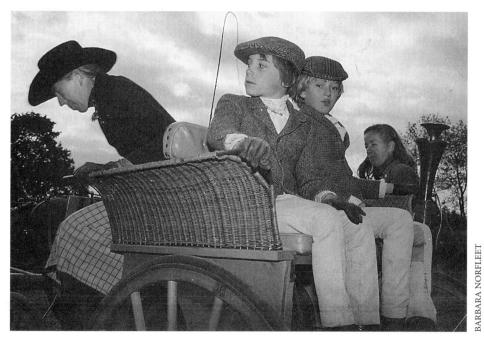

Flying Horse farm at Hamilton, Massachusetts, 1981.

Children sleeping on mattresses, Tennessee.

Glen, December 1989.

Edgartown Yacht Club, Edgartown, Massachusetts, 1983.

"I don't feel that Richie playing with guns will have a negative effect on his personality. (He already wants to be a policeman.) His childhood gun-playing won't make him into a cop-shooter. By playing with guns he learns to socialize with other children. I find the neighbors who are offended by Richie's gun, either the father hunts or their kids are the first to take Richie's gun and go off and play with it."

BILL OWENS

Linda and Shannon bathing in a creek near Chimney Rock, North Carolina.

Hunt Club's winter beach ride, Ipswich, Massachusetts, 1982.

Hermineo taking clothes home to his mother in their cardboard shack, October 1987.

"People throw away a lot of good things: clothes, toys, broken toasters, record players, and in the newer areas they throw out tables and chairs that don't fit in their new house. The ecology movement doesn't matter. I make over $250 in Coke bottles. People here can't realize there are poor people in the world. They can't think about the needs of other people."

Picnic, Hunt Club, The North Shore, Boston.

Salvaging after a fire on Hillside Avenue, November 1989.

BILL OWENS

"We have to move. My husband's been transferred to Southern California."

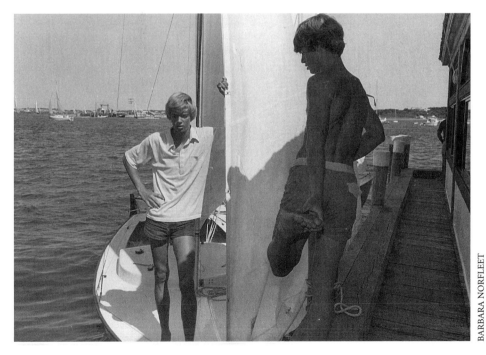

BARBARA NORFLEET

Edgartown Yacht Club, Edgartown, Massachusetts, 1981.

BILL OWENS

"*This is our second annual Fourth of July block party. This year 33 families came for beer, barbecued chicken, corn on the cob, potato salad, green salad, macaroni salad, and watermelon. After eating and drinking we staged our parade and fireworks.*"

Final club garden party at Harvard University, Cambridge, Massachusetts, 1984.

Chicago.

BILL OWENS

Long Island Shelter, Massachusetts.

Private house, Mississippi.

Calvin Tindal harvesting squash, Dana, North Carolina.

"I bought the lawn in six-foot rolls. It's easy to handle. I prepared the ground and my wife and son helped roll out the grass. In one day you have a front yard."

Master of the fox hounds training the hounds, Myopia Hunt Club, Hamilton, Massachusetts, 1982.

Private house, New Providence Island, The Bahamas, 1982.

CHAPTER 12

The Architecture of Inequality:
Race and Ethnicity

- *Oppression and Inequality: Stories through the Years*
- *Assimilation versus Multiculturalism: One Culture, One People?*
- *Racial and Ethnic Relations*
- *The Cultural Ideology of Racism*
- *Institutional Racism: Injustice Built into the System*
- *Global Perspectives on Racism*

In the months leading up to the 1996 presidential primary elections, the rumor mills buzzed with assessments of the political aspirations of the retired chairman of the Joint Chiefs of Staff, General Colin Powell. Was he going to run for president? If so, would he run as a Republican or an Independent? When it became clear that he didn't wish to be a presidential candidate, questions turned to the possibility of a vice-presidential candidacy. He was painted by many—in particular, by conservative Republicans—as a veritable savior for the country and the Republicans' best chance for regaining the White House. Each day brought a new rumor or revelation about Powell's intentions.

Such political vigils are nothing new. There have always been popular but reluctant public figures in whom the voting populace invests its political hopes and dreams. Furthermore, retired military figures have frequently captured the country's fancy. George Washington, Ulysses Grant, and Dwight Eisenhower were all war heroes who rode a wave of popular support into the White House.

What made General Powell's situation particularly noteworthy was the relative lack of attention paid to the fact that he is an African American. If you had told an abolitionist in the 1860s, or even a civil rights worker in the 1960s, that someday millions of Americans, even conservative Americans, would pin their hopes for the country on a black man running for president or vice president, he or she might have laughed in your face. Even 10 or 15 years ago, it probably would have been inconceivable. But there Powell was, making speeches to large enthusiastic audiences and giving interviews on national television, further fueling speculation about his intentions.

In the end, he didn't run, and many people were disappointed. But people's desire to see him in public office made me think about the tremendous gains that African Americans and other racial groups have made economically, politically, educationally, and culturally. The number of middle- and upper-class African Americans, Asian Americans, and Hispanics has increased significantly over the past decade. Some of today's highest-paid entertainers and athletes are African American. African Americans sit on the Supreme Court and along with Hispanics, serve in presidential cabinet positions. The African-American presence in art, music, film, fashion, mass marketing, and pop culture is ubiquitous. More Hispanics and Native Americans are in elected offices than ever before. Asian Americans have achieved tremendous economic and educational success. One popular book even proclaimed that racism in the United States is, for all intents and purposes, over (D'Souza, 1995).

Yet as I watched the color-blind enthusiasm that surrounded General Powell's every move, my mind kept pulling me back to a different reality. Despite progress, African Americans, Hispanics, and Native Americans remain the poorest and most disadvantaged of all groups in this country; their average annual income is about half that of whites (U.S. Bureau of the Census, 1995a). Almost half of all black babies are born into poverty, compared to fewer than one in eight white babies (Edelman, 1988; Morganthau, 1992). A little over half of all Hispanic students complete high school, and one-quarter of all Hispanic families have zero net wealth (Blackwell, 1990; U.S. Bureau of the Census, 1995a). A third of all black men between the ages of 20 and 29 are embroiled in the criminal justice system, and the leading cause of death among this segment of the population is gunshot wounds.

I thought of specific events that also belie the image of racial progress:

■   The numerous and highly publicized incidents of black citizens and Mexican immigrants being harassed, humiliated, and beaten by white police officers.
■   The 30-odd African-American churches that were burned in 1995 and 1996.
■   The high school couple in Alabama who were not allowed to attend their senior prom because he was white and she was black.
■   The two soldiers at Fort Bragg, North Carolina, who were murdered by fellow soldiers because they were black.

I also thought of many college campuses that in the past few years have experienced a flurry of incidents stemming from long-dormant racial hatred. Ten black law students at Yale University received anonymous "nigger" notes in their dormitory mailboxes after a reported rape. At the University of Connecticut, a group of white students taunted and spit at Asian-American students who were on their way to a dance. At Olivet College, a small, quiet campus in rural Michigan, a racial brawl ensued following a rash of rumors about black men and white women. At the University of Southern California, following the O. J. Simpson verdict, someone circulated a flier that read: "I need to alert all the whites that the niggers are taking over. Take up arms and defend yourselves, my brothers" (Applebome, 1995, p. B8). Students at the University of Wisconsin held a mock slave auction.

How far have we really come? Which is the real United States? Is it the one that Martin Luther King Jr. dreamed about in 1963, a place where race and ethnicity are losing their status as major criteria for judging the content of one's character? Or is it the one perpetually torn apart by economic inequality, prejudice, and hatred?

In the previous two chapters I examined America's class stratification system. But social class isn't the only thing that influences social status and life chances. Chapter 12 focuses on another important determinant of social inequality: race and ethnicity.

Oppression and Inequality: Stories through the Years

Racial and ethnic problems have been a defining feature of the American social landscape from the very beginning. In 1835, the French scholar Alexis de Tocqueville (1835/1969) wrote that racial conflict perpetually haunts the American imagination. More than a century later, Gunnar Myrdal, the Swedish economist, saw that America's racial problems were a severe threat to our collective definition as a people. He observed that despite the "American Creed"—our stated values of liberty and equality—white Americans could not treat other racial groups as their equals (Myrdal, 1944). Even as the 20th century winds down, we still can't seem to decide the place that racial and ethnic diversity ought to have in our society.

A glance at the history of America reveals that our story is not just one of freedom, justice, and equality, but one of conquest, discrimination, and exclusion. Racial and ethnic inequality has manifested itself in such phenomena as slavery, the seizure of vast tracts of land from Native Americans and Mexicans, the exclusion of Chinese and Japanese workers in the 19th century, widespread economic, educational, and political deprivation, the violent and nonviolent protests of the civil rights movement, and racially motivated hate crimes in the 20th century. Along the way it has affected people's access to the basic necessities of life, including housing, health care, family stability, and occupations. For some, racial inequality has served as a rallying cry and a source of solidarity for the oppressed; for others it has served as a justification for that very oppression.

Every racial or ethnic minority has its own story of persecution. When they first arrived in significant numbers in the United States, white European immigrants—Irish, Italians, Poles, Jews, Greeks—were all objects of varying degrees of hatred, suspicion, and discrimination. Jews, for instance, were refused admission to many American universities until the middle of the 20th century. The National Origins Act of 1924 placed restrictions on immigration from southern Europe—mainly Greece and Italy—up until the 1960s. Newspaper want ads from the 19th century routinely carried the message "No Irish need apply."

Because these groups were the same race as the dominant white Protestants, however, they were able eventually to overcome most of these obstacles and gain entry into mainstream society. But for people of color—namely, Native Americans, Hispanics, African Americans, and Asian Americans—racial equality and destigmatization have been more difficult to achieve.

Native Americans

The story of Native Americans has been one of racially inspired massacres, the takeover of their ancestral lands, confinement on white-run reservations, and unending governmental manipulation. Successive waves of westward expansion in the 18th and 19th centuries pushed them off any land white settlers considered desirable. Native Americans "started off with everything and have gradually lost much of what they had to an advancing alien civilization" (U.S. Commission on Human Rights, 1992). A commonly held European belief that Native Americans were "savages" who should be displaced to make way for white civilization provided the ideological justification for conquering them.

Despite their history of severe oppression, though, Native Americans have shown a remarkable ability to endure and in some cases promote their own economic interests. In the Pacific Northwest, for instance, some Indian tribes have been successful in protecting their rights to lucrative fishing waters (F. G. Cohen, 1986). Elsewhere, organizations have been formed to advance the financial concerns of Native Americans in industries like gas, oil, and coal, where substantial reserves exist on Indian land (Snipp, 1986). However, intense struggles between large multinational corporations and Native American tribes continue today over control of these reserves.

Hispanic Americans

The history of Hispanics, particularly Mexican Americans, has also been one marked by hostility and oppression. When the United States expanded into the Southwest, white Americans moved into areas that had already been settled by Mexicans. After a war that lasted from 1846 to 1848, Mexico lost half of its national territory, including what is now Arizona, California, Colorado, New Mexico, Texas, Nevada, and Utah, as well as parts of Kansas, Oklahoma, and Wyoming.

In theory, Mexicans living on the American side of the new border were to be given all the rights of U.S. citizens. In practice, however, their property rights were violated and they lost control of their mining, ranching, and farming industries. The exploitation of Mexican workers coincided with a developing economic system that was built around mining and large-scale agriculture, activities that demanded a large pool of cheap labor (Farley, 1982). Today, the average annual income for Hispanics is approximately half that of whites (U.S. Bureau of the Census, 1995a). Nevertheless, in some areas of the country, Hispanics have become quite successful. Cubans, for example, have achieved substantial economic and political power in a number of cities in south Florida. Most large cities have successful Spanish-language TV stations, radio stations, and newspapers.

African Americans

African Americans have historically been the most visible target of racial hostility. From 1619, when the first black slaves were sold in Jamestown, Virginia, to 1865, when the Thirteenth Amendment was passed outlawing slavery, several million blacks in this country endured the brutal reality of forced servitude. Even after slavery was abolished, the conditions of life for blacks in this country showed little improvement. "Jim Crow" laws established rigid lines between the races. In 1896 the Supreme Court ruled that segregation was constitutional. Unequal access to public transportation, schools, hotels, theaters, restaurants, campgrounds, drinking fountains, the military, and practically every other aspect of social life continued until the middle of the 20th century.

The quality of life for most African Americans remains below that of whites. In 1993 the average annual income for black families was $21,542, compared to $39,300 for whites (U.S. Bureau of the Census, 1995a). According to a 1992 survey, over half of African Americans think that their lives have gotten worse over the last decade (Morganthau, 1992). Nevertheless, blatant discrimination has declined in the last four decades and some economic, educational, and political advances have been made. For instance, between 1987 and 1992, the number of black-owned businesses grew 46% while the total number of U.S. businesses grew only 26% (Key, 1996).

Asian Americans

Asian Americans have also experienced treatment that calls into question the American declaration that all people are created equal. The Chinese were brought to this country in the second half of the 19th century as laborers to work on the expanding railroad system. Although the Chinese, and later the Japanese, population in this country was not very large, anti-Asian sentiment began to grow. Asians were seen by working whites as economic competitors for the scarce jobs that existed. As a result, laws were passed that put limits on and even prohibited Asian immigration. These attitudes culminated in the internment of hundreds of thousands of Japanese Americans following the bombing of Pearl Harbor in 1941.

The irony of race for Chinese, Japanese, Koreans, Vietnamese, Cambodians, Laotians, and other Asian groups is that they are often perceived as "model minorities" or "America's greatest success story." Almost twice as many Asian Americans as whites complete college. The average income for Japanese and Chinese

Americans is actually higher than that of the population as a whole (U.S. Bureau of the Census, 1995a).

But the expectations and resentment associated with being the "model minority" can be just as confining and oppressive as those created by more negative labels. During the mid-1980s some university administrators openly worried about what they perceived as the overrepresentation of Asian students among their student bodies. The University of California at Berkeley, Stanford University, and Brown University used discriminatory quotas or increased the English-language-proficiency requirements for admission to limit the enrollment of Asian-American applicants. At the University of California alone, Asian enrollment dropped 21% from 1983 to 1984 (Takagi, 1990). A report by the Federal Civil Rights Commission found that Asian Americans still face widespread discrimination in the workplace (Dugger, 1992). And a recent study concluded that anti-Asian hate crimes increased 35% between 1994 and 1995 (Noble, 1995).

Opportunities to achieve "life, liberty, and the pursuit of happiness" have always been distributed along racial and ethnic lines in this country. Although some groups have been able to transcend the status of "despised minority," others continue to suffer.

Assimilation versus Multiculturalism: One Culture, One People?

The United States is in a period of unprecedented ethnic diversity (see Table 12.1). Soon the presumption that the "typical" American is someone who can trace her or his ancestors to Europe will be a thing of the past.

Over the past decade there has been a 38% increase in residents for whom English is a foreign language (Barringer, 1993). Nationwide, of the 43.6 million children attending public school, 2.6 million (or 5%) don't speak English as their first language—an increase of 76% in the past decade (Hornblower, 1995). In states such as New York and New Mexico, as many as 25% of students in the schools don't speak English. In one elementary school in Brooklyn, 40% of the children are immigrants whose families speak any one of 26 languages (Leslie, 1991). Schools in Arlington, Virginia, now need to offer bilingual education or other language support for children in as many as 100 different languages. What effect will these changes in racial and ethnic configuration have on our personal lives, our culture, and our social institutions?

The "Melting Pot"

One of the bedrock goals of the American value system has always been the ultimate assimilation of racial and ethnic groups into mainstream society. **Assimilation** is the process by which members of minority groups change their ways to conform to those of the dominant culture. I can recall as a child learning of 19th-century descriptions of America as the great "melting pot," a place where immi-

Table 12.1   *Projected Changes in Racial and Ethnic Composition of the U.S. Population*

	1995	2030	2050
White	73.6%	60.5%	52.8%
Black	12.0	13.1	13.6
Hispanic origin	10.2	18.9	24.5
Asian	3.3	6.6	8.2

Note: Figures do not sum to 100% because of rounding and because Native Americans are not shown.
Source: Holmes, 1996.

grants of varied racial and ethnic backgrounds willingly and happily blended to create a brand-new national identity. Most people believed that opportunities for inclusion into the larger society as well as high-paying, stable jobs could come about only if people from different cultures gradually lost their differences and adopted the lifestyle of the majority.

It sounded good, particularly when the image of full assimilation was spiced with stories of my own grandparents, who arrived in this country as penniless immigrants but worked hard and eventually "became" proud Americans. However, the inherent trap of assimilation is that although it may signal an ethnic or racial group's inclusion in mainstream society, it also requires the group to transcend its status as a disliked minority by conforming to the dominant—in our society, European-American—way of life.

Assimilation has sometimes been systematically forced on groups whose beliefs conflict with those of the dominant white culture. Native Americans, for instance, were forced to abandon a lifestyle that was built on values unacceptable to whites. When blacks were brought to America as slaves, they were forced to take new names, families were split apart, and they were forbidden to practice any of the traditions of their native cultures. For them, and for other minority groups, assimilation is sometimes an undesirable goal.

Multiculturalism and Social Institutions

In contrast to the melting pot model, many people today feel that the maintenance of a pluralistic or multicultural society—in which groups maintain not only their ethnic identity but also their own language, art, music, food, literature, and religion—enriches American civilization. With the massive influx of foreign-born, non-English-speaking people into this country, it has become especially difficult to think of America as one culture and Americans as one people.

Many of our social institutions are struggling with the question of how to represent the different histories and cultures of all these diverse groups. In the educational system, the traditional emphasis on the history and culture of white European civilization is now being attacked as racist and incomplete. Over the past 25 years, most universities have created what are known as ethnic studies programs: African-American Studies, Latino/Latina Studies, Asian Studies, Native-American Studies.

Multiculturalism has also become an issue in the workplace. Employers are finding that they need assistance managing an ever-expanding, diverse workforce in which members of minority groups and immigrants now hold a significant proportion of the jobs (L. Williams, 1992b). Only a few years ago the idea of adjusting to ethnic and racial diversity in the workplace was being dismissed by employers as irrelevant to production and profit and as threatening to the white male workforce. Today, however, more employers view diversity as good business. Companies that set aside time and money and hire expensive consultants to cultivate diversity hope to prevent costly lawsuits over unfair treatment and to provide a more tolerant and innovative work environment. Employers are being taught how to accommodate cultural differences. For instance, a manager may be encouraged to realize that an Asian employee's reluctance to give an oral presentation at a staff meeting is motivated by that individual's adherence to cultural norms of modesty and not by professional inadequacy (L. Williams, 1992b).

Ironically, at a time when ethnic diversity and tolerance for that diversity is at an all-time high, the inaccurate "melting pot" metaphor may be closer than ever to reality. Mass forms of communication and transportation are powerful forces breaking down the unique aspects of cultures and compressing them into common forms, with only slight ethnic variations. The same basic billboard that pictures white people and is written in English in Iowa is slightly altered to feature blacks in Detroit and to express its message in Spanish in Miami (Marger, 1994). Moreover, as the population becomes more ethnically varied, especially in major cities, cultures begin to fuse in curious combinations:

> Just as the Irish, Poles, Jews and Italians, who had rubbed shoulders and more in the wake of the European immigration of 1900, had, by the 1950s and '60s, begun to intermarry en masse, so the process is beginning to take place among recent arrivals in L.A. One can find every sort of nonwhite combination in the city now: Hmong and Salvadoran, Ethiopian and Taiwanese, Mexican and Filipino. (Rieff, 1991, p. 20)

Though more and more groups celebrate the need to retain their ethnic culture, societal trends continue to make the maintenance of those differences difficult. For instance, the recent movement to make English our official language is a backlash against multiculturalism.

Racial and Ethnic Relations

Given our society's long history of racial inequality, it is likely that the increasing size of racial and ethnic minorities, the growing influx of non-English-speaking immigrants, and the subsequent heightened competition and conflict over scarce economic resources will threaten to perpetuate our society's racist past. **Racism** is the belief that humans are subdivided into distinct groups that are different in their social behavior and mental capacities and that can therefore be ranked as superior or inferior. The presumed inferiority and superiority is then used to legitimate the unequal distribution of society's resources, such as various forms of wealth, prestige, and power (Marger, 1994). Racism can be expressed at the personal level through individual attitudes and behavior, at the cultural level in our language and collective ideologies, and at the macro-structural level in our social institutions.

Personal Racism

Personal racism is the expression of racist attitudes or behaviors by individual people. This is the most obvious form of racism and includes the use of derogatory names, biased treatment during face-to-face contact, avoidance, and threats or acts of violence. Personal racism receives the most media attention when it is violent and brutal, such as racially motivated hate crimes or the organized hatred of white supremacist groups. However, subtle forms of personal racism, like the high school guidance counselor who steers minority students away from "hard" subjects toward those that do not prepare them for higher-paying jobs, are much more common. Whether blatant or subtle, personal racism rests on two important psychological constructs: stereotypes and prejudice.

Stereotypes

The word **stereotype** was first used by the political commentator Walter Lippmann in 1922. He defined it as an oversimplified picture of the world, one that satisfies our need to see our social environment as a more understandable and manageable place than it really is. It is the overgeneralized belief that a certain trait, behavior, or attitude characterizes all members of some identifiable group. Casual observations easily refute the accuracy of common racial or ethnic stereotypes. Not all African Americans are on welfare, not all Jews are greedy, not all Italians belong to the Mafia, not all Asian Americans are excellent math students, and so on. Overgeneralizations like these can never be true for every member of that group.

Yet despite their obvious inaccuracy, stereotypes remain a common part of our everyday thinking. We all know what the stereotypes are, even if most of us choose not to express them. Today it seems clear that stereotypes aren't the irrational beliefs they were once thought to be. The modern view of stereotypes is that they are natural categories and an essential, universal aspect of human thought (Hamilton, 1981). Our brains have a tendency to divide the world into distinct categories: good and bad, strong and weak, them and us (Rothenberg, 1992). By allowing us to group information into easily identifiable categories, stereotypes make the processing of information and the formation of impressions more efficient. As we saw in chapter 6, our lives would be utterly chaotic if we weren't able to quickly categorize people in terms of sex, race, age, ethnicity, and so on.

In short, it is unrealistic to condemn stereotypical thoughts. We all have them, we all know them, and we all must employ stereotypes to organize the "kaleidoscopic flow of events" around us (McCall & Simmons, 1978, p. 110). Stereotypes, in and of themselves, are inescapable.

Nevertheless, stereotypes must be learned. One of the most potent sources of racial and ethnic stereotypes is the media. Television, films, and literature provide large audiences with both real and fantasized images of people, events, and situations. In so doing, they offer representations of racial, religious, and ethnic groups that impersonally form the basis of many people's attitudes and beliefs. Consider the skewed images of certain ethnic groups served up on television: the savage Indian, the Jewish-American Princess, the obnoxious Japanese tourist, the fanatic Arab terrorist, and so on. Hispanics have historically been cast as "Latin lovers," "banditos," "greasers," or "lazy good-for-nothings" (Reyes & Rubie, 1994).

Although all racial and ethnic groups suffer from stereotypical media portrayal, most of the attention focuses on African Americans. Early television shows of the 1950s, including "Amos 'n Andy" and "The Beulah Show," depicted blacks either as lazy clowns, opportunistic crooks, or happy, docile servants. Most blacks realized, even then, that the rest of the country was receiving inaccurate and dangerous images of them. Henry Louis Gates (1992) recalls what it was like in the early 1950s:

> I can remember as a child sitting upstairs in my bedroom and hearing my mother shout at the top of her voice that someone "*colored . . . colored!*" was on TV and that we had all better come downstairs at once. And, without fail, we did, sitting in front of our TV, nervous, full of expectation and dread, praying that our home girl or boy would not let the race down. (p. 311)

Television representations have not always been blatantly negative. "Sanford and Son," "Good Times," "What's Happening," and the other so-called ghetto sitcoms of the 1970s tried to represent blacks more positively by showing slums and housing projects as places where people could lead happy, loving, even humorous lives. When American society itself could not achieve social reform through civil rights, television solved the problem by inventing symbols of black success and racial harmony (Gates, 1992). Shows like "Julia" or "I Spy" in the 1960s, "Roots" and "The Jeffersons" in the 1970s, "Benson," "A Different World," and "The Cosby Show" in the 1980s, and "The Fresh Prince of Bel-Air" and "Family Matters" in the 1990s seemingly overcame these harmful stereotypes by depicting blacks as strong, smart, and successful. They played an unmistakable role in showing that blacks and whites often share the core values of American culture.

But critics have charged that these portrayals are also fantasies, which may be just as harmful to African Americans as the negative stereotypes of the 1950s.

They feel that the characters in these shows, which were designed to overcome past images and tell America that blacks can be "just like" whites, amounted to what some call the "white Negro" in television. The message seemed to be that the more black characters resembled whites, the more acceptable they would be to the viewing audience. The George Jefferson character from "The Jeffersons" began his TV existence as the working-class neighbor of Archie Bunker. But through dogged commitment to the American values of hard work and determination, he and his family were able to "move up" into the new black upper class and, not surprisingly, into a white neighborhood.

Such representations feed the cultural belief that blacks are personally responsible for their poor social conditions, with little or no acknowledgment of the structural reality most black people face that restricts life opportunities. Once we come to believe that "anyone can be successful"—like Cliff and Claire Huxtable on "The Cosby Show"—we are provided the luxury of seeing no need to change societal conditions. To no surprise, "Cosby" was one of the most popular television shows in South Africa during the 1980s (Gates, 1992). Thus the blame for black poverty is thrown back onto the impoverished. White America was exposed to the idealized image of the black American, while the social and economic conditions of many blacks were bleaker than they had been in years. The underlying message is that racism will end when blacks become as successful as whites (Jhally & Lewis, 1992).

In fairness, however, such shows and the popularity of many black celebrities and athletes do have a beneficial effect. Their visibility helps to bring certain aspects of black culture—such as language patterns, values, sense of humor, tastes in fashion, music and theater—into the larger American culture. Many things that we identify as "American," such as jazz music and dedication to civil rights, have roots in the black experience.

Prejudice and Discrimination

When stereotypes are used to form a set of rigidly held, unfavorable attitudes, beliefs, and feelings about members of a racial or ethnic group, they constitute **prejudice** (Allport, 1954). In one study a group of whites was shown a photograph of a white person holding a razor blade while arguing with a black person on a New York subway. They were shown the picture for a split second and then asked to write down what they saw. More than half of them saw the black man holding the razor against the white man's throat (cited in Helmreich, 1992). The belief that all blacks are violent was so powerful that it distorted people's perceptions.

Prejudiced beliefs like this would be of little significance if they weren't linked, from time to time, to discrimination. **Discrimination** refers to the unfair treatment of people based on some social characteristic such as race, sex, or ethnicity. The 1964 Civil Rights Act prohibits discrimination or segregation on the grounds of race, color, religion, or national origin. This act has produced tremendous progress in American race relations. Nevertheless, discrimination—expressed as hate-inspired violence, avoidance, suspicions of wrongdoing, and denied privileges—still exists.

In 1993, the Denny's Restaurant chain agreed to a settlement with the U.S. Justice Department regarding allegations of discrimination against black customers. A group of customers sued Denny's, claiming that the restaurant required black customers to pay a cover charge or pay in advance for meals, refused to honor its free Birthday Meal offer to blacks, subjected blacks to racially derogatory remarks, threatened or forcibly removed black customers, and locked the doors so blacks couldn't enter. One Denny's manager was told by a supervisor that

> "A-A's"—in-house code for African-Americans—posed a problem because they could not be counted on to follow the protocols of restaurant-going; they offended other customers by being boisterous; they alienated waitresses by leaving skin-flinty tips; they cost the company money by skipping out on the bill. . . . "We were told we should take whatever measures we could to keep A-A's to a minimum. . . . [We] were to eliminate them from [the] restaurant. No questions asked. Just get it done."
> (Kohn, 1994, p. 44)

The company denied the charges but agreed to provide racial sensitivity training to its employees and managers, post notices of its policy of nondiscrimination in its restaurants, and include 20 blacks in its television and newspaper ads ("Denny's Restaurant hit with discrimination suit," 1993). In a 1995 ad that appeared in newspapers nationally, the president of Denny's stated that the organization had made considerable changes in the way it did business. For instance, 12% of its annual food and paper purchases are now from minority suppliers, and 28% of its franchises are now minority-owned ("It's a new day," 1995).

Most of the time discrimination is much more subtle; in fact, the person engaging in it may not even realize he or she is doing so. Psychologists Carl Word, Mark Zanna, and Joel Cooper (1974) created an experimental situation in which white subjects were led to believe they were interviewing applicants for a team position in a group decision-making experiment. Their behavior was secretly being observed by the researchers. The applicants, who were really confederates of the researchers, were both black and white.

The results showed that the "interviewers" treated black applicants very differently from white ones. For instance, they placed their chairs at a significantly greater distance from the black interviewees. They leaned forward less and made less eye contact with the black applicants. In addition, they ended the interview sooner and tended to trip over their words.

In a second experiment Word, Zanna, and Cooper sought to determine the effect such behavior would have on the applicants. In this experiment, the interviewers were now confederates of the experimenters. These new interviewers were trained to mimic the behaviors found among interviewers in the first experiment. This time, applicants who encountered the "less-friendly" behavior—that is, reduced eye contact, greater physical distance, and so on—performed less adequately and showed less composure during the interview than others.

These experiments illustrate the process by which racism operates, even in people who are not self-consciously racist. We are generally so unaware of our own nonverbal behavior that if we unwittingly give off signs of our dislike, we don't interpret others' subsequent behavior as reactions to our nonverbal cues. Rather, we attribute it to some inherent trait in them. We may unknowingly create the very actions that we then use as evidence of some flaw or deficiency in that group.

As such behavior becomes common among large numbers of people, prejudice and discrimination become mutually reinforcing. If one group is defined as inferior by another and treated that way, the resulting discrimination in the form of denied access to jobs and inferior education becomes self-fulfilling in that it will produce the very inferiority that the group was believed to possess in the first place.

It's worth noting that prejudice and discrimination can sometimes occur *within* the same racial group. For example, many black immigrants from the West Indies refuse to call themselves "black" when they come to this country. They often try to distance themselves as much as possible from American blacks, whom they feel are socially, culturally, and financially inferior. West Indian immigrants generally make substantially more money than American blacks, live in better neighborhoods, and have stronger families (Gladwell, 1996). Not having experienced the debilitating effects of discrimination, West Indian immigrants often have difficulty understanding why American blacks have such a difficult time "making it" in American society. Hence they, like whites, can focus on the inferior characteristics of American blacks as the reason for their lack of success. The effect, according to one observer, is to reinforce, even legitimate, prejudice against blacks:

> The success of West Indians is not proof that discrimination against American blacks does not exist. Rather, it is the means by which discrimination against American blacks is given one last, vicious twist: I am not so shallow as to despise you for the color of your skin, because I have found people your color that I like. Now I can despise you for who you are. (Gladwell, 1996, p. 79)

Class, Race, and Discrimination

Some sociologists have argued that discriminatory treatment, as well as the unequal economic, social, and political status of some racial groups, is more a function of social class than of race (for example, W. J. Wilson, 1980). If this were true, the lives of middle- and upper-class members of racial minorities should be relatively free of discrimination. Yet this is far from the case. For many highly successful minority professionals, lack of respect, faint praise, low expectations, shattered hopes, and even outright harassment and exclusion are common features of their lives. The result is often utter despair:

> I have done everything I was supposed to do. I have stayed out of trouble with the law, gone to the right schools, and worked myself nearly to death. *What more do they want?* Why in God's name won't they accept me as a full human being? Why am I pigeonholed in a "black job"? Why am I constantly treated as if I were a drug addict, a thief, or a thug? Why am I still not allowed to aspire to the same things every white person in America takes as a birthright? Why, when I most want to be seen, am I suddenly invisible? (Cose, 1993, p. 1)

Sociologist Joe Feagin (1991) conducted in-depth interviews with 37 middle-class black Americans to determine the extent of discrimination directed against them in public situations. These 37 people, who were all college educated and held professional or managerial jobs, reported a total of 62 discriminatory incidents in public places like hotels, jewelry stores, and restaurants. The incidents consisted of avoidance, poor service, closer scrutiny, verbal epithets, "hate stares," and police threats and harassment.

The events disturbed the subjects not only because of the racist attitudes that lay behind them but also because they had come to believe that their upward social mobility protected them from such treatment. A 28-year-old New York lawyer sums up such experiences this way:

> When I walk into a store they don't see my Princeton undergraduate degree, my Harvard law degree, my associate law status. They see a black man. Credentials do not make your blackness invisible no matter how impressive they may be. (quoted in L. Williams, 1991b)

Feagin concludes that the stigma of color is still very important in the lives of African Americans, including affluent ones. They remain vulnerable targets of deprivation and discrimination. This modern form of racism within public, economic settings is rooted in deep racial prejudices:

> Blacks are seen as shoplifters, as unclean, as disreputable poor. No matter how affluent and influential, a black person cannot escape the stigma of being black even while relaxing or shopping. (quoted in L. Williams, 1991b)

The days of "No Negroes" and "No Coloreds" may be gone, but the expressions of personal racism described here serve as a constant reminder that, as the 20th century draws to a close, African Americans and other racial minorities are still being stereotyped, prejudged, and discriminated against on the basis of their race. Taken as individual incidents, racial slurs, "hate stares," and poor service in restaurants may seem to be just trivial inconveniences. However, these forms of discrimination reflect the reality to which racial and ethnic minorities of all classes are exposed on a daily basis.

What whites may see as "minority paranoia" is a response to discrimination and humiliation that has accumulated over the years and has become part of everyday life. One middle-class black woman interviewed by Feagin pointed out that whenever she leaves her home she must put on her "shield" and be prepared for the insults and discrimination she expects to receive in public places.

From the point of view of those discriminated against, subtle forms of personal racism are harder to fight than the overt bigotry of the past. If you are excluded from a job because you're Asian or denied membership in a club because you're Jewish, you can fight to open those doors. Today, some people have made it through these doors (Blauner, 1992), but once inside, they have found new barriers to overcome.

A New Form of Racism

The nature of public attitudes toward racial and ethnic groups has changed, prompting many sociologists to rethink their ideas of what constitutes personal racism. Attitudes toward the principle of racial equality and the rejection of absolute segregation in schools, housing, and jobs have improved markedly over the past three or four decades (Citrin, 1996; Schuman, Steeh, & Bobo, 1988). However, concrete efforts to change the racial status quo don't appear to be equally favored (McClendon, 1985). For instance, although most whites feel that schools should be integrated and that people of all races should have equal opportunities to enter any occupation, overwhelming majorities in national surveys oppose special government economic assistance to minorities and government efforts to desegregate schools, such as court-ordered busing. Recent national polls show that nine out of ten whites oppose preferential hiring and promotion of blacks (Citrin, 1996).

This paradox has led some to argue that a new form of racism has emerged (Sniderman & Tetlock, 1986). **Symbolic racism** is linked to the traditional forms of personal racism by common negative feelings toward certain groups. However, symbolic racism is expressed indirectly through opposition to programs that seek to improve the status of minorities in society (McClelland & Auster, 1990). The symbolic racist would tend to disagree strongly with a statement like "Mexican Americans are not generally as smart as Anglos" but at the same time would likely agree with a statement like "Mexican Americans are getting too demanding in their push for Spanish-language services." They justify their opposition to government programs for minorities on the grounds that one's achievements should be based on merit. What complicates the situation even more is that this type of personal racism is often expressed by people who consider themselves liberal, unbiased, and nonprejudiced. They are likely to sympathize with the victims of past injustice; support public policies that, in principle, promote racial equality . . . ; identify more generally with a liberal political agenda; regard themselves as non-prejudiced and non-discriminatory; but, almost unavoidably, possess negative feelings and beliefs about [minority groups]. (Gaertner & Dovidio, 1990, p. 271)

The feelings common to symbolic racism are not hate or hostility but discomfort, uneasiness, and sometimes fear, which tend to motivate avoidance rather than outright destructive acts. Symbolic racists are people who maintain that it is wrong to discriminate against a person because of his or her race or ethnicity but who nonetheless cannot entirely escape the cultural forces that give rise to racist beliefs in the first place.

You can see how symbolic racism can be more insidious than overt personal racism. Social and legal pressures have a significant impact on traditional expressions of bigotry; however, such techniques cannot alleviate symbolic racism because these people already believe in egalitarian, nondiscriminating values. They are acutely aware of the social undesirability and the unfairness of their feelings, but they hold them anyway.

The changing face of racism has serious institutional consequences as well. When racism remains hidden, people are tempted to assume that it has disappeared, forestalling the perceived need to help groups that have traditionally been the objects of discrimination. Most whites in our country believe that the socioeconomic status of blacks has vastly improved and see no need to continue federal programs to assist them (Kluegel & Smith, 1986). Recent efforts to eliminate affirmative action programs exemplify this trend. Many whites now believe that the only reason so many blacks are unsuccessful is that they aren't committed to "white" values—hard work, individualism, delayed gratification, and so on. Although these beliefs are more subtle than overt acts of bigotry, they have the same effect by promoting prejudice toward individuals on the basis of stereotypes.

The Cultural Ideology of Racism

If I stopped here in my discussion of racism and its constituent elements, you might be inclined to consider it a phenomenon of individuals that could best be stopped by changing the way people think and act. But the sociologically important thing about racism is that it exists not just in individuals' minds and actions but in a cultural ideology that both justifies the domination of some groups over others and provides a set of social norms that encourages differential treatment for these groups (O'Sullivan See & Wilson, 1988). From a conflict perspective, the cultural ideology of racism that exists in our language and in our prevailing collective beliefs maintains racial and ethnic inequality.

Racism in Language

If we accept that the dominant white culture in this country is racist, then we would expect our language—the transmitter of culture—to be racist as well (Moore, 1992). Certainly racial slurs and derogatory words reflect underlying racism. But racism doesn't just lie in spoken or written language. As recently as 2 or 3 years ago, American Sign Language relied on visual stereotypical representations as signs for certain racial and ethnic groups. For instance, the sign for "Japanese" was a twisting of the little finger next to the eye. The sign for "Negro" was a flattening of the nose. The sign for "stingy" was derived from the sign for "Jewish" (stroking an imaginary beard). Such signs have fallen out of polite usage with increased sensitivity to their harmful effects (Senior, 1994).

What is particularly important about language is the extent to which the seemingly neutral or even positive content of our everyday words perpetuates racism. Consider the use of common terms to refer to diverse ethnic groups. Today we use the general terms *Native Americans* and *Asian Americans* to refer to a variety of peoples whose traditions and lifestyles are quite different from one another. Similarly, *Hispanic* refers to all people whose backgrounds are from such culturally diverse areas as Mexico, the Caribbean, Central America, and South America.

When the first Europeans "discovered" Africans, they were quick to label them all "black" (Omi & Winant, 1992). Not only did this term mask the fact that they came from a variety of different cultures, it also maximized the perceived differences between "black" Africans and "white" Europeans (Fairchild, 1985). Furthermore, the word *black* capitalizes on a large set of negative connotations within the English language. For instance, good guys wear white hats and bad guys wear black hats. Among the definitions of *black* in *Webster's New Universal Unabridged Dictionary* are soiled and dirty, thoroughly evil, wicked, gloomy, marked by disaster, hostile, and disgraceful. The definition of *white*, on the other hand, includes fairness of complexion, innocent, favorable, fortunate, pure, and spotless.

The pervasive "goodness" of white and "badness" of black affects children by the age of 4 and provides white children with a false sense of superiority (Moore, 1992). Children know the difference between a *black lie*, which is harmful and inexcusable, and a *white lie*, which is small, insignificant, and harmless. A black mark on your academic record certainly will not help your chances of getting into medical school. Black cats crossing your path are bad luck. Black magic is sinister and devilish. The black sheep of the family causes everyone else shame and embarrassment by not conforming to generally accepted standards of behavior. To be blackballed or blacklisted is to be ostracized and identified as undesirable. Blackmail is a powerful way to force someone into an act he or she would rather avoid (Moore, 1992).

More important are the political implications of racist terminology. Terms like *culturally deprived, economically disadvantaged*, and *underdeveloped* mislead and distort our awareness of social phenomena. To apply the label "culturally deprived" to a Hispanic person, for instance, is to symbolically reinforce the belief that the only culture that really matters is the dominant white one. Similarly, the use of the term *nonwhite* to describe people of color implies that white is the standard against which all others are measured.

In 1992 we celebrated the 500th anniversary of Columbus's voyage to the Americas. Most of us were taught that this event was a positive step toward the creation of a civilized New World. Every 5-year-old in the country has been taught that Columbus "discovered" America in 1492. However, according to *Webster's Unabridged Dictionary*, to "discover" is to find something that was previously unknown or to gain sight of something previously unseen. Hence, a continent inhabited by millions of people for thousands of years cannot, logically, be "discovered." Nevertheless, we continue to use this term, ignoring the perspective of Native Americans who are likely to see this event not as the dawning of the civilized New World, but as the first step toward their subjugation and annihilation.

Certain adjectives that are usually used in a positive context can convey something very different when applied in a racial context. For instance, you may hear black athletes described on television or in newspapers as "intelligent" or "bright and articulate." Although such descriptions may be well-meaning, they imply that the person in question violates preconceived notions about the intellect and speaking abilities of "most blacks." White athletes are rarely described as "articulate." That a person feels compelled to use such qualifying adjectives illustrates how deeply embedded racist beliefs can be.

Racist language is just a small part of the overall problem of racist ideology in American society. It seemingly pales in comparison to more visible issues like racial violence and economic discrimination. We must remember, however, that language filters our perceptions. It affects the way people think from the time they first learn to speak. Efforts are being made today to address the issue of language and its crucial role in maintaining racism and oppression. People are becoming more aware of the capacity of words to both glorify and degrade others (Moore, 1992).

The Myth of Innate Racial Inferiority

The cultural ideology of racism is also supported by theories positing innate racial or ethnic inferiority. These theories have long been used to explain why certain racial groups, as a whole, lag behind whites in such areas as educational achievement and financial success. They combine with the belief in competitive individualism (see chapter 11) to provide "scientific" justification and a seemingly intellectual climate for the perpetuation of all forms of prejudice and discrimination.

Appeals to biology and nature have been used throughout history to define the existing stratification system as proper and inevitable (Gould, 1981). In the 18th and 19th centuries no one doubted the correctness of natural racial rankings: Indians below whites, and blacks below everyone else. Even some of our historical idols—Abraham Lincoln, Thomas Jefferson, Charles Darwin—held beliefs about the "natural inferiority" of some races that were common knowledge at the time but would be considered bigoted or racially insensitive today.

The approval given by scientists to conventional racial rankings arose not from objective data and careful research but from a shared worldview, a cultural belief that expressed the "goodness" of racial stratification. Such beliefs were then twisted into independent, "scientific" support. Scientists, like everybody else, have attitudes and values that shape what they see. Such thinking is not the result of outright dishonesty or hypocrisy; rather, it is the way human minds work and the generally accepted knowledge of the day.

The belief in innate racial inferiority is not just a historical curiosity. Recently, the idea reemerged in a book called *The Bell Curve: Intelligence and Class Structure in American Life* (Herrnstein & Murray, 1994). The authors argued that racial and ethnic differences in intelligence—as measured by IQ scores—must be due, at least in part, to heredity. The book set off a firestorm of debate that continues to this day.

From a functionalist perspective, cultural beliefs about innate racial inferiority provide advantages for the dominant group. These beliefs discourage subordinate groups from attempting to question their disadvantaged status. In addition, they provide moral justification for maintaining a society in which some groups are routinely deprived of their rights and privileges. Whites could justify the enslavement of blacks, and Nazis could justify the extermination of Jews and other "undesirables," by promoting the belief that those groups were inherently subhuman.

Races do differ in obvious, visible ways: skin color, anatomical structure, and so forth. But despite energetic searches over the centuries, the link between "inferior" race-based genes and intelligence, creativity, or other valued abilities has not yet been found (Hacker, 1992). Comparing racial groups on, say, intelligence, and discovering that one group performs better on average than the other overlooks the range of differences within and between groups. Many African Americans are more intelligent than the average white; many whites are less intelligent than the average Native American. Variations like these are difficult to explain genetically.

It makes more sense to argue that if certain races or ethnic groups do better in some areas than others, it is because they grew up in environments that prepared them for these endeavors. The importance of one's learning environment in affecting intelligence was illustrated several years ago by the finding that IQ scores for some groups have been rising for the past 50 years (cited in Goleman, 1984). Early tests of Jewish, Chinese, and Italian immigrants showed these groups to be far below average in intelligence. Their grandchildren, however, generally have average or above average IQ scores (Sowell, 1977). Such a large difference over the span of two generations cannot be explained by heredity.

Nevertheless, the idea that racial inferiority is innate is appealing. If observable, physical differences between races are inherited, why not differences in social behavior, intelligence, the ability to rule, and so on? Like the belief in competitive individualism, the belief in innate racial inferiority places the blame for suffering and economic failure on the traits of the individual rather than on the society in which that individual exists.

Racism flourishes in a culture with an ideology that creates and maintains racial inequality. That racism can exist well above the level of personal attitudes indicates that it won't disappear by simply reducing individual people's prejudices and stereotypes. This point becomes particularly important when we examine racism at the structural level of social institutions.

Institutional Racism: Injustice Built into the System

Anyone can be personally racist, and any racial group can develop a set of cultural beliefs or a vocabulary that denigrates outsiders. But one form of racism, less obvious and more dangerous perhaps, can work only to the advantage of those who wield power in society: institutional racism. **Institutional racism** consists of established laws, customs, and practices that systematically reflect and produce racial inequalities in society, whether or not the individuals maintaining these practices have racist intentions (J. M. Jones, 1986). Thus a society can be racist even if only a minority of its members are racist. Because it is a built-in feature of social arrangements, institutional racism is much more difficult to detect than acts of personal racism.

Institutional racism is the established and customary means by which some groups are kept subordinate (Eitzen & Baca-Zinn, 1989). Because Native Americans, African Americans, Hispanics, and other groups have historically been excluded from key positions of authority in social institutions, they often find themselves victimized by the routine workings of such structures. For example, when granting home mortgage loans, many banks use ZIP codes to mark off the neighborhoods they consider high risks—that is, where property values are low and liable to drop even further. Mortgages tend to be unavailable or very difficult to obtain in these areas. Unfortunately, these are precisely the areas that minorities, with lower average incomes, are able to afford.

Similarly, home-delivery businesses, like pizza restaurants, often refuse to deliver to some neighborhoods. Domino's Pizza distributes software to its outlets to let them mark addresses on computers as green (deliver), yellow (curbside only), or red (no delivery). Businesses defend these policies as a reasonable response to the threat of sending easy-to-spot delivery personnel with cash into high-crime areas ("The pizza must go," 1996).

Although these practices, called "red-lining," are considered a "good" business policy and are not intentionally racist, the consequences of using them make them racist because these high-risk neighborhoods tend to be inhabited predominantly by people of color. Institutional racism is difficult to address in these cases because there is no individual "bad guy," no identifiable bigot who is the source of intentional, hate-motivated discrimination.

Likewise, people in neighborhoods where hazardous waste treatment plants or other sources of industrial pollution exist are disproportionately exposed to unhealthful effects of air pollution, water pollution, and pesticides. The decisions on where to place such facilities are often based not on race but on factors like the cost of land, population density, and geological conditions. However, these decisions have the effect of discriminating against certain groups because the less-desirable residential areas (and hence more-desirable industrial areas) are disproportionately inhabited by minorities and other poor people. The nation's largest hazardous waste dump is located in Emelle, Alabama, a small rural community that is 90% black (Bullard & Wright, 1992). A study of toxic emissions along the lower Mississippi River by the Environmental Protection Agency showed that 9 out of the 10 major sources of industrial pollution in Louisiana are in predominantly black neighborhoods. In the town of Carville, an area that is 70% black, 353 pounds of toxic material per person per year is released into the environment. That compares to an average 105 pounds in the rest of the state (Cushman, 1993).

Racism in one institution tends to be accompanied by racism in another. For instance, the traditional exclusion of certain racial and ethnic groups from the upper levels of education will affect their economic opportunities, which in turn will affect their access to other basic necessities like quality health care and housing. I described in chapter 11 how poverty has become geographically concentrated, leaving poor communities more isolated and without access to the institutions, resources, and values necessary for success in modern society (Wilson, 1987). Residential segregation based on class and race is so prevalent in this society that one sociologist refers to the situation as "American apartheid" (Massey, 1990).

Throughout the 1970s laws were established to prevent housing discrimination and thereby promote integration. Indeed, white attitudes toward neighborhood integration have become more favorable over the years. In a 1976 survey, 57% of white respondents who were asked to imagine they lived in a neighborhood that was one-third black said they would be uncomfortable there, and 41% said they'd try to move out. By 1992, only 44% indicated they'd be uncomfortable, and only 29% said they try to move away (Farley & Frey, 1994). During the 1980s and early 1990s, residential segregation decreased slightly in large cities, particularly in the West and South. But most of these cities have also seen substantial increases in their Hispanic and black populations and an accompanying decrease in the white population (Kasarda, 1985). Consequently, overall levels of segregation—

especially between blacks and whites—remains quite high (Farley & Frey, 1994). Hispanics are slightly less residentially segregated than blacks, and Asians are substantially less segregated than blacks (Harrison & Bennett, 1995). Still, if laws prohibit residential segregation and personal racism has eased, why does segregation continue to exist at such high levels? Certainly the distribution of races in a whole city involves more than just individual bigotry and personal discrimination.

■ ■ ■ ■ ■ ■ ■ ■

DIANA PEARCE
Institutional Racism and Real Estate

Sociologist Diana Pearce (1979) was interested in how a structural phenomenon like residential segregation is maintained. She randomly selected about a hundred real estate agents in the greater Detroit area to be in her study. Each agent was visited at different times by a white couple and a black couple who were looking to purchase a house. The couples were similar in terms of education level, occupation, income, family size, and the type of house they wanted. The agents were unaware that the couples were trained and paid accomplices of the researcher.

Pearce found that the chances of actually being shown a house on the first visit to the real estate agent were one in four for the black couples and three in four for the white couples. Even when the black couples were shown homes, they were shown fewer than the white couples. The efforts of the black homeseekers to see homes were not met with strong, blatant refusal. Instead they were met with reasonable sounding excuses like "I don't have the key" or "I need to make an appointment ahead of time." Finally, when black couples were shown homes, they were subtly "steered" into poorer neighborhoods. This lack of overt insult and mistreatment masks the discriminatory treatment to which the black homeseekers were subjected.

Pearce concluded that such practices were not isolated instances of personal racism; in fact, they occurred in a variety of different communities across the entire metropolitan area. There seems to be a high level of consensus in the real estate field about what the racial composition of Detroit neighborhoods ought to be. This study shows that racism embedded in an entire industry can be manifested at the personal level. But the fact that the actions of these agents were "typical" of all agents characterizes their practices as institutional racism.

■ ■ ■

The irony of institutional racism is that while it may not be the result of conscious bigotry on the part of individual people and therefore not motivated by outright personal hatred, it is likely to be more harmful than personal racism in the long run and more difficult to stop. If tomorrow all Americans were to wake up with all hatred, prejudice, and animosity toward other groups gone from their hearts and minds, institutional racism would still exist:

> All that is needed for job opportunities to remain unequal is for employers to hire those with the most conventional training and experience and to use machines when they seem more . . . economical than manual labor. All that is needed to ensure that poor children get an inferior education is to continue . . . using class-biased tests, . . . rewarding children who conform to the teachers' middle-class concepts of the "good student," and paying disproportionately less for education. In other words, all that is needed to perpetuate discrimination in the United States is to pursue a policy of "business as usual." (Eitzen & Baca-Zinn, 1989, pp. 218–219)

Institutions have a permanent, inevitable quality. Once they are in operation, it is extremely difficult to change them except through massive, sometimes revolutionary means.

Racism in the Economic System

Institutional racism is readily apparent throughout our economic institutions. Consider participation in the labor force. Despite recent advances, workers from racial and ethnic minorities tend to be concentrated in lower-paying jobs (see Table 12.2). African Americans make up 10% of the entire American workforce, but they make up 31% of nursing aides and orderlies, 25% of all taxi drivers, 25% of hotel maids, and 22% of janitors and cleaners (National Committee on Pay Equity, 1995). They are severely underrepresented in the fields of law (3.2%), medicine (3.0%), and engineering (3.2%) (Hacker, 1992). Only about one-quarter of Hispanics have managerial, technical, and administrative jobs compared to one-half of non-Hispanic whites (Valdivieso & Davis, 1991). In the microelectronic manufacturing industries of Silicon Valley, people of color make up 26% of the total workforce but 80% of the lower-paying production jobs (Hossfeld, 1990). Ninety-seven percent of senior managers in Fortune 500 companies are white (DeWitt, 1995). With the exception of Asian Americans, the rate of unemployment for people of color is twice as high as that of whites (U.S. Bureau of the Census, 1995a).

Because minorities are occupationally concentrated in low-paying jobs and geographically concentrated in poor inner-city neighborhoods, they are particularly vulnerable to economically motivated business changes, such as plant shutdowns, the automation of lower-level production jobs, and corporate relocations. When a factory in a predominantly black or Hispanic section of an inner city moves to an all-white suburb, current minority employees tend to face greater problems than white employees in securing housing in the new location or higher transportation costs in commuting to the new work location (Squires, 1980).

We can see evidence of institutional racism in common employment policies,

Table 12.2 *Occupations with Highest Concentration by Race/Ethnicity/Sex*

Black Women:	Social workers; postal clerks; dieticians; child-care workers and teacher's aides; private household cooks and cleaners; nursing aides and orderlies
Black Men:	Vehicle washers and equipment cleaners; bus drivers; concrete workers; guards; sheriffs, bailiffs, and other law enforcement
Hispanic Women:	Private household cleaners and servants; child-care workers; janitors and cleaners; health service occupations; sewing machine operators
Hispanic Men:	Janitors and cleaners; construction trades; machine operators; cooks; drivers; laborers and helpers; roofers; groundskeepers, gardeners, farm and agricultural workers
White Women:	Physical therapists; dental hygienists; secretaries; bookkeepers; accounting and auditing clerks
White Men:	Marketing, advertising, and public relations managers; engineers, architects, and surveyors; dentists; firefighters; construction supervisors; tool and die makers
Asian Women:	Marine-life workers; electrical assemblers; dressmakers; launderers
Asian Men:	Physicians; engineers; professors; technicians; cooks; launderers; longshore equipment operators
Native American Women:	Welfare aides; child-care workers; teacher's aides; forestry (except logging)
Native American Men:	Marine-life workers; hunters; forestry (except logging); fishers

Source: National Committee on Pay Equity, 1995.

too. If you've ever worked in a job for a long time, you know that continuous service is rewarded with certain privileges and benefits. People who have worked at a company the longest tend to get the highest salaries, even though their jobs might be no more demanding than those of more recent hirees. Moreover, they have better job stability because seniority rules usually include a "last hired, first fired" provision.

Again, nothing about seniority rules is inherently discriminatory. Most of us think that people who have been with a company longest ought to be entitled to certain benefits as a result. However, seniority rules become institutionally racist when they are applied to jobs for which only whites had been hired in the past. If a company has only recently begun hiring Asian Americans or Hispanics and finds itself in the position of having to lay off workers, the newest employees, a higher proportion of whom also tend to be minorities, will be the first to lose their jobs.

In addition, members of racial and ethnic minorities remain marginal participants in the economy as owners of their own businesses. Loan companies usually demand a credit history, some form of collateral, and evidence of potential success before they will lend money to prospective businesses. These are standard practices, but when they are applied to members of groups who may have a poor credit rating because of past exploitation and no collateral because of poverty, such practices serve to perpetuate racial stratification. Admittedly, poor people are greater credit risks, and businesses in poorer communities must pay more for insurance because of the greater likelihood of theft or property damage. But the higher costs of doing business not only make it more difficult for minorities to start their own businesses but also hurt consumers in these areas, who must pay higher prices for goods and services.

At an even broader level, market pressures also perpetuate institutional racism. Racial and ethnic discrimination in business settings is sometimes difficult to overcome precisely because it may occur for reasons other than personal hatred. On the surface you would think that discrimination would be self-destructive for employers. A company that refuses to hire Hispanics, for instance, not only is losing out on a broader pool of labor but also is running the risk of driving away a group of potential customers. As customers and prospective employees drift to nondiscriminatory companies, you would think that the discriminating ones would eventually be driven out of business (Sunstein, 1991, p. 22).

The fact that racial discrimination continues to exist in business situations is therefore puzzling. However, if we look at it not as a problem of personal racism but as a function of the competitive, profit-driven nature of the economic marketplace, then it starts to make sense. As we saw earlier with the Denny's Restaurant example, businesses sometimes discriminate not because of some deepseated racism but because of financial concerns. Senior executives at Denny's, convinced that black customers were costing them money, issued orders that were widely interpreted by employees to mean they had to discriminate to improve profits or they would lose their jobs (Kohn, 1994).

An employer who is intent on introducing norms of equality into the workforce may actually be financially punished for doing so. From his or her point of view "discrimination is in fact neutral, a quite ordinary form of profit-maximization through catering to consumer demand" (Sunstein, 1991, p. 25). As long as the economic marketplace is driven by consumer preferences that happen to be racist, institutional discrimination will continue.

Through such business practices, the disadvantage of certain groups becomes self-perpetuating. Members of racial minorities are sometimes reluctant to enter occupations previously closed to them (Pettigrew & Martin, 1987). For instance, relatively few African Americans are likely to invest in the lengthy education needed to become a doctor as long as white patients remain uneasy about being treated by African-American doctors. But with few African-American doctors in practice, white people may never have the chance to learn tolerance and acceptance. The result is a further perpetuation, perhaps even an increase, in discriminatory hiring practices.

There are, of course, exceptions. We all know of situations in which members of a racial or ethnic minority invested a great deal of themselves in a profession that treated them inhospitably. In general, however, the discouraging reception for most perpetuates the exclusion of these groups from certain sectors of the economy (Sunstein, 1991).

Interestingly, just as racist actions may be motivated by economic forces and not personal prejudice, so are nonracist actions. Network television in the 1990s has had more series than ever featuring black characters. At one point in 1993, the Fox network had nine black-oriented series. On the surface the entertainment industry appears to be finally attempting to eradicate a long tradition of racial inequality. On closer inspection, though, this trend appears to really be driven by economic considerations. A recent Nielsen study showed that black households average 70 hours a week of television watching compared with 47 hours in nonblack households (Hammer, 1992). The decision to represent more blacks on television is a financially motivated one, reflecting the industry's need to cater to the perceived tastes of the viewership, whoever that viewership happens to be.

As long as individuals are motivated to maximize their own interests (and profits), they are likely to adapt to market tastes. To the extent that those tastes reflect underlying prejudice, discrimination will continue. This functionalist explanation of institutional racism is important because it enables us to see why discrimination is so difficult to end. The problem is not individual bigotry; it is the mistreatment that has been built into the system so effectively that it is sometimes difficult to see, let alone remove.

Racism in the Educational System

In 1954 the U.S. Supreme Court ruled, in *Brown* v. *Board of Education of Topeka*, that racially segregated schools were unconstitutional because they were inherently unequal. A recent study by the Harvard Project on School Desegregation, however, found that 66% of all African-American public school students and 74% of Hispanic students still attend predominantly minority schools, defined as those schools with more than 50% of their enrollment made up of either African-American or Hispanic students (Celis, 1993). The percentage rises to 94% in the nation's large inner cities. These figures represent the highest rates of school segregation reported in the last 25 years.

The racial mix of the classroom has important implications for the quality of education. Although the gap is closing, blacks and Hispanics continue to have lower educational attainment than whites and Asian Americans. About 82% of whites and 94% of Asian Americans earn a high school diploma, but only 73% of blacks and 62% of Hispanics do so (U.S. Bureau of the Census, 1995a). Unfortunately, lower educational achievement interacts with other economic forces to present a major barrier to social advancement for minorities.

Schools in poor communities lack the financial and therefore educational resources that more affluent communities have (see chapter 11). In 1989 the city of Chicago spent $5,000 for each student in its secondary schools. This average compares to $9,000 in some of the wealthy suburbs a few miles to the north (Kozol, 1991). These differences are a function of the value of property in these communities and not race per se. The consequences are nonetheless linked to race, because of the high concentration of racial and ethnic minorities in poor school districts. Furthermore, these districts face increasing financial pressures because of reductions in federal assistance programs. The rising cost of higher education also reduces the number of minority students who are able to attend college.

Lack of money isn't the only problem. Common practices within the educational system may perpetuate institutional discrimination. According to the National Coalition of Advocates for Students, poor, black, or Hispanic children are more likely to be physically punished, suspended, expelled, or forced to repeat a grade than white students. These forms of treatment go beyond personal mistreatment and humiliation; they all increase the likelihood that a child will drop out of school (cited in Eitzen & Baca-Zinn, 1991).

Consider also the common use of standardized intelligence tests (IQ, SAT, and so on). Many elementary and secondary schools use IQ tests as the basis for tracking students—that is, assigning them to different educational programs based on their intellectual abilities. In principle, tracking allows every student to receive an education that is consistent with his or her talents. In practice, however, students from privileged backgrounds are likely to be placed in higher tracks, while those from less-privileged backgrounds, who are disproportionately members of minority groups, are likely to be placed in lower tracks (Bowles & Gintis, 1976; Oakes, 1985).

IQ tests supposedly measure innate intelligence. Many educational experts agree, though, that these tests are culture-bound, tapping an individual's familiarity with a specific range of white, middle-class experiences rather than indicating innate intelligence (Curran & Renzetti, 1990). Here is a typical IQ question:

Tennis is to racquet as golf is to:
a. club
b. strike
c. bat
d. swing

This question does not just measure mental skills like insight or creativity; instead, it measures a specific piece of knowledge that must be learned from the environment. To the extent that a child's environment does not include such knowledge—that is, he or she has never been exposed to tennis or golf—that child will not be able to answer this question, and the IQ score will suffer (Goleman, 1984). Such a child is not necessarily less intelligent, only lacking in the social experiences necessary to answer the question correctly.

Imagine taking an IQ test consisting of questions that reflect a culture about which you know very little. People from that culture will probably score significantly higher than you on this test. One researcher developed an intelligence test based on knowledge found within Chicano culture (Ramirez, 1988). Among the questions included were the following:

That part of the southwestern United States from which it is believed the Aztecs migrated before they settled in Mexico City is:
a. San Diego
b. Aztlan
c. Colorado
d. Santa Barbara

Chicano term for the police:
a. *la migra*
b. *la chota*
c. *el gabacho*
d. *el pachuco*

When this test was administered to white and Chicano college students, Chicanos scored significantly higher on average than whites: 93.3 out of a possible 140 points compared to 36.4 for the white students. (The correct answer to both questions, by the way, is "b.")

■ ■ ■ ■ ■ ■ ■ ■

CLAUDE STEELE
Stereotype Vulnerability and Educational Performance

A lot of scholarly work examines where stereotypes come from, but less attention has been paid to how they affect the object of the stereotypical thinking. According to social psychologist Claude Steele, in the institutional setting of universities, stereotypes function much like self-fulfilling prophecies and may account for why some groups—blacks and Hispanics, in particular—don't fare as well academically as others.

Steele became interested in how stereotypes affect students when he found that 80% of black students at the University of Michigan—some of whom were extremely bright—were enrolled in remedial programs (Gose, 1995). Still, their dropout rate far exceeded that of white students. He wondered whether many capable students were dropping out not because they were innately intellectually inferior (see Herrnstein & Murray, 1994) but because the institutional practice of enrolling them in remedial classes was essentially labeling them as "dumb." When people are confronted with a negative stereotype about their intellectual skills before they take tests—what Steele calls "stereotype vulnerability"—they tend to perform according to the stereotype (Steele & Aronson, 1995). Whether they believe the stereotype or not, the mere threat that they might be judged in terms of it is enough to hurt academic performance. If true, the gap between whites and blacks on standardized tests—which is estimated to be 15 points on IQ tests and 140 points on the Scholastic Aptitude Test—would disappear if blacks are taught that they have the same academic potential as whites.

To test his ideas, Steele conducted an experiment in which groups of black and white students at Stanford University were given portions of the Graduate Record Exam. In the section asking for personal information, half the tests asked the students to indicate their race; the other half did not. Steele found that the blacks asked to identify their race scored significantly lower than whites who were asked their race. In contrast, blacks and whites who were not asked to identify their race scored about the same. In another experiment, blacks who were told they were taking a test that would evaluate their intellectual skills scored much lower than whites. Blacks who were told the test didn't evaluate intellectual ability scored the same as whites.

Steele has put his ideas into practice. He now runs a freshman transition program at Stanford in which incoming students from a variety of racial and ethnic backgrounds participate in workshops and seminars about adjustment to college. The emphasis of the program is on intellectual challenge, not remediation. Students are not led to believe they are in the program to compensate for some perceived intellectual deficiency. He has found that black students in the program earn slightly better grades than white students who aren't in the program (Gose, 1995).

Steele's research shows how longstanding and well-meaning practices of large educational institutions like remedial education programs may unintentionally harm the very people they are designed to help.

▪ ▪ ▪

Racism in Law and Politics

Despite a decline in the overall crime rate, about 5,000 of every 100,000 black men are in prison or jail—a rate five times higher than the rate of imprisonment of black men during the apartheid years in South Africa. In comparison, the prison rate for the general population is 500 per 100,000 (Cockburn, 1995). One of the reasons for this imbalance is certainly the personal biases of individual police officers, attorneys, and judges. Over the past few years, for instance, we've seen several highly visible instances of police officers harassing, humiliating, and sometimes beating blacks and Hispanics. Few of us will soon forget the virulent bigotry of one of the Los Angeles police officers investigating the O. J. Simpson case.

But we must also examine the possibility that racial discrimination exists at the institutional level. Consider, for instance, discrepancies in prison sentences for certain types of drug offenses. The average length of a sentence for selling crack cocaine is 133 months; for powdered cocaine it is 94 months. According to federal law, it would take 500 grams of powdered cocaine (or 5,000 doses) to draw the same mandatory minimum sentence of 5 years in prison that a person convicted of possessing 5 grams (or 10 doses) of crack cocaine would get (Cockburn, 1995). Crack is the only drug that carries a mandatory prison sentence for possession without the intent to sell it. Many law enforcement officials argue that the different levels of punishment are justified because crack cocaine is more closely associated with violence than powdered cocaine and more dangerous to the user.

But some sociologists argue that the problems associated with crack have as much to do with poverty, unemployment, and homelessness as the drug itself. And others point to the skewed racial distribution of the users of crack versus the users of powdered cocaine. The common perception is that the typical powdered cocaine user is a white suburbanite and the typical crack user is a young, urban black man. Official crime statistics support this perception. In 1994, 95% of those convicted of federal crack offenses were black or Hispanic; only 3.5% were white. By contrast, 29.7% of those convicted in federal powdered cocaine charges were black, 25.9% were white, and 42.8% were Hispanic (cited in C. Jones, 1995).

In this federal drug policy, we see a clear example of institutional racism. Although the law itself is well intentioned and not meant to be racist, its consequences are. Blacks are serving longer prison sentences for drug offenses not because of their race but because they are more likely to use a drug that is punished more severely than any other.

Race is also a key issue within the American political system. For one thing, members of racial minorities are not as involved in the political process as whites. Perhaps minorities take less of an interest because in the past blacks in the South and Hispanics in the Southwest were deliberately prevented from voting or even registering to vote. It wasn't until 1965, when Congress passed the Voting Rights

Act, that minorities were assured the right to vote in elections. Nevertheless, cynicism and disillusionment with the system still keep many minority voters away from the polls. In the 1992 presidential election, 64% of whites voted compared to 54% of blacks and 29% of Hispanics. Only when a viable black candidate ran for president (Jesse Jackson in 1984) did the percentage of blacks who voted approach that of whites.

When minority voters don't vote, minority representation in the government remains low. In 1985, fewer than 5% of U.S. Representatives were black, 2% were Hispanic, and 1% were Asian (U.S. Bureau of the Census, 1995a). Only 2 out of 108 congressional representatives from the South were black, even though blacks composed 20% of the population in those states. In 1991, under pressure from the U.S. Justice Department to strengthen minority voting power, several state legislatures adopted plans to redraw the boundaries of congressional districts so they would be majority black or Hispanic (N. Bernstein, 1996). The state of Texas, for instance, used a computer program that provided racial and ethnic information at the block level so that black streets could be sorted into one district and white streets into another. By 1995, the number of black and Hispanic congressional representatives had doubled.

Opponents of this process—known formally as *redistricting*—called it a form of political apartheid that splits neighborhoods by race; supporters argued that it was the best way to integrate the political process. In 1996, after years of debate, the U.S. Supreme Court ruled that redistricting is unconstitutional because it classifies citizens by race (Greenhouse, 1996b). The Court immediately voided race-based congressional districts in North Carolina, Texas, and Georgia. In one Georgia district, a 60% black majority became a 60% white majority overnight, placing into doubt the reelection of its black representative.

Whether minority participation and representation in our political institutions increase or decrease remains to be seen. What is clear, however, is that race is still a crucial factor by which people are included or excluded, hindered or helped, valued or devalued within the political system.

Ways to Overcome Institutional Racism

Clearly, overcoming institutional racism will take more than the good will of individual people. The most far-reaching and controversial structural solution to the problem of institutional racism has been a governmental policy referred to as **affirmative action**. Affirmative action is a program that seeks out members of minority groups for educational or occupational positions from which they had previously been excluded. The assumption is that organizations will not change racist policies unless they are forced to do so. Another assumption is that past discrimination has left certain people ill equipped to compete as equals today.

Contrary to popular belief, the goal of affirmative action is not to enact hiring quotas. Employers are not compelled to hire unqualified persons or compromise standards to meet these goals. They are simply required to gather all relevant information on all qualified applicants, to interview minority candidates, and to make sure minorities have access to job information. Government agencies and private firms doing business with the government, for instance, are required to publicly announce job openings at least 45 days prior to the cutoff day for applications (Cherry, 1989). Quotas are only a last resort, reserved for situations in which organizations are not making good-faith efforts to seek out qualified minority candidates. If a firm announces a job opening in newspapers that reach only the white community or uses discriminatory procedures to eliminate minorities from employment, the government can then impose quotas.

Affirmative action policies have been used successfully in several areas of social life. Cities have been ordered to bus children to schools outside their neighborhoods to eliminate school segregation. Businesses, unions, universities, and local governments accused of discrimination in hiring or admission have been sued under the 1964 Civil Rights Act. In 1994, more than 40% of U.S. colleges and universities reported enrollment gains among African Americans and Hispanics (cited in Worsnop, 1996b). In part because of such action, people of color now hold a greater percentage of management, white-collar, and upper-level blue-collar jobs than ever before. Minority employment among firms doing business with the government grew by 20% between 1974 and 1980 (Pear, 1983). Wages and salaries relative to those of whites have also improved. Figure 12.1 shows the changes in household income of blacks and whites between 1967 and 1992.

Despite such advances, affirmative action came under fire starting in the 1980s. Critics argue that the constitutional protection of each person's right to life, liberty, and property means that all groups, including those whose rights have never been violated or neglected, must have their opportunities safeguarded and must be treated equally. Hence any preferential treatment of a group, even one whose rights have been historically unrecognized, amounts to a form of "reverse discrimination" that usually claims white males as its victims. Not only is reverse discrimination unfair, they suggest, but it will also create a "white backlash" and undermine the main goal of the policy, which is to reduce prejudice.

The catalyst for these criticisms was a case that went to the Supreme Court in 1978. A white male student named Alan Bakke was twice denied admission into a California medical school. He claimed that less-qualified applicants had been accepted under a special admissions program that saved 16 out of 100 places for minorities. The Supreme Court ruled in favor of Bakke, although it also stated that race or ethnicity could be used as one of several factors in evaluating applicants. The court reversed itself a year later, however, when it ruled that private employers could legally give special preference to black workers to eliminate "manifest racial imbalance" in jobs traditionally restricted to whites.

Figure 12.1 *Household Income by Race, 1967–1992 (percent making each amount)*

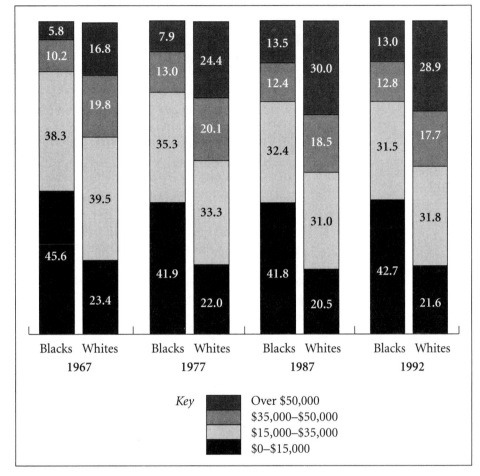

Source: J. Hochschild, 1995, p. 44.

After more than two decades of affirmative action, many whites have come to believe it should be abolished (Citrin, 1996). They argue that enough has been done and that now the deck is stacked against them. There has never been greater disagreement about whether past discrimination entitles racial and ethnic minorities to preferential treatment in education or hiring. Over three-fourths of whites now feel that qualified blacks should not receive preference over equally qualified whites in such matters as getting into college or getting jobs (Citrin, 1996).

Several recent organizational and legal decisions have threatened the continued existence of affirmative action. In 1995, the University of California Board of

Regents ended its 30-year-old affirmative action program when it decided to stop admitting students, hiring professors, and awarding contracts on the basis of race and sex. The university projects that under the new guidelines black enrollment could decrease by as much as 50% and Hispanic enrollment may go down by as much as 24% in the next few years (Worsnop, 1996b). In 1996, the U.S. Supreme Court let stand a lower court ruling that the University of Texas Law School could not use race as a factor in admissions, implying that race-based affirmative action plans—even if used for the purpose of correcting racial imbalances—are discriminatory and therefore unconstitutional.

Even some members of the African-American community argue that affirmative action is a mixed blessing and may actually hurt those groups it is intended to help (Loury, 1985). For instance, black students attending predominantly white universities often find that many of their white classmates assume they were admitted because of affirmative action and not their qualifications. Furthermore, some sociologists point out that affirmative action has enhanced the opportunities of middle-class blacks, but has done nothing to help the millions of poor blacks who have seen their situations worsen (Wilson, 1990). Others point out that many of the continuing problems blacks face today are a product of the cultivation and exploitation of the status of "victim." Programs like affirmative action simply reinforce inferiority, discourage initiative, and encourage blacks to claim victimization (Steele, 1990).

▪ ▪ ▪ ▪ ▪ ▪ ▪ ▪

MICRO-MACRO CONNECTION
Voluntary Resegregation

Dissatisfaction with affirmative action as a means of addressing institutional racism has led to other rather dramatic solutions. One such solution is voluntary resegregation.

Four decades after the *Brown* v. *Board of Education of Topeka* case declared that separate facilities could never be equal and that segregation hurt blacks, a new generation of politicians, activists, and social observers is questioning the notion that integration is always the best solution to the problem of racial inequality. The standard remedies for discrimination—busing, affirmative action, specially drawn voting districts—are under attack.

These ideas don't represent a rebirth of the sort of white bigotry that has historically plagued the nation. This time many blacks, convinced that integration hasn't been successful and may have even been a mistake, are looking more favorably at the idea of racially segregated institutions. Integration and equality, they feel, are not synonymous. Hence they are choosing to live in segregated neighborhoods or work in segregated businesses.

Voluntary segregation is particularly popular in the educational system. The belief that black students will automatically benefit academically by being in classes with whites is, some contend, racist. Indeed, research suggests that African-American students who are forced to attend racially mixed schools show only small gains in academic achievement (Entwisle & Alexander, 1994). Some advocates of voluntary segregation feel attention ought to be directed toward enhancing institutions that are predominantly black, making them "separate *and* equal."

Consequently, many black parents are sending their children to race-segregated, or "Afrocentric," schools (Innis, 1993). A deepening sense of alienation and frustration with the educational system has led to calls for a new education policy that emphasizes black recognition, self-help, pride, and empowerment. The curricula in these schools often place Africa at the center of the development of civilization and attempt to amend traditional history by including contributions made by African people. The emphasis on African-American and African history is meant to give black students a better appreciation for their own life experiences.

Critics, however, argue that attempts to promote African culture and history as superior simply shift the weight to favor a different culture instead of instilling balance, stability, and an appreciation of all groups. Although the desire for a more honest representation of the past is understandable, they feel that Afrocentric curricula have simply become another form of ethnocentrism, driving a deeper wedge between racial and ethnic groups in American society (Schlesinger, 1992).

■ ■ ■

In a society with a tradition of racial stratification, what is the best way to overcome institutional and personal inequality? Is resegregation in *equal but separate* institutions necessary to create self-sufficiency? Does it take discriminating in the opposite direction to "make things equal," or is it enough simply to treat people equally from this point on?

Imagine a fictitious final game of the NCAA Basketball Championship Tournament between University A and University B. The rules of the game clearly favor University A. They are allowed five players on the court, while Team B is allowed only four. Team A gets four points for every basket made; Team B gets two. Team A is given two points for each free throw made; Team B gets one. Team A is allowed to physically impede the progress of the opposing players without being called for a foul, and so on.

At halftime Team A leads Team B by a score of 70 to 15. During halftime the NCAA Rules Committee, responding to pressure from the referees, the fans, and players from both teams, decides that the current rules have made the game completely unfair and have harmed the interests of Team B. The committee declares that the second half of the game will use a new system of rules that makes the game more just. Each team has the same number of players on the court and receives the same number of points per basket. The inequality of the game has been successfully eliminated, and fairness rules the day.

But there's a slight problem: the score is still 70 to 15! In other words, just because opportunities have been equalized doesn't mean that disadvantages of the past have been entirely erased. Such is the problem we face today. We can legislate hiring or admission polices that do away with unfair advantages to any group, but does that action address a long history of exclusion? For a long time to come, members of certain groups will continue to be underrepresented in traditionally white positions. Is it possible to achieve complete equality without forcing those who have benefited historically to give up some of their advantages? The answer to this question is complex, controversial, and emotionally charged and will have a great impact on the nature of American race relations as we enter the 21st century.

Global Perspectives on Racism

Given the focus of this chapter so far, it would be tempting to conclude that racism and racial inequality are purely American phenomena. Certainly these problems are most obvious in a society like ours, which is so ethnically and racially diverse and which has had such a long history of bitter racial conflict. But racial and ethnic tension is the worldwide rule, not the exception.

In Mexico, for example, all citizens are considered equal under the country's constitution. The National Commission of Human Rights has never received a racial discrimination complaint. Yet it is a society deeply divided along racial lines, particularly between dark-skinned people of Indian descent and light-skinned people of Spanish descent. Most Mexicans are of mixed lineage, so that nearly all of them could be considered at least part Indian. Indeed, the degree of "Indianness," or the darkness of one's skin, determines one's status in society. Because darkness is associated with low status, many Mexicans, especially in the larger cities, use hair dyes, skin lighteners, and blue or green contact lenses to appear more European (DePalma, 1995).

Mexicans who are considered Indians are the object of severe discrimination. Although 1 in 10 Mexicans is Indian, none serve in the presidential cabinet and only a handful are in the congress. More than 80% of Mexico's Indian communities suffer high levels of poverty; nearly half of all Indians are illiterate, and only 14% complete sixth grade. The Indians even refer to themselves as "Mexico's most forgotten people" (DePalma, 1996a).

The 1994 armed uprising by Mayan Indians in the state of Chiapas was an attempt to force the government to acknowledge its unjust treatment and abandonment of its Indian people. They were protesting against years of poverty and their long-standing status as second-class citizens. The catalyst for the uprising was the Mexican government's signing of the North American Free Trade Agreement (NAFTA), which ended state subsidies for crops that the Indians depend on for their survival. Despite this rebellion, racism in Mexico remains, by and large, unaddressed, and the cultural assault on people of Indian descent continues.

In some countries, prejudice and discrimination against a particular minority group have nothing to do with actual racial differences. The most disadvantaged minority in Japan, for instance, are the *Burakumin*, who represent about 2% of the Japanese population and are biologically, religiously, and ethnically indistinguishable from other Japanese. Nevertheless, a national poll found that more than two-thirds of Japanese people consider the Burakumin a completely different race (Hane, 1982). Their low status dates back to the 17th century, when their occupations dealt with killing animals and disposing of their remains, which violated Buddhist principles. These jobs were necessary for society but considered so degrading that only "subhuman" outcasts would do them, forever contaminating those who engaged in them (Kristof, 1995).

The innate inferiority of the Burakumin is beyond question to many Japanese. They are widely believed to be mentally inferior, aggressive, impulsive, and dirty (Neary, 1986). Before a marriage or the hiring of a new employee, some Japanese will have a detective agency check the background of a person for Burakumin ancestors. In the past, some shopkeepers accepted money from Burakumin customers in baskets with long handles and then washed the coins afterward (Mihashi, 1987).

The treatment and perception of the Burakumin have recently improved somewhat. Today almost two-thirds say they've never encountered discrimination, although many children are never told by their parents that they are Burakumin. Over 70% now marry non-Burakumin, and most believe they are treated fairly by the police (Kristof, 1995). The Japanese government has invested large sums of money to improve Burakumin neighborhoods so they are no longer unlivable slums.

But like disadvantaged ethnic or racial groups in the United States, the Burakumin still suffer from institutional discrimination. They have the lowest income and educational attainment and the highest rates of poverty, crime, alcoholism, single parenthood, and welfare dependency in Japanese society. And like minority groups in the United States, their dependence on government assistance has created resentment from a public that believes they are getting special, undeserved help.

In both Mexico and Japan, as in many other countries, racism has deep historical roots. Sociologists once believed that such traditions would gradually succumb to the global forces of industrialization and modernization, which would create racially diverse societies where people's loyalty would be directed to the national society rather than their racial or ethnic community (Deutsch, 1966). But the opposite has happened. At a time when people from every corner of the globe are linked technologically, economically, and ecologically and mass migrations mix people from different races, religions, and cultures in unprecedented numbers, racial and ethnic hostilities are at an all-time high (Barber, 1992).

Judging by what we see going on in the world today, we might conclude that hostility of one group for another is among the most universal of human feelings

(Schlesinger, 1992). Look at the front page of the newspaper and you will see stories of conflict and violence between Jews and Palestinians in Israel, Hutus and Tutsis in Rwanda and Burundi, Serbs and Muslims in Bosnia, English-speaking Canadians and French-speaking Canadians in Quebec, Tamils and Sinhalese in Sri Lanka, Azerbaijanis and Armenians or Russians and Chechens in the former Soviet Union, or Hindus and Sikhs in India. Racial and ethnic hatred around the world costs the lives of millions of people each year. In 1993 alone, there were more than 50 wars in progress, most of them ethnic, racial, tribal, or religious in character (Binder & Crossette, 1993).

Immigration and global financial instability have also created strains between racial and ethnic groups as they compete for scarce economic opportunities. When people's survival is threatened, they often blame others—particularly newly arrived others who look and act differently—for their problems. In Great Britain, France, and Germany, loud and sometimes violent resentment is directed toward immigrants from Africa, Eastern Europe, and Asia. In the United States such animosity is likely to be directed toward immigrants from Latin America and Asia (see chapter 14 for more detail).

But global forces don't always increase racial tension and inequality. In South Africa, for example, the end of apartheid—the system of legal segregation and discrimination against blacks—was the result of an international boycott of companies that did business there. In the 1980s, the global media brought the world pictures and stories of the brutal treatment of South African blacks. When consumers in the United States and other industrial nations stopped buying products from companies that held investments in South Africa, the companies began to withdraw their money. The minority white government felt the sting as domestic economic problems mounted. As a result of these pressures, the white population of South Africa voted to abolish apartheid. Shortly thereafter, the first black president, Nelson Mandela, was elected. In 1996, a new constitution was adopted that officially and peacefully completed South Africa's transition from white supremacy to nonracial democracy. The document renounces the racism of the past and guarantees all South Africans broad freedoms of speech, movement, and political activity (Daley, 1996). Although serious inequalities and animosities remain, the country is well on its way toward unity and stability.

Conclusion

On April 16, 1963, Martin Luther King Jr. allowed himself to be arrested and jailed for leading a civil rights demonstration in Birmingham, Alabama. Birmingham at the time was perhaps the most thoroughly segregated city in the country. Not only were blacks subjected to daily doses of fear, violence, and humiliation, they also had to constantly fight what Dr. King called "a degenerating sense of nobodiness." Torn between the brutal reality of a racist society and a fierce optimism for the future, he wrote from his jail cell:

Let us all hope that the dark clouds of racial prejudice will soon pass away and the deep fog of misunderstanding will be lifted from our fear-drenched communities and in some not too distant tomorrow the radiant stars of love and brotherhood will shine over our great nation with all of their scintillating beauty. (King, 1991, p. 158)

Some 30 years later Dr. King's words continue to fall on deaf ears. Our society—and most societies around the globe—still struggle with the debilitating effects of personal and institutional discrimination based on race, religion, and ethnicity. In the United States, lynchings and state-supported segregation have given way to a quiet, almost polite racism that resides not in bloodshed and flagrant exclusion but in the day-to-day workings of our major social institutions.

With a few exceptions, minority groups still suffer noticeable disadvantages in economics, education, politics, employment, vulnerability to crime, health care, and so on. Three decades after racial segregation was ruled unconstitutional, the complete integration of such fundamental social institutions as public schools, government, and business remains largely unachieved. Some question the very value of integration. When opportunities to learn, legislate, and make a living are unequally distributed according to race, all facets of life remain unequal.

One reason why race relations are so problematic today is that public debate over the issue confuses the various types of racism. While one person might use "racism" to refer to personal forms of bigotry, another might use it to refer to broader forms of institutional racism. Different types of racism require different solutions. We cannot put an end to economic deprivation or massive residential segregation by trying to convince people not to hold stereotypical beliefs about other groups.

I realize this chapter has been rather depressing. After reading it, it's hard to imagine a multiracial society without racial stratification. We must remember, however, that differences do not have to imply inequality. The transformation from difference to disadvantage is a social construction. We as a culture have decided that some differences should be irrelevant while others should be the primary criterion for making social and legal distinctions between groups of people. Because we construct these differences, we can tear them down.

CHAPTER HIGHLIGHTS

▪ The history of race in American society is an ambivalent one. Our famous sayings about equality conflict with the experiences of most racial and ethnic minorities: oppression, violence, and exploitation. Opportunities for life, liberty, and the pursuit of happiness have always been distributed along racial and ethnic lines.

▪ American society is built on the assumption that different immigrant groups will ultimately assimilate, changing their way of life to conform to that of the dominant culture. But the increasing diversity of the population has shaped people's ideas about what it means to be an American and has influenced our relationships with one another and with our social institutions.

▪ Personal racism is manifested in the form of bigotry, prejudice, and individual acts of discrimination. Symbolic racism is not expressed directly but rather indirectly through avoidance or opposition to programs designed to improve the status of minorities in society.

▪ Racism can also be found in a language and cultural ideology that justifies a set of social norms prescribing differential treatment of certain groups.

▪ Institutional racism exists in established institutional practices and customs that reflect, produce, and maintain racial inequality. Institutional racism is more difficult to detect than personal racism, hence it is more difficult to stop. Because such racism exists at a level above personal attitudes, it will not disappear simply by reducing people's prejudices.

▪ Racial and ethnic conflict is not just an American phenomenon. It is a global reality.

YOUR TURN

In this chapter I examined the personal and institutional forms that racism takes. A curious and disturbing feature of prejudice is that many of our beliefs and attitudes about other racial or ethnic groups are formed without any direct contact with members of those groups. The media—most notably television—play a significant role in providing the public with often inaccurate and oversimplified information about racial and ethnic groups that indirectly shapes public attitudes.

For one week, observe several prime-time television shows that feature prominent African-American, Hispanic, and Asian characters. The shows can be either comedies or dramas. Note the number of characters on each show that are people of color. Pay particular attention to the way the characters are portrayed. What is their apparent social class standing? How does their behavior conform to common stereotypes associated with members of these groups? How frequently do they refer to their own race? Do the plots of the shows revolve around what you might consider "racial" themes? That is, how often does the issue of race come up during the course of the show?

Interpret your observations sociologically. What are the implicit messages communicated by the portrayal of racial/ethnic minorities? Are characters who do not act in stereotypical ways conforming instead to a white, middle-class standard? If so, how will this portrayal ultimately affect public perceptions of race?

CHAPTER 13

The Architecture of Inequality: Gender

- *Sexism at the Personal Level: From Objectification to Victim Blaming*
- *The Ideology of Sexism*
- *Institutions and Sexual Inequality*

At a women's rights convention held in Seneca Falls, New York, participants created a modified version of the Declaration of Independence. They called it the Declaration of Sentiments and Resolutions. Here are some excerpts from that document:

> We hold these truths to be self-evident: that all men and women are created equal.
> . . . The history of mankind is a history of repeated injuries . . . on the part of man
> toward woman, having in direct object the establishment of an absolute tyranny over
> her:
>
> - He has compelled her to submit to laws, in the formation of which she had no
>   voice.
> - He has monopolized nearly all profitable [occupations], and from those she is
>   permitted to follow, she receives but a scanty remuneration. He closes against her
>   all the avenues to wealth and distinction which he considers most honorable to
>   himself.
> - He has endeavored, in every way that he could, to destroy her confidence in her
>   own powers, to lessen her self-respect, and to make her willing to lead a depen-
>   dent and abject life.
>
> In view of their social degradation and in view of the unjust laws above mentioned,
> and because women do feel themselves aggrieved, oppressed, and fraudulently
> deprived of the most sacred rights, we insist that they have immediate admission to
> all the rights and privileges which belong to them as citizens of the United States.

The women who wrote this declaration were not the women's libbers of the 1960s and 70s or the radical feminists of the 1980s and 90s. They were participants in the first meeting in support of women's rights ever held in our country—in 1848.

Many of us are inclined to believe that the battle against sexual inequality is a relatively recent phenomenon that emerged along with the civil rights movement of the 1960s and the so-called sexual revolution of the 1970s. We tend to think that women of the past were either content with their second-class status or unaware that it could be otherwise. As you can see from the above declaration, though, early American women were anything but passive, ignorant victims of discrimination. They were as angry, humiliated, and frustrated by social mistreatment as many women are today. The purpose of their struggle—to overcome economic, legal, and social inequality—was as relevant and urgent in 1848 as it is in the 1990s.

Along with economic and racial inequality, sexual inequality has been a fundamental part of the historical development of our national identity. It has influenced the lives and dreams of individual people, shaped popular culture, and created and maintained social institutions. Chapter 5 discussed how we learn to become boys and girls, men and women within the appropriate social and cultural context. Being placed in a category based on your gender affects everything you do in life. But gender is more than just a source of personal identity that sets societal expectations; it is a major criterion for the distribution of important resources in most societies. Therefore, gender is perhaps the most important determinant of stratification worldwide.

In this chapter I explore the lives and experiences of women living in a society constructed by and for men. Several important questions are addressed: What is sexism? How is it expressed and felt at the personal level? How is sexual inequality supported by cultural beliefs and symbols? At the institutional level, how is it related to family and work roles? What are its legal and economic consequences?

Sexism at the Personal Level: From Objectification to Victim Blaming

What do you think of when you hear the word *sexism*? The husband who won't let his wife work outside the home? The construction worker who whistles and shouts sexual comments at female passersby? The office worker who tells lewd jokes about women around the water cooler? It is all those things, but sociologically speaking, **sexism** refers to a system of beliefs that assert the inferiority of one sex and that justify sexual inequality. In a male-dominated society, or **patriarchy**, cultural beliefs and values give higher prestige and importance to men than to women. Sexual inequality exists throughout such a society, from the perceptions, thoughts, and social interactions of men and women to the organization of social institutions. Above all, sexual inequality provides men with privileged access to socially valued resources and furnishes them with the ability to influence the political, economic, and personal decisions of others.

In chapter 12, I discussed the differences between personal and institutional racism. A similar distinction can be made between personal and institutional sexism. At the personal level, sexism refers to attitudes and behaviors communicated in everyday interaction. Research on sex stereotypes, for instance, has consistently shown that women are perceived as more passive, emotional, easily influenced, and dependent than men (Broverman, Vogel, Broverman, Clarkson, & Rosenkrantz, 1972; Deaux & Kite, 1987; Tavris & Offir, 1984). Sex stereotypes like these have changed little over the years (Berger & Williams, 1991). Others have noted the myriad ways personal sexism can be expressed, both overtly and subtly, in micro-level interactions such as physical domination, condescending comments, sabotage, and exploitation (Benokraitis & Feagin, 1993). Such attitudes and behaviors not only place women in a lower status position vis-à-vis men but also channel them into unequal social opportunities.

Men aren't the only ones who can be personally sexist. Certainly many women dislike men, judge them on the basis of stereotypes, hold prejudiced attitudes toward them, consider them inferior, and even discriminate against them socially or professionally. We must keep in mind, though, that male sexism occupies a very different place in society than female sexism. The balance of power in this society has historically allowed men as a group to subordinate women socially and sometimes legally to protect their own interests and privileges. Because men tend to dominate this society, male sexism has more cultural legitimacy and more serious consequences than female sexism.

Consider the following quote from a female newspaper columnist:

> By whistling and yelling at attractive but insecure young men, we women may actually help them feel better about themselves, and give them new appreciation of their bodies. Some might say women were descending to the level of male street-corner oafs, but I'm willing to take that risk. If, with so little effort, I can bring joy to my fellow man, then I am willing to whistle at cute guys going down the street. (Viets, 1992)

If you're a man, these actions don't sound so bad, do they? So why do women get so upset when such behavior is directed toward them? The answer simply is that this behavior means different things to men and women.

Verbal harassment might be an enjoyable, esteem-enhancing experience for men because it doesn't have the weight of a long tradition of subordination attached to it; nor is it linked in any way to the threat of violence. Men aren't **objectified**—that is, treated like objects rather than people—as much as women are. In other words, a whistle is just a whistle. Their entire worth is not being condensed into a crude assessment of their physical appearance. To women who must still fight to be taken seriously in all areas of their social, private, and professional lives, however, whistles and lewd comments reinforce their lowly status in the stratification system. These actions serve as a reminder that their social value continues to be based primarily on their looks. Men have the luxury of knowing that, for them, this will never be so.

Sexism and Social Interaction

Social interaction has always been a more perilous venture for women than men. Sex-role stereotypes put them at a disadvantage in any exchange with men. Communication is one area of social interaction that clearly shows the effects of sexism. Women and men carry on conversations in different ways (Parlee, 1989; Tannen, 1990). For instance, women are more likely than men to use a questioning intonation at the end of a statement like, "She's a good professor, *don't you think?*" They are also more likely to use modifiers and hedges like *sort of* and *kind of*, and be excessively polite and deferential in their speech (Lakoff, 1975). Such techniques may make the speaker sound less powerful and therefore call into question the credibility and qualifications of women who happen to occupy positions of authority. Imagine if your math professor said, "The answer to the problem is 3x + y, *isn't it?*" or if your boss said, "We're going to pursue the Johnson account, *is that OK?*"

The implicit, nonverbal messages of social interaction—body movements, facial expressions, posture—also have more serious implications and consequences for women than for men. Recall from chapter 6 that nonverbal cues play an important role not only in preserving social order but in providing people with information about our social worth. Nonverbal behavior also serves to keep women "in their place." For instance, the fact that men can more freely touch women than vice versa serves as a reminder that women's bodies are free property for everyone's use:

> I have seen women swung painfully dizzy at square dances, chased by playful gangs of men and thrown in water, carried, spanked, or dunked at the beach, all clearly against their will. The cheek- and hair-patting, chin-chucking, and bottom patting and pinching continue as part of many women's daily experiences. (Henley, 1977, pp. 121–122)

In addition, women's bodily demeanor must be restrained and restricted (Henley, 1977). Femininity is gauged by how little space women take up; masculinity is judged by men's expansiveness and the strength of their gestures. What is considered "ladylike"—crossed legs, folded arms—is also a closed expression of submission. Men's freedom of movement—feet on the desk, legs spread, straddling a chair—conveys power and dominance.

Such interactional norms place women who are in authoritative positions in a no-win situation. If, on the one hand, they meet cultural definitions of femininity by being passive, polite, submissive, and vulnerable, they fail to meet the requirements of authority. If, on the other hand, they exercise their authority by being assertive, confident, dominant, and tough, their femininity is called into question (J. L. Mills, 1985).

Sexual Violence

The epitome of sexual domination expressed at the personal level is, of course, rape. Forcible rape is the most frequently committed but least reported violent crime in America today. A study funded by the U.S. Department of Health and Human Services found that 683,000 women had been raped in 1990, a figure more than five times as high as the 130,260 sexual assaults officially reported to the police that same year. Studies consistently show that close to 60% of college-aged women have been sexually assaulted after the age of 14 (Abbey, Ross, McDuffie, & McAuslan, 1996). More than 70% of rape victims in one study said they were concerned about their families discovering they had been raped, and about two-thirds worried that they might be blamed (cited in Johnston, 1992). Rape also has one of the lowest conviction rates of any violent crime: Only about 1 in 150 suspected rapists is ever found guilty (Renzetti & Curran, 1989).

Rape as a Means of Social Control

According to conflict theorists, sex stratification has long distorted our society's understanding of rape. Throughout history women have been viewed socially and legally as the property of men, either fathers or husbands. In the past, rape was seen as a crime against men or, more accurately, against men's property (S. Griffin, 1986). Any interest a husband had in a sexual assault on his wife reflected a concern with his own status, the loss of his male honor, and the devaluation of his sexual property.

According to some feminist theorists, rape and the threat of rape have also been used throughout history to keep women in their place (Brownmiller, 1975). The existence of rape limits women's freedom, denies them the right of self-determination, makes them dependent on men, and subordinates and oppresses them (S. Griffin, 1986). All forms of oppression, whether against blacks in South Africa, peasants in South America, or women in the United States, employ the threat of violence to ensure compliance (Sheffield, 1987). The subordination of women depends on the power of men to intimidate and punish sexually.

The fear of rape goes beyond simply making life uncomfortable for women. It also affects them economically by restricting opportunities. Women may avoid some neighborhoods where there is affordable housing because of potential danger. If a woman has a job that requires night work, she may be forced to buy a car to avoid walking at night or using public transportation. The threat of sexual assault limits where and when she is able to work, thereby limiting her money-earning choices and perhaps keeping her financially dependent on others.

Women are also harmed by the larger cultural ideology surrounding rape and rapists. I think most of us are inclined to believe that men who rape must be insane. The stereotypical image is one of the sex-crazed stranger hiding in bushes or in the back seat of a parked car. He is the wild-eyed psychopath bent on harming and humiliating women because of some deep-seated psychological defect. All one has to do to avoid being raped, then, is to avoid strange guys.

There is little evidence, however, that rapists as a group are any more disturbed or crazy than nonrapists (S. Griffin, 1986; Warshaw, 1988). In fact, most rapists are quite "normal" by usual societal standards. Furthermore, most are not strangers but friends or acquaintances of their victims (Abbey et al., 1996). But when rape is perceived as the fault of a small number of defective strangers, it doesn't have any effect on the dominant culture and established social arrangements. In other words, it's not the fault of society, it's the fault of flawed individuals who can't abide by society's rules. This assumption may explain why date or acquaintance rape, marital rape, and other forms of sexual violence that don't fit the typical image have, until quite recently, been ignored or trivialized.

The crime of rape must be examined within the broader cultural context that encourages certain types of behavior between men and women (Jackson, 1995). Rape then becomes less an act of deviance and more an act of overconformity to cultural expectations; less an act of defective individuals and more an act of "normal" men. As one author wrote, rape is the "All-American Crime," involving precisely those characteristics traditionally regarded as desirable in men: strength, power, domination, and control (S. Griffin, 1989).

Victim Blaming

To no one's surprise, the legal response to rape tends to be consistent with men's interests, focusing on women's complicity or blameworthiness. In rape cases, unlike any other crime, victims typically must prove their innocence rather than the state having to prove the guilt of the rapist. This situation is partly a consequence of the definition of rape, which is based on a traditional model of sexual intercourse—vaginal-penile penetration—rather than the violent context within which the act takes place. Rape is still largely viewed in terms of women's sexuality rather than men's coercion (Sheffield, 1987).

The exclusive focus on the sexual component of the crime requires that information about the circumstances of the act and about the relationship between the people involved be taken into consideration. Victims must provide some evidence that they were "unwilling" and tried to resist. No other crime requires that the victim prove lack of consent. People aren't asked if they wanted their car stolen or if they consented to being robbed. The rape laws in several states still have what are called "corroboration rules," which require that rape charges be confirmed by evidence other than the victim's testimony (Tong, 1984).

If women cannot prove that they resisted or cannot find someone to corroborate their story, consent is presumed. Anything short of vigorous and repeated resistance calls the victim's motives into question. In 1992 in Austin, Texas, a man forcibly entered a woman's apartment. The woman fled and locked herself in the bathroom. He broke down the door, held a knife to her, and demanded sex. Fearing for her life, not only because of the knife but also because of the chances of contracting a sexually transmitted disease, she begged the man to put on a condom. He agreed and went on to assault her for over an hour. The next day he was arrested for burglary with intent to commit sexual assault. In a sworn deposition he admitted that he had held a knife to her and had had sex with her. The grand jury originally refused to indict the man because the victim's act of providing a condom was taken to mean consent. Only after widespread public outrage was the man tried, convicted, and sentenced to 40 years.

Not only are women sometimes accused of not doing enough to stop rape, they are occasionally suspected of actually doing something to invite or "precipitate" it (Amir, 1971). Many people regard situations in which a woman places herself at risk—by hitchhiking, acting seductively, wearing provocative clothing, or telling dirty jokes—as a form of victim-precipitated rape. Historically, jurors in rape trials have used such thinking in their deliberations. Accused rapists have been acquitted in cases in which victims had been raped during beer-drinking parties, had willingly entered a car with several men, had hitchhiked, or had gone dancing with the men who later assaulted them (Wood, 1975). Consider this statement by a California Court of Appeals in overturning the conviction of a man who had been convicted in a lower court of picking up and raping a hitchhiker:

> The lone female hitchhiker in the absence of an emergency situation, as a practical matter, advises all who pass by that she is willing to enter the vehicle with anyone who stops and in so doing advertises that she has less concern for the consequences than the average female. Under such circumstances it would not be unreasonable for a man in the position of the defendant here to believe that the female would consent to sexual relations. (quoted in Hills, 1980, p. 65)

Research reveals a pervasive cultural belief that women provoke rape. One survey of 400 teens (Goodchilds, Zellman, Johnson, & Giarusso, 1988) found that approximately half of the boys and about 30% of the girls felt it was acceptable for a man to force sex on a woman when

- She is going to have sex with him and changes her mind.
- She has "led him on."
- She gets him sexually excited.
- They have dated for a long time.
- She lets him touch her above the waist.

In another study, male and female high school students were given a list of statements and asked to indicate the extent to which they agreed with them

(Kershner, 1996). Fifty-two percent agreed that most women fantasize about being raped by a man. Forty-six percent felt that women encourage rape by the way they dress, and 53% said they felt that some women provoke men into raping them. Thirty-one percent agreed that many women falsely report rapes. Thirty-five percent felt that the victim should be required to prove her innocence during a rape trial.

The important sociological point of these findings is that many men and even some women don't always define violent sexual assault as wrong. They think it is what men are expected to do under certain circumstances. These views have become so entrenched in this culture's view of rape that many women have internalized the message, blaming themselves for their own victimization. Outside of fear, self-blame is the most common reaction to rape and is more frequent than anger (Janoff-Bulman, 1979). When rape victims say things like, "I shouldn't have walked alone," "I should have locked my windows," or "I shouldn't have worn that dress to the party," they are at least partly taking the blame for a crime they didn't commit.

The crucial consequence of victim blaming is that women must bear most if not all of the responsibility for preventing rape. I frequently pose this question to students in my classes: What can people do to stop rape from occurring? Their responses always contain advice like: Don't hitchhike. Don't walk alone at night. Don't get drunk at parties where men are present. Don't initiate sex play. Don't engage in foreplay if you have no intention of "going all the way." Don't miscommunicate your intentions. Don't wear provocative clothing. Don't accept invitations from strangers. Note how these suggestions focus exclusively on things that women should avoid in order to prevent rape and say nothing about the things men can do to stop it.

I don't mean to imply that one ought to ignore this advice. It certainly makes sense, given the violent nature of today's society, to communicate intentions clearly and not to put oneself in dangerous situations. Indeed, some authors argue that if women don't take responsibility for protecting themselves, they're perpetuating the image of the helpless, passive victim (Roiphe, 1993). The implication of such instructions, however, speaks volumes about the nature of rape and the place of women in this society. Confining discussions of rape prevention to women's behavior suggests that if a woman doesn't take these precautions, she is "inviting trouble." And "inviting trouble" implies that violent male behavior either is a natural response or is likely to happen if certain things aren't done to discourage it. Hence, a woman cannot dress the way she wants, walk where and when she wants, talk to whom she wants, or change her mind about having sex.

Without a fundamental restructuring of society, no significant reduction in rape is likely to occur. Such a change would require a transformation of male-female relationships and childhood socialization, as well as a more equitable sharing of political and economic power. The recent increase in attention paid to rape, particularly to acquaintance or date rape, has increased public awareness. Myths are being debunked, the sexual exploitation of women in the media is being protested, and the rules governing admissible evidence in rape trials are being changed. However, as long as a deeply ingrained sexist ideology that objectifies women and glorifies male assertiveness continues to exist, so too will sexual violence.

The Ideology of Sexism

The domination of one group over another is always endorsed by a set of beliefs that explains and justifies that domination. With racism, it is the belief in innate racial inferiority; with sexism, it is the belief that biology is destiny, which leads to the subsequent cultural devaluation of women.

Biology as Destiny

You will recall from chapter 5 that sex is commonly defined in terms of the biological characteristics that distinguish males from females. The unique physiology and biological functioning of women have been used for centuries to advance the view that women's disadvantaged status in society is a function of their anatomy (Holstrom, 1982). For 19th-century physicians, few facts were more incontestable than the fact that women were the products and prisoners of their reproductive systems. Women's place in society was thought to be linked to and controlled by the existence and function of the uterus and ovaries (Scull & Favreau, 1986). Everything "abnormal" about women could be explained by their reproductive anatomy: the predominance of the emotional over the rational, the capacity for affection, the love of children and aptitude for child rearing, the preference for domestic work, and so on (Ehrenreich & English, 1979; Scull & Favreau, 1986).

Scholars at the time warned that young women who studied too much were struggling against nature, would badly damage their reproductive organs, and perhaps even go insane in the process (Fausto-Sterling, 1985). The exclusion of women from higher education was not only justifiable but necessary for health reasons and for the long-term good of society.

Such beliefs about the undesirable effects of women's biological functioning are not just a thing of the past. Many contemporary physicians and psychiatrists argue that the normal biological process of menstruation predisposes women to certain personality disorders. The Board of Trustees of the American Psychiatric Association continues to debate the inclusion of a psychiatric diagnosis called "premenstrual dysphoric disorder" in its official manual of mental disorders. (At the time of this writing it appears in the manual as a "proposed category in need of further investigation.") There is no denying that women around the world recognize irritability, moodiness, and other symptoms related to menstruation. The issue, however, is whether these symptoms ought to be labeled as a medical problem

(Lander, 1988). To do so fosters a belief that women's bodies are weak and in need of medical attention and promotes the selling of drugs to healthy women (C. A. Bailey, 1993).

Functionalist sociologists have also used the observable physical differences between men and women as the basis of their explanation of sexual inequality. The fact that men tend to be physically stronger and that women bear and nurse children has created many culturally recognized and necessary sex-segregated roles, especially at work and in the family (Parsons & Bales, 1955).

This specialization of roles is the most effective way to maintain societal stability, functionalists believe. By giving birth to new members, by socializing very young children, and by providing affection and nurturance, women make invaluable contributions to the reproduction of society. The usual occupations that women have outside the home—teacher, nurse, day care provider, maid, social worker, and so on—tend simply to be extensions of their "natural" tendencies.

Similarly, men's physical characteristics better suit them for the roles of economic provider and protector of the family. Because they are assumed to be "naturally endowed" with traits like strength, assertiveness, competitiveness, and rationality, they are best qualified to enter the serious and competitive world of work and politics (Kokopeli & Lakey, 1992). As one social scientist matter-of-factly put it, men inevitably occupy the most prestigious positions in society because they possess more testosterone—the hormone most of us associate with aggression—and therefore have a competitive advantage over women in the occupational marketplace (S. Goldberg, 1974). In short, men are assumed to be the natural power wielders and societal leaders. One study, however, has found that the higher the level of testosterone in men, the lower their occupational status (Dabbs, 1992).

By depicting masculinity and femininity as natural, biological phenomena, however, functionalists confuse sex with gender. Their message is simple and clear: Nature cannot change, so we ought not try to change it. But the assumption that gender is unchangeable overlooks the fact that extensive similarities between the sexes and extensive variation within each sex exist. The distributions of men and women on most personality and behavioral characteristics generally overlap. For instance, it's true that men as a group tend to be more aggressive than women. Yet some women are much more aggressive than the average man and some men are much less aggressive than the average woman. Indeed, social circumstances may have a greater impact on aggressive behavior than any innate, biological traits. Some studies show that when women are rewarded for behaving aggressively, they are just as violent as men (Hyde, 1984).

This assumption also overlooks the power of socialization to shape behavior. In just the past few decades, for instance, women have been socialized to be more assertive and ambitious. The rapidity of this change is inconsistent with the slow pace of evolutionary, biological changes.

Furthermore, the reliance on biology overlooks the wide cultural and histori-cal variation in conceptions of masculinity and femininity. For instance, every known society has a division of labor based on sex. But what's considered "men's work" and "women's work" differs from society to society. In most societies, men fish, hunt, clear land, and build boats and houses; but in some societies these tasks are performed regularly by women. In most societies women do the cook-ing; but in some societies this is typically a male responsibility (Eitzen & Baca-Zinn, 1991).

▪ ▪ ▪ ▪ ▪ ▪ ▪ ▪

MARGARET MEAD

Sex and Temperament

The famous anthropologist Margaret Mead (1963) believed that masculine and feminine characteristics are based mostly on cultural conditioning. She set out to support her theory by studying three cultures in New Guinea. Among the moun-tain-dwelling Arapesh, men and women displayed similar attitudes and actions. They showed traits we would commonly associate with femininity: cooperation, passivity, sensitivity to others. Mead described both men and women as being "maternal." These characteristics were linked to broader cultural beliefs about people's relationship to the environment. The Arapesh didn't have any conception of "ownership" of land, so there were never conflicts over possession of property.

South of the Arapesh were the Mundugumor, a group of cannibals and head-hunters. Here, too, males and females were similar. However, both displayed traits that we in the West would associate with masculinity: assertiveness, emotional in-expressiveness, insensitivity to others. Women, according to Mead, were just as violent, just as aggressive, and just as jealous as men. Both were equally virile, without any of the "soft" characteristics we associate with femininity.

Finally, there were the Tchambuli. This group did distinguish between male and female traits. However, their gender expectations were the opposite of what we have here. Women were the ones who were dominant, shrewd, assertive, and managerial; men were submissive, emotional, and seen as inherently delicate.

Mead's work is important because it shows that definitions of the natural ten-dencies of men and women vary from culture to culture. Women need not be the nurturers of children; men need not be the aggressors. Both engage in behaviors different from those in Western cultures yet are still considered men and women.

▪ ▪ ▪

In sum, the biological rationale for sexual inequality is difficult to justify. Tech-nological advances, including bottled baby formula and contraceptives that reduce women's childbearing and child-rearing responsibilities, and improved mechanization that lessens the need for sheer physical strength, have made the biological imperative for gender-based role responsibilities obsolete (Gough, 1971). Nevertheless, as long as people believe that gender-linked roles and societal contributions are determined by nature, they will continue to accept sexual inequality in opportunities, expectations, and outcomes. If it is considered "natural" for women to play nurturant, weak, and dependent roles, then structurally limiting them to such positions seems neither unfair nor oppressive.

The Cultural Devaluation of Women

If biology is not destiny, then we must look to culture to explain the unequal treatment of women. Anthropologists agree that despite cross-cultural differences in gender expectations, most societies devalue women to some extent (Stockard & Johnson, 1992). At first glance, it may appear that women have been making tremendous advances around the world—becoming more economically independent, better educated, and more involved in national politics than ever before. Nevertheless, women represent 70% of the 1.3 billion people living in poverty worldwide, even though they work an average of 13% more hours than men in every country ("Vital signs," 1995). About 585,000 women around the world die each year in pregnancy and childbirth, and perhaps as many as 18 million more suffer debilitating illnesses or injuries as a consequence of childbearing (Crossette, 1996a). Women make up the vast majority of global factory workers in multinational corporations, often working under unsafe and unhealthy conditions at extremely low pay.

In some societies the extreme consequences of female devaluation affect not only their economic well-being, but their health and even their survival. As you read in chapter 4, perhaps as many as 100 million women worldwide have undergone female genital mutilation. In Bangladesh, land laws dictate that a family's property can be passed down only through males. A daughter's inheritance automatically goes to her husband upon marriage. Families short on food will commonly see to it that the male children are well fed, often at the expense of female children. Nationwide, girls get 16% less food than boys, even though their nutritional needs are the same. As a result, girls grow up sicker. Many female babies are so undernourished that they die within the first year (Bryjak & Soroka, 1992).

The cultural devaluation of women can have even more violent consequences. One of the most pernicious forms of wife abuse—known locally as "bride burning" or "dowry deaths"—takes place in India (Heise, 1989; Van Willigen & Channa, 1991). Dowry traditionally referred to the gifts that a woman received from her parents upon marriage. Even though it was officially banned in 1961, dowry is still an essential part of premarital negotiations and now refers to the wealth that the bride's family pays the groom. In many cases it has become a get-rich-quick scheme for men and their families. Young brides, who by custom live with their new husbands' parents, are commonly subjected to severe abuse if promised money is not paid. Sometimes dowry harassment ends in suicide or murder. In 1994, about 6,200 wives—an average of 17 a day—were killed by their husbands for not providing adequate dowries ("Vital signs," 1995). Often the husband and his family try to disguise the murder as an accident by setting the wife on fire and then claiming she died in a kitchen mishap. In the city of Bombay, 19% of all deaths among women 15 to 44 years old are due to "accidental burns" (Heise, 1989).

In our society the cultural devaluation of women is not usually so life threatening. Here devaluation is manifested in beliefs that women are less capable than men in performing many tasks outside the home (Wagner, Ford, & Ford, 1986). People still find female doctors or dentists unusual and debate the role of female soldiers in combat. The controversy in both the Episcopal and Catholic churches over whether or not women should be ordained as ministers illustrates the depth and intensity of people's feelings about gender-appropriate career pursuits. Female devaluation, however, is not just a matter of men subjugating women. Women also come to expect certain things in their lives that affect not only the perceptions of others but their self-perceptions as well.

Moreover, the qualities we consider feminine are usually seen as less socially valuable than those considered masculine. Girls do suffer sometimes when their behavior is considered "boylike." But for a boy to be called a girl is the ultimate schoolyard insult because it implies weakness, frailty, and lack of ability. Even today, many men can be easily whipped into anger by accusations of femininity, as when drill sergeants or football coaches call their male soldiers or players "girls" or "ladies" to draw out their aggressiveness.

The devaluation of women, and therefore all things "feminine," even influences the cultural value of certain emotions. We think of love as involving emotional expressiveness, verbal self-disclosure, and affection (Cancian, 1987). Clearly these are qualities associated with women. The desirable masculine traits—independence, competence, emotional inexpressiveness—usually imply the antithesis of love. It is no coincidence, then, that our society tends to glorify achievement and downplay emotional expression as overly sentimental and foolish. When we think of love in such a way, men's power over women is strengthened. Women are encouraged to specialize in and be emotionally responsible for romantic relationships, whereas men are expected to specialize in work activities, which are more highly regarded in society.

■ ■ ■ ■ ■ ■ ■ ■

MICRO-MACRO CONNECTION

Women in Japan

Sometimes, the public devaluation of women hides a very different private reality. In Japan, for instance, women have historically occupied a visibly subservient position in society. A woman may still walk several steps behind her husband so as not to offend his dignity by stepping on his shadow (Kristof, 1995). Wives are legally prohibited from using different surnames than their husbands.

In the 1980s, Japan's equal rights movement and a booming economy sent many women surging into the workplace, although most were "office flowers"—submissive part-time workers who smiled sweetly, talked softly, poured tea, and answered telephones. The current economic slump in Japan, however, has forced many women back out of the workforce and into their prior domestic roles. Those who remain in the workforce suffer discrimination in hiring, salary, and promotion despite an equal opportunity law. One company newsletter advises women who are thinking about getting married to "submit a letter of resignation one month before the wedding" (quoted in WuDunn, 1995, p. 3).

Yet, things now look very different within the Japanese home. Even though women are still expected to clean, cook, and tend to the needs of their husbands, they exercise a surprising degree of power and authority. Many wives dominate their husbands completely, referring to them as "oversize trash." Typically, they control the household finances, giving their husbands monthly allowances as they see fit. Recent surveys have found that about half of Japanese men are dissatisfied with the amount of their allowances. Many wives refuse to give their husbands cash cards for the family account. If a man wants to withdraw money from the account, the savings bank will usually phone the wife to get her approval. Japanese men are even starting to take on some of the housework responsibilities, a development that would have been unthinkable a decade ago. One man summed up the situation this way: "Things go best when the husband is swimming in the palm of his wife's hand" (quoted in Kristof, 1995, p. A6).

■ ■ ■

Sexism and Cultural Symbolism

An explanation of sexist ideology wouldn't be complete without some mention of the cultural images that contribute to the subordination and devaluation of women. In large part, these images come from the media. You saw in chapter 5 that the media's portrayal of men and women contributes to early gender socialization. But, as women are underrepresented and, more important, misrepresented in the media, these images can also be dangerous and demeaning (Cantor, 1987).

A glimpse at the portrayal of women in advertising, fashion, television, music videos, and films today reveals that the image of the modern woman is a dual one (Sidel, 1990). On the one hand, there is the successful woman of the nineties: the perfect wife/mother/career woman, the triumphant professional who leaps gracefully about the pages of fashion magazines. Like the popular television character Murphy Brown, she is outgoing, bright, attractive, and assertive. No occupation is beyond her reach: She can be a lawyer, doctor, politician, executive, police officer, or entrepreneur.

On the other hand, there is the stereotypical image of the exhibited woman. She is the seductive sex object displayed in beer commercials, magazine advertisements, soap operas, and the swimsuit issue of *Sports Illustrated.* According to a recent study by the National Commission on Working Women, television continues to present stereotypes that show women as shallow, vain, and materialistic characters whose looks still count for more than their brains (cited in Sidel, 1990). The sex object is the most dangerous media image of all because conventional beauty is her only attribute: "Women are constantly exhorted to emulate this ideal, to feel ashamed and guilty if they fail, and to feel that their desirability and lovability are contingent upon physical perfection" (Kilbourne, 1992, p. 349).

It is no surprise, then, that beauty pageants, the epitome of the exhibition of women, continue to be popular in our country. Tens of thousands of women compete in local and state pageants for a shot at the title of Miss America. An estimated 55 million people, 75% of whom are women, tune in each year to watch the Miss America Pageant (Sidel, 1990). Many women watch to find out what an attractive female is supposed to look like (Freedman, 1986).

The image of beauty presented by the exhibited woman is artificial and largely unattainable. For instance, the body sizes of the winners of the Miss America Pageant have been steadily decreasing over the past 20 years, reaffirming the cultural value of thinness (Garner, Garfinkel, Schwartz, & Thompson, 1980). Women are encouraged to view themselves as in constant need of alteration, improvement, and disguise. Hence they will go to great lengths to change their faces and bodies (Kilbourne, 1992). Any doubt that such images have an effect on the activities and self-concepts of young women is quickly dispelled by the statistics on eating disorders in America and the number of school-age girls who diet.

It is conservatively estimated that one in five young American women today has an eating disorder. A recent survey of students in Chicago-area schools found that more than half the fourth-grade girls were dieting and three-quarters felt they were overweight (cited in Kilbourne, 1992). A *Glamour* magazine survey in 1984 found that over 75% of the respondents considered themselves overweight. What is more telling is that nearly half of the women in this survey, who were in reality underweight, reported feeling too fat and wanting to diet. Sticklike standards of beauty have become an ideal many young women are ready to starve themselves to attain (cited in Kilbourne, 1992).

These media messages are confusing and can be, as in the case of eating disorders, lethal. Young women today not only must achieve at unprecedented levels, but they also must look sexy doing it. These images create the illusion that success or failure is purely a personal, private achievement and ignore the complex social, economic, and political forces that continue to operate and prevent real-life women from achieving the success that artificial media images seem to enjoy so easily.

Institutions and Sexual Inequality

The subordination of women that is part of the workings of social institutions (or **institutional sexism**) has far greater consequences for women as a group than personal sexism or media images do. As we have seen throughout this book, the experiences of individuals must always be located within an institutional structure. The law, the family, and the organization of work all have a role in producing gender stratification (M. Brinton, 1988). Most institutions have historically been developed by men, dominated by men, and interpreted by men. The only institution in which women have had a central role is the family, but as we will see, that role has traditionally been a subordinate one (Acker, 1992). When sexism in social institutions becomes part of the ongoing operation of large-scale organizations, it perpetuates and magnifies women's structural disadvantages, making social equality all the more difficult to attain.

Not only are social institutions sexist—in that women are sometimes segregated, exploited, or excluded—they are also gendered. In other words, institutions and organizations themselves are structured along gender lines. Take sports, for example. Most of us would agree that to compete successfully an athlete must be aggressive, strong, and powerful—attributes typically associated with men. By celebrating these traits, a sport like football symbolically declares an arena that women cannot or should not enter. But even sports like gymnastics that have traditionally valued more "feminine" traits like grace, beauty, and balance have changed their rules to accommodate more power and strength. Simply being graceful is no longer enough for a woman to be a world-class gymnast. She must also exhibit explosive acrobatic power. Indeed, the recent growth in the popularity of women's sports in this country (basketball, soccer, softball, and so on) coincides with the increasing physical strength and competitive vigor of female athletes.

Similarly, most bureaucracies in institutional areas like business, politics, and the military operate according to masculine principles:

> This "masculine ethic" elevates the traits assumed to belong to men . . . to necessities for effective organizations: a tough-minded approach to problems; analytic abilities to abstract and plan; a capacity to set aside personal, emotional considerations in the interests of task accomplishment; a cognitive superiority in problem-solving and decision making. (Kanter, 1975, p. 43)

Successful leaders and organizations are usually portrayed as aggressive, goal oriented, competitive, and efficient, all characteristics we associate with masculinity in this society. Rarely are prosperous businesses or efficient departments in the military described as supportive, nurturant, cooperative, kind, and caring (Acker, 1992).

Sexism and the Law

Historically women have been denied many of the legal rights that men take for granted. In 1894, for instance, the U.S. Supreme Court heard the case of Belva Lockwood, who was denied a license to practice law even though the state of Virginia permitted any "person" licensed as an attorney in any other state to practice there. The court ruled against Lockwood, stating that the word *person* meant "male" (Renzetti & Curran, 1989).

In the past, when women got married, they lost many of the legal rights they enjoyed as single women: legal title to their property, the right to execute contracts, and so forth. Husbands could chastise their wives, force them to stay at home, and even rape them without legal sanction. Such laws were based on the English common law doctrine of "coverture," under which a married woman's legal identity was submerged into that of her husband (Baron, 1987).

We don't have to go back a century to find attempts at limiting the legal rights of women. In 1981 a bill called the Family Protection Act was introduced in Congress. Although the bill was never passed, its objective was to dismantle many of the legal achievements of the women's movement. Among its proposals were eliminating federal laws supporting equal education, forbidding the "intermingling of the sexes in any sport or other school-related activities," requiring marriage and motherhood to be taught as the proper career for girls, denying federal funding to any school using textbooks portraying women in nontraditional roles, repealing all federal laws protecting battered wives from their husbands, and banning all federally funded legal aid for any women seeking abortion counseling or divorce (Faludi, 1991). In addition, through an extra tax on spouses who file separate income tax returns, the bill encouraged a family structure with a working husband and nonworking wife (Ruether, 1980).

To counteract a long history of legal inequality, Congress has passed many laws aimed at improving the situation of women in this society. The 1964 Civil Rights Act focused on sexism in employment. The 1974 Educational Amendments Act focused on gender equality in education. Obstacles to equality have been removed in other areas like housing, eligibility for credit, and hiring practices (Eitzen & Baca-Zinn, 1989). The 1993 Family Leave Act guarantees some working mothers (as well as fathers) up to 12 weeks of unpaid sick leave per year to care for a new child or a sick relative.

The courts have also made several noteworthy decisions that addressed women's concerns. In 1993, the U.S. Supreme Court ruled that victims of workplace harassment could win lawsuits without having to prove that the offensive behavior left them psychologically damaged—which in the past meant either a documented nervous breakdown or psychiatric hospitalization—or unable to do their jobs. Now workers only need prove that as a result of harassment the workplace environment "would reasonably be perceived as hostile or abusive" (Greenhouse, 1993). In 1996, the Court ruled that all-male public colleges and universities have to admit women.

But these court decisions and laws haven't been entirely effective. Occupations are still highly segregated along gender lines; female workers still earn a fraction of what male workers earn; college athletic budgets are still highly skewed toward men's sports; and a woman's right to control her own body through legal abortion continues to be challenged.

Even laws explicitly designed to protect women's rights have created unforeseen disadvantages. Divorce laws, which were written to make the termination of marriages more fair, have actually increased the number of women who become poor after a divorce (Arendell, 1984; Weitzman, 1985). As we discussed in chapter 10, divorced husbands typically experience an increase in their standard of living, while divorced wives suffer a decrease. In California, for instance, after no-fault divorce laws were enacted, only 13% of mothers with preschool children received spousal support (cited in Tavris, 1992). The situation for divorced women, particularly older women, was so bad that the California legislature had to pass the Displaced Homemakers Relief Act, which required judges to consider the future earning potential of each spouse before awarding a settlement.

Not all legislation aimed at giving women equal legal rights has met with public approval. In 1982 the Equal Rights Amendment, which would have made unconstitutional state and federal laws that treat men and women unequally, was defeated. The defeat of the ERA is a classic example of how powerful the control of perceptions of reality and definitions of situations can be. The amendment consisted of a single sentence: "Equality of rights under the law shall not be denied or abridged by the United States or any State on account of sex." Opponents claimed the amendment would destroy American life by, among other things, integrating public bathrooms, forcing women to fight in the military, and destroying the family. One group called the amendment one of "the most destructive pieces of legislation ever to pass Congress" and referred to feminists as "moral perverts" and "enemies of every decent society" (Spretnak, 1982).

Sexism and the Family

Much of the sexual inequality found in the law revolves around the traditional family role of women as the producer and socializer of children. Women have always retained the responsibility of reproduction; it is one of the few areas in society where women can exert tremendous societal influence (Rowland, 1990). Motherhood has always been considered the pinnacle of a woman's social identity and her God-given and socially expected duty. This role can be the source of pride, joy, and a sense of accomplishment, but it can also be the source of pain, exploitation, and discrimination.

Reproductive Technology and Fetal Rights

Although the institution of family is idealized in our society, reproduction is relatively invisible and devalued until it fails to function, and then it is likely to become the focus of criticism (Acker, 1992). Traditionally, the only reproductive issue facing women was choice: the right to have or not to have children. Thirty years ago, feminists fought to protect women's right to have children by opposing organized efforts at the forced sterilization of some women. Later, they fought to ensure women's right *not* to bear children by fighting for universal access to contraception and abortion.

Today the issue of reproductive choice is much more complicated. Technological developments like in vitro fertilization and surrogate motherhood have allowed thousands of infertile women to conceive children. Although access is limited primarily to the affluent—some procedures can cost as much as $20,000—these techniques have the potential of increasing the reproductive choices and opportunities available to women (B. K. Rothman, 1987; Rowland, 1990).

Ironically, such advances, coupled with our culture's inability to accept infertility, make it increasingly more difficult for women to choose not to have children and may in fact actually take away their reproductive control. Increased technological intervention into the processes by which women conceive has allowed the male-dominated medical profession to control the reproductive process (Rowland, 1990; Woliver, 1989).

Men tend to benefit professionally and economically from these developments. Because of the cultural value placed on children, fertility research has faced virtually no criticism and has been allowed to expand with little community debate (Rowland, 1990). After all, who would criticize research that could provide infertile couples with the miracle of a baby? Consequently, the predominantly male field of high-tech fertility is flourishing. In only a decade the industry has grown from 30 clinics to more than 300. It is a $350-million-a-year business that is largely exempt from government regulation and immune to the downward pressure on costs that insurance companies exert (Gabriel, 1996). At some hospitals, fertility doctors earn more than the hospital presidents.

Unfortunately, women are the ones who serve as experimental subjects. Their bodies become "alternative reproductive vehicles," "human incubators," or "uterine environments" within which "harvested" eggs can be planted (Raymond, 1993). Women must also face most of the emotional and physical risks, which include infection, painful side effects, permanent physical injury, or the heartbreak of failure.

When women become pregnant, they often find that their rights are considered secondary to those of their unborn children. The contemporary debate that pits fetal rights against women's rights illustrates the growing public desire to place women's reproductive capacities under governmental control. In the 19th century, women were restricted from all sorts of activities (including higher education) out of concern that too much knowledge might affect their ability to reproduce. We no longer hold such beliefs, but a vast array of policies, laws, and practices still protect fetal rights over and above women's rights. Employers, hospitals, and local, state, and federal governments have even imposed new limits on pregnant women (C. R. Daniels, 1993).

The emphasis on fetal rights gives the fetus an individual identity, asserting its equality with the woman—and perhaps, according to some, its superiority (Roth, 1993). Women are seen to have a moral, societal, and legal responsibility to ensure a healthy birth. Consequently, pregnant women are often denied the rights of bodily integrity and self-determination that all competent adults in this society are granted (Tavris, 1992). Consider these recent court cases:

- A Washington, D.C., judge ordered a pregnant woman seriously ill with cancer to undergo a cesarean section against her wishes and those of her husband, her parents, and her doctor, in order to save the life of her 25-week-old fetus. She and the fetus died during the procedure, which was performed hastily, before her lawyers could appeal.
- A Wisconsin woman was charged with attempted murder for giving birth to a baby with a blood alcohol level twice the threshold for a legal finding of intoxication. The mother had long had a drinking problem and had been drinking heavily the night of the birth (Terry, 1996).
- A South Carolina woman was convicted of child abuse and sentenced to eight years in prison for using cocaine while pregnant ("Prenatal drug use," 1996).

Cases like these show the extent to which society has come to define women as the major threat to the health of their newborns. Since the late 1980s more than 200 women in 30 states have been prosecuted for behavior while pregnant that posed a danger to their fetuses, the vast majority involving the use of illegal drugs (Terry, 1996). Women's behavior has thus become the most urgent political target in the fight to protect children.

From an institutional perspective, focusing solely on pregnant women allows us to ignore other dangers and other threats to the well-being of children that lie outside the mother's body: poverty, inadequate health care, poor housing, environmental hazards, racism, and so on. One in five pregnant women today lack access to any sort of prenatal health care (Pollitt, 1991), yet such facts are overlooked in the pursuit of fetal rights. Controlling the behavior of mothers allows the government to appear concerned about babies without having to spend any money, change any priorities, or challenge any vested interests (Pollitt, 1991). But as we become more obsessed with pregnant women's behavior, the health and well-being of American children continues to decline. Like poverty, homelessness, and crime, the health of children is construed as a matter of freely chosen individual behavior: "We have crime because we have lots of bad people, poverty because we have lots of lazy people . . . and tiny, sickly, impaired babies because we have lots of women who just don't give a damn" (Pollitt, 1991, p. 243).

Once a problem is defined this way, coercion and punishment come to be seen as justifiable and necessary responses. I'm not suggesting that using drugs or smoking cigarettes while pregnant is a good thing to do. But the problem of infant sickness must be placed in the larger institutional context:

> The concept of fetal rights . . . posits a world in which women will be held accountable, on sketchy or no evidence, for birth defects; . . . in which courts, employers, social workers and doctors—not to mention nosy neighbors and vengeful male partners—will monitor women's behavior. It imposes responsibilities without giving women the wherewithal to fulfill them, and places upon women alone duties that belong to both parents and to the community. (Pollitt, 1991, p. 251)

Housework and the Domestic Division of Labor

One of the major consequences of the Industrial Revolution of the late 19th and early 20th centuries was the separation of work and home. Prior to industrialization, the nation's economy was primarily agricultural. People's lives centered around the farm, where husbands and wives were partners not only in making a home but in making a living (Vanek, 1980). The farm couple was interdependent; each needed the other for survival. Women therefore played a crucial role in the family economy by producing the basic necessities. It was taken for granted that women provided for the family along with men (Bernard, 1981). Although the relationship between husbands and wives on the farm was never entirely equal—wives still did most if not all of the housekeeping and family care—complete male dominance was offset by women's indispensable contributions to the household economy (Vanek, 1980).

With the advent of industrialization, things began to change. New forms of technology and the promise of new financial opportunities and a good living drew men away from the farms and into cities and factories. For the first time in American history, the family economy was based outside the household. Women no longer found themselves involved in the day-to-day supervision of the family's business as they had once been. Instead, they were consigned to the only domestic responsibilities that remained: the care and nurturance of children and the maintenance of the household. Because this work was unpaid and because visible goods were no longer being produced at home, women quickly found that their work was devalued in an industrial economy (Hareven, 1992).

The devaluation of women's work is also the result of the difference in power between the public and private spheres (Sidel, 1990). As long as men have a monopoly over the public sphere, they will wield greater economic and political power within society and also be able to translate that power into authority at home. "Women's work" within the relatively powerless private sphere will continue to be hidden, free, and of little social value.

It's not that housewives don't work, it's that they work outside the mainstream economy, in which work is strictly defined as something one is paid to do (Ciancanelli & Berch, 1987; Voyandoff, 1990). If a woman were to be paid for all her labor as mother and housekeeper according to the actual pay scales for the jobs she does—chauffeur, nurse, day care worker, maid, cook, therapist—her yearly salary would be over $50,000, substantially more than the salaries of most male full-time workers. In 1990 unpaid household work was equal to about 44% of the gross national product, or over $1 trillion (Strong & DeVault, 1992). However, because societal and family power are a function of who earns the money, such work does not afford women the prestige it might if it were paid labor.

Despite significant shifts in attitudes toward gender roles and the accelerated entry of women into the paid labor force, housework continues to be predominantly female (Brines, 1994). Husbands do play a more prominent role in the raising of children than they did two decades ago, but they've made smaller changes in the area of housework. Research has consistently shown that women spend about 50 hours a week doing housework, while men contribute a maximum of about 11 hours (Cowan, 1991; Levant, Slatter, & Loiselle, 1987). Moreover, the housework men do tends to be quite different from the work their wives are doing:

> They take out the garbage, they mow the lawns, they play with children, they occasionally go to the supermarket or shop for household durables, they paint the attic or fix the faucet; but by and large, they do not launder, clean, or cook, nor do they feed, clothe, bathe, or transport children. These . . . most time-consuming activities . . . are exclusively the domain of women. (Cowan, 1991, p. 207)

One could argue that traditional gender disparities in household responsibilities actually reflect an equitable, functional, interdependent division of labor. That is, the husband works in the paid labor force and supports the family financially; the wife takes care of the household work and child care. Each person provides essential services in exchange for those provided by the other. But if this were the case, you would expect housework to be shared equally if both partners work full-time. Research in this area, though, indicates that the gender discrepancy in housework responsibilities does not diminish when women work full-time. Several recent national studies have found that, on average, working women spend over 33 hours a week on housework compared to 18 hours a week for their husbands (Lennon & Rosenfield, 1994; South & Spitze, 1994). The discrepancy is especially large among married couples (see Figure 13.1).

Working women continue to be primarily responsible for housework and end up working what amounts to two full-time jobs. Even if a husband is unemployed, he does much less housework than a wife who puts in a 40-hour week. Interestingly, this is the case even among couples who profess egalitarian, nonsexist values. Husbands who say that all the housework should be shared still spend significantly less time doing it than their wives (Blumstein & Schwartz, 1983).

The fact that housework is still predominantly women's work gives us some sense of how pervasive and powerful our sexist ideology continues to be. Men's aversion to housework may be so intense that it can sour a relationship. The

Figure 13.1   *Mean Hours Spent Doing Housework, by Gender and Marital Status*

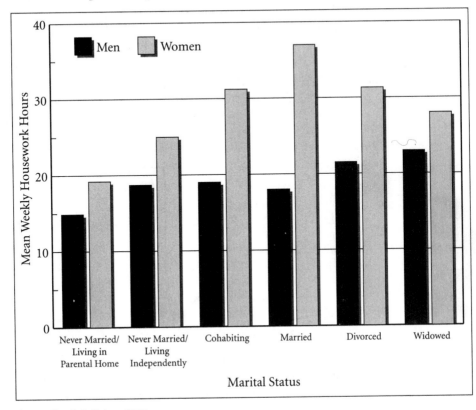

Source: South & Spitze, 1994.

more housework married men do, the more conflict there is in the marriage (Blumstein & Schwartz, 1983). Such a pattern may serve as a significant barrier to the reorganization of gender roles within the family.

Sexism and the Economy

Family obligations that keep women out of the paid labor force or that restrict their opportunities once they enter it promote economic inequality between men and women (Acker, 1988). In turn, economic well-being influences many aspects of a person's life, including political power, access to education, relationship satisfaction, and physical and emotional health.

Women have historically been prevented from taking advantage of the occupational opportunities and rewards to which most men have had free access. Today women continue to have much less earning power in the American labor market than men (Blood, Tuttle, & Lakey, 1992). About two-thirds of all poor people in this country are women. Institutional sexism is most vividly felt within the work sphere, for that is where discrimination can be measured in dollars and career mobility.

The unequal economic status of women not only results from personal expressions of sexism but is tied to larger economic structures and institutional forces. The standard assumptions that drive the typical workplace often work against women. Think of the things you have to do in order to be considered a good worker by your boss: You may have to work extra hours, travel to faraway business meetings, go to conferences, attend training programs, be willing to work unpopular shifts, or entertain out-of-town clients. These activities assume you have the time and the freedom from familial obligations to do them. Because women, especially mothers, still tend to have the lion's share of responsibility at home, they have more difficulty making time for these activities and therefore are less able to "prove" to management that they are good, committed employees. Because of the built-in assumptions about what one needs to do to get ahead, women are less likely than men to possess the qualities commonly associated with an "ideal worker."

Sex Segregation in the Workplace

In view of the persistence of sexism, women have made remarkable progress in overcoming traditional obstacles to employment. Today, over 70% of all women between the ages of 18 and 64 work in the paid labor force (Baca-Zinn & Eitzen, 1993). Close to half of all American workers today are female (Reskin & Padavic, 1994). These workers make a significant contribution to their families. In a recent survey, more than half of employed women said they provided at least half of their household income, and 18% said they were their household's sole provider (cited in Lewin, 1995). Today one-third of all U.S. businesses, employing over 13 million people, are owned by women (U.S. Bureau of the Census, 1996).

Over the past several decades women have increased their representation in the paid labor force worldwide (see Figure 13.2). In the United States, this increase has been particularly dramatic in male-dominated fields like engineering, medicine, law, and administration (Reskin & Hartmann, 1986). The representation of women in skilled trades has increased by over 80% (Sidel, 1986). Figure 13.3 shows the increase in the number of women in a variety of professional occupations.

Although such figures are encouraging, sex segregation in the workplace is still the rule and not the exception. Almost half of all employed women work in occupations that are at least 80% female—as librarians, nurses, elementary school teachers, secretaries, and so on (Philipson, 1993; Reskin & Hartmann, 1986). According to the U.S. Bureau of the Census (1995a), women constitute 98% of all secretaries, 93.8% of all registered nurses, 97.3% of all child care workers, 100% of all dental hygienists, and 75% of all teachers, excluding those in colleges and universities. On the other hand, women make up only 13.3% of all

Figure 13.2 *Worldwide Women's Share in Major Occupational Groups, 1980 and 1990*

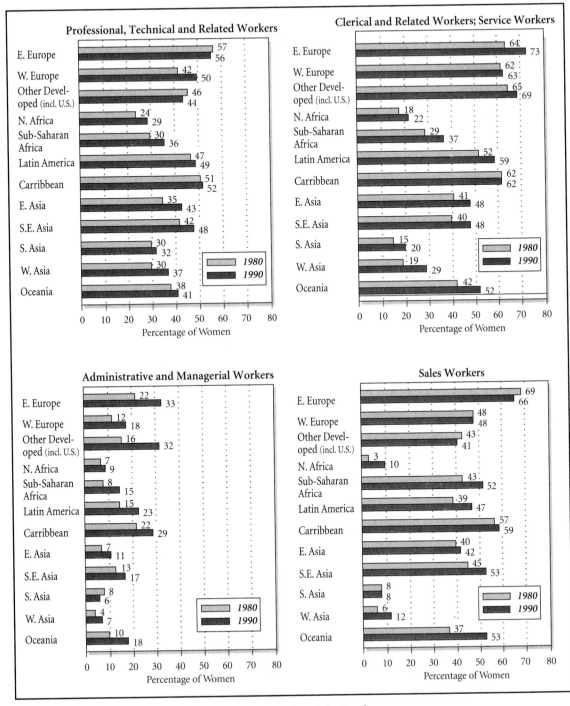

Source: United Nations Secretariate, Women's Indicators and Statistics Database.

Figure 13.3   *Trends in Proportion of Women in Managerial and Professional Jobs*

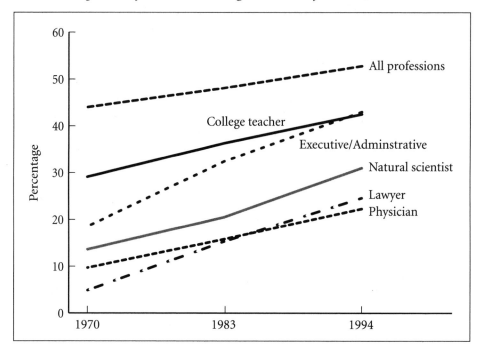

Source: U.S. Bureau of Labor Statistics, 1985, 1989; U.S. Bureau of the Census, 1995a.

dentists, 22.3% of all physicians, 8.3% of all engineers, 24.8% of all lawyers and judges, and 15.6% of all police officers. It's estimated that about two-thirds of American men and women would have to change jobs today in order to achieve equal gender distribution across occupations, a figure that was the same in 1900 (Philipson, 1993).

Most of the changes that have taken place in the sex distribution of different occupations have been due to women entering male lines of work. Although women have entered traditionally male occupations at a steady clip since the 1970s, men have not noticeably increased their representation in female-dominated occupations. The number of male nurses, kindergarten teachers, librarians, and secretaries has increased only minimally, if at all (Reskin & Hartmann, 1986). One recent study found that some men would rather suffer unemployment than accept "women's jobs," even if they are high-paying ones, because of the potential damage to their masculinity (Epstein, 1989).

This kind of "one-way" occupational shift may ultimately lead to the resegregation of the workforce. Historically, when large numbers of women enter a particular occupation previously closed to them, there is an accompanying decrease in the number of men in that occupation. Given the fact that in this society greater value is usually awarded to male pursuits, such occupations become less prestigious as men leave them. In fact, the higher the proportion of female workers in an occupation, the less both male and female workers earn (Reskin & Padavic, 1994).

During the early part of this century, for example, the job of bank teller was a well-respected and exclusively male occupation. Between World War I and World War II, however, bank telling was de-skilled, meaning that what started as a relatively complex job was broken down into simpler tasks. Within the bank structure, a hierarchy of jobs was created, which meant a hierarchy in salaries. Women were more willing than men to work for lower wages and were viewed by employers as appropriate for the work assignments at the lower end of the hierarchy. By the beginning of World War II, women had come to hold 37% of all bank teller positions (Philipson, 1993). This figure increased even more during the war as women were hired to replace men who had entered the military.

The nature of banking was also changing. Prior to World War II, banks primarily served corporations and wealthy individuals. Few people had checking accounts. During the Depression and war years, however, banks began offering services to larger segments of the population in order to provide people with greater access to funds. They introduced economy checking accounts with no minimum balance requirements, made installment loans for consumer purchases, real estate, and small business investments, and began accepting phone and utility payments (Philipson, 1993). Between 1939 and 1952 the number of checking accounts in the United States nearly doubled. Consequently, banks expanded their number of branches and, in turn, the number of bank employees.

This shift from "class" to "mass" banking further eroded the status of bank telling; as its status declined, so too did the bank tellers' wages. Bank telling ultimately lost its attractiveness to male employees. After the war, men did not reclaim these jobs. By 1950 women filled almost half of all bank telling positions. By 1990, 90% of bank tellers were women (Philipson, 1993; Reskin & Padavic, 1994).

Greater female entry into a traditionally male line of work doesn't necessarily mean gender equality. A recent report by the American Bar Association states that the average annual incomes of women lawyers are significantly lower than men's at every level of experience and at all types of legal practice (cited in N. Bernstein, 1996). Their rate of promotion is lower than that of their male counterparts, and they remain underrepresented in high positions like judges on the federal courts, district courts, and circuit courts of appeals.

Furthermore, segregation within occupations is still strong. For instance, although half of all assemblers in the manufacturing industry are now women—a fact that suggests occupational integration—they make up 75% of electrical assemblers but only 17% of motor vehicle assemblers, which is a higher-paying job (Reskin & Hartmann, 1986). Women who work as sales clerks in department stores are likely to be in the lower-paying departments (for example, clothing and housewares), whereas men are likely to be in the more lucrative departments (for example, furniture and large appliances). Female physicians are substantially over-represented in specialties like pediatrics, obstetrics, and gynecology and under-represented in more prestigious and lucrative areas like neurosurgery (Patterson & Engelberg, 1978).

Such within-occupation segregation reinforces gender stereotypes. A study of jobs in a McDonald's restaurant found that despite roughly the same number of male and female workers, most of the women worked at the counter or the drive-up window and most of the men worked at the grill. Many of the workers found this arrangement unremarkable. They simply assumed that women were more interested in working with people and that the job requirements of smiling and showing deference to customers was best suited to a feminine style of interaction (Leidner, 1991).

Many women who "buck the system" and enter traditionally male occupations find they must continuously battle their marginal status and the differential treatment resulting from it. They may also find that they have been hired for highly visible positions only to give the business the outward appearance of equality.

■ ■ ■ ■ ■ ■ ■ ■
MICRO-MACRO CONNECTION
Tokenism in the Workplace

In the early years of the women's liberation movement, sociologist Rosabeth Moss Kanter (1977) observed and interviewed over a period of five years employees at a large industrial supply company she called Industrial Supply Corporation. She used the word *tokens* to refer to the relatively few women given prominent positions in a particular occupational setting.

Whether they are women, minorities, people with handicaps, or the elderly, tokens are often treated as symbols or representatives of the marginal social group to which they belong. As a result, their thoughts, beliefs, and actions are likely to be taken as typical of all in their social group. Some women at Industrial Supply Corporation were even told that their job performance could affect the prospects of other women in the company. In short, the token is less an individual than a social category.

Tokens must perform their jobs under conditions very different from those facing other workers. Consequently, token status has important social and psychological consequences. The token doesn't have to work hard to be noticed, but she does have to work hard to have her achievements noticed. Many of the women Kanter studied told of situations in which their abilities were eclipsed by their physical appearance, creating additional performance pressures.

Token women also experienced the added pressure of trying not to make male co-workers look bad, of trying not to perform too well on group tasks. But because of their visibility, their actions can never be hidden. The irony is that, while they must work twice as hard just to be seen as competent, they also feel that their successes should be kept to themselves. There is a fine line between doing just well enough and too well (Kanter, 1977).

The choice is either to turn their noticeability to their advantage or to try to become socially invisible. To limit visibility is to risk being overlooked; to take advantage of publicity is to risk being labeled a troublemaker.

Kanter also found that tokens are constantly being reminded of their outsider status. Their presence actually increases group solidarity and camaraderie among men. Typical male behavior—telling tales of sexual adventure, sharing off-color jokes, talking about sports—becomes more dramatic and is acted out more fervently in the presence of token women. This reinforces the feeling that the tokens are not part of the "club."

Kanter also discovered that in more formal settings like meetings and conferences men would often preface their acts with apologies or questions about appropriateness directed toward the token woman, such as, "I probably shouldn't say this in mixed company" or "Can we still use technical jargon?" The token then feels as though she is "interrupting" the usual course of events. Rarely does a token woman feel comfortable enough to prevent a large number of men from engaging in an activity they consider normal. By saying these things, men make their dominant culture clear to the tokens and effectively state the terms under which they will be allowed to participate as outsiders.

Tokens can never be seen as who they really are. They must always fight stereotypes and tailor their actions to the desires and tastes of others. We can see the self-fulfilling prophecy at work here. Stereotypical assumptions about what tokens "must be like" force them into playing limited and caricatured roles. This situation serves the interests of those in the dominant group, who can fall back on preexisting expectations and traditional behaviors.

The courteous, polite, gentlemanly behavior of men toward women, such as opening doors for them or expressing excessive concern for their safety, implies, on the surface, respect and affection. But this behavior not only subordinates women, it also limits their employment opportunities because it reinforces the notion that women are in need of special protection:

> [Mary's] male counterparts in the company frequently were invited to out-of-town business meetings and social functions from which she was excluded. These occasions were a source for information on business trends and store promotions and were a rich source of potentially important business contacts. When [Mary] asked why she was not invited to these meetings and social gatherings, the response was that her employer thought it was "too dangerous for her to be driving out of town at night by herself. . . . " (quoted in Benokraitis & Feagin, 1993, p. 335)

Kanter argues that the implications of token status can apply to people of any social category who find themselves few of a kind among a majority of others.

This is an important point sociologically because it shows that the treatment of certain social groups is not fixed by inflexible characteristics but can depend on their relative numbers vis-à-vis the majority. Workplace discrimination is a product of the system as much as it is a product of individuals within it.

Nevertheless the actual experience of tokenism can vary between social groups. For instance, men in traditionally female jobs (for example, male nurses, librarians, elementary school teachers) and women in traditionally male jobs (for example, physicians, engineers, carpenters) both face prejudice and discrimination. But the nature and consequences of such treatment can be quite different (C. L. Williams, 1992). The discrimination token women workers face is the kind that first comes to mind when we consider sexism on the job: difficulties getting hired, earning promotions, and getting respect from supervisors and colleagues. These obstacles come from within the job itself, either from its basic organizational structure or from the people in it. However, the prejudice men feel from working in nontraditional occupations is more likely to come from outside the job. Men often encounter stigmatizing negative stereotypes when they come into contact with clients and people outside of work. Male nurses are assumed to be gay, and male librarians or social workers might be considered feminine. Male elementary school teachers often have to confront suspicions that they are potential child molesters (C. L. Williams, 1992).

Although such outside prejudice is enough to prevent large numbers of men from entering traditionally female professions, those that do enter them often find that they receive fair, sometimes even preferential, treatment. For many men, their token status as males in predominantly female professions works to their advantage in hiring and promotions. As opposed to the "glass ceiling" encountered by women, the set of invisible obstacles that prevent them from moving up in a company, many men in female occupations encounter a "glass escalator": invisible pressures to move up in their professions (C. L. Williams, 1992). In sum, men are able to take their culturally derived gender privilege with them when they enter predominantly female professions, despite the fact that they make up only a small percentage of all people in that profession.

▪ ▪ ▪

The institutional structure of contemporary American labor markets segregates women into relatively low-wage occupations or excludes them entirely. Although the motivation for such discrimination may be primarily economic, the role of sexist ideology and gender stereotypes cannot be overlooked. Employers as well as the public at large still believe women and men are naturally inclined toward certain jobs (Reskin & Hartmann, 1986).

Sociologist Richard Levinson (1975) had male and female undergraduate sociology students make job inquiries in response to 256 classified advertisements. The jobs were categorized as "male" (security guard, truck driver, car sales, etc.)

or "female" (receptionist, hostess, cosmetic sales, etc.). Working in male-female pairs, one partner made a telephone inquiry about a "sex inappropriate" job—for example, a man asking about a receptionist position or a woman asking about a truck driver job. About 30 minutes later, the other partner called about the same job. This time the person was "sex appropriate"—the woman called about the receptionist job or the man called about the truck driver opening. The students were instructed to be polite and to use identical words in their inquiries.

Levinson found clear-cut discrimination in 35% of the cases. The sex-inappropriate caller might be told that the person doing the hiring was out of town or that the position had already been filled. However, when the sex-appropriate caller phoned a half hour later, he or she might be told that the position was still open or was even encouraged to come in for an interview. Ambiguous discrimination was found in another 27% of the cases. This type of discrimination ranged from expressions of surprise to subtle attempts on the part of employers to discourage the sex-inappropriate caller from applying for the job. A more recent replication of this study found that these forms of sex discrimination, although not as common as they were in Levinson's study, still exist (Winston, 1988).

Such thinking about the sex-appropriateness of certain jobs also leads employers to make personnel decisions on the basis of characteristics believed to be typical of a group. Consider the different reactions employers commonly have toward their male and female employees getting married. For a man, marriage is likely to be seen as a "stabilizing" influence. From the point of view of management, his "settling down" will make him a better, more dependable worker. He might even need a raise, since fatherhood is probably looming not far down the road.

But for women, marriage is still likely to be seen as disruptive to their careers. The employer may jump to the conclusion that a newly married woman will soon be seeking maternity leave or quitting altogether. Rather than making her a more dependable worker, marriage actually may make her less dependable in the eyes of management. These beliefs subtly influence hiring and promotion decisions (Reskin & Hartmann, 1986).

We continue to have one set of jobs that employs almost exclusively women and another that employs almost exclusively men. Such segregation has consequences that extend beyond its mere existence (Reskin & Hartmann, 1986). When people are allocated jobs on the basis of sex rather than ability to perform the work, chances for self-fulfillment are limited. Society also loses, because neither men nor women are free to do the jobs for which they might best be suited. Sex segregation represents a failure of the economy to use the available labor force most efficiently. However, segregation is most harmful to women, primarily because the occupations they predominantly hold tend to be less desirable than those held predominantly by men. In particular, occupational segregation contributes to the lower wages earned by women.

The Wage Gap

> The Lord spoke to Moses and said, "When a man makes a special vow to the Lord which requires your valuation of living persons, a male between twenty and sixty years old shall be valued at fifty silver shekels. If it is a female, she shall be valued at thirty shekels. (Lv. 27:1–4, cited in Corcoran, Duncan, & Hill, 1986)

You don't have to go back to the Bible to find evidence of the practice of setting women's pay at about three-fifths that of men's. In 1973, for instance, women on average earned only 56.6 cents for every dollar a man earned. Advances in work experience and job-related skills have enabled some women—particularly middle- and upper-class women—to improve their income levels relative to men's. However, obvious discrepancies still exist. In 1993 men working full-time year-round earned an average salary of $31,077 per year; women working full-time year-round earned an average salary of $22,469 per year (U.S. Bureau of the Census, 1995a). To put it another way, for every dollar a man earns, a woman earns approximately 72 cents. The differences are even more pronounced for African-American and Hispanic women, who earn 65 and 55 cents respectively for every dollar a man earns. Some sociologists argue that the wage gap has narrowed somewhat not because women's earning power has improved but because men's has worsened (Bernhardt, Morris, & Handcock, 1995).

The discrepancy between men's pay and women's pay has proved remarkably resilient over the years. The 1963 Equal Pay Act guaranteed equal pay for equal work, and Title VII of the 1964 Civil Rights Act banned job discrimination on the basis of sex (as well as race, religion, and national origin). Yet the gap still persists.

I should point out that the wage gap is not an exclusively American phenomenon. To varying degrees, in every country around the world men earn more than women. In the developing countries of Latin America, Africa, and Asia, women commonly earn 25% or less of what men earn (Tiano, 1987). In Korea and Japan, women earn barely half of men's income. In some countries, however, such as France, Sweden, Australia, and Denmark, the wage gap is actually much narrower than it is here, with women earning 80% to 90% of what men earn (Reskin & Padavic, 1994).

Multinational corporations frequently export our wage gap abroad by paying female factory workers in developing countries as little as half of what they pay men. In many countries, women constitute over three-quarters of unskilled assembly workers. This preference for women is sometimes rationalized by beliefs that they have a high tolerance for monotonous work, an inherent dexterity that suits tasks that involve tiny parts, and a docile nature that allows them to withstand the pressure of closely supervised production (Tiano, 1987).

Why does the wage gap continue to exist? One reason, of course, is occupational segregation and the types of jobs women are most likely to have. Studies suggest that occupational segregation accounts for about 40% of the gender differ-

Table 13.1   *Average Monthly Income, by Sex and Educational Attainment, 1993*

	Monthly Income	
Level of Educational Attainment	Male Workers	Female Workers
All workers	$2,230	$1,186
High school dropout	1,211	621
High school graduate	1,812	1,008
Some college, no degree	2,045	1,139
Associate degree	2,561	1,544
Bachelor's degree	3,430	1,809
Master's degree	4,298	2,505
Professional degree	6,312	3,530
Doctorate	4,421	4,020

Source: U.S. Bureau of the Census, 1995a.

ences in average earnings (Reskin & Hartmann, 1986). For the five "most female" jobs (that is, those more than 96% female)—which are secretary, receptionist, licensed practical nurse, private household worker, and child care worker—the average weekly salary is $219. For the five "most male" jobs (those less than 3% female)—which are airplane pilot, construction worker, truck driver, firefighter, and miner—the average weekly salary is $506 (adapted from Barrett, 1987).

Some economists and policy makers argue that the wage gap is essentially an institutional by-product that exists because men on the whole have more work experience, more training, and higher education than women. The U.S. Bureau of the Census, however, reports that gender differences in education, labor force experience, and seniority—factors that might make discrepancies in salary justifiable—account for less than 15% of the wage gap between men and women (cited in National Committee on Pay Equity, 1995). For instance, the average income of full-time female workers is significantly lower than men's with the same level of educational training. In fact, women with a bachelor's degree can expect to earn slightly less than men with only a high school diploma ($1,809 per month for women compared to $1,812 for men) (U.S. Bureau of the Census, 1995a). These statistics are shown in Table 13.1.

There are also broader economic reasons for the existing wage gap. Because of the type of occupations women tend to have, their labor force participation is more likely to be determined by the fluctuating needs of the economy. Women are easily exploited and are used as cheap labor and quickly dispensed with when no longer needed (J. Smith, 1981). More than two-thirds of temporary or part-time workers in this country are women (Baca-Zinn & Eitzen, 1993). During hard times these workers are the first ones pushed out of employment, not because they're women but because their jobs are the most expendable.

Comparable Worth: Overcoming Economic Discrimination

You have seen the various ways in which women are economically discriminated against in American society. What can be done about it? How would you reduce the large gap between men's and women's earnings? One controversial policy to achieve pay equity is called comparable worth.

Comparable worth is the principle that different jobs that are of equal value to society and require equal levels of training ought to be paid equally. This principle rejects the premise that women's work is inherently worth less than men's and the related assumption that workers are paid according to their needs and that women need less money than men (Feldberg, 1984). The ultimate goal is to raise the wages of underpaid, female-dominated occupations.

Going beyond the principle of "equal pay for equal work," comparable worth acknowledges that women and men do not do the same work and that sex segregation is the rule, not the exception (Ciancanelli & Berch, 1987). The assumption is that to achieve any equality in a work world already structured around difference, it is necessary to use comparability as a criterion for judging the relative worth of certain occupations. Consequently, any gender disparity in wages between jobs deemed comparable must be addressed (Ames, 1995).

Comparable worth is now used routinely to set pay scales in corporations. A job is broken down into the various skills required of the jobholder: education, special abilities, and experience. The job is also broken down in terms of difficulty: Does it require physical labor, manual dexterity, responsibility for important decisions, supervision of others? Then these skills and requirements are valued in dollar amounts across different jobs (P. Simpson, 1983). Panels of experts assign point values to jobs based on their judged "worth." If, for example, nurses are paid less than tree trimmers, can such a difference be justified by the skills and training required for these different jobs? Or is the wage difference simply illustrative of a pattern of discrimination against women?

At present, all but five states have addressed the issue of pay equity (National Committee on Pay Equity, 1995). Almost half of all states have conducted job evaluation studies to determine if their systems for setting the wages of state workers are discriminatory. In Minnesota, a job evaluation study found a 20% gap between comparable male-dominated and female-dominated jobs. Adjustments are being phased in over a 4-year period.

Critics claim that comparable worth attacks free market capitalism and destroys economic competition (Aaron & Lougy, 1986). They feel employers should be free to pay workers the "going market rate." Women's low wages, they say, are simply the result of economic forces dictating that higher wages ought to be paid to workers in the more socially valuable or useful positions. If these forces were truly at work, however, the drive to maximize profits by using cheap labor would create a uniform wage structure in which everyone was paid poorly, not one characterized by huge gender differences. Instead, the low wages women earn must be the result of a socially constructed labor market that incorporates history, customs, prejudices, and belief systems that connect the worth of different jobs with ideas about the inherent worth of the people who perform them (Feldberg, 1984).

Even those who wish to implement comparable worth pay policies acknowledge some practical difficulties. For example, such policies may actually discourage women from seeking jobs in what are considered to be traditionally male occupations: Why should they put up with the difficulties of breaking into male occupations if they can earn the same salary in traditionally female occupations? Comparable worth may end up establishing wage equality but still not end the sex segregation of occupations (Kelly & Bayes, 1988). There is some merit to this argument. Setting salaries according to an occupation's worth will reduce the gender gap in wages only if women have access to the jobs that society values (Feldberg, 1984). If men continue to dominate the jobs deemed to be most socially "worthy," then pay equity will never be achieved.

This raises a larger point regarding cultural perceptions. The skills required in many predominantly female occupations are often not socially recognized as skills and therefore are not included in the formal evaluation of the worth of those occupations. For instance, much of the work teachers, nurses, and secretaries do is geared toward recognizing and responding to subtle cues from others and understanding other people's needs (Feldberg, 1984). These skills are difficult to quantify and may not be perceived as compensable because they are likely to be viewed as an extension of women's unpaid household skills. When these skills are overlooked, strange rankings may result, as when the job of nursery school teacher is rated lower than that of a dog trainer (Feldberg, 1984).

In sum, comparable worth is a useful tool in reducing wage discrimination. However, because of practical issues of implementation as well as continuing prejudices and cultural stereotypes, it has not produced full equality. It seems that comparable worth, at present, may have more symbolic than practical value. Nevertheless, it is an honest attempt to overcome sexual inequality at the institutional rather than personal level.

Conclusion

Sexual inequality goes beyond the degrading media and cultural images of women, face-to-face interactions that reinforce the devaluation of women, and the stereotypes of individual people. It is woven into the institutional and cultural fabric of our society. It is as much a part of the American scene as baseball, apple pie, and the Fourth of July. Every woman in the country has felt sexism at some level, whether as personal violence, sexually suggestive leers and comments, fear of going out at night, job discrimination, legal obstacles, or subtle encouragement toward "appropriate" sports, hobbies, and careers.

We have seen in this chapter that men tend to benefit from living in a society where language, identity, intimacy, history, culture, and institutions are built on gender distinctions, even if the men themselves do not support such inequality. Thus most men do not see sexual inequality as their problem; it's a "women's issue." Like most people whose interests are being served by the system, men are largely unaware of the small and large advantages the social structure provides them (W. J. Goode, 1981). Therefore, men are less likely to seek change.

The first step toward sexual equality is that men will have to come to understand their role in the process, even in the absence of blatant, personal sexism. We are all tacitly involved in the oppression of women each time we automatically giggle at sexist jokes, mistake female doctors for nurses, see women in purely physical terms, expect less from them on the job or in school, or expect more of them at home.

The next step will require a fundamental transformation of institutional patterns and cultural values. Such a solution sounds too massive to be possible. But today we are seeing early steps in that direction: changing conceptions of familial roles, increasing (though not yet equal) labor force participation, growing political power, and greater awareness of sexual exploitation and violence. How far these changes will take us in the future remains to be seen.

CHAPTER HIGHLIGHTS

▪ Personal sexism is most apparent during the course of everyday interaction in the form of communication patterns and gestures. It can be particularly dangerous when expressed in the form of sexual harassment and sexual violence.

▪ Sexual stratification is perpetuated by a dominant cultural ideology that devalues women on the basis of inherent biological differences between men and women. This ideology overlooks the equally important role of social forces in determining male and female behavior.

▪ Institutional sexism exists in the law, in the family (in terms of reproductive choices, fetal rights, and the domestic division of labor), and in economics. Women have entered the paid labor force in unprecedented numbers, but they still tend to occupy jobs that are typically considered "female" and still earn significantly less than men.

▪ Not only are social institutions sexist in that women are systematically segregated, exploited, and excluded, they are also "gendered." Institutions themselves are structured along gender lines so that traits associated with success are usually stereotypically male characteristics: tough-mindedness, rationality, assertiveness, competitiveness, and so forth.

YOUR TURN

To understand how beliefs are translated into action, it is important to examine how sexism influences people's activities. One fruitful area of examination is the home. Locate at least one of each of the following types of couples in which both partners work full-time outside the home:

■ newly married without children (married less than one year)
■ married without children (married 10 years or more)
■ married (older or younger) with at least one child living at home
■ cohabiting (heterosexual or homosexual)

Ask each person to make a list of all the household chores that need to be done during the course of a week. Ask each to be as specific and exhaustive as possible (for example, "cleaning windows" rather than "cleaning the house"). After the lists are completed, ask each person to indicate which of these tasks he or she is primarily responsible for, which his or her partner is responsible for, and which are shared. Ask the participants also to estimate the total amount of time spent each week on all these tasks combined. Finally, ask them if they are employed outside the home and, if so, about how many hours they work during a typical week. (Note: It is important that partners are not in each other's presence when answering these questions.)

In comparing responses, see if there are any differences—in terms of time spent doing housework and the number of tasks for which each one is responsible—between

■ partners in the same couple
■ men and women
■ younger and older couples
■ married and cohabiting couples

Do women who work outside the home still bear the primary responsibility for housework? Are there certain types of couples for which this is not the case? If partners within the same couple had different ideas about housework responsibilities, to what can you attribute this lack of agreement? Describe the tensions men and women experience when trying to balance work and home responsibilities.

GENDER VIOLENCE

DOUGLAS HARPER with photographs by DONNA FERRATO*

"…This is violence against women…violence because of a personal argument…violence against the social role that women occupy…."

This chapter includes much information about what can best be called "gender violence." This is violence against women, but rather than violence because of a personal argument, it is violence against the social role that women occupy. As you have learned from this chapter, there is gender violence in most societies, including hidden murder in India as well as the sadly common rape and battering that are part of our own social fabric.

This visual essay is excerpted from the book *Living with the Enemy* by Donna Ferrato (Aperture, 1991). After first witnessing violence against women in a routine magazine assignment, she took as her special mission the documentation of gender violence. None of these extraordinary photographs is staged.

Her book, as well as the essay we have selected from it, shows the process of violence, a social narrative of violent behavior. Women are hit, run over, burned, and raped as a result of men's sense of their natural superiority, as a result of men's socialization to violence, and

A woman is struck by her husband in the course of an argument.

because society takes a moderate, even ambivalent view of violence toward women.

Not all women, however, passively accept this violence. Some fight back (and are often imprisoned, even if they have acted in self-defense). Women often leave punishing relationships; they establish counterinstitutions and help one another find a social environment in

*Photographs © Donna Ferrato/Domestic Awareness Abuse Project from the book *Living with the Enemy* (Aperture).

A battered wife sneaks her belongings out of her house while her husband is gone.

A woman bloodied by her husband.

which they are not physically threatened. Some men are sentenced to counseling and thereby gain insights that defer future violence. Disturb-

ing as this essay is, we must face the reality of these social narratives as a common part of our social landscape.

Mother with two kids in her room at the Women Against Abuse shelter in Philadelphia, after leaving her abusive husband.

Children are terribly affected by spouse abuse. Studies relate the experience of observing violence to a greater likelihood of becoming violent in later life. The published caption for this photo is: "'I hate you! Never come back to my house,' screamed an eight-year-old at his father as police arrested the man for attacking his wife."

After Mary's husband, Lawson, held a shotgun to her head and threatened to blow it off, Mary took her three daughters and ran to a shelter. The next day she filed a complaint against him, secured a restraining order, and sued him for divorce and custody of their children. Charged with assault, Lawson was given two days in jail, a $165 fine, and a year's probation. Said Mary, "I tried to press attempted murder charges because he tried to kill me that night. But the lawyer said he couldn't do it, that it was only domestic assault, since I'm his wife." Lawson was seen driving around in the neighborhood of the shelter. Mary was terrified her husband would try to punish her. With help from some of the other women in the shelter, she dyed her brown hair blonde in the hope that Lawson wouldn't recognize her.

In a Boston self-defense course, women learn to fight back effectively.

Around midnight, when the children are finally asleep, women take time off for themselves. Over cigarettes and coffee, with the music turned up loud, they let loose, laugh, and talk about what they've been through and what the future will bring. Sharing information helps them overcome.

Counseling programs for abusive men...teach men to take responsibility for their behavior and to change it. Most participants are ordered by the court to join the group. Often programs last only a few weeks. Bill (right) cried as he admitted to the group that beating his wife reminded him of his father, a violent man who sometimes turned his attack on Bill....Now, in front of his therapy group, Bill wept because he recognized there was little difference between the man he had become and the man he had dreaded as a young boy.

Becca Jean Hughes shot her husband in self-defense as he tried to choke her to death. During the first eight years of being together, Don "never raised his voice, never swatted me, never slapped a child. He was the type of husband you would have given a medal to. But it just went from good to bad to worse. I got everything from broken bones to skull fractures. I was hit with chainsaws. There were many beatings not bad enough to send me to the hospital, but when they were, he always drove me there." She had made plans to leave the state, but her husband returned early from a trip. She told him of her plans to leave, and he beat her and tried to choke her. Photos of her bruises were not allowed in court. The presiding judge did not allow information regarding abuse to enter the case. The gun she used to kill her husband, which she grabbed from under the seat of the truck cab in the middle of her struggle not to be choked to death, was the same gun admitted as evidence in a trial 23 years earlier in a domestic quarrel her husband had had with his previous wife. Becca Jean's sentence was life without parole for premeditated murder. (The average murderer in America serves six years.) She remains in jail.

This is not an untypical story. Women receive such stiff penalties for killing their abusers that in some states governors have released prisoners. For example, in 1990 Ohio Governor Celeste released 25 battered women from state prison who had been denied fair trials precisely because expert testimony about battering was excluded from the proceedings.

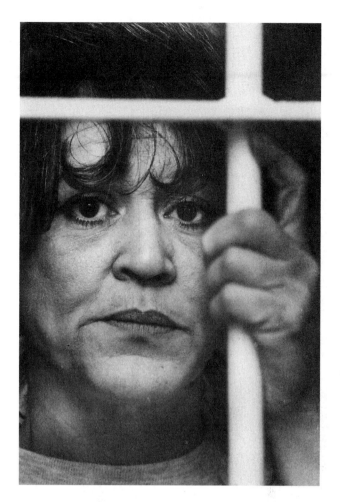

CHAPTER 14

The Dynamics of Population: Demographic and Global Trends

- ■ *The Influence of Birth Cohorts*
- ■ *Demographic Dynamics*
- ■ *The Impact of Population Trends on U.S. Institutions*

In his novel *Generation X: Tales for an Accelerated Culture*, Douglas Coupland (1991) describes the experiences of three friends in their 20s who quit their "low-pay, low-prestige, low-benefit, no-future jobs" and move to Palm Springs, California, in search of new experiences they hope will give meaning to their lives. In one scene Andy, the narrative voice of the book, describes an experience with his friend Dag:

> Just after 2:00 A.M., Dag got off of shift at Larry's Bar where along with me he is a bartender. While the two of us were walking home, he ditched me right in the middle of a conversation we were having and darted across the road, where he then scraped a boulder across the front hood and windshield of a Cutlass Supreme. This is not the first time he has impulsively vandalized like this. The car was the color of butter and bore a bumper sticker saying WE'RE SPENDING OUR CHILDREN'S INHERI-TANCE, a message that I suppose irked Dag . . .
> "I don't know, Andy," he said . . . "whether I feel more that I want to punish some aging crock for frittering away my world, or whether I'm just upset that the world has gotten too big—way beyond our capacity to tell stories about it, and so all we're stuck with are these blips and chunks and snippets on bumpers. . . . I feel insulted either way." (p. 5)

The disillusionment and frustration voiced by Dag symbolizes the fears and anxieties of a specific segment of the American population. But this is not a group of people characterized by common skin color, ethnicity, religion, or sex; nor is it a social group brought together by the same occupation or an emotional political issue. These individuals are bonded by one simple and unchangeable fact: They are members of the same **birth cohort**—a set of people who were born during the same time period and who must face similar societal circumstances brought about by their position in the age structure of the population.

In the past several chapters I have examined the various interrelated sources of social stratification: class, economic resources, race, and gender. We have seen how the distance between the haves and the have-nots continues to grow wider as a result of their different levels of access to important resources. We have seen how race and gender continue to determine access to cultural, economic, and political opportunities. But we have not yet examined another source of inequality that has enormous local, national, and global significance: the changing size and shape of the human population. Globally, population imbalances between richer and poorer societies underlie most if not all of the other forces for change that are taking place today. In the United States, the domestic population imbalances between various age and ethnic groups will be our defining feature in the decades to come.

This chapter examines the relationship between population trends and everyday life. First I describe how the time in which we were born influences our everyday experiences. Next, I look at three population trends occurring across the globe today: population growth, changing age structures, and migration. I then turn my focus to some of the key population trends occurring in our society. How are the changing age structure of American society and the growing number of legal and illegal immigrants affecting our ability to provide people with the resources they need for a comfortable life? How are our important social institutions functioning as a result of population shifts? Do these institutions now benefit some cohorts at the expense of others?

The Influence of Birth Cohorts

You've no doubt asked yourself questions like: What career will I pursue? Where will I live? Will I be able to afford a house? Will I have a spouse? children? The answers to these questions are influenced by your personal desires, traits, values, ambitions, and abilities as well as your social class, gender, race, religion, and ethnicity. But they are also affected by your place in the population at a given point in time. The sheer number of people living in a society will affect the availability of affordable houses, high-paying jobs, attractive potential mates, and so on. More than that, the shape of your birth cohort or "generation" and its position and size relative to other cohorts will be tremendously influential. Each cohort has distinctive properties—such as initial size, ethnic composition, age-specific birth rates, and average life expectancies—that set it apart from other cohorts.

Cohorts and Everyday Life

Cohorts influence the everyday lives of individuals in two fundamental ways (Riley, 1971):

■ People born at roughly the same time tend to experience life course events or social rites of passage at the same time, including puberty, marriage, childbearing, graduation, entrance into the workforce, and death. Sociologists call this life course dimension **cohort effects**. Think of it as the collective experience of aging.

▪ People born at the same time also share a common history. A cohort's place in time tells us a lot about the opportunities and constraints placed on its members. Historical events and major social trends, called **period effects**, contribute to the unique shape and outlook of each cohort. Many historians, for instance, believe that a period of drought and famine caused the abandonment of the great cities of the Mayan civilization nearly a thousand years ago. Those who were young when this period began enjoyed comfortable lives, reveled in the high culture of the Mayans, and had tremendous prospects for the future. But for their children, born just a generation later, starvation, death, and social dislocation were basic facts of life (Clausen, 1986).

Cohort and period effects combine to profoundly affect the lives of cohorts. Cohort members experience the same major societal or world circumstances at about the same stage in their lives. Consider what people born just prior to 1920 have experienced: They survived World War I and the flu epidemic of 1919-1920 as infants; they lived through the Depression era of the 1930s as young teens; they experienced World War II, perhaps even firsthand, as young adults; and they witnessed the Vietnam War in middle age. They have also seen the advent of airplanes, radio, television, space travel, and computers, not to mention dramatic changes in sexual, political, educational, and religious values (Clausen, 1986).

It's not only exposure to these events that shapes cohort histories, it's also how old people are when these events occur that distinguishes them from other cohorts (Soldo & Agree, 1988). For instance, cohorts who experienced the Great Depression during their peak childbearing years have the lowest birth rate of any cohort observed so far in this century. Therefore, people born between 1900 and 1910 have smaller families to rely on and similar worries about how they will be cared for in their old age. These experiences contrast sharply with people born only 10 years later or earlier, who either were past their prime childbearing years during the Depression or were too young to have children and therefore tend to have larger families today (Soldo & Agree, 1988).

Your cohort may be as influential in forming your worldview and self-concept as your race, class, gender, or family. Think how different your goals and ambitions would be had you experienced childhood during the Depression as opposed to a period of relative affluence. Rights and privileges considered unattainable dreams by one cohort are likely to be taken for granted by a future one. Similarly, the differences in attitudes and values between people who became adults during the Vietnam War and people who became adults during the Persian Gulf War are not only a function of simple age differences but a function of differences in prevailing social and historical conditions. Think how different your perceptions of the world and your ideas about solving international conflicts would be if your most vivid teenage memory was one of angry crowds jeering soldiers going off to fight an unpopular war as opposed to an image of adoring crowds cheering soldiers going off to fight a popular one.

As we grow older, we develop and change in a society that itself is developing and changing. We start our lives in one historical period with a distinct age pattern of behavior and set of social norms, and we end our lives in another. Throughout most of the 20th century, for instance, each succeeding generation has received substantially more schooling than the previous one. Early in the century most people went to school for only 6 or 7 years, which yielded an adequate education for the sorts of jobs their parents and older siblings held. Today, most people are in school 12 years or more. As a result, older cohorts on the whole tend to score substantially lower on standardized intelligence tests than younger ones. Because of such a trend, it was long assumed that intelligence declined markedly with age. But we now know that these differences are not the result of aging but of changing societal values regarding education (Clausen, 1986).

Even the way people experience the aging process is affected by the character of the cohort to which they belong and by the social, cultural, and environmental changes to which their cohort is exposed in moving through the life course. People are living longer, and advancements have been made in nutrition, education, sanitation, and other areas. As a result, cohorts experience the physical consequences of aging in different ways (Riley, Foner, & Waring, 1988). For instance, the average age of menarche (a girl's first menstrual period) has gradually lowered from about 14 a century ago to 12.5 today (Darton, 1991). When combined with changing social norms, values, and cultural beliefs, such a change will inevitably speed up the point at which young people become sexually curious and explorative.

In sum, to understand the impact cohorts exert on everyday life, we must place them within their relevant historical and social contexts. Birth cohorts are more than just a collection of individuals born within a few years of each other; they are distinctive generations tied together by historical circumstances, population trends, and societal changes. However, we must also realize that when many individuals in the same cohort are affected by social events in similar ways, the changes in their collective lives can produce changes in the social structure. Each succeeding cohort leaves its mark on the prevailing culture. Each helps create and is shaped by its own *zeitgeist*—the intellectual, moral, and cultural spirit of the time (Mannheim, 1952). In other words, cohorts are not only affected by social changes, they contribute to them as well (Riley, Foner, & Waring, 1988).

Baby Boomers and Generation X

The birth cohort that has received the most national attention is, without a doubt, the baby boom generation, those 76 million or so people born between 1946 and 1964. They now make up almost one-third of the entire U.S. population. Preceded and followed by much smaller cohorts, they stand in sharp political, economic, and cultural contrast to those around them:

> They grew up as the first standardized generation, drawn together by the history around them, the intimacy of television, and the crowding that came from the sheer onslaught of other Baby Boomers. They shared the great economic expectations of the 1950's and the fears that came with Sputnik and the dawn of the nuclear era. They shared the hopes of John F. Kennedy's New Frontier and Lyndon Johnson's Great Society, and the disillusionment that came with the assassinations, Viet Nam, Watergate, and the resignations. (P. Light, 1988, p. 10)

The passing of this massive cohort through the life course has been described metaphorically as "a pig in a python." If you've ever seen one of those *National Geographic* films of snakes digesting small animals, you can see how apt the metaphor is. As this cohort bulge works its way through the life course, it stretches the parameters of the relevant social institutions at each stage. Baby boomers packed hospital nurseries as infants, school classrooms as children, and college campuses, employment lines, and the housing markets as young adults (P. Light, 1988).

As the baby boomers reach their golden years, those institutions concerned with later life—pension plans, Social Security, medical and social care—will be seriously stressed, leading one gerontologist to call the baby boomers a "generation at risk" (Butler, 1989). By the year 2030, one out of every three Americans will be over 65. At that time, there will be more than 50 million retired baby boomers, about twice the number of retirees there are today. Some have even predicted a huge surge in business for the funeral industry by then as this generation reaches the end of its collective life cycle (Schodolski, 1993).

Baby boomers have also left a particularly influential mark on the institution of the family. Their generation was the first to redefine families to include a variety of living arrangements, like cohabitation, domestic partnerships, and never-married women with dependent children (Wattenberg, 1986). They were also the first to acknowledge the expectation of paid work as a central feature of women's lives. And they were the first to grow up with effective birth control, making delayed childbearing and our present low birth rate possible.

Hence baby boomers are responsible for the smaller families we have today. Consequently, as they reach old age, they will have fewer children to turn to for the kind of help they gave in earlier years (Butler, 1989). This, along with the trend toward greater mobility and independent living, means that the baby boom elders will be more likely to turn to social service and health care organizations to care for them.

While the baby boomers have dominated the cultural spotlight, American society is just beginning to take notice of its next generation, known in the media as "twentysomethings," "baby busters," or "Generation X." Today there are roughly 48 million people either in or approaching their 20s, a sort of lost cohort tucked between the massive baby boom generation and their offspring. The birth rate during the 1970s, when these individuals were born, was about half as large as it was during the post-World War II years of the baby boomers.

These young people are less likely to get married than other generations and more likely to delay marriage if they do. In 1970, 55% of men and 36% of women between the ages of 20 and 24 had never married. In 1994 the figures were 81 and 66%, respectively (U.S. Bureau of the Census, 1995a). Furthermore, the high divorce rate over the past several decades has had a direct and lasting impact on this cohort. Roughly 40% of people in their 20s are children of divorce. Even more of them were so-called latchkey children, the first generation of children to experience the wholesale effects of two working parents. For many, childhood was marked by dependence on secondary relationships—teachers, friends, day care.

Like the fictional Dag at the beginning of this chapter, members of this cohort are disillusioned over shrinking opportunities due to poor economic times and angry that they have inherited a variety of gargantuan crises, from the national debt and the savings and loan bailout to the degradation of the natural environment and growing urban decay. Resentful of the wasteful excesses of their elders, they are experiencing unprecedented apprehension about their own futures. Many sense they are destined to become society's sacrificial "clean-up crew."

But rather than evoke sympathy from other cohorts, they have instead become a symbol of a nation in decline. This generation is described in dismal terms:

> They have trouble making decisions. . . . They have few heroes, no anthems, no style to call their own. They crave entertainment, but their attention span is as short as one zap of a TV dial. They hate yuppies, hippies and druggies. They postpone marriage because they dread divorce. They sneer at Range Rovers, Rolexes and red suspenders. . . . They possess only a hazy sense of their own identity but a monumental preoccupation with all the problems the preceding generation will leave for them to fix. (D. M. Gross & Scott, 1990, p. 57)

From the perspective of older generations, Generation X has become a metaphor for despair over the state of American culture and fear for our collective future (Howe & Strauss, 1992).

Demographic Dynamics

Many aspects of your personal life are influenced by your birth cohort, but your life is also affected by macro-level population trends. All of us are born, age, and eventually die. These seemingly private, biological events are part of the social fabric of societies. Practically every sphere of activity is influenced by population trends. The sociologists who study these trends in population characteristics are called **demographers**. Demographers examine several important and interrelated population processes in order to explain current social problems or project future ones: birth or fertility rates (changes in the number of children people are having), death or mortality rates (changes in people's life expectancy), and patterns of migration (the movement of people in and out of a society). These three processes influence a population's growth, overall age structure, and distribution.

Population Growth

The most fundamental population characteristic is size. No other phenomenon has the ability to touch the lives of everyone on the planet as profoundly as the growth of the human population. Changes in population size are a function of birth and death rates. As long as people are dying and being born at similar rates, the size of the population stabilizes (barring large changes due to migration). But when birth rates increase and death rates decrease, the population grows.

It took hundreds of thousands of years, from the beginning of humanity to the early 19th century, for the earth's population to reach 1 billion. However, it took only an additional hundred years to reach 2 billion. Three billion was reached 30 years later; 4 billion, 16 years later; and 5 billion, a little over 10 years after that. Today we are fast approaching 6 billion and will exceed 7 billion by 2010.

Ten thousand years ago the world's population was 8 million. Today it takes a little over a month for the population to grow by that much (Farley, 1991). Figure 14.1 charts world population growth since 7000 B.C.

The bulk of the growth is occurring in developing countries. The annual rate of growth worldwide between 1990 and 2000 will be approximately 1.5%. But that figure masks dramatic differences, from Europe's tiny 0.22% per year to Africa's massive 3.0% per year. In 1950 Africa's population was half that of Europe. By 2025 its population is expected to be three times as large as that of Europe, and about 95% of all global population growth will take place in Africa alone. Today 78% of the world's population resides in the developing countries of Africa, Asia, and Latin America. By the year 2030 that figure will rise to 86% ("World population growth," 1995). World population growth by region is shown in Figure 14.2.

There is no denying that the world's population is growing at unprecedented speed. However, there is some disagreement as to what the consequences of that growth will be. In the past, large numbers of people were seen as a precious resource. The Bible urged humanity to be fruitful and multiply. One 18th-century British scholar, referring to the strategic importance of a large population, called a high birth rate "the never-failing nursery of Fleets and Armies" (quoted in Mann, 1993, p. 49).

Although few people today sing the praises of massive population growth, some argue that it isn't particularly troublesome. A larger population creates greater division of labor and a larger market to support highly specialized services.

Figure 14.1   *World Population Growth since 7000 B.C.*

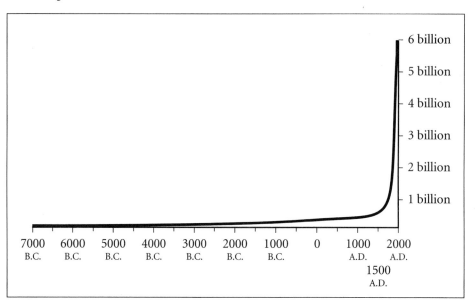

Source: Farley, 1991.

More people are available to contribute to production. A study in the early 1980s concluded that by using modern agricultural technology, developing countries could support an additional 30 billion people (cited in Mann, 1993). The Food and Agriculture Organization estimates that nearly 80 billion acres of usable farmland are lying idle, four times what is now being cultivated (Percival, 1989). Pollution is decreasing, resources are becoming more available, average food consumption levels are improving, and people are living longer (J. Simon, 1983).

Others, however, haven't been so optimistic. Population growth can compound, magnify, or even create a wide variety of problems, such as food shortages, pollution, housing shortages, high inflation, energy shortages, unemployment, illiteracy, and the loss of individual freedom (Weeks, 1994). Thousands of years ago, philosophers in ancient China worried about the need to shift the masses to underpopulated areas. Plato said that cities with more than 5,040 landholders were too large (Mann, 1993). According to some contemporary demographers, global population growth will destroy the onetime bonanza of environmental resources like fossil fuel, rich soil, and certain plant and animal species; widen the gap between rich and poor nations; perpetuate social and economic inequality within nations; give rise to racial and ethnic separatism, as we are seeing today in the former Soviet Union and Yugoslavia; and increase already high levels of world hunger and unemployment (Ehrlich & Ehrlich, 1993). When a

Figure 14.2   *World Population Growth by Region*

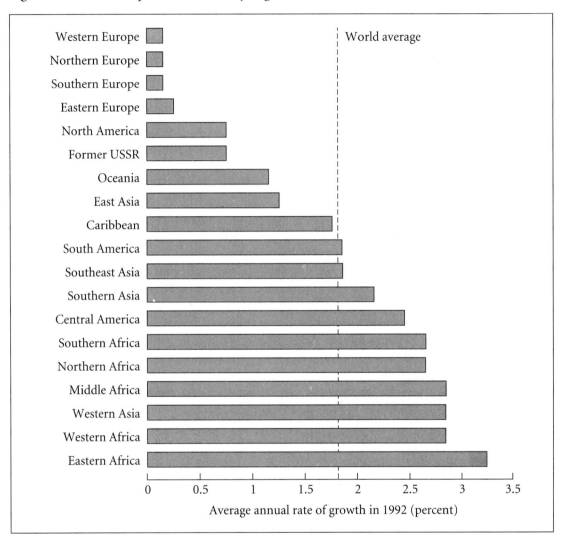

Source: Weeks, 1994.

particular population is excessively large, individuals are forced to compete for limited food, space, jobs, and salaries. People's ability to achieve a standard of living they feel they are entitled to is hampered by the size of the population.

On balance, the problem seems to be not so much that the earth's population is expanding but that different countries are experiencing vastly different rates of growth. Populations in poor, developing countries of the world are rapidly expanding, while those in wealthy, developed countries have either stabilized or are declining. These imbalances influence how people view one another, affect global and domestic policies, and determine the availability of food, energy, and adequate living space (P. Kennedy, 1993).

The Demographic Transition

In 1972 a group of researchers at the Massachusetts Institute of Technology predicted that because of rapid population growth, the world would run out of gold by 1981, oil by 1992, and usable farmland by 2000; civilization itself would collapse by 2075 (Mann, 1993). If Nigeria were to continue at its present rate of population growth (around 3.4% annually), in 140 years its population would be equal to that of the entire world today (Keyfitz, 1989). Needless to say, none of these things has happened or is going to happen. Sooner or later growth will have to stop. But why?

An 18th-century English clergyman named Thomas Malthus argued that populations always grow faster than food supplies. As the gap widens, starvation ensues. Famines, combined with wars, plagues, diseases, and the like eventually act as natural limits to population growth. Malthus assumed that food supplies were the ultimate population check. But he couldn't have foreseen the ability of trade and technology to solve the food supply problem. Japan's population, for instance, would have started dying off long ago if it had to rely on its own food production instead of imports from other countries. In addition, agricultural progress over the last two decades has enabled societies to produce food more abundantly and more efficiently than was possible during Malthus's time. Global food production actually rose more than 10% between 1968 and 1990 (Mann, 1993). Many of the nations today that are experiencing famines actually have food surpluses (Keyfitz, 1989). The starvation is not being caused by a lack of food per se but by maldistribution, which is often made worse by politics or civil war.

A less grim and more popular theory of population growth and contraction is what demographers call the **demographic transition**. Underlying this model is the assumption that all societies go through similar stages of economic and social development. During the first, preindustrial stage of development, both birth and death rates tend to be quite high. People have lots of children, but life expectancy is so low that roughly the same number of people die as are born each year. Hence the size of the population remains fairly stable.

The second stage occurs when societies begin to industrialize and living conditions improve. The first demographic phenomenon to improve is usually the death rate. New technology often means better food supplies and increased knowledge about disease. Societies learn how to keep their water supplies clean and how to dispose of garbage and sewage. But for a considerable period of time after the death rate begins to fall, there isn't an accompanying drop in the birth rate. The end result is a dramatic increase in the size of the population. Many demographers feel that most of the world's developing countries are in this second stage of the demographic transition. In these countries women will bear an average of 3.6 children in their lifetimes, and the number reaches an astronomical 7.3 in Malawi. In industrialized countries women on average will have a statistical 1.9 children in their lifetimes (in Japan, the figure is 1.6; in the United States it is 2.1) (Elliot & Dickey, 1994).

You might find it hard to understand why poor parents in developing countries who already face enormous difficulties would continue to produce more mouths to feed. Part of the reason is the lack of access to effective birth control. In Pakistan, for instance, only 12% of married women use some form of contraception (compared to 74% in the United States and 80% in France) (Elliot & Dickey, 1994). In addition, for some time during this stage of the demographic transition, traditional beliefs about the importance of large families remain. Often established laws, customs, and religious norms continue to exert strong influence on people's reproductive behavior. In developing nations children are likely to be perceived as economic assets. They are the "Social Security" of traditional cultures and a form of savings few people can do without (Mann, 1993).

As countries modernize, they reach the third and final stage, which is marked by a low birth rate and a low death rate. People moving into cities soon begin to realize that large families are an economic liability rather than an asset. They discover that raising large numbers of children in a crowded city is exceedingly difficult. Traditional and religious beliefs become weaker as a result. Therefore, population growth in modern countries like the United States and the countries of Western Europe is quite a bit slower than that in the developing countries of Africa, Latin America, and Asia.

Although the demographic transition model is useful in understanding the unequal rates of population growth, it has its drawbacks. The model is based on processes of urbanization and modernization that characterized 18th-century Europe but may not apply to developing countries today. Death rates fall at a much more accelerated rate in today's developing countries than they did 200 years ago because immunizations, antibiotics, pesticides, and other health advances are likely to be imported from more advanced countries instead of arising from economic and scientific development within a country. As a result, declining mortality is not always accompanied by an increase in the standard of living, as it was in the past. And because birth rates tend to fall when standards of living increase, there is currently less pressure in developing countries today to drive down their birth rates. Hence developing countries are stalled in the second stage of the model with no realistic chance of moving on to the final stage.

Signs indicate, however, that this assessment may be too pessimistic. Many people are beginning to seek more active ways to curb the global population explosion. Representatives from 182 nations attended the 1994 International Conference on Population and Development. Despite opposition from some Islamic countries and the Vatican, they agreed that promoting health care and reproductive education—particularly for women—is the best way to keep populations in developing countries in check (Ching, 1994). The conference draft plan stated, "Advancing gender equity and the empowerment of women is a cornerstone of population programs" (quoted in Elliott & Dickey, 1994, p. 22).

A study by the Population Crisis Committee found that overall access to birth control has indeed increased worldwide ("World progress in birth control," 1993). Of the 87 developing nations studied, 57 had improved birth control substantially over the last 5 years. Forty percent of the countries surveyed had decreased their average family size by a third, and another 42% exhibited smaller but noticeable differences.

We must keep in mind, however, that although the rate of population growth may be declining, annual absolute increases in the number of people continue to mount in many countries and will continue to be large for several decades to come (Merrick, 1986). When a country has a large and young population base, several generations may pass before a declining rate of growth can offset the sheer number of people produced by the high rates of the past. Even though individual people might be producing fewer children, so many of them are having kids that the population continues to grow anyway.

Politics, Culture, and Population Growth

You might get the impression from the above discussion that population growth is a "natural" process working relentlessly and inevitably on unsuspecting populations. Yet human intervention—government intervention, more specifically—has at times purposefully altered the size or even the configuration of a population for political or economic reasons.

Take China, for example. Because of this country's massive population of more than 1.2 billion and its limited resources, China's leadership has been struggling for decades to limit family size. One out of every five humans alive today is Chinese, but China has only 7% of the earth's farmland, much of it of poor quality. In response, the government enacted a strict birth policy. Couples must wait until their mid-20s to marry. Provinces and cities are assigned yearly birth quotas. Neighborhood committees determine which married couples can have a baby and when they can start trying. The committees also oversee contraceptive use and even record women's menstrual cycles (Ignatius, 1988). In some areas, groups of family planners visit each village once or twice a year and take all women who have already had children to a nearby clinic to be sterilized (Kristof, 1993b). Couples who have only one child are rewarded with salary bonuses, educational opportunities, and housing priorities. Penalties are imposed on couples who have more than one child. For instance, a couple may be fined more than a year's salary, lose access to apartments, schools, and free education, or be fired from their jobs (Ignatius, 1988).

The effectiveness of China's birth policy has amazed demographers. Population targets have been reached that weren't expected until 2010. The average number of births per woman has decreased from more than seven in the 1960s to fewer than two in 1992 (P. Kennedy, 1993; Kristof, 1993a). In contrast, the average woman in India, a country with similar population problems, still gives birth to four children in her lifetime. Only 9% of all Chinese births in 1992 were third, fourth, or subsequent children, down from over 15% in 1988. Over 80% of all Chinese couples of childbearing age are sterilized.

At the same time people are being encouraged to limit the size of their families, cultural tradition continues to express a deep preference for male children, forcing some couples, especially peasants, to illegally have more than one baby if the first one is a girl. Sons are preferred because only they can perpetuate the family line. Sons also represent an economic asset to the family and a source of security for parents in old age (Heise, 1989).

Such devaluation of female children in China and other countries can lead to extreme acts. A few years ago I was stunned by the following passage in a newspaper article:

> At least 60 million females in Asia are missing and feared dead, victims of nothing more than their sex. Worldwide, research suggests, the number of missing females may top 100 million. (Kristof, 1991)

Reading this, I tried to imagine 40% of the entire American population gone and presumed dead. If this many people were missing because of a war, earthquake, tidal wave, or plague, we surely would have heard something about it. How could something as massive and hideous as this happen so quietly?

Before I address this question, let me describe how demographers arrive at such an estimate in the first place. These figures are based on a few fundamental facts about the natural gender configuration of human populations. Worldwide there are 5% or 6% more male babies born than female babies. But under normal circumstances males die at higher rates at every age thereafter. In the United States and Europe, the number of men and women evens out by the time a cohort reaches its 20s or 30s (Kristof, 1991). Later in life, though, there is a higher number of women because women tend to live longer than men. The overall sex ratio in developed countries is approximately 105 women for every 100 men.

The figures in many developing countries contrast sharply with these demographic expectations. In India, for instance, the figure is only 92 females for every 100 males. In China, it is 84 females for every 100 males (Kristof, 1993b). Similar shortages of women have been found in Pakistan, Bangladesh, Nepal, and Papua New Guinea. Hence the 100 million estimate cited represents the difference between the actual number of females in the world and the number that should be expected under normal demographic circumstances.

The "missing" females may include children of all ages who are aborted, killed at birth, abandoned, neglected, given up for foreign adoption, or hidden (Kristof,

1993b). Some girls die because they are given less food than boys or because family members view a sick daughter as a nuisance but a sick son as a medical crisis requiring immediate attention. In Punjab, India, parents spend more than twice as much on medical care for boy infants as for girls (Heise, 1989).

Ironically, although countries like China see their future in reducing the size of their populations, other countries are starting to worry that their populations aren't growing enough. The developed, industrialized countries of the world, which tend to have higher standards of living and superior health care, enjoy low mortality rates. But these countries have also experienced drastically lower fertility rates over the past 30 years. Taiwan has experienced a dramatic drop in its birth rate over the last 30 years from 5.3 births per woman in 1963 to 1.8 today (U.S. Bureau of the Census, 1995a; Weeks, 1994). Because of the high cost of living, childlessness and singlehood have become more popular, even fashionable lifestyles. The government, fearing a future population with too many old people and not enough young people, is trying to reverse its approach to population growth and adopt a low-key "pro-baby" policy that, among other things, encourages early marriage and procreation and offers inexpensive specialist advice to infertile couples ("Taiwan's little problem," 1993).

In other cases governments have used much more drastic measures in an attempt to increase the size of their populations. In 1966, Romanian dictator Nicolae Ceausescu decided that his country's strength lay in its numbers. He called for a plan to increase the country's population from 23 million to 30 million by the year 2000. Ceausescu declared that "the fetus is the property of the entire society. Anyone who avoids having children is a deserter who abandons the laws of national continuity" (quoted in Breslau, 1990).

Within several years Romania's birth rate nearly doubled. However, because the country still provided virtually no prenatal care and was ravaged by poor nutrition, the infant mortality rate soared to 83 deaths for every 1,000 births (to give you an idea of how high that is, the infant mortality rate for most Western European countries is less than 10 deaths per 1,000 births). This population growth plan also contributed to the increased institutionalization of children, the spread of infant AIDS, and large-scale international trafficking in babies and children through adoption.

But Ceausescu pressed on with his plan. He outlawed sex education, classifying books on sexuality and reproduction as state secrets (Breslau, 1990). Women under the age of 45 were rounded up at their places of work every 2 or 3 months and taken to clinics, where they were examined for signs of pregnancy in the presence of government agents. A pregnant woman who had a miscarriage would automatically be suspected of arranging an illegal abortion and could be summoned for questioning. If a child died in a doctor's district, that doctor could lose 10% to 25% of his or her salary.

The world was given its first glimpse of this policy when Ceausescu was overthrown in 1989. The consequences of his "program" have been tragic. Not only have thousands, perhaps millions of women suffered through unwanted pregnancies and self-induced illegal abortions, but the country's orphanage system is bulging today with unwanted and unhealthy children.

Age Structure

In addition to affecting the size of the population, birth and death rates also combine to affect that society's **age structure**, the balance of old and young people. For areas in which recent population growth is exceedingly rapid and in which life expectancy remains low, as in Southeast Asia, Latin America, the Indian subcontinent, the Middle East, and Africa, the age structure will be increasingly dominated by young people. In Pakistan, Nigeria, Egypt, Turkey, Mexico, India, and most other developing countries, 40% to 50% of the population is now under the age of 15 (U.S. Bureau of the Census, 1995a). On the other hand, those countries that are experiencing low birth rates coupled with increasing life expectancy have a much different age structure (see Figure 14.3): More old people are living, and fewer young people are being born. In the United States, for instance, only 22% of the population is under 15.

The international implications of these different age structures are worth mentioning. When young people become numerous in a particular country, they are likely to achieve higher visibility and overwhelm social institutions like the economy and the educational system (K. Davis, 1976). The resulting economic stresses generate political conflict as well. A steady decline in living standards will no doubt mean growing unrest, which can have an impact on our lives here in the United States if the unrest takes place in countries we depend on for certain resources, goods, or services. According to one columnist:

> Given what is coming—unemployed youths roaming the streets in countries where half the population often is under 18 years of age, and looking to irregular leaders to lead them in new and as yet unpredictable movements—there is little question that even more political explosions are on the immediate horizon. (quoted in L. R. Brown, 1988, p. 33)

The obvious consequence of today's population trends is that developing nations will have the burden of trying to support millions of people under the age of 15, while developed nations will have the burden of trying to support millions of people over the age of 65. As the prosperous societies of the world struggle with the problem of allocating more resources to the elderly, the rest of the planet must deal with the demands of growing numbers of children and infants.

Immigration

In response to these problems, many people will be motivated to move to another place where prospects for a comfortable life are brighter. Therefore, large-scale

Figure 14.3   *Age Distribution in Less Developed and Developed Countries*

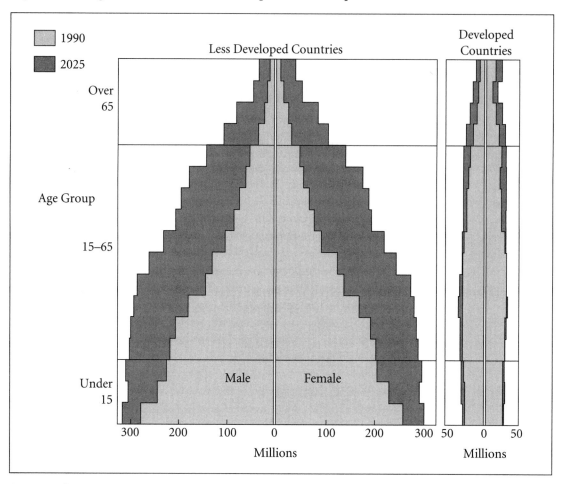

Source: Keyfitz, 1989.

migration, the third major demographic process, is an important factor to consider in the growth and decline of populations. According to a recent report from the United Nations, more than 100 million people worldwide have left their homes in search of a better life somewhere else. In the process, they bring together an extraordinary diversity of ethnicities and cultures:

> A woman gynecologist from Romania sells bananas in a downtown supermarket [in the U.S.]. Polish engineers pick grapes in Swiss alpine vineyards. . . . Thai bar girls in Tokyo ride the Japanese economic boom together with 700,000 workers from Korea. . . . Among the 2.8 million foreign workers . . . in the Middle East last year were 17,000 Vietnamese. Hundreds of thousands of Indonesians harvest rubber and copra in Malaysia for the same pocketbook reasons that Mexicans pump gasoline in Los

Angeles. In Germany, there are more than 1,000 mosques for resident Turkish workers. (McMichael, 1996, p. 187)

The growing pressures that encourage migration fundamentally arise from disparities in opportunities. Poverty, political instability, famine, environmental deterioration, high unemployment, and the lure of richer countries continue to drive the world's poorest people to seek safety and a better life in more prosperous nations. Consider, for instance, the situation in Mexico. Between 1994 and 1995, the Mexican peso was devalued by 73%, throwing millions into unemployment and poverty. As Mexico's agricultural system modernizes, millions more will be forced off their land. Economists estimate that the country will need a million new jobs each year just to maintain the poor level of employment that exists today. Until that unlikely time, many Mexicans will continue to cross the border into the U.S. seeking employment (Graham, 1996).

Whereas in the past migration meant moving to uncharted or newly developed areas, today it means pushing into territories already occupied by others. The United Nations estimates that by the year 2005 over half the world's population will live in urban areas; less than 50 years ago, only a third of the world's population lived in cities (Crossette, 1996b). Even developing countries are experiencing widespread growth of already overcrowded cities as people move in from rural areas. Today 1.4 billion people in the world live in the cities of developing countries; by 2025 there will be 4.1 billion. Of the 20 "megacities" with populations of over 11 million that will exist by the end of the century, 17 will be in the developing world, including such places as Mexico City, São Paulo, Calcutta, Bombay, and Shanghai. It is estimated that by the year 2000, 90% of the poorest people in Latin America will live in cities (Honebrink, 1993).

This transformation illustrates more than just a shift of living tendencies; it has changed our assumptions about what urban living means worldwide. In the past, cities were meccas of great wealth, cultural activities, fine houses, impressive streets, and so on. Today, however, urban life is associated with environmental and social devastation. Ninety percent of raw sewage from urban areas in developing countries pours into streams and oceans. Of India's 3,000 cities, only 8 have full water treatment plants (Crossette, 1996b). Cities have much higher rates of poverty, crime, violence and sexually transmitted diseases than rural areas. The sheer number of people crammed into these large cities makes life difficult. At 11,480 people per square mile, you may think New York City is crowded. But it is a veritable open prairie compared to Bombay, India, where there are 127,461 people per square mile (see Figure 14.4).

It would seem that when people migrate from underdeveloped, overcrowded countries to more developed, technologically advanced countries, everyone would benefit. After all, migration lowers population pressures and unemployment at home while offsetting the problems of negative population growth and an aging workforce in developed countries. As one author puts it:

Figure 14.4   *Urban Overcrowding Worldwide*

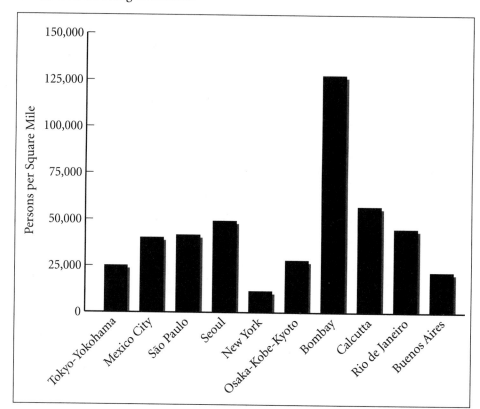

Source: U.S. Bureau of the Census, 1993a.

Why . . . should North America not allow the influx of millions of families from south of the Rio Grande; or labor-short Japan admit vast numbers of willing workers from Southeast Asia; or the European Community, with its graying populations, welcome the millions of unemployed of North Africa? Since most of Europe has a negative replacement fertility rate and the populations of Algeria, Morocco, and Tunisia are expected to double over the next few decades this seems . . . "the perfect match." (P. Kennedy, 1993, pp. 42–43)

From a sociological point of view, however, people in receiving countries perceive the influx of immigrants and their economic impact in personal rather than societal terms. Instead of being seen in terms of their contribution to the overall economy, immigrants are seen as an immediate threat. They seek to satisfy the same needs as everyone else. They require housing, education, and medical attention, all of which are in short supply. They also bring with them foreign habits, traditions, norms, and cultural ways.

Even though laws in most countries ban discrimination against foreigners, deep-seated resentment and prejudice is growing. In Great Britain the resentment is directed against Indians and Pakistanis; in France it's Algerians and Moroccans; in Germany it's the Turks; in Sweden it's Iraqis and Kurds; and in the United States it's immigrants from Latin America and Asia.

Industrialized countries face an uncontrollable tide of people from poorer countries, and many are closing their gates. In 1991 there were more than 1,500 attacks in Germany against foreigners. Even though such violence is carried out by a relatively small number of extremists, up to 40% of the German population can be characterized as "silent sympathizers," people who express at least some sympathy for issues of "racial purity" and "foreigners out" raised by extremists. In France, mounting resentment against Muslim Arab immigrants forced the government to place tight restrictions on immigration. One survey found that 76% of French citizens believe too many Arabs are in the country. In Italy, 75% of the population favor closing the borders to all new immigrants (Levin, 1993).

These responses show that migration is quickly becoming one of the world's major social and political issues. To some, the consequences of current migratory trends are nothing short of apocalyptic:

> The most potent political force shaping the civilization of the future may well be one that has no place in any ideology: the sheer movement of people from one place to another. It is changing the face of the world, rendering old boundaries and policies obsolete, and laying the foundation for a "new world order" quite unlike anything foreseen by any political leader or theorist—a boundary-less world in which people live where they choose. (quoted in Honebrink, 1993, p. 47)

Immigration creates a variety of cultural fears: the fear that a nation can't control its own boundaries, the fear that an ethnically homogeneous race will be altered through intermarriage, the fear of an influx of a "strange" way of life with religious rituals and cultural habits, and the fear that newcomers will encroach upon property, clog the educational system, and suck up social benefits owned and largely paid for by natives (Kennedy, 1993). Many people also express concern that immigrants are responsible for outbreaks of diseases like AIDS, measles, and cholera, which strain health care systems and create even more resentment. Above all, there is the fear that immigrants might one day become a statistical majority, rendering the "natives" powerless in their own country.

The Impact of Population Trends on U.S. Institutions

How are these demographic processes affecting the population in our country? It is difficult to talk about common effects because different ethnic, religious, and gender groups experience population trends differently. Hispanic Americans, for instance, have a significantly higher birth rate than whites. Catholics and Mormons have higher birth rates than other religions (Weeks, 1994). American women, on average, can expect to live longer than American men.

Nevertheless, two important demographic trends in the United States will exert a profound effect on the entire population in years to come: the growing proportion of nonwhite, non-English-speaking immigrants and their children and the shifting age structure of the population, marked by a growing proportion of elderly and a shrinking proportion of young people. These two trends together strain America's social fabric, raising questions about the fair distribution of social resources.

Immigration and the Changing Face of the United States

Because we live in a society where the population grows at a manageable rate, it is hard for us to understand how population explosions in other countries can affect us. But as populations burst the seams of national boundaries elsewhere, many of those seeking better opportunities end up here in the United States. Some arrive legally by plane, boat, or train. Others arrive illegally by foot or are smuggled in the backs of trucks or the bottoms of boats.

The Immigrant Tide

In the mid-1980s the U.S. Census Bureau predicted that by the year 2050 the United States would have a population of 300 million (there are roughly 265 million Americans today). In the early 1990s, however, the Bureau revised its estimate, projecting instead a population of 383 million by 2050 (Pear, 1992). Part of the reason these projections were adjusted was that immigration has played a more significant role in our population growth over the last several years than had been anticipated. About a million documented immigrants enter this country each year (U.S. Bureau of the Census, 1995a). One of every 11 people who live here was born somewhere else. In California alone, immigrants represented 37% of the population growth during the 1980s and early 1990s (Reinhold, 1993). The Census Bureau predicts that over 90% of the growth in the U.S. population by the year 2050 will be due to immigration that occurred after 1991 (cited in Honebrink, 1993).

This isn't the first time our country's population has been radically increased by a flood of immigration. In the first decade of the 20th century, nearly 9 million immigrants entered the country. What makes contemporary immigration different, though, is that relatively few of these newcomers will be of European descent (see Figure 14.5). In the late 19th century, 90% of the immigrants who came to this country were from northern and southern Europe. But by 1990 only 10% were from Europe; 38% were from Asia, and 46% from Latin America (U.S. Bureau of the Census, 1995a). The vast majority of the estimated 3 million illegal immigrants who enter the country each year come from Latin America (U.S. Bureau of the Census, 1995a).

Figure 14.5   *Legal Immigration to the United States by Region*

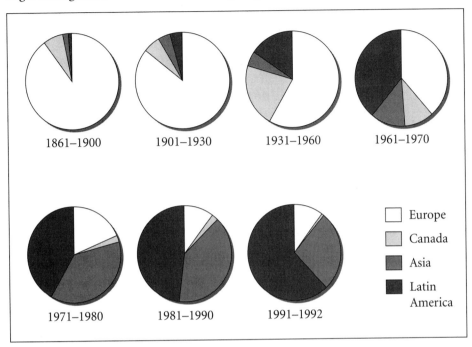

Source: Daniels, 1990; U.S. Bureau of the Census, 1995a.

Not surprisingly, the racial and ethnic composition of the country has changed more quickly and dramatically in the past decade than at any previous time in the 20th century. Experts estimate that by the year 2000 the Hispanic population will increase by 21%, the Asian-American population by 22%, and the African-American population by 12%. In contrast, the white population will increase by about 2% (Baca-Zinn & Eitzen, 1993).

The strains of high immigration levels are likely to continue for some time. Most people who immigrate to this country are pulled by the lure of employment and a better life. Until population and economic pressures ease in other regions of the world, the United States will remain an appealing destination. And as long as U.S. employers are willing to hire illegal immigrants, then it seems unlikely that enhanced efforts to seal the borders against them or to limit their access to education and social programs will be successful (R. L. Clark & Passel, 1993).

Social Responses to Immigrants

As their numbers grow, immigrants find that they are becoming the targets of a variety of social anxieties, from economic tension to outright anger (Sontag, 1992). Although immigrants contribute to the economy through their work and the taxes they pay, they are widely perceived to be an economic drag on society, using health, school, and police services while spreading crime, drug trafficking, and disease (Reinhold, 1993). One study estimates that the millions of immigrants, legal and illegal, who will enter the country in the next decade will cost taxpayers approximately $668 billion dollars in welfare, primary and secondary education, and Medicaid (Huddle, 1993).

The problem is particularly acute in California. In a 1992 survey, 76% of Californians felt there were too many immigrants entering their state; 78% said immigrants had become a financial burden on the state; and 80% thought steps should be taken to limit immigration (cited in Miles, 1992).

Given these perceptions, we should not be too surprised that violence against immigrants, or "immigrant bashing," is becoming more common throughout the United States:

- In Los Angeles, a television news crew videotaped the clubbing of two illegal Mexican immigrants by sheriff's deputies.
- A Salvadoran dishwasher was beaten and robbed; his attackers told him, "You steal our jobs, we steal your money."
- A Mexican immigrant who sells flowers on a street corner was routinely spat upon by passersby and told to return to her country.
- A 15-year-old Vietnamese boy was stomped to death by two skinheads in Houston. As he was dying, he reportedly cried out, "God forgive me for coming to this country!" (Sontag, 1992).
- In Detroit, a Chinese American was beaten to death with a baseball bat as his assailants shouted, "It's because of you that we're out of work!" (Levin, 1993).

The changing ethnic configuration of the population is not just heightening tensions between immigrant groups and whites but may also increase animosity *between* minority groups. As discussed in chapters 11 and 12, we have a two-tiered occupational structure in which jobs on the lower rung tend to belong to members of racial minorities. To the extent that vast waves of immigration mean greater competition for unskilled jobs, those most affected by the presence of immigrants may well be other people of color. For instance, janitorial companies serving downtown Los Angeles have almost entirely replaced their unionized black workforce with nonunionized, and therefore less expensive, immigrants from Latin America and Asia. African Americans are also being forced out of jobs as gardeners, busboys, construction workers, and nannies (Miles, 1992).

New immigrants also face animosity from members of their own racial or ethnic groups who arrived earlier. According to the 1992 Latino National Political Survey, over 70% of the respondents—which included people of Cuban, Mexican, and Puerto Rican descent—felt that too many Hispanic immigrants were coming into this country (Suro, 1992). About two-thirds of them felt that special preferences should not be given to Latin American immigrants. The researchers concluded that the strain of competing with recent Hispanic immigrants is felt as strongly by Hispanics as it is by whites.

Our country has always had a love-hate relationship with immigrants. In good times they have been inexpensive and welcome contributors to the economy. Their labor helped build our rail system and our roads. They filled unwanted jobs, opened businesses, and improved the lives of many Americans by working cheaply as housekeepers, dishwashers, and gardeners. When times are bad, however, or when the political winds shift, the inclination is to shut the door and blame them for many of the country's economic and social woes.

■ ■ ■ ■ ■ ■ ■ ■ ■

MICRO-MACRO CONNECTION
The Peculiar Politics of Immigration

The growing hostility directed toward immigrants lately has been fueled, to a large degree, by anti-immigrant sentiments voiced by politicians, lobbyists, academics, and writers who have capitalized on the frustration of some Americans over increasing competition for jobs and social services.

In 1996 the conservative Republican Pat Buchanan ran his unsuccessful but influential presidential campaign on a theme that immigrants were overrunning the country and would soon "dilute" our European character. He called for the immediate deportation of all illegal aliens and advocated an impenetrable barrier along the border between the United States and Mexico to keep them out.

You might think that harsh, anti-immigrant rhetoric would be the exclusive domain of conservative politicians. But these sentiments stem from divergent concerns and interests and cross traditional party lines. For instance, both presidential candidates in 1996 supported limits on immigration. Liberal Democratic politicians—like California's Senator Dianne Feinstein—have also called on the government to seal the nation's border. Their concern is that immigration, both legal and illegal, hurts poor Americans. According to one liberal journalist, competition with immigrants has accounted for roughly half the recent decline in wages among unskilled workers (Lind, 1996). The greatest gains in income by middle- and working-class Americans came between 1920 and 1960, an era of immigration restriction. In addition, some environmentalist groups—typically associated with politically liberal causes—oppose immigration on the grounds that it will render an already overcrowded country unable to protect its environment (Holmes, 1995).

In 1994, California voters overwhelmingly approved a measure that would have denied illegal immigrants a broad array of welfare benefits and social services, including nonemergency medical care and schooling. The referendum has since been tied up in a series of lawsuits. In 1996, the U.S. Senate passed a bill, the

Immigration and Financial Responsibility Act, which authorized the hiring of an additional 4,700 U.S. border patrol agents, made it more difficult for those here illegally to gain employment, and set limits on social services available to illegal immigrants (Graham, 1996). Other legislation is directed toward limiting the rights of *legal* immigrants. The 1996 welfare bill slashes the number of legal immigrants using government programs that provide services such as prenatal care, job training, college loans, Medicaid, and supplemental security income (Schmitt, 1996b).

But not everyone involved in politics is so fervently anti-immigrant. On this issue, too, we see rather odd coalitions of groups at vastly different ends of the political spectrum. Some Christian fundamentalists, for instance, assert that proposals to restrict immigration preferences for parents and siblings of naturalized American citizens is "antifamily." The National Rifle Association and the American Civil Liberties Union—as politically opposite as two organizations could be—are opposed to a proposal that immigrants be required to carry a national identification card containing a photograph and fingerprints. For many civil rights organizations and advocates of ethnic minorities, immigration is a human rights issue, and hostility toward immigrants is seen as fundamentally racist (Holmes, 1995).

Some conservative economists have even taken a pro-immigration stance, arguing that immigrants are directly responsible for the economic recoveries some areas experienced in the mid-1990s. In California, for example, the number of Latino-owned companies grew from 70,000 in 1982 to 280,000 in 1996. California immigrants are more likely to be self-employed, start their own businesses, and experience quick advances in income than their American-born counterparts (Kotkin, 1996). Real estate developers there credit immigrants with saving the faltering real estate market:

> Indians and Vietnamese . . . now anchor the housing market in the middle-class areas. . . . Latinos . . . have been buying up properties in more working class areas. . . . And many Asians, particularly Chinese, have become important, perhaps even leading, buyers of high-priced homes in upscale areas. (Kotkin, 1996, p. A14)

Furthermore, many wealthy owners of manufacturing facilities and agricultural businesses that employ large numbers of workers believe that the free flow of people across national borders leads to prosperity. Immigration, especially by easily exploited undocumented workers, provides abundant, cheap labor (Graham, 1996).

This issue illustrates a clash of political and economic forces. To politicians of all stripes, immigration is a valuable, hot-button campaign issue. But as long as powerful business interests see a need for a pool of cheap, mobile labor that is willing to work outside union and regulatory constraints, attempts to "close the borders" will remain ineffective. Until U.S. laws barring the employment of illegal aliens are fully enforced, poor foreigners will continue to come here. The conflict-ing interests have produced a stalemate:

> We now live in a time when everything crosses national borders—images, capital, technology, disease, ideas—and as the century draws to a close, there will no doubt be more dramatic demands that the border be properly policed. These demands our government will oblige with grand operations and congressional bills designed to pacify the populace until after the next election. We should, however, expect little by way of substantive change—just more empty gestures and more aliens. (Graham, 1996, p. 50)

▪ ▪ ▪

The "Graying" of America

At the same time that the United States must deal with the changing ethnic and racial configuration of its population, it also has to address a monumental shift in its age structure. The age structure of a society is one of the key factors determin-ing the need for various social resources. Very young people require physical care and protection. Use of educational resources is based, in large part, on the age of individuals. Workers at the beginning and end of their careers are more suscep-tible to unemployment than those at midcareer. And age is the major determi-nant of decisions to retire.

The age structure can even influence certain social problems in ways that are not immediately apparent. Take crime, for instance. According to the FBI, almost 50% more arrests were made in the United States in 1980 than in 1970. To some this statistic showed that society had fallen apart. To others it was proof that the country had turned into a police state. Actually, neither was true. The large baby boom cohort had reached its late teens and early 20s, a period in the life course when criminal activity is most common (L. E. Cohen & Land, 1987). The crime rates went up not because crime became a more desirable pursuit or because Americans as a whole became less respectful of the law but simply because there were more people at the age when criminal activity is statistically more likely to take place.

Perhaps the most important and most problematic demographic trend in this country today involves the increasing average age of the population. Two hun-dred years ago, the median age for Americans was 16. Today it is about 34.6. It is expected to be close to 39 by the middle of the next century, as the massive baby boom cohort reaches old age (U.S. Bureau of the Census, 1995d).

Two developments in the 1960s and 1970s changed the age structure of the United States in dramatic ways (Preston, 1984). The first was a decrease in the number of children being born. From 1960 to 1982, the number of children un-der 15 fell by 7%. During this period the birth rate dropped from 3.7 births per

Figure 14.6   *Percent Distribution of the Population, by Age: 1990–2050*

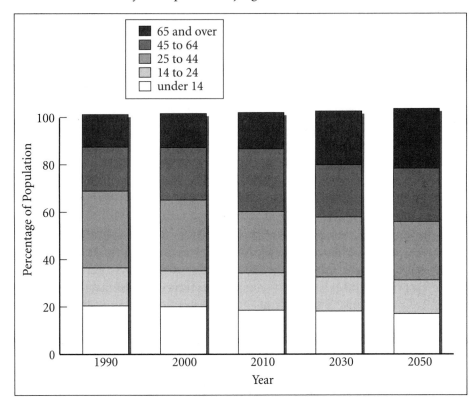

Source: U.S. Bureau of the Census, 1993a.

woman to about 2.0 (Yorburg, 1993). Furthermore, more families than ever chose to have only one child.

The other development was a rapid increase in the number of people surviving to old age. Between 1960 and 1980, the proportion of people over 65 grew by 54%. By 2030 there will be more old people in this country than children (see Figure 14.6). The number of people over 85, an age group for which health care costs are exceptionally high, will grow fastest of all, doubling to 6.5 million by 2020 and soaring to 17.7 million by 2050. More than one million people will be over the age of 100 by then as well (Pear, 1992). Technological advances in medicine and nutrition have extended the lives of countless numbers of Americans who would have routinely died several decades ago. Life expectancy has risen from 70.8 in 1970 to 75.5 in 1993 and is projected to be 78 by the year 2010 (U.S. Bureau of the Census, 1995d).

Why should we be concerned about the "graying" of the American population? The answer is that a society with an aging population will inevitably experi-

ence increased demands for pensions, health care, and other social services catering to the needs of the elderly (OECD, 1988). Moreover, aging populations
change the assumptions we make about our economy, the family, and the larger
culture.

Effects on the Economy

One of the key concerns arising out of this trend is whether society, and in particular the working population, will be able and willing to bear the additional
burden of caring for the growing number of elderly people. This concern has led
demographers to look at the statistical relationship between the elderly and the
rest of the population. This relationship tells us a great deal about the social, political, and economic effort society may be asked to make in support of its elderly
(Kart, 1990). By 2030 the ratio of elderly people (that is, those over 65) to people
of working age (18 to 64) will be three times greater than it was in 1950, meaning
that workers, on average, will have to support three times as many older people.

This figure is probably exaggerated. Not all people over 65 are retired, nor are
they all in poor health. And not all people between the ages of 18 and 64 are
working, nor are they all in good health (Friedland, 1989). Nevertheless, the re-
tirements of older people will be directly or indirectly financed by the working-
age population through Social Security and other pension programs. Unless the
future's elderly are better able to support themselves financially than today's elderly, the government, through tax dollars, will have to play an even larger role in
providing health care and other services.

The graying of America is challenging employers to restructure the workplace. Many more workers have been choosing early retirement, and fewer young
workers are available to replace them. As a result, the cost of labor is likely to go
up in the future. Some employers will be forced to focus more attention on employee productivity, perhaps turning to machines to replace workers. On the
positive side, however, because of the impending labor shortage, employers will
have to pay attention to the needs of their valuable employees and find better
ways to attract and retain them (Friedland, 1989). We may see more employers
providing assistance with child and elder care. Employers may also have to find
ways to keep older workers interested in working longer rather than retiring by
offering bonuses for continued employment or by creating prestigious and well-
paid part-time positions.

Effects on the Family

The growth of the elderly population will have an enormous impact on the
American family as well. In the distant past it was quite rare for a child to know,
let alone grow up with, his or her grandparents. It made sense to focus on the

nuclear family. However, with many families today having four or even five generations alive at the same time, it becomes increasingly difficult to conceptualize the family simply in terms of parents and children. Today over half of all people over 65 have great-grandchildren (Baca-Zinn & Eitzen, 1993).

One important familial consequence of increasing longevity is prolonged marriage. When life expectancy was lower, the average marriage ended as a result of the death of one of the spouses after only 20 or so years of marriage. At the turn of the century, more than half of all marriages were ended by the death of one spouse before the last child had left home (Kart, 1990). Today, the average couple could live 30 years or more after the last child has left home. It's estimated that, apart from divorce, one out of every five married couples will celebrate their 50th anniversary (Glick & Norton, 1977).

In a graying society, married couples have more time to compile extensive common experiences and share broad historical changes, but they also have more time to get on each other's nerves (Preston, 1976). Divorce among older people— a segment of the population typically assumed to be beyond the reach of national trends in divorce—has more than doubled since 1960 (Uhlenberg & Myers, 1981). Between 1980 and 1994, the number of divorced individuals over the age of 65 increased from 3.5 million to 5.6 million (U.S. Bureau of the Census, 1995a). Now, in a sense, people are "outliving" their marriages.

Increased longevity also extends the amount of time parents spend with their children. It will not be uncommon in the near future for a significant number of parents and children to spend 60 years together, of which only 18 are in the traditional parent-child relationship (Riley, 1983). A government study found that one or both parents are still alive for 44% of people between the ages of 58 and 66 (Kolata, 1993). Certainly such longevity increases the number of important experiences that parents and children can share. However, it also increases the financial and emotional burdens on the children when they reach adulthood, resulting in role conflict. The likelihood that one's parents will live well into their 80s means that, for many people, their role as someone's child and the accompanying responsibilities will long overlap their roles as someone's spouse and parent.

Effects on Culture

Care of the growing numbers of the very old will be one of the country's most urgent social issues over the next several decades. It is further complicated by the low cultural value traditionally placed on the elderly in this society. For many of us, the elderly represent precisely what we spend a significant portion of our lives trying to deny: our own mortality. Old people symbolize disease, disability, and death (Butler, 1975). As a result, they are one of the most excluded age groups in American society today.

Elderly people are likely to experience prejudice, discrimination, and residential segregation simply because they are old. Common stereotypes about the elderly—that they're sick, slow-witted, senile, mean, depressed, and drive too slowly—reinforce the public perception that they are socially worthless (Neugarten, 1980). As with other forms of prejudice, these perceptions are usually translated into action, that is, discrimination. The Age Discrimination Employment Act of 1967 prohibits hiring, firing, wage determination, or other privileges and conditions of employment on the basis of age. It is clear, however, that age discrimination in employment practices still exists today. Mandatory retirement policies in some businesses operate on the assumption that all people experience a decrease in mental and physical capabilities when they reach a certain age. As long as the elderly are perceived to be rigid, unhealthy, unhappy, and unemployable, discriminatory treatment accorded them will continue to be justified. It will also be difficult to convince younger people that tax dollars ought to be spent on supporting the elderly.

Cohort Inequality and the Tarnished American Dream

In all societies, different age groups have different rights, duties, and privileges (Riley, Johnson, & Foner, 1972). They are subjected to different societal expectations and accorded different access to social resources. Such age stratification is as influential as class, income, race, and gender stratification.

You might think that a change in America's age structure would help young people and hurt old people. Fewer young people should mean less competition for resources and greater availability of social services; an increase in old people should strain institutions such as nursing homes, hospitals, and Social Security. However, the economic well-being of the elderly has actually been steadily improving since the 1960s, while that of the younger cohorts—baby boomers and Generation X alike—has been steadily deteriorating (Preston, 1984). According to the U.S. Census, real income for people over 65 increased 52.6% between 1967 and 1987; the increase for all others was about 7%. During the 1980s the only age group to suffer a drop in real income—10.8%—were people under 25.

In the early 1970s a typical 30-year-old male made 6% more than a typical 60-year-old male; today he makes 14% less. Although most teens today expect to have an annual income over $30,000 by the time they're 30, according to the U.S. Census Bureau in 1990, the number of Americans between ages 25 and 29 who made less than $30,000 outnumbered those who made more by eight to one (Howe & Strauss, 1992).

For people beginning their families and careers in the late 1980s and early 1990s, inflation widened the gulf between their quality of life and that of their parents and grandparents. The average price of a new house went up 294% during the 1980s. Federal income taxes went up 175%, and state taxes increased by 520%. Social Security taxes went up 331%. The cost of having a baby in a hospital increased 233%. Tuition costs at private universities doubled or even tripled

(P. Light, 1988). On virtually every available economic indicator, today's young people lag behind previous generations.

Consequently, over the past several decades there have been dramatic changes in the proportion of young people who live in poverty relative to the proportion of elderly. In 1970, 16% of children under age 16 lived in poverty compared to 25% of those older than 65 (Preston, 1984). By 1994 the situation had been completely reversed: 22% of children lived in poverty compared to 12% of the elderly (U.S. Bureau of the Census, 1995a). Sixty-nine percent of the wealthiest 400 people in this country are 65 years of age or older ("The Forbes four hundred," 1990). Certainly not all old people are this wealthy, but their economic status as a group does continue to improve.

Not surprisingly, many young people today feel that the American Dream is unattainable, at least for them. They fear they will be the first generation to fail to match their parents' economic success (Shapiro, 1993). In a 1990 poll, two out of three Americans between the ages of 18 and 29 thought it would be much harder for people in their generation to live as comfortably as previous generations. Sixty-nine percent believe they will have more trouble buying a house, 52% feel they will have less leisure time, and 53% are worried about their future (D. M. Gross & Scott, 1990). Today, 75% of Americans between the ages of 18 and 24 still live at home—the largest percentage since the Great Depression of the 1930s (D. M. Gross & Scott, 1990). These so-called boomerang kids are finding independent life away from home difficult, if not impossible, to sustain.

■ ■ ■ ■ ■ ■ ■ ■

RUTH SIDEL
"Twenty-something" Women on Their Own

To examine the life outlooks of today's young people, sociologist Ruth Sidel interviewed 150 women in their late teens and early 20s. She wanted to know what members of this generation thought about family, work, and women's roles in contemporary society. Sidel found that many young women today believe very strongly in the basic tenets of the American Dream: that with enough hard work they will "make it." As she put it, "They have bought into the image of a bright future" (1990, p. 18).

Such dreams are quite different from those held by young women only two generations ago. Those women, for the most part, did not perceive themselves as independent individuals with their own futures and their own needs. Their identities were determined by their ability to satisfy the needs of others, usually as wives or mothers. But by the 1970s and 1980s women had come to feel that they were entitled to play roles formerly reserved for men. They saw no reason they couldn't contribute to fields like medicine, law, or politics. Most agreed that if they were ever to gain the same recognition and respect as men, they would have to enter the male-dominated public sphere, for that is where the real money, power, and status lie.

The young women in Sidel's research had a strong commitment to career, material wealth, success, and independence. One of the common desires of all of the women interviewed was to be affluent. In fact, the dreams of these women were remarkably similar across racial and ethnic groups, class lines, and levels of education. Today's young women are the first generation to take for granted that they, like men, deserve their fair share of the American Dream.

But Sidel found lurking behind all these dreams and ambitions an almost overwhelming sense of despair. The young women she interviewed consistently expressed the belief that they are essentially on their own. They are convinced that if they are to "make it" they will have to do it by themselves. Their dreams of success have become symbols of identity in an era of "fragmented family life, insecure, often transient work relationships, and a vanishing sense of community" (Sidel, 1990, p. 223).

On the one hand, this focus on individualism signals a growing sense of independence and personal responsibility among young women, a sign that they have acquired the voice of hearty American individualism that had long been suppressed. On the other hand, Sidel speculates that perhaps the women of this generation have been hoodwinked into believing that they can do it all, have it all, and be it all while society itself remains largely unchanged in its neglect of youth. In other words, is the self-sufficiency this generation perceives to be necessary possible within the current structure of American society? Clearly the dilemmas facing young women today are as much a function of their times as of their gender. The baby boomers raised women's expectations to unprecedented levels. Yet the increasing economic burdens on today's young women limit their ability to fulfill these expectations. We can see the enormous generational relevance of the subtitle of Sidel's book: *Growing Up in the Shadow of the American Dream*. The dream looms large—casting a broad shadow over all aspects of life—yet it remains a shadow, something that can be seen but not grasped.

■ ■ ■

Conclusion

The interconnectedness of private experiences and macro-structural forces is clearly felt in the relationship between population trends and everyday life. You have seen in this chapter that our destinies, whether positive or negative, can be profoundly influenced by the size, ethnic makeup, and age structure of the population in our country as well as in other countries. You have also seen how the experiences of your birth cohort are shaped by the processes, events, and social changes that occur in society as you progress through the life course. In sum, the process of growing older is much more complex than simply adding a year to your age each birthday. It involves the private experience of major world events, cultural trends, and shifts in population characteristics.

In discussing current and future demographic trends, I can't help but think about my own children and their as yet unnamed generation. As I write this book they are 7 and 10. Their generation will be the first to reach the teen years during the 21st century. I wonder what kind of impact being born in the late 1980s and growing up in the 1990s will have on their lives. Will the world's population reach the predicted catastrophic proportions, or will we figure out a way to control population growth and enable all people to live quality lives? Will the growing ethnic diversity of this society continue to create tension and conflict, or will we eventually learn how to be a truly multicultural nation? What will be their cohort's single, most definitive "punctuating" event: a war, an assassination, a severe economic depression, or some other unimaginable catastrophe? Or will it be world peace, an end to hunger and homelessness, or a cure for AIDS?

I also wonder how well our important social institutions will serve their generation. What will their experience in higher education be like? Will jobs be waiting for them when they are ready to go to work? What will be their share of the national debt? How will they perceive family life? Will marriage be an outdated mode of intimacy by the time they reach adulthood? What will be a desirable family size?

As a parent, of course, I'm more than a little curious about how these questions will be answered. I want to know the answers right now! But as a sociologist, I realize that they will emerge only from the experiences and interactions of my kids, and others their age, as they progress through their lives. Herein lies the unique and fundamental message of the sociological perspective. As powerful and relentless as the demographic and generational forces described in this chapter are in determining my children's life chances, the responsibility for shaping and changing this society in the 21st century ultimately rests in the hands of their generation. It is this topic—the ability of individuals to change and reconstruct their society—that will serve as the theme for the final chapter.

CHAPTER HIGHLIGHTS

■ Often overlooked in our quest to identify the structural factors that shape our everyday experiences are the effects of our birth cohort. Birth cohorts are more than just a collection of individuals born within a few years of each other; they are distinctive generations tied together by historical events, national and global population trends, and large-scale societal changes.

■ The earth's population is growing at an unprecedented rate. But different countries experience different rates of growth. Poor, developing countries are expanding rapidly, while the populations in wealthy, developed countries have either stabilized or, in some cases, declined.

■ When the population of a country grows rapidly, the age structure is increasingly dominated by young people. In slow-growth countries with low birth rates and high life expectancy, the population is much older.

■ As conditions in developing countries grow worse, pressures to migrate increase, creating a variety of cultural, political, and economic fears in countries experiencing high levels of immigration.

■ All societies have a system whereby different age groups are stratified and given different rights, duties, and privileges. The changing age structure of the American population—more older people and fewer younger people—has meant that the gap between rich and poor has increasingly become a gap between old and young.

YOUR TURN

Demographers often use "population pyramids" to graphically display the age and sex distributions of a population (refer back to Figure 14.3). These pictures are often used to draw conclusions about a population's most pressing economic, educational, and social needs. Using information from the most recent U.S. Census (available in the government documents section of your school's library), construct population pyramids for several different types of cities:

■ a college town (for example, Ann Arbor, Michigan; Iowa City, Iowa)
■ a military town (for example, Norfolk, Virginia; Annapolis, Maryland)
■ a large urban city (for example, New York, Chicago, Los Angeles)
■ a small rural town
■ an affluent suburb
■ a city with a large elderly retirement community (for example, St. Petersburg, Florida; Sun City, Arizona)

The pyramids should use the following structure:

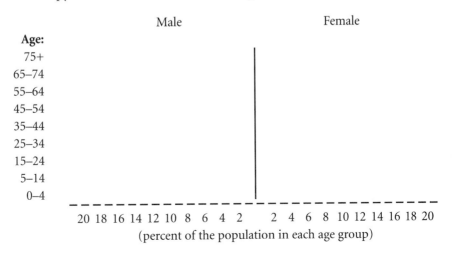

Describe how the age and sex profiles of these cities differ. What other characteristics of these cities would be different as a result of the shape of their populations? Consider the following:

- the nature of the educational system
- the types of businesses that would succeed and fail
- the sorts of recreational opportunities available
- important political issues and the degree of citizen involvement in political activity
- important health care issues
- crime rates
- divorce rates
- suicide rates

From these differences draw some general conclusions about how people's lives are influenced by the age and sex distribution of the population in their cities.

THE SOCIOLOGY OF THE CONTEMPORARY IMMIGRANT

DOUGLAS HARPER with photographs © KEN LIGHT[*]

"Discrimination and violence against immigrants are worldwide phenomena....fueled by fear of outsiders by outright racism...."

The photos in this essay are taken from the book, *To the Promised Land,* by Ken Light and Richard Rodriguez (Aperture, 1988). As you study this visual narrative, reflect on the following themes drawn from the chapter:

- Immigration is a function of global imbalances. These imbalances are increasing; gaps between the rich and the poor in almost all countries are growing larger, and gaps between rich and poor countries are becoming greater.

- There is rapid population growth in developing countries, and there are stable or declining rates of growth in developed countries.

- In most Third World countries, there is widespread migration from rural areas to urban areas, where the quality of life is particularly poor.

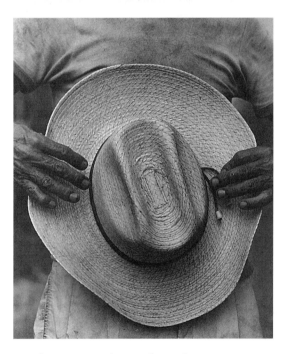

Handwoven campesino *sombrero, Oaxaca.*

Discrimination and violence against immigrants are worldwide phenomena, particularly acute in Europe as well as America. They are fueled by fear of outsiders or by outright racism. America is a land of immigrants, yet those who arrived only a generation or two ago treat the more recently arrived as aliens and outsiders. Although it would be rational for

[*]Detail in top photograph on this page cropped from photograph by Ken Light appearing on page 532.

Father and his sons looking al Norte *from Cañon Zapata.*

developed countries, with stable or declining birth rates, to welcome immigrants from developing countries to participate in a growing economy, few individuals in the developed countries see the situation in societal terms. Rather, people in developed countries see immigrants as a personal threat against their own economic security.

Immigrants (legal or illegal) have two primary functions in the labor market. First, they become servants, cooks, and nannies for the middle class, providing the middle class with the accoutrements of the rich. Second, immigrants compete with the most disadvantaged in developed countries for the least desirable jobs. Thus their participation in the labor force keeps wages low and lessens the pressure to address the particular problems of agricultural and other labor. In this way, the U.S. consumer has the benefit of products made with cheap labor.

The photo essay reproduced here shows that the Mexican "illegal immigrants" were members of a close-knit village life before economic pressures drove them across the border. Whether or not we approve of the illegal flight across the border, we must recognize the danger and humiliation it represents. Immigrants in the United States adapt to a servile, oppressed, and

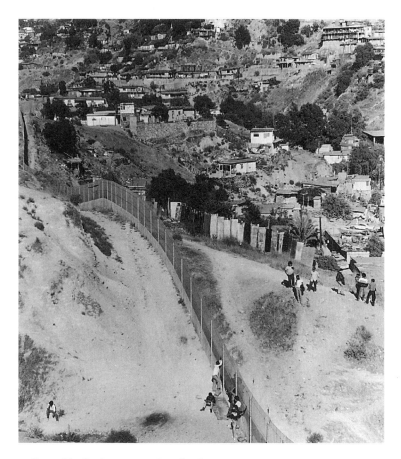

La linea *(the line), U.S.-Mexican border.*

"*I can only talk about the way I came across. It was very difficult for me. I'm not used to doing that—run all night, hide, jump. It's like the cat and the mouse, with the fear of being caught.*"
—LEONOR R., 23, Tepejillo, Oaxaca

exploited culture. They live in substandard housing and perform many of the hardest jobs in the economy for some of the worst wages. In the back of their minds they remember the cul-ture they have left behind, supportive networks of family and village. In Mexico, say the immi-grants, the men are allowed to sing, and they sing love songs.

Mother and nursing child,
Acaquizapan, Oaxaca.

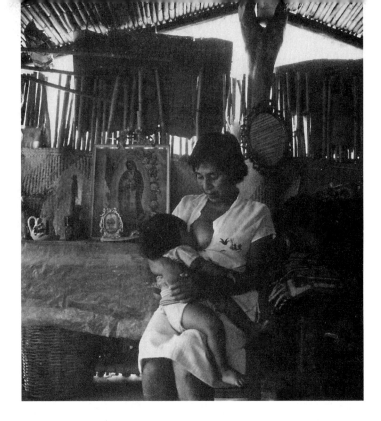

Leaving Cañon Zapata for
el Norte.

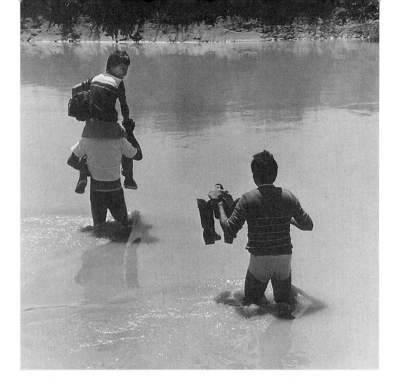

"Wetbacks" crossing the Rio Bravo (Rio Grande), El Paso, Texas.

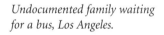

Undocumented family waiting for a bus, Los Angeles.

"El aqujero international" *("the
international hole"), Tijuana/San Ysidro.*

Caught running from
la migra *(Border patrol),*
San Ysidro.

Indocumentados discovered in the trunk of a car abandoned by their coyote (a person who helps others cross the border illegally), San Ysidro.

Border patrol agent with "la perrera" ("van for the dogs") and men apprehended at "Japs Drive," San Ysidro.

Room with a sink, 6th Street, Los Angeles.

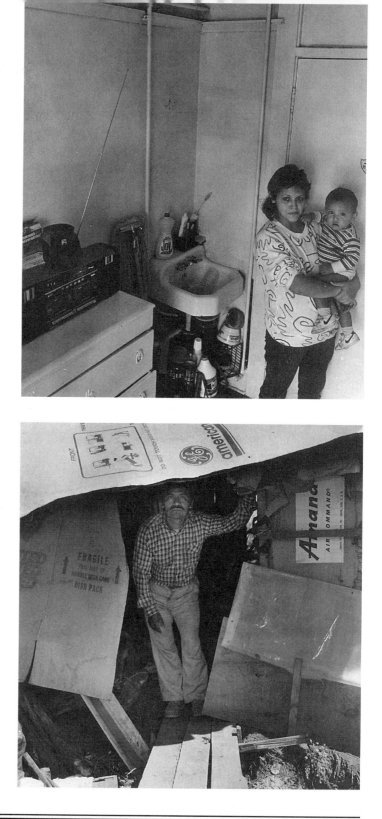

Makeshift home, northern San Diego County.

CHAPTER 15

Architects of Change: Reconstructing Society

- *The Elements of Social Change*
- *Collective Action and Change*
- *Social Movements*
- *Reconstructing Society: The Sociological Imagination Revisited*
- *Conclusion and Farewell*

The 1992 film *Lorenzo's Oil* dramatized the true story of a couple, Augusto and Michaela Odone, who discover that their son, Lorenzo, is suffering from a rare disease known as adrenoleukodystrophy (ALD). ALD destroys the protective coating around nerve fibers, progressively impairing victims' ability to talk, walk, and care for themselves. Death is slow, painful, and certain. Frustrated by doctors' overwhelming pessimism and inability to treat their son's disease, and having no scientific training whatsoever, the Odones launched a two-person crusade to find a treatment. They read obscure medical journals and managed to find a few medical and chemical experts who were willing to help them. They eventually discovered that a combination of two natural oils would stop the physical decline brought about by ALD. The film ends with a visual testimony to the many other children who used the Odones' oily concoction and were spared the debilitating effects of the disease.

As with all films derived from real-life events, there is some debate as to whether the facts of Lorenzo's life and the actions of his parents are different from what were portrayed in the film. Nevertheless, the message is sociologically compelling: Two individuals were able to overcome the institutional indifference of the medical establishment to find their own solution to a seemingly insoluble problem.

The Odones succeeded in helping their son precisely because the medical establishment could not. From an institutional perspective, there is little profit for pharmaceutical companies that invest in so-called *orphan diseases*, ailments that affect only a small percentage of the total population. Furthermore, new drugs must be tested meticulously to determine their effectiveness and to identify all potentially dangerous side effects. A sharp line must be drawn between the need to satisfy the principles of sound scientific method and the desire to help individual people (D. J. Rothman & Edgar, 1992). As we have seen throughout this book, institutions must operate in a highly structured, standardized, and impersonal way, at a level above the interests and personalities of the individual people they are created to serve. Imagine the chaos that would ensue if all parents with sick children went around challenging medical science and creating their own treatments. The entire health care system would quickly collapse.

But such institutional needs are often little comfort to the individuals whose lives operate under the influence of that institution. Lorenzo's story, while illustrating the inherent tension between individuals and institutions, also shows that individuals can overcome bureaucratic lethargy and actually change a part of their social structure. As a result of the Odones's actions, the standard medical approach to ALD will probably never be the same again.

The Odones aren't the only individuals who have succeeded in "altering the system." AIDS activists, frustrated by mounting deaths and a government drug-approval process that often takes years to get drugs into the hands of the people who need them, have succeeded in changing the way drugs are developed and regulated for AIDS so that potentially helpful treatments can be produced more quickly (Arno & Feiden, 1992). Unlike Lorenzo's parents, however, AIDS activists are members of an organized social movement.

This theme, the power of individuals acting collectively to influence the structural elements of their society, guides us through this final chapter of the book. I have spent the previous 14 chapters discussing how our society and everything in it is socially constructed and how these social constructions, in turn, impact the lives of individuals. At times the message has been pessimistic, even downright gloomy. It's hard not to feel a little helpless when discussing the control that culture, bureaucracies, institutions, and systems of social stratification have over our lives. And it's hard to be upbeat when discussing things like poverty, racial and sexual inequality, and the global population explosion. It's only fitting, then, to end on a positive note with a discussion of social change and how individuals can reconstruct their society.

The Elements of Social Change

Whether it occurs in our personal relationships, in our cultural norms and values, in our systems of stratification, or in our institutions, change is the preeminent characteristic of modern human societies. Political challengers running for elected office often base their campaigns on the concept of change. Bill Clinton in 1992 and Bob Dole in 1996 frequently used terms like *a new age, revolutionary,* and *a time of great excitement.* Granted, these phrases may simply have been hollow campaign rhetoric. But beyond politics they do seem to characterize all corners of human life as we approach the 21st century.

The world in which you are living at this precise moment is undoubtedly different from the one I experienced when I wrote this book. I've had to revise several examples at the last minute because some things have changed so abruptly. It seems that everywhere you look—your relationships, your school, your job, your home, your entertainment equipment, your diet, your clothes, and your government—institutional and cultural change is the rule, not the exception.

Consider family life in America over the past 30 or 40 years. Divorce rates skyrocketed, then stabilized. Women have entered the workforce in unprecedented numbers. People are waiting longer to get married, and once they do, they are having fewer children. Cultural concerns over gender equality have altered the way men and women relate to one another inside and outside the home. Social and sexual rules that once seemed permanent have disintegrated: Unmarried couples can live openly together, unmarried women can have and keep their babies, remaining single and remaining childless have become acceptable lifestyle options (Skolnick & Skolnick, 1992). In short, today's American family bears little resemblance to the cultural ideal of the 1950s.

These changes have, in turn, affected other institutions. Because so many families are headed by dual-earner couples, children spend less time with their parents than they did in the past, forcing them to depend on secondary relationships: paid caregivers, friends, teachers. Schools are being called on to address many of society's social problems by providing students with training in moral values and technological "literacy," the provision of adequate nutrition, and practical instruction to help them avoid drug and alcohol abuse, teen pregnancy, and AIDS. It's not surprising that the very nature of childhood is also changing.

Contemporary social critics argue that childhood has all but disappeared. Children today are exposed to events, devices, and ideas that would have been inconceivable to their baby boom parents. The cultural "secrets" of adulthood—death, illness, violence, and sexuality—are revealed to them in their homes, in their schools, in their neighborhoods, on their computer networks, and on television. We read about sixth graders who have to pass metal detectors to enter their schools; 12-year-olds becoming pregnant; 7-year-olds being tried for such crimes as rape and drug smuggling. Recently prosecutors in a northern California county charged a 6-year-old boy with attempted murder for dumping a neighbor's four-week-old infant out of its bassinet and beating it nearly to death. (The charges were eventually dropped.)

Recent studies have unearthed some startling findings:

- 1 in 6 children between the ages of 10 and 17 has seen someone shot or knows someone who has been shot.
- 1 in 12 high school students has attempted suicide, and 1 in 4 has seriously considered it.
- 1 in 8 high school students carries a weapon to school, and 1 in 9 stays away from school because of fear.
- 1 in 3 13-year-olds uses drugs.
- The number of children under 18 arrested for violent crimes has more than doubled since 1970; the number arrested for weapons violations has tripled.

Kids today worry about everything from contracting AIDS to drive-by shootings to not being able to find a good job (Adler, 1994; Applebome, 1996b; Kantrowitz, 1993).

Psychologists estimate that children today are about 2 to 3 years ahead of children their age 25 years ago:

> The idea of childhood as a sheltered time, free from adult anxieties, is becoming a nostalgic luxury in a world where young people die of AIDS and TV newscasts are filled with stories of child-pornography rings, kidnappings and the sorrowful faces of abused children. (Darton, 1991, p. 62)

The fundamental nature of work in American society has changed, too. If you had taken this course 30 years ago, your instructor would have needed only a few tools: a well-stocked collection of books, a manual typewriter, some pencils, a stack of carbon paper, and a love of the discipline. Good instructors today still need a love of the discipline (I hope), but it's becoming increasingly difficult to teach interestingly, effectively, and efficiently without taking advantage of state-of-the-art technology: a high-speed desktop computer, electronic mail, on-line databases, computerized test banks, colorful overhead projections, a video library, and access to photocopy and fax machines.

In the 1950s no one doubted that technology would dramatically improve their work lives. The automated future was going to be efficient, clean, and beautiful. Machines would take the drudgery out of virtually every task. However, no one foresaw the real impact of automation. Sophisticated machines and computers have reduced or, in some cases, completely displaced the need for human labor in many areas of manufacturing and business.

As a result, we have become what sociologists call a **postindustrial society**, one in which knowledge, the control of information, and the provision of services are more important than manufacturing and production (Bell, 1976). An economic way of life that once centered around factories and the production of material goods now revolves around information and service industries, including public relations, tourism, advertising, insurance, banking and finance, and computer systems.

Sources of Social Change

Where do all these technological, cultural, and institutional changes come from? Sociologists tell us that social change can come from a variety of sources.

Environmental and Population Pressures

The increasing degradation of the land, sea, and air due to pollution has not only fostered changes in individual and community behavior, such as recycling and conservation, but has also served as the motivation behind innovations in environmentally safe products and services (low-watt light bulbs, low-flow shower heads, biodegradable detergent, and so on). Likewise, natural disasters like earthquakes and tornadoes often inspire improvements in home safety products and architectural design.

Consider also how the shifting size and shape of our population creates change in society. In the previous chapter I discussed how the movement of the baby boom cohort through the life course has and will continue to force all relevant social institutions to change along the way.

Cultural Innovation

Sometimes change is spurred by scientific discoveries and technological inventions within a society. The discovery of fire, electricity, and disease processes changed the nature of human lives and cultures for all time. The invention of the internal combustion engine, television, the microchip, and effective birth control have been instrumental in determining the course of history in the 20th century.

Social institutions can sometimes be slow to adjust to scientific and technological innovation. Artificial insemination, in vitro fertilization, surrogate motherhood, and other medical advances in the area of infertility have increased the number of people who can now have children. Yet these technological developments were changing the face of parenthood well before society began to recognize and address the ethical, moral, and legal issues raised by them.

Technological innovation can sometimes cause unforeseen negative consequences. Helmets and other safety and protective gear have actually made football a more dangerous sport; low-tar, low-nicotine cigarettes encourage people to continue smoking; lines at automated teller machines in the evening are longer than they used to be at bank tellers' windows during working hours (Tenner, 1996).

Similar problems have been created by the growth of computer technology. On a personal level, "Internet addiction" and "carpal tunnel syndrome" (a nerve disorder in the hands caused by too much keyboard use) are directly related to the spread of computers. Computers are indeed an indispensable tool in our postindustrial society and will no doubt have a lasting effect on the culture. They now keep track of vast quantities of crucial information in practically every area of society, including banks, schools, hospitals, credit companies, the military, and the government. Certainly our day-to-day lives have become more efficient as a result. But it didn't take long for clever "hackers" to figure out how they could use their own personal computers for nefarious purposes, breaking into larger systems to alter important and highly confidential information like bank accounts and credit ratings. When these acts were first recognized as a potentially dangerous problem, there were no laws against them. The legal system had not yet adjusted to this new activity. It took several years for a new body of criminal law to evolve that specifically focused on computer crimes (Hollinger & Lanza-Kaduce, 1988).

Diffusion of Technological or Cultural Practices

Another source of social change is diffusion: the process by which beliefs, technology, customs, and other cultural items are spread from one group or society to another. Most of the taken-for-granted aspects of our lives originally came from somewhere else. For instance, pajamas, clocks, toilets, glass, coins, newspapers, soap, even our alphabet and language were initially imported from other cultures (Linton, 1937). More recently, Japanese innovations in microelectronics have dramatically altered the patterns of communication, transportation, and personal entertainment in American society. At the same time, American culture, as expressed in fashion, art, music, and food, is being incorporated into the lives of many young Japanese.

Like cultural innovation, technological diffusion sometimes causes unforeseen problems. The worldwide use of antibiotics has created drug-resistant strains of bacteria that require the dispersion of new drugs. The heavy increase in international transportation—cars, trains, planes—has enabled destructive pests to migrate (Tenner, 1996).

Moreover, the diffusion process is not always friendly, as you recall from the discussion of colonization and forced assimilation in chapter 10. When one society's territory is taken over by another society, people may be required to adapt to new customs and beliefs. When the Europeans conquered the New World, Native American people were forced to abandon their traditional ways of life and become more "civilized." Hundreds of thousands of Native Americans died in the process, not only from warfare but also from new diseases inadvertently brought over by their conquerors.

The Speed of Social Change

Whatever the source of change, it is clearly a feature of all societies. But change is not always immediately apparent to individuals within a society. In the distant past, change tended to be slow, almost imperceptible, during the course of one's lifetime. Family and community traditions typically spanned many generations:

> From the time of the great pyramids in Egypt, built 4,700 years ago, to the time of Cleopatra, a bit over 2,000 years ago, the pace of change was so slow that few people in Egypt were aware of it. During that time there were significant advances in metallurgy, agriculture, ship building, astronomy, mathematics, statecraft, historiography and much more. But most Egyptian peasants in the Nile valley and delta were largely ignorant of these changes; for them life continued much as it was hundreds, even thousands of years before. (Chirot, 1994, p. 14)

Throughout the centuries, change has become more accelerated. You can see evidence in the way we characterize separate periods of history. We frame distant eras—periods with their own distinct cultures and social structures—in chunks of time hundreds of years long: the Middle Ages, the Dark Ages, the 19th century, and so forth. More recent eras, however, are packaged in terms of decades (the Roaring Twenties, the turbulent sixties). In fact, today it may take as little as half a decade for the culture to adopt a new set of characteristics and a new identity: the early 1980s versus the late 1980s. Many communities now hold "'80s revivals" complete with 1980s theme parties and radio shows. As one columnist put it, "We've sped up to the point where we're looking back to three years ago. Everything is happening faster in popular culture" (quoted in Silver, 1992, p. B4).

Because we live in a world that is in a constant state of flux, it's tempting to see concern with rapid social change as an exclusively contemporary issue. Keep in mind, however, that sociologists and other scholars have always expressed deep concern over the effects these changes have on people. Victorian social observers, for example, linked accelerated social change with 19th century England's high incidence of insanity:

> I doubt if ever the history of the world, or the experience of past ages, could show a larger amount of insanity than that of the present day. It seems, indeed, as if the world was moving at an advanced rate of speed proportionate to its approaching end; as though, in this rapid pace of time, increasing with each revolving century, a higher pressure is engendered on the minds of men and with this, there appears a tendency among all classes constantly to demand higher standards of intellectual attainment, a faster speed of intellectual traveling, greater fancies, greater forces, larger means than are commensurate with health. (quoted in Showalter, 1985, p. 25)

The 19th-century sociologist Émile Durkheim argued that rapid social change created a normative vacuum—what he called **anomie**—in which the old cultural rules that governed people's lives no longer applied. When things change quickly, through sudden economic shifts, wars, natural disasters, population explosions, or rapid transitions from a traditional to a modern society, people become disoriented and experience anomie as they search for new guidelines and rules.

Widespread anomie affects the larger society as well. When norms are disrupted by rapid social change, our naturally greedy impulses are unleashed. Without moral norms to constrain our unlimited aspirations and with too few resources to satisfy our unlimited desires, we are in a sense doomed to a frustrating life of striving for unattainable goals (Durkheim, 1897/1951). The result, Durkheim felt, is higher rates of suicide and criminal activity as well as weakened ties to family, neighborhood, and friends. What Durkheim considered rapid social change, though, would appear sluggish by contemporary standards.

The velocity of change today has affected the way sociologists go about their work. When American society was understood to be relatively stable, sociological study was fairly straightforward. Most social researchers in the 1950s believed that one could start a 5- or 10-year study of some social institution, like the family or work, and assume that that institution would still be much the same when the study ended (A. Wolfe, 1991). Today, such assumptions about the staying power of society are dubious at best. There is no such thing as a permanent social institution.

Collective Action and Change

One of the dangers of talking about the structural sources of social change or its cultural, environmental, and institutional consequences is that we then tend to see change as a purely macro-structural phenomenon, something that happens to us rather than something we create. But social change is not some huge, invisible hand that descends from the heavens to arbitrarily disrupt our routine way of life. It is, in the end, a phenomenon driven by human action.

In chapter 10 I discussed the fact that some segments of the population have greater access to important social and financial resources and therefore have greater power than other segments of the population. Don't conclude that only powerful people have the wherewithal to change society. People without access to such resources are rarely completely powerless. By acting collectively, ordinary people can sometimes create sweeping, historic changes in our culture and in the structure of our major social institutions.

Collective action is group behavior that is not derived from, and may even be opposed to, the institutional norms of society (J. Lofland, 1981). The term encompasses spontaneous as well as organized group behavior.

Collective actions vary in terms of their goals, shape, and duration. The goal of collective action may be expressive (to publicly display emotions such as joy or hostility) or instrumental (to achieve some concrete goal like the redistribution of power in society). Collective actions also range from unorganized, such as street riots, to highly organized, such as social movements with formal leadership, bureaucratic organization, and a planned program of action. Finally, collective actions vary in terms of duration. Some activities, such as victory celebrations, last a few hours; others, like riots, last for days; still others, like the civil rights movement, may last for years.

Whether expressive or instrumental, organized or diffuse, short-term or long-term, all types of collective action require a redefinition of a situation from one that is routine to one that is problematic. This shared redefinition of right and wrong prompts a relatively large number of people to begin to feel that events in a community or in society as a whole are not proceeding as they should.

The norms that emerge rationalize activity that would not be acceptable under ordinary conditions. One of the key features of collective action is that citizens acting in groups do things they would not usually do. They may panic, riot, loot from stores, march, demonstrate, engage in civil disobedience, or launch terrorist campaigns because they find immediate social support for the view that what they are doing is the right thing given present circumstances (Turner & Killian, 1987).

Of course, incorrect redefinitions may predominate. Take, for instance, the mass hysteria that resulted from the discovery of the AIDS virus in the mid-1980s. Panic and anxiety over the deadly disease spread quickly. Misinformation about how it is transmitted was disseminated nationwide and took on the appearance of fact. People began to believe that it could be passed on merely by being near or touching someone with the disease. Homosexuals, the subset of the population most closely identified with the disease, were fired or denied housing and, at worst, became the objects of violent attacks. Children diagnosed with the AIDS virus were forced out of school by their classmates' parents and school officials. Some doctors, dentists, and hospital workers refused to treat not only AIDS patients but all homosexuals; undertakers refused to embalm AIDS patients; police officers wore rubber gloves and masks when arresting anyone they thought was homosexual (Conrad, 1992; A. G. Johnson, 1992). A legitimate and tragic medical emergency had been made even worse by widespread hysterical fears created by the spread of false definitions.

Social Movements

Collective action directed toward an issue of concern to large numbers of people can be continuous and organized and extend beyond the immediate confines of groups or mobs. These actions are called **social movements** (Zurcher & Snow, 1981). Underlying all social movements is change: the desire to enact it, stop it, or reverse it. Social movements tend to involve a variety of activities, from signing petitions, participating in demonstrations, donating money, protesting in the streets, and campaigning during elections to more violent means like rioting and staging government coups d'etat.

Types of Social Movements

On the basis of their size and the magnitude of their goals, social movements can be categorized as either reform or revolutionary movements. A **reform movement** attempts to change limited aspects of a society but does not seek to alter or replace major social institutions. Take the civil rights movement of the 1960s. It did not call for an overhaul of our economic system (capitalism) or our political system (two-party democracy). Instead, it advocated a more limited change: opening up existing institutions to full and equal participation by members of minority groups (DeFronzo, 1991). Similarly, the anti–Vietnam War movement sought to change government policy rather than change the form of government itself. Other recent examples of reform movements include the women's movement, the nuclear freeze movement, the union movement, and the environmental movement.

Because reform movements seek to alter some aspect of existing social arrangements, there will always be people and groups opposed to such changes. Reform movements typically spawn organized **countermovements** designed to prevent or reverse the changes sought or accomplished by an earlier movement. Countermovements are most likely to emerge when the reform movements against which they are reacting become large and effective in pursuing their goals and therefore come to be seen as threats to personal and social interests (Chafetz & Dworkin, 1987; Mottl, 1980).

The emergence of the conservative and religious New Right in the 1980s and 1990s was provoked by a growing perception of enormous social upheaval, breakdown of traditional roles and values, and challenge to existing institutions like education, religion, and the family brought about by the civil rights, anti-war, student, and women's movements of the 1960s and 1970s (Klatch, 1991). The women's movement in particular is perceived by the New Right as having launched an ideological attack on the family. Indeed, the leaders of the New Right were the first to articulate that women's equality was responsible for women's unhappiness and the weakening of the American family (Faludi, 1991). The rising divorce rate and the increased number of working mothers are seen as eroding the moral bases of family life (Klatch, 1991). One New Right minister said, "We're not here to get into politics. We're here to turn the clock back to 1954 in this country" (quoted in Faludi, 1991, p. 230).

Through organizations such as the Moral Majority, the Heritage Foundation, the Eagle Forum, the Christian Coalition, and many smaller religious groups around the United States, the New Right has sought to restore the faith, morality, and decency they feel America has lost in recent years. Over the past two decades the New Right has been successful in shifting the political and social mood of the country. It first gained legitimacy in 1980 when Ronald Reagan and several senate candidates it supported won election; it reaffirmed its influence in 1994 with the Republican takeover of Congress. Many of its most notable triumphs have been at the state and local levels, where it has succeeded in influencing public school curricula as well as antiabortion and anti–gay rights legislation.

Both reform movements and countermovements operate within the existing social system. **Revolutionary movements** are attempts to overthrow the entire system itself, whether it be the government or the existing class structure, in an effort to replace it with another (Skocpol, 1979). The American Revolution of 1776, the French Revolution of 1789, the Russian Revolution of 1917 and the Iranian Revolution of 1979 are examples of movements that toppled existing governments and created a new social order. Although revolutionary change in basic social institutions can be brought about through nonviolent means (peaceful labor strikes, democratic elections, civil disobedience, etc.), most successful revolutions have involved some level of violence on the part of both movement participants and groups opposing revolution (DeFronzo, 1991).

The Development of a Social Movement

Whether reform or revolutionary, social movements occur when unsatisfied people see their condition as resulting from society's inability to meet their needs. Many movements develop when certain segments of the population conclude that society's resources—access to political power, higher education, legal justice, medical care, a clean and healthy environment, and so on—are distributed unequally and unfairly (R. Brown, 1986). People come to believe that they have a moral right to the satisfaction of their unmet expectations and that this cannot or will not occur without some effort on their part. This perception is often based on the experience of past failures of working within the system.

As individuals and groups who share this sense of frustration and unfairness interact with one another, the existing system begins to lose its perceived legitimacy (Piven & Cloward, 1977). In large numbers, individuals who ordinarily might have considered themselves helpless come to believe they have the capacity to change things and significantly alter their lives and the lives of others.

The Role of Ideology

A social movement must have an **ideology**, a coherent system of beliefs, values, and ideas that justifies its existence (R. W. Turner & Killian, 1987; Zurcher & Snow, 1981). Consider the antiabortion movement. Its ideology rests on several assumptions about the nature of childhood and motherhood (Luker, 1984). For instance, each conception is an act of God, and so abortion violates God's will; life begins at conception; the fetus is an individual who has a constitutional right to life; and every human life should be valued (Michener, DeLamater, & Schwartz, 1986). Believing that every child is wanted, the antiabortion movement subscribes to the belief that everyone can "make room for one more," reinforcing the view that abortion is both evil and self-indulgent (Luker, 1984). Anyone who favors continued legal abortion is automatically defined as immoral.

An ideology fulfills several functions. It defines the group's interests and helps to identify people as either supporters or enemies, creating an identifiable group of "good guys" and "villains." An ideology also provides participants with a collective sense of what the goals of the movement are or should be.

Misdirected or ill-conceived ideologies can sometimes break a social movement: It has been argued that organized opposition to the 1991 Persian Gulf War was ineffective primarily on ideological grounds. Antiwar activists were committed to an ideological script that had been used successfully in the movement against the war in Vietnam 20 years earlier: Portray the United States as the hostile aggressor (Goertzel, 1993). But given the reports of Iraqi atrocities and the unsavory actions of Saddam Hussein, it was difficult to convince the public that the American military response was wrong. Indeed, 90% of Americans supported President Bush's handling of the crisis. There was no "innocent victim" the United States was attempting to destroy, as had been the case in Vietnam. This antiwar movement was therefore caught between two conflicting ideological positions: opposing Iraqi aggression on the one hand but wanting to paint the United States as the bad guy. By acting against only American military action, those involved in the movement became, for all intents and purposes, allies of Hussein. In a speech broadcast on CNN on January 28, 1991, Hussein stated:

> All the people of Iraq are grateful to all the noble souls amongst the United States people who are coming out into the street demonstrating against this war. We follow with keenness this sublime level of humanity, which comes out to counter the policies of aggression. (quoted in Goertzel, 1993, p. 143)

The leadership of the U.S. Army was, in fact, quite reluctant to go to war, and there was considerable public reluctance as well. In addition, the congressional vote authorizing the use of force passed by only a narrow margin. If the movement had focused its support on legislators who favored stronger economic sanctions against Iraq rather than military intervention, it might have been more effective. But this approach would have required the movement to abandon its "America as the hostile aggressor" stance. The movement failed to make a clear ideological distinction between opposition to war and selective opposition to only those wars conducted by the United States (Goertzel, 1993).

Although the content of an ideology might be what attracts people to a movement, the ideology must be spread through social networks of friends, family, coworkers, and so on (Zurcher & Snow, 1981). For some people, in fact, the ideology of the movement is secondary to other social considerations. Potential participants in a social movement usually are unlikely to join without being informed about it and introduced to it by someone they know. The ideological leaders of a social movement might want to believe that participants are there because of "the cause," but chances are that participants have a friend or acquaintance who convinced them to be there (Stark & Bainbridge, 1980; Gerlach & Hine, 1970).

Ironically, social movements sometimes require the involvement of individuals from outside the group of people whose interests the movement represents. Those individuals who are the most deprived and most in need of massive changes in social arrangements are not necessarily those who are most likely to subscribe to the ideology that sustains the movement. People who are already disadvantaged may also lack the money, time, skills, and connections that successful movements require. For instance, the people who would stand to benefit the most from environmental improvement (individuals in poor, polluted communities) have historically been uninvolved in the environmental movement. They are often skeptical of the "environmentalists," who they feel are taking away their jobs rather than protecting their interests. Recently, however, many members of these communities have joined the movement, motivated not by a desire to "save the earth" but by an ideology that is more relevant to their everyday lives.

■ ■ ■ ■ ■ ■ ■ ■

ROBERT BULLARD AND BEVERLY WRIGHT
The Environmental Justice Movement

In chapter 12 I mentioned that environmental degradation disproportionately affects minority communities. Urban black ghettoes, rural Latino "poverty pockets," and economically destitute Native American reservations face the worst environmental devastation in the nation. In Los Angeles, over 71% of the African Americans and 50% of the Latinos live in areas with the most polluted air, compared to only 34% of the white population (Bullard, 1993). A report by the Commission for Racial Justice (1987) concluded that the racial makeup of a community is the best predictor of where toxic waste sites in the United States are located.

For the most part, African Americans and other people of color have been underrepresented in the mainstream environmental movement. The ideological supporters of this movement tend to be middle- and upper-middle class whites whose environments are relatively unpolluted. They are likely to focus on such goals as wilderness and wildlife preservation, wise resource management, and population control (Bullard, 1993). The environmental degradation of poor, minority communities has been largely overlooked.

These communities are often on the brink of economic catastrophe, places where providing jobs for residents is of utmost concern. In many instances, bringing jobs to the community has been achieved only at great risk to the health of the workers and the surrounding areas. Nobody wants garbage dumps, landfills, incinerators, or polluting factories in their backyards. But if these are the only ventures that will provide steady employment for residents, the communities are left with little choice but to support them. The result has been a form of environmental job blackmail: You can get a job, but only if you're willing to do work that will harm you, your family, and your neighbors (Bullard, 1993).

Hence one of the biggest obstacles to getting people in poor, minority communities involved in the environmental movement has been an economic one: the fear of job loss or plant closure. How do you get people to protest against a dangerous, polluting factory when that factory is the only source of their economic survival? To answer this question, sociologists Robert Bullard and Beverly Wright (1992) examined environmental activism within African-American communities in the South, the region with the largest ecological disparities between black and white communities in the nation. They interviewed activist leaders in five communities involved in environmental disputes: Institute, West Virginia; Alsen, Louisiana; Emelle, Alabama; and black neighborhoods in Houston and Dallas, Texas. In addition, they examined newspaper articles, editorials, and feature stories concerning the disputes.

In the 1980s and early 1990s, communities like these began to challenge both the industrial polluters and the often indifferent mainstream environmental movement by actively fighting environmental threats in their neighborhoods. The key, according to Bullard and Wright, was that these movements framed environmental degradation within a social justice ideology rather than an exclusively ecological one. In other words, they were able to band together to fight for their own interests by painting pollution and environmental danger as a form of racial discrimination. The movements made environmental quality a basic civil right of all individuals. Consequently, they adopted the confrontational strategies of the earlier civil rights movement. For instance, all the communities used local protest demonstrations, petitions, and press lobbying to publicize their plight.

Bullard and Wright found that all these movements were spearheaded by local people—church leaders, community improvement workers, and civil rights activists—who had very little previous experience with environmental issues. Many of them had worked in other organizations that fought discrimination in housing, employment, and education. They played a pivotal role in organizing, planning, and mobilizing opposition activities. Mainstream environmental leaders, referred to as "outside elites," played only a minor role. Indeed, many residents were suspicious of the motives of outside environmentalists and the largely white national environmental movement.

All of the environmental justice movements Bullard and Wright examined achieved some level of success. In West Dallas, individuals were able to convince the city and state to join in a lawsuit against an industrial polluter that routinely pumped more than 269 tons of lead particles into the air each year. The plant was eventually shut down, and some residents won a $20 million out-of-court settlement against the company.

In Houston, the city council, after intense pressure from the African-American community, passed a resolution opposing the placement of a garbage dump nearby. However, a federal court ruled against the plaintiffs, and the dump was eventually built. Nevertheless, the city council passed ordinances that prohibited city-owned solid waste trucks from dumping at the controversial site and regulated the distance between the landfill and schools, parks, and playgrounds.

In Alsen, Emelle, and Institute, protesting residents were able to convince government officials to fine facilities for pollution and safety violations. In addition, they were able to extract some concessions from the firms, such as technical modifications, updated pollution monitoring systems, and reduced emission levels.

In sum, the driving force around which these movements organized was the imbalance between the small financial benefits derived from the jobs provided by polluting firms and toxic dump sites and the excessive costs borne by minority communities. Reducing environmental inequities was consistent with the struggle to end other forms of discrimination throughout society.

It's unlikely that we'll see a massive influx of people of color into national environmental groups in the near future. However, multiracial, grassroots environmental groups have been the fastest-growing segment of the environmental movement over the past decade. These groups are increasingly forming alliances with one another and with other community-based groups to increase their power (Bullard, 1993). Distant are the days when minority communities would remain silent or refuse to question the nature of new jobs being promised them by companies manufacturing dangerous products (D. E. Taylor, 1993). And the successes of these groups have caught the attention of mainstream environmental organizations which now provide support in the form of technical advice, expert testimony, direct financial assistance, fundraising, research, and legal assistance. The "environmental" community and the "social justice" community are beginning to take steps toward reducing the artificial barriers that have historically kept them apart.

■ ■ ■

Sometimes the activities required to promote or sustain a particular movement run counter to the ideological goals of the movement itself. The leaders of successful political revolutions, for example, soon realize that in order to run the country they now control they must create highly structured bureaucracies not unlike the ones they have overthrown.

Individuals in reform movements may also be forced to engage in behaviors that conflict with the ideological tenets of the movement. The New Right movement was organized, in part, as a backlash against the women's movement. Its pro-family, pro-motherhood, and anti–equal rights for women positions are clearly designed to turn back the feminist agenda. However, early in the movement it became clear that in order to be successful it would have to enlist high-profile women to campaign against feminist policies. New Right women had to abandon their families, travel the country to make speeches, and display independent strength—characteristics that were anything but the ideal models of passive womanhood they were publicly promoting. Phyllis Schlafly, a woman who has vehemently argued that a woman's natural place is to be a wife and mother in a household supported by her husband, is a Harvard-educated lawyer, an author of nine books, and a two-time congressional candidate (Faludi, 1991).

The Role of Rising Expectations

You might think that major social movements, particularly revolutionary ones, would be most likely to occur when many people's lives are at their lowest and most desperate point. Certainly huge numbers of disadvantaged people, who see little chance that things will improve and who perceive the government as unwilling or unable to meet their needs, are necessary for any massive movements for change (Tilly, 1978).

But some sociologists argue that social movements are actually more likely to arise when social conditions are getting better than when they are at their worst (C. Brinton, 1965; Davies, 1962). Constant deprivation does not necessarily make people want to revolt. Instead, they are more likely to be preoccupied with daily survival than with demonstrations and street protests. Improvements in living conditions, however, show those who are deprived that their society is capable of being different, raising their expectations and sparking a desire for large-scale change. When these expectations aren't met, deprived people become angry. The gap between what they expect and what they have now seems intolerable. Although they may actually be better off than they had been in the past, their situation relative to their expectations now appears much worse (Davies, 1962). Such frustration makes participation in protest or revolutionary activity more likely.

Consider the short-lived pro-democracy movement in China in 1989. During the early 1980s the Chinese government began to introduce economic reforms that would open up markets and create faster growth and political reforms to provide citizens with more freedom. These reforms inspired a popular demand for even greater freedom and democracy, a movement that was violently squashed in Tiananmen Square.

Resource Mobilization and Movement Organization

At any point in time, numerous problems in a society need fixing. And yet at that same point in time, relatively few major social movements exist. If widespread dissatisfaction and frustration were all that is needed to sustain a social movement, "the masses would always be in revolt" (Trotsky, 1959). What allows a social movement to get started, gain support, and achieve its goals?

According to *resource mobilization theory*, effective organization keeps a movement going and enables it to be successful. How far a movement goes in attaining its goals depends on its ability to expand its ranks, acquire large-scale public support, and transform those who join into committed participants (Zurcher & Snow, 1981). Thus, no social movement can exist unless it has an organized system for acquiring the necessary resources for operation, like money, labor, participants, legal aid, access to the media, and so on (McCarthy & Zald, 1977).

■ ■ ■ ■ ■ ■ ■ ■
DOUGLAS MURRAY
The Abolition of the Short-Handled Hoe

Some social movements become successful only when they secure broad organizational support. Sociologist Douglas Murray examined the process by which a simple farm tool, the short-handled hoe, came to symbolize the exploitation of California farm workers and served as a focal point for a successful social movement. During the early 20th century, the short-handled hoe became the principal tool used by farm laborers for thinning and weeding crops. Growers claimed that it was more accurate and efficient than the long-handled hoe. However, farm laborers saw another motive in growers' desire to change: increased supervision and control of the workers. With the long-handled hoe, supervisors sometimes couldn't tell when a worker was working or just leaning on the hoe. With the short-handled hoe it became easier to see when they were working, because they had to stand up to rest.

Use of the short-handled hoe came to be called "squat labor" or "stoop labor" because of the bent-over position one had to be in to use the tool correctly. Numerous physicians and medical experts pointed out that use of this tool over long periods of time caused a degeneration of the spine, leading to permanent disabilities. According to one farm worker:

> When I used the short-handled hoe my head would ache and my eyes hurt because of the pressure of bending down so long. My back would hurt whenever I stood up or bent over. I moved down the rows as fast as I could so I could get to the end and rest my back for a moment. (quoted in Murray, 1982, p. 29)

As early as the 1920s farm workers engaged in isolated protests and work stoppages over the use of the short-handled hoe. During the Depression, though, poor people from Oklahoma, Arkansas, and elsewhere flocked to California willing to do any work, including using the short-handled hoe, for lower wages. Hence the protests of the 1920s were rendered ineffective.

It wasn't until the early 1970s, when the civil rights movement was in full swing and the United Farm Workers union had been organized, that the issue of the short-handled hoe was resolved:

> Late one afternoon in the spring of 1973, farm workers leaving the fields of the fertile Salinas Valley in Central California gathered beside the buses which would take them to the nearby labor camps for the night. They moved nervously about a large pile of short-handled hoes which they had been using that day to thin and weed long rows of lettuce. One farm worker quickly doused the hoes with gasoline; another tossed a match, setting them ablaze. Cries of protest swept through the crowd as the farm workers served their bosses with a defiant notice: no longer would they work with "el cortito," the short-handled hoe. (Murray, 1982, p. 26)

The protesters were finally able to mobilize state and legal organizations to bring the growers to court. Because of heightened access to the media, farm worker strikes drew national attention. With the help of national labor unions, government agencies such as the Office of Economic Opportunity, and legal assistance agencies for the disadvantaged, the short-handled hoe was eventually declared to be in violation of federal worker health and safety protections.

Since the short-handled hoe was banned, farm worker conditions have improved and growers report fewer worker compensation claims for back injuries. The success of the case, along with the powerful organizational structure representing farm workers, encouraged labor protests over other conditions, such as exposure to dangerous pesticides. In sum, the protest over this little tool, made more effective by the use of government and legal organizations, spawned the farm workers movement that exists to this day.

▪ ▪ ▪

Most large, long-term social movements involve a national, even international coalition of groups. Such widespread organization makes the movement more powerful by making the mobilization of resources, in the form of people and fund-raising, more efficient. For example, environmental degradation is perceived by many to be today's most urgent national and global issue. Yet most of the movement's successes are accomplished not by highly visible parades, protests, and concerts but by the quieter activities of several large bureaucratic organizations, including the Sierra Club, the Audubon Society, the National Wildlife Federation, the National Parks and Conservation Association, and Greenpeace.

In addition, highly organized social movements must have established networks of communication (McCarthy & Zald, 1977). The ability to quickly mobilize people for, say, a march on the nation's capital depends on extensive communications networks: phone systems, direct mailing systems, and computers. Movements need both an effective system of mass communications for recruiting and fund-raising and a way for information to get to all participants when face-to-face interaction is impossible (Tarrow, 1994).

Moreover, a social movement must mobilize the media to help validate and enlarge the scope of its cause. The media serve as a vital political tool in the construction of a particular social reality. The media spotlight sends the message that the movement is an important force in society. Achieving standing in the media is often a necessary condition before those who are the targets of influence will grant a movement recognition and deal with its claims and demands (Gamson & Wolfsfeld, 1993). A protest march with no media coverage at all is a non-event.

In sum, social movement activities are neither spontaneous nor disorganized (Ferree, 1992). The movements that succeed in enacting substantial social change are not necessarily those with the most compelling ideological positions or the highest emotional appeal. Instead, they are the ones with the necessary high-level organization and communication networks to mobilize supporters and the necessary media access to neutralize the opposition and transform the public into sympathizers. Those movements that historically have been the longest lasting—the women's movement, the civil rights movement, and the environmental movement—are those that are supported by large organizations. The National Organization for Women, the National Association for the Advancement of Colored People (NAACP), the Sierra Club, and the like have full-time lobbyists or political action committees that connect them to the national political system. Few movements can succeed without such connections, because achieving social change often requires changing laws or convincing courts to interpret laws in particular ways.

The Bureaucratization of Social Movements

It makes sense that the most successful social movements are the ones that are best organized. However, high-level organization is not necessarily a guarantee of success, especially when it leads to the rigidity and turf wars common to any bureaucracy. When constituent organizations differ in their philosophies and tactics, tremendous infighting and bickering may break out among groups ostensibly working toward the same goal. For instance, the civil rights movement during the 1950s and 1960s included many diverse, seemingly incompatible organizations: The NAACP was large, racially integrated, legalistic, and bureaucratic in form; the Student Non-Violent Coordinating Committee was younger, more militant in its tactics, and after a while excluded whites from participation; the Southern Christian Leadership Conference was highly structured, had a religious ideology, and was dominated by male clergy; the Black Muslims and the Black Panthers advocated extreme, sometimes violent methods to achieve civil rights. The goals and methods of these diverse civil rights groups often conflicted, which arguably slowed down the extension of civil rights to African Americans.

No matter what their shape, size, or motive, social movements require sustained activity over a long period of time (R. W. Turner & Killian, 1987). Thus, unlike riots, which are of limited duration, social movements may become permanent, bureaucratic fixtures in the political and social environment. Ironically, a social phenomenon whose goal is a large-scale alteration of some aspect of society can become part of the establishment.

In addition, people who devote their lives to the movement come to depend on it for their own livelihood. Hence social movements organized for the purposes of enacting social change actually provide structure and order for the lives of their members, acting as sources of opportunities, careers, and rewards (Hewitt, 1988).

Political Opportunity Structure

Social movements also depend on conditions outside their reach. One such condition is the structure of existing political institutions. Movements won't develop if the political structure does not provide opportunities for change: "Rational people do not often attack well-fortified opponents" (Tarrow, 1994, p. 86).

Political systems are more or less vulnerable and more or less receptive to challenge at different points in time (McAdam, McCarthy, & Zald, 1988). These ebbs and flows of political opportunities produce cycles of protest and movement activity (Tarrow, 1994). When political systems are firm, unyielding, and stable, people have to resort to individual coping mechanisms or existing channels for airing their grievances. But when a system opens up and people realize it is vulnerable—that they can actually make a difference—movements are likely to develop.

Sometimes these opportunities are unintentional and exist quite independently from the actions of movement members. For instance, similar antinuclear movements arose about the same time in the 1970s in Germany and France. Both had similar ideologies and used similar techniques. However, the German movement flourished and remains highly influential in German politics today. The French movement was weak and ineffectual and quickly atrophied. Why were the outcomes for these two movements so different? In Germany, the government procedure for reviewing nuclear power facilities provided opportunities for those opposed to nuclear power to legally intervene. The procedure in France was closed and unresponsive to public sentiment (Nelkin & Pollack, 1981). Similarly, the emergence in the 1970s of the contemporary environmental movement in this country was possible because of a political system that included government agencies already sympathetic to environmental concerns (Gale, 1986).

The idea that unintentional political opportunities can encourage social movements for change was dramatically supported by the 1989 pro-democracy movement in the former Soviet Union and Eastern Europe. In the mid-1980s, the Soviet government under Mikhail Gorbachav embarked on a massive program of economic and structural reforms (*perestroika*) as well as a relaxation of constraints on freedom of expression (*glasnost*). The ensuing liberties encouraged open criticism of the political order and created new opportunities for political action (Tarrow, 1994). Protest movements took advantage of these opportunities, fomenting the sometimes violent struggles for independence on the part of small, ethnically homogeneous republics that we saw in the early 1990s. In other words, only when the political structure became less repressive could these monumental changes take place.

Political instability can sometimes spawn less dramatic reform movements. The changing fortunes of a government create uncertainty among supporters and encourage challengers to try to take advantage of the situation. Take, for instance, the civil rights movement in this country in the 1950s and 1960s. During the 1950s, as the first, early calls for racial equality were being heard, many conservative southern Democrats defected to the Republican party, where their segregationist leanings met with more sympathy. The ensuing decline of southern white support for the Democratic party, coupled with the movement of African Americans to large cities where they were more likely to vote, forced the Democrats to seek black support in the presidential election of 1960. The black vote is widely credited with John Kennedy's narrow victory (McAdam, 1982). Hence the Kennedy administration (and later, the Johnson administration) was compelled to seize the initiative for civil rights (Tarrow, 1994). Increased political power, in turn, enhanced the bargaining position of civil rights forces, culminating in two landmark pieces of legislation: the Civil Rights Act of 1964 and the Voting Rights Act of 1965.

At other times existing political regimes intentionally create or actively support structural opportunities for change. For example, in the 1980s the Reagan administration accepted political support from Christian fundamentalist groups and organizations. In return, it made some efforts to limit abortion access and appoint judges who opposed legal abortions. These reforms, in turn, encouraged the growth and development of the pro-life movement (R. Garner, 1996).

Similarly, the anti–drunk driving movement is strong and influential today because it enjoys substantial support from federal, state, and local governments; state and federal highway agencies; and state and local police departments (McCarthy & Wolfson, 1992). When the movement advocated a national drinking age of 21 in the 1980s, many state legislatures balked, fearing a backlash from powerful alcohol producers, distributors, and retailers. However, the federal government enacted legislation threatening to withhold significant amounts of federal highway funds from states that didn't establish the 21-year-old drinking age. This proved to be a strong incentive for states to pass such a law.

In sum, political opportunities provide the institutional frame within which social movements operate. Movements form when ordinary citizens respond to changes in the opportunity structure that lower the costs of involvement and reveal where the authorities are vulnerable. Unlike money and power, these conditions are external to the movement. If political opportunities exist, then even groups with fairly mild grievances or few resources can develop a successful movement (see also Jenkins & Perrow, 1977). In contrast, groups with deep grievances and ample resources—but few political opportunities—may never get their movements off the ground (Tarrow, 1994).

Reconstructing Society: The Sociological Imagination Revisited

In the summer of 1981 I had the good fortune to visit Florence, Italy. While there I made a point of visiting the Galleria dell' Accademia, the museum where one of my favorite works of art, Michelangelo's statue of David, resides. The statue stands in a bright rotunda at the end of a long hallway. To my eye it is truly a masterpiece in sculpture, nearly flawless in its detail.

I stood there admiring this amazing work of art for close to 2 hours. Afterward, as I contentedly made my way back down the hallway, I noticed a series of sculptures that had escaped my attention when I first entered the museum. I found out that they, too, were created by Michelangelo. What made them particularly interesting was that they were all unfinished. Some were obviously near completion, but others looked to me like shapeless blocks of granite.

There was something astounding in these pieces. As I looked closer it wasn't difficult to see the actual chisel marks that the great sculptor had made. I could imagine the plan Michelangelo had in his head as he worked. I could envision him toiling to bring form to the heavy stone. These imperfect slabs of rock showed evidence of human creation in a way that the perfect finished statue of David never could. At that moment I realized that Michelangelo was a real person who fashioned beauty from formlessness. I began to admire the genius of the creator and not just the creation. I went back to look at David again with a new-found appreciation.

Society isn't nearly as perfect as Michelangelo's artwork, yet it is easy to see social structure as a product that exists on its own and not as something that people collectively chiseled. We sometimes forget that many of the realities of our lives that we take for granted were the result, at some point in history, of the handiwork of individuals. One generation's radical changes become another's common features of everyday life. The fact that you can't be forced to work 70 or 80 hours a week, can't be exposed to dangerous working conditions without your knowledge, and are entitled to a certain number of paid holidays a year are a result of the actions of real people in early labor union movements.

Because we take many of our freedoms, rights, and desires for granted, we may not only overlook the struggles of those who came before us but also downplay the extent to which inequities and injustices existed in the past. For instance, many young women today have never even considered that they might have to struggle to get into the college of their choice, put their own careers on hold in order to provide the support their husbands need to succeed, or be the sole caregivers for their children. Like most beneficiaries of past movements, they simply take their freedoms and opportunities for granted, sometimes even expressing contempt for the movement responsible for the rights they so casually enjoy (Stacey, 1991).

The irony of social movements, then, is that the more profound and far-reaching their accomplishments, the more likely it is that the efforts of the individuals who produced them will eventually be forgotten. Like Michelangelo's sculpture, these achievements ultimately become objectified and begin to exist independently of the individuals and groups who created them. Changing mainstream society is the ultimate goal of any social movement, but the cultural and historical price is that the efforts and sacrifices made by real individuals to re-create our society will ultimately fade into collective oblivion.

Fundamentally, not only the nature of social movements but also the nature of human society itself—whether stable or rapidly changing—must be understood by examining what people do and think. We must remember that societies remain stable because enough individuals define existing conditions as satisfactory and that societies change because enough individuals define situations that were once tolerable as problems that must be acknowledged and solved. As one author wrote regarding the antiwar movement during the 1960s and 1970s:

Ten years and 12 days after the first busloads of demonstrators rolled into Washington to protest U.S. involvement in Indochina, the last planeloads of Americans left Saigon.... The standard American histories of the Vietnam War, when they are culled from the memoirs of the generals and politicians ... are unlikely to record this coincidence. But the decisions about the pursuit of those generals' and politicians' objectives in Indochina were not made only in their carpeted offices. They were also made in the barracks, in the schools, in the streets, by the millions of Americans—Blacks and whites, students, workers, nuns and priests, draftees and draft resisters—who made up the Anti-War Movement. (Cluster, 1979, p. 131)

Some influential acts of individuals may at first blush appear rather insignificant. Early in 1960, four black students at North Carolina Agricultural & Technical State University in Greensboro engaged in a series of discussions in their dormitory rooms about the state of the civil rights movement. They came to the conclusion that things weren't progressing quickly enough in the still-segregated South and that it was time for action. They decided to go to the lunch counter at the local Woolworth's department store and order coffee and doughnuts. In the 1960s South, it was forbidden by law to serve blacks at public eating facilities that weren't for blacks only.

After purchasing some school supplies in another part of the store, they sat down at the lunch counter and placed their orders. As anticipated, the reply was "I'm sorry, we don't serve you here" (McCain, 1991, p. 115). They remained seated for 45 minutes, citing the fact that they had been served in another part of the store without any difficulty. They returned the next week with more demonstrators. Word of their actions spread quickly. Within 2 months sit-ins had spread to 9 states and 54 cities in the South as well as to areas in the North, where sympathetic pickets of department stores took place. The sit-ins eventually proved to be one of the most effective tactics of the civil rights movement.

Some social observers argue that many of the political movements for change that burst onto the scene in the 1960s—including the women's movement, the antiwar movement, and the student free speech movement—could trace their philosophical and tactical roots to this small act by four students (Cluster, 1979). That's not to say that those movements wouldn't have developed had these four men been served coffee and doughnuts. The point is, the collective movement that arose from the actions of these seemingly insignificant individuals had an enormous impact on the massive changes that occurred in our country during that decade.

We re-create society not only through acts of defiance and organized social movements but also through our daily interactions. The driving theme throughout this book has been that society and its constituent elements are simultaneously human creations and phenomena that exist independently of us, influencing and controlling our private experiences at every turn.

Organizations and institutions exist and thrive because they implicitly or explicitly discourage individuals from challenging the rules and patterns of behavior that characterize them. Imagine what would happen to the system of higher education if you and others like you challenged the authority of the university. You could establish a new order in which students would dictate the content of courses, take control of the classroom, abolish grading or any other evaluative mechanism used for assessing student performance, do away with tuition, and so on. But because you have an education and a career to gain from the institutional structure as it stands, it's not very likely you'd do something to jeopardize it.

Are we then to believe that we are all helpless leaves in the wind, buffeted here and there by the powerful and permanent forces of a structure that dwarfs us? To some extent the answer is yes. I subscribe to the sociological imagination and strongly believe that to fully understand our lives we must acknowledge that processes larger than ourselves determine some of our private experiences. Along the way, though, we sometimes lose sight of our important role as shapers of society:

> We know when to tear down a building that has ceased to serve any useful function and may even be a source of danger. However, we sometimes rattle around in dusty old social institutions that are cracked and crumbling simply because we fail to realize that it is within our power to step beyond the confines of this structure and build others. . . . What may have served as a useful basis for achieving some particular end becomes an ideology and an end in itself. When this occurs our social constructions may cease to serve any useful function but we may persist in maintaining them simply because they have become permanent, hardened features of our social landscape. (Kollock & O'Brien, 1993, p. 503)

Although society presents itself as largely unchangeable, our culture is based at least in part on the value of the American "can do" attitude. I recall, as a child, sitting in a darkened living room with my parents on a warm July evening in 1969. The only light in the room came from the gray-blue glow of the television. I watched with great amazement the fuzzy, almost imperceptible image of astronaut Neil Armstrong taking the first tentative steps on the moon and stating: "That's one small step for man, one giant leap for mankind." I didn't realize then how the power of that statement stretched beyond the space program. People *can* influence the world in which they live.

In this chapter you've seen that we do have some influence in shaping and changing our dusty old institutions. Individuals, bound together by only the thin strand of an idea that things ought not to be the way they are, can change the course of social history. We are active participants in the construction of our realities. Yes, we are affected by social forces. Yes, our lives are influenced, maybe even determined, by social institutions. But we have the ability and the obligation to be aware of that influence, to analyze it, and to act on it. And, as the efforts of the four young men in Greensboro proved, one small act can change society.

Conclusion and Farewell

Sociology is not one of those disciplines that draws from a long-standing body of scientific facts and laws. We do have some good explanations for why certain important social phenomena happen, and we can make reasonable predictions about future developments, but sociology is not inherently a discipline of answers. It's a discipline of questions, one that provides a unique and useful method for identifying the puzzles of your life and your society.

This discipline scrutinizes, analyzes, and dissects institutional order and its effects on our thinking. It exposes the vulnerable underbelly of both objective and official reality and, by doing so, prods us into taking a closer look at ourselves and our private worlds, not an easy thing to do. Sociology makes everyday life an unsafe place. I don't mean that it makes people violent or dangerous, I mean that it makes perceptions of social stability unstable or at least fair game for analysis. We don't want to admit that our reality may be a figment of our collective minds and just one of many possible realities. We live under a belief system that tells us our unchallenged assumptions are simply the way things are.

Sociology is a "liberating" perspective (Liazos, 1985). It forces us to look at the social processes that influence our thoughts, perceptions, and actions and helps us see how social change occurs and the impact we can have on others. In doing so, sociology also points out the very limits of liberation. We are aware of the chains that restrict our "movements," but we also have the tools to break those chains. The sociological imagination goes beyond a description of powerful social forces to a questioning of them and ultimately a push toward social action. Sociology gives us a glimpse of the world both as it is and as it could be. To be a sociologically astute observer of the world as it is, you must be able to strip away fallacies and illusions and see the interconnected system underneath. Only then can you take full advantage of your role as a co-creator of society.

I leave you with one final thought: If you now look at your life and the lives of those around you differently, if you now question things heretofore unquestionable, if you now see where you fit in the bigger societal picture, if you now see orderly patterns in areas you previously thought were chaotic or chaos in areas you previously thought were orderly, then you are well on your way to understanding the meaning—and the promise—of sociology.

CHAPTER HIGHLIGHTS

- Whether at the personal, cultural, or institutional level, change is the preeminent feature of modern societies.
- Social change has a variety of sources: adaptation to environmental pressures, the importation of cultural practices from other countries, internal population changes, and technological discoveries and innovations.

▪ Social change is not some massive, impersonal force that arbitrarily disrupts our routine way of life; it is a human creation.

▪ Social movements are long-term collective actions that address an issue of concern to large numbers of people.

▪ The nature of society, from its large institutions to its tiny, unspoken rules of everyday life, can be understood only by examining what people do and think. Societies remain stable because enough people define existing conditions as satisfactory, and they change because enough people define once-accepted conditions as problems that must be solved.

YOUR TURN

It's one thing to read about people taking an active role in reconstructing a part of their personal lives or of their society, but it's quite another to see such people in action. Most communities contain people who were at one time active in a major movement for social change: the labor movement, the antiwar movement, the women's movement, the civil rights movement, and so forth. Find a few people who were involved in one such movement. Ask them to describe their experiences. What was their motive for joining the movement? What sorts of activities did they participate in? What were the goals they wanted to accomplish? Looking back, do they feel the movement accomplished those goals? If not, why not? What else needs to be done? What did they feel they accomplished?

For purposes of historical comparison, see if you can identify a movement that is currently under way in your community. It might be a drive to promote environmental or AIDS awareness, an antiabortion movement, or a group organized to address an issue of local interest such as a neighborhood improvement drive or an attempt to stop the construction of a factory or business.

Try to attend a gathering in which the movement is involved. It might be an organizational meeting, a town council meeting, a protest march, or a demonstration. What happened at the gathering? What seemed to be the overall atmosphere? Was it festive? solemn? angry? businesslike? Was any opposition present?

Interview some of the participants. Ask them the same questions you asked the participants who were in past movements. Do people get involved in social movements for the same reasons they did in the past?

Relate your observations and the information from the interviews to the discussion of social movements in this chapter. What are the most effective tactics and strategies? How are resources mobilized? Why do some movements succeed and others fail?

Social Change
The Example of the American Ghetto

DOUGLAS HARPER with photographs by CAMILO JOSÉ VERGARA

"...social change emerges through social movements: people with similar interests organizing, often courageously and against great odds, to change the system...."

The book ends with a mixed message. Social change is everywhere; things get better for some elements of society but not for all. The sources of change are technological, political, and cultural. If people become involved in social movements, they may become creators of their social worlds.

This visual essay offers an excerpt of a recent photographic study by Camilo José Vergara (1995) to explore these themes. Vergara used the method called "rephotography"—photographing the same setting over time—to show us how ghettos in American cities are changing. We see in these images that poverty itself is not a fixed characteristic of people or places; it too is a social process.

When looking at these photographs in the context of the last chapter, ask yourself:

- Does social change necessarily bring progress?

- If there is progress, who is it for and under what circumstances?

- What was the role of modern technology in creating these changes?

- How did social movements affect the trends shown in these photographs?

Of these questions, the first is perhaps the most complex. Most of us deplore the violence, the terrible housing conditions, the social disorganization and disorder of American ghettos. Yet real people inhabit these spaces. Most of these people are not in legal trouble, and they find a way to create community amid the great challenges of their lives. When ghettos are torn down, these communities are destroyed. The poor who lived in the dilapidated housing projects are dispersed into other parts of the city. Their friends and extended families go in other directions. The services they depended on disappear or become more difficult to access.

When the ghettos are torn down, the poor often lose. If another class gentrifies the old dwellings or buys new developments, then that class obviously wins. The meaning of social change for the two groups indeed differs greatly.

Technology figures heavily in all the decision-making processes that these changes represent. Who has access to this technology? If the poor were computer literate and had access to the Internet, would they have been able to envision a form of change that would better represent their interests?

Finally, we note in this chapter that a great deal of social change emerges through social movements: people with similar interests organizing, often courageously and against great odds, to change the system. We must recognize that despite many vital social movements among the poor, they have not organized to force changes that would benefit them more than do the changes represented in these images. How does one inspire, among those most defeated in the system, the urge for collective action?

Empty lots scatter across once busy, urban, downtown Detroit. Most of the skyscrapers are empty or almost empty. Many are ruined.

A church congregation holds a yard and barbeque sale for the homeless on the east side of Detroit.

This scene of a clapboard house amid a field of wildflowers could be in rural Indiana, but it is in fact a residential location in the city of Detroit.

(October 1987) The Thirteenth Avenue Presbyterian Church was constructed in Newark, New Jersey, in 1888. It served Newark's oldest black congregation between 1910 and 1967.

(February 1990) By the 1970s, after more and more congregation members left the neighborhood, the church was disbanded. Over the years, its walls were weakened by scavengers, or "brickeaters." In 1987, what was left of the old building was occupied by squatters.

(February 1992) Entrance to the Thirteenth Avenue Presbyterian Church surrounded by townhouses.

(October 1992) Now townhouses occupy the site, and all that remains of the Romanesque brickwork is a curved section serving as a memento of an elegant past.

The U.S. Post Office is the main symbol of the federal government in American cities. But where you might expect a classical building decorated with eagles and images of the Pony Express, here in the ghetto you find instead concrete blocks, high fences, and windows covered by iron grates.

At this nursing home in Detroit an iron gate and barbed wire separate the inhabitants from the neighborhood, and vice versa.

> *"Fortification epitomizes the ghetto in America today. . . . Buildings grow claws and spikes, their entrances acquire metal plates, their roots get fenced in, and any additional openings are sealed, cutting down light and ventilation."*
> —VERGARA, 1994

Many commercial establishments in ghettos are heavily fortified. Locked grates around this hairstyling salon on Chicago's South Side render those alluring pictures difficult to comprehend.

Views along Charlotte Street, South Bronx, March 1981. Although running only three short blocks, Charlotte Street was the most famous ghetto in the country; with great fanfare, Jimmy Carter in 1977 and Ronald Reagan in 1979 visited this national symbol of "urban decay."

Here is Charlotte Street in August 1989, part of a "reclaimed ghetto." Photographer Vergara asks: Are such efforts leading to the elimination of ghettos or toward the creation of mini-cities of exclusion within a larger urban wasteland?

The same forces of abandonment that can open the way for urban decay can also free land for new homes. Under the leadership of churches, community organizations, and private developers, many such ghettos have kicked out the dependent poor and refused to admit the enterprises that serve them (such as homeless shelters, methadone clinics, prisons, and incinerators). Instead they focus on attracting working families, keeping out drug dealers, and building guarded enclaves.

Aaron, H. J., & Lougy, C. M. 1986. *The comparable worth controversy.* Washington, DC: Brookings Institution.

Abbey, A., Ross, L. T., McDuffie, D., & McAuslan, P. 1996. "Alcohol and dating risk factors for sexual assault among college women." *Psychology of Women Quarterly, 20,* 147–169.

Acitelli, L. 1988. "When spouses talk to each other about their relationship." *Journal of Social and Personal Relationships, 5,* 185–199.

Acker, J. 1978. "Issues in the sociological study of women's work." In A. H. Stromberg & S. Harkees (Eds.), *Women working.* Palo Alto, CA: Mayfield.

———. 1988. "Class, gender and the relations of distribution." *Signs, 13,* 473–497.

———. 1992. "From sex roles to gendered institutions." *Contemporary Sociology, 21,* 565–569.

Adamec, C., & Pierce, W. L. 1991. *The encyclopedia of adoption.* New York: Facts on File.

Aday, D. P. 1990. *Social control at the margins.* Belmont, CA: Wadsworth.

Adler, J. 1994. "Kids growing up scared." *Newsweek,* January 10.

Ahrons, C. R., & Rodgers, R. H. 1987. *Divorced families: A multidisciplinary developmental view.* New York: Norton.

Ainlay, S. C., Becker, G., & Coleman, L. M. 1986. *The dilemma of difference.* New York: Plenum.

Aldous, J., & Dumon, W. 1990. "Family policy in the 1980's: Controversy and consensus." *Journal of Marriage and the Family, 52,* 1136–1151.

Allon, N. 1982. "The stigma of overweight in everyday life." In B. B. Wolman (Ed.), *Psychological aspects of obesity.* New York: Van Nostrand Reinhold.

Allport, G. 1954. *The nature of prejudice.* Reading, MA: Addison-Wesley.

American Association of University Women. 1991. *Shortchanging girls, shortchanging America: A call to action.* Washington, DC: American Association of University Women.

American Psychiatric Association. 1987. *Diagnostic and statistical manual of mental disorders* (3rd ed.). Washington, DC: Author.

"America's poor showing." 1993. *Newsweek,* October 18.

Ames, L. J. 1995. "Fixing women's wages: The effectiveness of comparable worth policies." *Industrial and Labor Relations Review, 48,* 709–724.

Amir, M. 1971. *Patterns of forcible rape.* Chicago: University of Chicago Press.

Ammerman, N. T. 1987. *Bible believers: Fundamentalists in the modern world.* New Brunswick, NJ: Rutgers University Press.

Anderson, E. 1990. *Streetwise: Race, class and change in an urban community.* Chicago: University of Chicago Press.

Andrews, E. L. 1992. "Broadcasters, to satisfy law, define cartoons as education." *New York Times,* September 30.

Applebome, P. 1995. "On once liberal campuses, racial divide grows wider." *New York Times,* October 25.

———. 1996a. "Holding parents legally responsible for the misbehavior of their children." *New York Times,* April 10.

———. 1996b. "Crime fear is seen forcing changes in youth behavior." *New York Times,* January 12.

Archer, D. 1985. "Social deviance." In G. Lindzey & E. Aronson (Eds.), *Handbook of social psychology* (3rd ed., Vol. 2). New York: Random House.

Arendell, T. 1984. "Divorce: A woman's issue." *Feminist Issues, 4,* 41–61.

Arendt, H. 1963. *Eichmann in Jerusalem: A report on the banality of evil.* New York: Viking Press.

Aries, P. 1962. *Centuries of childhood: A social history of family life.* New York: Vintage Books.

Armstrong, P. J., Goodman, J. F. B., & Hyman, J. D. 1981. *Ideology and shop-floor industrial relations.* London: Croom Helm.

Arno, P. S., & Feiden, K. L. 1992. *Against the odds: The story of AIDS drug development, politics and profits.* New York: HarperCollins.

Asch, D. A. 1996. "The role of critical care nurses in euthanasia and assisted suicide." *New England Journal of Medicine, 334,* 1374–1379.

Asch, S. 1958. "Effects of group pressure on the modification and distortion." In E. E. Maccoby, T. M. Newcomb, & E. L. Hartley (Eds.), *Readings in Social Psychology.* New York: Holt, Rinehart, & Winston.

Auletta, K. 1982. *The underclass.* New York: Random House.

Babbie, E. 1986. *Observing ourselves: Essays in social research.* Belmont, CA: Wadsworth.

———. 1992. The practice of social research. Belmont, CA: Wadsworth.

Baca-Zinn, M., & Eitzen, D. S. 1993. *Diversity in families.* New York: HarperCollins.

———. 1996. Divesity in families. New York: HarperCollins.

Bagdikian, B. H. 1991. "Missing from the news." In J. H. Skolnick & E. Currie (Eds.), *Crisis in American institutions.* New York: HarperCollins.

———. 1992. *The media monopoly.* Boston: Beacon Press.

Bailey, B. L. 1988. *From front porch to back seat: Courtship in 20th century America.* Baltimore: Johns Hopkins University Press.

Bailey, C. A. 1993. "Equality with difference: On androcentrism and menstruation." *Teaching Sociology, 21,* 121–129.

Bailey, W. C. 1990. "Murder, capital punishment, and television: Execution publicity and homicide rates." *American Sociological Review, 55,* 628–633.

Bailey, W. C., & Peterson, R. 1989. "Murder and capital punishment: A monthly time series analysis of execution policy." *American Sociological Review, 54,* 722–743.

Ballard, C. 1987. "A humanist sociology approach to teaching social research." *Teaching Sociology, 15,* 7–14.

Bandura, A., & Walters, R. H. 1963. *Social learning and personality development.* New York: Holt, Rinehart & Winston.

Bane, M. J., & Ellwood, D. T. 1983. "The dynamics of dependence: The routes to self sufficiency." Report prepared for Assistant Secretary For Planning and Evaluation, Office of Evaluation and Technical Analysis, Office of Income Security Policy, U.S. Department of Health and Human Services. Washington, DC.

Banfield, E. 1970. *The unheavenly city.* New York: Little, Brown.

Barber, B. 1992. "Jihad vs. McWorld." *Atlantic Monthly,* March, pp. 53–65.

Baron, A. 1987. "Feminist legal strategies: The powers of difference." In B. Hess & M. M. Ferree (Eds.), *Analyzing gender: A handbook of social science research.* Newbury Park, CA: Sage.

Barrett, N. 1987. "Women and the economy." In S. E. Rix (Ed.), *The American woman,* 1987–88. New York: Norton.

Barringer, F. 1992. "Whether it's hunger or 'misnourishment,' it's a national problem." *New York Times,* December 27.

———. 1993. "Immigration in the '80's made English a foreign language for millions." *New York Times,* April 28.

Basch, C. E., & Kersch, T. B. 1986. "Adolescent perceptions of stressful life events." *Health Education,* June/July, 4–7.

Beaman, A. L., Klentz, B., Diener, E., & Svanum, S. 1979. "Objective self awareness and transgression in children: A field study." *Journal of Personality and Social Psychology, 37,* 1835–1846.

Beck, M. 1990. "Be nice to your kids." *Newsweek,* March 12.

Becker, H. 1952. "Social class variations in the teacher–pupil relationship." *Journal of Educational Sociology, 25,* 451–466.

———. 1963. *The outsiders.* New York: Free Press.

Becker, H. S., & Geer, B. 1958. "The fate of idealism in medical school." *American Sociological Review, 23,* 50–56.

Bedard, M. 1991. "Captive clientele of the welfare supersystem: Breaking the cage wide open." *Humanity and Society, 15,* 23–48.

Beeghley, L. 1984. "Illusion and reality in the measurement of poverty." *Social Problems, 31,* 322–333.

Begley, S. 1994. "One pill makes you larger, and one pill makes you small . . ." *Newsweek,* February 7.

———. 1995. "Three is not enough." *Newsweek,* February 13.

Belkin, L. 1990. "Airport anti-drug nets snare many people fitting 'profiles.'" *New York Times,* March 20.

Bell, D. 1976. *The coming of post-industrial society.* New York: Harper & Row.

Bell, D. J., & Bell, S. L. 1991. "The victim-offender relationship as a determinant factor in police dispositions of family violence incidents: A replication study." *Policing and Society, 1,* 225–234.

Bellah, R., Madsen, R., Sullivan, W. M., Swidler, A., & Tipton, S. M. 1985. *Habits of the heart.* New York: Harper & Row.

Belsky, J. 1988. "The effects of infant day care reconsidered." *Early Childhood Research Quarterly, 3,* 235–272.

Bennett, N. G., Bloom, D. E., & Craig, P. H. 1986. *Black and white marriage patterns: Why so different?* (Discussion Paper No. 500). New Haven, CT: Economic Growth Center, Yale University.

Benokraitis, N. V., & Feagin, J. R. 1993. "Sex discrimination: Subtle and covert." In J. Henslin (Ed.), *Down to earth sociology.* New York: Free Press.

Ben-Yehuda, N. 1990. *The politics and morality of deviance.* Albany: State University of New York Press.

Berg, B. 1992. "The guilt that drives working mothers crazy." In J. Henslin (Ed.), *Marriage and family in a changing society.* New York: Free Press.

Berger, D. L., & Williams, J. E. 1991. "Sex stereotypes in the United States revisited: 1972–1988." *Sex Roles, 24,* 413–423.

Berger, P. L. 1963. *Invitation to sociology.* Garden City, NY: Anchor.

Berger, P. L., & Kellner, H. 1964. "Marriage and the construction of reality: An exercise in the microsociology of knowledge." *Diogenes, 46,* 1–23.

Berger, P. L., & Luckmann, T. 1966. *The social construction of reality.* Garden City, NY: Anchor.

Bernard, J. 1972. *The future of marriage.* New York: Bantam.

———. 1981. "The good provider role: Its rise and fall." *American Psychologist, 36,* 1–12.

Berndt, T. J., & Heller, K. A. 1986. "Gender stereotypes and social inferences: A developmental study." *Journal of Personality and Social Psychology, 50,* 889–898.

Bernhardt, A., Morris, M., & Handcock, M. S. 1995. "Women's gains or men's losses? A closer look at the shrinking gender gap in earnings." *American Journal of Sociology, 101,* 302–328.

Bernstein, M. F. 1996. "Racial gerrymandering." *The Public Interest,* Winter, 59–69.

Bernstein, N. 1996. "Equal opportunity recedes for most female lawyers." *New York Times,* January 8.

Bernstein, S. 1990. "Getting it done: Notes on student fritters." In J. W. Heeren & M. Mason (Eds.), *Sociology: Windows on society.* Los Angeles: Roxbury.

Berscheid, E., and Walster, E. 1974. "Physical attractiveness." In L. Berkowitz (Ed.), *Advances in experimental social psychology.* New York: Academic Press.

Bertenthal, B. I., & Fischer, K. W. 1978. "Development of self-recognition in the infant." *Developmental Psychology, 14,* 44–50.

Best, J. 1990. *Threatened children: Rhetoric and concern about child-victims.* Chicago: University of Chicago Press.

Best, R. 1983. *We've all got scars: What boys and girls learn in elementary school.* Bloomington: Indiana University Press.

Binder, D., & Crossette, B. 1993. "As ethnic wars multiply, U.S. strives for a policy." *New York Times,* February 7.

Birenbaum, A., & Sagarin, E. 1976. *Norms and human behavior.* New York: Praeger.

Bishop, K. 1991. "Ads on Holocaust 'hoax' inspire campus debates." *New York Times,* December 23.

Bjerklie, D., Cole, P. E., & Cray, D. 1995. "Age of the road warrior." *Time,* Spring.

Blackman, A. et al. 1994. "When violence hits home." *Time,* July 4.

Blackwell, J. E. 1990. "Current issues affecting blacks and Hispanics in the educational pipeline." In G. E. Thomas (Ed.), *U.S. race relations in the 1980's and 1990's.* New York: Hemisphere.

Blakely, E. J., & Snyder, M. G. 1995. "The walling and gating of American suburbs." *Nation's Cities Weekly,* October 2.

Blau, J. 1992. *The visible poor.* New York: Oxford University Press.

Blau, P. M. 1964. *Exchange and power in social life.* New York: Wiley.

Blau, P. M., & Duncan, O. D. 1967. *The American occupational structure.* New York: Wiley.

Blau, P. M., & Meyer, M. W. 1987. "The concept of bureaucracy." In R. T. Schaeffer & R. P. Lamm (Eds.), *Introducing sociology.* New York: McGraw-Hill.

Blauner, R. 1964. *Alienation and freedom.* Chicago: University of Chicago Press.

———. 1992. "The ambiguities of racial change." In M. L. Anderson & P. H. Collins (Eds.), *Race, class and gender: An anthology.* Belmont, CA: Wadsworth.

Block, J. H. 1983. "Differential premises arising from differential socialization of the sexes: Some conjectures." *Child Development, 54,* 1335–1354.

Blood, P., Tuttle, A., & Lakey, G. 1992. "Understanding and fighting sexism: A call to men." In M. L. Anderson & P. H. Collins (Eds.), *Race, class and gender: An anthology.* Belmont, CA: Wadsworth.

Blumstein, P. 1975. "Identity bargaining and self-conception." *Social Forces, 53,* 476–485.

Blumstein, P., & Kollock, P. 1988. "Personal relationships." *Annual Review of Sociology, 14,* 467–490.

Blumstein, P., & Schwartz, P. 1983. *American couples.* New York: Morrow.

Bohlen, C. 1989. "Holtzman may appeal probation for immigrant in wife's slaying." *New York Times,* April 5.

Bonnie, R. J., & Whitebread, C. H. 1974. *The marijuana conviction.* Charlottesville: University of Virginia Press.

Booth, A., Johnson, D. R., Branaman, A., & Sica, A. 1995. "Belief and behavior: Does religion matter in today's marriage?" *Journal of Marriage and Family, 57,* 661–671.

Bot, M. 1985. *Miserere: The great pilgrimages of penance in Europe.* Rotterdam [English edition].

Bowles, S., & Gintis, H. 1976. *Schooling in capitalist America: Educational reform and the contradictions of economic reform.* New York: Basic Books.

Bradley, G. W. 1978. "Self-serving biases in the attribution process: A reexamination of the fact or fiction question." *Journal of Personality and Social Psychology, 36,* 56–71.

Bradshaw, Y. W., & Wallace, M. 1996. *Global Inequalities.* Thousand Oaks, CA: Pine Forge Press.

Bradsher, K. 1993. "Mark Twain would understand the water crisis that's corrupting Iowans." *New York Times,* July 22.

———. 1995a. "Sluggish income figures show modest gains for some groups." *New York Times,* October 6.

———. 1995b. "Gap in wealth in U.S. called widest in west." *New York Times,* April 17.

———. 1996. "Rich control more of U.S. wealth, study says, as debt grows for poor." *New York Times,* June 22.

Braun, D. 1991. *The rich get richer: The rise of income inequality in the United States and the world.* Chicago: Nelson-Hall.

Breslau, K. 1990. "Overplanned parenthood." *Newsweek,* January 22.

Bridges, J. S. 1988. "Sex differences in occupational performance expectations." *Psychology of Women Quarterly, 12,* 75–90.

Brim, O. 1968. "Adult socialization." In J. A. Clausen (Ed.), *Socialization and society.* Boston: Little, Brown.

Brines, J. 1994. "Economic dependency, gender and the division of labor at home." *American Journal of Sociology, 100,* 652–688.

Brinton, C. 1965. *The anatomy of revolution.* New York: Vintage.

Brinton, M. 1988. "The social-institutional bases of gender stratification." *American Journal of Sociology, 94,* 300–334.

Brody, J. E. 1991. "Children of divorce: Actions to help, can hurt, study finds." *New York Times,* July 23.

Brooke, J. 1985. "The unexplained lost years of Gladys Burr." *New York Times,* July 11.

Brophy, B. 1995. "Kindergartners in the Prozac nation." *U.S. News & World Report,* November 13.

Broverman, I., Vogel, S., Broverman, D., Clarkson, F., & Rosenkrantz, P. 1972. "Sex role stereotypes: A current appraisal." *Journal of Social Issues, 28,* 59–78.

Brown, J. L. 1987. "Hunger in the U.S." *Scientific American, 256,* 37–41.

Brown, L. R. 1988. "Analyzing the demographic trap." *Current,* March/April.

Brown, R. 1986. *Social psychology.* New York: Free Press.

Brownmiller, S. 1975. *Against our will: Men, women and rape.* New York: Simon & Schuster.

———. 1984. *Femininity.* New York: Fawcett.

Bryjak, G. J., & Soroka, M. P. 1992. *Sociology: Cultural diversity in a changing world.* Boston: Allyn & Bacon.

Bullard, R. D. 1993. "Anatomy of environmental racism and the environmental justice movement." In R. D. Bullard (Ed.), *Confronting environmental racism*. Boston: South End Press.

Bullard, R. D., & Wright, B. H. 1992. "The quest for environmental equity: Mobilizing the African-American community for social change." In R. E. Dunlap & A. G. Mertig (Eds.), *American Environmentalism: The U.S. environmental movement, 1970–1990*. Philadelphia: Taylor & Francis.

Bullington, B. 1993. "All about Eve: The many faces of United States drug policy." In F. Pearce & M. Woodiwiss (Eds.), *Global crime connections*. Toronto: University of Toronto Press.

Bumpass, L., & Sweet, J. 1989. "Children's experience in single-parent families: Implications of cohabitation and marital transitions." *Family Planning Perspectives, 21,* 256–260.

Bumpass, L., Sweet, J., & Castro Martin, T. 1990. "Changing patterns of remarriage." *Journal of Marriage and the Family, 52,* 747–756.

Burawoy, M. 1979. *Manufacturing consent.* Chicago: University of Chicago Press.

Burton, T. M. 1996. "Lilly sales rise as use of Prozac keeps growing." *Wall Street Journal,* January 31.

Butler, R. 1975. *Why survive? Being old in America.* New York: Harper & Row.

———. 1989. "A generation at risk: When the baby boomers reach Golden Pond." In W. Feigelman (Ed.), *Sociology Full Circle.* New York: Holt, Rinehart & Winston.

Butterfield, F. 1995a. "More blacks in their 20's have trouble with the law." *New York Times,* October 5.

———. 1995b. "More in U.S. are in prisons, report says." *New York Times,* August 10.

Campbell, A. 1987. "Self-definition by rejection: The case of gang girls." *Social Problems, 34,* 451–466.

Campbell, A., Converse, P. E., & Rodgers, W. L. 1976. *The quality of American life.* New York: Russell Sage Foundation.

Cancian, F. 1987. *Love in America: Gender and self-development.* New York: Cambridge University Press.

Cantor, M. G. 1987. "Popular culture and the portrayal of women: Content and control." In B. B. Hess & M. M. Ferree (Eds.), *Analyzing gender: A handbook of social science research.* Newbury Park, CA: Sage.

Carr, J. 1988. *Crisis in intimacy.* Pacific Grove, CA: Brooks/Cole.

Carter, H., & Glick, P. C. 1976. *Marriage and divorce: A social and economic study.* Cambridge, MA: Harvard University Press.

Celis, W. 1993. "Study finds rising concentration of black and Hispanic students." *New York Times,* December 14.

Cetron, M. J., Rocha, W., & Luckins, R. 1991. "Into the 21st century: Long term trends affecting the United States." In L. Cargan & J. H. Ballantine (Eds.), *Sociological footprints* (5th ed.). Belmont, CA: Wadsworth.

Chafetz, J. S. 1978. *A primer on the construction and testing of theories in sociology.* Itasca, IL: Peacock.

Chafetz, J. S., & Dworkin, A. G. 1987. "In the face of threat: Organized anti-feminism in comparative perspective." *Gender and Society, 1,* 33–60.

Chalfant, H., & Prigoff, J. 1987. *Spraycan art.* New York: Thames and Hudson.

Chambliss, W. 1964. "A sociological analysis of the law of vagrancy." *Social Problems, 12,* 66–77.

———. 1974. "The state, the law and the definition of behavior as criminal or delinquent." In D. Glaser (Ed.), *The handbook of criminology.* Chicago: Rand McNally.

Chambliss, W., & Nagasawa, R. H. 1969. "On the validity of official statistics: A comparative study of white, black and Japanese high-school boys." *Journal of Research in Crime and Delinquency, 6,* 71–77.

Chapman, G. 1996. "The Internet: Promise and peril in cyberspace." *Microsoft Encarta Encyclopedia.*

Charon, J. 1992, *Ten questions: A sociological perspective.* Belmont, CA: Wadsworth.

Cherlin, A. 1978. "Remarriage as an incomplete institution." *American Journal of Sociology, 84,* 634–650.

———. 1992. *Marriage, divorce, remarriage.* Cambridge: Harvard University Press.

Chernin, K. 1981. *The obsession: Reflections on the tyranny of slenderness.* New York: Harper & Row.

Cherry, R. 1989. *Discrimination: Its economic impact on blacks, women and Jews.* Lexington, MA: Lexington Books.

Ching, F. 1994. "Talking sense on population." *Far Eastern Economic Review,* October 6.

Chirot, D. 1994. *How societies change.* Newbury Park, CA: Pine Forge Press.

"Christian faith in the age of Prozac." 1995. *Harper's Magazine,* December.

Ciancanelli, P., & Berch, B. 1987. "Gender and the GNP." In B. B. Hess & M. M. Ferree (Eds.), *Analyzing gender: A handbook of social science research.* Newbury Park, CA: Sage.

Cicirelli, V. G. 1983. "Adult children and their elderly parents." In T. H. Brubaker (Ed.), *Family relationships in later life.* Beverly Hills, CA: Sage.

Cirino, R. 1973. "Bias through selection and omission: Automobile safety, smoking." In S. Cohen & J. Young (Eds.), *The manufacture of news.* Beverly Hills, CA: Sage.

Citrin, J. 1996. "Affirmative action in the people's court." *The Public Interest,* Winter, 39–48.

Clark, B. 1960. "The 'cooling out' function in higher education." *American Journal of Sociology, 65,* 569–576.

Clark, R. D., III, & Word, L. E. 1972. "Why don't bystanders help? Because of ambiguity." *Journal of Personality and Social Psychology, 24,* 392–400.

Clark, R. L., & Passel, J. S. 1993. "Studies are deceptive." *New York Times,* September 3.

Clausen, J. A. 1986. *The life course: A sociological perspective.* Englewood Cliffs, NJ: Prentice-Hall.

Clifford, M. M., & Walster, E. 1973. "The effect of physical attractiveness on teacher expectations." *Sociology of Education, 46,* 248–258.

Clinard, M. B., & Meier, R. F. 1979. *Sociology of deviant behavior.* New York: Holt, Rinehart & Winston.

Cloward, R., & Piven, F. F. 1993. "The fraud of workfare." *The Nation,* May 24, 693–696.

Cluster, D. 1979. *They should have served that cup of coffee.* Boston: South End Press.

Cobb, N. J., Stevens-Long, J., & Goldstein, S. 1982. "The influence of televised models on toy preference in children." *Sex Roles, 8,* 1075–1080.

Cockburn, A. 1995. "The white man's answer." *The Nation,* November 27.

Cockerham, W. C. 1992. *Sociology of mental disorder.* Englewood Cliffs, NJ: Prentice-Hall.

Coe, R. M. 1978. *Sociology of medicine.* New York: McGraw-Hill.

Cohen, A. K. 1955. *Delinquent boys: The culture of the gang.* New York: Free Press.

———. 1966. *Deviance and control.* Englewood Cliffs, NJ: Prentice-Hall.

Cohen, A. M., & Brawer, F. 1982. *The American community college.* San Francisco: Jossey-Bass.

Cohen, B. 1991. "Taking time off: Leave provision in the European community for parents of school age children." *Women's Studies International Forum, 14,* 585–598.

Cohen, F. G. 1986. *Treaties on trial: The continuing controversy over Northwest Indian fishing rights.* Seattle: University of Washington Press.

Cohen, L. E., & Land, K. C. 1987. "Age structure and crime: Symmetry vs. asymmetry and the projection of crime rates through the 1990's." *American Sociological Review, 52,* 170–183.

Colburn, D. 1992. "A vicious cycle of risk." *Washington Post Health Magazine,* July 28.

Collins, R. 1971. "Functional and conflict theories of educational stratification." *American Sociological Review, 36,* 1002–1019.

———. 1981. "On the microfoundations of macrosociology." *American Journal of Sociology, 86,* 984–1014.

Collins, R., & Makowsky, M. 1984. *The discovery of society.* New York: Random House.

Comer, J. P., & Poussaint, A. F. 1992. *Raising black children.* New York: Plume.

Commission for Racial Justice. 1987. *Toxic waste and race.* New York: United Church of Christ.

Conrad, P. 1975. "The discovery of hyperkinesis: Notes on the medicalization of deviant behavior." *Social Problems, 23,* 12–21.

———. 1992. "The social meaning of AIDS." In J. W. Heeren & M. Mason (Eds.), *Sociology: Windows on society.* Los Angeles: Roxbury.

Conrad, P., & Schneider, J. W. 1980. *Deviance and medicalization: From badness to sickness.* St. Louis: C. V. Mosby.

Cookson, P., & Persell, C. 1985. *Preparing for power.* New York: Basic Books.

Cooley, C. H. 1902. *Human nature and social order.* New York: Charles Scribner's Sons.

Coontz, S. 1992. *The way we never were.* New York: Basic Books.

Cooper, M. H. 1994. "Prozac controversy." *CQ Researcher,* August 19.

Corcoran, M., Duncan, G. J., & Hill, M. S. 1986. "The economic fortunes of women and children: Lessons from the panel study of income dynamics." In B. C. Gelpi, et al. (Eds.), *Women and poverty.* Chicago: University of Chicago Press.

Cose, E. 1993. *The rage of the privileged class.* New York: HarperCollins.

Coser, L., & Coser, R. 1993. "Jonestown as a perverse Utopia." In K. Finsterbusch & J. S. Schwartz (Eds.), *Sources: Notable selections in sociology.* Guilford, CT: Dushkin.

Coulson, M. A., & Riddell, C. 1980. *Approaching sociology.* London: Routledge & Kegan Paul.

Coupland, D. 1991. *Generation X: Tales for an accelerated culture.* New York: St. Martin's Press.

"Court rules city may oust unwed couple." 1986. *Seattle Times,* 19:6, November 8.

Cowan, R. 1991. "More work for Mother: The postwar years." In L. Kramer (Ed.), *The sociology of gender.* New York: St. Martin's Press.

Cowley, G. 1994. "The culture of Prozac." *Newsweek,* February 7.

Crittenden, K. S. 1991. "Asian self-effacement or feminine modesty? Attributional patterns of women university students in Taiwan." *Gender and Society,* 5, 98–117.

Crittenden, K. S., & Wiley, M. G. 1985. "When egotism is normative: Self-presentational norms guiding attributions." *Social Psychology Quarterly,* 48, 360–365.

Cross, J., & Guyer M. 1980. *Social traps.* Ann Arbor: University of Michigan Press.

Crossette, B. 1995. "Female genital mutilation by immigrants is becoming cause for concern in U.S." *New York Times,* December 10.

———. 1996a. "New tally of world tragedy: Women who die giving life." *New York Times,* June 11.

———. 1996b. "Hope, and pragmatism, for U.N. cities conference." *New York Times,* June 3.

Cummings, S., & Taebel, D. 1978. "The economic socialization of children: A neo-Marxist analysis." *Social Problems,* 26, 198–210.

Curran, D. J., & Renzetti, C. M. 1990. *Social problems.* Boston: Allyn & Bacon.

Cushman, J. H. 1993. "U.S. to weigh Blacks' complaints about pollution." *New York Times,* November 19.

———. 1996. "Western governors back on-line university to offer e-mail degrees to cyberstudents." *New York Times,* June 25.

Dabbs, J. M. 1992. "Testosterone and occupational achievement." *Social Forces,* 70, 813–824.

Dahl, R. 1961. *Who governs? Democracy and power in an American city.* New Haven, CT: Yale University Press.

Dahrendorf, R. 1959. *Class and class conflict in industrial society.* Stanford, CA: Stanford University Press.

Daley, S. 1996. "A new charter wins adoption in South Africa." *New York Times,* May 9.

Daniels, C. R. 1993. *At women's expense: State power and the politics of fetal rights.* Cambridge, MA: Harvard University Press.

Daniels, R. 1990. *Coming to America.* New York: HarperCollins.

Darton, N. 1991. "The end of innocence." *Newsweek* [special summer issue].

Darwin, C. 1871/1971. *The descent of man.* Adelaide, Australia: Griffin Press.

Davies, J. C. 1962. "Toward a theory of revolution." *American Sociological Review,* 27, 5–19.

Davis, A. J. 1984. "Sex-differentiated behaviors in nonsexist picture books." *Sex Roles,* 11, 1–16.

Davis, F. J. 1991. *Who is black?* University Park: Pennsylvania State University Press.

Davis, J. A., & Smith, T. 1986. *General social survey cumulative file 1972–1982.* Ann Arbor, MI: Inter-University Consortium for Political and Social Research.

Davis, K. 1937. "The sociology of prostitution." *American Sociological Review,* 2, 744–755.

———. 1976. "The world's population crisis." In R. K. Merton & R. Nisbett (Eds.), *Contemporary social problems.* New York: Harcourt Brace Jovanovich.

Davis, K., & Moore, W. 1945. "Some principles of stratification." *American Sociological Review,* 10, 242–247.

Deaux, K., & Kite, M. E. 1987. "Thinking about gender." In B. B. Hess & M. M. Ferree (Eds.), *Analyzing gender.* Newbury Park, CA: Sage.

DeCoursey, J. 1995. "Maidenform fashions Wonderbra challenger." *Advertising Age,* February 20.

DeFronzo, J. 1991. *Revolutions and revolutionary movements.* Boulder, CO: Westview.

Della Fave, L. R. 1980. "The meek shall not inherit the Earth: Self evaluation and the legitimacy of stratification." *American Sociological Review, 45,* 955–971.

"Denny's Restaurant hit with discrimination suit," 1993. *Jet Magazine,* April 12.

Denzin, N. 1977. *Childhood socialization: Studies in the development of language, social behavior, and identity.* San Fransisco: Jossey-Bass.

———. 1989. *The research act: A theoretical introduction to sociological methods.* Englewood Cliffs, NJ: Prentice-Hall.

DePalma, A. 1995. "Racism? Mexico's in denial." *New York Times,* June 11.

———. 1996a. "For Mexico's Indians, new voice but few gains." *New York Times,* January 13.

———. 1996b. "Income gulf in Mexico grows and so do protests." *New York Times,* July 20.

DeParle, J. 1990. "In debate over who is poor, fairness becomes the issue." *New York Times,* September 3.

———. 1991. "Suffering in the cities persists as U.S. fights other battles." *New York Times,* January 27.

Derber, C. 1979. *The pursuit of attention.* New York: Oxford University Press.

Deutsch, K. W. 1966. *Nationalism and social communication.* Cambridge, MA: MIT Press.

DeWitt, K. 1995. "Panel's study cites job bias for minorities and women." *New York Times,* November 23.

Diamond, J. 1994. "Race without color." *Discover,* November, 82–89.

Dillon, D. 1994. "Fortress America." *Planning.* June.

DiMaggio, P. J., & Powell, W. W. 1983. "The iron cage revisited: Institutional isomorphism and collective rationality in organizational fields." *American Sociological Review, 48,* 147–160.

———. 1991. "Introduction." In W. W. Powell & P. J. Dimaggio (Eds.). *The new institutionalism in organizational analysis.* Chicago: University of Chicago Press.

Dion, K. K. 1972. "Physical attractiveness and evaluations of children's transgressions." *Journal of Personality and Social Psychology, 24,* 207–213.

Dion, K., Berscheid, E., & Walster, E. 1972. "What is beautiful is good." *Journal of Personality and Social Psychology, 24,* 285–290.

Dobash, R. E., & Dobash, R. P. 1979. *Violence against wives: A case against the patriarchy.* New York: Free Press.

"Doctors implicated in Tutsi genocide." 1996. *The Lancet, 347,* p. 684.

Domhoff, G. W. 1983. *Who rules America now? A view from the eighties.* Englewood Cliffs, NJ: Prentice-Hall.

Donath, J. S. 1997. "Identity deception in the virtual community." In P. Kollock & M. Smith (Eds.), *Communities in cyberspace.* Berkeley: University of California Press.

Dowd, M. 1994. "Americans like G.O.P. agenda but split on how to reach goals." *New York Times,* December 15.

Doyle, R. 1994. *Atlas of contemporary America.* New York: Facts on File.

Drucker, S. 1996. "Who is the best restaurateur in America?" *New York Times Magazine,* March 10.

D'Souza, D. 1995. *The end of racism.* New York: The Free Press.

Dugger, C. W. 1992. "U.S. study says Asian-Americans face widespread discrimination." *New York Times,* February 29.

———. 1996a. "Woman's plea for asylum puts tribal ritual on trial." *New York Times,* April 15.

———. 1996b. "U.S. grants asylum to woman fleeing genital mutilation rite." *New York Times,* June 14.

———. 1996c. "Immigrant cultures raising issues of child punishment." *New York Times,* February 29.

Duncan, G. J. 1984. *Years of poverty, years of plenty.* Ann Arbor: University of Michigan Press.

Durkheim, E. 1951. *Suicide.* New York: Free Press. (Original work published 1897)

———. 1954. *The elementary forms of religious life* (J. Swain, Trans.). New York: Free Press. (Original work published 1915)

———. 1958. *The rules of sociological method* (G. E. G. Catlin, Ed.; S. A. Solovay & J. H. Mueller, Trans.). Glencoe, IL: Free Press.

Eagly, A. H., Wood, W., & Fishbaugh, L. 1981. "Sex differences in conformity: Surveillance by the group as a determinant of male nonconformity." *Journal of Personality and Social Psychology, 40,* 384–394.

Ebaugh, H. R. F. 1988, *Becoming an ex.* Chicago: University of Chicago Press.

Edelman, M. W. 1988. "Growing up black in America." In J. Skolnick & E. Currie (Eds.), *Crisis in American institutions.* Glenview, IL: Scott, Foresman.

Edney, J. 1979. "Free riders en route to disaster." *Psychology Today,* August, pp. 80–102.

Edney, J. J., & Harper, C. S. 1978. "The commons dilemma: A review of contributions from psychology." *Environmental Management, 2,* 491–507.

Egan, T. 1993. "A cultural gap may swallow a child." *New York Times,* October 12.

———. 1995. "Many seek security in private communities." *New York Times,* September 3.

Ehrenreich, B. 1989. *Fear of falling: The inner life of the middle class.* New York: Harper.

———. 1990. "Is the middle class doomed?" In B. Ehrenreich (Ed.), *The worst years of our lives.* New York: Harper.

Ehrenreich, B., & English, D. 1979. *For her own good: 150 years of the experts' advice to women.* Garden City, NY: Anchor.

Ehrlich, P. R., & Ehrlich, A. H. 1993. "World population crisis." In K. Finsterbusch & J. S. Schwartz (Eds.), *Sources: Notable selections in sociology.* Guilford, CT: Dushkin.

Eitzen, D. S., & Baca-Zinn, M. 1989. *Social problems.* Boston: Allyn & Bacon.

———. 1991. *In conflict and order: Understanding society.* Boston: Allyn & Bacon.

Eitzen, D. S., Jung, M. A., & Purdy, D. A. 1982. "Organizational linkages among the inner group of the capitalist class." *Sociological Focus, 15,* 179–189.

Elder, G. H., & Liker, J. K. 1982. "Hard times in women's lives: Historical influences across 40 years." *American Journal of Sociology, 88,* 241–269.

Elliot, M., & Dickey, C. 1994. "Body politics." *Newsweek,* September 12.

Emerson, R. 1962. "Power-dependence relations." *American Sociological Review, 27,* 31–41.

Emmet, H. L. 1989. *Fruit tramps.* Albuquerque: University of New Mexico Press.

Engelhardt, T. 1992. "The Gulf War as total television." *The Nation,* May 11.

English, C. 1991. "Food is my best friend: Self-justifications and weight loss efforts." *Research in the Sociology of Health Care, 9,* 335–345.

Entwisle, D. R., & Alexander, K. L. 1994. "Winter setback: The racial composition of schools and learning to read." *American Sociological Review, 59,* 446–460.

Epstein, C. F. 1989. "Workplace boundaries: Conceptions and creations." *Social Research, 56,* 571–590.

Erickson, P. G., & Goodstadt, M. S. 1979. "Legal stigma for marijuana possession." *Criminology, 17,* 208–216.

Erikson, K. 1966. *Wayward puritans.* New York: Wiley.

Ervin-Tripp, S. 1964. "Interaction of language, topic and listener." *American Anthropologist, 66,* 86–102.

Eskenazi, G. 1992. "The plan no one wants to use." *New York Times,* May 22.

Evans-Pritchard, E. E. 1937. *Witchcraft, oracles and magic among the Azande.* Oxford: Oxford University Press.

Evered, R. 1983. "The language of organizations: The case of the Navy." In L. R. Pondy, P. J. Frost, G. Morgan, & T. C. Dandridge (Eds.), *Organizational symbolism.* Greenwich, CT: JAI Press.

Ewen, S., & Ewen, E. 1982. *Channels of desire: Mass images and the shaping of the American consciousness.* New York: McGraw-Hill.

Ewing, W. 1992. "The civic advocacy of violence." In M. S. Kimmel & M. A. Messner (Eds.), *Men's Lives.* New York: Macmillan.

"The facts about figures." 1996. *People,* June 3.

Fairchild, H. H. 1985. "Black, Negro or Afro-American? The difference is crucial!" *Journal of Black Studies, 16,* 47–55.

Faludi, S. 1991. *Backlash: The undeclared war against women.* New York: Crown.

Farb, P. 1983. *Word play: What happens when people talk.* New York: Bantam.

Farhi, P. 1992. "Number of U.S. millionaires soars." *Washington Post,* July 11.

Farley, J. 1982. *Majority-minority relations.* Englewood Cliffs, NJ: Prentice-Hall.

———. 1991. *Sociology.* Englewood Cliffs, NJ: Prentice-Hall.

Farley, J. E. 1991. *American social problems: An institutional analysis,* 2nd ed. Upper Saddle River, NJ: Prentice-Hall.

Farley, R., & Frey, W. H. 1992. *Changes in the segregation of whites from blacks during the 1980s: Small steps toward a more racially integrated society.* Ann Arbor: Population Studies Center, University of Michigan.

————. 1994. "Changes in the segregation of whites from blacks during the 1980s: Small steps toward a more integrated society." *American Sociological Review, 59,* 23–45.

Fausto-Sterling, A. 1985. *Myths of gender: Biological theories about women and men.* New York: Basic Books.

————. 1993. "How many sexes are there?" *New York Times,* March 12.

Feagin, J. R. 1975. *Subordinating the poor.* Englewood Cliffs, NJ: Prentice-Hall.

————. 1991. "The continuing significance of race: Anti-black discrimination in public places." *American Sociological Review, 56,* 101–116.

Featherstone, M. 1990. *Global culture: Nationalism, globalization and modernity.* Newbury Park, CA: Sage.

Federal Bureau of Investigation. 1991. *Uniform crime reports for the United States.* Washington, DC: U.S. Government Printing Office.

Fee, E., & Fox, D. M. 1992. *AIDS: The making of a chronic disease.* Berkeley: University of California Press.

Feigelman, W., & Silverman, A. B. 1984. "The long-term effects of transracial adoption." *Social Service Review, 58,* 588–602.

Feldberg, R. L. 1984. "Comparable worth: Toward theory and practice in the United States." *Signs, 10,* 311–328.

Felmlee, D., Sprecher, S., & Bassin, E. 1990. "The dissolution of intimate relationships: A hazard model." *Social Psychology Quarterly, 53,* 13–30.

Ferraro, K. J., & Johnson, J. M. 1983. "How women experience battering: The process of victimization." *Social Problems, 30,* 325–339.

Ferrato, D. 1991. *Living with the enemy.* New York: Aperture.

Ferree, M. M. 1992. "The political context of rationality." In A. D. Morris & C. M. Mueller (Eds.), *Frontiers in social movement theory.* New Haven: Yale University Press.

Festinger, L., Riecken, H., & Schacter, S. 1956. *When prophecy fails.* New York: Harper & Row.

Fincham, F., & Bradbury, T. N. 1987. "The impact of attributions in marriage: A longitudinal analysis." *Journal of Personality and Social Psychology, 53,* 510–517.

Fine, G. A. 1990. *Talking sociology.* Boston: Allyn & Bacon.

Fineman, H. 1991. "The new politics of race." *Newsweek,* May 6.

Finlay, B. 1985. "Right to life vs. right to die: Some correlates of euthanasia attitudes." *Sociology and Social Research, 69,* 548–560.

Fitchen, J. M. 1992a. "Homelessness in rural places: Perspectives from upstate New York." *Urban Anthropology, 20,* 177–210.

————. 1992b. "On the edge of homelessness: Rural poverty and housing insecurity." *Rural Sociology, 57,* 173–193.

Flynn, L. 1996. "Prototypes of virtual shoppers." *New York Times,* March 4.

"The Forbes four hundred." *Forbes Magazine,* 1990, 147, 318–327.

Foucault, M. 1965. *Madness and civilization.* New York: Vintage.

Fox, M. F. 1989. "Women and higher education: Gender differences in the status of students and scholars." In J. Freeman (Ed.), *Women: A feminist perspective.* Mountain View, CA: Mayfield.

Frank, A. G. 1969. *Capitalism and under-development in Latin America.* New York: Monthly Review Press.

Frank, M., Ziebarth, M., & Field, C. 1982. *The life and times of Rosie the Riveter.* Emeryville, CA: Clarity Educational Productions.

Franklin, C. W., II, 1988. *Men and society.* Chicago: Nelson-Hall.

Freedman, R. 1986. *Beauty bound.* Lexington, MA: Lexington Books.

Freiberg, P. 1991. "Self-esteem gender gap widens in adolescence." *APA Monitor, 22,* 29.

Friedland, R. 1989. "Questions raised by the changing age distribution of the U.S. population." *Generations, 13,* 11–13.

Friedson, E. 1970. *Profession of medicine.* New York: Dodd, Mead.

Frieze, I. H., Parsons, J. E., Johnson, P. B., Ruble, D. N., & Zellman, G. L. 1978. *Women and sex roles: A social psychological perspective.* New York: Norton.

Frisbie, W. P., & Kasarda, J. D. 1988. "Spatial processes." In N. J. Smelser (Ed.), The handbook of sociology. Newbury Park, CA: Sage.

Funicello, T. 1993. *Tyranny of kindness: Dismantling the welfare system to end poverty in America.* New York: Atlantic Monthly Press.

Furstenberg, F. F., & Cherlin, A. J. 1991. *Divided families.* Cambridge, MA: Harvard University Press.

Gabriel, T. 1996. "High-tech pregnancies test hope's limit." *New York Times,* January 7.

Gaertner, S., & Dovidio, J. 1990. "The aversive form of racism." In A. G. Halberstadt & S. L. Ellyson (Eds.), *Social psychology readings: A century of research.* New York: McGraw-Hill.

Gailey, C. W. 1987. "Evolutionary perspectives on gender hierarchy." In B. B. Hess & M. M. Ferree (Eds.), *Analyzing gender: A handbook of social science research.* Newbury Park: Sage.

Galambos, N. L., & Maggs, J. L. 1991. "Children in self-care: Figures, facts and fictions." In J. V. Lerner & N. L. Galambos (Eds.), *Employed mothers and their children.* New York: Garland.

Gale, R. P. 1986. "Social movements and the state: The environmental movement, countermovement and governmental agencies." *Sociological Perspectives, 29,* 202–240.

Galles, G. M. 1989. "What colleges really teach." *New York Times,* June 8.

Gamson, W. A., Fireman, B., & Rytina, S. 1982. *Encounters with unjust authority.* Homewood, IL: Dorsey Press.

Gamson, W. A., & Wolfsfeld, G. 1993. "Movements and media as interactive systems." *Annals of the American Academy of Political and Social Science, 528,* 114–125.

Gans, H. 1971. "The uses of poverty: The poor pay for all." *Social Policy,* Summer, 20–24.

———. 1996. "Positive functions of the undeserving poor: Uses of the underclass in America." In J. Levin & A. Arluke (Eds.), *Snapshots and portraits of society.* Thousand Oaks, CA: Pine Forge Press.

Garfinkel, H. 1967. "Common sense knowledge of social structures: The documentary method of interpretation in lay and professional fact finding." In H. Garfinkel (Ed.), *Studies in ethnomethodology.* Englewood Cliffs, NJ: Prentice-Hall.

Garment, L. 1996. "Christian soldiers." *New York Times,* June 27.

Garner, D. M., Garfinkel, P. E., Schwartz, D., & Thompson, M. 1980. "Cultural expectations of thinness in women." *Psychological Reports, 47,* 483–491.

Garner, R. 1996. *Contemporary movements and ideologies.* New York: McGraw-Hill.

Garson, B. 1988. *The electronic sweatshop.* New York: Penguin.

Gates, H. L. 1992. "TV's black world turns—but stays unreal." In M. L. Anderson & P. H. Collins (Eds.), *Race, class and gender: An anthology.* Belmont, CA: Wadsworth.

Gaubatz, K. T. 1995. *Crime in the public mind.* Ann Arbor: University of Michigan Press.

"Gay men and lesbians find a home on Internet services." 1996. *New York Times,* June 16.

Gelles, R. J., & Cornell, C. P. 1990. *Intimate violence in families.* Newbury Park, CA: Sage.

Gelles, R. J., & Straus, M. A. 1988. *Intimate violence.* New York: Simon & Schuster.

Gergen, D. 1991. "Not in my backyard." *U.S. News & World Report,* July 22.

Gergen, K. J. 1991. *The saturated self.* New York: Basic Books.

Gerlach, P., & Hine, V. H. 1970. *People, power, change: Movements of social transformation.* Indianapolis: Bobbs-Merrill.

Gerson, K. 1985. *Hard choices: How women decide about work, career, and motherhood.* Berkeley: University of California Press.

Gertsel, N. 1987. "Divorce and stigma." *Social Problems, 34,* 172–186.

Gibbons, D. C. 1992. *Society, crime and criminal behavior.* Englewood Cliffs, NJ: Prentice-Hall.

Gibbons, F. X. 1986. "Stigma and interpersonal relations." In S. C. Ainlay, G. Becker, & L. M. Coleman (Eds.), *The dilemma of difference.* New York: Plenum.

Giddens, A. 1984. *The construction of society: Outline of the theory of structuration.* Berkeley: University of California Press.

Giddens, A. 1996. *Introduction to sociology.* New York: Norton.

Gillen, B. 1981. "Physical attractiveness: A determinant of two types of goodness." *Personality and Social Psychology Bulletin, 7,* 277–281.

Gillespie, C. K. 1989. *Justifiable homicide.* Columbus: Ohio State University Press.

Gilligan, C. 1990. "Teaching Shakespeare's sister: Notes from the underground of female adolescence." In C. Gilligan, N. P. Lyons, & T. J. Hanmer (Eds.), *Making connections.* Cambridge: Harvard University Press.

Gitlin, T. 1979. "Prime time ideology: The hegemonic process in television entertainment." *Social Problems, 26,* 251–266.

Gladwell, M. 1996. "Black like them." *The New Yorker,* April 29 & May 6.

Glantz, S. A. 1996. "The anti-smoking campaign that tobacco loves." *Harper's Magazine,* July, 26–28.

Gleason, H. A. 1961. *An introduction to descriptive linguistics.* New York: Holt, Rinehart & Winston.

Glenn, N. 1982. "Interreligious marriage in the United States: Patterns and recent trends." *Journal of Marriage and the Family, 44,* 555–566.

Glick, P. C., & Norton, A. J. 1977. "Marrying, divorcing, and living together in the U.S. today." *Population Bulletin, 32.* Washington, DC: Population Reference Bureau.

Godson, R., & Olson, W. J. 1995. "International organized crime." *Society, 32,* 18–29.

Goertzel, T. G. 1993. "Some observations on psychological processes among organized American opponents to the Gulf War." *Political Psychology, 14,* 139–146.

Goetting, A. 1982. "The six stations of remarriage: Developmental tasks of remarriage after divorce." *Family Relations,* April, 213–222.

Goffman, E. 1952. "On cooling the mark out: Some aspects of adaptation to failure." *Psychiatry, 15,* 451–463.

———. 1959. *The presentation of self in everyday life.* Garden City, NY: Doubleday.

———. 1961. *Asylums.* Garden City, NY: Anchor.

———. 1963. *Stigma: Notes on the management of spoiled identity.* Englewood Cliffs, NJ: Prentice-Hall.

———. 1967. *Interaction ritual.* Chicago: Aldine.

Goldberg, C. 1996. "Homeless in San Fransisco: A new policy." *New York Times,* May 20.

Goldberg, S. 1974. *The inevitability of patriarchy.* New York: Willam Morrow.

Goldberg, S., & Lewis, M. 1969. "Play behavior in the year-old infant: Early sex differences." *Child Development, 40,* 21–31.

Goleman, D. 1984. "Rethinking IQ tests and their value." *New York Times,* July 22.

———. 1986. "Perception of time emerges as a key psychological factor." *New York Times,* December 30.

———. 1989. "Sensing silent cues emerges as key skill." *New York Times,* October 10.

———. 1990. "The group and the self: New focus on a cultural rift." *New York Times,* December 25.

———. 1991a. "When ugliness is only in the patient's eye, body image can reflect a mental disorder." *New York Times,* October 2.

———. 1991b. "Parents' warmth is found to be key to adult happiness." *New York Times,* April 18.

———. 1993. "Therapists find some patients are just hateful." *New York Times,* May 4.

Goodchilds, J., Zellman, G., Johnson, P., & Giarusso, R. 1988. "Adolescents and the perceptions of sexual interaction outcomes." In A. W. Burgess (Ed.), *Sexual assault.* New York: Garland.

Goode, E. 1994. *Deviant behavior.* Englewood Cliffs, NJ: Prentice-Hall.

———. 1989. *Drugs in American society.* New York: McGraw-Hill.

Goode, W. J. 1971. "World revolution and family patterns." *Journal of Marriage and the Family, 33,* 624–635.

———. 1981. "Why men resist." in B. Thorne & M. Yalom (Eds.), *Rethinking the family: Some feminist questions.* New York: Longman.

Gordon, D. M., Edwards, R., & Reich, M. 1982. *Segmented work, divided workers: The historical transformation of labor in the United States.* Cambridge: Cambridge University Press.

Gordon, M. M. 1964. *Assimilation in American life.* New York: Oxford University Press.

Gose, B. 1995. "Test scores and stereotypes." *Chronicle of Higher Education,* August 18.

Gottfredson, M., & Hirschi, T. 1989. "Why we're losing the war on crime." *Washington Post Magazine,* September 10.

Gottfried, A. E. 1991. "Maternal employment in the family setting: Developmental and environmental issues." In J. V. Lerner & N. L. Galambos (Eds.), *Employed mothers and their children.* New York: Garland.

Gottlieb, M. 1995. "Plan would give doctors new ways to make money." *New York Times,* October 31.

Gough, K. 1971. "The origin of the family." *Journal of Marriage and the Family, 33,* 760–770.

Gould, S. J. 1981. *The mismeasure of man.* New York: Norton.

Gove, W., Hughes, M., & Geerkin, M. R. 1980. "Playing dumb: A form of impression management with undesirable effects." *Social Psychology Quarterly, 43,* 89–102.

Gove, W., Style, C. B., & Hughes, M. 1990. "The effect of marriage on the well-being of adults." *Journal of Family Issues, 11,* 34–35.

Gracey, H. L. 1991, "Learning the student role: Kindergarten as academic boot camp." In J. Henslin (Ed.), *Down to earth sociology.* New York: Free Press.

Graham, W. 1996. "Masters of the game." *Harper's Magazine,* July.

Granovetter, M., & Tilly, C. 1988. "Inequality and labor processes." In N. J. Smelser (Ed.), *Handbook of sociology.* Newbury Park, CA: Sage.

Grant, L. 1984. "Black females' 'place' in desegregated classrooms." *Sociology of Education, 57,* 98–111.

Green, M. 1984. "When money talks, is it democracy?" *The Nation,* September 15, pp. 200–204.

Greencastle Banner Graphic. 1992. Letter to the editor. March 7.

Greenhouse, L. 1986. "The rise and rise of McDonald's." *New York Times,* June 8.

———. 1990. "Use of illegal drugs as part of religion can be prosecuted, high court says." *New York Times,* April 18.

———. 1993. "Court, 9–0, makes sex harassment easier to prove." *New York Times,* November 10.

———. 1996a. "Christian Scientists rebuffed in ruling by Supreme Court." *New York Times,* January 23.

———. 1996b. "High court voids race-based plans for redistricting." *New York Times,* June 14.

Griffin, J. L. 1993. "Domestic partners getting benefits." *Indianapolis Star,* November 28.

Griffin, S. 1986. *Rape: The power of consciousness.* New York: Harper & Row.

———. 1989. "Rape: The all American crime." In L. Richardson & V. Taylor (Eds.), *Feminist frontiers II.* New York: Random House.

Griswold, W. 1994. *Cultures and societies in a changing world.* Thousand Oaks, CA: Pine Forge Press.

Gross, D. M., & Scott, S. 1990. "Proceeding with caution." *Time,* July 16.

Gross, E. 1984. "Embarrassment in public life." *Society, 21,* 48–53.

Gross, E., & Etzioni, A. 1985. *Organizations and society.* Englewood Cliffs, NJ: Prentice-Hall.

Gross, E., & Stone, G. P. 1964. "Embarrassment and the analysis of role requirements." *American Journal of Sociology, 70,* 1–15.

Gruber, K. J., & White, J. W. 1986. "Gender differences in the perceptions of self's and others' use of power strategies." *Sex Roles, 15,* 109–118.

Gruenbaum, E. 1993. "The movement against clitoridectomy and infibulation in Sudan: Public health policy and the women's movement." In C. B. Brettell & C. F. Sargent (Eds.), *Gender in cross-cultural prospective.* Englewood Cliffs, NJ: Prentice-Hall.

Gusfield, J. R. 1963. *Symbolic crusade: Status politics and the American temperance movement.* Urbana: University of Illinois Press.

Hacker, A. 1992. *Two nations: Black and white, separate, hostile, unequal.* New York: Charles Scribner's Sons.

Hafferty, F. W. 1991. *Into the valley: Death and socialization of medical students.* New Haven, CT: Yale University Press.

Hagan, J. 1985. *Modern criminology: Crime, criminal behavior and its control.* New York: McGraw-Hill.

Hall, E. T. 1969. *The hidden dimension.* Garden City, NY: Doubleday.

———. 1983. *The dance of life.* Garden City, NY: Anchor.

Hall, P. 1990. "The presidency and impression management." In J. W. Heeren & M. Mason (Eds.), *Sociology: Windows on society.* Los Angeles: Roxbury.

Hall, R. M., & Sandler, B. R. 1985. "A chilly climate in the classroom." In A. G. Sargent (Ed.), *Beyond sex roles.* New York: West.

Hall, W. 1986. "Social class and survival on the S.S. Titanic." *Social Science and Medicine, 22,* 687–690.

Halle, D. 1984. *America's working man: Work, home, and politics among blue-collar property owners.* Chicago: University of Chicago Press.

Hallin, D. C. 1986. "We keep America on top of the world." In T. Gitlin (Ed.), *Watching television.* New York: Pantheon.

Hamilton, D. L. 1981. *Cognitive processes in stereotyping and intergroup behavior.* Hillsdale, NJ: Erlbaum.

Hammer, J. 1992. "Must Blacks be buffoons?" *Newsweek,* October 26.

Hancock, L., & Kalb, C. 1996. "A room of their own." *Newsweek,* June 24.

Handy, C. 1995. "Trust and the virtual organization." *Harvard Business Review,* May–June, 40–50.

Hane, M. 1982. *Peasants, rebels and outcastes: The underside of modern Japan.* New York: Pantheon

Hardin, G., & Baden, J. 1977. *Managing the commons.* New York: W. H. Freeman.

Hareven, T. K. 1978. *Transitions: The family and the life course in historical perspective.* New York: Academic Press.

———. 1992. "American families in transition: Historical perspectives on change." In A. S. Skolnick & J. H. Skolnick (Eds.), *Family in transition.* New York: HarperCollins.

Harper, D. 1996. Personal communication.

"Harper's Index." 1986. *Harper's Magazine,* December.

———. 1996. *Harper's Magazine,* July.

Harris, K. M. 1996. "Life after welfare: Women, work, and repeat dependency." *American Sociological Review, 61,* 407–426.

Harris, M. 1964. *Patterns of race in the Americas.* New York: Norton.

Harrison, B., & Bluestone, B. 1988. *The great U-turn: Corporate restructuring and the polarizing of America.* New York: Basic Books.

Harrison, R. J., & Bennett, C. E. 1995. "Racial and ethnic diversity." In R. Farley (Ed.), *State of the Union: America in the 1990s.* New York: Russell Sage.

Hartmann, H., Kraut, R. E., & Tilly, L. A. 1989. "Job content: Job fragmentation and the deskilling debate." in D. S. Eitzen & M. Baca-Zinn (Eds.), *The reshaping of America.* Englewood Cliffs, NJ: Prentice-Hall.

Heise, L. 1989. "The global war against women." *Washington Post Magazine,* April 9.

Helmreich, W. B. 1992. "The things they say behind your back: Stereotypes and the myths behind them." In H. F. Lena, W. B. Helmreich, & W. McCord (Eds.), *Contemporary issues in sociology.* New York: McGraw-Hill.

Henley, N. 1977. *Body politics.* Englewood Cliffs, NJ: Prentice-Hall.

Henslin, J. 1991. *Down-to-earth sociology.* New York: Free Press.

Henslin, J., & Biggs, M. A. 1978. "Dramaturgical desexualization: The sociology of the vaginal examination." In J. Henslin & E. Sagarin (Eds.), *The sociology of sex: An introductory reader.* New York: Schocken.

Henwood, D. 1994. *The state of the USA atlas.* New York: Simon & Schuester.

Herbert, B. 1993. "The real jobless rate." *New York Times,* August 4.

———. 1996. "Nike's pyramid scheme." *New York Times,* June 10.

Herrnstein, R. J., & Murray, C. 1994. *The bell curve: Intelligence and class structure in American life.* New York: Free Press.

Hertz, R. 1986. *More equal than others: Women and men in dual-career marriages.* Berkeley: University of California Press.

Hewitt, J. P. 1988. *Self and society: A symbolic interactionist social psychology.* Boston: Allyn & Bacon.

Hewitt, J. P., & Hewitt, M. L. 1986. *Introducing sociology: A symbolic interactionist perspective.* Englewood Cliffs, NJ: Prentice-Hall.

Hewitt, J. P., & Stokes, R. 1975. "Disclaimers." *American Sociological Review, 40,* 1–11.

Hiller, D. V., & Philliber, W. W. 1986. "The division of labor in comtemporary marriage: Expectations, perceptions and performance." *Social Problems, 33,* 191–201.

Hiller, E. T. 1933. *Principles of sociology.* New York: Harper & Row.

Hills, S. 1980. *Demystifying social deviance.* New York: McGraw-Hill.

Hilts, P. J. 1995. "Pessimism is hazardous to health, a study says," *New York Times,* November 29.

Hirschi, T. 1969. *Causes of delinquency.* Berkeley: University of California Press.

Hochschild, A. 1983. *The managed heart.* Berkeley: University of California Press.

Hochschild, J. L. 1995. *Facing up to the American dream.* Princeton, NJ: Princeton University Press.

Hodson, R. 1991. "The active worker: Compliance and autonomy at the workplace." *Journal of Contemporary Ethnography, 20,* 47–78.

Hofferth, S. 1983. *Updating children's life course.* Bethesda, MD: Center for Population Research, National Institute for Child Health and Human Development.

Hollinger, R. C., & Lanza-Kaduce, L. 1988. "The process of criminalization: The case of computer crime laws." *Criminology, 26,* 101–126.

Holmes, S. A. 1991. "Homelessness rises, but not as an issue." *New York Times,* December 25.

———. 1995. "The strange politics of immigration." *New York Times,* December 31.

———. 1996. "Income disparity between poorest and richest rises." *New York Times,* June 20.

Holstrom, N. 1982. "Do women have a distinct nature?" *The Philosophical Forum, 14,* 25–42.

Holtzworth-Munroe, A., & Jacobson, N. S. 1985. "Causal attributions of married couples: When do they search for causes? What do they conclude when they do?" *Journal of Personality and Social Psychology, 48,* 1398–1412.

Honebrink, A. 1993. "Migrants create a new world order with their feet." *Utne Reader,* May/June, pp. 46–49.

Hornblower, M. 1995. "Putting tongues in check." *Time,* October 9.

Hossfeld, K. J. 1990. "'Their logic against them': Contradictions in sex, race and class in Silicon Valley." In K. Ward (Ed.), *Women workers and global restructuring.* Ithaca, NY: ILR Press.

House, J. 1981. "Social structure and personality." In M. Rosenberg & R. H. Turner (Eds.), *Social psychology: Sociological perspectives.* New York: Basic Books.

Howard, J. A., Blumstein, P., & Schwartz, P. 1986. "Sex, power and influence tactics in intimate relationships." *Journal of Personality and Social Psychology, 51,* 102–109.

Howe, N., & Strauss, W. 1992. "The new generation gap." *Atlantic Monthly,* December.

Huber, B. 1994. *Internal memorandum of the American Sociological Association,* February 10.

Huber, J., & Form, W. H. 1973. *Income and ideology.* New York: Free Press.

Huddle, D. L. 1993. "Immigrants: A cost or a benefit?" *New York Times,* September 3.

Hughes, L. 1958. *The Langston Hughes reader.* New York: George Braziller.

Humphry, D. 1991. *Final exit: The practicalities of self-deliverance and assisted suicide for the dying.* Eugene, OR: Hemlock Society.

Hunt, J. 1985. "Police accounts of normal force." *Urban Life, 12,* 315–341.

Hunt, J. G., & Hunt, L. L. 1990. "The dualities of careers and families: New integrations or new polarizations?" In C. Carlson (Ed.), *Perspectives on the family: History, class and feminism.* Belmont, CA: Wadsworth.

Hunter, J. D. 1987. *Evangelicalism: The coming generation.* Chicago: University of Chicago Press.

———. 1991. *Culture wars: The struggle to define America.* New York: Basic Books.

Hurst, C. 1979. *The anatomy of social inequality.* St. Louis: C. V. Mosby.

Huston, T. L. 1983. "Power." In H. Kelley et al. (Eds.), *Close relationships.* New York: W. H. Freeman.

Hyde, J. S. 1984. "How large are gender differences in aggression? A developmental meta-analysis." *Developmental Psychology, 20,* 722–736.

Ignatius, A. 1988. "China's birthrate is out of control again as one-child policy fails in rural areas." *Wall Street Journal,* July 14.

Inciardi, J. A. 1992. *The war on drugs II.* Mountain View, CA: Mayfield.

"Infant deaths tied to poverty, study confirms." 1995. *New York Times,* December 12.

Innis, L. 1993. "School desegregation: Too high a price?" *Social Policy, 24,* 6–16.

Institute on Hunger and Development. 1992. *Hunger 1992: The 2nd annual report on the state of world hunger.* Washington, DC: Author.

Instone, D., Major, B., & Bunker, B. B. 1983. "Gender, self-confidence, and social influence strategies: An organizational simulation." *Journal of Personality and Social Psychology, 44,* 322–333.

"Is there a Santa Claus?" 1897, *New York Sun,* September 21.

"It's a new day at Denny's." 1995. *New York Times,* December 12.

Jackall, R. 1988. *Moral mazes: The world of corporate managers.* New York: Oxford University Press.

Jackman, M. R., & Jackman, R. W. 1983. *Class awareness in the United States.* Berkeley: University of California Press.

Jackson, S. 1995. "The social context of rape: Sexual scripts and motivation." In P. Searles & R. J. Berger (Eds.), *Rape and society.* Boulder, CO: Westview Press.

Jacobs, P. 1988. "Keeping the poor, poor." In J. H. Skolnick & E. Currie (Eds.), *Crisis in American institutions.* Glenview, IL: Scott, Foresman.

Jacquet, C. H., & Jones, A. M. 1991. *Yearbook of American and Canadian churches.* Nashville: Abingdon.

James, W. 1890. *Principles of psychology.* New York: Holt.

Janis, I. 1991. "Groupthink." In L. Cargan & J. H. Ballantine (Eds.), *Sociological footprints.* Belmont, CA: Wadsworth.

Janoff-Bulman, R. 1979. "Characterological versus behavioral self-blame: Inquiries into depression and rape." *Journal of Personality and Social Psychology, 37,* 1798–1809.

Jaynes, G. 1982. "Suit on race recalls lines drawn under slavery." *New York Times,* September 30.

Jencks, C. 1994. *The homeless.* Cambridge, MA: Harvard University Press.

Jencks, C., Bartlett, S., Corcoran, M., Crouse, J., Eaglesfield, D., Jackson, G., McClelland, K., Mueser, P. Olneck, M., Schwartz, J., Ward, S., & Williams, J. 1979. *Who gets ahead?* New York: Basic Books.

Jenkins, J. C., & Perrow, C. 1977. "Insurgency of the powerless: Farm worker movements (1946–1972)." *American Sociological Review, 42,* 249–268.

Jensen, C., & Project Censored. 1995. *The news that didn't make the news—and why.* New York: Four Walls Eight Windows.

Jhally, S., & Lewis, J. 1992. *Enlightened racism: The Cosby Show, audiences, and the myth of the American Dream.* Boulder, CO: Westview.

Johnson, A. B. 1990. *Out of bedlam: The truth about deinstitutionalization.* New York: HarperCollins.

Johnson, A. G. 1992. *Human arrangements.* Fort Worth, TX: Harcourt Brace Jovanovich.

Johnson, D. 1991. "Polygamists emerge from secrecy, seeking not just peace but respect." *New York Times,* April 9.

Johnson, D. 1996a. "Students still sweat, they just don't shower." *New York Times,* April 27.

———. 1996b. "No-fault divorce is under attack." *New York Times,* February 12.

Johnson, P. 1976. "Women and power: Toward a theory of effectiveness." *Journal of Social Issues, 32,* 99–110.

Johnson, R. 1987. *Hard time: Understanding and reforming the prison.* Pacific Grove, CA: Brooks/Cole.

Johnston, D. 1992. "Survey shows number of rapes far higher than official figures." *New York Times,* April 24.

Jones, C. 1995. "Crack and punishment: Is race the issue?" *New York Times,* October 28.

Jones, E. E., Farina, A., Hastorf, A. H., Markus, H., Miller, D. T., & Scott, R. A. 1984. *Social stigma: The psychology of marked relationships.* New York: W. H. Freeman.

Jones, E. E., & Pittman, T. S. 1982. "Toward a general theory of strategic self-presentation." In J. Suls (Ed.), *Psychological perspectives on the self* (Vol. 1). Hillsdale, NJ: Lawrence Erlbaum.

Jones, J. M. 1986. "The concept of racism and its changing reality." In B. P. Bowser & R. G. Hunt (Eds)., *Impacts of racism on white Americans.* Beverly Hills, CA: Sage.

Kagan, J. 1976. *Raising children in modern America: Problems and prospective solutions.* Boston: Little, Brown.

Kagay, M. R., & Elder, J. 1992. "Numbers are no problem for pollsters. Words are." *New York Times,* August 9.

Kain, E. 1990. *The myth of family decline.* Lexington, MA: Lexington Books.

Kalmijn, M. 1994. "Assortive mating by cultural and economic occupational status." *American Journal of Sociology, 100,* 422–452.

Kamerman, S. B. 1985. "Time out for babies." *Working Mother, 4,* 80–82.

Kanter, R. M. 1975. "Women and the structure of organizations: Explorations in theory and behavior." In R. M. Kanter & M. Millman (Eds.), *Another voice.* New York: Doubleday.

———. 1977. *Men and women of the corporation.* New York: Basic Books.

Kanter, R. M., & Stein, B. A. 1979. *Life in organizations: Workplaces as people experience them.* New York: Basic Books.

Kantrowitz, B. 1993. "Wild in the streets." *Newsweek,* August 2.

Karabel, J. 1972. "Community colleges and social stratification." *Harvard Educational Review, 42,* 521–559.

Kariya, T., & Rosenbaum, J. E. 1987. "Self selection in Japanese junior high schools: A longitudinal study of students' educational plans." *Sociology of Education, 60,* 168–180.

Karp, D. A., & Yoels, W. C. 1976. "The college classroom: Some observations on the meanings of student participation." *Sociology and Social Research, 60,* 421–439.

———. 1985. *Sociology and everyday life.* Itasca, IL: Peacock.

Kart, C. S. 1990. *The realities of aging.* Boston: Allyn & Bacon.

Kasarda, J. D. 1985. "Urban change and minority opportunities." In P. E. Peterson (Ed.), *The new urban reality.* Washington, DC: Brookings Institution.

———. 1989. "Urban industrial transition and the underclass." In W. J. Wilson (Ed.), *The ghetto underclass: Social science perspectives.* Newbury Park, CA: Sage.

Katz, J. 1975. "Essences as moral identities: Verifiability and responsibility in imputations of deviance and charisma." *American Journal of Sociology, 80,* 1369–1390.

Kaufman, M. 1987. *Beyond patriarchy: Essays by men on pleasure, power, and change.* Toronto: Oxford.

Kearl, M. C. 1980. "Time, identity and the spiritual needs of the elderly." *Sociological Analysis, 41,* 172–180.

———. 1989. *Endings: A sociology of death and dying.* New York: Oxford University Press.

Kearl, M. C., & Gordon, C. 1992. *Social psychology.* Boston: Allyn & Bacon.

Kelley, R. D. G. 1996. "Freedom riders (the sequel)." *The Nation,* February 5.

Kelly, R. M., & Bayes, J. 1988. *Comparable worth, pay equity and public policy.* Westport, CT: Greenwood Press.

Kennedy, D. J. 1995. "Residential associations as state actors: Regulating the impact of gated communities on non-members." *The Yale Law Journal, 105,* 761–793.

Kennedy, P. 1993. *Preparing for the 21st century.* New York: Random House.

Kerbo, H. R. 1991. *Social stratification and inequality.* New York: McGraw-Hill.

Kershner, R. 1996. "Adolescent attitudes about rape." *Adolescence, 31,* 29–33.

Kessler, S. J., & McKenna, W. 1978. *Gender: An ethnomethodological approach.* Chicago: University of Chicago Press.

Key, P. 1996. "Black expo looks back to its source." *Indianapolis Star,* July 7.

Keyfitz, N. 1989. "The growing human population." *Scientific American,* September.

Kilborn, P. T. 1993. "New jobs lack the old security in time of 'disposable workers.'" *New York Times,* March 15.

Kilbourne, J. 1992. "Beauty and the beast of advertising." In P. S. Rothenberg (Ed.), *Race, class & gender in the United States.* New York: St. Martin's Press.

King, M. L., Jr. 1991. "Letter from Birmingham City Jail." In C. Carson, D. J. Garrow, G. Gill, V. Harding, & D. Clark Hine (Eds.), *Eyes on the Prize civil rights reader.* New York: Penguin.

Kirk. M. O. 1996. "The virtual office bumps into some very real limits." *New York Times,* March 3.

Kirk, S. A., & Kutchins, H. 1992. *The selling of DSM: The rhetoric of science in psychiatry.* Hawthorne, NY: Aldine deGruyter.

Klatch, R. 1991. "Complexities of conservatism: How conservatives understand the world." In A. Wolfe (Ed.), *America at century's end.* Berkeley: University of California Press.

Kleck, R. 1968. "Physical stigma and nonverbal cues emitted in face to face interaction." *Human Relations, 21,* 19–28.

Kleck, R., Ono, H., & Hastorf, A. 1966. "The effects of physical deviance and face to face interaction." *Human Relations, 19,* 425–436.

Kleck, R., & Strenta, A. 1980. "Perceptions of the impact of negatively valued physical characteristics on social interaction." *Journal of Personality and Social Psychology, 39,* 861–873.

Kligman, G. 1992. "Abortion and international adoption in post-Ceausescu Romania." *Feminist Studies, 18,* 405–419.

Kluegel, J. R., & Smith, E. R. 1986. *Beliefs about inequality: Americans' views of what is and what ought to be.* New York: Aldine deGruyter.

Kobrin, F. E. 1976. "The fall in household size and the rise of the primary individual in the United States." *Demography, 31,* 127–138.

Kohlberg, L. A. 1966. "A cognitive-developmental analysis of children's sex-role concepts and attitudes." In E. Maccoby (Ed.), *The development of sex differences.* Stanford, CA: Stanford University Press.

Kohn, H. 1994. "Service with a sneer." *New York Times Magazine,* November 6.

Kohn, M. L. 1979. "The effects of social class on parental values and practices." In D. Reiss & H. A. Hoffman (Eds.), *The American family: Dying or developing.* New York: Plenum.

Kokopeli, B., & Lakey, G. 1992. "More power than we want: Masculine sexuality and violence." In M. L. Anderson & P. H. Collins (Eds.), *Race, class and gender: An anthology.* Belmont, CA: Wadsworth.

Kolata, G. 1993. "Strong family aid to elderly is found." *New York Times,* May 3.

———. 1996. "Boom in Ritalin sales raises ethical issues." *New York Times,* May 15.

Kollock, P., Blumstein, P., & Schwartz, P. 1985. "Sex and power in interaction: Conversational privileges and duties." *American Sociological Review, 50,* 34–46.

Kollock P., & O'Brien, J. 1993. *The production of reality.* Newbury Park, CA: Pine Forge Press.

Kotkin, J. 1996. "New fuel for California's engine." *Wall Street Journal,* March 25.

Kovel, J. 1980. "The American mental health industry." In David Ingleby (Ed.), *Critical psychiatry.* New York: Pantheon.

Kozol, J. 1988. *Rachel and her children: Homeless families in America.* New York: Crown.

———. 1991. *Savage inequalities: Children in America's schools.* New York: Harper & Row.

Kramer, P. 1993. *Listening to Prozac.* New York: Penguin.

Krantowitz, B., & Witherspoon, D. 1987. "The December dilemma: How to reconcile 2 faiths in one household." *Newsweek,* December 28.

Kristof, N. D. 1991. "Stark data on women: 100 million are missing." *New York Times,* November 5.

———. 1993a. "China's crackdown on births: A stunning and harsh success." *New York Times,* April 25.

———. 1993b. "Peasants of China discover new way to weed out girls." *New York Times,* July 21.

———. 1995. "Japanese outcasts better off than in past but still outcasts." *New York Times,* November 30.

Kurtz, L. R. 1995. *Gods in the global village.* Thousand Oaks, CA: Pine Forge Press.

Labalme, J. 1995. "Parents opposed removal of life support." *Indianapolis Star,* December 1.

Ladner, J. 1978. *Mixed families: Adopting across racial boundaries.* Garden City, NY: Anchor Press.

Lakoff, R. 1973. "Language and woman's place." *Language and Society, 2,* 45–80.

———. 1975. *Language and woman's place.* New York: Harper & Row.

Lamanna, M. A., & Reidmann, A. 1994. *Marriages and families: Making choices and facing change.* Belmont, CA: Wadsworth.

Lander, L. 1988. *Images of bleeding: Menstruation as ideology.* New York: Orlando.

Landler, M. 1996. "Corporate insurer to cover cost of spin doctors." *New York Times,* September 10.

Langston, D. 1992. "Tired of playing monopoly?" In M. L. Anderson & P. H. Collins (Eds.), *Race, class and gender: An anthology.* Belmont, CA: Wadsworth.

Lasch, C. 1977. *Haven in a heartless world.* New York: Basic Books.

Laslett, B., & Warren, C. A. B. 1987. "Losing weight." In E. Rubington & M. S. Weinberg (Eds.), *Deviance: The interactionist perspective.* New York: Macmillan.

Latané, B., & Darley, J. 1970. *The unresponsive bystander: Why doesn't he help?* New York: Appleton-Century-Crofts.

Latané, B., & Rodin, J. 1969. "A lady in distress: Inhibiting effects of friends and strangers on bystander intervention." *Journal of Experimental Social Psychology, 5,* 189–202.

Lauderdale, P. 1980. *A political analysis of deviance.* Minneapolis: University of Minnesota Press.

Lauer, R., & Handel, W. 1977. *Social psychology: The theory and application of symbolic interactionism.* Boston: Houghton Mifflin.

Lawson, C. 1992. "Who believes in make-believe? Not these new toys." *New York Times,* February 6.

———. 1993. "Stereotypes unravel, but not too quickly, in new toys for 1993." *New York Times,* February 11.

Leape, L. L., et al. 1995. "Systems analysis of adverse drug events." *Journal of the American Medical Association, 274,* 35–43.

Leary, W. E. 1996. "Even when covered by insurance, black and poor people receive less health care." *New York Times,* September 12.

Leidner, R. 1991. "Serving hamburgers and selling insurance: Gender work and identity in interactive service jobs." *Gender and Society, 5,* 154–177.

Leinberger, P., & Tucker, B. 1991. *The new individualists: The generation after the organization man.* New York: HarperCollins.

Lekachman, R. 1991. "The specter of full employment." In J. H. Skolnick & E. Currie (Eds.), *Crisis in American institutions.* New York: HarperCollins.

Leland, J. 1996. "Tightening the knot." *Newsweek,* February 19.

Lemert, E. 1972. *Human deviance, social problems, and social control.* Englewood Cliffs, NJ: Prentice-Hall.

Lennon, M. C., & Rosenfield, S. 1994. "Relative fairness and the division of housework." *American Journal of Sociology, 100,* 506–531.

Lerner, M. 1970. "The desire for justice and reactions to victims." In J. Macauley & L. Berkowitz (Eds.), *Altruism and helping behavior.* New York: Academic Press.

Leslie, C. 1991. "Classrooms of Babel." *Newsweek,* February 11.

Levant, R. F., Slatter, S. C., & Loiselle, J. E. 1987. "Fathers' involvement in housework and child care with school age daughters." *Family Relations, 36,* 152–157.

Levin, J. 1993. *Sociological snapshots.* Newbury Park, CA: Pine Forge Press.

Levine, H. G. 1992. "Temperance cultures: Concern about alcohol problems in Nordic and English-speaking cultures." In G. Edwards, et al. (Eds.), *The nature of alcohol and drug related problems.* New York: Oxford University Press.

Levine, R., & Wolff, E. 1988. "Social time: The heartbeat of culture." In E. Angeloni (Ed.), *Annual edi-*

tions in anthropology 88/89. Guilford, CT: Dushkin.

LeVine, R. A., & White, M. 1992. "The social transformation of childhood." In A. S. Skolnick & J. H. Skolnick (Eds.), *Family in transition.* New York: HarperCollins.

Levinson, M. 1991. "Living on the edge." *Newsweek,* November 4.

Levinson, R. M. 1975. "Sex discrimination and employment practices: An experiment with unconventional job inquiries." *Social Problems, 22,* 533–543.

Lewin, T. 1989. "Aging parents: Women's burden grows." *New York Times,* November 14.

———. 1990. "Suit over death benefits asks, what is a family?" *New York Times,* September 21.

———. 1991. "Jobless pay for mother." *New York Times,* March 13.

———. 1994. "Outrage over 18 months for man who killed his wife in 'heat of passion.'" *New York Times,* October 21.

———. 1995. "Study says more women earn half their household income." *New York Times,* May 11.

Lewis, M. 1978. *The culture of inequality.* New York: New American Library.

Lewis, M. M. 1948. *Language in society.* New York: Social Science Research Council.

Lewis, N. A. 1988. "For New York City, the lessons are hard and the gold stars are few." *New York Times,* September 4.

Lewis, O. 1968. "The culture of poverty." In D. P. Moynihan (Ed.), *On understanding poverty: Perspectives from the social sciences.* New York: Basic Books.

Liazos, A. 1985. *Sociology: A liberating perspective.* Boston: Allyn & Bacon.

Light, D., & Keller, S. 1985. *Sociology.* New York: Knopf.

Light, K., with introduction by R. Rogriguez. 1988. *To the promised land.* New York: Aperture.

Light, P. 1988. *Baby boomers.* New York: Norton.

Lind, M. 1996. "Huddled excesses." *The New Republic,* April 1.

Lindesmith, A. R., Strauss, A. L., & Denzin, N. K. 1991. *Social psychology.* Englewood Cliffs, NJ: Prentice-Hall.

Link, B. G., Cullen, F. T., Frank, J., & Wozniak, J. F. 1987. "The social rejection of former mental patients: Understanding why labels matter." *American Journal of Sociology, 92,* 1461–1500.

Link, B. G., Mirotznik, J., & Cullen, F. T. 1991. "The effectiveness of stigma coping orientations: Can negative consequences of mental illness labeling be avoided?" *Journal of Health and Social Behavior, 32,* 302–320.

Linton, R. 1937. "One hundred percent American." *The American Mercury, 40,* 427–429.

Lippmann, L. W. 1922. *Public opinion.* New York: Harcourt Brace Jovanovich.

Lips, H. M. 1993. *Sex and gender: An introduction.* Mountain View, CA: Mayfield.

Lofland, J. 1981. "Collective behavior: The elementary forms." In M. Rosenberg & R. H. Turner (Eds.), *Social psychology: Sociological perspectives.* New York: Basic Books.

Lofland, L. H. 1971. "Self-management in public settings, Part I." *Urban Life and Culture, 1,* 93–117.

———. 1973. *A world of strangers: Order and action in urban public space.* New York: Basic Books.

Lopez, G. A. 1991. "The Gulf War: Not so clean." *Bulletin of the Atomic Scientists, 47,* 30–35.

Lorber, J. 1989. "Dismantling Noah's Ark." In B. J. Risman & P. Schwartz (Eds.), *Gender in intimate relationships: A microstructural approach.* Belmont, CA: Wadsworth.

Lord, W. 1956. *A night to remember.* New York: Bantam.

Lott, B. 1987. *Women's lives: Themes and variations in gender learning.* Pacific Grove, CA: Brooks/Cole.

Loury, G. C. 1985. "Beyond civil rights." *The New Republic,* October.

Lubeck, S., & Garrett, P. 1990. "Child care 2000: Policy options for the future." In C. Carlson (Ed.), *Perspectives on the family.* Belmont, CA: Wadsworth.

Luker, K. 1984. *Abortion and the politics of motherhood.* Berkeley: University of California Press.

Lytton, H., & Romney, D. M. 1991. "Parents' differential socialization of boys and girls: A meta-analysis." *Psychology Bulletin, 109,* 267–296.

MacAndrew, C., & Edgerton, R. B. 1969. *Drunken comportment: A social explanation.* Chicago: Aldine.

MacDonald, K., & Parke, R. D. 1986. "Parent-child physical play: The effects of sex and age on children and parents." *Sex Roles, 15,* 367–378.

Makinson, L. 1993. *Open secrets: The encyclopedia of congressional money and politics.* Washington, DC: Congressional Quarterly Inc.

Makinson, L. 1995. *The price of admission: Campaign spending in the 1994 elections.* Washington, DC: The Center for Responsive Politics.

Mann, C. C. 1993. "How many is too many?" *Atlantic Monthly,* February.

Mannheim, K. 1952. "The problem of generations." In P. Kecskemeti (Ed. and Trans.), *Essays on the sociology of knowledge.* London: Routledge & Kegan Paul.

Mannon, J. 1990. *American gridmark.* Tucson, AZ: Harbinger House.

Mantsios, G. 1995. "Media magic: Making class invisible." In P. S. Rothenberg (Ed.), *Race, class and gender in the United States.* New York: St. Martin's Press.

Marger, M. N. 1994. *Race and ethnic relations: American and global perspectives.* Belmont, CA: Wadsworth.

Margolick, D. 1990. "Death and faith, law and Christian Science." *New York Times,* August 6.

"Marriage and divorce." 1996. *CQ Researcher,* May 10.

Martin, M. K., & Voorhies, B. 1975. *Female of the species.* New York: Columbia University Press.

Martin, T. C., & Bumpass, L. L. 1989. "Recent trends in marital disruption." *Demography, 26,* 37–51.

Marx, K. 1963. *The 18th Brumaire of Louis Bonaparte.* New York: International Publishing Co.

Marx, K., & Engels, F. 1982. *The communist manifesto.* New York: International Publishers. (Original work published 1848)

Massey, D. 1990. "American apartheid: Segregation and the making of the underclass." *American Journal of Sociology, 96,* 329–357.

Mathews, L. 1996. "More than identity rides on a new racial category." *New York Times,* July 6.

Matthews, J. 1989. "Rescue plan for Africa." *World Monitor,* May, 28–36.

Mauro, J. 1994. "And Prozac for all . . ." *Psychology Today, 27,* 44–52.

Mayo, J. M. 1990. "Propaganda with design: Environmental dramaturgy in the political rally." In D. Brissett & C. Edgley (Eds.), *Life as theater: A dramaturgical sourcebook.* New York: Aldine deGruyter.

McAdam, D. 1982. *Political process and the development of black insurgency, 1930–1970.* Chicago: University of Chicago Press.

McAdam, D., McCarthy, J. D., & Zald, M. N. 1988. "Social movements." In N. J. Smelser (Ed.), *Handbook of sociology.* Newbury Park, CA: Sage.

McCain, F. 1991. "Interview with Franklin McCain." In C. Carson et al. (Eds.), *The Eyes on the Prize civil rights reader.* New York: Penguin.

McCall, G. J. 1982. "Becoming unrelated: The management of bond dissolution." In S. Duck (Ed.), *Personal relationships 4: Dissolving personal relationships.* London: Academic Press.

McCall, G. J., & Simmons, J. L. 1978. *Identities and interactions.* New York: Free Press.

McCarthy, J. D., & Wolfson, M. 1992. "Consensus movements, conflict movements, and the cooptation of civic and state infrastructures." In A. D. Morris & C. M. Mueller (Eds.), *Frontiers in social movement theory.* New Haven: Yale University Press.

McCarthy, J. D., & Zald, M. N. 1977. "Resource mobilization and social movements: A partial theory." *American Journal of Sociology, 82,* 1212–1241.

McClelland, K. E., & Auster, C. J. 1990. "Public platitudes and hidden tensions: Racial climates at predominantly white liberal arts colleges." *Journal of Higher Education, 61,* 607–642.

McClendon, M. J. 1985. "Racism, rational choice and white opposition to racial change: A case study of busing." *Public Opinion Quarterly, 49,* 214–233.

McHugh, P. 1968. *Defining the situation.* Indianapolis: Bobbs-Merrill.

McLanahan, S., & Booth, K. 1991. "Mother-only families." In A. Booth (Ed.), *Contemporary families: Looking forward, looking back.* Minneapolis: National Council on Family Relations.

McMichael, P. 1996. *Development and social change: A global perspective.* Thousand Oaks, CA: Pine Forge Press.

McPhee, J. 1971. *Encounters with the archdruid.* New York: Noonday.

McRoy, R. G., & Zurcher, L. A. 1983. *Transracial and inracial adoptees: The adolescent years.* Springfield, IL: Charles Thomas.

Mead, G. H. 1934. *Mind, self and society.* Chicago: University of Chicago Press.

Mead, M. 1963. *Sex and temperament in three primitive societies.* New York: William Morrow.

Medvedev, Z. A., & Medvedev, R. A. 1971. *A question of madness.* New York: Norton.

Mehan, H., & Wood, H. 1975. *The reality of ethnomethodology.* New York: Wiley.

Merrick, T. W. 1986. "World population in transition." *Population Bulletin, 41,* 2.

Merrow, J. 1995. "Reading, writing and Ritalin." *New York Times,* October 21.

Merton, R. 1948. "The self fulfilling prophecy." *Antioch Review, 8,* 193–210.

———. 1957. *Social theory and social structure.* New York: Free Press.

Messick, D. M., & Brewer, M. B. 1983. "Solving social dilemmas: A review." In L. Wheeler & P. Shaver (Eds.), *Review of personality and social psychology.* Beverly Hills, CA: Sage.

Meyer, J. W., & Rowan, B. 1977. "Institutionalized organizations: Formal structure as myth and ceremony." *American Journal of Sociology, 83,* 340–363.

Miall, C. E. 1989. "The stigma of involuntary childlessness." In A. S. Skolnick & J. H. Skolnick (Eds.), *Family in transition.* Boston: Little, Brown.

Michener, H. A., DeLamater, J. D., & Schwartz, S. H. 1986. *Social psychology.* San Diego, CA: Harcourt Brace Jovanovich.

Mies, M. 1982. *The lace makers of Narsapur.* London: Zed Press.

Mihashi, O. 1987. "The symbolism of social discrimination." *Current Anthropology, 28,* S19–S24.

Miles, J. 1992. "Blacks vs. browns." *Atlantic Monthly,* October.

Milgram, S. 1974. *Obedience to authority.* New York: Harper & Row.

Miller, C. L. 1987. "Qualitative differences among gender-stereotyped toys: Implications for cognitive and social development." *Sex Roles, 16,* 473–488.

Miller, J. 1984. "Culture and the development of everyday explanation." *Journal of Personality and Social Psychology, 46,* 961–978.

Miller, T. M., Coffman, J. G., & Linke, R. A. 1980. "Survey on body-image, weight and diet of college students." *Journal of the American Dietetic Association, 77,* 561–566.

Millman, M. 1980. *Such a pretty face.* New York: Norton.

Mills, C. W. 1940. "Situated actions and vocabularies of motive." *American Sociological Review, 5,* 904–913.

———. 1956. *The power elite.* New York: Oxford University Press.

———. 1959. *The sociological imagination.* New York: Oxford University Press.

Mills, J. L. 1985. "Body language speaks louder than words." *Horizons,* February.

Minzesheimer, B. 1989. "PACs play both sides of fence." *USA Today,* May 9.

Mitford, J. 1963. *The American way of death.* Greenwich, CT: Fawcett Crest.

Moffatt, M. 1989. *Coming of age in New Jersey.* New Brunswick, NJ: Rutgers University Press.

Mokhiber, R. 1989. "Crime in the suites." *Greenpeace, 14,* 14–17.

Molotch, H., & Lester, M. 1974. "News as purposive behavior: On the strategic use of routine events, accidents, and scandals." *American Sociological Review, 39,* 101–112.

———. 1975. "Accidental news: The great oil spill as local occurrence and national event." *American Journal of Sociology, 81,* 235–260.

Moore, R. B. 1992. "Racist stereotyping in the English language." In M. L. Anderson & P. H. Collins (Eds.), *Race, class and gender: An anthology.* Belmont, CA: Wadsworth.

Moorhead, G., Ference, R., & Neck, C. 1991. "Group decision fiascoes continue: Space shuttle Challenger and a revised groupthink framework." *Human Relations, 44,* 539–550.

Moorman, J. E. 1987. "The history and future of the relationship between education and first marriage." Unpublished paper. Washington, DC: U.S. Bureau of the Census.

Morgan, G. 1986. *Images of organizations.* Newbury Park, CA: Sage.

Morgan, M. 1982. "Television and adolescents' sex role stereotypes: A longitudinal study." *Journal of Personality and Social Psychology, 48,* 1173–1190.

———. 1987. "Television sex role attitudes and sex role behavior." *Journal of Early Adolescence, 7,* 269–282.

Morganthau, T. 1992. "Losing ground." *Newsweek,* April 6.

Morris, M., & Williamson, J. B. 1987. "Workfare: The poverty/dependence tradeoff." *Social Policy,* Summer, 13–16, 49–50.

Mottl, T. L. 1980. "The analysis of countermovements." *Social Problems, 27,* 620–635.

Murdock, G. 1957. "World ethnography sample." *American Anthropologist, 59,* 664–687.

Murray, D. L. 1982. "The abolition of el cortito, the short-handled hoe: A case study in social conflict and state policy in California agriculture." *Social Problems, 30,* 26–39.

Murty, K. S., Roebuck, J. B., & Armstrong, G. R. 1994. "The black community's reaction to the 1992 Los Angeles riot." *Deviant Behavior, 15,* 85–104.

Mydans, S. 1995. "A shooter as vigilante, and avenging angel." *New York Times,* February 12.

Myrdal, G. 1944. *An American dilemma.* New York: Harper & Row.

Nanda, S. 1990. *Neither man nor woman: The Hijras of India.* Belmont, CA: Wadsworth.

———. 1994. *Cultural anthropology.* Belmont, CA: Wadsworth.

National Alliance to End Homelessness. 1995. Annual Report.

National Center for Education Statistics. 1989. *1989 education indicators.* Washington, DC: U.S. Government Printing Office.

———. 1993. "Time in the classroom." *The conditions of education, 1993.* Washington, DC: U.S. Government Printing Office.

National Committee on Pay Equity. 1995. "The wage gap: Myths and facts." In P. S. Rothenberg (Ed.), *Race, class and gender in the United States.* New York: St. Martin's Press.

National Public Radio. 1995. "L.A. gated communities." In A. Etzioni (Ed.), *Rights and the common good: The communitarian perspective.* New York: St. Martin's Press.

Navarro, V. 1992. "The middle class—a useful myth." *The Nation,* March 23.

Neary, I. J. 1986. "Socialist and communist party attitudes towards discrimination against Japan's Burakumin." *Political Studies, 34,* 556–574.

Nelkin, D., & Pollack, M. 1981. *The atom besieged.* Cambridge, MA: MIT Press.

Neubeck, K. 1986. *Social problems: A critical approach.* New York: Random House.

Neugarten, B. L. 1980. "Grow old along with me! The best is yet to be." In B. Hess (Ed.), *Growing old in America.* New Brunswick, NJ: Transaction Books.

"A new divide between haves and have-nots." 1995. *Time,* Spring.

Newman, K. 1988. *Falling from grace: The experience of downward mobility in the American middle class.* New York: Free Press.

Niebuhr, G. 1996. "Public supports political voice for churches." *New York Times,* June 25.

Njeri, I. 1990. *Every good-bye ain't gone.* New York: Random House.

Noble, K. B. 1995. "Attacks against Asian-Americans are rising." *New York Times,* December 13.

Norfleet, B. 1986. *All the right people.* Boston: Little, Brown.

Norton, A. J. 1987. "Families and children in the year 2000." *Children Today,* July/August, 6–9.

Novac, V. 1988. "Formula for profit: How private corporations grow fat from a program designed to feed the poor." *Seeds,* August, 22–25.

Oakes, J. 1985. *Keeping track: How high schools structure inequality.* New Haven: Yale University Press.

OECD (Organization for Economic Co-operation and Development). 1988. *Aging populations: The social policy implications.* Washington, DC.

Olsen, M. 1965. *The logic of collective action.* Cambridge: Harvard University Press.

Omi, M., & Winant, H. 1992. "Racial formations." In P. S. Rothenberg (Ed.), *Race, class and gender in the United States.* New York: St. Martin's Press.

O'Neill, M. 1992. "As the rich get leaner, the poor get french fries." *New York Times,* March 18.

Oreskes, M., & Toner, R. 1989. "The homeless at the heart of poverty and policy." *New York Times,* January 29.

Ostrander, S. 1980. "Upper class women: Class consciousness as conduct and meaning." In G. W. Domhoff (Ed.), *Power structure research.* Beverly Hills, CA: Sage.

O'Sullivan See, K., & Wilson, W. J. 1988. "Race and ethnicity." In N. Smelser (Ed.), *Handbook of sociology.* Newbury Park, CA: Sage.

Owens, B. 1973. *Suburbia.* San Francisco: Straight Arrow Press.

Parenti, M. 1986. *Inventing reality.* New York: St. Martin's Press.

———. 1988. *Democracy for the few.* New York: St. Martin's Press.

———. 1995. *Democracy for the few.* New York: St. Martin's Press.

———. 1996. "The make-believe media." In M. J. Carter (Ed.), *Society and the media.* New York: HarperCollins.

Parlee, M. B. 1989. "Conversational politics." In L. Richardson & V. Taylor (Eds.), *Feminist frontiers II.* New York: Random House.

Parsons, T. 1951. *The social system.* New York: Free Press.

———. 1971. "Kinship and the associational aspect of social structure." In F. L. K. Hsu (Ed.), *Kinship and culture.* Chicago: Aldine.

Parsons, T., & Bales, R. F. 1955. *Family, socialization and interaction process.* Glencoe, IL: Free Press.

Parsons, T., & Smelser, N. 1956. *Economy and society.* New York: Free Press.

Passell, P. 1993. "Like a new drug, social programs are put to the test." *New York Times,* March 9.

Patterson, M., & Engelberg, L. 1978. "Women in male-dominated professions." In A. H. Stromberg & S. Harkess (Eds.), *Women working.* Palo Alto, CA: Mayfield.

Paulos, J. A. 1995. *A mathematician reads the newspaper.* New York: Basic Books

Payer, L. 1988. *Medicine and culture.* New York: Penguin.

Pear, R. 1983. "Study says affirmative action rule expands hiring of minorities." *New York Times,* June 19.

———. 1992. "New look at the U.S. in 2050: Bigger, older and less white." *New York Times,* December 4.

———. 1993a. "Wide health gap, linked to income, is reported in the U.S." *New York Times,* July 8.

———. 1993b. "Poverty in U.S. grew faster than population last year." *New York Times,* October 5.

———. 1995. "Proposed definition of indigence could expand number of poor." *New York Times,* April 30.

Pearce, D. 1979. "Gatekeepers and homeseekers: Institutional patterns in racial steering." *Social Problems, 26,* 325–342.

Percival, R. 1989. "Malthus and his ghost." *National Review,* August 18.

Perin, C. 1988. *Belonging in America*. Madison: University of Wisconsin Press.

Perlez, J. 1991. "Madagascar, where the dead return, bringing joy." *New York Times,* August 31.

Perlman, D., & Fehr, B. 1987. "The development of intimate relationships." In D. Perlman & S. Duck (Eds.), *Intimate relationships: Development, dynamics and deterioration*. Newbury Park, CA: Sage.

Perrow, C. 1986. *Complex organizations: A critical essay*. New York: Random House.

Perrow, C., & Guillen, M. 1990. *The AIDS disaster: The failure of organizations in New York and the nation*. New Haven, CT: Yale University Press.

Pescosolido, B. A. 1986. "Migration, medical care and the lay referral system: A network theory of role assimilation." *American Sociological Review, 51,* 523–540.

Pescosolido, B. A., & Georgianna, S. 1989. "Durkheim, suicide, and religion: Toward a network theory of suicide." *American Sociological Review, 54,* 33–48.

Peters, T. J., & Waterman, R. H. 1982. *In search of excellence*. New York: Harper & Row.

Petersilia, J. 1985. *Probation and felony offenders*. Washington, DC: U.S. Department of Justice.

Peterson, J., & Kim, P. 1991. *The day America told the truth*. New York: Prentice-Hall.

Peterson, P. 1991. "The urban underclass and the poverty paradox." In C. Jencks & P. Peterson (Eds.), *The urban underclass*. Washington, DC: Brookings Institution.

Peterson, R. R. 1996. "A re-evaluation of the economic consequences of divorce." *American Sociological Review, 61,* 528–536.

Peterson, S. B., & Lach, M. A. 1990. "Gender stereotypes in children's books: Their prevalence and influence in cognitive and affective development." *Gender and Education, 2,* 185–197.

Petrunik, M., & Shearing, C. D. 1983. "Fragile facades: Stuttering and the strategic manipulation of awareness." *Social Problems, 31,* 125–138.

Pettigrew, T. F., & Martin, J. 1987. "Shaping the organizational context for black American inclusion." *Journal of Social Issues, 43,* 41–78.

Pfohl, S. J. 1977. "The discovery of child abuse." *Social Problems, 24,* 310–323.

———. 1985. *Images of deviance and social control*. New York: McGraw-Hill.

Philipson, I. J. 1993. *On the shoulders of women: The feminization of psychotherapy*. New York: Guilford.

"Physical traits affect earning power, study says." 1994. *New York Times,* July 13.

Piliavin, I., & Briar, S. 1964. "Police encounters with juveniles." *American Journal of Sociology, 70,* 206–214.

Piore, M. J. 1994. "The dual labor market: Theory and implications." In D. B. Grusky (Ed.), *Social stratification: Class, race and gender in sociological perspective*. Boulder, CO: Westview Press.

Piven, F. F., & Cloward, R. A. 1977. *Poor people's movements: Why they succeed, how they fail*. New York: Vintage.

"The pizza must go through: It's the law in San Francisco." 1996. *New York Times,* July 14.

Pollitt, K. 1991. "Fetal rights: A new assault on feminism." In J. H. Skolnick & E. Currie (Eds.), *Crisis in American institutions*. New York: HarperCollins.

Powell, W. W. 1991. "Expanding the scope of institutional analysis." In W. W. Powell & P. J. DiMaggio (Eds.), *The new institutionalism in organizational analysis*. Chicago: University of Chicago Press.

Pratkanis, A., & Aronson, E. 1991. *Age of propaganda*. New York: W. H. Freeman.

"Prenatal drug use is ruled child abuse." 1996. *New York Times,* July 17.

Preston, S. H. 1976. *Mortality patterns in national population: With special references to recorded causes of death*. New York: Academic Press.

———. 1984. "Children and the elderly in the U.S." *Scientific American,* December, 44–49.

Pryor, J. B., & Ostrom, T. M. 1981. "The organization of social information: A converging-operations approach." *Journal of Personality and Social Psychology, 41,* 628–641.

Pugliesi, K. 1987. "Deviation in emotion and the labeling of mental illness." *Deviant Behavior, 8,* 79–102.

Putnam, R. D. 1995. "Bowling alone: America's declining social capital." *Journal of Democracy, 6,* 65–78.

Quinn, J. B. 1993. "What's for dinner, Mom?" *Newsweek,* April 5.

Quinney, R. 1970. *The social reality of crime.* Boston: Little, Brown.

Ramirez, A. 1988. "Racism toward Hispanics: The culturally monolithic society." In P. A. Katz & D. A. Taylor (Eds.), *Eliminating racism.* New York: Plenum.

Raymond, J. G. 1993. *Women as wombs.* New York: HarperCollins.

Reich, R. 1991. "The secession of the successful." *New York Times Magazine,* January 20.

Reiman, J. 1990. *The rich get richer and the poor get prison.* New York: Macmillan.

Reinarman, C. 1994. "The social construction of drug scares." In P. A. Adler & P. Adler (Eds.), *Constructions of Deviance.* Belmont, CA: Wadsworth.

Reinharz, S. 1992. *Feminist methods in social research.* New York: Oxford University Press.

Reinhold, R. 1993. "A welcome for immigrants turns to resentment." *New York Times,* August 25.

Renwick, T. J., & Bergmann, B. R. 1993. "A budget-based definition of poverty." *Journal of Human Resources, 28,* 1–24.

Renzetti, C. M., & Curran, D. J. 1989. *Women, men and society: The sociology of gender.* Boston: Allyn & Bacon.

Reskin, B., & Hartmann, H. 1986. *Women's work, men's work: Sex segregation on the job.* Washington, DC: National Academy Press.

Reskin, B., & Padavic, I. 1994. *Women, men and work.* Newbury Park, CA: Pine Forge Press.

Reyes, L., & Rubie, P. 1994. *Hispanics in Hollywood: An encyclopedia of film and television.* New York: Garland Press.

Reynolds, J. M. 1973. "The medical institution." In L. T. Reynolds & J. M. Henslin (Eds.), *American society: A critical analysis.* New York: David McKay.

Rheingold, H. 1994. *The virtual community.* New York: Harper Perennial.

Richards, E. 1987. *Below the line: Living poor in America.* New York: Consumers Union Press.

Richardson, L. 1987. "Gender stereotyping in the English language." In L. Richardson & V. Taylor (Eds.), *Feminist frontiers II.* New York: Random House.

Rieff, D. 1991. "The new face of L.A." *Los Angeles Times Magazine,* September 15.

Riesman, D. 1950. *The lonely crowd.* New Haven, CT: Yale University Press.

Rifkin, J. 1996. "Civil society in the information age." *The Nation,* February 26.

Riley, M. W. 1971. "Social gerontology and the age stratification of society." *The Gerontologist, 11,* 79–87.

———. 1983. "The family in an aging society: A matrix of latent relationships." *Journal of Family Issues, 4,* 439–454.

Riley, M. W., Foner, A., & Waring, J. 1988. "Sociology of age." In N. J. Smelser (Ed.), *Handbook of sociology.* Newbury Park, CA: Sage.

Riley, M. W., Johnson, M., & Foner, A. 1972. *Aging and society III: A sociology of age stratification.* New York: Russell Sage Foundation.

Ritzer, G. 1993. *The McDonaldization of society.* Newbury Park, CA: Pine Forge Press.

Roberts, S. 1995. "Alone in the vast wasteland." *New York Times,* December 24.

Robins, L. N., & Regier, D. A. 1991. *Psychiatric disorders in America: The epidemiologic catchment area studies.* New York: Free Press.

Robinson, R. V., & Bell, W. 1978. "Equality, success and social justice in England and the United States." *American Sociological Review, 43,* 125–143.

Robinson, R. V., & Kelley, J. 1979. "Class as conceived by Marx and Dahrendorf: Effects on income inequality and politics in the United States and Great Britain." *American Sociological Review, 44,* 38–58.

Rodin, J. 1985. "The application of social psychology." In G. Lindzay & E. Aronson (Eds.), *The handbook of social psychology.* New York: Random House.

Rodman, H., Pratto, D. J., & Nelson, R. S. 1985. "Child care arrangements and children's functioning: A comparison of self care and adult care children." *Developmental Psychology, 21,* 413–418.

Roethlisberger, F. J., & Dickson, W. J. 1939. *Management and the worker.* Cambridge: Harvard University Press.

Rohter, L. 1993. "Miami meals tax to aid homeless." *New York Times,* August 3.

Roiphe, K. 1993. *The morning after: Sex, fear and feminism on campus.* Boston: Little, Brown.

Roof, W. C. 1993a. *A generation of seekers: The spiritual journeys of the baby boom generation.* San Francisco: Harper.

———. 1993b. "Toward the year 2000: Reconstructions of religious space." *The Annals of the American Academy of Political and Social Science, 527,* 155–170.

Rosenhan, D. 1973. "On being sane in insane places." *Science, 179,* 250–258.

Rosenthal, R., & Jacobson, L. 1968. *Pygmalion in the classroom.* New York: Holt, Rinehart & Winston.

Ross, C. E., Mirowsky, J., & Goldstein, K. 1990. "The impact of family on health: The decade in review." *Journal of Marriage and the Family, 52,* 1059–1078.

Rossi, A. 1968. "Transition to parenthood." *Journal of Marriage and the Family, 30,* 26–39.

Rossi, P. 1988. *Down and out in America: The origins of homelessness.* Chicago: University of Chicago Press.

Roth, R. 1993. "At women's expense: The costs of fetal rights." *Women and Politics, 13,* 117–135.

Rothenberg, P. S. 1992. *Race, class and gender in the United States.* New York: St. Martin's Press.

Rothman, B. K. 1987. "Reproduction." In B. B. Hess & M. M. Ferree (Eds.), *Analyzing gender: A handbook of social science research.* Newbury Park, CA: Sage.

Rothman, D. J. 1994. "Shiny happy people." *The New Republic,* February 14.

Rothman, D. J., & Edgar, H. 1992. "Scientific rigor and medical realities: Placebo trials in cancer and AIDS research." In E. Fee & D. M. Fox (Eds.), *AIDS: The making of a chronic disease.* Berkeley: University of California Press.

Rothschild, N. 1990. *New York City neighborhoods.* New York: Academic Press.

Rowland, R. 1990. "Technology and motherhood: Reproductive choice reconsidered." In C. Carlson (Ed.), *Perspectives on the family: History, class and feminism.* Belmont, CA: Wadsworth.

Rubin, J. Z., Provenzano, F. J., & Luria, Z. 1974. "The eye of the beholder: Parents' views on sex of newborns." *American Journal of Orthopsychiatry, 44,* 512–519.

Rubin, L. 1976. *Worlds of pain.* New York: Basic Books.

Ruether, R. 1980. "Politics and the family: Recapturing a lost issue." *Christianity and Crisis, 40,* 261–267.

Ruggles, P. 1990. "The poverty line—too low for the 90's." *New York Times,* April 26.

Rusbult, C. E., Zembrodt, I. M., & Iwaniszek, J. 1986. "The impact of gender and sex-role orientation on responses to dissatisfaction in close relationships." *Sex Roles, 15,* 1–20.

Ryan, W. 1976. *Blaming the victim.* New York: Vintage Books.

Salholz, E. 1986. "Too late for Prince Charming?" *Newsweek,* June 2.

Sapir, E. 1929. "The status of linguistics as a science." *Language, 5,* 207–214.

———. 1949. *Selected writings* (D. G. Mandelbaum, Ed.). Berkeley: University of California Press.

Sarkis, M. 1995. World Wide Web Home Page.

Satchell, M. 1991. "Poisoning the border." *U.S. News & World Report,* May 6.

Saul, L. 1972. "Personal and social psychopathology and the primary prevention of violence." *American Journal of Psychiatry, 128,* 1578–1581.

Saunders, J. M. 1991. "Relating social structural abstractions to sociological research." *Teaching Sociology, 19,* 270–271.

Schacter, S. 1951. "Deviation, rejection, and communication." *Journal of Abnormal and Social Psychology, 46,* 190–207.

Scheer, C. 1995. "'Illegals' made slaves to fashion." *The Nation,* September 11.

Schlesinger, A. 1992. *The disuniting of America.* New York: Norton.

Schmitt, E. 1996a. "Adoption bill facing battle over a provision on Indians." *New York Times,* May 8.

———. 1996b. "Provisions on legal immigrants jeopardize bill on illegal aliens." *New York Times,* May 28.

Schodolski, V. J. 1993. "Funeral industry, pitching videos, 2-for-1 specials to baby boomers." *Indianapolis Star,* December 26.

Schofield, J. 1982. *Black and white in school.* New York: Praeger.

Schor, J. B. 1991. "Global equity and environmental crisis: An argument for reducing working hours in the north." *World Development, 19,* 73–84.

Schuman, H., Steeh, C., & Bobo, L. 1988. *Racial attitudes in America: Trends and interpretations.* Cambridge: Harvard University Press.

Schur, E. M. 1984. *Labeling women deviant: Gender, stigma and social control.* New York: Random House.

Schwartz, B. 1973. "Waiting, exchange and power: The distribution of time in social systems." *American Journal of Sociology, 79,* 841–870.

Schwartz, R. D., & Skolnick, J. H. 1962. "Two studies of legal stigma." *Social Problems, 10,* 133–138.

Schwarz, J. E., & Volgy, T. J. 1993. "Above the poverty line—but poor." *The Nation,* February 15.

Scott, M., & Lyman, S. 1968. "Accounts." *American Sociological Review, 33,* 46–62.

Scott, R. 1967. "The selection of clients by social welfare agencies: The case of the blind." *Social Problems, 14,* 248–257.

Scull, A., & Favreau, D. 1986. "A chance to cut is a chance to cure: Sexual surgery for psychosis in three nineteenth century societies." In S. Spitzer & A. T. Scull (Eds.), *Research in law, deviance and social control* (Vol. 8). Greenwich, CT: JAI Press.

Scully, D., & Marolla, J. 1984. "Convicted rapists' vocabulary of motive: Excuses and justifications." *Social Problems, 31,* 530–544.

Seedman, A. A., & Hellman, P. 1975. *Chief.* New York: Avon.

Segall, A. 1987. "Sociocultural variation in sick role behavioral expectations." In H. D. Schwartz (Ed.), *Dominant issues in medical sociology.* New York: Random House.

Senior, J. 1994. "Sign language reflects changing sensibilities." *New York Times,* January 3.

Sennett, R. 1984. *Families against the city: Middle class homes in industrial Chicago.* Cambridge, MA: Harvard University Press.

Sennett, R., & Cobb, J. 1972. *The hidden injuries of class.* New York: Vintage Books.

Shakin, M., Shakin, D., & Sternglanz, S. H. 1985. "Infant clothing: Sex labeling for strangers." *Sex Roles, 12,* 955–964.

Shanker, A. 1990. "The Family Medical Leave Act." *New York Times,* June 24.

Shapiro, J. P. 1993. "Just fix it." *U.S. News & World Report,* February 22.

Sheffield, C. J. 1987. "Sexual terrorism: The social control of women." In B. B. Hess & M. M. Ferree (Eds.), *Analyzing gender: A handbook of social science research.* Newbury Park, CA: Sage.

Sherman, S. R., Ward, R. A., & LaGory, M. 1988. "Women as caregivers of the elderly: Instrumental and expressive support." *Social Work,* March–April, 164–167.

Sherraden, M. 1988. "Rethinking social welfare: Toward assets." *Social Policy,* Winter, 37–43.

Shibutani, T. 1961. *Society and personality: An interactionist approach to social psychology.* Englewood Cliffs, NJ: Prentice-Hall.

Shilts, R. M. 1987. *And the band played on: Politics, people and the AIDS epidemic.* New York: St. Martin's Press.

Shireman, J. F., & Johnson, P. R. 1986. "A longitudinal study of black adoptions: Single parent, transracial and traditional." *Social Work, 31,* 172–176.

Shon, S. P., & Ja, D. Y. 1992. "Asian families." In A. S. Skolnick & J. H. Skolnick (Eds.), *Family in transition.* New York: HarperCollins.

Shotland, R. L., & Straw, M. K. 1976. "Bystander response to an assault: When a man attacks a woman," *Journal of Personality and Social Psychology, 34,* 990–999.

Showalter, E. 1985. *The female malady.* New York: Penguin.

Sidel, R. 1986. *Women and children last.* New York: Penguin.

———. 1990. *On her own: Growing up in the shadow of the American Dream.* New York: Penguin.

Signorielli, N. 1990. "Children, television and gender roles." *Journal of Adolescent Health Care, 11,* 50–58.

Silver, V. 1992. "Barely gone, the 80's are ripe for a revival." *New York Times,* December 15.

Silverman, D. 1982. *Secondary analysis in social research: A guide to data sources and methods with examples.* Boston: Allen & Unwin.

Simon, J. 1983. "Life on earth is getting better." *The Futurist,* August.

Simon, R., Alstein, H., & Melli, M. S. 1994. *The case for transracial adoption.* Washington, DC: The American University Press.

Simons, M. 1995. "Dutch doctors to tighten rules on mercy killings." *New York Times,* September 11.

Simpson, I. H. 1979. *From student to nurse: A longitudinal study of socialization.* Cambridge: Cambridge University Press.

Simpson, P. 1983. "The fight for pay equity." *Working Woman*, April.

Singleton, R., Straits, B. C., & Straits, M. M. 1993. *Approaches to social research*. New York: Oxford University Press.

Siwek, J. 1992. "Plight of the homeless shows flaws in the system." *Washington Post Health Magazine*, July 28.

Skocpol, T. 1979. *States and social revolutions: A comparative analysis of France, Russia and China*. New York: Cambridge University Press.

Skolnick, A. S. 1981. "Married lives: Longitudinal perspectives on marriage." In D. H. Eichorn, J. A. Clausen, N. Haan, M. P. Honzik, & P. H. Mussen (Eds.), *Present and past in middle life*. New York: Academic Press.

———. 1987. *The intimate environment: Exploring marriage and the family*. Boston: Little, Brown.

———. 1991. *Embattled paradise*. New York: Basic Books.

———. 1996. *The intimate environment: Exploring marriage and the family*. New York: HarperCollins.

Skolnick, A. S., & Skolnick, J. H. 1992. *Family in transition*. New York: HarperCollins.

Smeeding, T., Torrey, B. B., & Rein, M. 1988. "Patterns of income and poverty: The economic status of children and the elderly in eight countries." In T. Smeeding, J. L. Palmer, & B. B. Torrey (Eds.), *The vulnerable*. Washington, DC: Urban Institute Press.

Smelser, N. J. 1988. "Social structure." In N. J. Smelser (Ed.), *Handbook of sociology*. Newbury Park, CA: Sage.

Smith, D. A. 1993. "Technology and the modern world system: Some reflections." *Science, Technology and Human Values, 18*, 186–195.

Smith, J. 1981. *Social issues and the social order: The contradictions of capitalism*. Cambridge, MA: Winthrop.

Smolowe, J. 1993. "Giving the cold shoulder." *Time*, December 6.

———. 1996. "The stalled revolution." *Time*, May 6.

Smothers, R. 1996. "As Olympics approach, homeless are not feeling at home in Atlanta." *New York Times*, July 1.

Sniderman, P. M., & Tetlock, P. E. 1986. "Symbolic racism: Problems of motive attribution in political analysis." *Social Forces, 42*, 129–150.

Snipp, C. M. 1986. "American Indians and natural resource development." *American Journal of Economics and Sociology, 45*, 457–474.

Snow, D. A., Baker, S. G., Anderson, L., & Martin, M. 1986. "The myth of pervasive mental illness among the homeless." *Social Problems, 33*, 407–423.

Snow, D. A., Robinson, C., & McCall, P. 1991. "'Cooling out' men in singles' bars and nightclubs." *Journal of Contemporary Ethnography, 19*, 423–449.

Soldo, B. J., & Agree, E. M. 1988. "America's elderly." *Population Bulletin, 43*, 1–45.

Solomon, J. 1988. *The signs of our times: The secret meanings of everyday life*. New York: Harper & Row.

Sontag, D. 1992. "Across the U.S., immigrants find the land of resentment." *New York Times*, December 11.

Sontag, S. 1979. *Illness as metaphor*. New York: Random House.

Sorohan, E. G. 1995. "Soundbite." *Training and Development, 49*, 11–12.

South, S. J., & Lloyd, K. M. 1995. "Spousal alternatives and marital dissolution." *American Sociological Review, 60*, 21–35.

South, S. J., & Spitze, G. D. 1994. "Housework in marital and nonmarital households." *American Sociological Review, 59*, 327–347.

Sowell, T. 1977. "New light on black IQ." *New York Times Magazine*, March 27.

Spanier, G. B. 1989. "Cohabitation in the 1980's: Recent changes in the United States." In A. S. Skolnick & J. H. Skolnick (Eds.), *Family in transition*. Boston: Little, Brown.

Spence, J. T., Deaux, K., & Helmreich, R. L. 1985. "Sex roles in contemporary American society." In G. Lindzey & E. Aronson (Eds.), *The handbook of social psychology*. New York: Random House.

Spickard, P. R. 1989. *Mixed blood*. Madison: University of Wisconsin Press.

Spitze, G. 1988. "Women's employment and family relations: A review." *Journal of Marriage and the Family, 50*, 595–618.

Spretnak, C. 1982. "The Christian Right's 'holy war' against feminism." In *The politics of women's spirituality*. New York: Anchor.

Sproull, L., & Kiesler, S. 1991. *Connections: New ways of working in the networked organization*. Cambridge, MA: MIT Press.

Squires, G. D. 1980. "Runaway factories are also a civil rights issue." *In These Times*, May, 14–20.

Stacey, J. 1991. "Backward toward the postmodern family." In A. Wolfe (Ed.), *America at century's end*. Berkeley: University of California Press.

Staples, R. 1992. "African American families." In J. M. Henslin (Ed.), *Marriage and family in a changing society*. New York: Free Press.

Staples, R., & Mirande, A. 1980. "Racial and cultural variations among American families: A decennial review of the literature on minority families." *Journal of Marriage and the Family, 42,* 157–173.

Stark, R., & Bainbridge, W. S. 1980. "Networks of faith: Interpersonal bonds and recruitment in cults and sects." *American Journal of Sociology, 85,* 1376–1395.

Starr, P. 1982. *The social transformation of American medicine.* New York: Basic Books.

Steele, C., & Aronson, J. 1995. "Stereotype threat and the intellectual test performance of African Americans." *Journal of Personality and Social Psychology, 69,* 797–811.

Steele, S. 1990. *The content of our character: A new vision of race in America.* New York: HarperCollins.

Stein, L. I. 1967. "The doctor-nurse game." *Archives of General Psychiatry, 16,* 699–703.

Steinfels, P. 1992. "Apathy is seen toward agony of the homeless." *New York Times*, January 20.

Steinmetz, S. K., Clavan, R., & Stein, K. F. 1990. *Marriage and family realities: Historical and contemporary perspectives.* New York: Harper & Row.

Stephens, G. 1994. "The global crime wave." *The Futurist, 28,* 22–28.

Stephens, W. N. 1963. *The family in cross cultural perspective.* New York: University Press of America.

Stevenson, R. W. 1992. "Maker is accused of faulty tests on parts for missiles and aircraft." *New York Times*, April 23.

Stewart, J. E. 1980. "Defendant's attractiveness as a factor in the outcome of criminal trials: An observational study." *Journal of Applied Social Psychology, 10,* 348–361.

Stockard, J., & Johnson, M. M. 1992. *Sex and gender in society.* Englewood Cliffs, NJ: Prentice-Hall.

Stokes, R., & Hewitt, J. P. 1976. "Aligning actions." *American Sociological Review, 41,* 837–849.

Stone, G. P. 1981. "Appearance and the self: A slightly revised version." In G. P. Stone & H. A. Farberman (Eds.), *Social psychology through symbolic interaction.* New York: Wiley.

Stone, L. 1979. *The family, sex and marriage in England 1500–1800.* New York: Harper Torchbooks.

Straus, M. A. 1977. "A sociological perspective on the prevention and treatment of wife beating." In M. Roy (Ed.), *Battered women.* New York: Van Nostrand.

Straus, M. A., & Gelles, R. J. 1986. "Societal change in family violence from 1975 to 1985 as revealed by two national surveys." *Journal of Marriage and the Family, 48,* 465–479.

Straus, M. A., Gelles, R. J., & Steinmetz, S. K. 1980. *Behind closed doors.* New York: Bantam.

Strong, B., & DeVault, C. 1992. *The marriage and family experience.* St. Paul, MN: West.

Strube, M. J., & Barbour, L. S. 1983. "The decision to leave an abusive relationship: Economic dependence and psychological commitment." *Journal of Marriage and the Family, 45,* 785–793.

Stryker, S. 1980. *Symbolic interactionism.* Menlo Park, CA: Benjamin/Cummings.

Stummer, H. 1994. *No easy walk.* Philadelphia: Temple University Press.

Sudnow, D. 1965. "Normal crimes: Sociological features of the penal code in a public defenders' office." *Social Problems, 12,* 255–264.

Sunstein, C. 1991. "Why markets don't stop discrimination." In E. F. Paul, F. D. Miller, & J. Paul (Eds.), *Reassessing civil rights.* Cambridge, MA: Blackwell.

Suro, R. 1992. "Poll finds hispanics desire to assimilate." *New York Times*, December 15.

Sutherland, E., & Cressey, D. 1955. *Criminology.* Philadelphia: Lippincott.

Swanson, G. 1992. "Doing things together: On some basic forms of agency and structuring in collective action and on some explanations for them." *Social Psychology Quarterly, 55,* 94–117.

Sweet, J. A., & Bumpass, L. L. 1987. *American families and households.* New York: Russell Sage.

Sykes, G., & Matza, D. 1957. "Techniques of neutralization: A theory of delinquency." *American Sociological Review, 22,* 664–670.

Szasz, T. 1984. *The therapeutic state.* Buffalo, NY: Prometheus Books.

———. 1990. *Insanity: The idea and its consequences.* New York: Wiley.

"Taiwan's little problem." 1993. *The Economist,* June 5.

Takagi, D. Y. 1990. "From discrimination to affirmative action: Facts in the Asian-American admissions controversy." *Social Problems, 37,* 578–592.

Tannen, D. 1990. *You just don't understand: Women and men in conversation.* New York: Ballantine.

Tannenbaum, F. 1938. *Crime and community.* New York: Ginn.

Tarrow, S. 1994. *Power in movement.* New York: Cambridge University Press.

Tavris, C. 1992. *The mismeasure of woman.* New York: Touchstone.

Tavris, C., & Offir, C. 1984. *The longest war: Sex differences in perspective.* New York: Harcourt Brace Jovanovich.

Tauber, M. A. 1979. "Parental socialization techniques and sex differences in children's play." *Child Development, 50,* 225–234.

Taylor, D. E. 1993. "Environmentalism and the politics of inclusion." In R. D. Bullard (Ed.), *Confronting environmental racism.* Boston: South End Press.

Taylor, R. J., Chatters, L. M., Tucker, M. B., & Lewis, E. 1990. "Developments in research on black families: A decade review." *Journal of Marriage and the Family, 52,* 993–1014.

Taylor, S. J., & Bogdan, R. 1980. "Defending illusions: The institution's struggle for survival." *Human Organization, 39,* 209–218.

Tenner, E. 1996. *Why things bite back.* New York: Alfred A. Knopf.

Terry, D. 1995. "Heat death toll rises to 436 in Chicago." *New York Times,* July 20.

———. 1996. "In Wisconsin, a rarity of a fetal-harm case." *New York Times,* August 17.

Thoits, P. 1985. "Self-labeling process in mental illness: The role of emotional deviance." *American Journal of Sociology, 91,* 221–249.

Thomas, D. L., Franks, D. D., & Calonico, J. M. 1972. "Role taking and power in social psychology." *American Sociological Review, 37,* 605–614.

Thompson, P. 1989. *The nature of work.* London: Macmillan.

Thompson, R. A. 1991. "Infant day care: Concerns, controversies, choices." In J. V. Lerner & N. L. Galambos (Eds.), *Employed mothers and their children.* New York: Garland.

Thorne, B., & Luria, Z. 1986. "Sexuality and gender in children's daily worlds." *Social Problems, 33,* 176–190.

Thorne, B., & Yalom, M. 1982. *Rethinking the family: Some feminist questions.* New York: Longman.

Thornton, A. 1989. "Changing attitudes toward family issues in the United States." *Journal of Marriage and Family, 51,* 873–893.

Thurow, L. 1995. "Companies merge, families break up." *New York Times,* September 3.

Tiano, S. 1987. "Gender, work and world capitalism: Third world women's role in development." In B. B. Hess & M. M. Ferree (Eds.), *Analyzing gender: A handbook of social science research.* Newbury Park, CA: Sage.

Tilly, C. 1978. *From mobilization to revolution.* Reading, MA: Addison-Wesley.

Timms, E., & McGonigle, S. 1992. "Psychological Warfare." *Indianapolis Star,* April 5.

Tobin, J. J., Wu, D. Y. H., & Davidson, D. H. 1989. *Preschool in three cultures: Japan, China and the United States.* New Haven, CT: Yale University Press.

Tocqueville, A. de. 1969. *Democracy in America.* New York: Doubleday. (Original work published 1835)

Toennies, F. 1963. *Community and society.* New York: HarperCollins. (Original work published 1887).

Tong, R. 1984. *Women, sex and the law.* Totowa, NJ: Rowman & Allanheld.

Torrey, E. F. 1988. *Surviving schizophrenia.* New York: Harper & Row.

Trepanier, M. L., & Romatowski, J. A. 1985. "Attributes and roles assigned to characters in children's writing: Sex differences and sex role perceptions." *Sex Roles, 13,* 263–272.

Triandis, H. C., McCusker, C., & Hui, C. H. 1990. "Multimethod probes of individualism and collectivism." *Journal of Personality and Social Psychology, 59,* 1006–1020.

Trice, H. M., & Roman, P. M. 1970. "Delabeling, relabeling and alcoholics anonymous." *Social Problems, 17,* 538–546.

Trotsky, L. 1959. *The history of the Russian Revolution* (F. W. Dupee, Ed.). Garden City, NY: Doubleday.

Trudgill, P. 1972. "Sex, covert prestige and linguistic change in the urban British English of Norwich." In B. Thorne & N. Henley (Eds.), *Language and society.* Cambridge: Cambridge University Press.

Tumin, M. 1953. "Some principles of stratification: A critical analysis." *American Sociological Review, 18,* 387–393.

Turkle, S. 1994. "Constructions and reconstructions of self in virtual reality: Playing in the MUDs." *Mind, Culture and Activity, 1,* 158–167.

Turner, J. H. 1972. *Patterns of social organization.* New York: McGraw-Hill.

Turner, R., & Edgley, C. 1976. "Death as theater: A dramaturgical analysis of the American funeral." *Sociology and Social Research, 60,* 377–392.

———. 1983. "From witchcraft to drugcraft: Biochemistry as mythology." *Social Science Journal, 20,* 1–12.

Turner, R. W., & Killian, L. M. 1987. *Collective behavior.* Englewood Cliffs, NJ: Prentice-Hall.

Uchitelle, L. 1993. "Use of temporary workers is on rise in manufacturing." *New York Times,* July 6.

Uchitelle, L., & Kleinfield, N. R. 1996. "On the battlefields of business, millions of casualties." *New York Times,* March 3.

Uhlenberg, P., & Myers, M. A. 1981. "Divorce and the elderly." *The Gerontologist, 21,* 276–282.

"Uninsured hospital patients found far more likely to die." 1991. *New York Times,* January 16.

United Nations Development Program. 1996. *Human Development Report, 1996.* New York: Oxford University Press.

United Nations Research Institute, 1995. *States of disarray: The social effects of globalization.* London: UNRISD.

United States Bureau of Justice Statistics. 1983. *Report to the nation on crime and justice: The data.* Washington, DC: U.S. Government Printing Office.

———. 1993. *Sourcebook of criminal justice statistics—1992.* Washington, DC: U.S. Government Printing Office.

United States Bureau of Labor Statistics. 1985. *Handbook of labor statistics.* Washington, DC: U.S. Government Printing Office.

———. 1989. *Handbook of labor statistics.* Washington, DC: U.S. Government Printing Office.

United States Bureau of the Census. 1990a. "Marital status and living arrangements." *Current population reports.* Washington, DC: U.S. Government Printing Office.

———. 1990b. "Poverty in the United States: 1990." Current population reports. Washington, DC: U.S. Government Printing Office.

———. 1991a. *Statistical abstract of the United States.* Washington, DC: U.S. Government Printing Office.

———. 1991b. *Census and You, 26,* September, p. 3.

———. 1991c. "Money income and poverty status of persons and families in the U.S." *Current population reports.* Washington, DC: U.S. Government Printing Office.

———. 1992a. *Statistical abstract of the United States.* Washington, DC: U.S. Government Printing Office.

———. 1992b. *Census and You, 27,* November, p. 7.

———. 1992c. "Educational attainment in the United States: March 1991 and March 1990." *Current population reports.* Washington, DC: U.S. Government Printing Office.

———. 1992d. *Population projections of the United States by age, sex, race and Hispanic origin: 1992 to 2050.* Washington, DC: U.S. Government Printing Office.

———. 1993a. *Statistical abstract of the United States.* Washington, DC: U.S. Government Printing Office.

———. 1993b. *Census and You, 28,* April, p. 14.

———. 1993c. *Census and You, 28,* January, p. 1.

———. 1994. *Statistical abstract of the United States.* Washington, DC: U.S. Government Printing Office.

———. 1995a. *Statistical abstract of the United States.* Washington, DC: U.S. Government Printing Office.

———. 1995b. *Census and You, 30,* June, p. 1.

———. 1995c. *Census and You, 30,* November/December, p. 3.

———. 1995d. "Population projections of the United States by age, sex, race and Hispanic origin: 1995–2050." *Current Population Reports,* Series P25, 1130.

———. 1996. *Census and You, 31,* April, p. 4.

United States Commission on Human Rights. 1992. "Indian tribes: A continuing quest for survival." In P. S. Rothenberg (Ed.), *Race, class and gender in the United States.* New York: St. Martin's Press.

United States Department of Health and Human Services. 1988. "The health consequences of smoking." *Nicotine addiction: A report of the Surgeon General.* Washington, DC: U.S. Government Printing Office.

———. 1996. *National household survey on drug abuse, 1995.* Washington, DC: U.S. Government Printing Office.

———. 1990. *Report of the United States Advisory Board on Child Abuse and Neglect.* Washington, DC: U.S. Government Printing Office.

United States Department of Health, Education and Welfare. 1973. *Work in America: Report of a special task force to the Secretary of Health, Education and Welfare.* Cambridge, MA: MIT Press.

United States Senate Committee on Governmental Affairs. 1978. *Interlocking directorates among the major U.S. corporations.* Washington, DC: U.S. Government Printing Office.

Useem, M. 1978. "The inner group of the American capitalist class." *Social Problems, 25,* 225–240.

Valdivieso, R., & Davis, C. 1991. "U.S. Hispanics: Challenging issues for the 1990's." In J. Skolnick & E. Currie (Eds.), *Crisis in American institutions.* New York: HarperCollins.

van den Haag, E. 1975. *Punishing criminals: Concerning a very old and painful question.* New York: Basic Books.

Vanek, J. 1980. "Work, leisure and family roles: Farm households in the United States: 1920–1955." *Journal of Family History, 5,* 422–431.

Van Willigen, J., & Channa, V. C. 1991. "Law, custom and crimes against women: The problem of dowry death in India." *Human Organization, 50,* 369–377.

Vaughan, D. 1986. *Uncoupling.* New York: Vintage.

———. 1996. *The Challenger launch disaster.* Chicago: University of Chicago Press.

Veblen, T. 1953. *The theory of the leisure class: An economic study of institutions.* New York: Mentor. (Original work published 1899)

Vega, W. A. 1990. "Hispanic families in the 1980's: A decade of research." *Journal of Marriage and the Family, 52,* 1015–1024.

Vergara, C. J. 1994. "Our fortified ghettos." *The Nation,* January 31.

———. 1995. *The new American ghetto.* New Brunswick, NJ: Rutgers University Press.

Verhovek, S. H. 1993. "A Klansman's black lawyer and a principle." *New York Times,* September 10.

Viets, E. 1992. "Give a whistle, he'll love it." *St. Louis Post-Dispatch,* November 29.

"Vital signs." 1995. *The Nation,* September 11.

Vojejda, B. 1996. "Study rebuts 'danger' of day care." *Indianapolis Star,* April 21.

von Baeyer, C. L., Sherk, D. L., & Zanna, M. P. 1981. "Impression management in the job interview: When the female applicant meets the male (chauvinist) interviewer." *Personality and Social Psychology Bulletin, 7,* 45–51.

Voyandoff, P. 1990. "Economic distress and family relations: A review of the eighties." *Journal of Marriage and the Family, 52,* 1099–1115.

Wagner, D. G., Ford, R. S., & Ford, T. W. 1986. "Can gender inequalities be reduced?" *American Sociological Review, 51,* 47–61.

Walker, A., & Parmar, P. 1993. *Warrior marks: Female genital mutilation and the sexual blinding of women.* New York: Harcourt Brace.

Wallerstedt, J. F. 1984. "Returning to prison." *Bureau of Justice Statistics special report.* Washington, DC: U.S. Government Printing Office.

Wallerstein, I. 1974. *The modern world system.* New York: Academic Press.

Walsh, E. J., & Warland, R. H. 1983. "Social movement involvement in the wake of a nuclear accident: Activists and free riders in the TMI area." *American Sociological Review, 48,* 764–780.

Walton, J. 1990. *Sociology and critical inquiry.* Belmont, CA: Wadsworth.

Warshaw, R. 1988. *I never called it rape.* New York: Harper & Row.

Wattenberg, E. 1986. "The fate of baby boomers and their children." *Social Work, 31,* 20–28.

Watzlawick, P. 1976. *How real is real?* Garden City, NY: Doubleday.

———. 1984. "Self-fulfilling prophecies." In P. Watzlawick (Ed.), *The invented reality: How do we know what we believe we know? Contributions to constructivism.* New York: Norton.

Webb, E. J., Campbell, D. T., Schwartz, R. D., Sechrest, L., & Grove, J. B. 1981. *Nonreactive measures in the social sciences.* Boston: Houghton Mifflin.

Weber, M. 1946. "Bureaucracy." In H. H. Gerth & C. W. Mills (Eds.), *From Max Weber: Essays in sociology* (pp. 196–244). New York: Oxford University Press.

———. 1947. *The theory of social and economic organization.* New York: Free Press.

———. 1968. *Economy and society* (G. Roth and C. Wittich, Eds.). New York: Bedminster Press.

———. 1970. *From Max Weber: Essays in sociology* (H. H. Gerth & C. W. Mills, Eds.). New York: Oxford University Press.

———. 1977. *The Protestant ethic and the spirit of capitalism.* New York: Macmillan. (Original work published 1904)

Weeks, J. 1995. *Population: An introduction to concepts and issues* (updated 5th ed.). Belmont, CA: Wadsworth.

Weinstein, E. A., & Deutschberger, P. 1963. "Some dimensions of altercasting." *Sociometry, 26,* 454–466.

Weitzman, L. 1985. *The divorce revolution: The unexpected consequences for women and children in America.* New York: Free Press.

Weitzman, L., Eifler, D., Hodada, E., & Ross, C. 1972. "Sex-role socialization in picture books for preschool children." *American Journal of Sociology, 77,* 1125–1150.

"Welfare mistrust." 1996. *USA Today,* July 2.

Welsh, J. F. 1984. "The presentation of self in capitalist society: Bureaucratic visibility as a social source of impression management." *Humanity and Society, 8,* 253–271.

Weston, K. 1991. *Families we choose: Lesbians, gays, kinship.* New York: Columbia University Press.

Whalen, C. K., & Henker, B. 1977. "The pitfalls of politicization: A response to Conrad's 'The discovery of hyperkinesis: Notes on the medicalization of deviance.'" *Social Problems, 24,* 590–595.

White, L., & Brinkerhoff, D. 1981. "The sexual division of labor: Evidence from childhood." *Social Forces, 60,* 170–181.

"Whites retain negative view of minorities." 1991. *New York Times,* January 10.

Whorf, B. 1956. *Language, thought and reality.* Cambridge, MA: MIT Press.

Whyte, M. K. 1990. *Dating, mating and marriage.* New York: Aldine deGruyter.

Whyte, W. H. 1956. *The organization man.* Garden City, NY: Doubleday.

Wiesel, E. 1986. *Night.* New York: Bantam Books.

Wilkerson, I. 1991a. "As interracial marriage rises, acceptance lags." *New York Times,* December 12.

———. 1991b. "Shift in feelings on the homeless: Empathy turns to frustration." *New York Times,* September 2.

Wilkinson, L. C., & Marrett, C. B. 1985. *Gender influences in classroom interaction.* Orlando, FL: Academic Press.

Will, J., Self, P., & Datan, N. 1976. "Maternal behavior and perceived sex of infant." *American Journal of Orthopsychiatry, 46,* 135–139.

Williams, C. L. 1992. "The glass escalator: Hidden advantages for men in the 'female' professions." *Social Problems, 39,* 253–267.

Williams, L. 1991a. "In a 90's quest for black identity, intense doubts and disagreements." *New York Times,* November 30.

———. 1991b. "When blacks shop bias often accompanies sale." *New York Times,* April 30.

———. 1992a. "Girls' self-image is mother of the woman." *New York Times,* February 6.

———. 1992b. "Scrambling to manage a diverse workforce." *New York Times,* December 12.

Wilson, W. J. 1980. *The declining significance of race.* Chicago: University of Chicago Press.

———. 1987. *The truly disadvantaged.* Chicago: University of Chicago Press.

———. 1990. "Race-neutral programs and the Democratic coalition." *The American Prospect, 1,* 75–81.

Winick, C., & Kinsie, P. 1991. *The lively commerce: Prostitution in the United States.* Chicago: Quadrangle Books.

Winston, N. A. 1988. "Sex-bias response to telephoned job inquiries, Tampa, 1987." *Sociology and Social Research, 72,* 121–124.

Wolfe, A. 1991. *America at century's end.* Berkeley: University of California Press.

Wolfe, S. M. 1991. *Women's health alert.* Reading, MA: Addison-Wesley.

Woliver, L. R. 1989. "The deflective power of reproductive technologies: The impact on women." *Women and Politics, 9,* 17–47.

Wood, P. L. 1975. "The victim in a forcible rape case: A feminist view." In L. G. Schultz (Ed.), *Rape victimology.* Springfield, IL: Charles Thomas.

Wooton, A. 1975. *Dilemmas of discourse.* London: Allen & Unwin.

Word, C. O., Zanna, M. P., & Cooper, J. 1974. "The nonverbal mediation of self-fulfilling prophecies in interracial interaction." *Journal of Experimental Social Psychology, 10,* 109–120.

World Almanac. 1996. "Infant mortality rates." (p. 963). Mahwah, NJ: World Almanac Books.

World Health Organization. 1995. "World health report 1995—Executive summary." World Health Organization World Wide Web site.

World Monitor. 1992. "The Map." *World Monitor,* September 11.

"World population growth." 1995. *The Futurist,* January-February.

"World progress in birth control." *The Futurist,* 1993. August.

Worsnop, R. 1996a. "Helping the homeless." *CQ Researcher,* January 26.

———. 1996b. "Getting into college." *CQ Researcher,* February 23.

Worthington, R. 1996. "Doctoral degree holders face daunting job shortages." *Indianapolis Star,* May 26.

Wright, E. O. 1976. "Class boundaries in advanced capitalist societies." *New Left Review, 98,* 3–41.

Wright, E. O., Costello, C., Hachen, D., & Sprague, J. 1982. "The American class structure." *American Sociological Review, 47,* 709–726.

Wright, E. O., & Perrone, L. 1977. "Marxist class categories and income inequality." *American Sociological Review, 42,* 32–55.

Wright, R. 1995. "Who's really to blame?" *Time,* November 6.

Wrong, D. 1988. *Power: Its forms, bases, and uses.* Chicago: University of Chicago Press.

WuDunn, S. 1995. "In Japan, still getting tea and no sympathy." *New York Times,* August 27.

———. 1996. "In Japan, even toddlers feel the pressure to excel." *New York Times,* January 23.

Wuthnow, R. 1994. *Sharing the journey.* New York: Free Press.

Yorburg, B. 1993. *Family relationships.* New York: St. Martin's Press.

Young, T. R. 1993. "Dress, drama and self: The tee shirt as text." In P. Kollock & J. O'Brien (Eds.), *The production of reality.* Thousand Oaks, CA: Pine Forge Press.

Zastrow, C. 1977. *Outcome of black children–white parents transracial adoptions.* San Francisco: R & E Research Associates.

Zborowski, M. 1952. "Cultural components in responses to pain." *Journal of Social Issues, 8,* 16–30.

Zelizer, V. 1985. *Pricing the priceless child.* New York: Basic Books.

Zerubavel, E. 1985. *The seven day circle: The history and meaning of the week.* New York: Free Press.

Zimbardo, P. 1971. "The pathology of imprisonment." *Society, 9,* 4–8.

Zola, I. 1986. "Medicine as an institution of social control." In P. Conrad & R. Kern (Eds.), *The sociology of health and illness.* New York: St. Martin's Press.

Zuboff, S. 1988. *In the age of the smart machine.* New York: Basic Books.

Zucker, L. G. 1991. "The role of institutionalization in cultural persistence." In W. Powell & P. DiMaggio (Eds.), *The new institutionalism in organizational analysis.* Chicago: University of Chicago Press.

Zurcher, L. A., & Snow, D. A. 1981. "Collective behavior: Social movements." In M. Rosenberg & R. H. Turner (Eds.), *Social psychology: Sociological perspectives.* New York: Basic Books.

Zweigenhaft, R. L. 1987. "Minorities and women of the corporation." In G. W. Domhoff & T. R. Dye (Eds.), *Power elites and organizations.* Newbury Park, CA: Sage.

GLOSSARY/INDEX